THE OFFICIAL PRICE GUIDE TO

DOLLS

Antique • Vintage • Modern

By Denise Van Patten

House of Collectibles
New York London Toronto Sydney Auckland

Copyright © 2005 by Denise Van Patten

Important Notice: All the information, including valuations, in this book has been compiled from reliable sources, and efforts have been made to eliminate errors and questionable data. Nevertheless, in a work of such immense scope, the possibility of error always exists. The publisher will not be responsible for any losses that may occur in the purchase, sale, or other transaction of items because of information contained herein. Readers who feel they have discovered errors are invited to write and inform us, so they may be corrected in subsequent editions.

All rights reserved. No part of this book may be reproduced in any form or by any means, electronic or mechanical, including photocopying, recording, or by any information storage and retrieval system, without the written permission of the publisher. Published in the United States by House of Collectibles, an imprint of The Random House Information Group, a division of Random House, Inc., New York, and simultaneously in Canada by Random House of Canada Limited, Toronto.

 House of Collectibles and colophon are registered trademarks of Random House, Inc.

RANDOM HOUSE is a registered trademark of Random House, Inc.

This book is available for special discounts for bulk purchases for sales promotions or premiums. Special editions, including personalized covers, excerpts of existing books, and corporate imprints, can be created in large quantities for special needs. For more information, write to Special Markets/Premium Sales, 1745 Broadway, MD 6-2, New York, NY, 10019 or e-mail *specialmarkets@randomhouse.com*.

Please address inquiries about electronic licensing of any products for use on a network, in software, or on CD-ROM to the Subsidiary Rights Department, Random House Information Group, fax 212-572-6003.

Visit the House of Collectibles Web site: www.houseofcollectibles.com.

Library of Congress Cataloging-in-Publication Data is available.

First Edition

Printed in the United States of America

10 9 8 7 6 5 4 3 2 1

ISBN: 0-375-72036-7

TABLE OF CONTENTS

ACKNOWLEDGMENTS

This book would not have been possible without the contribution of many people. My love and endless thanks go to my husband, Russ, for his support and encouragement, plus endless hours searching for auction and Internet prices (not to mention the fantastic gourmet meals . . .). My children, Alex and Katie, get thanks and credit for putting up with a doll-obsessed mother, and for allowing me the many, many hours of work that were needed to create this book.

I also could not have completed this book without Theriault's, the world-famous doll auction house. Special thanks are due to Stuart Holbrook, president of Theriault's, and Florence Theriault, and I do forgive them for all of the fabulous dolls they have tempted me to purchase from them over the years. Also to Theriault's, great thanks for the several hundred amazing photographs they contributed to this book, including the lovely color photographs of dolls that grace much of the mid-section of this book.

My acknowledgment section would not be complete without thanks to the UFDC (United Federation of Doll Clubs) for the years of doll education, research, and inspiration that they have shared with me. Thanks also to About.com for the unparalleled soapbox they gave me on the Internet to explore dolls and doll collecting with my community of doll collectors at Doll Collecting at About.com—by far the best and most enthusiastic group of doll collectors on the Internet, and perhaps in the world.

Thanks also goes to the Just About Dolls Club of Northern California for tolerating the whirlwind that is me and for the wealth of dolls and doll knowledge that the members of the club let me tap. Special thanks to Arleen Niblett, our club president, and Marsha Cumpton, our club secretary and my devoted employee at my doll shop for many years.

Thank you to the following people who let me photograph dolls in their private collections: Marsha Cumpton, Ellen Johnson, Janet Lawrence, Clara Robbins and Martha Robbins, Geneva Wallen, and Dana Probert, plus many others who allowed me to photograph their beautiful dolls.

Thank you to my mother and father, Robert and Joan Di Lello, who indulged me as a child with nearly every popular doll sold in the 1960s. Thank you also to my sister, Michele Bernstein, who discovered doll collecting long before I did, and who definitely stirred the collecting "gene" in me. Thanks to my mother-in-law, Patricia Van Patten, for all her love and help with the children, and to all of my wonderful sisters at Beta Sigma Phi (especially my chapter, Xi Pi Nu) for their understanding and support during the last few months before my book was delivered.

Thanks also goes to Lindsey Glass at Random House for her great help in putting together this book. She never flinched when I'd call her for the thirtieth time in one day when trying to organize the 900 photos in the book.

And finally, but not least, my thanks to my editor, Dottie Harris, for suggesting the madness that is a 600-page book on dolls in the first place, and then for the support and encouragement she gave me along the way which has enabled me to complete it so beautifully.

To Russ, Alex and Katie,
without whom there would be
no joy in my dolls.

INTRODUCTION

Welcome to the world of doll collecting. There is no other hobby that combines so many varied and fascinating pursuits—antiques, art, history, fashion, textiles, popular culture, and collecting, to name just a few.

This book is your passport to this world. If you are new to doll collecting, this book will provide you with an overview of the hobby, extensive information on dolls from antique to modern, and thousands of prices for dolls taken from auctions, shops, shows, and the Internet over the past two years.

If you are already involved in the hobby of doll collecting, this book will provide you with vital information about the massive changes to the collecting landscape that have taken place during the last few years. You'll find extensive information on the Internet and how it has reshaped doll collecting, plus the latest trends and new areas of collecting. You have in this book a powerful, comprehensive price guide covering dolls from the early 1800s through the beginning of the 21st century.

MY LIFELONG INVOLVEMENT WITH DOLLS

I have been a collector of dolls my whole life, from the moment my godmother gave me a Madame Alexander Christening doll the week of my birth (a doll that I still have!). For each Christmas as a child in the 1960s and early 1970s, my parents always had the latest dolls under the tree—Barbie, Tammy, Penny Brite, Liddle Kiddles, Crissy, Dawn, Madame Alexanders, and many others. All my childhood dolls are now avidly collected by baby boomer collectors.

As I grew older and out of "playing" with dolls (well . . . I never really grew out of playing with dolls, as this book proves . . .), the dolls shifted more toward collectible dolls. I took a small hiatus from doll collecting while at college and as a young adult, but then reconnected with dolls as a young married woman while trying to replace my childhood Barbies, which my mother had (tragically!) given to Goodwill while I was at college. As it is with many

The author as a child with a favorite Yogi Bear doll.

Home page of www.collectdolls.about.com.

women of my generation, it's the search for lost childhood dolls that leads them to dolls as an adult, and then to doll collecting as a hobby.

I will never forget the day I found replacements for my childhood Talking Barbie (and Casey, her cousin) in a doll store in L.A. Something clicked. Before you knew it, I was also collecting vintage Barbie outfits. Then, the collectible Barbie dolls. Next thing, my mother found some of my childhood dolls and returned them to me—my Tammy, Penny Brite, Mary Poppins, Crissy, and Dawn. It wasn't long after that and I was off researching and learning about 1960s dolls.

My growing interest in antique dolls was not far behind. First, I started to look for them in antique stores, then I started attending doll shows and auctions. I also studied porcelain dollmaking, including reproduction antique dollmaking which helped me delve deeply into the history and manufacture of antique dolls. All this was happening in the early 1990s.

In 1994, something earth-shattering happened. I was on bed rest due to a difficult pregnancy. And I was bored. My husband got me a computer in my bedroom, and for the first time I hooked up to the Internet. The first thing I found was the CompuServe doll forums, where I immediately found a like-minded group of doll collectors. A few months later, I found the AOL forums for doll collecting.

My child was born, and one thing led to another. In early 1996, I was one of the first buyers and sellers of dolls on eBay (at the time, called AuctionWeb). I also started a rudimentary website for my doll business. In the late 1990s, I started lecturing on the burgeoning subject of doll collecting and the Internet at national UFDC (United Federation of Doll Clubs) conventions. By 1997 I had joined About.com, where I am still the guide to doll collecting.

I continue to be an avid doll collector. Currently, my personal collection consists of more than 2,000 dolls including antique, vintage, fashion, and modern dolls, although throughout my life I have owned many thousands of dolls. I am an active member of a UFDC doll collector's club called Just About Dolls. I also own a doll store called Katherine's Cottage (after my daughter), which you can find at www.katherinescottage.com and which carries all the latest modern dolls as well as antique and vintage dolls. I have written articles for many magazines, and I lecture on various doll topics, including the history of fashion dolls, Barbie, and, of course, dolls and the Internet. In other words, I live and breathe dolls, and I absolutely love it.

DOLL COLLECTING AT ABOUT.COM AND THE OFFICIAL WEBSITE FOR THIS BOOK

The About.com doll collecting site is the largest informational site about doll collecting any-where in the world. There are over six years of articles, news, information, and facts about dolls and doll collecting on the site—literally, thousands of pages of information. For nearly two years, the website was also the official website for *Doll Reader* magazine. Additionally, there are active communities of doll collectors in our popular doll forums for doll collectors of all types, including antique doll collectors, modern doll collectors, and Barbie doll collec-tors. There are links to over 1,300 doll sites on the Internet, and the site is updated with doll news on a nearly daily basis. Our popular (and free) About Doll Collecting e-mail newsletter goes out to over 10,000 collectors on a weekly basis. The website is at www. collectdolls.about.com. Since links to information on the site may change before publication of this book, you can access all of the major links to that site plus updates to this book and much more at www.officialpriceguidetodolls.com, the official website for this book.

1 HOW TO COLLECT DOLLS: THE ADVENTURE OF DOLL COLLECTING

Doll collecting has been the greatest adventure of my life. It has led me to lifelong friends, worldwide travel, and research into historical periods and topics that I might never have considered otherwise. I have been to dozens of cities in the United States for doll conventions and auctions, I have enjoyed many a fine dawn at flea markets and garage sales, I've had the thrill of wins (and losses) at auctions, and I've had my life enriched beyond measure by having dolls and all of their history, art, and drama in my life.

If you are reading this book, you have some interest in dolls. Perhaps you simply want to know the value of some old family dolls. Perhaps you've been gently bitten by the doll-collecting bug, are starting to frequent flea markets and eBay, and are trying to find out more. Perhaps you are already a full-fledged doll collector who cannot get enough of dolls! Wherever you are on this continuum, I hope that this book will help you along on your journey, and pull you even further into the great adventure of doll collecting.

What is a Doll?

How do you define what a doll is? There is a great debate in the doll-collecting community about what qualifies as a doll. For many years, you could define a doll as a representation of the human form created for a child's play. However, with the advent of collectors and dolls made especially for the collector's market, that definition is no longer inclusive enough. And, if you just define dolls as three-dimensional representations of the human form, that definition is *too* broad—it includes figurines, statues, and other items that are clearly not thought of as dolls.

For many collectors, and for purposes of this book, a doll is defined as a three-dimensional representation of the human form with some sort of jointing. Therefore, a figurine is not a doll. Therefore, a three-dimensional representation of an animal is, generally, not a doll. Of course, definitions being what they are, certain dolls that do not fit the definition are included in this book—notably, half dolls, bathing beauties, Frozen Charlottes, and piano babies. The only reason for this is that these items have generally been classified as dolls by collectors and are eagerly collected along with traditional dolls. Another exception to the rule is paper dolls, which are two dimensional. There will be a section on paper dolls, since so many doll collectors also have paper dolls in their collections. Finally, due to collecting customs and space limitations, other human representations such as Santa Clauses, fantasy figures, and action figures will not be included in this book.

Why Collect Dolls?

Why do so many people collect dolls? There are almost as many reasons as there are collectors. Some of the most compelling reasons include:

Art: People unfamiliar with dolls might regard collecting dolls as a superficial, inconsequential, even childish pursuit. After all, dolls have been mainly children's playthings

Group of Santa Claus figures. Are they dolls?

The author, age one, with a favorite baby doll.

Antique lawyer's bookcase converted into display cabinet for small all-bisque and dollhouse dolls in the home.

throughout history—not objects of attention for grown women and men.

What such people miss is that each doll, even one originally created for children, is an individual work of art and craftsmanship. The art of dolls is sometimes most evident in modern one-of-a-kind artist dolls, where artists individually sculpt, dress, and finish each doll individually by hand, and then sell the doll for several thousand dollars. But art is apparent in nearly every type of doll, even those manufactured by the millions. These dolls are art because each doll starts as a sculpture—sometimes elegant sculpture for a doll like the antique Bru or Jumeau, sometimes whimsical sculpture (think Liddle Kiddles, Whimsies, Reminder Angels), and sometimes representative sculpture, where the essence of the human form and face is captured and stylized by the artist (think Kewpies, Martha Chase Dolls, even Barbie dolls).

Doll costuming is also art—textile art, through use of fabric and through design. A well-designed doll costume can capture the essence of a decade sometimes better than a photo from the period.

Investment: Many collectors are attracted by the value of dolls, and their potential to increase in value over time. Some collectors are fascinated that a doll costing $3 in their childhood (such as the first Barbie doll) can be worth many thousands of dollars today. Others understand the historic value and rarity of early dolls such as Hurets and Brus from the second half of the 1800s, with prices often exceeding $10,000 per doll.

Others, of course, are simply interested in the investment value of dolls. It's true that many, many dolls have increased greatly in value over time. Take the example of the above-mentioned first (#1) Barbie doll. Originally retailing for $3, that doll today is worth, in mint condition with the original box, between $5,000 and $7,000. Bisque antique dolls such as Jumeau and German character dolls that sold for under $100 in the 1970s can easily bring $3,000 and up today. Even some modern dolls have greatly appreciated in value; for instance, the first Happy Holiday Barbie, which sold for $29.99 in 1988, now costs $400 on the secondary market, and the first Gene doll by Mel Odom, "Premiere," which cost $69 at issue in 1995, is now $300 on the secondary market.

To think, however, that all dolls simply escalate in value would be a huge mistake. There have been many "crashes" in doll prices—the notable crashes of the prices of modern

Madame Alexander dolls in the 1980s and the crash of Collectible Barbie doll prices in the late 1990s come to mind. The down economy from 2001 to 2003 adversely affected prices on many dolls. And, overall, the Internet has had a substantial downward effect on many doll prices (including the aforementioned 1990s Barbie dolls)—but much more on this later.

So the question remains—can you still collect for investment? Of course! If a collector has a good eye and can select uncommon, quality dolls which have great or growing collector demand, that collector can see a good return on their investment over time. BUT the oldest and most often-repeated advice about doll collecting is "buy what you love" and that advice bears repeating here. If you buy dolls that you love and want to own, then you can't go wrong if the economy, Internet, or the whims and fashions of doll collectors later reduce the value of your purchase. If you buy only with an eye to investment, then you really do have nothing if the investment value isn't there.

Nostalgia: As already mentioned, many adults become doll collectors when they get nostalgic for the dolls of their youth. As adults, these collectors seek to replace the dolls from their childhood—baby boomers often collect the dolls of the 1950s and 1960s, Generation Xers the dolls of the 1970s and early 1980s, and so on. Often, it doesn't take these same collectors very long to branch out into dolls of other eras.

Collectors have also embraced reproductions of their childhood dolls—numerous dolls have been reproduced in the last 15 years, including vintage Barbie, Ginny, Betsy McCall, Betsy Wetsy, Patti Playpal, Terri Lee, Cissy, Strawberry Shortcake, Dawn, and countless others.

Finally, dolls also depict the clothes and lifestyles of earlier eras, which draws people nostalgic for those eras to them.

Fun/Play: Dolls are fun! With our over-packed, stressful lives, dolls are a refuge of fun and play. As it becomes more acceptable for adults to have toys (yes, electronics, sporting equipment, and all other forms of collectibles are definitely toys) adults—mostly women—have become more comfortable with owning and playing with dolls. Of course, not all women are comfortable with buying themselves a doll. I cannot tell you how many times women come into my doll shop and exclaim "if only I had a little girl to buy these dolls for" and then how shocked they look when I tell them that the dolls aren't made for little girls at all, but are made for adult collectors. This book is part of my unofficial crusade to make such people open their eyes to doll collecting as a respectable adult hobby. Millions of women (and, yes, men) collect dolls, and doll collecting is the second biggest collecting hobby after stamps. If you are a bit sheepish about picking up this book and/or collecting dolls, now is the time to put those qualms to rest.

And, to get back on point, this respectable adult hobby is FUN! Some collectors are happy to simply own their dolls, and they wouldn't dream of taking a modern Barbie out of its box or redressing an 1890s Simon & Halbig bisque doll. But more and more collectors enjoy and play with their dolls—antique collectors will often sew for their dolls or buy them additional clothing, and modern doll collectors will often go so far as to repaint, rewig, recostume, and re-everything else their dolls! Doll clubs are a form of social play (sharing and learning about dolls as a group) as are online doll communities.

Thrill of the Hunt: Collectors often enjoy the process of adding dolls to their collections—the thrill of the hunt. Hunting grounds can include garage sales, estate auctions, family and neighbor's attics, thrift stores, doll shows, doll shops, antique stores, and auctions. The enjoyable process of discovery—and, sometimes, getting something wonderful for nearly nothing—is often the reason that some collectors collect.

History: Some collectors who love history are drawn to collecting general antiques or vintage collectibles, but it would be hard to find any antique or collectible that can tell us as much about history as a doll. Dolls can teach us about the style of dress of a particular time period. Their costumes can teach us about fashion and textile history, their accessories can teach us about the lifestyles and activities of an era, their wigs about the hairstyles of their day. When you study vintage and antique dolls, you learn much about the lives of the children who owned the dolls, and you also learn about manufacturing history—in fact, about history itself. Most major world events, including World Wars I and II and even 9/11, have had profound impacts on the doll industry.

Owning dolls is like owning a piece of history in your hands. The early 1960s Barbie doll is a true historical artifact of the 1960s, as is a French bébé of the 1870s. They embody their time and place in history.

Display: There are collectors who have no interest in history, investment, or playing with dolls. These collectors like the way dolls look, and they make dolls an integral part of their homes. Antique dolls can be desirable accents to Victorian or earlier era homes. Modern fashion dolls look sleek and sculpture-like in a modern home. And charming childhood dolls are perfect for the nursery. Collectors who collect for decoration and display are often not as interested in doll research or prices for their dolls as are traditional doll collectors.

Community: When you start to collect dolls, you become part of a worldwide community of collectors. This alone can be a powerful reason to continue to collect dolls. On the Internet, there are communities centered around discussion boards or forums. Doll clubs are local communities, and many collectors meet friends from around the nation and the world at yearly collectors' conventions.

Fashion: Some collectors are barely interested in the dolls. They view them as necessary hangers for the far-more-interesting (to them!) clothing. And, the clothing on dolls is fascinating. It is hard to look at an intricately

embroidered, perfectly hand-sewn garment for a French fashion doll of the 1860s, or a tiny, detailed luncheon suit for Barbie from 1965 and not be completely enchanted. Doll clothing also reflects, usually with extreme accuracy, the fashions of the era the doll is from.

Finally, doll fashions can be wish-fulfillment. In our jeans and sweatshirts world, owning couture evening gowns with our modern fashion dolls, or an elaborate, embroidered christening outfit with a baby doll, may by far be the closest we come to owning and enjoying elaborate clothing and fashion.

Where to Collect Dolls

In the past decade, the Internet has brought a huge world of doll collecting, doll knowledge, and doll purchasing right to your door. The Internet provides a large marketplace and an amazing resource for doll collectors. But it is important not to put Internet blinders on. The Internet is not the only game in town, and if all your collecting energy is focused on the Internet, it can narrow and stagnate your collection. Even if you are a veteran Internet collector, I truly believe that the Internet should supplement real-world doll collecting and not be the whole focus of your collecting experience. If you focus only on collecting on the Internet, you'll miss out on all the knowledge, friends, and experience that you can gain only by attending doll shows and auctions, visiting doll shops, and attending doll club meetings and conventions.

Plus (and this is a very important point, one that permeates this book where you see differences between Internet and real-world doll prices) seeing a photo of a doll is **not** the same a seeing a doll in person. Ever. The opportunity to be affected by a doll emotionally and the opportunity to examine a doll in person is far superior to viewing a photo, especially a relatively low-resolution photo on the Internet. This is true for both antique and modern dolls, where there can be slight differences in doll expression, face painting,

Katherine's Cottage, author's doll shop in Chico, CA.

hair, and other details from doll to doll that are not evident when you cannot see the doll in person.

Doll Shops—The Heart of Doll Collecting:
I once won an online eBay auction for a vintage Miss Revlon from the 1950s, MIB. The doll looked incredible in the online auction photos. When I received the doll, she was just as lovely when I took her out of the box—until I looked at the *back* of the doll, where the entire dress of the doll was severely faded. Evidently, the doll had spent quite a long time standing in someone's window, and the online seller failed to disclose this or hadn't noticed. In any event, I did get my money back from the transaction.

This type of online peril is one very good reason why you should *not* ignore doll shops. Local doll shops are a very important source of dolls. Without your local doll shop, there would be no place to see new dolls in person. Doll shop owners and staff are often knowledgeable about a wide variety of dolls from a wide variety of manufacturers, artists, and eras (including antique and vintage dolls if the store sells them). Without shops, artists and manufacturers would have fewer places to sell their dolls and showcase their dolls, leading to fewer dolls being produced.

A beautiful doll shop can be place of inspiration and discovery. Perhaps you collect only modern dolls, and that's fine, but you might get exposed to (and fall in love with) antique dolls at your local shop after seeing them in person. Or vice-versa! At shops, collectors can find new dolls from previously undiscovered artists and manufacturers and also new types and eras of dolls to collect. Sure, you can see photos of dolls all over the Internet, but did you ever fall in love with a doll from a photo? Doll shops also usually support their local doll clubs in many ways, and they often offer doll repair. Doll shops have collector events. Plus one of the most important things about doll shops is that they bring new collectors into our hobby on a regular basis—this is why I call doll shops the heart of doll collecting.

You can find local doll shops in your local yellow pages, through all major doll magazines, and in the Doll Shop Directory at www.officialpriceguidetodolls.com.

Doll Shows and Dealers: Doll dealers often don't have a physical doll shop, but they offer their dolls via doll shows, magazines, mail, and the Internet, and they are an invaluable source for vintage and antique dolls. In many cities and towns there are periodic doll shows. Shows are usually organized by a doll club or a show promoter. They bring many doll dealers into one place at one time, which makes comparison of dolls for sale easy and convenient, and it also affords the same type of inspiration and discovery that a doll shop can. Plus the great variety of dolls all in one location at a large doll show, usually including rare and unusual dolls, is a fantastic learning experience that is hard to duplicate in any other way. Doll shows and doll dealers can be found through doll magazines, in local advertisements, and via online searches.

Doll Clubs: If you have more than just a passing interest in dolls, then I implore you to join your local doll club! There are many types of doll clubs—clubs for Barbie and fashion doll collectors, clubs for antique collectors, and clubs for collectors of all types of dolls. My recommendation for a doll club would be a general doll collecting club affiliated with the UFDC, the United Federation of Doll Clubs. These clubs offer educational and research resources, as well as fun. Local clubs often have commercial sections during their meetings where collectors can buy, sell, and trade dolls and where they can showcase through show and tell the new dolls they have obtained. If there is no club in your area, you can also join an online doll club affiliated with the UFDC, or you can even start your own. You can often find an existing club via www.ufdc.org. If you cannot attend doll club meetings and you are not interested in an online doll club, you can join the UFDC as a MAL (member at large). MALs get the UFDC magazine and newsletters, and they can attend all UFDC events and conventions.

Television Shopping Channels: Television shopping channels have created thousands of new doll collectors. Dolls from major modern doll artists and manufacturers such as Marie Osmond, Lee Middleton, Donna RuBert, Seymour Mann, Fayzah Spanos, Mattel, Rustie, Richard Simmons (Collection of the Masters), Lee Middleton, Boyds, Kingsgate, Pauline, Zapf, and many, many others can be found on QVC and HSN, the

two major television shopping networks. And what could be better than sitting at home in your fuzzy slippers and pj's, and purchasing dolls with a quick phone call?

Antique Shops: Antique shops and antique malls are good sources of older vintage and antique dolls, especially if you don't have a doll shop or doll dealer carrying older dolls in your area. It is getting harder and harder to find hidden treasures since the advent of eBay, as many dolls that would have been put in antique shops and antique malls in the 1980s and early 1990s now go directly to eBay. As for pricing, beware—often a general antiques dealer will price a doll at full "book" price for an excellent condition doll, even if the doll has major flaws, replaced clothing, or other problems.

Flea Markets: Flea markets are a source for all types of dolls—antique through modern. The same caveats on availability and pricing apply to flea markets as to antique shops, and over the past 20 years the selection of good dolls at these markets has definitely decreased. However, you can often find interesting dolls from the second half of the 20th century at flea markets, even if they are not expensive dolls in pristine condition. Remember to get to the flea market early, since it's true that the best dolls are snapped up before the latecomers arrive.

Garage/Estate Sales: Garage and estate sales are still a popular and fun way to obtain dolls. Wake up early, get there first, and think fast! The best dolls can be gone in minutes.

Live Doll Auctions: Auctions are an exciting and educational way to obtain dolls. You can find auctions featuring dolls close to home, at local estate auctions, and you can also find auctions specializing in dolls in major cities. For example, Theriault's, www.theriaults .com, is a leading international auction house that specializes in dolls. The majority of the photos in the color section of this book are photos of dolls that Theriault's has auctioned over the years, and several hundred other photographs of dolls in this book are also of dolls they have auctioned. Theriault's holds several auctions each year in cities around the United States.

It is important to know your prices before you attend a live auction—at an auction, two determined collectors with a good reserve of cash is all it takes to have a doll bring a price well over what it is worth. Plus it is easy to lose your head in the heat of the auction battle with the excitement of so many beautiful dolls in the room! Here are some tips for attending a live doll auction:

- **Obtain the Catalog in Advance of the Auction:** The more time you have to look over the dolls in the auction catalog, the smarter your bidding decisions will be. You can research market values prior to the auction using this book, previous auction prices, and online prices. You can also narrow down the dolls you are truly interested in bidding for and save your preview time for a close examination of those dolls. If you are attending an uncataloged auction, sometimes you can get a list of dolls faxed to you just prior to the auction.

- **Dress Comfortably and Don't Forget to Eat:** Auctions can run many hours, and you will want to be as comfortable as possible so you are not distracted from the bidding, plus comfortable shoes will help you survive being on your feet at the auction preview. Don't forget to eat something prior to the auction, since auctions often run all day, and you don't want to make poor bidding decisions due to lightheadedness from lack of food.

- **Pack the Following Items:** A snack, a small flashlight (to check for hairlines and damage), this book (for checking values, especially at an uncataloged auction), pen and paper for notes, your checkbook, a seller's ID if you are buying for a business, and your identification to establish your bidder's account.

- **Get to the Preview When It Opens:** No matter how good (or bad!) a doll looks in a catalog, it will always look different in person. This is why time spent at the auction preview prior to the auction is essential. You may mark ten dolls in your catalog, and then bid on five completely different dolls after seeing and examining the dolls at the preview. Plan to arrive early, since previews are often two hours or less, and there can be hundreds of auctiongoers all crowded in a small room trying to preview several hundred dolls. Time before the crowd builds can be valuable.

- **Save a Seat:** Auctions can be very crowded! As soon as you arrive, use your pad or your doll value book, a sweater, or something to save a seat.

- **Check the Dolls Carefully Prior to Auction:** Try not to bid on dolls you have not examined prior to the auction. Try to inspect the condition of all dolls you intend to bid on. For a bisque doll, remove the wig and put your flashlight inside to reveal any repairs, hairlines, or damage. Consider if the body of a doll, or perhaps its arms or legs, have been replaced. If a lot of dolls are in boxes, and the boxes are stacked and rubber-banded, take the whole thing apart and look at each doll! You get the idea. Remember, uncataloged auctions are buyer beware, although, obviously, not all dolls sold at uncataloged auctions are fatally flawed. Personally, I've purchased UFDC blue ribbon–winning dolls at uncataloged auctions, and you can too, if you are careful.

- **Set Spending Limits:** You should determine your high bid for each doll, and stick to it. Your high bid does not necessarily mean your bid will be in the range of the presale estimate. You might be interested only in certain dolls if they are a bargain and come in under the presale estimate. For other dolls, your predetermined high bid could be double the presale estimate if you want the items badly enough. An overall budget is important as well—remember, it is easy to get carried away in the heat of bidding when you see so many beautiful dolls!

Display of Muffie dolls at 2003
Modesto UFDC Doll Convention.
With permission of Elaine Pardee.

- **Don't Forget the Buyer's Premium:** During the auction, when you are bidding and when you are adding up what you have spent, don't forget the buyer's premium. The amount of the premium can vary, generally from 10% to 15%, and they can quickly make a doll that seems like a bargain not such a great bargain after all.

- **When You Win a Doll, Check It Carefully:** Generally, you must check all items you purchase at a doll auction when the doll is delivered to you or at the checkout—not later back in your room or at home. For cataloged auctions, if you find a flaw that was undisclosed in the catalog (such as a hairline crack or a missing finger) the auction house will generally take the item back. For uncataloged auctions, auction houses may take back bisque dolls with undisclosed flaws as well.

- **If You Are Traveling By Air:** Special Advice: Since 9/11, it has become much more difficult to transport dolls via the major airlines. Right now, the best way to transport dolls when flying is in your carry-on luggage. Even then, be prepared to have your dolls unwrapped and handled when going through the security line. If you plan to check your luggage with dolls in it, you need to know that you can no longer lock your luggage, since most airports now randomly hand-screen luggage, sometimes out of the view of passengers. Also, most airlines will not insure luggage with antiques.

- **Go to the Auction Even if You Don't Plan to Buy Anything:** If you are a collector of vintage or antique dolls, or if you are a dollmaker, do not miss a chance to go to a doll auction! Other than museums, doll conventions, and doll shows, there generally isn't a better opportunity to see rare and unique dolls than at a doll auction.

Doll Conventions: Imagine hundreds or even thousands of doll collectors who share your collecting interests at a giant party that lasts several days. Imagine that there is a huge salesroom with thousands of dolls for sale, and lunches and dinners with very limited dolls as souvenirs. Imagine doll competitions, seminars and lectures by doll experts, and a grand banquet to end the party. You've just imagined a doll convention! There are general doll conventions such as the UFDC and Collectors United conventions that are held yearly and attended by thousands of collectors. There are also conventions that focus on a particular category of dolls, such as the Modern Doll Collector's convention, the Fashion Doll Collector's convention, and the Paper Doll Collector's convention. And, there are conventions for individual types of dolls—Barbie, Gene, Nancy Ann Storybook, Madame Alexander, Tonner Dolls, Dawn—and many of these are also held yearly. Doll conventions are exciting opportunities to cram as much doll fun and education as you can possibly imagine into a few days, and their doll salesrooms often offer remarkable varieties of dolls for sale. You'll also make lifelong friends who share your hobby. You can find conventions easily on the Internet, or through the resources listed in Appendix 2 of this book.

Internet: The Internet has changed the face of doll collecting. The Internet has had a profound impact on doll pricing and availability, and has permeated nearly every aspect of doll collecting. See the section on the Internet below for detailed information on how to collect dolls on the Internet, and for more information on the impact of the Internet on the hobby of doll collecting.

Factors in Doll Pricing: What Makes a Desirable Doll

There are numerous factors that make a doll desirable to collect. Although desirability is, to some extent, an individual thing (an antique doll collector might not think a modern Robert Tonner doll is desirable, and a modern Robert Tonner doll collector might not think old, antique dolls are desirable) there are some overall factors that most collectors consider.

Face of the Doll: The head and face of a doll are the heart of a doll. An attractive and well-molded head is essential for making a doll desirable. For instance, when collecting antique dolls, you can see huge differences in the molding and detail in dolls' heads depending on when they came out of the mold—the newer the mold, the better the detail and modeling. Dolls that have come out of old molds can have a dull, flat, and less three-dimensional appearance than dolls from the same mold that were produced when the mold was new. Another factor is the painting of the face of the doll. Most vintage and antique dolls have hand-painted faces, and you can see huge differences in techniques and style for face painting on the same doll. For instance, one of the most common antique dolls is the Armand Marseille 390 from Germany, which was in production for well over 30 years. Some of these dolls have rudimentary painting, with single-stroke eyebrows, and no painted upper eyelashes at all. Other 390s can have beautifully feathered, painted eyebrows and individually painted lashes that rival the painting on more expensive French bisque. Therefore, the painting and molding on any particular doll can affect the value of that doll either upward or downward from book value for a typical doll.

Damage: Any damage to a doll will lower the value and the desirability of that doll. Some damage may be expected in an older doll—as an example, most composition dolls from the mid-20th century have minor crazing (tiny cracks which form in the composition surface over time). Minor crazing doesn't detract very much from the desirability or value of such dolls, since it is such a common occurrence caused by the age of the doll. However, deep or extensive crazing, or wide cracking or lifting of the composition, affects value. Also, most antique bisque dolls have wear from age—this is to be expected in the clothing and bodies of the dolls, and doesn't detract from their desirability.

Actual damage to antique bisque dolls, such as hairline cracks (cracks in the bisque that are hard to see with the naked eye) or actual cracks, repairs, or major body repainting or patches lowers the desirability of the doll and therefore the pricing. One interesting effect of the healthy antique doll market of the last few years is that as the prices for antique dolls continue to rise, it gets harder and harder to find dolls in original condition and minor damage such as hairline cracks do not make dolls as undesirable as they used to be. At auctions and in shops, collectors used to refuse to purchase dolls with hairline cracks except at deep discounts. Now, more and more of these dolls sell for good prices (al-

The beauty of a doll's face is all-important in determining value. Madame Alexander Babs Skater doll. Courtesy Cathy Messenger.

though generally below book value), especially when the hairlines are barely noticeable and not on the face of the dolls. Buying slightly damaged dolls for personal enjoyment, if the discount is fair, can help a collector afford rarer examples of dolls that might not be affordable otherwise. If you do buy damaged dolls, remember that location of damage on the doll is paramount—if the doll's face is visibly damaged, most of the value of a doll is gone, but damage to the body, the back of the head under the wig or the lower back of a doll shoulder plate will have much less of an effect on value. Minor damage that is not noticeable when a doll is displayed has a smaller downward effect on value.

As for most modern dolls, the effect of any damage on a modern doll can make the doll lose most of its value no matter where the damage on the doll is located, because modern dolls, in mint condition, are generally in plentiful supply.

Originality: As it gets harder and harder to find antique and older vintage dolls in completely original condition, dolls found with original clothing, or dolls found with original extras such as boxes, tags, and accessories continue to greatly outpace the pricing for other dolls. More and more of a premium is

added for dolls in all-original conditions. Sometimes, a mint antique doll found in undeniably original clothing, and sometimes with an original box or extra, can easily double or triple book value. Mint store presentations of very common dolls have become more highly valuable and desirable as fewer and fewer of them are available to collectors. For mint vintage dolls in all-original presentations with boxes and accessories, the same is true. One caveat—frequently, antique dolls are sold in clothing that is "original," but often all that can be fairly determined without other examples or documentation is that the old clothing the doll is wearing is of the time period and appropriate to the doll.

For modern dolls, complete originality is expected, and a doll *not* in original clothing or in its original box will greatly reduce the value and desirability of that doll.

Condition: Perhaps this section should start with condition, as it is the most important thing to consider when considering the desirability of a doll, but looking at damage and originality first is important, as they are aspects of condition. However, condition is more than considering damage and originality. When valuing the price or desirability of a doll, it is important to look at how much the doll has been played with, and how much aging has happened to the doll over time—the condition of a doll.

Again, here we have a double standard, with mint condition (unplayed-with condition) being expected in most modern dolls (1980s–2000s) and with less than mint condition being fine with antique or vintage dolls. Book values for antique and vintage dolls generally are for dolls in excellent condition, with appropriate clothing. Book values for modern dolls are for mint dolls. Of course, there is a sliding scale depending on the exact age of a doll. Any doll surviving from the 1700s tends to be valuable and desirable no matter what the condition, yet common dolls in mint condition from the last two decades might not have any value or desirability at all. See more on condition in the section "How To Use This Book."

Rarity: The rarity of a doll affects its desirability and value, but it is not paramount. A very, very rare doll, if it is ugly or if it doesn't appeal to collectors for other reasons (such as a rubber-head doll from the 1800s), may be priced well below a very common, but heavily collected doll (such as a Shirley Temple or a Tête Jumeau, which are actually fairly common dolls which have heavy collector demand). However, generally speaking, dolls that are rarer are valued higher, when demand is present.

Demand and Internet Effects on Prices: This is one of the variables that most heavily affects the value and desirability of a doll today. Thanks to the Internet, if a doll is common and in plentiful supply, everyone knows it, since the doll will have multiple auctions, nearly every day, on eBay. For some common dolls, the demand is there to meet the supply, and prices remain steady—dolls such as 1950s Ginny dolls, or Shirley Temple dolls. For other dolls, supply has increased well beyond the demand for the doll, and the desirability and prices for the doll have plummeted. For instance, the Gene fashion doll produced by Ashton Drake from 1996 to 2003 has been a popular collector doll, but it has been overproduced and

despite continued collector demand, there is too great a supply of the doll, especially at Internet auctions. Therefore, most prices for Gene are now below the retail prices that the doll originally sold for.

Another example of how great supply can outstrip demand for a doll is with vintage Barbie (Barbies produced from 1959 to 1972). Vintage Barbie prices peaked in the 1990s, before the onslaught of Internet auctions. There are many, many vintage Barbie collectors, and when the dolls could be obtained only from dealers, auctions, and shows, competition was fierce and prices were high. Now, everyone can take their old Barbies out of their garage or attic and put them on eBay. This has caused prices to drop drastically. However, vintage Barbies are still a desirable collectible, and mint or NRFB examples still bring high prices. It's the common dolls in average condition that have suffered the most, price-wise, due to excessive supply.

Overall, that's the most important thing to remember about supply and demand—common dolls in average condition, in the age of the Internet, are not as desirable to collectors as they once were, thanks to the Internet, and their prices reflect that. The plus side of this equation is that it allows collectors to build lovely collections at good prices, especially if they are handy and have skills that allow them to fix up these common, average dolls.

Perceived Value: If a doll is too easy to obtain, or if a doll is sold again and again at heavily discounted prices, a doll (especially a modern one) can lose its cachet as a desirable collectible.

Modern Dolls—Limited Editions, Store Specials, Convention Dolls: Most modern dolls made for collectors are in plentiful supply. If you collect modern dolls, the smaller the edition of the doll, generally, the more desirable it is. For modern large-size fashion dolls (Tyler Wentworth, Gene, Brenda Starr, Willow, and Daisy) the average size of an edition is 1,000 to 2,000 dolls. Certain dolls

This Angelina doll by the Tonner Doll Co. was a limited edition of only 400 dolls, issued for the Tonner dinner at the 2003 UFDC National Convention.

are produced in even smaller editions. You can find small editions through store specials (dolls created for one store only), through conventions (dolls produced as favors for events, in very small editions) and sometimes through happenstance (in the last year of production, the Willow and Daisy dolls were produced in very small numbers, and sometimes a manufacturer doesn't produce an entire edition due to fabric shortages or other problems).

Overall Appeal—The "Look": Some dolls just have "it." For whatever reason—the way their face is painted, their costuming, extras like hang tags and accessories, or a combination of several factors, some dolls simply look more appealing to doll collectors than others. They have "the look" of iconic dolls of their type, and therefore, they are more desirable to a greater number of collectors. Collectors will pay more for this appeal.

Collectible Dolls Today

Modern collectible dolls are a relatively new phenomenon. Dolls produced for collectors, and not for children, really began to be made only in the 1980s. Until that time, most collectors collected dolls originally made for children—almost all vintage and antique dolls were originally children's playthings.

Modern collectible dolls have vastly changed doll collecting, and have brought many collectors into the hobby. These collectors are not looking to replace the dolls from their childhood, and they are not necessarily attracted to older dolls and their history. These collectors want to collect dolls for many of the reasons we discussed in the beginning of this book—because they are art, because they are fun, because they are (or could become) valuable, or because they are pretty and look great at the collector's home.

Modern Doll Editions: Most modern collectible dolls are produced in some type of limited edition, limited either by the time of production, or the number of dolls produced. Here are some popular edition types:

- **One of a Kind Dolls (OOAK):** A doll produced by an artist, in an edition of one. Generally an "art" doll, one that is individually sculpted and dressed by the doll artist.

- **Artist Limited Editions:** Dolls also individually made by a doll artist, but in a small edition of anywhere from 3 to 25 dolls.

- **Limited Edition Manufactured Dolls:** Manufactured dolls, created in a defined, limited number. Can be any amount of dolls; generally from 500 to thousands. Most limited edition dolls are numbered and have a certificate which shows the number of the doll, such as #842 of 1,000, in an edition of 1,000 dolls. This is the most common way that modern collector dolls are produced. Barbie dolls are an exception to the small numbers of limited edition dolls—because there is such great worldwide collector demand for Barbie, her limited editions can be as high as 35,000 dolls (as of the latest definition—this number had changed several times in the last decade). Limited edition Barbie dolls generally are not individually numbered, nor do they come with an individually numbered certificate, nor do Robert Tonner dolls.

- **Annual Editions:** Dolls limited to one year of production. Dolls can also be limited to one day or one week of production. The Lee Middleton Doll Company, which produces collectible baby dolls, often limits its editions to one day or one week.

- **Open Editions:** No limit on the edition. Not recommended for collecting, since if the doll is popular, the manufacturer can simply produce and produce until all collector demand is met—even for ten years!

Discounting and eBay: Rampant discounting of modern collectible dolls by doll retailers has hurt the collectibility and value of some modern lines of dolls. Doll manufacturers are fighting back, with new contracts with dealers that don't allow discounting beyond a certain percentage and that prohibit sales on eBay, or otherwise limit eBay sales. This can only be good, overall, for the modern collectible doll industry, and therefore also good for modern doll collectors, since perceived value of a doll is important for keeping the value of the doll high.

Home Shopping Networks: Home shopping networks have been a great boon to modern doll collecting. Home shopping networks have brought thousands of new collectors to the hobby of doll collecting— collectors who might never have been exposed to modern collectible dolls in any other way. Many modern doll manufacturers, including Charisma Dolls which produces Marie Osmond Dolls, have built their businessees on the home shopping network shows. These shows are here to stay. When collecting from QVC, HSN, or any other shopping channel, keep the section on doll desirability and value in mind, and also how large an edition of dolls is. Also keep in mind that even a small edition of dolls, say 500 dolls, may be too large an edition if the collector base for that doll just isn't there.

Reproduction Dolls—Manufactured Vintage Reproductions: Another large trend in doll collecting is to reproduce desirable dolls from earlier eras. Dolls such as vintage Barbie, Tiny Tears, Patti Playpal, Terri Lee, and many, many others have been reproduced in recent years. Generally, the reproduction of these dolls has not adversely affected doll prices for the original dolls, since reproductions never seem to completely or perfectly replicate the original doll. Also, reproductions are often priced lower than the original vintage dolls, and can often appeal to a different type of collector than the older dolls (some collectors don't want preowned or old dolls of any type!). Most reproductions have different markings or are clearly marked reproductions so there is not any confusion between the original vintage dolls and the reproduced dolls.

Reproduction Dolls—Antique Artist Reproductions: Other types of reproductions that are currently popular are reproductions of antique bisque and china dolls. These should not be confused with fakes or frauds, which are reproduced with the intent to deceive the purchaser. A legitimate reproduction doll will always be signed by the artist, either on the head or the shoulder plate, incised into the bisque, usually with the date of production. Many of these reproduction antique dolls are works of art in their own right, and command prices in the several-hundred-dollar range. The most popularly reproduced dolls are ones that are very expensive—Jumeaus, Brus, character German dolls—but nearly every type of antique doll is reproduced. I've seen small, inexpensive Frozen Charlottes reproduced, and penny

Dollmaking tools and reproduction bisque doll heads.

store all-bisque dolls. All can be very delightful and fun to make and collect.

If you are interested in making reproduction antique dolls, you can find a studio that teaches this art through the Doll Artisan Guild, at http://dollartisanguild.org.

Doll Customization and Fashion Doll Makeovers: Another hot area of modern doll collecting involves customized, repainted, made over, and "reborn" dolls. These are dolls that have been redone by collectors—some dolls are simply repainted (the original face paint is removed, and new face painting applied), some dolls are also redressed, others even are rewigged or the hair is reapplied completely. The most common dolls that are customized or given makeovers are fashion dolls, such as Barbie, Gene, and Tyler. However, even baby dolls are remade—Berenguer Baby dolls are popular dolls to be "reborn." Reborn baby dolls are customized by being either reassembled with a new body, or tinted and sometimes weighted for a realistic feeling. The painting and the hair is always redone.

Most doll companies have allowed makeover and customization artists to sell their remade dolls, as long as no company trademarks are used. These doll companies realize that the remade dolls are good for business and can drive sales of the original, underlying dolls. Dolls that have been repainted or remade by well-known artists can often sell for several hundred dollars. The majority of the market for customized dolls is on the Internet.

Displaying Dolls

For any collector of dolls, displaying dolls is a joy as well as a challenge. There are many things to consider when you display your dolls so that they don't end up looking like little soldiers, all standing together in the same boring row.

Props: Displaying dolls using props can help bring your dolls to life! One of the nicest displays of antique dolls I have ever seen had dolls placed around a guest room, with several dolls having a tea party, one doll riding a toy horse while another doll held the reins, and other dolls riding in antique toy carriages. The way the props were used brought the viewer into the charming world of these dolls and the children who played with them at the time they were made. You can also find tiny antique vanity sets, tiny antique stoves and pots, and many, many other types of antique accessories and toys to display with antique dolls. Some of the most popular props to display with older dolls are antique and vintage bears.

Selection of French fashion doll clothing, late 1800s.

Dolls displayed with various props.

Tyler Wentworth dolls, clothing, and accessories in wardrobe case.

Any type of doll display can be enhanced using props. Barbie dolls can be displayed in small vignettes, using 1/24 scaled miniatures as accessories, or you can use many of the wonderful Barbie branded accessories that have been produced by Mattel throughout the years (especially during the vintage Barbie period). Baby dolls can be displayed in old cradles, with quilts and baby care accessories. Large fashion dolls often have accessories available in their outfit packs.

Clothing and Accessories: A wonderful display can be made of clothing and accessories made for dolls—without any dolls! If you have extra clothing and accessories, you can display clothing on mannequin stands, and hats on hat stands. Small purses and other tiny things can be displayed on appropriately sized doll furniture. And dolls and accessories displayed alongside the appropriate antique doll can be wonderful.

Almost any fashion doll lends itself to a display with its things—an antique French fashion doll can be displayed with her trunk and its contents—antique white underwear, sewing necessaries, leather handbags, perfect leather shoes. Most modern fashion dolls have clothing and accessories of many types made for them—it's a shame to store it all out of sight in drawers.

Wardrobes and Cases: You can display your doll in its wardrobe or case, with clothing and accessories in the case on view as well. Or wardrobe cases make a nice backdrop to a display of related dolls—for instance, vintage Ginny cases with 1950s Ginny dolls, or 1960s vinyl Barbie cases with vintage Barbie.

Furniture: Doll furniture can be one of the most powerful display objects for your dolls. Antique doll furniture is perfect for antique dolls, as is newer doll furniture made to look antique. Baby dolls look great in cradles and high chairs (baby or doll size) and even tinier dolls such as Madame Alexander Wendy or Ginny have had furniture made especially for them.

Limiting Number of Dolls on Display: While a room filled with dolls can create an enticing display, sometimes the best way to have impact in your doll display is to limit the number of dolls on active display. Many collectors will rotate their dolls—displaying a small portion of their collection to its best advantage, and then storing those dolls and taking out another group to display. Some collectors will rotate based on doll theme—this month, celebrity dolls, next month, dolls dressed in red and green for Christmas. Other collectors rotate based on doll type

Vintage Barbie doll wardrobe case.

Large cabinets with glass fronts
protect dolls from dust, bugs, pets,
and other potential problems.

(for three months, they'll have a baby doll display, and then switch to antique character dolls and then to modern Barbies). Choices are endless, and each time you change your doll display, you will see your dolls in a new light.

Specific Rooms: Some collectors prefer to display their dolls in a separate room in their house. A guest room is often a popular choice, and dolls in a guest room can create a charming retreat for your guests—like a room at a bed and breakfast inn! Collectors who don't have to worry about pets and small children, or disapproving husbands (or wives!) might choose the family room or living room where the dolls can be enjoyed at all times. If collectors have home offices where they spend a majority of their time, they can create inviting working environments where they can be surrounded by the dolls they love. Finally, a garage or attic or workroom can be converted into a doll room. The only requirement is your imagination, and, for the best conservation of your dolls, a temperature-controlled room (see more on conservation below).

Display Everywhere in Your House: Of course, dolls don't have to be segregated into a separate display area or room. You can beautifully display dolls all throughout your house. Bathing or vanity-themed dolls can be in the bathroom, a showstopper-type doll in your entryway, perhaps some antique or modern collectible dolls on the shelves in your living or family room. Of course, if your house has children or pets, you might not want to display your most expensive dolls in this manner. If you are short on room in your home, you can find creative ways to incorporate your dolls throughout your home—one collecting friend I know has a shelf in the kitchen where she displays dolls baking cookies!

Cabinets: Many collectors choose to display their dolls in closed cabinets, and this has several advantages. First, it keeps dolls out of the prying hands of children and the prying paws of cats, dogs, and other pets. Dolls are nearly irresistible to children, and you might have a well-behaved pet, but some cats find mohair (made from goat's fur) wigs nearly irresistible as well. Second, cabinets will help conserve your dolls, protecting them from dust. You can make lovely displays in cabinets, using some of the display techniques in this section. Cabinets are available in a wide variety of styles to complement nearly any type of doll. Antique cabinets are wonderful with antique dolls, and modern cabinets in clean lines often work best with modern dolls, especially fashion dolls. If you cannot find an appropriately sized cabinet for your collection, you might try stores selling shop fixtures, where a wide variety of cabinet styles can be found, often for reasonable prices.

Artifacts of Childhood: This has been partially covered in the discussion on displaying dolls with props, but it deserves another mention, especially for collectors of antique dolls. Vintage collectibles and antiques that relate to childhood are hot collectibles, and they display beautifully with dolls. Teddy bears and other old plush, old games (with great graphics on the boxes), children's books, vintage tin pails, toy horses, and many other similar items are collectibles in their own right, and they truly bring displays of dolls to life.

Seasonal Displays: You can change your doll display by adding seasonal items—Easter bunnies and chicks for Easter, red, white and blue accessories for the Fourth of July, small Christmas trees and Santas for Christmas, and vintage pumpkins and witches for Halloween. Many vintage and antique holiday collectibles are popular in their own right. If you are a modern doll collector, craft stores such as Michaels often have small ornaments and holiday decor items perfectly sized for display with dolls. Even doll manufacturers have made holiday items for display with dolls—Ashton Drake has made their Gene fashion doll a doll-size tree, complete with doll-size ornaments.

Conservation Considerations: However you choose to display your dolls, make sure you read the section on doll conservation. Dust, dirt, light, humidity, and excessively high or low temperatures are the enemies of your dolls and their condition, and you must protect against these things when you display your dolls. This doesn't mean you cannot enjoy your dolls and cannot display them free of cabinets if you wish, but you should take these factors into account and protect against them as best you can. For instance, you might have your dolls charmingly displayed around your sewing room, but if your sewing room lets direct sunlight stream into the room, your dolls will quickly fade and have sun damage. Shades or curtains might be all you would need to make your room conservation friendly.

Focusing a Collection

Many collectors, over time, have their collecting activities hampered by practical factors. Perhaps they are running out of display space for their dolls, perhaps they have limited funds to spend on their collections, perhaps they have limited time to collect. One way to deal with almost all of these practical factors is to focus your collection on a particular era, type of doll, or theme. This will help you limit your collecting choices and perhaps spend your valuable collecting time gaining expertise in a smaller field of a very large collecting universe. There are almost endless ways to devise a focus for your collection, here are some of the most popular ones:

Focus By Era: Collectors who focus on era might pick something broad, like dolls from the 19th century (due to the expense of antique dolls, this might be enough of a focus) or they can pick something more defined, like dolls from the 1920s (bisque, bathing beauties, and composition). A collector who grew up in the 1960s might want to focus on the dolls of their childhood—Barbie, Liddle Kiddles, Chatty Cathy, and Patti Playpal. A collector who grew up in the 1980s, or any other decade, might want to do the same thing. Aficionados of large-size modern fashion dolls such as Gene and Tyler might only collect dolls from 1995 to today. Focusing on an era can still give you a diverse collection, yet limit your collecting choices enough so that you are not overwhelmed.

Manufacturer: You can also pick a favorite doll manufacturer, and focus on their dolls. For instance, antique doll collectors might only collect dolls from Kestner, Simon & Halbig, or Jumeau. A vintage doll fan might pick Ideal or Horsman, and a modern doll fan might pick Mattel or Robert Tonner. Again, although your universe of dolls to collect may be in the hundreds, if you focus on one manufacturer, it's no longer in the hundreds of thousands as it would be if you didn't focus.

Type of Doll: By type of doll, I don't mean Barbie or Bye-Lo Babies (see below) I mean genre—baby dolls or fashion dolls or toddler dolls. One of my collections centers on all-bisque dolls from all eras. Perhaps you also love dollhouses—you could pick dollhouse dolls. If you absolutely love composition dolls, you can focus on those. Again, you have a broad range of collecting possibilities, in most areas from antique to modern, yet your collection will take on a certain organization and you, again, have narrowed the collecting universe.

One-Doll Focus: For a more narrowly focused collection, try a collection of one type of doll! Many dolls have been produced in so many variations that a one-doll collection can be very interesting. Some of the best collections in the world focus on one type of doll, where the collector tries to find every possible variation. Perhaps you want to collect Ginny, who has been in production since the 1950s. An obvious choice is Barbie, but she has been created in so many countless varieties that you can focus even narrower for a large Barbie collection—vintage Barbies, or only Silkstone Barbies, or career Barbies, or high-fashion Barbies. Maybe you want to have the world's best collection of Kamkins. Or Raggedy Ann. Or Shirley Temple. A one-doll focused collection can be very large and endlessly interesting.

Theme (Celebrity, International, Wizard of Oz, Peter Pan, Christmas): Finally, you can choose to focus and organize your collection along a theme. Some themes are endlessly popular with doll manufacturers. Celebrity dolls have been made since the late 1800s, and are a very popular area—Shirley Temple, Deanna Durbin, Charlie Chaplin, and a whole host of television and movie stars and characters have been made into dolls. You can even focus narrower than that—perhaps only dolls that were television stars of the 1970s, or movie stars from the golden age of Hollywood.

You can even collect dolls based on one popular movie—there have literally been hundreds of dolls made representing the characters from *The Wizard of Oz*. Other popular movie-based doll collections include *Peter Pan* and *Gone With the Wind*.

Storybook characters are also a popular doll theme—collections can be centered on characters such as Little Red Riding Hood, Goldilocks, Hitty, Eloise, Olivia (the pig, made into a doll by Madame Alexander), and others.

Some collectors collect international dolls—dolls in costumed dress from countries around the world. Some collectors collect dolls by ethnicity—perhaps only Black dolls or Asian or Native American.

Finally, you could collect dolls associated with one holiday. Many modern manufacturers (and some vintage ones) have made Christmas-themed dolls, with Christmas clothing and/or Christmas names. Other holidays might be harder, but it would not be impossible to put together a Fourth of July doll collection or an Easter doll collection.

A Note about Teddy Bears

Teddy bears came into existence in 1902, when they were first manufactured in both the United States and Germany. They have been a companion collectible to dolls ever since. It is very common to see shops that specialize in both dolls and bears as well as auctions that have both dolls and bears, and it is very common for collectors of all types of dolls to display teddy bears with their dolls. Although modern collectible teddy bears are not as popular as they were a few years back, the markets for vintage and antique teddy bears continue to increase, with very rare and desirable antique bears sometimes valued in excess of $10,000. Whatever your collecting style or collecting budget, there are teddy bears that can fit in well with your dolls and which will display well with them. The value of teddy bears, for the most part, is beyond the scope of this book.

Steiff teddy bear and bird and
1960s Dakin Dream Pet displayed
with antique German bisque doll.

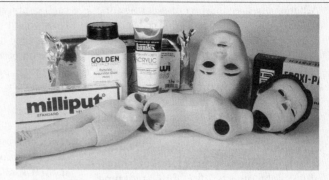

Doll restoration supplies.

A Note about Crossover Collectibles

Crossover collectibles are collectibles that can be at home in several collections. Dolls with Coca-Cola themes fit in both doll collections and Coca-Cola collections. *Wizard of Oz* dolls can be in *Wizard of Oz* collections as well as doll collections. The same with Shirley Temple dolls—there are collectors of Shirley Temple memorabilia that collect Shirley dolls not because they are dolls, but because they are part of the Shirley Temple world. Crossovers can be combined with dolls for strong and interesting displays. Additionally, dolls that are themselves crossover collectibles can often maintain their value better than other dolls, because the universe of collectors of those dolls is exponentially larger. Look for movie dolls (*Wizard of Oz, Gone With the Wind*), dolls of popular characters (Mickey and Minnie Mouse) and dolls with licensed product themes (Harley Davidson, Disney, Coca-Cola) to be strong crossover collectibles.

Doll Restoration: Necessity and Ethics

There is an epidemic in doll collecting—an epidemic of doll restoration. This epidemic has been fostered by the easy, open market of eBay and other online auction houses, which has allowed collectors to easily sell items from their collections (as well as their garage sale and estate sale finds). Naturally, a vintage or antique doll that is photo-ready with a perky dress, bright painted features, and a neat hairdo is going to sell more quickly than a doll with aged-looking clothing, faded paint, and flaws. So collectors by the thousands are taking their vintage and antique dolls that are not in mint condition, and they are doing everything in their power to make the doll and its outfit more perfect, by curling and styling the hair, washing, bleaching, and starching the doll costume (or replacing it entirely, whether it is original to the doll or not), and by even repainting facial features.

Now, I am not *necessarily* saying there is anything wrong with this, what I *am* saying is that there is a right way to restore a doll that preserves its originality, historical value, and that does not damage a doll. On the other hand, careless restoration can actually damage the value of the doll, and also destroy any historical value it might have. I agree strongly with, and cannot emphasize enough, the importance of the UFDC motto on doll conservation and restoration: **"Do nothing that cannot be undone."**

Additionally, a vital aspect of doll collecting is often overlooked by eager doll collectors—conservation of their dolls. To conserve a doll is to treat something that has already happened to the doll and halt the problem—for instance, restringing a doll with loose limbs, treating an insect infestation, resetting eyes that have fallen out, or stopping further melting of silk in a costume. Conservation goes hand in hand with preservation—to fight against the damaging forces of temperature, light, insects, dirt, dust, and time. Conservation, properly done and understood, will help your treasures last your lifetime, and hopefully also last for generations to come. Doll conservation and preservation will be discussed in the next section.

The mechanics of doll restoration are beyond the scope of this book. You can find an eight-article series on doll restoration through my website, www.officialpriceguidetodolls.com. The articles cover a multitude of topics including how to wash and style doll hair, cleaning bisque dolls, filling in the missing pieces of a doll, stringing, painting, clothing repair and restoration, safely washing doll clothing, and tips for restoring vintage Barbie dolls.

Ethics of Selling a Restored Doll: If you sell a doll, it is proper to disclose any changes made to the doll—any repainting, repairs, or added materials (new eyes, wig). For certain vintage dolls such as vintage Barbie, even restyling the hair affects the value and should be disclosed; so does washing the clothing. However, you do not have to disclose basic conservation measures such as cleaning dolls, combing hair, or restringing. For antique dolls, washing of clothing and restyling of wigs is generally not required to be disclosed.

Doll Preservation and Conservation

Of course, if you collect vintage or antique dolls, preservation and conservation of those dolls should be uppermost in your mind. However, even modern doll collectors can benefit from knowing the basics of preservation and conservation, since modern dolls can be subject to light, dust, and other problems which destroy and devalue the dolls, just as they destroy and devalue older dolls. But with older dolls already facing fragility due to age, preservation and conservation of those dolls is a pressing concern.

Light: Light damages dolls. Sunlight quickly fades doll clothing and will also fade skin tones on vinyl dolls. Sunlight also quickly degrades rubber dolls. It is best to keep all natural sunlight away from your dolls. Do not display dolls in windows, and keep display cases out of direct sunlight. The heat from natural light can also be damaging, especially to composition and vinyl dolls.

Artificial light also fades dolls and doll clothing. So your best course of action is to have all lighting be indirect. Do not have lights directly over or under your dolls. If you have lighted display cases, put the lights on only when showing your dolls. In general, incandescent lights are less damaging than fluorescent lights, as long as you keep the incandescent lights far enough away from your dolls so that they aren't affected by the heat of the lights. Fluorescent lights can turn some vinyl dolls green, such as vintage Barbies. One way to help protect your dolls is to buy UV lighting sleeves from an archival company (see Appendix 2, "Resources"). Another possibility, if you must display your dolls in a well-lighted room, is to drape sheer curtains over your display cases so the dolls are not affected by the light when they are not being viewed.

Temperature: The ideal temperature for dolls is somewhere between 65 and 72 degrees, although studies have shown that variance of the temperature up or down 10% will not cause permanent damage to most dolls. Practically, this means that the worst thing you can do is store your dolls in a nontemperature-controlled environment. Attics and garages are the most popular storage spots for dolls that are not on display, and these are the worst places for dolls, with their wide swings in temperature and humidity. If at all possible, any dolls in storage should be in an inner closet in your house or apartment.

Humidity: High humidity can lead to mold problems on many doll surfaces, and excessively low humidity can cause cracking of wood and composition dolls. This is another reason to store your dolls in a temperature-controlled environment. Also, don't store your dolls in closed plastic bags or boxes where humidity cannot escape.

Dust: It is optimal to store your dolls in a closed glass case, since dust and dirt make dolls look dingy, will destroy fabrics over time, and can also attract bugs. Also consider air pollutants—outside air pollution through open windows and inside air pollution from chemicals such as rug-cleaning solutions and oil paint. If your dolls do become dusty or dirty, they can be partially cleaned with a mini vacuum or compressed photographic air.

Insects: Moths. Wood-boring beetles. Carpet beetles. All these insects, and others, can infest your dolls. Moth larvae can feast on wool doll clothing and mohair wigs, wood-boring beetles can make their way into wood and composition dolls, and carpet beetles have larvae that enjoy mohair, various clothing fibers, and feathers. To control bugs, there are several things you can do. First, always have clean hands when handling your dolls. Oils, food particles, and hand creams from your hands can transfer onto dolls and their clothing and wigs, and many bugs will find those oils, food particles, and hand creams to be excellent food sources. Some owners of expensive antique dolls will only handle them with gloves on. You can also use moth crystals in a doll cabinet, but if you do, make sure that the crystals do not touch the dolls or come in close contact—the best place to place the crystals would be toward the top of a case, loosely wrapped in a cloth. Use caution, since vinyl dolls can have a bad chemical reaction with moth crystals, and should not be in a case with them.

If you *do* get a bug infestation, attack it as soon as possible so it doesn't transfer to other dolls. You can try freezing clothing or wig items to kill bugs (sometimes that works, sometimes it doesn't). Some people swear by microwaving an item (carefully) and you can microvacuum items to suck up bug eggs. You can also place a moth-infested doll in a box with moth crystals (again, not touching the doll) if the doll isn't plastic or vinyl.

Proper Storage: Finally, your best overall strategy to fight the enemies of doll preservation is proper display and storage of the dolls. A closed cabinet, away from strong light sources and in a temperature-controlled room is your best option. If the cabinet is wood, make sure that your dolls don't come into direct contact with the wood, which contains acids. Also, if you store your dolls in boxes, make sure that you wrap them in acid-free tissue paper (also available from archival supply houses) which will prevent the dolls from coming into contact with the acids in cardboard boxes.

Having said all of this regarding proper preservation and conservation of dolls, I am now going to tell you that I don't follow all of my own advice. I *do* protect my dolls from direct light, and I *do* keep them in a temperature-controlled environment. However, I want to enjoy my dolls, and so many of them sit all around my doll room, freely enjoyed by me and my family, but also freely available to dust, dirt, and my lovely but rather clumsy dog. Basically, I feel you should balance your preservation and conservation needs with truly enjoying your collection.

From Modern Collectible Doll Collecting to Vintage and Antique Collecting

Many new doll collectors come to the hobby by first collecting modern dolls. Whether their first love is the modern collectible Barbie dolls, the beautiful fashion dolls of Robert Tonner, Marie Osmond's sweet toddlers and babies, or dolls by Madame Alexander, Wendy Lawton, and a host of others, their first exposure as a collector is to modern dolls, and they are barely aware of the universe of vintage and antique dolls.

After a while, many of these collectors start to notice other dolls—dolls from earlier eras, perhaps dolls from their childhood, or their mother's childhood. Perhaps their exposure to other, earlier dolls first occurs at a doll show, or while surfing doll-related websites or online auction sites. Sometimes, these collectors would like to start collecting the older dolls, but it's intimidating—unlike new-issue modern dolls, where pricing is exact and easily known (you have a manufacturer's suggested retail price for guidance) there is no "price" for a vintage or antique doll—only prices in price guides such as this are available for guidelines. And, as pointed out elsewhere in this book, each vintage and antique doll is unique.

Here are some tips to make the jump from modern doll collecting to vintage and antique doll collecting less intimidating:

Knowledge is Power: Read, read, read! This book is a good start, but be sure to check the bibliography at the end of this book, with nearly 200 books on dolls listed, the majority of them on vintage and antique dolls. The more you know, the smarter your purchasing decisions will be. You can also learn from the doll information websites, such as www.officialpriceguidetodolls.com.

Focus on One Type of Doll: There are so many types of vintage and antique dolls out there, it can be overwhelming! For your first foray into older dolls, pick one and stick to that till you get the hang of it. For instance, you might pick Liddle Kiddles if you had them as a child, or vintage Georgene Raggedy Ann dolls if you cannot resist their charms.

Don't Prejudge. All Vintage and Antique Dolls Are Not Expensive: Many modern doll collectors are afraid to get involved with vintage, and especially antique dolls, because they believe they cannot afford them. Although there are certainly many dolls that *do* sell for hundreds or thousands of dollars each, there are also many, many very desirable vintage and antique dolls that can be had for the same price as or even less cost than many

modern dolls today. For instance, many German antique bisque dolls are available for under $200–$300—Armand Marseille, Ernst Heubach, Revalo—and many other similar dolls come to mind. As for vintage dolls, many delightful dolls, in excellent condition, can be purchased for less than even $100! They may not be the most popular brand names, but sometimes they are—think of Liddle Kiddles MOC (mint on card) or Bubble Cut Barbies, in excellent condition. Or, how about one of the lesser-known brands of hard plastic or composition dolls? Another way to cut cost is to get dolls with flaws that won't show on display, as long as you pay an appropriate discount for that doll.

Join a Doll Club (or Form One Yourself!): There is no better way to learn about dolls than to join a doll club. See Appendix 2 for more information.

See Dolls in Person: Yes, you can learn a lot from books and websites and auctions. But nothing beats the amount you can learn from seeing dolls in person, or holding a doll in your hand. Before you start purchasing vintage and antique dolls, attend live doll events—shows, auctions (go to their previews!), and conventions. If you are lucky enough to have a doll shop with vintage and antique dolls in your area, visit often.

Selling Your Dolls

Perhaps you have purchased this book because you aren't interested in collecting dolls—perhaps, you have inherited dolls or otherwise suddenly acquired or found them, and you want information on the value of your dolls only so you can sell them. Or, perhaps you are a collector who is ready to part with some of your dolls—many collectors, in fact, constantly sell dolls so they can "upgrade" their collection. Other collectors simply find that their tastes change, and yet others find themselves having to "downsize" a collection when moving into smaller living quarters. Whatever your reason for selling your dolls, here are some things to keep in mind, and some typical outlets for selling your dolls.

Doll Dealer/Doll Shop: The dealer or shop-keeper will have the expenses of his or her business to consider when reselling *your* doll to a collector. These expenses include storage, employee salaries, insurance, advertising, rent, and much more. A doll shop owner or dealer also generally has a list of clients who can be customers for your doll, no matter how specialized, and the knowledge and background to present your doll in the best light to customers. Taking all this into account, you can generally expect 40% to 60% of the "book" value for a doll when selling to a doll shop or doll dealer.

Online Auction: Of course, you could try to sell the doll yourself to a collector via an on-line auction, figuring that you might be able to do better. However, when you take into consideration the costs and time of selling the doll yourself (including fees to the online auction company, costs of photography, shipping, etc.) *plus* the time spent learning how to sell your doll online, how to create attractive and appropriate photos and get them online, plus the research needed to sell the doll for the best price (what category to list in? Is the outfit original? What needs to be described?) things look very different. Given all that, you might not do much better than the price that the dealer was going to give you for your doll, and with a whole lot less trouble. If you would like to sell the doll yourself via an online auction, read "Tips For Selling Dolls on eBay," below.

Auction House: If you have a high-value doll, or a large collection of vintage or an-tique dolls, you might consider selling the dolls via a specialty doll auction house, such as Theriault's. The advantage of selling via a doll auction house is that the auction house generally has an extensive customer list, and can find a buyer for your doll no matter how rare, expensive, or unique it is. Usually, an auction house will keep a percentage of your doll's sale as compensation for selling your doll—the fee varies.

Estate Sale: Dolls can also be sold via local estate sales. Estate sales are held all over the United States by small auction houses. However, you cannot generally expect to receive top dollar for your dolls at an estate sale unless you know there is a core of devoted local doll collectors who frequent the local estate sales.

General Antiques Dealer: General antiques dealers will sometimes purchase dolls. Be aware that some antiques dealers do not have enough knowledge about dolls to appropriately appraise your doll to make you a fair offer.

Direct to a Collector Via a Magazine or Newspaper Ad: You can sell directly to a collector. If you are confident about your knowledge of the doll, and you can set a fair asking price, this can be a way to get top dollar for your doll. You can find doll collectors through newspaper or doll magazine ads. The disadvantage of this method of selling your dolls is that it can take you much longer to sell your doll than if you sold to a dealer, or through an auction or estate sale.

2 DOLL COLLECTING AND THE INTERNET

Doll Collecting And The Internet—Introduction

Before collecting on the Internet became possible in the mid-1990s, supply and demand for dolls was affected, and often limited, by many factors, including geography, lack of knowledge on the part of noncollectors, and limited sources for dolls—generally, you could find dolls only via dealer lists, doll shops, doll shows, and conventions. Collectors in rural areas had an especially difficult time either buying or selling dolls, with few avenues available to them. Collectors also faced personal limitations on collecting. Mothers of young children, working women, and older collectors with physical limitations had difficulty visiting shows, shops, conventions, or attending regular doll club meetings, because of a lack of time or access. All this limited collecting opportunities.

Before the Internet—Limited Doll Collecting Resources: Besides limited collecting opportunities, there were also limited sources of doll collecting information. All information pre-Internet was from magazines, shops, clubs, books, and mail. Information was available, but more expensive to obtain, and not as timely as on the Internet. Of course, all the traditional methods of doll collecting are still vitally important (nothing replaces looking at a doll in person!). You can *never* replace the experience of attending a doll convention as I've described above, and you also cannot replace the thrill of a great doll show, or of having a doll shop in your area where you have knowledgeable staff and the continuing opportunity to see

dolls in person. Books and magazines are irreplaceable for always-available, hands-on information and photos of dolls. However, this is all now enhanced, and has been greatly changed, by Internet resources for buying and selling dolls online, and for Internet research.

After the Internet—24-Hour Doll Collecting: With the advent of the Internet as a resource for doll collecting in the mid-1990s and its complete explosion into the 21st century, every collector now has access to an overwhelming number of dolls for sale, reams of information about dolls, communities of doll collectors, and nearly every doll company and club online. You now have 24-hour collecting, with millions of doll collectors online worldwide.

The Internet Explodes—Impact on Doll Collecting: Back in 1994, the doll collecting community on the Internet was just forming, and was very small, with a few rudimentary discussion boards. In 1995, the eBay Internet auction site was started (as AuctionWeb), and the explosion of doll collecting on the Internet began. Soon there were online doll communities everywhere, doll companies created websites in droves, new only-online doll companies formed by the hundreds, and thousands of Internet auctions for dolls took place on eBay every day. At first, the impact on doll collecting was only positive—a greater supply of dolls led to more demand. But, eventually, the explosion—especially the gargantuan growth of eBay—started to completely change doll collecting. On the plus side, it has brought a whole new generation of young, Internet-savvy collectors to doll collecting as a hobby. On the down side, the effect of Internet auctions has caused an oversupply of certain categories of dolls that has led to a downward effect on prices for those dolls. This situation continues today. Many doll shows have had their doors closed, as more dealers and collectors alike have turned to the Internet as their doll marketplace.

The Internet Bubble Bursts—But The Growth in Online Doll Collecting Continues: Nearly everyone reading this is aware that the Internet bubble burst in 2000. This had a definite effect on many free, information-only doll collecting sites, which went out of business, as did large retail doll and toy sites such as iDolls and eToys. However, the bubble bursting had no adverse effect on Internet auctions—they have actually picked up steam since 2000, with more dolls available online via Internet auctions than ever before.

The Internet and the Official Guide to Doll Collecting: Many doll price guides have chosen to ignore or downplay prices for dolls on the Internet, and specifically Internet auctions. Internet auctions in general, and eBay in particular, have irrevocably changed the marketplace for dolls, and the pricing of dolls, especially for vintage and modern dolls (dolls from 1925 through today). To ignore Internet pricing is to ignore the true market values of many dolls today, and trends in popularity and pricing. In several categories of dolls, where there is an overabundance of supply (such as Madame Alexander dolls from the 1980s to 1990s and modern Barbie dolls from the late 1990s), there has been a severe downward pressure on prices, with many more MIB or NRFB examples of these dolls for sale than there are collectors for these dolls at this time. For other dolls, the Internet has created a hot international market that might not exist otherwise, with very high prices. Examples of this include Blythe dolls, Terri Lee dolls, and fine examples of 1920s–1930s boudoir dolls. Internet prices have been presented along with show and shop prices in this book, and in the "Online/Offline" and "Market Reports" sections in each category of dolls, Internet trends are discussed. Chapter 3, Using This Book, further explains how to use this book for Internet, dealer, shop, and show pricing.

Doll Collecting on the Internet: The remainder of this section is a primer on how to collect dolls on the Internet, with information and tips on buying, selling, auctions, and doll collecting communities.

Buying And Selling Dolls Online

Buying from Web Pages of Small Business Owners and People Selling Their Collections: Small doll shops and individuals that sell dolls from their collections often sell dolls from their own websites. Some of these sites are sophisticated, with fancy graphics and links to large pictures of the dolls; others are rudimentary, with text lists only. For individual doll collectors, you generally contact the website owner via e-mail, and complete transactions with checks or money orders and often PayPal, an online credit card service. Most doll shops now allow purchases online using credit cards on a secure server, since the shopping cart technology has come down in price in the last few years. If you do shop online using a credit card, make sure that the page which asks for your credit card information has an "https" beginning, or the page is *not* on a secure server.

- **Buying Modern Dolls:** Buying a modern doll is a rather straightforward transaction. If someone lists a NRFB Barbie doll with a mint box, you know exactly what you are getting, and you can also get many valid price comparisons in magazines, at shows, and on eBay. Make sure, if boxes matter to you, that you get a good description of the condition of the box, because that can vary greatly depending on the seller, and box condition matters greatly to the prices of modern dolls such as Barbies and Madame Alexanders. Also, be careful about return policies, since some sellers will not take returns on NRFB dolls.

- **Buying Antique and Vintage Dolls:** This is obviously more difficult via the Internet because of the wide range of conditions these dolls are in, and the subjectivity of such conditions. A completely mint flat-top china doll might sell for $600, yet one with a hairline, replaced arms, wear, and other flaws might only be worth $150 or less. Remember, condition is everything when pricing dolls, and what is "mint" to one collector might barely rate a "good" condition with most other doll collectors. Please read the section on "Protecting Yourself in Online Transactions" to deal with this potential problem. In any event, get as much information as you can. Ask lots of questions, get complete descriptions, doll marks, and as many photos as possible.

- **Have a Dollar Limit:** Put a limit on the amount you will spend on a doll online. This is personal, since the limit should be what *you* can "afford" to lose on a doll, if the person selling the doll is dishonest, or disappears after selling a doll not honestly described. But remember that many people *do* successfully trade expensive dolls online—I am constantly bemused by the $5,000 Jumeaus and $15,000 Brus that are constantly bought and sold on eBay. You need to make your own decisions based on your computer, collecting experience, and financial situation. Your online limit could be $50, or $5,000.

Online Shopping at Large Doll Company Sites: You can find modern dolls at doll company websites such as www .barbiecollector.com or www.collectibles today.com (Ashton Drake) as well as at online shops of well-known large doll retailers as www.toysrus.com. You search the site for the doll you want, you then purchase through the online shopping cart, and in a few days, you receive the item. This saves you a trip to a store, or a long time holding on the phone.

- **Hot Dolls:** For "hot" dolls, you can see pictures, and have the dolls ordered even before the catalog is printed. Sometimes you can get hot limited edition dolls before they sell out or even reach the actual stores. Also some dolls are Internet exclusives (for instance, certain Barbie Collector Club dolls are available only from www.barbiecollector.com).

- **You're Just an Order Number:** Do note, however, that you will always be just a "number" with a big store online—it's impossible to develop a personal relationship with anyone there, as you can at a small local store or with a good salesperson at a branch of a large retail store.

- **Stores Go Out of Business:** You may come to rely on a "big" online store for your doll purchases only to see it go out of business, like eToys and iDolls.

- **Security of Online Credit Card Use:** Many people will not shop online using a credit card because they fear for the security of their accounts. I have bought countless dolls via the Internet with no problems. Technology is such right now that it is probably safer to order online with a credit card than it is to give the unknown 18-year-old clerk at the local corner store your Visa card to buy some milk. Millions more people buy merchandise on the Internet each year, and there has been no explosion of credit card fraud online. Of course, credit card fraud does exist, and card numbers can be taken via hackers, so *always* look for a secure web page for orders.

Web Pages—Selling Dolls From Your Own Web Page: Perhaps you have a collection that has become too large for your home—perhaps your doll room is beginning to look like the inside of Yankee Stadium, because you have too many dolls stuffed inside. One option for selling your collection, especially if you are not a fan of online auctions, is to sell your collection online via your own web page.

To do this, you must have a website, either through a free service like Yahoo/Geocities or free through your online service provider (such as AOL) or you will need to purchase a website domain name and pay a monthly fee for hosting your site. Putting the site together will require knowledge of HTML, or a good WYSIWYG (What You See Is What You Get) web editor like Front Page. You will also have to get your website noticed among the many thousands of websites with dolls to sell, either through online advertising or through search engines such as Google. In any event, the following tips will help you sell your dolls via a web page:

- **Photos Sell!:** Dolls with photos will sell remarkably faster than dolls without photos, even if you give the dolls extensive online descriptions. If you do list a doll with just a text description, your customer will most likely ask for photos of the doll anyway, so you might as well start with large, clear photos.

- **Disclose All Flaws:** Disclose all doll flaws and all positive points. If you are honest and forthcoming with information, you will have mostly happy customers.

- **Have Policies on Payment:** Post your payment and shipment policies online, and stick to them. Do you offer layaway? What is your shipping charge? What kinds of payment do you accept? If you cannot accept credit cards, it is helpful to accept PayPal, at www.paypal.com.

- **Offer a Return Policy:** Offer a return for anything that is *not* as described in your listing on your website. You can offer an even more liberal return policy if asked for it up front. State whether or not you refund shipping charges (most sellers don't).

- **Be Prompt:** Nothing loses an online customer faster than a slow response to an inquiry on a doll. The Web is a very immediate medium, and shoppers are using the Web partly for that immediacy, so don't dawdle answering e-mails.

- **Make Your Site Appealing and Offer Something New:** Try to make your website visually attractive without excess clutter. Do not put music on your site, which many Web shoppers find annoying. And offer your visitors a reason to come back and see what you have for sale next month; offer changing information, weekly updates, a fun page, something!

Online Auctions: By far the most popular way to buy or sell dolls online is through Internet auctions, at eBay.com and several others. As mentioned, the growth of eBay as a venue for buying and selling dolls has changed the hobby like no other modern development has. It would be hard to write a book about dolls today and not mention eBay.

What Is an Online Auction?: For those that are new to the concept of online auctions, there are many Internet sites which conduct auctions over a period of days (up to two weeks) that accept bids via a Web page. Generally, as a buyer of dolls, you find a listing for an item that interests you with its bid price, closing time, and the number of bids so far. You can then click on the item and read a detailed description of it, see a picture or pictures, and then place your bid (many auction sites allow you to place your maximum bid, and will automatically place higher bids for you as other bidders increase the bidding).

eBay: The Most Trafficked Auction Site on the Web for Dolls: No other site on the Internet comes close to eBay, www.ebay.com, for the number of dolls bought and sold, the number of doll categories, and the amount of traffic to the site. This makes eBay certainly the best site for sellers, and, due to the wide variety of dolls offered, for buyers as well. It also makes eBay a 2,000-pound gorilla—many longtime sellers feel that eBay is now so powerful it can do anything it wants, and that it has changed not only doll collecting but the entire collectibles industry. Many collectors fear that eBay, overall, wields too much influence on the doll market, and also that any changes made by eBay in its service, such as raising prices or adding or discontinuing services, have immediate ripples that can be felt throughout the world of doll collecting.

Using eBay Auctions: The eBay home page is the jump-off point for the eBay auction experience, where thousands of sellers auction off items of every description, including thousands of dolls, to thousands of buyers (at no cost to the buyers). On the eBay home page, you can see listings for some of the major auction categories—dolls and bears, toys and hobbies, collectibles, antiques, books, computers, etc. The main page for buying and selling dolls is at http://dolls .ebay.com. Today, the eBay community includes over 100 million registered users and is the most popular shopping site on the Internet. In 2003, the eBay community transacted more than $204 billion in gross merchandise sales. Every day there are over 19 million (!!) items for sale listed on eBay, across 27,000 categories. On high-traffic days, eBay receives over 580 million page views and 7.1 million bids. As you can see, this is a busy place for collectors! Here are some tips for using the eBay service to buy and sell dolls:

How Does eBay Work? Individual sellers put items up for sale to the highest bidder, and the seller pays eBay two small fees: (1) a fee for inserting the item in eBay's listings ($.30 up to $3.30 for most items, depending on the "starting bid" or reserve price for the item); and (2) a percentage of the winning bid—5.25% of the winning bid up to $25, and 2.75% of the winning bid over $25 and up to $1,000 and then 1.50% after that. For "reserve" items (we will get to reserves later) the insertion fee is based on the reserve price of the item, so it is more expensive to list a reserve ($.50 for a reserve price under $25, $1 for a reserve price over $25, and 1% of the reserve on an item over $1—this is on top of the other fees but is refunded if the item sells). Additional fees are levied for many things, including "gallery" photos next to the listing, featured or bold items, and scheduling auctions at a later date. Once the bidding is completed, the seller and the buyer contact each other and complete the transaction.

Bidding, Selling—the Basics: Bids are made through the individual item pages for a period of three, five, seven, or ten days (ten-day auctions cost an additional fee of 10 cents). Highest bidder by the closing time of the auction wins the item (except for "reserve auctions," where the winning bid must be over the "reserve" in order for the high bidder to win the item). Sellers and bidders must register at eBay. For sellers, this requires credit card information and bank account information. This is, in a very rudimentary manner, the basics on eBay. For full information on eBay basics please go to eBay's own basics course, at http://pages.ebay .com/help/index.html, which covers registration, searching for items, bidding, selling and much more.

Tips for Bidding on eBay: There are two strategies that seem to be used by most eBay bidders:

- **Wait Until the Last Day (or Minute) to Snipe:** One strategy is to not bid on a doll until the last day of an auction. Some people believe that they will not drive up the price of the doll they want to win if they do this. This can be a foolhardy strategy—first, real life often intervenes, and you can simply be too busy to remember to bid at that last moment. Also sometimes several people wait until the last day and then a fierce, last-minute bidding war escalates (and, in the heat of battle, people lose their heads—okay, I'll admit it—I love when this type of bidding war happens to a doll I am selling!). Some people "snipe," which means carrying this strategy so far that they won't place a bid until the last five minutes, or even last five seconds, of an auction. This is very risky, since there can be too much Internet or site traffic to get through to eBay, or the existing bidders may have already placed large maximum bids. The last-minute bidder can run out of time trying to get in the highest bid (umm—I have tried this, and it is not fun to run out of time or not be able to get through). So I have decided that the second bidding strategy is the soundest:

- **Place Your Maximum Bid the First Time You Bid:** It seems much sounder, both fiscally and to improve your chances of getting a doll, to place your maximum bid the first time you view the doll, and then forget about your bid until the auction is over. Remember, eBay will not go to your maximum bid unless someone bids you up to it—if you bid, say, $110 on a vintage Bubble Cut Barbie on the first day of the auction, and the minimum bid is $50, your bid is listed at only $50, and there is where it will stay unless someone bids higher than $50. If only one other person bids, and their maximum bid is $70, you will get the item for $71.

Now some people do not like this strategy because they fear last-minute snipers (see below) will swoop in and get the doll for $111 one minute prior to the close of the auction. Well, that is very possible, but what I do is decide what the true maximum I would pay for a doll is, then I add 10% and make that my maximum bid. If someone outbids me by $1 with such a bid, then I know they didn't get a bargain, and I can sleep well at night. If it is an item that, irrationally, I cannot live without (a doll I have been looking for for years, let's say) then I put my maximum bid at 20% over my "rational" maximum. It works for me, and with this strategy you will spend a lot less time watching last-minute bidding, and more time collecting.

- **But I WANT to Snipe!:** Nevertheless, human nature being what it is, chances are that you at least want to try sniping. Okay, here's how! To snipe like a pro, the first thing you need to do is synchronize your clock exactly to the eBay clock. Next, decide how strong your constitution is. If you are a knock-kneed sniper (sort of like me) you may want to start your sniping activities as much as five to ten minutes before the end of the auction (to see who has bid lately and how much, to see how the server is responding, etc.). If you have a constitution of steel, you may choose not to open the auction-page window until two or three minutes before the close of the auction (you will need time to enter your bid, at least!).

Next, you will want to open two windows in your browser on whatever doll you are bidding on. The first window is where you will repeatedly hit the "reload" button to see updated prices for any new bids made. The second window is where you will set up your snipe bid. You will want to enter your bid amount, your ID, and your password on this second page, and then click to the "review bid" page. You will minimize this, and keep reloading your *other* window to see where the

bid stands, until you are ready to place your snipe bid! Again, some brave souls have this down to a science, and will do this with less than a minute to spare. I generally do this two or three minutes before the close of auction (on the rare occasions that I snipe) to allow for computer or server glitches or power outages, or time to snipe VERY fast in case my bid isn't the highest and I really want to try again.

If you have followed these instructions, and barring any last-minute snipers or people with large preplaced maximum bids, you should now be the winner of the doll!

- **Use "My eBay":** You can use "My eBay," www.myebay.com, to keep track of all of the auctions you are bidding on, plus feedback and more. You can also watch auctions that you are not yet bidding on. This very versatile tool is free to all registered eBay users.

Selling Dolls on eBay: What Price Can I Expect? Should I Sell Via eBay at All?: When you sell a doll on eBay, you will generally (except for very hot dolls) get less for your doll than a dealer would get, but you don't have the overhead of a dealer selling an item when you sell on eBay. You could say that the expected eBay price is somewhere between the buy-from-dealer price and the sell-to-dealer price. If you sell your doll directly to a dealer, you are generally paid about 40% to 60% of what the dealer can expect to sell the doll for. This is very fair because the dealer must pay rent, employee salaries, insurance, electricity, and much more in order to make a profit on your doll.

Because prices on common dolls sold on eBay have been so depressed lately, chances are you will do better selling your dolls directly to a dealer instead of on eBay. Often, if the doll dealer has a developed clientele, 40–50% of the dealer's expected selling price can often be nearly as good, or better, than the eBay price. Also, you shouldn't underestimate the amount of work and the costs associated with selling your dolls on eBay. Selling on eBay is a time-consuming process. For each doll sold, you need a detailed description and photos. You have to pay fees, have an eBay account, deal with questions, create good digital photos and have those photos loaded onto the Internet, pack and ship the doll, etc.

Why You Need to Follow My Selling Tips if You Sell Dolls on eBay: On eBay lately, the large glut of sellers means that very good items at very good prices can get overlooked. Prices for more common items on eBay (Barbies, common antiques, lesser-quality composition dolls, etc.) have definitely been lower in the past year—bad for sellers, great for buyers. In fact, an article in the *New York Times* in mid-2003 claimed that the average price of a collectible sold on eBay had fallen by 38% since 2000. The good news is that the decline is slowing, and was only 3% in 2002.

Another statistic from the *New York Times* article is that only 45% of items put up for auction were sold in 2003, down from 55% in 2002 and 72% in 2000. I haven't seen the numbers for the past year, but my instinct tells me that an even smaller percentage is now selling. However, my sell-through rate still far exceeds 70%, and if you follow the suggestions in this book, stay away from unrealistic reserves, and start your auction at a fair price, your sell-through rate can be much greater than 45%, too.

Tips for Selling Dolls on eBay: There are certain things you can do to maximize your profits and improve your sell-through rate when you list items for sale on eBay.

- **Check Completed Auction Prices for the Doll:** Before you place an item up for bid, search for the same item in a completed auctions search. You can search completed listings for dolls (right from a main listing page from a box at the side of the page) and see what prices have been realized for that item. If you are selling a modern Barbie, for instance, or a modern Robert Tonner doll, chances are you will see many completed auctions for the same item. The prices can be all over the map, depending on condition of the item, or traffic patterns. As time goes by on eBay, I find the range of prices gets wider and wider (from high to low) as more sellers and items are added, and as the

buyers for items get diluted further and further among too many items. However, you will get an idea of the general selling range (make sure you do not count auctions where reserves were not met—those sometimes have a low "final bid" appearing in the completed-auction listings, but they do not really reflect a market price, since the auction wasn't completed). The range of prices your completed-auction search turns up can give you a good idea of what you will realize for your item, and this can help you decide if you want to sell your doll via eBay. You can also short-circuit this process for many vintage and modern dolls listed in this price guide, where the majority of price listings have been taken from online auction sales.

Also note that sometimes one person will list an item that sells at a high price, and the next week 20 sellers will list the same item, temporarily creating a supply imbalance that lowers prices on the next 20 of that item. Additionally, if you have a more offbeat item for sale (perhaps a rare Raggedy Ann) chances are you won't see many completed auction prices for that item, and you will have to try to find similar items on which to base your starting price and reserve.

- **"Buy It Now":** I highly recommend using this feature, which allows a buyer to immediately purchase your doll. Often, a doll will sit without any bids until near the auction closing time. Most people snipe, and there can be no sense of urgency to place a bid. The "Buy It Now" feature does create a sense of urgency to bid or buy. When you list an item with this feature, you list the price that you would immediately sell the item for. That price is only good until the first bid is made—if bidding starts, the "Buy It Now" price disappears. This works for you in two ways—one, you might sell your item almost immediately for your desired price. Or the "Buy It Now" feature may encourage an early bid by someone who wants the "Buy It Now" to disappear! You can combine the feature with an "instant purchase" using PayPal and the bidder can buy and pay for your item immediately. Instant selling gratification.

If your item has a reserve and you use the "Buy It Now" feature, your "Buy It Now" remains available to bidders until the reserve is met, again creating a sense of urgency to either buy now or meet the reserve.

- **Check Traffic Patterns:** When are the best prices realized in your category? Maybe the Nancy Ann Storybook doll collectors are a weekend bunch, with the heaviest bidding and best prices realized for auctions ending on the weekend. Or maybe the Terri Lee doll collectors are a weeknight group. Or maybe so many auctions end on a weekend in a particular doll category that your item will get lost in the shuffle and you are better off ending your auction on a weeknight. Get to know the category you are selling in, and then decide when you want your auction to end.

- **Three, Five, Seven, or Ten-Day Auctions:** I always used to conduct seven-day auctions for maximum exposure to bidders. Now I find that the volume on eBay is so heavy that most people check items only on the first and last days. So sometimes a three-day or five-day auction will bring the same price. However, a seven-day auction can have the benefit of beginning and ending on the weekend, if you decide that is the best time for posting a doll in your chosen category. If you are selling a very specialized doll or a doll people are only likely to see using eBay's search, then a seven-day or even a ten-day auction gives you more exposure.

- **Use Photos and Make Them as Good as Possible:** Photos help sell items, especially for vintage or antique dolls, which can vary so much in condition, but really, for any doll, because dolls have such a strong visual component. You should add as many photos as possible to your auction—taking care, however, that your photos are compressed so that they do not take forever to load. To add photos you either need to have an online website to store the photos (recommended for advanced users, since it's free and you have total control) and an FTP client or you can use eBay's Picture Services. Picture Services can be accessed directly from the eBay listing pages. One photo per listing is free, and there are fees for additional photos, slide shows, and "supersize" pictures. The service is easy to use and a boon for beginners who struggle with adding photos. The photos are limited in size, however, and are sometimes less dramatic than doll photos you can host yourself.

Your photos should be well lighted. The dolls should be placed against a clutter-free background, and you should come in as tightly as you can for the photos. The biggest mistake I see in eBay photos of dolls are dolls with dull lighting. The second biggest mistake I see in eBay photos are photos where the camera is too far from the doll to show the doll's detail, or photos that have lots of wasted "white space" that isn't cropped out. To light your photos properly, you should either take your photos outdoors on a sunny day or, if you can afford it, buy stationary studio lights. Flash often makes the dolls too flat. I also recommend a good digital camera which doesn't have to be an expensive one (mega-pixels are not required—you won't need them on the Internet!).

- **Give a Detailed Description:** "Blonde Bubble Cut Barbie, good condition" tells a buyer nothing about the doll for sale. A better description would be: "Blonde Bubble Cut Barbie, great facial paint, hair slightly combed out, good body with two scratches on lower thigh." A detailed description is always preferable. Photos cannot detail all defects in a doll, and if you do not describe all doll defects you will have an unhappy buyer. Also, detailed descriptions will help you realize better prices—vague descriptions leave too much to the imagination, and the imagination usually decides you are hiding something when the description isn't detailed enough. Of course, all positive features of the doll should be pointed out as well. Stay away from hyperbole, however—nothing turns a buyer off more than a seller claiming a doll is "rare" when the doll isn't!

- **Decide on a Sound Minimum Bid:** Remember, you are agreeing to sell your item for this minimum, so if you cannot part with an item for less than $50, don't list it with a lower minimum. However, from experience, I can tell you that the free market is alive and well for unique or mint vintage and antique items, and that low minimum bids encourage active bidding—people cannot turn away from a bargain, so try a low minimum bid and let the free market take over. Another advantage is that the lower the minimum bid, the lower your listing fee. And, yes, you may end up selling some items for very low prices with low minimum bids, so be prepared for that eventuality if you use this strategy.

If you are selling a very common modern doll, a very unusual, or a very, very expensive item with a limited bidding audience, then you truly must consider a higher minimum bid to protect your investment in the doll. Remember, for very common dolls, your eBay auction might simply be overlooked and you could end up selling a doll worth $50 for your opening bid of $9.99. For the rarer or limited audience doll, you might also want to consider a reserve (see below), since very high opening bids can be even more daunting than a reserve auction.

- **Carefully Craft Your Listing Title:** With the huge number of auctions on eBay right now, how you word your title (so that it can be brought up by buyers in title-only searches for your item) can mean the difference between lots of page views and bidders and a good price, or an item that gets lost in the shuffle. Try a few searches for your type of item, and see which phrases work. Also, get as much info in the title as you can without resorting to meaningless abbreviations. If you are not running a reserve auction, try fitting in the title *no reserve, n/res,* or even *N/R* to indicate no reserve, since I am convinced no reserve auctions do better and command higher prices than reserve auctions, which turn off many bidders. A free-for-all auction is fun and has definite entertainment value.

- **Credit Cards and PayPal:** Some people won't bid on auctions if you don't take credit cards—they hate writing checks or getting money orders. Now with PayPal almost all sellers accept credit cards and you are at a disadvantage if you don't.

- **When to Use Reserve Auctions:** I rarely use reserves. I am sure that they turn off bidders, and in fact they turn me off, since many times people use reserve auctions to test the market by listing dolls with unrealistically high reserves. I dislike bidding on these dolls, wasting my time, and then when the doll does not sell, I still don't know the undisclosed reserve price. Many items with reserves do not meet the reserve, so I think many bidders share my feelings on reserve auctions. I do use reserves (and you should too) with very expensive or rare dolls, since sometimes very high minimums turn off bidders (see above), and, if the doll is special enough, it will probably still sell. Plus reserves protect your investment in a doll when you must protect it.

- **Expect the Unexpected!:** Remember, this is an auction—anything can happen and that is part of the fun! You may get an irrationally high or an irrationally low price, and you have to be able to accept this (if you can't accept an irrationally low price, see "Reserve Auctions," above!). Once, I sold a doll book on eBay that I had expected to sell for $15 or $20 for $85! Another time, I sold a pristine mint vintage Barbie outfit (Patio Party) that I was convinced was going to bring at least $90, and received a paltry $45 for it (the buyer was thrilled).

- **A Note on Payment and Shipping:** Have a clear payment, shipping, and handling policy spelled out in your listing. Buyers appreciate that. For your own protection, do not send out merchandise until a personal check has cleared. If you are sending merchandise to a post office box address, make sure you also get a street address and/or phone number in case the check bounces. In your auction listing, discuss clearly any handling charges, how you compute postage or shipping and insurance. Clearly indicate your accepted methods of payment. When it's time to ship the dolls, pack them well, using appropriate bubble wrap, Styrofoam peanuts, etc. Don't be tempted to skimp on packing materials, since a doll damaged in shipping is a hassle for both the buyer and the seller. Charge more for handling hard-to-pack pieces (such as an antique bisque doll or a 1988 Happy Holidays Barbie doll—remember, half the value of a doll like that is in the box, so double box it— one dent, and you have a returned item!). I highly recommend that you get your buyer to pay for postal insurance in case something goes wrong.

eBay Shipping Services: Various shipping services, including shipping calculators, are available at http://pages.ebay.com/ services/buyandsell/shipping.html.

International: Note in your auction listing if you accept international bids. Some of my best sales have been to international buyers, but there is extra hassle (shipping overseas, language problems) involved in these transactions. Also, there have been some problems with fraud using PayPal and international transactions. You might want to limit your international shipments to certain territories and avoid territories (like Malaysia or Nigeria) where some fraudulent credit card rings are known to operate.

- **Glut of Sellers:** Just be aware when listing dolls for sale that the game has changed on eBay in the last few years. As already mentioned, there is a glut of sellers, and common merchandise often fetches way below retail or book values. The market is now super-liquid, and not only doll collectors, but all sorts of garage-sale aficionados are out there buying up dolls to sell them on eBay and some doll dealers are even selling modern dolls thanks to lax wholesale account policies. If an item is very common, expect a very low price because you will see the item (modern collectible dolls, 1970s and 1980s Madame Alexanders) coming and going on eBay. However, good quality, mint vintage items (mint 1950s Ginny and 1950s Madame Alexander dolls, Liddle Kiddles, fine mint all-bisque antique dolls, etc.) do fetch good prices because demand is high and supply is limited.

- **My eBay:** I cannot say enough good things about My eBay, the free service that eBay offers both buyers and sellers. You can cus-

tomize your page and keep track of all auctions you are running, invoices, payments received (if by PayPal), your eBay account, and feedback . My eBay can be accessed at the top of all eBay pages.

- **Auction Management Software:** If you are going to list more than a handful of dolls for sale on eBay, I highly recommend that you purchase auction management software to help you with your auctions. Most of the auction management software will help you craft attractive listings, help you keep track of your listings, and help you craft listings offline (and on one convenient page, instead of the multipage listing process on eBay). With such software, you only have to enter basic information like shipping and payment policies once and then they are automatically added to your auctions. eBay has its own auction management software available for a monthly subscription fee.

- **Fancy Listings/Music:** Don't use overly fancy graphics which bloat the load time for your listings. And never add music to your listings—it is annoying and some computers can't handle it. You don't want to crash the computer of a potential customer, do you?

- **About Me:** This is a free Web page that is linked to from all your eBay sales pages. Definitely use this—you can promote your own online business here, which is something that eBay now prohibits directly in eBay sales listings.

- **Gallery Pictures:** For an extra $.25 per listing, you can have a picture of your doll show up in the "Gallery," which buyers can browse, and on the title bar for your listing. Use this—it's a powerful tool for the price. When buyers browse eBay listings, your listing is at a great disadvantage if you do not have a Gallery photo available before bidders click on your eBay listing.

- **eBay Stores:** For $9.99 a month, you can have an eBay store. This is useful only if you are a high-volume seller, but very useful if you are, because you can list dolls for sale for only $.06 each, including a Gallery listing, for 30 days.

- **Other Online Auctions:** There are many other online auction websites trying to compete with eBay right now, but NONE of these sites gets the same amount of traffic that eBay does in the dolls categories. However, there are several auction houses that will let you attend their live auctions via your computer. Theriault's allows online attendance and bidding via an association with Proxibid. As for traditional online auctions, there is only one site worth checking out, Amazon.com (don't waste your time with Yahoo! auctions—they don't even have a separate category for dolls!), at http://auctions.amazon.com. The auctions have an easy-to-read interface. There are many auction categories and a fair number of listings, with a good buzz among bidders (there are 20 main doll categories plus subcategories—not as numerous as eBay, but more than many sites). Fees are competitive with eBay and Amazon guarantees that you will receive a materially accurately described item, for items which close at $250 or less. It will be interesting to see how this site grows over time.

Protecting Yourself In Online Transactions

It is a sad fact of life that some people are dishonest, others forgetful, and others simply misinformed about dolls. Just like in a real-life transaction at a doll show or shop, you need to protect yourself from being "taken" by the less-than-scrupulous. Unlike real life, when you purchase a doll online, you can't inspect it yourself. As a buyer, you must protect against getting a doll that is not as described in the listing, or not getting your doll at all. As a seller, your biggest fears are someone not paying you after the doll is sent, or someone returning a doll to you that is in worse condition than when you sent it. Here are some things you can do to help protect yourself in online transactions:

Protecting Yourself When Buying Online

Feedback: Check the feedback rating of the seller of an item you want to buy. eBay provides a service for users where people who have completed auction transactions leave "feedback," which are positive, negative or neutral comments on the person on the other side of the transaction. Positive comments are worth one point each, negative comments are -1 point each, and neutral comments, have no effect on the rating. However, look at the comments, since you cannot tell by the raw number next to a user's ID how many negatives have been given versus positives, nor the quality of the comments. Be aware that feedback doesn't always tell the whole story because some eBay users may not post a negative feedback if they fear retaliation in *their* feedback (a growing problem, where an unjustified person reneges on a bid or sends out unfairly described merchandise and threatens to ruin someone's record with retaliatory negative feedback should that person be given his justly deserved negative feedback). If a person has many negative comments, or hidden feedback, don't bid.

References: If you are in a situation with an unknown seller online but not on eBay, then ask for names of other people who have had successful online transactions with the seller and contact them, either via e-mail or phone.

Checks: Send a check, and not a money order, whenever possible (this is the reverse of what you would prefer as a seller). You can stop a check, but there is little you can do about a money order if things go bad in the middle of a deal.

Extensive Descriptions: Get extensive descriptions. Make sure that the description is detailed and fairly sets forth all defects, if any, even if a photo is listed. Ask questions if the initial description is not detailed enough, and make sure you receive answers. If you sense resistance, or receive evasiveness or vague answers, don't bid or buy.

Photos: Obtain photos. Photos can be very helpful in determining whether a doll has been correctly identified, or is in reasonably good condition; however, remember that many types of doll defects will not be picked up on the resolution of a computer screen.

Return Privilege: Dolls and many other collectibles are very subjective; if a doll is not NRFB, the seller should offer a return if the doll is *not as described*. Sellers do not have to offer returns if the buyer simply changes her mind, but if defects are not disclosed, any seller should offer a full refund.

Common Sense: Use your common sense! If something feels "off" about the doll, the seller, or the transaction, or you just get a bad feeling, *listen* to your inner self and pass on the doll. It isn't worth taking a chance, and your inner warning system is usually reliable. The few times I have been "burned" on a doll, if I had paid attention to my misgivings, I wouldn't have been!

Don't Be Rushed: If the seller is in an undue rush (desperate for money; family emergency, raising cash), your warning system should go off. Another doll will come along, so pass on this doll.

Keep Correspondence: Keep all computerized correspondence until the doll is delivered, in case there is a dispute.

Phone Number and Address: Don't rely on an e-mail address and a post office box; both can be ignored or disappear.

Does the Transaction Sound too Good to Be True? Is someone offering you a perfect Tête Jumeau for $500? Run, quickly, in the opposite computerized direction.

Very Expensive Dolls: Don't buy very expensive dolls online unless you know the seller. Set a limit on how much you are comfortable spending online and stick to it.

Shipping Insurance: It is a good idea to have this, in case your doll is lost or damaged in transit.

International Seller?: More and more sellers are international, so double-check before placing a bid or an order. The cost of returning items overseas is high, and there can be communication problems when languages don't mesh.

Protecting Yourself when Selling Online

Money Orders and Check Clearance: When you sell, money orders are best. If you accept checks, make 100% sure each check has cleared your bank before you ship the doll. This can take up to three weeks!

Disclose All Flaws: As mentioned above, disclose all flaws in the doll you are selling. Be 100% honest, or you will end up with unsuccessful transactions and returns.

Payment Policies: Have payment policies, also as mentioned above, and stick to them.

Return Policy: I offer return for any doll that is *not* as described (purchaser finds a flaw I didn't describe, etc.) and a more liberal policy if asked for it up front. You should, too.

Keep Correspondence, Documentation, and Pictures: Keep all documents until the transaction has been successfully completed.

Shipping Insurance: Make the buyer purchase shipping insurance. It will help you have peace of mind, in case the box doesn't arrive. Also, it gives you proof of successful delivery. Note that UPS insures automatically up to $100, and that the cost of postal insurance has increased greatly to a ridiculous $1.10 up to $50 and $2 up to $100, so you may chose to skip USPS insurance, and just self-insure inexpensive dolls.

Ship Promptly: Ship promptly, and let your customer know when to expect shipment. If you are going on a one-week vacation and can't ship that week, let your buyers know in advance, preferably in the auction listing, so they don't get nervous when their e-mails to you aren't answered.

UPS vs. US Mail?: This is a personal choice; I have had good luck with Priority Mail, insured. My UPS packages are often received more mangled than my post office ones, because UPS ships so many heavy packages, but UPS has a marvelous tracking service which enables you to track a package with your computer. They also have great software for your home computer that enables you to print your own shipping labels, and this is very useful if you sell many dolls.

Pack Well: Pack the dolls well as mentioned in my eBay section. You do not want to have an expensive doll ruined in transit. You will have a headache to deal with, a ruined sale, and an unhappy customer.

For Both Buyers and Sellers

Safe Harbor: If something goes wrong with an eBay transaction, contact eBay's Safe Harbor. There is a list of what problems they will handle and what they won't—they are notoriously unresponsive about feedback disputes, and many users say they are not responsive about much. However, the one time I contacted Safe Harbor about a suspected shill bidding ring, the culprits were kicked off eBay within a week.

Insurance: eBay (and some other online auction houses) now offer some insurance for deals gone bad—on eBay, you are covered up to $200 with a $25 deductible, as a seller if payment is not received and you ship, or as a buyer if you get something that is much less than described (a copper bracelet instead of a gold one . . .). Be aware, however, that this protection is not per transaction but *per seller or buyer,* so if many buyers are defrauded by one seller, it's useless. Amazon.com offers similar insurance protection per transaction.

Escrow: Escrow on eBay is available, and probably a good idea for very expensive items. Fees are expensive, and can be up to 4% of the value of an item. If you use another escrow service, be sure you know the company is legitimate, since some very legitimate-looking escrow sites have been fronts for Internet scams in the past.

Other Useful Sites: AuctionWatch, www .auctionwatch.com (rates online auction services, has multiple site search and FREE auction management tools) and Honesty .com, www.andale.com (free auction services including picture listing space, auction counters, and message boards about the auction communities) are both useful sites.

Online Doll Communities

You can do more than just buy and sell dolls on the Internet. The Internet has hundreds of online doll collecting communities, where you can make doll collecting friends, learn about dolls, or just hang out with others that share your interests.

Message Boards and Forums: Message boards and online forums are online areas (sorted by topics) in which collectors discuss dolls. Doll Collecting at About.com has two main Forums and 50 doll topic folders for message posting. America Online also has many doll collecting message boards, including boards for antique dolls, artist dolls, Barbie, Gene, Madame Alexander, composition and many others. eBay has its own message board devoted to doll collecting but it isn't separated into folders. Forums and message boards are terms used interchangeably—they are the same thing.

- **Doll Collecting at About.com Forums:** My doll collecting website at About.com currently has two main forums for doll collecting organized by topic. The main forum is organized by doll type (Madame Alexander, antique, 50s dolls, composition, etc.) at http://forums.about.com/ab-collectdolls and one is devoted exclusively to Barbie dolls and fashion doll collecting at http://forums.about.com/ab-collectdoll2.

- **Doll Message Boards Organized by Topics:** Messages are listed under a topic; you can then respond to the topic—all messages are listed with their date of posting, screen name posted by, and topic, and all members of the forum can read them. Your forum service remembers the posts you have read, so you can scan only new message posts at the next session. On Doll Collecting at About.com, all unread posts show up with a little "new" icon by them. On About.com and AOL, messages are "threaded" by topic.

Doll collecting at About.com,
Raggedy Ann & Andy article.

What Kind of Content?: For current, modern dolls you can find up-to-the-minute information on new doll releases, doll sales, information on upcoming shows, reviews from doll collectors on dolls they have purchased, and names of stores which have hard-to-find dolls in stock. For vintage and antique dolls, you will find show listings, reviews of auctions and shows, people searching for research or needing help on identification of dolls, and you will find delightful stories of people finding the dolls of their dreams.

- **Speed of Online Information:** This is a major reason to engage in online collecting and to participate in online forums, especially if you collect any hard-to-get modern dolls. Very often, doll forums and doll information will break news about new doll releases before most stores even have their catalogs or information from the doll company.

- **Veracity of Online Information—Not Everything You Read Is True:** This is the flip side of the speed of online information. Remember, *anyone* can post *anything* on the Internet. Unlike a magazine, newspaper, or TV station (which must publish the truth from valid sources in order to maintain respect and stay in business), on the Internet, anonymous people have nothing to stop them from posting

lies, except their own conscience, and rumors abound. So take information on the Web with a grain of salt, unless you know your source is reliable.

Doll Mailing Lists: A doll mailing list, or "listserv" is a community of people online who communicate with the other members of the community through an e-mail list. When one member sends a message, all members receive it. So someone brings up a topic, and then others can discuss it by replying, and all members follow the discussion. You subscribe to these lists by sending e-mail to the "list server" who runs the list. Then you automatically receive in your mailbox all e-mail generated by list subscribers. This is a nice way to find specialty doll communities—there are lists for collectors of boudoir dolls, Blythe dolls, antique dolls—nearly every type of doll. Many of these lists can be found via Yahoo!, at www.yahoogroups.com. It is also a semiprivate way to be part of a doll community; only those on the lists see the messages; no one on the Internet sees them. You can also find doll mailing lists from posts on doll forums, and via the databases at http://lists.topica.com.

Newsletters: Free e-mail newsletters are one of the best ways to stay informed about dolls and the world of doll collecting. I have a weekly doll-collecting newsletter called *About Dolls*, with 10,000 subscribers. This newsletter provides weekly doll news, links to new articles on my site, and much more. I also have the *Official Dolls Price Guide Newsletter* which will keep you up-to-date on changes in the doll market and future editions of this book. To sign up for the free newsletter, follow the instructions at www.officialpriceguidetodolls.com. Many other sites and doll shops online also have e-mail newsletters.

Chats: Chatting online lets you, in real time, read the typed responses of other people in a "room" on the Web, and lets you type back to all the people in the "room." On AOL, you go to the keyword "chat" to get to the chat area. You can also chat in many chat rooms run on websites on the Internet, but often you must download special software that will allow you to do this, and the software can differ from site to site. Like any get-together with friends, chats can be informative or delightful, but, also like get-togethers, if you have them too often, they are very time-consuming! Chats can be scheduled and open to the public, or they can be private and by invitation only. Chat rooms are a fantastic tool for staying in touch with doll-collecting friends all over the world.

Doll Research: Online doll research is beyond the scope of this book. However, there is a wealth of doll information on my websites, www.officialpriceguidetodolls.com and www.collectdolls.about.com, as well as thousands of other doll websites (see the appendix at the back of this book for sites, as well as both websites listed here). If you are not already familiar with Google, you should be. Google, at www.google.com, is the most widely used search engine on the Internet. You can find almost anything you need to know about dolls by searching Google, and although Google's results are not always accurate or on point, they far outstrip other search engines for both accuracy and relevancy.

3 USING THIS BOOK

Antique, Vintage, Modern Dolls: Definitions for this Book

Any division of dolls is, by nature, arbitrary. The classic definition of an antique is an object that is at least 100 years old. Well, that is fine, but it doesn't really help doll collectors, because there are dolls, for instance, from 1895 that are completely similar to certain dolls from 1905—why should the demarcation for an antique doll be at 1905 this year and 1906 next year? Please note that the dates used to break up antique, vintage, and modern dolls are approximate, and any doll that straddles the date would fall into the category where the majority of its production took place. So, although Armand Marseille *did* produce German bisque dolls after 1920, the majority of their production was prior to 1920, so they are included as antique dolls. The same for Raggedy Ann and Andy—although they began production in 1918, and although they are still produced today, they have been in constant production for 75 years, and will be included in the Vintage Dolls chapter. For purposes of this book, here is how we broke down the world of dolls into three categories:

Antique: Dolls Up to Approximately 1925

For purposes of this book, all dolls created prior to approximately 1925 will be considered antique. The Antique Dolls chapter will encompass almost all the antique bisque dolls, as well as all-bisque dolls, china dolls, wax, and papier mâché dolls. However, although some composition dolls were made prior to 1925, the majority were made after 1920 and those dolls will be included in the Vintage Dolls chapter. Bathing beauty dolls, which were made throughout the 1920s, will be included in the Antique Dolls chapter because they are made of bisque. When in doubt as to classification, consult the index in the back of the book.

Vintage: Dolls from Approximately 1925 to 1979

Vintage dolls are those dolls that are not quite antique, but they are certainly not modern—for the most part, these are dolls that were dolls of childhood for the greater part of the 20th century. Vintage dolls include everything from composition and hard plastic dolls of the mid-20th century to the vinyl play dolls of the 1960s. Raggedy Ann and Andy are also included here—although their production started in 1918, and they are still produced today, the majority of their production was in the vintage era, and the dolls are therefore included in the Vintage Dolls chapter.

Modern: Dolls from 1980 to Today

Most dolls in this category are dolls that were produced *not* for child's play, but for adult collectors. Dolls for the adult collectible market is a relatively new phenomenon that started, in earnest, in the 1980s. Nevertheless, certain childhood dolls produced after 1980 are starting to be eagerly sought by collectors and will be included here—such dolls as Cabbage Patch, See Wees, Rainbow Brite, Jem, and Strawberry Shortcake (which began production in 1979). Notably, Barbie

Kämmer & Reinhardt Marie, 201, c. 1912.

Madame Alexander Cissy, c. 1957.

NY Yankees Barbie, c. 1999.

dolls have been split between the Vintage Dolls and Modern Dolls chapters, since Barbie dolls made from 1959 to 1980 were mostly for children, while many of the modern Barbie dolls from the late 1980s on are collector editions intended for adults. Madame Alexander dolls have also been split between the Vintage Dolls and Modern Dolls chapters.

Pricing in *The Official Price Guide to Dolls*

How the Prices in this Book Were Determined:

Research: The prices were compiled from actual sales of dolls during an approximately 18-month period. Internet prices are from actual Internet auction and website sales. Prices taken from doll shops and doll shows are, when available, taken from actual sales at doll shops and shows, although in certain instances dealer asking prices are used in the database of prices, where the number of sales in a category in the 18-month period were slim. There are also many price quotes from dolls sold at "land-based" auction houses used in the database. The prices are generally an average of multiple sales, but this is not always the case for very rare dolls, spe-cific examples of dolls in rare outfits or with special features, dolls in limited supply, or dolls where a great number of sales did not take place in the given time period. In any event, many, many thousands of individual sales have been the basis for the research in this book.

What Prices Mean, Condition of the Dolls: Pricing for antique dolls is for dolls in excellent condition, with old appropriate clothes. Pricing for vintage dolls is for dolls in excellent condition with original clothes. For modern dolls, all pricing is for mint dolls with all original clothing and accessories, and their original boxes. Any variations in the condition for quoted prices will be noted in the listings—see below in the "How the Doll Listings Work" section for more details.

A Note on "Book" Values: As mentioned in the section "Selling Your Dolls," if you are selling your doll to a dealer or a doll shop, you cannot expect to be paid the "book value" of the doll. The dealer/shopkeeper will have the expenses of their business to consider when reselling your doll to a collector. These include storage, employee salaries, insurance, advertising, rent, and much more. A doll shop owner or dealer also generally has a list of clients who can be customers for your doll, no matter how specialized, and has the knowledge and background to present your doll in the best light to customers. Taking all this into account, you can generally expect 40%–60% of the "book" value for a doll when selling to a doll shop or doll dealer.

Spikes in the Market for Hot Dolls: Sometimes a particular category of dolls will get very "hot," especially at online auctions, where a certain group of collectors goes head-to-head in that category of doll. This will cause, at least in the short term, prices in that category to spike much higher than the book values. Sometimes these market spikes will hold out over time and become the new pricing level for the dolls; sometimes they die out and pricing levels off.

Modern Dolls Sold Nude With Outfits Sold Separately: A new trend, especially for large size (15" to 16") dressed fashion dolls (Gene, Tyler, Brenda, Alex) is to sell the doll nude and the outfit for the doll separately in online auctions. Often, when these dolls are sold in two parts they can bring more than if sold in original condition. At first glance, this seems nonsensical, but the popularity of this method of selling has caught on because many collectors don't want additional dolls but they DO want a particular, limited outfit available only on a "dressed doll," so they sell the doll nude. These nude dolls are often purchased by doll repainters and customizers, who want the dolls for their art, but not the costumes.

The converse of this is that doll repainters and customizers often buy a dressed doll so they can repaint the doll, but they don't want the outfit, so they sell the outfit separately. These are bought by collectors wanting only the doll outfit! It will be interesting, over time, if enough dolls are broken up like this, to see if the remaining mint, complete dressed dolls will be valued higher.

Note on Children's Dolls vs. Collectible Market Dolls: The majority of dolls collected by collectors over the past 100 years have been the dolls of childhood. These are dolls, by definition, that were used, loved and sometimes gently abused by their owners. That is what, historically, has made mint condition dolls and dolls in their original packaging so valuable—there just weren't that many of them out there! Now collectors buy dolls and they always keep the packaging for the dolls, and the clothing, and the doll (for the most part) in mint condition. Time will tell how this affects the market for these dolls. On the other side of the equation, many millions of a particular play doll are usually produced, but often only a few thousand (or fewer) of a particular collectible doll are produced. That may even out the market for these collectible dolls in the future, if their popularity climbs.

My point here is: If everyone saves the boxes for their modern Madame Alexander dolls and keeps their modern collectible Barbie dolls NRFB (never removed from box) that isn't a special condition—that just becomes the standard condition for the dolls produced for the collector markets.

My second point here is: Don't overlook modern play dolls. As the children of the 1980s and 1990s get older, their dolls will become collectible and rise in value in the near future, just as the dolls of the baby boomers did in the 1980s and 1990s.

Building a Collection on Any Budget: Although this book certainly highlights some very expensive dolls, you will find dolls of all prices listed in this book. This was a conscious decision, to show that a fine doll collection can be built on nearly every budget. It is a misconception that doll collecting is an expensive hobby—surely, it *can* be an expensive hobby, but in certain categories of vintage and modern dolls, you can find literally thousands of dolls under $25—for instance, large collections of celluloid dolls, foreign travel dolls, or vinyl dolls of the 1960s could be built for a relatively small investment per doll. Even with antique dolls, there are many categories that have a wide variety of dolls under $200.

Another way to build a collection on a budget is to fix up dolls that are not in mint condition. If you are good at cleaning up and restoring dolls, bargains on dolls in good or fair condition or needing restoration abound on eBay. In the "Market Report" and "Online/Offline" sections of the book, I will occasionally point out where opportunities exist for finding great dolls at reasonable prices.

First Edition and Legal Disclaimers

This Is the First Edition of *The Official Price Guide to Dolls*: **How You Can Help with Future Editions:** There are so many additional categories of dolls and types of dolls that I would have liked to include in *The Official Price Guide To Dolls*. There are also literally thousands of additional dolls I would have liked to have included prices for. However, there was a tight deadline for production of the book as well as a limitation on how long it could be. Future editions of this book will include many additional dolls and types and sizes of dolls that could not be included here, as well as additional photos and updated pricing information.

Actually, I'm already working on the next edition of *The Official Price Guide To Dolls*, and you can help! I'd love to hear from you—if you see any inaccuracies or misinformation, please let me know (keeping in mind that the pricing information for this book had to "go to press" over a year before the book was published). Also, if you know of dolls we haven't covered but which you would like to see in future editions, or have any other suggestions, let me know. I can be contacted via Random House at 1745 Broadway, New York, N.Y. 10019.

Pricing Advice: Use the prices in this book as a general guide. Many, many antique and vintage dolls are truly one-of-a-kind dolls in their look, outfit, and face, and that can affect the price in an individual transaction—prices for any unique doll can therefore be outside of the range quoted in this book for many reasons. Generally, the prices in this book are for dolls of excellent quality. Dolls of lesser condition will sell for less—sometimes considerably less—and very mint dolls will sell for more—sometimes considerably more. Also, if you are selling to a dealer or shop, expect less for your dolls—generally, expect 40%–60% of book value (please see the section "Selling Your Dolls" for further information).

Identification of Dolls: Tools in this Book

Although this is not primarily a doll identification book, there are many tools in this book that can help you identify your dolls.

Photos: There are 900 photos of dolls in this book—if you have no doll marks or clothing tags, and you truly don't have any other identification information to get you started, skimming the photos in this book can help you determine what type of doll you have.

- **Photo Captions:** The photo captions contain a wealth of information. Most entries list the material the doll is made from, the mark on the doll, the size of the doll, and the approximate date the doll was made. Although there was not enough space to include extensive detail about the doll characteristics (which are included in the price listings), I have included the type of doll body, because in many cases bodies are made from different materials than the doll heads, and you cannot often tell the exact body type from the photograph. Also included where possible is an actual recent sale price for the doll.

As for the date of the doll's production, it is often difficult to date dolls exactly. Rather than leave out dates for the dolls for fear of inaccuracies, I've given the best date I can determine given research, provenance information, known dates of production for a particular doll, and other indicia. This is true throughout the book.

Finally, for antique dolls, when the caption states "jointed composition body," the body includes jointing at the shoulders, elbows, wrists, hips, and knees, unless otherwise noted.

Marks: Wherever possible, doll marks are included in the introductory sections in the price listings, or in the price tables. There is also Appendix 4 with doll marks listed and cross-referenced at the end of this book. Look for marks on dolls generally on the back of the head (or neck), or the back. Also, many dolls have clothing that is tagged with the type of doll and/or maker of the doll (such as a Madame Alexander clothing tag, or a cloth "Barbie" tag sewn into vintage Barbie outfits). Generally, look both on the outside of the clothing, at the waist or a back seam, and inside the clothing, at the neck or waist, for doll clothing tags.

For the doll marks listed in this book, if a location for the mark is not given, the mark is on the back of the doll's head or neck. Where possible, line separations for marks are given, such as 1958 / MATTEL. Where a slash is not surrounded by a space, it is actually part of a mark. Not all separations are shown, since we could not personally examine every mark included here to ascertain all line separations.

Information in Each Doll Category: The introduction to each doll category will have identifying information—what the doll is made of, sometimes what to look for to aid in identification. Additionally, the "Prices and Characteristics" sections include information on individual doll characteristics.

Extensive Bibliography, Broken Down by Type of Doll: This book can only touch the surface of information existing for the thousands of dolls that have been produced over the last 200 years. However, we've included nearly 200 doll books in the bibliography in Appendix 3 for further research. The bibliography is broken down by type of doll. Many of these books can be found at your local bookstore or on the Internet; some are out of print but readily available on eBay or through sources for secondhand books online.

How the Doll Listings Work

Introductory Section: Each section in this book starts with an introductory section that will give you some basics on the category of dolls, including the history of the dolls, when the dolls were produced, and defining characteristics of the dolls.

Market Report: The second section is the "**Market Report**" which gives you important information on the state of the market for that type of doll—is the market declining or advancing? What are the most desirable dolls in that category—what are collectors looking for? The market report is my opinion of the state of the market. I base this opinion on the research I have done for this book, my watch of the market on a continuing basis, as the Doll Collecting Guide for About.com, my own buying and selling activity as a doll dealer, and discussions with doll collectors and dealers alike. The Market Report is not meant to be the last word—it's just a jumping-off point, especially for those new to doll collecting. Also remember that prices and trends can change very quickly, and the Market Report is a snapshot I've taken of the doll market at the time this book was written.

- **"Hot" Dolls:** As to what is or is not a "hot" doll, please don't be offended if I've described the type of doll that you collect as "not hot," decreasing in price, or not appreciating much in price over the last few years. Remember, trends come and go, and what is a doll languishing on the market today might be the next big thing! Trends and styles come and go, and there have been rises and falls in the fortunes of many doll categories in the last 30 years. Also, if you collect something that isn't particularly hot right now, that can be a great advantage—you can pick up great dolls at great prices, and be poised for the next upswing in collecting in that category of dolls. Even if the dolls never really become "hot," at least you can collect, at relatively reasonable prices, dolls that you love!

Online/Offline Report: The third short section is the "**Online/Offline Report**" which compares pricing trends for Internet auctions vs. dealer, show, and land-based auction house prices.

Prices and Characteristics: Finally, the "Prices and Characteristics" section contains prices for the dolls and, wherever available, the size of the dolls, characteristics of the dolls, doll marks, and the approximate dates the dolls were produced. All sizes are in inches. Doll material is the material that the doll head is made from—a bisque head doll has a head of bisque but may have a body made of composition, cloth, or kid leather, as noted.

As mentioned above, the prices given throughout this book are a mix of Internet, dealer (doll shops and shows), and auction house prices. Each section denotes whether the majority of prices are from the Internet or dealer/auction houses—for some sections, prices of both kinds will be listed. Where no source of prices is listed, the prices are an average of all prices found.

Throughout the book, "bisque" denotes unglazed bisque, and "porcelain" denotes glazed bisque, or what many collectors like to call a "china doll" finish. For more definitions, see Appendix I.

One more note about eBay/online auction pricing vs. dealer/shop/show pricing. When you buy a doll from a dealer, the dealer has sought out the doll and assumed the expense of putting it in their inventory. This gives you the ability to inspect the doll in person prior to purchase. This causes dolls (especially more common ones) to often sell above eBay prices, and rightly so—when you buy the doll, you know exactly what you are getting and the exact condition of the doll. eBay dolls have a built-in discount because there can be so many surprises when you buy dolls off of eBay, because of the difficulty of assessing the condition of the doll from eBay, and because of postage/handling charges.

As an example, right before this book was completed I obtained seven dolls from eBay for photos for this book. I found the following flaws, none of which were explained in the auction text or could be seen in the photos: one doll had light pen marks on the face, one doll had a broken original cello (NRFB 1960s doll), one doll had broken accessories, one doll was soiled, one doll was an all-bisque reproduction and not an antique as it was represented! That is, five dolls out of seven had undisclosed flaws.

This type of experience explains part of the difference in eBay vs. dealer pricing—had I bought the dolls from a dealer, I would have paid more but saved myself untold hassle. Most of the sellers made good on the problems, but it cost me time and effort as I had to find replacement dolls for the photos. I don't think any of these sellers were trying to rip me off—they were just inexperienced in selling dolls, or a bit careless. Of course, if you buy from doll dealers that you know and trust on eBay, these problems would most likely not occur.

Doll Condition and Prices Quoted

Antique Dolls: All prices quoted are for dolls in excellent condition with appropriate old clothing from the same time period as the doll. Dolls with original clothing bring more as do dolls in mint condition. Dolls with replaced new clothing or condition less than excellent will bring less. Wherever price quotes given are for dolls that differ from excellent with old clothing, such differences will be noted.

Vintage Dolls: Price quotes are for dolls in excellent condition in original clothing. Dolls in mint condition or dolls with original boxes, tags, and paperwork will bring more. Dolls in replaced clothing will bring less. Wherever price quotes given are for dolls that differ from excellent in original clothing, such differences will be noted.

- **Prices Vary Greatly Based on Condition of a Doll:** There are wild swings in pricing due to extreme condition variations for any individual doll. When you have a vintage or antique doll in fair condition or worse (played with, missing clothing, other flaws), you can expect only a fraction of the book value for the doll.

- **Extra-Mint and Original Vintage and Antique Dolls: The Sky Is the Limit:** For mint vintage or antique dolls, especially those that are completely original with all labels, boxes, and tags, the sky can be the limit on value—often, the value can be 100% or more over book value. This is because there are fewer and fewer truly mint and all-original older dolls available to collectors each year, and the competition to own those dolls is intense. In some of the price listings, especially for vintage dolls, prices are quoted at various condition levels to illustrate this and to help guide the reader.

Modern Dolls: As these dolls were created for collectors, it is expected that these dolls are mint and all-original, with their original boxes and paperwork. Dolls in lesser condition, without their boxes and paperwork will frequently have little if any value, because so many mint, complete examples of modern dolls exist. Of course, for very rare dolls in great demand, even fair condition modern dolls have value, but again, that value is a fraction of book value.

Most modern dolls lacking their original clothing sell for a tiny fraction of their original cost, except for modern fashion dolls such as Gene, Tyler Wentworth, and others, where dolls and clothing sold separately can bring prices approaching the original cost of the dressed doll. Modern Barbie doll prices quoted are for dolls NRFB (never removed from box), which is what the modern Barbie doll collector expects.

In general, grades of condition are as follows (note the abbreviations, which are used throughout this book, especially in the price listings):

- **NRFB:** For modern dolls, a doll that has never been removed from the original box. Doll should be mint. Factory fresh.

- **MIB:** Mint doll in its original box (also MIP: mint in package and MOC: mint on card).

- **Mint:** Totally unplayed with, generally in original clothing. Factory fresh.

- **NM:** Near mint

- **Excellent (Ex):** Perhaps played with to some degree, but no flaws. If antique or vintage, in age-appropriate clothing; if the doll is generally 1960s or later, in original clothing.

- **Very Good (VG) or Average (Av):** Definitely played with, with wear and/or minor flaws (mussy hair, clothes not crisp), possibly redressed.

- **Good (Gd):** Played with pretty hard, perhaps a major flaw or several small flaws.

4 ANTIQUE DOLLS

All-Bisque Dolls

Most bisque dolls have heads that are bisque, but bodies that are wholly or partially made of another material—commonly, cloth or composition. All-bisque dolls are exactly what they sound like—dolls made completely of bisque. All-bisque dolls tend to be small, since the weight of larger all-bisque dolls, and the danger of breakage due to heavy weight, makes them impractical. The majority of all-bisque dolls are under eight inches tall.

French and German Makers: Antique all-bisque dolls were made by many French and German doll companies starting from approximately 1880 on (although earlier German examples have been found). Many all-bisques cannot be identified to the exact manufacturer—the majority are simply marked "Germany," or have numbers on the back and sometimes limbs. Most French-made (or assumed French-made) early all-bisques have no marks at all.

German firms that made all-bisques include Kestner, Simon & Halbig, Alt, Beck & Gottschalck, Hertwig, Limbach, Kling, and many others.

Dates of Production: All-bisque dolls were produced from about 1880 to approximately the early 1930s. Sometimes referred to as "penny dolls," they were produced in infinite varieties, and in the millions.

Japanese and Late Models: Starting after World War I, by the early 1920s and into the 1930s, millions of cheaper all-bisque dolls were produced in Japan. Some of the German-made dolls in this period were also "budget" models (created to compete with the Japanese dolls that were flooding the market), and some cruder dolls that were earlier attributed to Japanese makers are now attributed to German companies such as Hertwig, after original samples and catalogs have been found in Germany. These dolls are often, but not always, marked with the country of origin.

Market Report: All-bisque dolls are hot! One popularity factor is definitely the size of the dolls—it is easy to have a large collection in a very small space. Another factor in their huge popularity is the display possibilities—whether posed with larger dolls, or on a shelf with small accessories such as tiny doll stoves or bathtubs, all-bisque dolls give collectors endless possibilities. Then there is simply the charm factor of "little"—the dolls tend to be adorable, and they fit in the palm of your hand. Finally many collectors enjoy sewing for these dolls—elaborate costumes can be made using only tiny amounts of the best antique fabrics and trims.

- **Hottest Dolls:** The hottest all-bisques right now are the well-made French and early German all-bisques. The French and French-style slim, early dolls with long limbs and sometimes bare feet can go for several thousand dollars. Anything by Kestner and Simon & Halbig is sought after, as are unusually large and chubby all-bisques.

- **Glass Eyes, Swivel Neck:** When considering all-bisques, generally, glass-eyed dolls are more highly sought after than painted-eye dolls, and dolls with more jointing are more desirable than stiff-limbed dolls—dolls with

All-bisque, German, Kestner.
Glass eyes, 1-piece torso/head.
Boots with bows, heels, and 2
straps. 5", c. late 1890s. Mark: 150
/ 2. $400, dealer.

All-bisque, French mignonette in
original dress, 5.25", c. 1880.
$2,900 with two original outfits at
auction.

swivel necks are always more sought after than stiff-necked (one-piece head/torso) dolls.

- **Pre-Tinted Bisque:** The dolls with pre-tinted bisque (pink coloring mixed right into the porcelain) are later dolls, generally from the 1920s and 1930s. You can determine if an all-bisque has pre-tinting by looking inside a limb—if the inside of the bisque is the same pink color as the outside, you have a later pre-tinted bisque doll. If it looks white, you have an earlier doll where skin coloring was applied later. Earlier dolls are more desirable.

Look out for dolls where the feature painting is NOT fired on—these later dolls can have the paint flake off, and are of lesser quality.

- **Artistry of Individual Doll and Condition:** Finally, when considering any all-bisque dolls, look at the artistry of the dolls. Even

dolls made in Japan, if the painting is artfully applied, are desirable to collectors today—always consider if the doll's painted features are applied with detail or roughly applied. Look for smooth vs. rough, pebbly bisque. All-bisque dolls, to be in excellent condition, should be free of chips or cracks and appropriately dressed. You can expect more than price-guide value for dolls with original clothing or fine presentation.

- **French and French-Type:** These dolls are the rarest (and oldest) of the all-bisque dolls. Once thought to be all produced in France, there has been evidence in the past few years that many of the dolls were actually produced in Germany for the French market. The French and French-type all-bisques cannot be mistaken, however—they are much more slender than the majority of their German cousins, and they have a very distinctive look.

All-bisque, Japanese. Jointed arms and legs. 5.25". $20, eBay.

- **German:** The majority of all-bisque dolls were produced in Germany. Tending to be chubby and childlike (at least until the 1920s, when flapper-type all-bisques with their more slender physiques and bobbed hairstyles were all the rage) these are the dolls that most doll collectors think of when they think of antique all-bisques. Produced in endless varieties, entire books have been devoted to all-bisque dolls in their multitude of styles.

- **Japanese:** The Japanese entered the all-bisque market after World War I. They made cheaper knockoffs of many popular German all-bisque styles, and flooded the market with low-quality dolls. These dolls are collected today both as historical objects and to round out collections of all-bisque dolls. Some of the better-quality Japanese all-bisques (well-painted nodders, bent-limb all bisque babies) can be quite charming in their own right.

Online/Offline Report: The market is strong both online and from dealers and shows; however, expect to find better, finer, and broader selections of all-bisque dolls at good antique doll shows, from dealers, and from auction houses than on the Internet. Online auction prices often run below dealer and show prices on more common examples, due to the difficulty of assessing bisque and flaws online.

Prices and Characteristics: Unless otherwise stated, the all-bisque dolls have jointed arms and legs. "1-piece head/torso" indicates that the head and torso is molded as one piece and the head does not swivel. All dolls represent children unless otherwise stated. All-bisque dolls are wigged, generally with mohair, but sometimes with human hair, unless otherwise stated, and they have painted lashes and brows. To identify and price your doll, look for characteristics such as glass or painted eyes, swivel neck, type of shoes, molded hair or other molded features. Dolls with pink-tinted bisque tend to be less expensive than similar, earlier dolls.

Slender French and French-type all-bisque dolls are sometimes referred to as "mignonettes." All French and French-type dolls are wigged and have closed mouths, and the majority are peg-strung. Prices for French all-bisques are from dealers and auctions, except as noted.

FRENCH ALL-BISQUE

French-Type, Bare Feet

Size: 5–7"   Date: 1880
Price: $2,000–$4,000
Swivel neck, bare feet, glass eyes, elongated limbs, slender body. More for larger sizes. Some possibly German made.

All-bisque, French mignonette, *jointed elbows, glass eyes, swivel neck with original trousseau and box. 5.5", c. 1877. $5,000. Courtesy Theriault's.*

All-bisque, French. *Mignonette, glass eyes, swivel neck, jointed. Original costume. 4", c. 1890. $475, auction.*

Pair, all-bisque, French. *Mignonette, original folklore costumes. Painted eyes, swivel heads. 2.5", c. 1890. $150 each, dealer.*

French-Type, Molded Shoes or Boots
Size: 5–7"   Date: 1880
Price: $1,500– $3,000
Swivel neck, glass eyes, elongated limbs, slender body, molded shoes or boots. More for larger sizes. Some possibly German made. Most of molded/painted shoes have 2 straps.
Mark: Sometimes a number, usually unmarked.

French-Type, Painted Eyes
Size: 4–5"   Date: 1885
Price: $700–$1,000
Painted-eye French-type dolls tend to be smaller than their glass-eye counterparts. Swivel neck.

Jointed Elbows
Size: 3.75–5"   Date: 1880
Price: $3,300–$5,000
Swivel neck, bare feet, glass eyes, ball-jointed elbows. Some made by Schmitt et Fils.
Mark: Sometimes marked BTE or BTR.

Later Doll, Provincial French Costume
Size: 6"   Date: 1920s
Price: $825
Glass eyes, swivel neck, molded high-heel shoes.

Mechanical Arm, Dressed as Dandy
Size: 5.75"   Date: late 1880s
Price: $530
Bent arm holding hat, other holds flowers and when legs pushed down arm tips hat. Glass eyes.

Mignonette Group in Original Presentation
Size: 2.5"   Date: 1885
                    Internet: $750
5 dolls, swivel necks, painted features. These tiny boxed dolls were offered in French department store catalogs at the end of the 19th century, sometimes labeled as "Lilliputians." Some dolls in these sets represented costumes of France or other nations.

Mignonette with Trousseau in Basket
Size: 5"   Date: 1880
Price: $2,400
Glass eyes, bare feet, not original basket, clothes include 2 added dresses and hankie.

Mignonette, Original Presentation Box
Size: 5.5"   Date: 1886
Price: $5,100
Black-painted bootines, white stockings, glass eyes, swivel neck, many outfits in original presentation box.

Swivel Neck, Bare Feet, Bride
Size: 5.25"   Date: 1880s
Price: $2,500
Original bride costume, glass eyes, swivel neck.
Mark: 0 (back of legs)

Swivel Neck, Glass Eyes, in Trousseau Box
Size: 5.5"
Price: $3,800
In paper-covered box with 3 extra outfits, lingerie, and accessories, possibly later assembled. Molded high-button blue boots.

Unusually Large, Bare Feet
Size: 10"   Date: 1880
Price: $5,200
Glass eyes, closed mouth, peg-strung, bare feet.
Mark: 8 (head and torso)

Pair of all-bisques, German.
*Glass eyes, swivel head. 4". Mark:
Made in Germany. $400 each,
dealer sale.*

All-bisque, German, Kestner.
*Glass eyes, 4-strap boots, swivel
head. 6", c. 1885. $1400, dealer
sale.*

GERMAN ALL-BISQUE, 1-PIECE HEAD/TORSO

Pink-Tinted Bisque, Painted Eyes, 1-Strap Shoes or Boots

Size: 4–6″   Date: 1920s
Price: $100–$175   Internet: $75–$125
Penny Doll-types. Some with light blue shoes,
often with blue-rim socks. More for better-
painted or larger dolls.
Mark: Germany or unmarked.

Glass Eyes

Size: 4–6″   Date: 1890s–early 1900s
Price: $150–$300
Painted shoes and socks. Higher values for
larger sizes, more unusual shoes, unusual stockings.
Mark: Various numbers or unmarked, some
with "Germany."

Glass Eyes, Body Elongated

Size: 7″
Price: $825

Like a skinny Wrestler-type, 2-strap painted
black shoes, painted white socks with rim.
Mark: 61 10

Impish, Googly-Type, Painted Eyes

Size: 11″   Date: 1915
Price: $700
Impish side-glancing eyes.

Mignonette-Type, Glass Eyes

Size: 9″   Date: 1885
Price: $1,000
1-strap black shoes, blue stockings, closed
mouth.
Mark: 2

Molded Hair, Painted Eyes

Size: 7.5″
Price: $150

Painted Eyes, Nurse Outfit

Size: 6″
Price: $290
Original nurse outfit.
Mark: P 607 / I Germany

All-bisque, German. Jointed arms and legs, painted eyes, original outfit. 4″. Mark: Germany (back). Private collection.

All-bisque, German, Simon & Halbig. Peg-jointed, glass eyes, swivel head, black stockings, original outfit. 7.25″, c. 1890. Mark: 890 / 3 (head & torso). Private collection.

All-bisque, German, Kestner. Modeled chemise, holding ball. Jointed arms only. 3.75″, c. 1890. Mark: 111.4. Private collection.

Legs Frozen, Arms Jointed, Glass Eyes, Pink Socks

Size: 6″   Internet: $200
Pink, waffled socks. Attributed to Alt, Beck & Gottschalck.
Mark: 2 / 0 on top of head, in circle

Painted Eyes

Size: 3–5.5″   Date: 1880s–1900
Price: $125–$200   Internet: $115–$160
Painted shoes, socks. More for larger sizes, unusually painted shoes and socks.
Mark: Various numbers, or unmarked, some with "Germany."

Painted Eyes, Poor Quality

Size: 3.5″   Date: 1920s
Price: $30–$50   Internet: $30–$50
Later dolls, crudely painted, sometimes with nonfired tint.

GERMAN ALL-BISQUE, ASIAN

Asian, Queue San Baby Dolls

Size: 5″   Date: 1900s
                              Internet: $40–$65
Kneeling or standing.

Asian, Simon & Halbig

Size: 5.5″   Date: 1900
                              Internet: $825
Swivel neck, glass sleep eyes, closed mouth. Peg-jointed limbs, painted shoes/socks. Human hair queue.
Mark: 1

Asian, Simon & Halbig

Size: 7″   Date: 1895
Price: $750
Swivel neck, glass eyes.
Mark: 3

Asian, Simon & Halbig Attributed

Size: 5″   Date: 1890
Price: $650
Swivel neck, glass eyes, closed mouth, painted white stockings and blue slippers.

Asian, Swivel Neck

Size: 5″   Date: 1890
Price: $500
Glass eyes, closed mouth, 1-stroke brows, bare feet.

GERMAN ALL-BISQUE, BABIES

1-Piece Head/Torso, Glass Eyes

Size: 4–6″   Date: 1910–1920s
Price: $200–$400   Internet: $200–$400
Bent baby arms and legs, painted hair, bare feet. More for larger examples, babies with finer painting.
Mark: Various numbers or unmarked, some with "Germany."

1-Piece Head/Torso, Painted Eyes

Size: 3–6″   Date: 1910–1920
Price: $100–$300   Internet: $40–$100
Bent baby arms and legs, painted hair, bare feet. More for larger examples, babies with finer painting.
Mark: Various numbers or unmarked, some with "Germany."

All-bisque, German, Gebrüder Kühnlenz. Glass eyes, swivel head, closed mouth. 6", c. 1895. $800, auction.

All-bisque, German. 1-piece head/torso, painted eyes, light blue-painted shoes and white socks with green rim. 4", c. early 1900s.

All-bisque, German. 1-piece head/torso, painted eyes. 3.25", c. late 1890s–early 1900s. Foot damage. $75, dealer sale.

1-piece Head/Torso, Painted Eyes, Later

Size: 3–4"　　　　Date: 1920s
Price: $60–$100　　Internet: $40–$80
Pink-tinted bisque, lesser quality than earlier all-bisque babies. Bent baby arms and legs, painted hair, bare feet.
Mark: Various numbers or unmarked, some with "Germany."

Baby, 1-Piece Head/Torso, Large

Size: 10"　　　　Date: 1915
Price: $600
Painted hair. very large example.
Mark: 830 / 13 (torso and arms)

Baby Bo Kaye By J. Kallus

Size: 5"　　　　Date: 1910
Price: $450　　　Internet: $825
Swivel neck, glass sleep eyes, painted hair.
Mark: unmarked

Baby, Presentation Box

Size: 4"　　　　Date: 1915
Price: $950
Several outfits, pillows, brush, teething ring, etc. Made for French market.
Mark: unmarked

Bonnie Babe, Averill

Size: 7"　　　　Date: 1926
　　　　　　　　Internet: $820
Sleep eyes, swivel neck.

Bye-Lo, 1-Piece Head/Torso, Glass Eyes

Size: 4"　　　　Date: 1925
　　　　　　　　Internet: $210
Jointed arms; sleep eyes, closed mouth.

Mark: Copr by GS Putnam, and '10-20' (legs and arms)

Bye-Lo, 1-Piece Head/Torso, Painted Eyes

Size: 5"　　　　Date: 1925
Price: $225
Mark: Copr. By G.S. Putnam

Bye-Lo, Swivel Neck, Glass Eyes

Size: 5–6"　　　Date: 1923
Price: $750–$800
Mark: Copr. By Grace S. Putnam

Bye-Lo, Swivel Neck, Glass Eyes

Size: 8"　　　　Date: 1923
　　　　　　　　Internet: $700
Original label on front torso. Swivel neck, glass eyes, painted baby hair.
Mark: 6-20-Copr by Grace S. Putnam-Germany

Baby, Swivel Neck, Glass Eyes

Size: 6–8"　　　Date: 1910–1920s
Price: $350–$600+　Internet: $300–$600+
Open mouth with teeth. Bent baby limbs, bare feet.
Mark: Sometimes marked as to maker; numbers or "Germany."

GERMAN ALL-BISQUE, VARIOUS

Amberg, Louis, MIBS

Size: 4.5"　　　　Date: 1918
Price: $250　　　Internet: $210
Maybe Hertwig. Pink-tinted bisque, painted eyes, molded hair and brown shoes/socks.
Mark: MIBS (on back)

All-bisque, German. Pre-tinted pink bisque, paint not fired on, 1-piece torso/head. 4.5", c. 1920s. Mark: 620 (head) Made / in Germany (back). $100, dealer sale.

All-bisque, German. Prize Baby. Sleep eyes, original label and marked box. Box mark: BISC. / PRIZE BABY / REG. U.S. PAT. OFF. $300+, private collection.

All-bisque, German. Kewpie-type. Painted eyes, 1-piece head/torso. 2.5", c. 1920. Mark: Germany (back). Possibly Hertwig.

Black Stockings, Painted Eyes

Size: 4.25"　　　　Date: 1890
　　　　　　　　　Internet: $325
1-piece head/torso, unsophisticated face painting.
Mark: 4 / 0

Black, Kestner

Size: 5"　　　　　Date: 1890
　　　　　　　　　Internet: $1,300
1-piece head/torso, glass eyes, closed mouth.
Mark: 164-4/0

Black, Kühnlenz, Gebrüder, Bare Feet

Size: 3"　　　　　Date: 1885
Price: $400
Peg joints, swivel neck, set enamel eyes.
Mark: 61.7

Black, Kühnlenz, Gebrüder, Bare Feet

Size: 6"　　　　　Date: 1895
Price: $850
Swivel neck, glass eyes.

Carl Horn, Attributed

Size: 1.5"　　　　Date: late 1800s
Price: $60–$80　　Internet: $40–$75
Commonly found in crocheted outfits; perfect doll for a doll.

Cat

Size: 2.25"　　　　Date: late 1800s
Price: $645
1-piece head/torso, molded white shoes.
Mark: Germany (torso)

Character, Glass Eyes

Size: 9"　　　　　Date: 1920s
Price: $950

Flapper-style body, open/closed smiling mouth.
Mark: 156 / 10 (head) 155 / 10 (limbs)

Character, Resembles Moritz

Size: 7"　　　　　Date: 1915
Price: $2,400
Painted hair and side-glancing eyes.

Chubby, 1-Piece Head/Torso, Glass Eyes

Size: 6.5"　　　　Date: 1915
Price: $400
Chunky girl, painted blue knee socks, black 1-strap shoes.

Chubby, 1-Piece Head/Torso, Glass Eyes

Size: 9–10"　　　Date: 1915
Price: $375–$425
Glass eyes, 1-strap black shoes, white socks with blue rim, open mouth.
Mark: unmarked or 329 / 25

Clown, Molded Clothes

Size: 2.75"　　　　Date: 1870
Price: $470
Painted eyes, wire jointed. Painted molded clown suit.

Cupid, Butler Bros. (male or female)

Size: 5"　　　　　Date: 1916
　　　　　　　　　Internet: $60–$70
Kewpie-type. 1-piece head/ torso. Painted side-glancing eyes, molded hair tufts, girl has bow.
Mark: 10283-Germany or unmarked

Galluba & Hoffmann, lady

Size: 5.5"　　　　Date: 1915
Price: $1,700

Immobiles, 2.25″ each. Yellow dress marked "Germany," red dress marked "Japan." Private collection.

All-bisque Snow Baby, German. 1.35″. $50, eBay.

All-bisque, Orsini, character. 1-piece head/torso. Glass eyes. 5″, c. 1920. Mark: J.I.O. $600, auction. Courtesy Theriault's.

Original costume, original long mohair wig.
Mark: unmarked

Geo. Studdy Bonzo Dog, Pair
Size: 3″
Price: $130

Googly, Hertel, Schwab, Jointed Elbows and Knees
Size: 4.5″ Internet: $1,525
Glass eyes. Painted black shoes, white socks.
Mark: unmarked

Googly, Hertel, Schwab, 1-Piece Head/Torso
Size: 7″ Date: 1915
Price: $550
For more googlies, see Googly section.
Mark: 410 (arms) 179 410 (legs)

Googly, Kestner
Size: 6″ Internet: $675
Mark: 217/17

HEbee-SHEbee, Horsman
Size: 4″ Date: early 1920s
Internet: $550
With original bib. Painted features, uniquely jointed legs.
Mark: Copyright by / HeBee SheBee / Chas Twelve Trees (oval label, foot) Germany (back) 50 (arms & legs)

Hertwig, "Swimming" Doll
Size: 3″ Internet: $75
As male or female in painted swim wear. Arms jointed. Pink-tinted, molded dark-blonde hair. Girls have red bow.
Mark: Germany

Hertwig, 1-Piece Head/Torso
Internet: $50–$65
Crude bisque, brown paint on shoes rubs off. Painted eyes.
Mark: 20-11-made in Germany

Hertwig, Boy, Molded Hair, 1-Piece Head/Torso
Size: 7.5″ Internet: $100
Pink-tinted bisque. Painted black shoes with blue socks.

Hertwig, Character Face, Molded Hair
Size: 8″ Internet: $120
1-piece head/torso, side-glancing painted eyes.
Mark: unmarked

Hertwig, Swivel Neck, Glass Eyes
Size: 5″ Date: early 1900s
Internet: $185
Pink-tinted bisque, loop strung, chubby. Good quality.

Heubach, Character, Molded Hair
Size: 8″ Date: 1915
Price: $750
1-piece head/torso. Painted eyes and brown shoes.
Mark: 10500

Kling, Glass Eyes, 1 Piece Head/Torso
Size: 6″
Price: $200
Painted socks with blue rim, 2-strap black shoes, closed mouth.
Mark: 36 / 15 B (head) K (in bell)

Immobile, 3". Mark: Germany (back hip). Private collection.

Nodder, Mr. Bailey, the Boss, from the Dagwood comic strip. 3.5", c. 1925. Mark: MR.BAILEY / THE BOSS / GERMANY (back). $50–$60, dealers.

Nodder, Tilda (on left), Auntie Blossom (right). 4", c. 1925. Mark: TILDA/GERMANY (back); AUNTIE BLOSSOM / GERMANY (back). $50–$60, dealers.

Man, Molded Helmet
Size: 2.75–3.75"   Date: late 1800s
Price: $165–$235
Painted features, black mustache, military uniform.

Max and Moritz, crude
Size: 4.5"   Date: 1915
Price: $410
Molded hair, 5-piece bisque bodies, fawn-colored shoes, wire limb attachment.

Max and Moritz
Size: 3–4"   Date: 1915
Price: $2,000+
Swivel neck, well molded and painted.

Older Woman, Molded Hair
Size: 2.75"   Date: late 1800s
Price: $235
Exaggerated features, molded gray hair, painted eyes.

Only Arms Jointed, Painted Eyes, Lustre Boots
Size: 5"   Date: 1885
        Internet: $160
Elongated body, pale bisque, Frozen Charlotte-type.
Mark: unmarked

Only Arms Jointed, Painted Eyes, Solid Dome Head
Size: 6"   Date: 1885
        Internet: $275

Attributed to Kestner. Painted 1-strap shoes, wigged.
Mark: unmarked

Orsini, Character Girl
Size: 5"   Date: 1920
Price: $600
Mark: J.I.O. c. 1919

Wide-Awake Doll, Butler Bros.
Size: 5"   Date: 1914
        Internet: $110
Only arms jointed, painted features with side-glancing eyes. Molded tufts of hair, painted black flat slippers, blue socks.
Mark: "The Wide Awake Doll-registered-Germany"

GERMAN ALL-BISQUE, MOLDED CLOTHING

Molded Clothing, Painted Eyes, Jointed Arms, Various
Size: 4–7"   Date: 1890–1910
Price: $100–$200
Varies depending on quality of molding of clothing and painting.
Mark: unmarked

Molded Clothing, Regional
Size: 2.75"   Date: late 1800s
Price: $400
Painted eyes, molded hair, detailed molded lace-up bodice and puffy blouse.

All-bisque babies. 3–4″, c. early 1900s–1920s. Mark: Middle baby: (peace-type symbol) / MADE IN JAPAN. Front baby: Germany (back). $30–$50 each, dealers.

Molded Clothing, Sailor Boy, Butler Bros.
Size: 4″   Date: 1908
                        Internet: $100
Painted eyes, pin-jointed arms, molded hair.

Molded Hat, Multi-Strapped Boots
Size: 7.5″   Date: 1870s
Price: $1,000+
Molded hat and hair, molded 9-strap black boots, stockings to above knees, peg strung.

Hertwig, Molded Hair and Clothes
Size: 4″   Date: 1920
                        Internet: $100
Pin-jointed arms, painted side-glancing eyes, pouty expression, molded/painted uniform, brown shoes, socks.
Mark: unmarked

Hertwig, Native American
Size: 7.5″
Price: $120
Jointed arms only, lesser quality, painted hair and headdress.

Immobile, Aviator Boy
Size: 4″   Date: 1920s
                        Internet: $90
Aviator with painted side-glancing eyes, molded hair, aviator jacket.
Mark: unmarked

Immobile, Bobby with Molded Cap
Size: 2.75″   Date: late 1800s
Price: $175
Molded and painted features, mustache, bobby uniform.

Immobiles
Size: 1–3″   Date: 1920s
                        Internet: $20–$40
1-piece, molded, painted clothing. More for better-painting, children, and hard-to-find styles.

Jockey with Molded Cap
Size: 2.75″   Date: late 1800s
Price: $150
Molded and painted features, molded hair and hat, original outfit.

Molded Underwear, Painted Eyes, Butler Bros.
Size: 6″   Date: 1890
                        Internet: $70
1-piece head/torso, crude bisque, painted eyes, molded hair. Molded 1-piece underwear trimmed in pink.
Mark: unmarked

Snow Baby, In Bear Costume
Size: 4″   Date: 1920
Price: $600

Snow Baby, Various
Size: 3.5″   Date: 1920s
Price: $35–$60
For common styles.

GERMAN ALL-BISQUE, KESTNER & KESTNER TYPES

Kestner Attributed, Bare Feet
Size: 8″   Date: 1890
Price: $2,200
Peg-jointed, swivel neck.
Mark: 153 10

Kestner Look, 1-Piece Head/Torso, Chubby

Size: 7.5″   Date: 1910
                             Internet: $330
Glass sleep eyes, painted black shoes and white socks.
Mark: unmarked

Kestner, 150

Size: 5–6″   Date: 1900
Price: $185–$225   Internet: $180
Chubby, glass sleep eyes, 1-piece head/torso, painted 1-strap black shoes.
Mark: 150 / 2/0

Kestner, 150

Size: 7″   Date: 1900
Price: $325   Internet: $270
Mark: 150.1

Kestner, 150

Size: 8.5–9″   Date: 1900
Price: $600–$700
Mark: 3 / 150 or 150 / 4

Kestner, 150

Size: 11″   Date: 1910
Price: $1,250–$1,550
Mark: 150 6 (head and arms)

Kestner, 150, 2-Strap Brown Shoes With Rosette

Size: 7.5″   Date: 1900
                             Internet: $500
Mark: 150-7 1/2

Kestner, 1-Piece Head/Torso, Glass Eyes

Size: 11″   Date: 1910
Price: $1,550
Very large size for all-bisque.
Mark: 130 14 (head, inside arms) 14 (inside legs)

Kestner, 208

Size: 4″   Date: 1910
Price: $200
1-piece head/torso, sleep eyes, painted 1-strap shoes with blue rims.
Mark: 208

Kestner, Baby

Size: 10″   Date: 1915
Price: $1,050
Swivel neck.
Mark: 211 JDK

Kestner, Bare Feet

Size: 6″   Date: 1885
Price: $1,700
Swivel neck, glass eyes, peg-jointed, curled fingers, chubby face.
Mark: 1

Kestner, Bare Feet, Swivel Neck

Size: 7.25″   Date: 1880
Price: $3,500–$4,000+
Glass eyes, closed mouth, peg joints.

Kestner, Bare Feet

Size: 9.5″   Date: 1880s
Price: $8,225
Unusually large size with frail original box.

Kestner, Bare Feet, Bent Elbows, Chubby

Size: 7″   Date: 1885
Price: $2,900+
Swivel neck, glass eyes, bent elbows.
Mark: unmarked

Kestner, Glass Eyes, Jointed Arms and Legs

Size: 7″   Date: 1900
                             Internet: $250–$300
Chubby body, 1-piece head/torso, open/closed mouth, black shoes, white socks.
Mark: 83.125.16 1/2 (neck), 83.125 (arms)

Kestner, Glass Eyes, Only Arms Jointed

Size: 6.5″   Date: late 1800s
Price: $400
Open/closed mouth

Kestner, Jointed Knees

Size: 5.25″   Date: 1880
Price: $8,225
Glass eyes, closed mouth, swivel neck, peg strung, wrestler arms, molded pink boots with 4 straps.
Mark: 111 (upper torso, back legs)

Kestner, Jointed Knees

Size: 6″   Date: 1885
Price: $4,400
Glass eyes, cupped hands, bent right arm, painted white stockings; blue laced ankle boots and heels.
Mark: 1

Kestner, Swivel Neck, 10-strap boots

Size: 5.5″   Date: 1890
                             Internet: $2,000

Kestner, Swivel Neck, Black Boots, Blue Tassels

Size: 10″   Date: 1885
Price: $2,600
Mark: 4

Kestner, Swivel Neck, Glass Eyes

Size: 5.5″   Date: 1890
                             Internet: $300
Pale bisque, glass sleep eyes, open mouth, upper teeth, molded white socks, brown shoes.
Mark: 620 4 (neck and torso)

Kestner, Swivel Neck

Size: 7.5–8″   Date: 1880–1885
Price: $1,500–$1,800
Glass eyes, may have fancy boots, or square-cut
teeth.
Mark: 3

Kestner, Swivel Neck. Wrestler-Type

Size: 5″   Date: late 1800s
Price: $2,500+
Glass eyes, chubby, peg strung, bent arms, heeled
4-strap high black boots.
Mark: 0 (heads and limbs)

Kestner, Wrestler-Type, Swivel Neck, Chubby (also by Simon & Halbig)

Size: 9–9.5″   Date: 1885
Price: $3,600   Internet: $3,950
Curved arms, glass eyes, swivel neck, molded
boots, pierced ears, white ribbed stockings.
Mark: unmarked or 4 (head, upper back)

GERMAN ALL-BISQUE, SIMON & HALBIG & SIMILAR TYPES

Simon & Halbig, 886, Peach Stockings

Size: 9″   Date: 1885
Price: $3,000
2-strap shoes, open mouth with 2 upper teeth
and 1 lower tooth.

Simon & Halbig, 886

Size: 9″   Date: 1890
Price: $1,300
Mignonette-type.
Mark: 886 S 5 H

Simon & Halbig, Mignonette for French Market, 5-Strap Boots

Size: 8″   Date: 1890
Price: $2,800
Elongated body, blue stockings, swivel neck,
glass eyes.
Mark: S 3 H

Black Stocking Girl, 887

Size: 5″   Date: 1890
Price: $800
Swivel neck, glass eyes, open mouth, brown 1-
strap shoes.
Mark: S & H 887 1

Black Stocking Girl, 890

Size: 5″   Date: 1890
Price: $800   Internet: $600
Black stockings to above knees, brown 1-strap
shoes, glass eyes, swivel neck.
Mark: 890 / 1½ or 890 / 0

Black Stocking Girl

Size: 6″   Date: 1890
Price: $1,300
Swivel neck, peg joints, black ribbed stockings to
above knee, brown 1-strap heeled shoes.
Mark: 3

Black-Stocking Girl in French Presentation Box

Size: 7″   Date: 1890
Price: $5,800
Elaborate presentation, many outfits, accessories,
fur muff and collar. At auction.
Mark: 890 / 3

Blue Stockings, Simon & Halbig-Type

Size: 7″   Date: 1890
Price: $1,600
Open mouth, peg joints, painted above-knee
blue stockings, black 1-strap shoes. swivel-neck,
glass eyes.
Mark: unmarked

Swivel Neck, Glass Eyes, Simon & Halbig-Type

Size: 9.5″   Date: 1885
Price: $2,300
Attributed to Simon & Halbig, open mouth.
Very large

Swivel Neck, Glass Eyes, Simon & Halbig-Type

Size: 7″   Date: 1890s
Price: $1,400
Early Kestner/Simon & Halbig-type, closed
mouth.
Mark: unmarked

GERMAN ALL-BISQUE, SWIVEL NECK

Edwardian Bride

Size: 5″   Date: early 1900s
Price: $550
Closed mouth, swivel neck, molded shoes, origi-
nal outfit, glass eyes. At auction.

Glass Eyes

Size: 3.5″   Date: late 1800s
Price: $265
Closed mouth.

Glass Eyes, Mignonette Style

Size: 6″   Date: 1890
Price: $1,550
Closed mouth, peg joints, painted white socks,
black 1-strap shoes.
Mark: unmarked

Glass Eyes, Bare Feet

Size: 5.5″   Date: 1890
Price: $1,900
Probably Kestner. Closed mouth, peg jointed, molded closed fingers on left hand.
Mark: unmarked

Glass Eyes, Bare Feet, Kühnlenz

Size: 7″   Date: 1890
Price: $2,000
Gebrüder Kühnlenz rare signature open mouth, peg joints.
Mark: 18.16 G.K.

Glass Eyes, in Presentation Box

Size: 4″   Date: 1890
Price: $1,600
In silk-covered wooden box with complete trousseau. At auction.
Mark: unmarked

Glass Eyes, Better Quality, Various

Size: 3–7″   Date: 1880s–1910s
Price: $300–$500   Internet: $200–$500
Excellent quality, closed mouth, molded/painted shoes (many shoes with bows) or boots, stockings. More for large size or unusual shoes.
Mark: Various numbers, or unmarked, some with "Germany."

Glass Eyes, Various

Size: 3–5″   Date: 1880s–1910s
Price: $200–$300   Internet: $150–$300
Standard quality, simple shoes, many makers.
Mark: Various numbers, or unmarked, some with "Germany."

Glass Eyes, Blue-Rim Shoes

Size: 4.5″   Date: 1920s
Price: $100
Socks with blue rim, usually indicates a later doll. Painted shoes.
Mark: 13.5

NODDERS

The nodders are from the 1920s. Paint is not fired on, so flaking and chipping of paint is common. The nodders are one-piece bisque with only the heads "strung" on separately, so that it moves.

Common Comic Characters, Paint Worn, Germany

            Internet: $20–$50
Mark: Unmarked, or stamped with "Germany" and/or name of character.

Made in Japan Nodders

            Internet: $10–$30
More for well-detailed Japanese nodders.
Mark: MADE IN / JAPAN

Andy Gump Nodder

Size: 4″
Price: $65

Asian Man

Size: 3″
Price: $30
Red and white outfit.
Mark: Germany

Black

Price: $300

Ching Chow

Size: 3.5″
Price: $80
Mark: CHING / CHOW / Germany

Jeff

Size: 3″
Price: $100
From the *Mutt and Jeff* comic.
Mark: JEFF / illegible (back)

Little Orphan Annie

Size: 3.25″
Price: $55

Max

Price: $375

Rachel

Size: 3.75″
Price: $100
From *Gasoline Alley,* black mammy.
Mark: RACHEL / Germany (back)

Uncle Bim

Size: 3.25″
Price: $45   Internet: $100

W.C. Fields

Size: 3.25″
Price: $100
Mark: Germany

JAPANESE ALL-BISQUE

The majority of the Japanese all-bisques are from 1915 to the early 1930s.

Baby, Black, "Topsy"-Type

Size: 4″   Internet: $30–$45
1-piece head/torso, jointed arms and legs.
Mark: MADE IN / JAPAN

All-bisque, Japanese. Only arms jointed, silver-painted hair. 5.5", c. 1920. Mark: (peace-type sign) / MADE IN JAPAN / 5 _. $40 each, dealer.

All-bisque, Japanese, baby. Jointed arms and legs, painted eyes. 5", c. 1920, Mark: Made in Japan (back). $25, eBay.

All-bisque, Japanese. Jointed arms and legs. Painted features not fired on. 5.25", c. 1920s–1930s. No mark. $20, eBay.

Betty Boop-Type
Size: 4–6"   Internet: $20–$40
Only arms jointed, painted/molded eyes and hair.
Mark: Japan

Happifat
Size: 4"
Price: $60
Cruder version of German Happifat. Jointed arms only, clothing molded, eyes and hair painted.
Mark: JAPAN

Immobiles, Various
Size: 3–5"
Price: $15–$30   Internet: $7–$25
Mostly painted with nonfired paints. Price depends on character, pose, amount of paint loss. More for intricately painted immobiles, immobiles holding dolls, rarer characters.
Mark: MADE IN / JAPAN (back) and JAPAN (feet)

Immobiles, Boxed Set
Size: 3–5"
Price: $100+   Internet: $75–$100
For choice sets; usually illustration on multicolored box will match dolls inside box. Some boxes marked "Geo. Borgfeldt Corporation." More for unusual themed boxes of immobiles.
Mark: MADE IN / JAPAN (backs of dolls, box) and JAPAN (feet)

Kewpie-Type, Molded Hat, Sword
Size: 5"   Internet: $150
Pale pink complexion, painted side-glancing eyes, brown painted hair wisps, jointed arms, bisque molded hat attached by band.
Mark: unmarked

Nippon, Baby, Molded, Painted Hair
Size: 4"
Price: $30   Internet: $20–$40
Painted eyes.
Mark: NIPPON

Nippon, Child, Jointed Arms, Painted Hair
Size: 3–6"
Price: $35–$50   Internet: $25–$50
Mark: NIPPON

Nippon, Immobile, Solider Boy With Backpack
Size: 4.25"   Internet: $215
Molded hat, backpack, and soldier's uniform. No jointing.
Mark: NIPPON

Nippon, Side-Glancing Boy, Painted Outfit
Size: 4"   Internet: $60
Blue painted/molded outfit. Looking to side, only arms jointed.
Mark: Nippon, 4

Alt, Beck & Gottschalck

Although this porcelain factory in the Thuringia region of Germany (a famous area of intensive dollmaking) started mak-

All-bisque, Japanese. *Jointed arms, pink-tinted bisque. 2.5″, c. 1920s. No mark; similar dolls were made by Hertwig. $45, dealer.*

All-bisque, Japanese. *Immobiles, Set of 6 in original box. 3.5″, c. late 1930s. Mark: JAPAN (back of several dolls). $90, eBay.*

ing porcelain household goods in 1854, there is some debate as to when it started making doll heads—dates range from 1860 to approximately 1880, and production of dolls continued until 1930. Alt, Beck & Gottschalck is especially known for bisque shoulder head dolls, and it also made china dolls, character dolls, and baby dolls.

(NOTE: Some dates of production for German doll manufacturers that are presented throughout this book are taken from the landmark two-volume *Collector's Encyclopedia of Dolls* by Dorothy S., Elizabeth A., and Evelyn J. Coleman. For more information, please see the Bibliography.)

Market Report: The market for Alt, Beck & Gottschalck dolls has been somewhat soft lately, as it has been with many of the lesser known German manufacturers. However, many of these dolls are beautifully made, and these dolls could easily come back into fashion if collectors' moods swing back to this type of German antique doll. When buying Alt, Beck & Gottschalck dolls, look especially for sweeter-faced dolls (especially on the shoulder heads), and for sturdy, well-made kid or cloth bodies.

Online/Offline Report: Online auction prices are below those for dolls from dealers,

auction houses, and shows at this time, due to the difficulty of assessing antique bisque via online photos.

Marks: Can be ABG (intertwined), Alt, Beck & Gottschalck, or often solely the mold number, sometimes with "Germany" and sometimes with size number.

Prices and Characteristics: All dolls are bisque. Shoulder-head dolls have kid or cloth bodies with bisque lower limbs, unless otherwise stated—allow more for kid bodies. Child dolls with swivel heads generally have fully jointed composition bodies. Babies/toddlers have five-piece composition bent-limb baby bodies. Most Alt, Beck & Gottschalck dolls can have either glass or painted eyes in the same mold; allow more for glass eyes. Dolls are wigged with mohair or human hair except where noted. Baby and toddler dolls are generally from the 1920s. Child dolls are from the 1880s to the early 1900s and later, and lady dolls are from the 1880s–1890s.

ALT, BECK & GOTTSCHALCK

All-Bisque, 100
Size: 5.5″
Price: $170–$200

Alt, Beck & Gottschalck Child, 1000, shoulder head. *Muslin body with leather arms. 24″, c. 1885. Mark: 1000 / #11. Courtesy Theriault's.*

Alt, Beck & Gottschalck, Character Toddler 1329. *Composition toddler body. 18″, c. 1915. Mark: 5 / AB&G / 1329. Courtesy Theriault's.*

1-piece head/torso, sleep eyes, chubby, 1-strap black shoes with painted white socks and blue sock rim, teeth.
Mark: 100

Baby/Toddler Character 1322
Size: 12″
Price: $275
Open/closed mouth.
Mark: ABG 1322/1 Deponiert

Baby/Toddler Character, 1322
Size: 19″   Internet: $270
Wobble tongue.
Mark: 5 / 1322 / 50

Baby/Toddler Character, 1352
Size: 14″
Price: $325
Dimples.
Mark: ABG 1352/34

Baby/Toddler Character, 1361
Size: 22″
Price: $350
Good condition; more for better.
Mark: ABG (intertwined symbol) / 1361 / 55 / Made In Germany

Bonnet Head
Size: 22″
Price: $3,250
Parian-type, molded hair/bonnet.

Child, 1028, Molded Hair
Size: 26″
Price: $625
Shoulder-head with blonde molded hair, painted eyes.

Child, 1123
Size: 24″
Price: $350
Shoulder-head, sleep eyes, open mouth.
Mark: 11 (head) 1123 1/2 made in / Germany N11 (shoulderplate)

Alt, Beck & Gottschalck, Child 639, shoulder head, solid dome. Kid body, bisque forearms. 16", c. 1885. Mark: 639 / #8. Courtesy Theriault's.

Child, 1362
Size: 26"
Price: $425
Open mouth, sleep eyes, pierced ears.

Child, 1362
Size: 34"
Price: $600

Child, 1362, Walker/Nodder
Size: 24"
All Markets: $400
Walks and nods head when you move legs with wooden dowel mechanism; c. 1930.
Mark: 1362 ALT, BECK & GOTTSCHALCK - 3 1/2

Child, 639
Size: 18"
All Markets: $300–$400
Turned shoulder head, solid dome, glass eyes, closed mouth.
Mark: 639 Germany

Child, 639
Size: 20–22"
All Markets: $250–$350
Turned shoulder head, kid body, closed mouth.
Mark: 639 Germany

Child, 639
Size: 27"
Price: $425
Shoulder head, closed mouth.
Mark: 639 13

Child, 698
Size: 20"
Price: $260
Turned Shoulder head, open mouth.
Mark: 698 Germany

Child, 880, Molded Hair
Size: 20"
Price: $400
New body. Blonde molded hair, glass eyes.
Mark: 880 #8 (bottom of shoulder plate)

Child, Molded Hair
Size: 18"
Price: $175
Shoulder head, molded blonde hair with bangs, painted features.

Child, No Mold
Size: 17"   Internet: $465
Turned shoulder head.

Lady
Size: 14"   Internet: $325
Shoulder head, open mouth.
Mark: 3 1/2

Lady, 996, Molded Hair, Purple Ruffled Scarf
Size: 6"
Price: $1,100
Shoulder head, painted eyes.
Mark: 996 #10

Turned Shoulder Head
Size: 18"
Price: $275
Open mouth.

Baby Peggy. Jointed composition body. 18", c. 1924. Rarer model with smiling expression. Mark: Germany / 1924 c. L.A. & Sons N.Y. 50 / 973/3. $2,400. Courtesy Theriault's.

Newborn Babe. Solid dome head, cloth body with celluloid hands. 16", c. 1914. Mark: L.A. & S. 1914 (more below body) Louis Amberg (stamp on body). $500, dealer.

Amberg, Louis, & Son

Louis Amberg & Son was one of the very first companies to manufacture dolls completely in the United States. Although they existed as a doll importer as early as 1878, they are mostly known as a producer of American-made composition dolls from 1910 to 1930, when the company was sold to Horsman. They also imported various all-bisque dolls.

Market Report: The well-made composition dolls of Louis Amberg & Son have generally held their own in a somewhat down market for composition dolls. Very mint examples with minimal or no crazing can sell for well-over the price-guide value. The strongest Amberg dolls include Baby Peggy and Vanta Baby.

Online/Offline Report: Demand and prices for excellent and mint dolls from online auctions and dealers, shops, and shows is roughly similar.

Marks: Most Amberg dolls are clearly marked with AMBERG or LA & S as part of the mark.

Prices and Characteristics: A few of the early baby dolls are bisque, the remainder are composition, with bodies as described in the listings.

Newborn Babe
Size: 12"   Date: 1914
Material: bisque
Price: $200–$300
Alt, Beck & Gottschalck. Cloth body, composition hands.
Mark: LA & S 1914 / #G44520 / Germany

Newborn Babe
Size: 14"   Date: 1914
Material: bisque
Price: $325–$400
Cloth body, composition hands.
Mark: L.A.& S.© 1914 45559 Germany

Charlie Chaplin
Size: 14"   Date: 1915
Material: composition
Price: $300
Cloth body with black shoes.
Mark: Amberg label on suit sleeve

Girl, Body Twist
Size: 14"   Date: 1920s
Material: composition
Price: $200–$330
Jointed waist, painted, molded hair and features.
Mark: Dress tagged "Amberg Doll / Body Twist / All, all its own"

Baby Peggy
Size: 20"   Date: 1924
Material: bisque
Price: $1,500
Shoulder head, wigged, kid body.

Baby Peggy

Size: 20″   Date: 1922
Material: composition
Price: $500
Molded hair.

Peter Pan

Size: 13–14″   Date: 1928
Material: composition
Price: $360–$445
All-composition body with swivel waist. Molded hair.
Mark: Amberg. / Pat. Pend. / L.A. & S. © 1928 (back)

Sue (or Edwina)

Size: 14″   Date: 1928
Material: composition
Price: $400–$500
Sue doll has round ball joint at waist that swivels freely (Edwina doesn't). Also called the "IT" doll. Molded hair.
Mark: Amberg. / Pat. Pend. / L.A. & S.© 1928. (back) BODY TAG: "AMBERG DOLL WITH / BODY TWIST / all, all its own."

Vanta Baby

Size: 19″   Date: 1927
Material: composition
Price: $275–$375
Chunky baby legs, doll can sit. Distributed by Sears as advertisement for Vanta baby garments. Molded hair, tin eyes. More for dolls in tagged pink Vanta romper.
Mark: Vanta Baby / AMBERG

Vanta Baby

Size: 22″   Date: 1927
Material: composition
Price: $375+
With tagged Vanta clothing.
Mark: Vanta Baby / AMBERG

Prices for this section are a mix from all venues.

Asian Dolls

This section includes dolls that are Asian but which were not made in Asia (see the Japanese Dolls and Ethnic/Travel Dolls sections for those). The first dolls made outside Asia to represent Asian people were made by German and French dollmaking companies, most after 1900, but a few rare examples were made prior to 1900, including very few French fashion dolls. Other dolls made in Asian likenesses included small all-bisque dolls and a few composition dolls including the Ming Ming baby from Quan-Quan Co. of California. "Oriental" is considered a derogatory term by some Asian people, and therefore, despite somewhat common industry nomenclature describing these dolls as "Oriental," these dolls should be referred to as "Asian."

Market Report: Asian bisque, all-bisque and composition dolls are relatively few in number compared to the number of Caucasian dolls produced. This has helped the market for these dolls remain strong.

- **German & French Bisque:** Demand is strong and supply relatively small for the desirable German and French bisque dolls portraying Asian children and women. Demand is also strong for early German all-bisque Asian children. Look for good color to the bisque and original Asian-style clothing when possible.

- **Ming Ming, Small All-Bisque Dolls:** The Ming Ming dolls, made in California in the 1940s, portray an Asian child in composition. Their value has increased in the last few years—just a few years ago, these dolls were plentiful in the $70 to $100 range, and now mint examples can bring close to $200. Small Queue San-type later all-bisque dolls are generally not of high quality and can usually be found in the $50 to $75 range.

Online/Offline Report: You will find a much greater selection of fine French and German all-bisque dolls and dolls portraying children and women from dealers and auction houses than you will find on the Internet due to the rarity of the dolls. Ming Ming and later small all-bisque dolls are easily found on the Internet and at doll shows.

Prices and Characteristics: All dolls in this section are bisque with amber-tinting or skin tone. Child and lady dolls have fully jointed composition bodies, babies have jointed bent-limb baby bodies, and both have glass eyes and are wigged with mohair or human hair, except where noted. The Simon & Halbig dolls represent children, except where noted.

Simon & Halbig. Child, 1329,
jointed composition body. 13″, c.
1910. Mark: Simon & Halbig /
Germany / 1329/3. $1200, auction.

Kestner, Baby 243. Socket head,
bent-limb composition baby body.
19″, c. 1912. Mark: K / Made in
Germany / 243 / 14 / JDK. Cour-
tesy Theriault's.

ASIAN DOLLS

All-Bisque, Attributed to Simon & Halbig
Size: 5″   Date: 1890
Price: $650
Swivel neck, glass eyes, painted white stockings
and blue slippers.

All-Bisque, Attributed to Simon & Halbig
Size: 5.5″   Date: 1900
All Markets: $825
Glass sleep eyes, swivel head, 5-part body, closed
mouth, peg-wood joints, painted socks, shoes
and human hair queue.

All-Bisque, German, Swivel Neck
Size: 5″   Date: late 1800s
Price: $500
Closed mouth, glass eyes, 1-stroke brows, swivel
neck, bare feet.

Armand Marseille, Baby, 353
Size: 13″   Date: 1920
Price: $1,200

Closed mouth.
Mark: AM Germany 353/3/K

Armand Marseille, Baby, 353
Size: 19″   Date: 1920
Price: $1,800
Closed mouth.
Mark: AM Germany 353/8 K

Armand Marseille, Character, Baby, Ellar
Size: 11″   Date: 1920
Price: $450
Dome socket head.
Mark: A.Ellar M. / Germany / 355./3 1/2 K

Belton-Type
Size: 11″   Date: 1880
Price: $1,250
Closed mouth, adult figure, solid dome head,
glass set eyes, 5-piece body.

French Fashion, Bru Attributed, Wood Body
Size: 15″   Date: 1870s
Price: $9,500
Fully articulated wood body, at auction.

Bähr & Pröschild, Child 220.
Socket head with flattened dome
(Sonneberg style), 5-piece papier-
mâché body with painted slippers.
11", c. 1890. Mark: 220 / 3. Courtesy Theriault's.

Lambert, French automaton,
"Chinese Tea Drinker." Papier-
mâché torso and legs, bisque hands.
When wound, music plays, doll
nods, turns head, and motions as if
to pour tea. 18", c. 1890. Mark: LB
(key). Courtesy Theriault's.

Armand Marseille babies, 353
(large); 351 (small). Bent-limb
baby bodies. 16" and 5", c. 1925.
Mark: AM / Germany / 353 / 4K
and AM / Germany 351 /10/0.
Courtesy Theriault's.

German Bisque, Children, Pair

Size: 4.25"
Price: $400
Painted eyes, dome heads with queues, painted
red slippers, 5-piece bodies.

German Bisque, Closed Mouth, Dome Head

Size: 4.25"
Price: $235
5-piece composition body with red painted slippers.

Kestner, Character Baby, 243

Size: 12–13"   Date: 1912
Price: $2,500–$3,500
Antique silk Asian costume.
Mark: F. made in Germany 10 243 JDK

Kestner, Character Baby, 243

Size: 15"   Date: 1915
Price: $3,100
Represents Chinese baby.
Mark: 9 243 JDK

Kestner, Character, Baby, 243

Size: 18"   Date: 1912
Price: $4,200
Represents Chinese baby. Open mouth.
Mark: K made in Germany 14 243 JDK

Kühnlenz, Child, Scowling

Size: 9"   Date: 1895
Price: $300
5-piece composition body.
Mark: 55.18

Lady, German Bisque, Belton-Type

Price: $1,500   Date: 1880s
Closed mouth, adult figure, solid dome head,
5-piece body, original outfit.

Simon & Halbig, 1099

Size: 15"   Date: 1900
Price: $1,700
Mark: SH 1099 dep 5 1/2

Simon & Halbig, 1129

Size: 10"   Date: 1900
Price: $1,300
Mark: SH 1129 dep 3 Germany

Simon & Halbig, 1199

Size: 12"   Date: 1895
Price: $1,900
Antique silk costume.
Mark: SH 1199 Dep 5

Simon & Halbig, 1199

Size: 15"   Date: 1895
Price: $1,800–$2,000
Open mouth, antique silk costume.
Mark: S H 1199 Germany Dep 6

Simon & Halbig, 1329

Size: 13"   Date: 1910
Price: $1,000
Mark: 1329 Germany Simon & Halbig S & H 4

Simon & Halbig, 1329

Size: 15"   Date: 1900
Price: $1,675

Simon & Halbig, Child 1329. *Jointed composition body. 24", c. 1900. Mark: Simon and Halbig / Germany / 1329 / 10. $3,000, auction. Courtesy Theriault's.*

Pair, unknown German bisque. *5-piece papier-mâché bodies. 9" and 10", c. 1905. Courtesy Theriault's.*

All-bisque, attributed to Simon & Halbig. *Glass eyes, swivel head. 6", c. 1890. Unmarked. $650, auction.*

Simon & Halbig, 1329

Size: 17–18"   Date: 1900
All Markets: $1,100–$1,400
Replaced, new clothing. more for original.
Mark: Simon & Halbig / Germany / 1329-5

Simon & Halbig, 1329

Size: 24"   Date: 1900
Price: $2,500–$3,000
Mark: Simon & Halbig / Germany / 1329 / 10

Simon & Halbig, Lady, 1129

Size: 16"   Date: 1900
Price: $3,600
Original outfit, Lady of the Imperial House of Manchu Dynasty, original hairstyle. At auction.
Mark: SH 1129 / Germany / DEP / 6 1/2

Simon & Halbig, Lady, 1329

Size: 15"   Date: 1900
Price: $3,500
Same as previous entry.

Simon & Halbig, Lady, 164

Size: 23"   Date: 1900
Price: $4,500
Mark: 80 / 164

Automata

Automata are a specialized area of collecting, but they deserve mention in this book for their uniqueness, rarity, and special charm. Automata are antique dolls that move, usually through a key-wind mechanism of some type, often with music playing. These dolls were generally made in France in the later half of the 19th century. According to Florence Theriault in her book *Dolls in Motion,* "although automata were presented to wealthy clientele in luxury toy stores in Paris, London and New York, often ostensibly for their children, the actual target market was the adult." That, of course, would make automata one of the first types of adult collectible dolls! Some of this is evident in the themes used for the dolls—smoking dolls, for instance, were not possibly aimed at children.

Market Report: The French antique automata were luxury items when first produced, and they are generally some of the most expensive antique dolls today, with prices often surpassing several thousand dollars for working rare models in excellent condition. Some of the most desirable models have heads by French dollmakers such as Bru and Jumeau; look also for automata by Leopold Lambert with deluxe couture costumes (designed by his wife, Eugénie Maria Bourgois). Obviously, models with working mechanisms are most desirable.

Online/Offline Report: Most fine automata dolls trade at shows, auction houses, and from dealers, although you do occasionally find them on the Internet.

Prices and Characteristics: Each doll listed has a bisque head. All the automata play

French automaton, "The Marquise with Fan and Lorgnette." On base, when wound, music plays, doll (Tête Jumeau head) looks to left and raises lorgnette, then looks to right and raises fan. 18″, c. 1890. Mark (doll). Depose Tete Jumeau Bte SGDG. Courtesy Theriault's.

French automaton, Bébé Nid by Lambert. Girl (bisque Tête Jumeau head) on base, holds bouquet in one hand, "holds" large papier-mâché egg in other on bird's nest. When wound, music plays, doll turns head, lifts hand to throw kisses, raises lid of egg. Inside egg, bird "awakens." 19″, c. 1890. Mark (doll): Depose Tete Jumeau Bte SGDG 4. Courtesy Theriault's.

music, but only some of the mechanical dolls do. The actions are started by winding the mechanism with a key except where noted. Generally, the automata were created for an adult audience while the mechanical dolls were meant as children's playthings. All prices are from dealers and auction houses, except where noted. All prices in this section are for individual sales, and the majority were sold with original costumes and mechanisms working. All automatons listed are French except where noted. Lambert is Leopold Lambert, and Zinner, Gottlieb & Söhne is a German company.

AUTOMATON

Exotic Lady Playing the Guitar
Size: 23″
Price: $6,000

German.
Mark: Germany S&H Simon & Halbig

Girl With Mirror and Powder Puff
Size: 18″
Price: $4,600
Doll turns and lowers head, powders nose, then looks at mirror in hand. Redressed.

Lady at Her Toilette
Size: 14″   Internet: $1,300
Lifts hand, holding fur powder puff, lowers face into puff, raises left hand holding silver mirror, raises head to look in mirror. Large hairline lowered price.

Lady With Egg
Size: 16″
Price: $4,875
Taps eggs with stick and top of egg opens revealing glass-eye monkey peeking out.

French mechanical pull-toy, "Playing Chinese," attributed to Zinner, Gottlieb & Söhne. When toy is pulled, boy walks and "pulls" cart. 13″ long, 9″ high, c. 1890. Mark (dolls): G.K. Courtesy Theriault's.

Lady With Harp
Size: 23″   Date: 1880
Price: $6,750
Plays harp.

Lambert, Bébé au Polchinelle
Size: 20″   Date: 1890
Price: $11,000
Jumeau portrait crying head. Doll turns head and lifts body and head as though imploring someone to fix broken polchinelle doll.

Lambert, Bébé Bouquetiere
Size: 20″   Date: 1890
Price: $6,500
Tête Jumeau head. Turns head, lifts bouquet, nods head to sniff flowers, raises lid of basket.

Lambert, Bébé Cage
Size: 20″   Date: 1890
Price: $11,500
Tête Jumeau Head. Doll turns head, nods, alternately bird flutters and she offers cherries on branch.

Lambert, Bébé Russe
Size: 20″   Date: 1890
Price: $6,000
Turns head, pours tea.

Lambert, Chinese Tea Server
Size: 20″   Date: 1890
Price: $9,000
Head modeled by Jumeau only for this piece. Lady turns, nods head, offers tea, pours.

Lambert, Espagnole Jouese de Mandoline
Size: 24″   Date: 1890
Price: $19,000
Lady nods and revolves head, strums mandolin and keeps time to music with crossed leg.
Mark: LB (key)

Lambert, Girl With Fan and Lorgnette
Size: 18″   Date: 1890
Price: $5,400
Turns head from side to side, up and down, alternately fans herself and lifts lorgnette.
Mark: Deposé Tete Jumeau 4 (artist's checkmarks)

Lambert, Lady With Mandolin
Size: 23″   Date: 1885
Price: $8,500
Turns head up, around, sideways, alternately moving hands on mandolin strings, and raises and lowers leg to keep time to music.
Mark: 7 (head) LB (key)

Lambert, Spanish Dancer
Size: 18″   Date: 1880
                             Internet: $5,900
Jumeau head.
Mark: Deposé Tete Jumeau Bte SGDG

Lambert, The Happy Patissier
Size: 20″   Date: 1892
Price: $11,000
Tête Jumeau head. Turns head, nods forward, lifts cake box where a kitten is hiding.

Lambert, Young Girl With Mirror,
Size: 19″   Date: 1890
Price: $5,250

Simon & Halbig head. Doll turns head, opens and closes eyes, and alternately lifts mirror and puff while music plays.
Mark: S & H 1300 2 dep (head LB (key)

Leopold Lambert, Young Girl With Birdcage

Size: 18"   Date: 1890
Price: $11,500
Doll turns head, alternately moving cage and teasing bird with branch of cherries in hand.
Mark: 203 (incised) Deposé Tete Jumeau Bte SGDG

Little Girl in Party Costume

Size: 10"   Date: 1890
Price: $5,000
Little girl turns her head and alternately powders nose and gazes into mini hand mirror.
Mark: E 2/0

Phalibois, Gypsy Dancers

Size: 29"   Date: 1870
Price: $13,500
Seated doll turns head, fans self, dancing doll twirls, man waves tambourine. Man is tiny "smiling" Bru; 1 doll is Jumeau portrait crying head. Very early.

Punch-Type Child With Cymbals

Size: 19"
Price: $5,000
Tête Jumeau head. Claps cymbals and nods head left to right.

Roullet et Decamps, The Gentleman Smoker

Size: 22"   Date: 1895
Price: $6,250
Tête Jumeau head. Doll brings cigarette to mouth, inhales and appears to exhale smoke, waves handkerchief.

Roullet et Decamps, Berger Watteau

Size: 28"   Date: 1885
Price: $16,500
Shepherd turns head, nods, lifts and plays flute.

Roullet et Decamps, Bouquetiere Surprise

Size: 24"   Date: 1890
Price: $13,000
Lady turns head, nods, lifts lid of basket to reveal surprise—little bisque doll that rises up. Tête Jumeau head.

Roullet et Decamps, Patissier à la Brioche

Size: 11"   Date: 1895
Price: $4,000

Rzebitschek, Automaton

                   Date: 1800–1820
Price: $10,500

Very early, from Prague maker of music boxes. On platform, papier-mâché lady plays piano and papier-mâché man conducts her with baton.
Mark: lengthy label mark identifying Rzebitschek

Schoenau & Hoffmeister, Figures Playing Instruments

Size: 11"
Price: $3,000
Redressed. Dolls play instruments when box is wound.
Mark: 600 13 / 2 PB (in star) H / Germany

Smoking Man

Size: 23"
Price: $6,600
Tête Jumeau head. Gentleman smokes, nods head, swivels, raises cigarette to mouth.

Vichy, Moves Forward and Glides in Circles

Size: 11"   Date: 1864
Price: $2,700

Vichy, Festive Man Riding Donkey

Size: 14"   Date: 1890
Price: $3,800
Simon & Halbig head. Platform propels forward and in circles while donkey nods and man lifts arm, urging donkey forward, or drinks from bottle.

Vichy, Waltzing Couple

Size: 22"   Date: 1875
Price: $23,000
Barrois and Gaultier bisque Poupée heads. When wound, couple waltzes.

Young Count Playing Violin, Vichy Attributed

Size: 13"   Date: 1865
Price: $6,200
Boy turns head, nods, plays violin.

Zinner, Gottlieb & Söhne, Christmas Morning

Size: 20"   Date: 1890
Price: $31,000
Stage represents Victorian parlor, 8 all-bisque children with toys on Christmas morning—girls with dolls, carriages, boys with dogs, puppets, drums. Decorated tabletop feather tree. When hand wound, all dolls play with toys.
Mark: unmarked

MECHANICAL DOLLS

Autoperipatetikos Walking Doll

Size: 10"
Price: $900

Parian-style shoulder head. Molded hair, closed mouth. Body has carton moule skirt with clock-work mechanism, 32 protruding brass feet.
Mark: unmarked

Doll on Cart

Size: 8″
Price: $500
Painted eyes, molded hair, composition body with jointed arms, wire upper arms, wood hands, doll stands on 3-wheel metal cart, cart moves in circle, doll hands go up and down.
Mark: unmarked

Governess With Baby Carriage

Size: 12″   Date: 1880
Price: $5,750
Doll walks, pushing forward carriage with bisque baby.
Mark: unmarked

Pull Toy, Farmer's Wife and Geese

Size: 16″   Date: 1890
Price: $3,800
French, 4-wheeled platform, 3 geese and doll in folklore costume, when pulled woman turns head, waves arms, and geese turn back and forth.
Mark: France Limoges 1

Roullet et Decamps, Mechanical Cat

Size: 12″
Price: $725
White fur cat, glass eyes, wooden coffee grinder, cat cranks coffee grinder, nods head.
Mark: Decamps France (paper label)

Roullet et Decamps, Walking Doll

Size: 14″   Date: 1900
Price: $2,000
Doll slowly walks by lifting up alternate feet. Key marked R.D.
Mark: 1078 Germany Simon & Halbig S & H 4 (doll)

Steiner, Gliding Lady

Size: 15″   Date: 1867
Price: $9,500
Original box and outfit, lady glides forward, turns and advances while arm goes up and down.
Mark: E. 3 B (shoulder plate)

The Mandolin Player

Size: 14″
Price: $1,100
French, nods and strums mandolin when torso squeezed. Open mouth, torso with bellows.
Mark: 33 4/0

Unknown Maker, 2 Dolls Playing Music

Size: 7″   Date: 1880
                 Internet: $1,400

2 bisque dolls seated on a bench on the top of wooden base, dolls play music. Dolls have composition lower limbs, wooden body.
Mark: unmarked

Vichy Attributed, Lady With Child in Carriage

Size: 12″   Date: 1880
Price: $7,250
Lady walks forward, carriage front wheels turn, head turns side to side.

Vichy Attributed, Lady With Girl on Swing

Size: 13″   Date: 1880
Price: $8,800
Platform moves forward, then in circular mo-tion, lady turns head and raises arm, swing moves back and forth.

Vichy, Girl With Hunting Hound

Size: 12″   Date: 1875
Price: $4,750
Girl moves arms up and down, turns head, wheels turn and toy moves.
Mark: G. Vichy Paris (mechanism)

Vichy, Milkmaid With Brown-Eyed Cow

Size: 13″   Date: 1880
Price: $5,250
Girl turns head, waves arms up and down, plat-form moves on wheels
Mark: G. Vichy Paris (mechanism)

Vichy, Violinist

Size: 13″   Date: 1870
Price: $3,700

Violinist on Base

Size: 9″   Date: 1880
Price: $3,200
French, when wound, music plays, boy nods and plays violin, foot taps.

Zinner, Gottlieb & Söhne, Mechanical Bellows Dolls

Size: 13″   Date: 1890
Price: $1,700
Bisque heads by Kühnlenz. When base is squeezed dolls bend forward and back as if ring-ing bells, while music plays.

Zinner, Gottlieb & Söhne, Balancing Jester

Size: 27″   Date: 1890
Price: $10,200
Music plays, jester strums mandolin, "balances" twirling doll posed on his cap.

Zinner, Gottlieb & Söhne, Boys and Rocking Horse and Cart

Size: 16″   Date: 1890
Price: $4,000

Pull toy. When cart pulled, wheels turn, jester turns side to side, waves horse whip, rocking horse bucks up and down.

Zinner, Gottlieb & Söhne, Pull Toy, Little Boy Drummer
Size: 12″   Date: 1890
Price: $3,700
When pull, little boy turns head from side to side, clangs cymbals onto drum.

Zinner, Gottlieb & Söhne, The Dance Party
Size: 12″   Date: 1900
Price: $5,800
Platform stage, wallpaper, circular disk of floor moves, 3 pairs of bisque dolls twirl to music.
Mark: unmarked

Bähr & Pröschild

Bähr & Pröschild is another German doll factory with long-term doll production, from 1871 to approximately 1930. Located in the Ohrdruf area of Germany, Bähr & Pröschild produced doll heads for many other German dollmakers, including Kley & Hahn. Bähr & Pröschild is known for both dolly-faced and character children.

Market Report: If you like German antique baby dolls, don't overlook the babies of Bähr & Pröschild—they are truly charming, and prices are still reasonable.

Online/Offline Report: Prices for appealing character baby dolls are the same for Internet and other sources, but Internet prices do lag behind dealer/show prices.

Prices and Characteristics: All dolls are bisque socket heads except where noted. Babies have 5-piece jointed composition bent-limb baby bodies. Toddler dolls have 5-piece jointed composition bodies with side-hip jointing. Child dolls have fully jointed composition bodies, except where noted. Dolls are wigged with mohair or human hair. Child dolls are from the 1880s through early 1900s. Character dolls are from about 1912 to 1920.

BÄHR & PRÖSCHILD

Character 585, Baby
Size: 10–11″
Price: $350   Internet: $330–$425

Open mouth, sleep eyes.
Mark: B & P/O (in crossed swords) / 585 / 0 / Germany

Character 585, Baby
Size: 20″   Internet: $700
Toddler body, straight wrists, jointed knees.
Mark: BP / 585 / 12 / Made in Germany

Character 585, Baby
Size: 24″
Price: $600

Character 585, Toddler
Size: 9.5″   Internet: $850
Factory original.

Character 585, Toddler
Size: 11″
Price: $1,200
Sleep eyes, closed mouth, white space between lips.
Mark: 585 B.P. (crossed swords) Germany

Character 585, Toddler
Size: 21″
Price: $650
Mark: BP (in heart) / 585 / 12 / Made in / Germany

Character 585, Toddler
Size: 27″
Price: $750
Open mouth, sleep eyes.
Mark: B & P 585 13 Germany

Character 592, Child
Size: 12″
Price: $2,800
With trunk and many costumes. Rarer fully jointed toddler body, glass eyes.
Mark: BP (inside crossed symbol) 592 2

Character 604, Toddler
Size: 22″
Price: $1,500
Closed mouth.
Mark: B.P. (crossed swords) 604 12

Character 620, Baby
Size: 16″
Price: $350
Mark: GB & Co. / Germany / BP (in crossed arrows) / 620-8

Character 624, Baby
Size: 17″
Price: $300
Sleep eyes.
Mark: B & P (crossed swords) / 624 / 8 / Germany

Bähr & Pröschild, Child 320.
Jointed composition body, 17".
Mark: 320-0/dep. Private collec-
tion.

Bähr & Pröschild, Child 204.
Jointed composition body, straight
wrists. 11", c. 1890. Mark: 204 / 2.
Courtesy Theriault's.

Character 624, Baby
Size: 19"   Internet: $770
Mark: GB & Co. / Germany / BP (in crossed arrows) / 624-8

Character 678, Toddler
Size: 21"
Price: $850
Made in Germany stamped body, open mouth.
Mark: 678 / 11 / BP

Child, 201
Size: 24"
Price: $400
Open mouth.

Child, 201
Size: 28"   Internet: $1,100
Open mouth, original clothing.

Child, 204
Size: 11"
Price: $950

Sonneberg composition body, straight wrists, open mouth.
Mark: 204 2

Child, 204
Size: 16.5"   Internet: $500
Mark: 204

Child, 224
Size: 16.5"   Internet: $700

Child, 246
Size: 18"   Internet: $255
Kid body.

Child, 340
Size: 19"
Price: $350
Mark: 340 DEP

Native American, 244
Size: 12"   Internet: $1,700
Closed mouth, flattened solid dome, light brown complexion, 5-piece body.

Bähr & Pröschild, Child 394. *Carton torso with muslin cover, composition and wood arms (rarer body style). 17″, c. 1890. Mark: 394 / 5. Courtesy Theriault's.*

Pair, Native American, Bähr & Pröschild 244. *5-piece composition bodies. 16″, c. 1890. Original costumes. Mark: 244 / 5 (both dolls). At auction, $1,200 (right), $800 (left). Courtesy Theriault's.*

Bähr & Pröschild, baby, character 585. *Bent-limb composition baby body. 13.5″, c. 1910. Mark: B(crossed swords) and / 0/ 585 / 4/ Germany (in box). $450, dealer.*

Native American, 244

Size: 16″
Price: $800–$1,200
Closed mouth, flattened solid dome, light brown complexion, 5-piece body.
Mark: 244 / 5

Bathing Dolls and Bathing Beauties

There is some debate as to whether or not bathing dolls are dolls at all—after all, they are stationary, more like a statue or figurine in many ways, than a doll. However, the UFDC classifies bathing dolls as dolls, and as they are most often sold and displayed with dolls, and collected by doll collectors, I have decided to include them here.

Bathing dolls were generally made in the United States and Germany (mostly in Germany) starting at the very end of the 19th century and picking up steam in the 1920s, when most of them were produced. Some were produced in Japan as well, and these are generally of lesser quality.

A product of the roaring twenties, bathing beauties were very cutting-edge for their time (although they seem very tame to us today). Some bathing beauties have molded or cloth clothing, others are completely nude, and some bathing beauties are actually mermaids with flippers instead of feet.

Market Report: There has been a supply glut of lesser-quality and more common bathing beauties on eBay, and that has caused their prices to decline, so that many examples can be found in the $75 to $200 range. However, demand remains strong for more unusual or artistic models, especially those with original clothing, fine painting, or unusual modeling, and these examples bring considerably more. Bathing beauties by Galluba & Hoffmann can easily bring four figures.

One caveat—sources on the Internet have reported that bathing beauties and mermaids currently being produced by The German Doll Company from old German molds have had their German Doll Company marks removed by a few unscrupulous dealers, and are being passed in the market as antique. The German Doll Company clearly marks all their pieces (with a fired-in blue mark which depicts a roly-poly clown. The unscrupulous dealers sand off or otherwise remove the mark. To protect yourself, visit www.germandollcompany.com to familiarize yourself with their line of reproductions.

German bathing beauty. Fish fins are original (instead of the more common feet). 1.5″, c. 1920s. Mark: GERMANY / 6399 (lower buttocks and leg). $100, dealer.

German bathing beauty. 1 arm away, original harem-style outfit. 3″, c. 1920s. $500, auction.

Schafer & Vater bathing beauty. 4.5″, c. 1920s. Mark: Crown with starburst beneath. $300, dealer.

Online/Offline Report: Except for the more common styles, prices on and offline are similar.

Prices and Characteristics: Bathing beauties are generally made in Germany, one-piece, and bisque, and made in the 1920s, except where indicated. Prices are a mix of dealer, auction house and Internet prices, as shown. Bathing beauties come in countless designs; the dolls listed here represent just a few models.

BATHING BEAUTY

Ballerina, Standing
Size: 8.5″   Internet: $750
High-quality painting.

Dressel & Kister, Nude Medieval Bathing Beauty
Internet: $700
Porcelain, reclining on front elbows with legs in air. Medieval style band in hair.
Mark: Dressel & Kister blue stamp mark.

Galluba & Hoffmann
Size: 11″   Internet: $2,400
Unusually large size.
Mark: 423M

Galluba & Hoffmann, Wigged, Reclining
Size: 6″   Internet: $500
Multilayered skirt; original outfit.

Hands Outstretched, Poised on One Leg
Size: 5″   Internet: $750
Wearing original beaded dress; doll in dance-type pose with painted-on dance shoes. On base with pin up into leg to hold doll in position.

Hatpin Holder, Emerging From Shell
Size: 4.25″   Internet: $180
Porcelain. Doll emerges from shell that is a hatpin holder.

In Shell
Size: 3.75″
Price: $190
Late 1800s. Porcelain.

Mermaid, Double Tail
Size: 6″   Internet: $250
Nude with painted light blue tail instead of feet.

Nude, Reclining, Blue Hat
Internet: $200
Painting not very detailed.

On Shell Dish, Molded/Painted Bathing Suit
Size: 3.5″
Price: $65
Porcelain.

Painted Hat and Shoes
Size: 5″
Price: $75
Typical, simple type.

Pincushion Top, ORAs Holding Shell
Size: 2.5″
Price: $200

German bathing beauties. *With modeled swimsuits and caps. 5″ length, c. 1925. Courtesy Theriault's.*

German bathing beauty. *1 arm away, original bathing suit and cap made out of miniature glass beads. 3.12″ long, 1.25″ high, c. 1920s. Mark: Germany, back of lower leg. $350, dealer.*

Hertwig bathing beauty. *Uplifted head. 4.4″ length, c. 1920s. Courtesy Theriault's.*

Pincushion, ORA, 1 Close
Size: 2″
Price: $225
Porcelain.
Mark: Germany

Reclining, Sea Foam Suit
Size: 3.5″   Internet: $75
1930s, typical painting, on elbow, lavender cap, painted blue slippers.
Mark: 5684 (incised)

Schafer & Vater, With Crowing Rooster
Size: 2.5″   Internet: $935
5″ length.

Sitting on Rock
Size: 7.5″   Internet: $380
Wearing blue painted clothing.
Mark: 9262

Snow Bathing Suit, Reclining
Size: 3.5″   Internet: $100
Crudely painted face. "Snow" bathing hat, painted shoes and straps.
Mark: Germany

Wigged, Sitting Back on Arms
Size: 3″   Internet: $355

Wigged, Taking Slipper Off
Size: 3″   Internet: $700
Original bathing suit.

Bergmann, C.M.

C.M. Bergmann was a German doll factory with a long period of production, from the end of the 1880s to approximately 1930. Many companies supplied doll heads to C.M. Bergmann, and they are especially known for their dolls made with Simon & Halbig heads. Most of the production of C.M. Bergmann were dolly-faced child dolls.

C.M. Bergmann, Child 1199. *Simon & Halbig head, jointed composition body. 28", c. 1890. $1,000, dealer.*

C.M. Bergmann, child. *Simon & Halbig head, jointed composition body. 23", c. 1910. Courtesy Theriault's.*

Market Report: C.M. Bergmann is not the highest priced maker of antique German dolls, but they are well-made and perfect for beginning German antique collectors. Right now, prices on these dolls are quite reasonable due to a constant supply in the market. The dolls with marked Simon & Halbig heads are the most sought after. As with all German dolly-faced dolls, look for dolls with lustrous bisque and finely painted features.

Online/Offline Report: Internet prices lag dealer, show, and auction house prices in some but not all cases, but especially for dolls in average condition. Dolls in newer clothing and poor wigs can be picked up at good bargains on the Internet.

Prices and Characteristics: All Bergmann dolls are bisque, in excellent condition, and circa the late 1880s to the early 1900s. All have open mouths, sleep eyes, mohair or human hair wigs, and jointed composition bodies except as indicated.

C.M. BERGMANN

Toddler, Character, 612
Size: 19"
Price: $10,000
Rare, laughing model on side-hip jointed toddler body. At auction, 612 Character babies generally sell for $2,000–$3,000.

Mark: Made in Germany / Simon & Halbig / C.M. Bergmann / 612 / 11

Child
Size: 22"
Price: $345–$500   Internet: $300–$400
Mark: C.M. Bergmann / Simon & Halbig / S & H / 3

Child
Size: 26"
Price: $425   Internet: $300–$400
Mark: C.M.Bergmann / Simon & Halbig / 12

Child
Size: 29–30"
Price: $450   Internet: $700
Mark: C.M. Bergmann / Simon & Halbig / 12 1/2

Child
Size: 32"   Internet: $800

Child, 1916
Size: 10"
Price: $375   Internet: $300

Child, 1916
Size: 14–20"
Price: $500
Mark: C M Bergmann / Waltershausen / 1916 / 6

Child, 1916
Size: 22–28"
Price: $400–$500   Internet: $450

Child, 1916
Size: 30"
Price: $450   Internet: $600
Mark: C M Bergmann / Waltershausen / 1916 / 12

Child, S & H head
Size: 14"
Price: $450   Internet: $250–$350

Child, S & H head
Size: 22"   Internet: $350
Mark: C.M. Bergmann / Simon & Halbig / 9 1/2

Child, S & H head
Size: 24–26"
Price: $300–$425   Internet: $450
Higher prices for old clothing and original wig.

Child, S & H head
Size: 39–30"
Price: $525   Internet: $700

Child, S & H head
Size: 32"
Price: $500–$750

3-Faced Doll
Size: 15"
Price: $840
Turn knob on top of head for
sleeping/crying/awake expressions.

Bisque, French, Various Companies

Nearly every doll collector, even those who collect only modern or vintage dolls, has heard of the "Big Two" in French bisque dolls—Jumeau and Bru, and possibly a few other popular companies, such as Steiner and Gaultier. However, there are many other companies that produced high-quality bébés and other bisque dolls from the 1870s–1890s. Some of these companies had very small production output, and therefore today have relatively few dolls on the market, especially in relation to Jumeau (or even Steiner). There were various reasons for the small production outputs of these firms—for instance, Danel & Cie produced dolls for only three years because they were successfully sued by Jumeau for design infringement and unfair competition. You can learn interesting details about the histories of these French doll companies and many others in *The Encyclopedia of French Dolls* by Francois and Danielle Theimer, English translation edited by Florence Theriault (see Bibliography).

Market Report: Interest in the dolls from these French firms remains strong by collec-

tors of French bisque, and so do prices. As for unmarked or unknown maker French bisque, it's a bit scarier to buy such dolls because of the much higher prices (and risk) than for unmarked or unknown German bisque. Just as with the German dolls, remember that fine painting and good bisque is the same no matter how a doll is marked. If you know your dolls, you can pick up some lovely unmarked French dolls at relatively bargain prices compared to a marked doll of the same quality.

Online/Offline Report: You will rarely find French bisque dolls by these companies for sale online. Most dolls are found at live auctions and from dealers.

Prices and Characteristics: Antique French bisque dolls have bisque socket heads, in excellent condition, on French fully jointed composition and wood bodies (some with straight wrists), with closed mouths and paperweight eyes, mohair or human hair wigs, except where noted. Earlier dolls tend to have pressed bisque heads. Prices are dealer and auction prices, except where noted.

ALEXANDRE, HENRI

Bébé
Size: 17"   Date: 1890s
Price: $2,500
Body wear and flaws.
Mark: H7A / 5

Bébé Phénix Star
Size: 14"   Date: 1895–1900
Price: $1,400
Body flaws.
Mark: Phenix /85

DANEL & CIE BÉBÉ

Danel & Cie, Bébé Francaise
Size: 24"   Date: 1890
Price: $3,300–$3,700
Mark: Paris Bébé Tete Dep (incised)

DENAMUR, ETIENNE (E.D. BÉBÉ)

Bébé, Closed Mouth
Size: 28"   Date: 1890s
Price: $2,500

Denamur, Bébé, French. French jointed composition and wood body. 27″, c. 1890. Mark: E. 12 D. Depose. Courtesy Theriault's.

Gaultier, block letter Bébé. French jointed composition and wood body. 24″, c. 1884. Mark: F. 10. G. Courtesy Theriault's.

Straight wrists.
Mark: E 12 D Deposé

Bébé, Open Mouth

Size: 22″   Date: 1890s
Price: $1,400
Later doll with crude 5-piece composition body.
Mark: E. 10 D. / Deposé

Bébé, Open Mouth

Size: 24″   Date: 1890s
All Markets: $2,700
New clothing.
Mark: E 9 D / Deposé

EDEN BÉBÉ

Bébé, Closed Mouth

Size: 17″   Date: 1890
Price: $3,200
Straight-wrist body.

Bébé, Open Mouth

Size: 22″   Date: 1890
Price: $1,300

Doll with flaws, straight-wrist body.
Mark: Eden Bébé / Paris / M

GAULTIER

These are dolls made by François Gaultier and later Frères Gaultier (the Gaultier brothers). See the "French Fashion Dolls" section for Gaultier lady dolls. They have bisque socket heads, fully jointed French composition-and-wood bodies with straight or jointed wrists, wigs, glass eyes, and closed mouths, except as noted. Dolls with the block-letter mark are from approximately 1880–1887; dolls with the scroll mark are from approximately 1887–1900.

Bébé, Block Letter

Size: 9.5″
Price: $3,200
Mark: F. 1 G.

Joanny, Bébé. *French jointed composition and wood body, straight wrists. 12", c. 1885. Mark: J 4. Courtesy Theriault's.*

Mothereau, Bébé. *Metal fully jointed body (rare body type). 12", c. 1885. Mark: M 2 B. Courtesy Theriault's.*

Petit & Dumontier, Bébé. *French composition and wood body, pewter hands. 20", c. 1882. Mark: P 3 D. $7000 (faint hairline), auction. Courtesy Theriault's.*

Bébé, Block Letter
Size: 13–15"
Price: $4,100–$4,600
Mark: F. 6. 3

Bébé, Block Letter
Size: 20–23"
Price: $4,700–$5,400
Early models have plumper facial features.
Mark: F. 8. G, F.9 G or F.10 G

Bébé, Block Letter, Gesland Body
Size: 22–25"
Price: $5,000–$6,500
Gesland body, metal armature under padded stockinette, wooden lower limbs. May have Gesland blue body stamp.
Mark: F.9 G or F.10 G.

Bébé, Scroll Mark
Size: 13–15"
Price: $2,000–$3,000
On jointed or straight-wrist body.
Mark: F.G. (scroll) 3 or FG (in scroll) / 6 or 4 F.G. (in scroll)

Bébé, Scroll Mark
Size: 18–22"
Price: $2,200–$3,000
Mark: F.G. (in scroll) / 8 (or 9)

Bébé, Scroll Mark
Size: 22–23"
Price: $3,000+
Mark: F.G. (within scroll banner) 9

Bébé, Scroll Mark
Size: 27–32"
All Markets: $3,800–$4,600
Mark: 10 F.G (back) or F.G. (in scroll) or 13 F.G. (in scroll)

Bébé, Scroll Mark, Gesland Body
Size: 21"
Price: $3,000+
Mark: F.G. (in scroll) / 8

Bébé, Scroll Mark, Gesland Body
Size: 28"
Price: $4,000+
Mark: 11 F.G. (scroll, on head) F. Gesland Bte SGDG Paris (body stamp)

Marotte
Size: 12"
Price: $220
Bone handle, open mouth.
Mark: F.G. (block letters)

HALOPEAU

Bébé
Size: 18"   Date: 1875+
Price: $32,000
Straight-wrist composition body.
Mark: 2H

Bébé
Size: 21"   Date: late 1870s
Price: $43,000
Very rare!
Mark: 3H

Raberry & Delphieu, Bébé. French jointed composition and wood body, straight wrists. 24″, c. 1885. Mark: R 3 D. Courtesy Theriaults.

Schmitt et Fils, Bébé. French 8 loose-ball jointed body, straight wrists. 16″, c. 1880. Mark: Sch (shield mark) 1. Courtesy Theriault's.

HURET

Bébé
Size: 16″   Date: early 1900s
Price: $7,600
Pinker coloring than earlier models, composition fully jointed body.
Mark: MA / HURET

Bébé, Wood Body
Size: 18″   Date: 1880
Price: $27,000
Articulated wood body, metal hands and joints.

Bébé, Wood Body
Size: 18″   Date: 1880
Price: $13,800
Articulated wood body.
Mark: unmarked

Portrait, Gentleman
Size: 18″   Date: 1910
Price: $5,500
Later Elisa Prevost era, very pale bisque. Wood body.
Mark: Huret 4

Portrait, Lady, Wood
Size: 17″   Date: 1910
Price: $4,500
Later Elisa Prevost era, very pale bisque. Wood body.
Mark: Huret

J.J. AND J.M.

J.J. Bébé
Size: 14″   Date: 1890
Price: $3,600
All original, complete.
Mark: J. 2. J (incised)

J.M. Bébé
Size: 19″   Date: 1890
Price: $3,200
Straight-wrist body.
Mark: J M / 2

Schmitt et Fils, Bébé. *French 8 loose-ball jointed body, straight wrists. 19″, c. 1882. Mark: Sch 2 (shield mark). $9,250, auction. Courtesy Theriault's.*

Bébé, unknown mark. *In man's costume of northern coast of Brittany. Jointed composition body. 19″, c. 1895. Mark: B (raised) 3. $850, auction.*

Thullier, Bébé, A. T. *Swivel head, shoulder plate, kid-gusseted body with bisque forearms. 17″, c. 1882. Courtesy Theriault's.*

J.M. Bébé

Size: 26″   Date: 1890
Price: $8,900
Straight-wrist body, body flaws.
Mark: J M

JOANNY

Bébé with Bisque Arms

Size: 27″   Date: 1885
Price: $19,500
Bisque arms.
Mark: 12 (raised)

Bébé

Size: 17″   Date: 1885
Price: $4,600
Straight-wrist composition body.
Mark: J. 1

JULLIEN

Jullien, Bébé

Size: 19″   Date: 1895
Price: $4,000

Jullien, Bébé

Size: 23″   Date: 1895
Price: $3,200
Character-like expression.
Mark: Jullien 9

Jullien Bébé, Long Face, Open Mouth

Size: 28″   Date: 1895
Price: $3,200
Mark: Jullien 10

MASCOTTE

Mascotte, Bébé

Size: 19″   Date: 1890
Price: $3,700

Mascotte, Bébé

Size: 15″   Date: 1890
Price: $5,000

Mascotte, Bébé

Size: 24″   Date: 1890
Price: $3,100
Mark: M 9

M MARKED BÉBÉ

Bébé, M mark

Size: 17″   Date: 1890s
Price: $1,675
All dolls priced in this section have some flaws; more for better dolls.
Mark: M

Bébé, M4 mark

Size: 14″   Date: 1890s
Price: $1,275–$1,300
Mark: M 4

Bébé, M5 mark

Size: 18″   Date: 1890s
Price: $1,600
Mark: M 5

Bébé, M7 mark

Size: 19″   Date: 1890s
Price: $1,700
Mark: M 7

MOTHEREAU

Bébé
Size: 12″   Date: 1880s
Price: $5,250
Original pewter lower arms and legs.
Mark: M 2 B

Bébé
Size: 22″   Date: 1880s
Price: $8,500
Unattractive face.

Bébé
Size: 28″   Date: 1880s
Price: $15,500
Mark: B. 10 M.

Bébé
Size: 33″   Date: 1884
Price: $28,000
Rare size, straight-wrist body.
Mark: B.M. 11. 13.

PETIT & DUMONTIER

Bébé
Size: 18″   Date: 1880s
Price: $11,700
Early, pale bisque, original metal hands.
Mark: P. 2 D.

Bébé
Size: 20″   Date: 1882
Price: $7,000
All original.
Mark: P. 3 D.

Bébé
Size: 26″   Date: 1880s
Price: $5,750
Incorrect body.
Mark: P. 5 D.

PINTEL & GODCHAUX

Bébé
Size: 17″   Date: 1880s
Price: $1,800

Bébé
Size: 24″   Date: 1880s
Price: $2,200
Bisque flaws.
Mark: P 11 G

Bébé, Open Mouth
Size: 19″   Date: 1880s
Price: $1,800

Open mouth, 5-piece composition body, elaborate original costume.
Mark: B P 9 G

RABERY & DELPHIEU

Bébé
Size: 10″   Date: 1880s
Price: $2,600
Mark: R. 6 / 0 D

Bébé
Size: 15″   Date: 1880s
Price: $1,500
Body damage.
Mark: R 2 / 0 D

Bébé
Size: 19″   Date: 1880s
Price: $2,900
Closed mouth has modeled space.
Mark: R. 1 D.

Bébé
Size: 28″   Date: 1885
Price: $2,500
Hairline.
Mark: R. 4 D.

Bébé, Open Mouth
Size: 20″   Date: 1880s
Price: $1,700

SCHMITT ET FILS

Bébé
Size: 10″   Date: 1882
Price: $19,500
Unusually high price. At auction.
Mark: Sch (shield mark), 9 (head and backside),
4 (head)

Bébé
Size: 11.5″   Date: 1880
Price: $8,000
Body also marked.
Mark: Bte. SGDG 3 / 0

Bébé
Size: 15″   Date: 1880s
Price: $11,500
Body also marked.
Mark: Schmitt shield / O

Bébé
Size: 18–20″   Date: 1882
Price: $9,00–$12,000
Body also marked.
Mark: Sch 2, shield mark

Bébé
Size: 23–25″ Date: 1880
Price: $12,000–$19,500
Body also marked.
Mark: 4 (and shield mark)

Bébé
Size: 24″ Date: 1880s
Price: $11,500
Slight space between lips, marked Schmitt body.

Bébé
Size: 31″ Date: 1880s
Price: $38,000

Bébé, Sculpted Teeth
Size: 26″ Date: 1882
Price: $29,000
Very rare.
Mark: Sch (in shield) 8

Bébé, Triste
Size: 26″ Date: 1882
Price: $14,000
Pressed bisque, long-faced modeling, straight wrists.
Mark: 6 (raised)

THUILLIER

Bébé
Size: 10.5″ Date: 1882
Price: $10,500
Kid-gusseted jointed bébé body, replaced bisque lower arms.
Mark: A.1 T.

Bébé
Size: 13″ Date: 1880s
Price: $20,000
Bisque lower arms, some flaws.
Mark: A. 3 T.

Bébé
Size: 15″ Date: 1880s
Price: $32,200
Straight-wrist composition body.
Mark: A 7 T

Bébé
Size: 18″ Date: 1885
Price: $38,000
Mint.
Mark: A. 9 T.

Bébé
Size: 22″ Date: 1888
Price: $15,500
Mark: A. 11 T.

Bébé
Size: 23–25″ Date: 1882
Price: $25,000–$38,000
Lower price for doll with flaws.
Mark: A. 11 T.

Bébé
Size: 30″ Date: 1880s
Price: $18,000–$21,000
Mark: A 14 T

Bébé, Wooden Body
Size: 17″ Date: 1882
Price: $33,000
Jointed wood body.
Mark: A. 7 T.

UNMARKED AND OTHER FRENCH BÉBÉS

Bébé, Closed Mouth
Size: 26″ Date: 1885
Price: $5,000
Antique outfit, excellent bisque. Mystery maker, possibly Joanny.
Mark: 12

Bébé, 136, Open-Closed Mouth
Size: 22″ Date: 1900
Price: $1,600
Simple, single-stroke brows; later doll.
Mark: 136 / 16

Bébé, Closed Mouth
Size: 20″ Date: 1880s
Price: $4,600
Straight-wrist French composition body.
Mark: unmarked

Bébé, Open Mouth
Size: 20″ Date: 1920s
Internet: $300
Later doll; 5-piece composition body. New clothes.
Mark: LC /c / 3

Bébé, Portrait, Unknown Mark
Size: 26″ Date: 1885
Price: $10,500
Mark: 5

Bébé, Shoulder Head, Closed Mouth
Size: 13.5″ Date: 1890s
Price: $1,000
Socket head, bisque shoulder plate, kid body with bisque lower arms, gusseted.
Mark: 136 / 3

Character Lady, Closed Mouth

Size: 24″　　　　Date: 1912
Price: $2,000
Mark: unmarked

Character, Child, Toto

Size: 13″
Price: $400
2 lines of teeth, smiling and showing them off.
Mark: unmarked

Character, Girl, Lois Aimee LeJeune

Size: 22″　　　　Date: 1910
Price: $10,500
Shoulder head, painted features, closed mouth,
kid body, bisque lower arms, price for doll with
flaws.
Mark: Wings and LL (back)

Child, Shoulder Head, Sculpted Hair

Size: 11″　　　　Date: 1870
Price: $800
Muslin body, original outfit.
Mark: 2 / 0

Falck & Roussel, Bébé, Closed Mouth

Size: 15″
Price: $5,500
Mark: FR / 5

Pan, Bébé

Size: 12.5″　　　　Date: 1887
Price: $5,800
Mark: PAN / 2

Van Rozen, Black Doll, Character

Size: 18″　　　　Date: 1912
Price: $12,000
Head from bisque-like material. Portrait of
young black man as marquis, powder human
hair wig, 3-corner hat, molded teeth, inset eyes.
Mark: Van Rozen France Deposé

Van Rozen, Portrait, Man

Size: 14″　　　　Date: 1915
Price: $13,000
Head from bisque-like material.
Mark: Van Rozen France Deposé

Verdier & Gutmacher, Bébé, Open Mouth

Size: 26″　　　　Date: 1890
Price: $5,250
Mark: V 12 G

Verlingue, Character, Liane

Size: 20″
Price: $375
Set eyes, human hair wig.
Mark: Petite Francaise J V (anchor symbol)
France 6 d Liane

Bisque, German, Unmarked and Unknown Marks

Dollmaking companies in the 1800s and early 1900s were not thinking of collectors or historical records when they created the bisque dolls—many, many quality makers did not mark their dolls at all, or only marked portions of their production. Or they did mark their dolls, and now the marks are indecipherable to us today because of records lost to history.

Therefore, many of the unmarked and unknown mark dolls are made by the same companies as marked bisque dolls. And every year research has helped collectors identify more and more of these dolls.

Market Report: In spite of the fact that the quality and artistry on many of these dolls is comparable to marked dolls, to many collectors, collecting unmarked antique bisque dolls is a bit like walking a high wire without a net. With no marks to guide them, collectors must rely on their eyes to determine quality and desirability of unmarked bisque dolls. However, since every antique doll is, in some sense, a "one of a kind" due to individualized feature painting, bisque quality differences, outfits, and other variables that collectors don't find in modern dolls, the same determination as to individual quality must be made with unmarked antique dolls as with marked dolls. Of course, it certainly helps as a frame of reference to know if a doll was made by Simon & Halbig or Hertwig.

If you become familiar with styles of feature painting on the dolls of well-known German porcelain companies such as Simon & Halbig, Kestner, and Kämmer & Reinhardt, and if you teach yourself to identify fine bisque, you will become comfortable buying unmarked or unknown maker German bisque dolls. Prices on these dolls should improve as prices in general continue to rise for antique bisque.

Overall, the market for unmarked bisque dolls remains slow due to the already mentioned tendency for collectors to buy known

Child, unknown maker. Shoulder-head, crude composition 5-piece body. Factory original outfit. 12", c. 1890. $799, dealer.

Child, character, Fl. Jointed composition body. 18", c. 1915. $700, dealer. Mark: Fl

Baby, character, unknown maker. Jointed composition bent-leg baby body. 14". Mark: 5.3.0 / Germany.

quantities when buying unmarked bisque. When buying, look for artistically painted features and good-quality bisque (no pits or other flaws) of good color—pale or rosy, not ruddy, and without overly applied cheek blush. Also look for antique outfits on these dolls.

Online/Offline Report: Fine unmarked bisque dolls, well-presented, tend to do better at live auctions and from doll dealers directly than at Internet auctions, where there is more educated information to guide a collector when buying these dolls, and where they can be examined in person.

BELTON-TYPE

Actually, there is no such thing as a "Belton" doll, although this term is used often to describe this class of dolls. Belton-type dolls have flat-topped bisque dome heads with two or three stringing holes, set glass or paperweight eyes, fully jointed composition bodies with straight wrists (except as noted), and closed mouths with an outlined white space between the lips. Belton dolls were made from 1875 to approximately 1900. Belton dolls can resemble either French or German dolls of the period.

Child, French-Type
Size: 12"
All Markets: $1,000

Child, French-Type, Bru-Like Face
Size: 12"
Price: $2,400
Mark: "137" or unmarked

Child, French-Type
Size: 14–15"
Price: $1,600–$2,000

Child, French-Type
Size: 23"
Price: $1,800–$2,500
Mark: 176 / 14

Child, German-Type
Size: 10–11"
Price: $550–$700
5-piece jointed composition body.
Mark: Unmarked or number like 208 or 117.

Child, German-Type
Size: 14–15"
Price: $500–$700
5-piece crude composition body or fully jointed (higher price).
Mark: 132 or 6 or similar or unmarked.

Child, German-Type
Size: 17"
Price: $700
Mark: 11 / TR / 809x

SONNEBERG-TYPE DOLLS

These dolls are by unknown makers, although clearly made in the Sonneberg region of Germany, mostly from 1880–1890.

All-bisque baby, unknown maker. 8". Mark: 833 / 10 (head) Germany (back).

Sonneberg child, unknown maker. Solid flattened-dome socket head, composition-and-wood jointed body. 20", c. 1885. Mark: 183. Courtesy Theriault's.

Some Sonneberg dolls can also be referred to as "Belton" dolls, although not all Sonneberg-type dolls have flattened solid dome heads with stringing holes as the Belton dolls do. All Sonneberg-type dolls have socket bisque heads, fully jointed wood and composition bodies with straight wrists and often loose-ball jointing, socket heads, set glass or paper-weight eyes, and closed mouths, except as noted. Most have a high quality of painting and often are made for the French market. Most are unmarked or marked only with numbers.

Child
Size: 10"   Date: 1888
Price: $900

Child
Size: 12–14"   Date: 1885–1890
All Markets: $1,200–$1,600
French look. Often with mold mark 183.4 or 136 / 5 or 183 / 8 or similar.

Child
Size: 16"   Date: 1885
Price: $1,000
Defined space between lips.
Mark: 8

Child
Size: 16"   Date: 1880
Price: $1,900
Flattened solid dome, high forehead. Attributed to Ernst Grossman.
Mark: unmarked

Child
Size: 18"   Date: 1880s
Price: $2,250
Paperweight eyes, early in Jumeau chemise.
Mark: 9

Child
Size: 21"   Date: 1880
Price: $2,000
Flattened solid dome, pale bisque, choice modeling.

Child, unknown maker. 5-piece composition body , painted shoes and socks, original clothing. 9˝. $300 private sale. Courtesy Dana Probert.

Sonneberg child, unknown maker. Solid flattened dome socket head, composition and wood 8 loose-ball jointed body. 21˝, c. 1880. Mark: 504 (slightly illegible). Courtesy Theriault's.

Sonneberg child, unknown maker. Solid flattened dome socket head, composition and wood jointed body, straight wrists. 23˝, c. 1885. Unmarked. Courtesy Theriault's.

Child, Resembles Bru

Size: 14˝   Date: 1885
Price: $2,700
Flattened solid dome, set eyes.
Mark: 7

Child, 117, Rare Swivel Waist

Size: 16˝   Date: 1885
Price: $2,200

Child, 132, Resembles Bru Breveté

Size: 12–15˝   Date: 1885
Price: $2,200–$2,800
Sometimes found with swivel head and shoulder plate on kid body.
Mark: "132 1/0" or "132.1"

Child, 217

Size: 12˝   Date: 1885
Price: $2,300

Child, Jumeau-Type

Size: 12˝   Date: 1885
Price: $1,100
Child, Jumeau-type.
Mark: 4

Child, Jumeau-Type

Size: 14˝   Date: 1885
Price: $1,800
Emulates Jumeau for French market.
Mark: 6

Child, Rare Body Type

Size: 7˝   Date: 1880
Price: $2,900

Sonneberg composition and wood body with shapely torso, painted high white stockings, blue high-laced heeled boots, bisque arms.
Mark: 117

Fashion Lady

Size: 18˝   Date: 1885
Price: $2,600
Shoulder plate, kid body with 1-piece arms and legs.

Fashion Lady, Corset Body

Size: 18˝   Date: 1890
Price: $3,400
Swivel neck, closed mouth, defined space between lips, kid body with attached red silk corset, pin jointed, long limbs, bisque arms.
Mark: 137.7

CHARACTER DOLLS, UNKNOWN MAKER

All dolls have glass eyes and fully jointed composition bodies except as noted. All of the unknown maker German bisque character dolls listed here were made between 1915–1925.

Baby

Size: 6˝
Price: $450
5-piece bent-limb baby body.

Baby

Size: 15˝
Price: $200

Sonneberg child, unknown maker. *Swivel head on shoulder plate, kid gusset-jointed body, bisque forearms. Emulates the Bébé Bru, for French market. 15", c. 1885. Courtesy Theriault's.*

Täufling baby, unknown maker. *Solid dome, flat-cut neck socket, painted hair, composition shoulder plate, hips, fabric-covered bellows at midriff which makes "mama" sound. Fabric-covered upper arms and legs, wooden lower arms and legs, porcelain feet and hands. Porcelain feet and hands are unusual for this doll, and this is an unusually small size. 6.5", c. 1855. Courtesy Theriault's.*

Molded, painted hair, 5-piece bent-limb baby body.
Mark: 4

Baby, Siegfried
Size: 16"
Price: $500
Solid dome head, painted hair, muslin stitch-jointed body, celluloid hands.
Mark: Siegfried Germany

Boy
Size: 11"
Price: $375
Solid dome, painted hair and eyes, open/closed mouth.
Mark: 159 0 1/2

Boy, Sculpted Hair
Size: 24"
Price: $3,200
Exceptional modeling, set eyes, open mouth, toddler body, side-hip joints.
Mark: made in Germany 267/50

Child, 1407
Size: 9"
Price: $2,600
Wistful look, closed mouth, chipmunk cheeks, may be ABG.
Mark: 1407 20 Germany

Child, 495, Portrait Features
Size: 24"
Price: $2,900
Sleep eyes, open mouth, slender young woman's composition body.
Mark: 485 12

Child, Open Mouth
Size: 20"
Price: $650
Mystery maker, rare signature.
Mark: B & O (in circle and triangle) / B-5 / Germany

Child, Open Mouth, French Market
Size: 19"
Price: $1,200
French composition body, straight wrists, square-cut teeth.

Moritz-Type
Size: 5.5"
Price: $1,100
5-piece body.
Mark: 296 / 13

BISQUE UNMARKED AND UNKNOWN MARK CHILD DOLLS

If no body type is stated, doll has a bisque socket head on fully jointed composition body, glass eyes, and is wigged. The majority of these dolls are from 1880–1910.

Closed Mouth
Size: 14–16"
Price: $400
Socket head, shoulder plate, gusseted kid body with bisque lower arms.
Mark: 174 / 5

Closed Mouth
Size: 17"
Price: $675
German look.
Mark: unmarked

Closed Mouth, Early, Long-Faced
Size: 31"
Price: $4,200
Possibly Simon & Halbig
Mark: unmarked

Closed Mouth, French-Type, 137
Size: 15"
Price: $2,100
Mark: 137 7

Closed Mouth, French-Type
Size: 16"
Price: $1,150
French look.
Mark: TR (together) / 808

Closed Mouth, French-Type, 136
Size: 19–24"
Price: $1,400–$2,100
Paperweight eyes, swivel head on shoulder plate,
kid body, bisque arms.

Closed Mouth, Shoulder Plate
Size: 11–12"
Price: $500–$650
Swivel neck, gusseted kid body or muslin com-
mercial body, bisque lower arms, appropriate old
clothes.
Mark: Unmarked, or 50/3 or similar.

Closed Mouth, Shoulder Head
Size: 16"
Price: $350–$400
Kid body, rivet jointed.
Mark: unmarked

Closed Mouth, Turned Shoulder Head
Size: 12"
Price: $470
Glass eyes, dome head, bisque lower arms.

Closed Mouth, Turned Shoulder Head
Size: 24"
Price: $325
Mark: K

Closed Mouth, Shoulder Head
Size: 20"
Price: $250
Dome head, cloth body with leather hands and
boots.

Open Mouth
Size: 23–24"
Price: $300–$500
Mark: Unmarked or unknown number.

Open Mouth
Size: 20"
Price: $800
French look, composition body with straight
wrists, Pale bisque.
Mark: H. 10. C

Open Mouth
Size: 14–17"
Price: $300–$400
Mark: 51/6 (back head) or C or unmarked or
similar.

Open Mouth, 62
Size: 25"
Price: $525
Fully jointed composition body, lashes.
Mark: 62 182.13

Open Mouth, 630
Size: 19"
Price: $450
Fully jointed composition body, straight wrists.

Open Mouth, 989
Size: 15"
Price: $1,000
Straight-wrist German body (early).

Open Mouth, DEP
Size: 21"
Price: $850
Paperweight eyes, heavy feathered brows.
Mark: DEP / 10

Open Mouth, French Market
Size: 29"
All Markets: $600
Jointed composition body with straight wrists.
Mark: DEP / 8

Open Mouth, Shoulder Head, 216
Size: 10"
Price: $200
Painted hair, cloth body, composition lower
limbs.

Open Mouth, Shoulder Head, 300
Size: 17"
Price: $300
Rivet-jointed kidolene body, bisque arms.

Turned Head, Blonde Molded Hair
Size: 13"
Price: $450
Pierced ears, turned and tilted head, cloth body.

UNMARKED GERMAN BISQUE LADY DOLLS

Unmarked lady dolls priced here are generally from 1870–1880s. All have closed mouths, and are on kid or muslin bodies. All lady dolls listed here are unmarked except as noted.

Lady, Shoulder Head
Size: 15″
Price: $600
Muslin body, bisque lower limbs, possibly Kling.

Lady, Shoulder Head
Size: 16″
Price: $400
Kid leather body with gusset joints, bisque lower arms.
Mark: DEP.

Lady, Shoulder Head
Size: 20″
Price: $550–$650
Muslin body.

Lady, Shoulder Head
Size: 22″
Price: $700
Kid body, bisque lower arms.

Lady, Swivel Head
Size: 11.5″
Price: $600
Cloth body, bisque lower arms shoulder plate, pale bisque.

Lady, Swivel Head
Size: 20″
Price: $850

Lady, Swivel Head
Size: 32″
Price: $1,200

UNMARKED, UNKNOWN MAKER GERMAN BISQUE, VARIOUS

Dolls listed here are from approximately 1880 into the early 1920s. Dolls have bisque socket heads on fully jointed composition bodies, glass eyes, and are wigged as otherwise noted.

American Schoolboy
Size: 7″
Price: $275

American Schoolboys have short molded, painted blonde hair and glass eyes. Shoulder head, cloth body.

American Schoolboy
Size: 12″
Price: $450
Jointed composition body.
Mark: 3

American Schoolboy
Size: 18″
Price: $250
Shoulder head, cloth body with composition lower limbs.
Mark: 30 B 6 Germany

Bonnet Head, Baby
Size: 5″
Price: $350
Little baby, jointed arms and legs with bonnet head, original presentation box.

Bonnet Head, Child
Size: 9–17″   Internet: $175–$250
Bisque shoulder head, closed mouth, painted molded hair and bonnet. Muslin body with bisque or china lower limbs. More for rare bonnets.
Mark: unmarked

Child
Size: 16″   Internet: $600
Open mouth.
Mark: 106-X

Christmas Fairy
Size: 10″
Price: $1,050
Dressed as Christmas Fairy, all original, muslin body with composition lower limbs, bare feet.
Mark: unmarked

Man, Molded Mustache
Size: 8″
Price: $300–$380
Cloth or composition 4-piece body.

Marotte, Open Mouth
Size: 13″
Price: $180–$300

Molded Blonde Hair
Size: 22″
Price: $425
Well detailed hair, painted eyes, kid body.
Mark: unmarked

Molded Blonde Hair
Size: 27"
Price: $325
Cloth body, leather lower arms and boots,
painted eyes.

Molded Blonde Hair and Hair Band
Size: 15"
Price: $650
Shoulder head, molded hair, black band, cloth
body, bisque lower limbs; molded 5-strap
bootines.
Mark: unmarked

Molded Blonde Hair With Blue Ribbon
Size: 11"
Price: $850
Pierced ears, glass eyes, muslin body, bisque
lower limbs, painted pink ankle boots.
Mark: unmarked

Molded Blonde Hair, Child
Size: 19"   Internet: $275
Cloth body, painted eyes.
Mark: 9 (back of shoulder plate)

Native American
Size: 17"
Price: $750
Portrait; outstanding face modeling.
Mark: 103

Native American
Size: 8–10"
Price: $125–$175
Cloth body with composition lower limbs or 5-
piece composition body. Open mouth, teeth.
Mark: 201

Tiny Child in Trousseau Box
Size: 7"
Price: $875
Sleep eyes, molded teeth, mohair wig, 5-piece
composition body, molded shoes, socks.

Toddler, SAH Mark
Size: 22"
Price: $1,300
Toddler jointed composition body, mohair wig,
wobble tongue.
Mark: SAH (entwined in circle) / 11

2-Faced Baby, Unmarked
Size: 12"
Price: $650

Viola
Size: 24"
Price: $350

Bisque, German, Various Companies

There is not really much to differentiate between some of the German companies listed
in this section compared with the companies
that received their own section in this book
(such as Kling or Ernst Heubach), other
than space constraints. When evaluating
dolls from these companies, just as with unmarked German bisque dolls, quality of the
bisque and painting of the doll and the overall presentation (body type, clothing) should
guide you.

Market Report: Some of the bisque dolls, especially the bisque dolly-faced dolls, can be
perfect dolls for the beginning doll collector
or a collector on a budget. Many dolls can be
found for under $400. Prices for these dolls
overall have declined slightly in the last few
years.

Online/Offline Report: You can definitely
find eBay bargains here, and dealers will
often have these dolls available reasonably at
shows and shops.

Prices and Characteristics: For all German
bisque companies listed in this section, prices
are for dolls in excellent condition, with
bisque socket heads and fully jointed composition bodies, glass eyes, and wigged, except
as noted. Where dates are not given, the dolls
were generally produced between the 1890s
and 1930.

ARNOLD, MAX OSCAR

Baby
Size: 12"   Internet: $200
5-piece bent-limb baby body.
Mark: MOA (in star) 150 / Made in Germany /
Welsch 0

Child, Open Mouth, 200
Size: 23"   Internet: $725
Well-painted features.
Mark: MOA (in 8-point star) 200 MADE IN
GERMANY / WELSCH 7

American Schoolboy child, un-
known maker. Composition and
wood jointed body. 12″, c. 1880.
$450, auction. Courtesy
Theriault's.

Max Oscar Arnold, child. 5-piece
crude composition body. 13″, c.
1920. Mark: MOA (in 8-pointed
star) / 200 / Made in Germany /
Welsh / 2/0. $100, eBay.

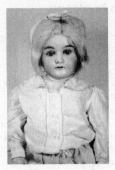

Karl H. Hartmann, child. From
original, 87-year owner, 2004.
Jointed composition body. 26″, c.
1911. Mark: K (in upper part of
large H) 3 (in lower part of H).
$300, eBay.

Child, Open Mouth

Size: 12″   Internet: $200
Crude cloth and composition body.

CATTERFELDER PUPPENFABRIK

Catterfelder Puppenfabrik dolls are from
1902 to approximately the 1920s.

Character, 201

Size: 8″
Price: $750
Painted eyes, 5-piece toddler body.
Mark: C.P. 201 23

Character, 201

Size: 14″
Price: $2,400
Painted hair and eyes, exceptional example.
Mark: C.P. 201 / 34

Character, 201

Size: 15″
Price: $850
Solid dome head, painted eyes, open/closed
mouth 5-piece toddler body.
Mark: C.P. 201 34

HANDWERCK, MAX

Max Handwerck dolls listed here are from
1900–1920.

Child, Open Mouth

Size: 24″
All Markets: $500

Child, Boy, Open Mouth

Size: 27″
Price: $625
Mark: Max Handwerck, Germany, 3

Googly, Helmet

Size: 12″
Price: $1,500
Mark: Dep Elite D1

Googly, Uncle Sam

Size: 12″
Price: $2,900
Mark: Dep Elite U.S. 1

K & K

K & K, Child, Shoulder Head

Size: 18–20″
Price: $250
Cloth body, composition arms, sleep eyes.
Mark: K & K / 58 /Made in Germany

K & K, Character, Baby, 122

Size: 16″
Price: $375
Open mouth, wigged, wobble tongue, sleep eyes.

K & K, Toddler, 60

Size: 23″
Price: $450

Gebrüder Kühnlenz, Child 165. Jointed composition body. 14.5″, c. 1890s. Mark: Gbr 165K / ½ / Germany. $499, dealer.

Gebrüder Kühnlenz, child. Composition and wood 8 loose-ball jointed body, straight wrists. Made to resemble the Bébé Bru to compete with doll. 13″, c. 1885. Mark: G.K. 34.24. Courtesy Theriault's.

KÖNIG & WERNICKE

Character, Child, 98
Size: 15″
Price: $425
Mark: made in Germany 98/3 or K & K / 98

Character, Toddler, 99
Size: 11″
All Markets: $860–$900
Sleep eyes, hair lashes, painted, fully jointed composition toddler body. Open mouth, teeth.

KÜHNLENZ, GEBRÜDER

All dolls have fully jointed composition bodies and are wigged with glass eyes. Gebrüder Kühnlenz dolls are from approximately 1885 to the early 1900s.

Child, 34, Black
Size: 7–9″
Price: $700–$900

Sleep eyes, open mouth, 5-piece composition body.
Mark: 34.10

Child, 34, Black, Resembles Bru
Size: 17″
Price: $3,600

Child, 38, Closed Mouth, Turned Shoulder Head
Size: 13″
Price: $500
Gusseted kid body, bisque lower arms.
Mark: G.K. / 38-23

Child, 39, Closed Mouth
Size: 9″   Internet: $650
Original Sonneberg-type composition jointed body.
Mark: GK / 39-20

Child, 39, Resembles Bru Breveté
Size: 14″
Price: $2,400

Schoenau & Hoffmeister, child.
*Shoulder-head, cloth body, bisque
hands, original outfit. 18", c. 1905.
Mark: S / PB (in 5-point star) H /
dep. Courtesy Dana Probert.*

König & Wernicke, toddler. *Composition-and-wood toddler body,
side-hip joints. 22", c. 1920.
Mark: KW (in circle). Courtesy
Theriault's.*

Attempts to imitate Bru Breveté for French
market.
Mark: 39.25

Child, 41

Size: 19"
Price: $1,100
Open mouth with square-cut teeth, solid dome
head, kid body, bisque lower limbs.
Mark: 41-4 DEP

Child, 44

Size: 9"
Price: $450
5-piece composition body, open mouth.
Mark: GK 44 / 18

Child, 47

Size: 14"
Price: $275
Shoulder head, kid body, bisque arms, cloth legs.
Mark: 47 / 22

Child, 89

Size: 14"
Price: $475
Mark: 89. 13

Child, 165

Size: 14"
Price: $500
Factory original. 165s have open mouths.
Mark: G br 165K / 0 1/2 / Germany

Child, 165

Size: 20"
Price: $350

Child, 165

Size: 28–29"
Price: $450–$500
Mohair lashes.
Mark: 32 GBR 165 K 13

Child, 165

Size: 34"
Price: $500

Schmidt, Bruno, Tommy Tucker.
Composition and wood toddler
body, side-hip joints. 21″, c. 1912.
Mark: 2048.5. Courtesy Theriault's.

Child, Boy
Size: 7″
Price: $150
Later boy, all composition.

PORZELLANFABRIK MENGERSGEREUTH (PM MARK)

Baby
Size: 10–12″
All Markets: $150–$170
Crude composition body, wigged, sleep eyes.
Mark: PM #914 Germany 1

Baby, Character, 914
Size: 11″
Price: $100–$200
5-piece composition baby body, open mouth.
Mark: PM 914 2

Baby, Character, 924
Size: 22″
Price: $200

Child, Character
Size: 16″
Price: $300

Child, Character
Size: 22″
Price: $825
Toddler body.

RECKNAGEL

Recknagel dolls are from the late 1880s through the 1930s.

Baby, 23
Size: 10″   Internet: $300
Sleep eyes, 5-piece composition baby body, wigged, open mouth with teeth.

Baby, 121
Size: 8″
All Markets: $100
Solid dome flange head, open mouth, molded, painted hair, cloth body with composition arms.

Child
Size: 9″   Internet: $150
Sleep eyes, open mouth, crude 5-piece composition body with painted shoes and socks.
Mark: R/A DEP 19/0

Child
Size: 22″
All Markets: $250
Open mouth, wood and composition body.
Mark: 21 / Germany / R4A

Child
Size: 12″
All Markets: $115
5-piece composition body.

Googly
Size: 6″   Date: 1914
                       Internet: $225
Painted, molded hair, painted eyes, crude 5-piece composition body.
Mark: R 45 / 13.0

Googly
Size: 8″   Internet: $400
Molded hair with blue bows, surprised look, 5-
piece crude composition body.
Mark: RA / 50

Recknagel, Doll in Presentation Trunk
Size: 8.5″
All Markets: $825
In trunk with clothing, ribbons, all original.
Composition body.
Mark: 21 Germany R.A.

SCHMIDT, BRUNO

Bruno Schmidt dolls were made from approximately 1900 through the 1920s.

All-Bisque, Flapper, 513
Size: 7″
Price: $500
Elongated limb flapper body, painted eyes, 1-
piece head/torso.
Mark: 513 17.Germany

Baby, Character, 2023
Size: 12″
Price: $375
Closed mouth, painted eyes.

Child, Character, 537, Wendy
Size: 11″
Price: $7,475
Rare in this size, sometimes called "Wendy."

Child, Character, 537, Wendy
Size: 16″
Price: $17,000
Rare character, glass eyes, closed mouth.
Mark: 2033 BSW (in heart) 537 5

Child, Character, 2097
Size: 34″
Price: $1,700
Unusually large size. Open mouth.
Mark: BP (crossed swords) BSW (in heart) 2097 /
7

Child, Open Mouth
Size: 11″   Internet: $650
Sonneberg composition body.
Mark: 687 / 2/0 / BSW-made in Germany

Child, Open Mouth
Size: 31″
Price: $650
Mark: Made in Germany / BS W (in heart)

Child, Open Mouth
Size: 35″
Price: $625
Mark: BSW in heart

Child, Pouty
Size: 23″
Price: $4,200
Attributed to Bruno Schmidt.
Mark: 13

Toddler, 2097
Size: 24″
Price: $500
Open mouth.
Mark: 14 / BSW (in heart) / 2097-6

Tommy Tucker
Size: 24″   Internet: $1,300
Several sizes. Painted hair, glass eyes.

SCHMIDT, FRANZ

Franz Schmidt dolls listed here are from the
1890s through the 1920s.

Baby, 1295, Open Mouth
Size: 23″
Price: $625
5-piece baby body.
Mark: 1295 / FS&C / Germany / 60

Baby, Character, 1272
Size: 20″
Price: $300
5-piece baby body.
Mark: F S & Co. 1272 Germany

Baby, Character, 1294
Size: 28″
Price: $1,000
Open mouth, mechanical key-wind flirt eyes, 5-
piece baby body.
Mark: 1294 72

Toddler, 1295
Size: 8″
Price: $500–$600
Socket head, open mouth, wigged, 5-piece tod-
dler body.
Mark: F S & C 1295

Toddler, 1295
Size: 22″
Price: $950
Socket head, open mouth, wigged, 5-piece tod-
dler body, wobble tongue.
Mark: 1295 / F.S. & C. / 50

Toddler, 1295, Flirty Eyes
Size: 24″
Price: $1,800
Mark: 1295 F.S. & C 55

SCHUETZMEISTER & QUENDT

Character, Baby
Size: 15″
Price: $700
Factory original. Sleep eyes, mohair wig, open mouth, 5-piece bent-limb baby body.

Character, Baby
Size: 19″
Price: $350
Open mouth, sleep eyes, 5-piece bent-limb baby body.
Mark: 201 S & Q 9

Character, Baby
Size: 24″
Price: $260
Open mouth, sleep eyes, 5-piece bent-limb baby body.
Mark: 201 SQ (cypher) Germany

STEINER, HERMANN

Herm Steiner dolls are from approximately 1910 to 1930.

Baby
Size: 15″
Price: $100
Flange neck, sleep eyes, closed mouth, cloth body, composition lower limbs.

Baby, Character, 128
Size: 7″
Price: $175
Open mouth, sleep eyes, wigged, baby body.

Child, Character, 128
Size: 11″
Price: $500
Open mouth, fully jointed composition body.
Mark: 128 / Herm Steiner / 9 0 / Germany

Child, Character, 128
Size: 21″   Internet: $1,000
Fully jointed composition body, factory original.

Child, Open Mouth
Size: 7″
Price: $150
Crude 5-piece composition body with painted shoes and socks, open mouth, wigged.
Mark: Herm / Steiner / 2/0

Child, Open Mouth
Size: 10″
Price: $450
Fully jointed French composition body, paperweight eyes.
Mark: 100 / Germany / Herm Steiner

Child, Open Mouth
Size: 14″
Price: $100
Crude 5-piece composition body.

SWAINE & CO.

Swaine & Co. dolls listed here are from approximately 1910 to the 1920s.

Baby Lori, Character
Size: 10″
Price: $800
Open mouth, composition baby body, glass eyes.
Mark: 232

Baby Lori, Character
Size: 22″
All Markets: $1,500
Closed mouth, 5-piece composition baby body, glass eyes.
Mark: D / Lori / 7 / GEschott / S&Co / Germany

Baby, DIP, Character
Size: 11″
Price: $550
5-piece composition baby body.

Baby, DIP, Character
Size: 16.5″
Price: $1,700
Sleep eyes, 5-piece composition baby body.
Mark: D.I.P. 4

Baby, DIP, Character
Size: 10–13″
Price: $800–$900
Closed mouth, sleep eyes, 5-piece composition baby body.
Mark: DIP 4 / GESCHUTZ S&Co (green stamp)

Child, Character, Smiling
Size: 9″
Price: $2,000
Painted hair, eyes.
Mark: B 3/0 (impressed) S&Co (green stamp)

Child, Character, Smiling
Size: 15″
Price: $1,675
Painted hair, eyes.

GERMAN BISQUE, VARIOUS COMPANIES

Most dolls from these companies are from the 1890s through the 1920s.

Bing, Child
Size: 6″
Price: $370

Goebel, Character, Baby
Size: 8″
Price: $300
5-piece composition baby body, sleep eyes, molded hair.

Carl Hartmann, Globe Baby
Size: 8.5″
Price: $225
5-piece composition body.
Mark: Globe Baby / DEP / Germany / C 3/0 H

Julius Hering Character Baby
Size: 12″
Price: $150
5-piece composition body, mohair wig.

Limbach, Child, Open Mouth
Size: 22″
Price: $575

Thüringer Puppen-Industrie, Baby
Size: 21″
Price: $350
5-piece composition baby body.
Mark: Waltershausen-TPI-10

Wiesenthal, Schindel & Kallenberg, Child, Open Mouth
Size: 18″
Price: $7,200
Mark: WSK 3

Wislizenus, Character, Boy
Size: 14″
Price: $425
Solid dome, painted hair, painted eyes, open/closed mouth, molded tongue and teeth.
Mark: 110 / 4 Germany

Black Dolls

This section includes Black antique dolls made mostly in Germany and France in the late 1800s and early 1900s, plus Black cloth folk dolls made in America in the same time period. Just like their Asian antique counterparts, many fewer Black antique dolls were made than their Caucasian counterparts. Refer to the Black Dolls section in the Vintage Dolls chapter for information on composition and hard-plastic dolls. Modern Black Dolls are covered under the various manufacturer sections in the Modern Dolls chapter.

Market Report: Black dolls is a hot collecting area, although perhaps not as hot as a few years ago. In most areas of vintage and antique doll collecting, prices for Black dolls outstrip those of nearly identical Caucasian dolls. In most categories, prices for Black dolls have gone up as collectors have recognized the relative rarity of these dolls. When collecting, look especially for even skin tones that are mid-range—not exaggerated dark tones, or dolls with wildly exaggerated features. Look also for rarer examples when possible—especially character dolls, and dolls from popular companies such as Simon & Halbig, Kestner, Kämmer & Reinhardt, Bru, and Jumeau.

One weak area price-wise is the simply done, more common Black cloth folk dolls which have no information available as to date or place of manufacture. These should not be confused with the earlier Black primitive dolls from the late 1800s to early 1900s—Black cloth dolls for which prices remain strong.

Online/Offline Report: Prices are equally strong online and at shops, shows, and live auctions. When buying or selling Black dolls on eBay, don't ignore possible cross-listing categories, such as Collectibles > Culture, Ethnicities > Black Americana > Dolls, Bears, or Antiques > Primitives, especially for cloth dolls.

Prices and Characteristics: Dolls have bisque heads with black or brown complexions, fully jointed composition bodies, glass eyes, and wigs, except as noted. All are in excellent condition. Prices generally are taken from non-Internet sources, with Internet pricing noted and overall Internet prices listed for celluloid and cloth dolls.

French, Bébé, Dep. Jointed composition body. 17", c. 1900. Mark:
Dep 6. Courtesy Theriault's.

French, Jumeau Bébé. French
composition-and-wood fully jointed
body. 17", c. 1900. From Jumeau to
S.F.B.J. transitional period. Mark: x
6. Courtesy Theriault's.

ANTIQUE BLACK BISQUE, FRENCH

Denamur, Bébé, Closed Mouth
Size: 20″   Date: 1890
Price: $4,600
Mark: E. 8 D.

French Fashion, Attributed to Bru
Size: 14″   Date: 1875
Price: $19,000
Open mouth, swivel head on shoulder plate,
wood body.
Mark: 2

French Fashion, Leather Body
Size: 17″
Price: $4,500
Leather body, open mouth with teeth, glass eyes.
Mark: unmarked

Paris Bébé
Size: 19″   Date: Early 1890s
Price: $5,400

Head attached to body with inverted wood
dowel, paperweight eyes.
Mark: 8

S.F.B.J., Bébé, 1907
Size: 12–14″   Date: 1907
Price: $1,300–$1,900
Open mouth.
Mark: 1907 2

S.F.B.J., Bébé, 60
Size: 14″
Price: $400
Open mouth.
Mark: SFBJ 60 Paris 4/0

S.F.B.J., Character, 226
Size: 17″   Date: 1910
Price: $1,100
Open/closed mouth.

S.F.B.J., Character, 237
Size: 22″   Date: 1910
Price: $16,500
Open, smiling mouth, 4 teeth.
Mark: SFBJ 237 Paris 8

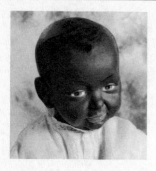

Kämmer & Reinhardt, baby, character 100. *Composition bent-limb baby body. 18″, c. 1910. Mark: K * R / 100 / 50. Courtesy Theriault's.*

German, Heubach characters. *Doll on left: laughing character, 14″, shoulder-head on muslin body, composition lower arms. Doll on right: character baby, 13″, composition bent-limb baby body. Both, c. 1910. Marks: Heubach (sunburst mark) 7657. Baby: Heubach (sunburst mark) Germany 4 / 76. Courtesy Theriault's.*

Steiner, Bébé, Series A, Closed Mouth
Size: 10″   Date: 1880s
Price: $6,100
Fully jointed Steiner composition body.

Steiner, Bébé, Series A, Open Mouth
Size: 14–15″   Date: 1880s
Price: $2,000–$3,500
Fully jointed composition Steiner body, paperweight eyes.
Mark: A7

Van Rozen, Character Doll, Young Man
Size: 18″   Date: 1912
Price: $12,000
Bisque-like material. Young black man as marquis.
Mark: VAN ROZEN, FRANCE Deposé

ANTIQUE BLACK BISQUE, GERMAN

Painted Bisque
Size: 8.5″
Price: $160
5-piece papier-mâché body.

Sonneberg, Closed Mouth
Size: 15″   Date: 1882
Price: $2,000
Resembles Circle-Dot Bru, flattened solid dome socket head, defined space between lips, pouty, Sonneberg body.
Mark: 8

Sonneberg, Open Mouth
Size: 18″   Date: 1885
Price: $2,500
Characterized features, flattened solid dome head, glass eyes, Sonneberg body.
Mark: 4

Googly, Oscar Hitt, Snowflake
Size: 3″
Price: $275–$300
Moving eyes, one piece doll.
Mark: Snowflake copr. Oscar Hitt / Germany

Handwerck, Heinrich, Child, Open Mouth
Size: 17″   Date: 1890s
Price: $1,100
Mark: Germany / Heinrich Handwerck / Simon & Halbig

Ernst (Koppelsdorf), Character, 418
Size: 8″   Date: 1920
Price: $725
Mark: Heubach Koppelsdorf 418 14/0

Heubach, Ernst, Baby 399, a.k.a. "South Seas Baby"
Size: 9–10″   Date: 1930
All Markets: $325 –$450
5-piece baby body, solid dome head, painted hair, sleep eyes. Often in a "South Seas" outfit. May have label with country name or "South Seas Baby."
Mark: Heubach / Koppelsdorf / 399 / 13/0 / DRGM / Germany

German, Kämmer & Reinhardt, toddler. 5-piece jointed composition toddler body. 9", c. 1920. Mark: K * R / Simon & Halbig / Germany / 126-2. Courtesy Theriault's.

German, Kestner, child. Jointed composition body, straight wrists. 10", c. 1900. Mark: made in Germany / 5. Courtesy Theriault's.

German, Simon & Halbig, Character Child 1368. Composition-and-wood jointed body. 13", c. 1912. Mark: 1368 / Germany / Simon & Halbig / S&H 4. Courtesy Theriault's.

Heubach, Ernst, Baby 399, a.k.a. "South Seas Baby"

Size: 12"   Date: 1920
Price: $550
Mint in original straw skirt, label.
Mark: Heubach Koppelsdorf 399 6/0 Germany DRGM

Heubach, Ernst, Baby 463, a.k.a. "South Seas Baby"

Size: 9"   Date: 1920
Price: $575
Mark: Heubach Koppelsdorf 463 15/0 Germany DRGM

Heubach, Ernst, Toddler

Size: 8"
Price: $175
Crude 5-piece body, as native.

Heubach, Gebrüder, Candy Container, Boy With Piglet in Egg

Size: 7"   Date: 1915
Price: $1,400
Mark: Heubach (sunburst)

Kämmer & Reinhardt, Character Baby, 100

Size: 18"   Date: 1910
Price: $1,350
Mark: K * R 100 50

Kestner, Baby, Hilda, 245

Size: 10"   Date: 1914
Price: $1,750
Sleep eyes, wobble tongue, bent-limb baby body.
Mark: 5 245 J.D.K. Jr. 1914© Hilda

Kühnlenz, Gebrüder, Character

Size: 6"   Date: 1895
Price: $375
5-piece papier-mâché body.
Mark: 34.14

Kühnlenz, Gebrüder, Character

Size: 9"   Date: 1895
Price: $675
5-piece papier-mâché body.
Mark: 34.17

Kühnlenz, Gebrüder, All-Bisque, Child, Closed Mouth

Size: 6"   Date: 1890
Price: $950
Swivel head, glass eyes, peg joints.
Mark: 61 / 17

Kühnlenz, Gebrüder, Child

Size: 9"   Date: 1890
Price: $700
5-piece body, open mouth, glass eyes.
Mark: 34-18

Marseille, Armand, Baby, 341

Size: 10–13"   Date: 1910+
Price: $220–$310
Results are a mix of Internet and other prices.
Composition bent-limb baby body, glass eyes, painted hair.

Marseille, Armand, Baby, 351

Size: 17"   Date: 1910+
Price: $375

German, Simon & Halbig, Child 949. *Composition-and-wood jointed body. 20", c. 1890. Mark: S 12 H 949. Courtesy Theriault's.*

French fashion, attributed to Bru. *Shoulder-head on kid gusset-jointed body. 15", c. 1868. $4,800, auction.*

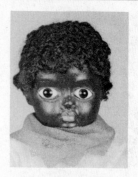

German, papier-mâché, child. *Twill-stuffed body, papier-mâché lower arms and legs. 12", c. 1890. Unmarked. $200, dealer.*

Dome head, open mouth, painted hair, glass eyes.
Mark: A.M / Germany / 351 / 5K

Marseille, Armand, Dream Baby, Black
Size: 18"   Date: 1925
All Markets: $300
Dome head, open mouth, painted hair, glass eyes.

Painted Bisque, Child
Size: 8.5"
Price: $200
Papier-mâché body, black glass eyes, caracul wig.

Schoenau & Hoffmeister, Hanna
Size: 6–7"   Date: 1910+
Price: $200–$300
5-piece composition baby body, sleep eyes, wigged.
Mark: S PB (in star) H / Hanna

Schuetzmeister & Quendt, Baby
Size: 16"   Date: 1920
Price: $1,300
Open mouth, 5-piece composition baby body.
Mark: 251 SQ (intertwined) Germany

Scootles, Composition Scootles
Size: 13"   Date: 1912–1920s
Price: $460

Simon & Halbig, Character, Child, 1538
Size: 22"   Date: 1912
Price: $10,300
Open mouth with teeth.

Simon & Halbig, Child
Size: 15"   Date: 1900
Price: $1,000
No mold number, glass eyes, open mouth.
Mark: Simon & Halbig S&H 6

Simon & Halbig, Child, 1009
Size: 15"   Date: 1890
Price: $1,200
Glass eyes, open mouth.
Mark: St. S 6 H 1009 dep.

Simon & Halbig, Child, 1009
Size: 22"   Date: 1890
Price: $1,675

Simon & Halbig, Child, 1039
Size: 20"   Date: 1900
Price: $1,200
Glass eyes, open mouth.

Simon & Halbig, Child, 1079
Size: 26"   Date: 1900
Price: $2,400
Glass sleep eyes, open mouth.
Mark: S & H 1079 dep 13

Simon & Halbig, Child, 1358
Size: 22"   Date: 1900
Price: $8,700
Harder to find larger size, open mouth with teeth.
Mark: 1358 Germany Simon & Halbig S & H 9

Simon & Halbig, Child, 1358
Size: 12"   Date: 1910
Price: $3,300

Cloth. Handmade Aunt Jemima doll. Sewn arm and leg joints, felt features. 14˝. $75, dealer.

Open mouth with teeth, pierced ears, glass sleep eyes.
Mark: 1358 Germany Simon & Halbig S&H 2

Simon & Halbig, Child, 1368

Size: 14˝   Date: 1900
Price: $3,500–$3,900
Open mouth with 4 teeth, glass sleep eyes.
Mark: 1368 Germany Simon & Halbig S&H 4

Simon & Halbig, Child, 739

Size: 14˝   Date: 1880s
Price: $1,700
Open mouth, glass eyes.
Mark: S & H / 739

Simon & Halbig, Child, 2-Faced, 900 Series

Size: 11˝   Date: 1892
Price: $3,000
White and black faces. Head revolves from cardboard cap with metal pivot ring. Using Carl Bergner Multifaced system.
Mark: 902 dep 3 (forehead)

Sonneberg, Child, Resembles Circle-Dot Bru

Size: 15˝   Date: 1882
Price: $2,000
Flattened solid dome socket head, closed mouth, defined space between lips.
Mark: 8

Unknown, Characterized Features

Size: 18˝   Date: 1885
Price: $2,500
Solid dome socket head, open mouth, Sonneberg composition body, set eyes.
Mark: 4 ˉ

ANTIQUE BLACK CELLULOID DOLLS

The Black celluloid dolls presented here are from the 1920s and 1930s.

German, Turtle Mark, Black Boy or Girl

Size: 13–15˝
Price: $150   Internet: $180–$225
Painted hair or wigged, glass eyes, 5-piece body, swivel neck. Rheinische Gummi und Celluloid Fabrik Co.
Mark: Turtle (in triangle) / 34 / 35

Kewpie, Celluloid

Size: 3˝
Price: $125   Internet: $100
Jointed arms.
Mark: Made In Germany (label, back)

Googly, Celluloid

Size: 6˝   Internet: $200
German, molded white clothes, 1 piece.

Kewpie, Japan, Celluloid

                         Internet: $10–$30
Made in Japan, lesser quality, often thin celluloid.

ANTIQUE BLACK CLOTH

All in excellent condition, but with acceptable wear. Almost all are unmarked.

Bruckner

Size: 14˝   Date: 1901
                         Internet: $450

Cloth-Mask Face, Georgene
Size: 12″   Date: 1930s
                             Internet: $200
With original label, body is sewn flowered-print cloth.

Cloth-Mask Face, Mammy
Size: 16″   Date: 1930s
                             Internet: $200
Original clothing

Golliwog, English
Size: 16–23″   Date: 1920s
Price: $350–$550   Internet: $250–$400

Magel Burgard, Pair
Price: $550   Date: late 1800s
Flat faces, painted features.

Mammy Doll
Size: 10–15″   Date: 1930s–1940s
Price: $30–$100   Internet: $40–$80
Handmade, simple, painted features, wool yarn hair, head scarf, embroidered features.

Mammy Doll
Size: 14.5″   Date: 1900
Price: $300
Oil-painted features and hair, oil-painted orange legs.
Mark: The Dark Kids….Sanitary -Old Mammy (torso stamp).

Primitive, American, Handmade
Size: 18–24″   Date: late 1800s
Price: $500–$900
Sewn or embroidered features.

Primitive
Size: 25″   Date: late 1800s
Price: $1,100
Exaggerated embroidered features, lots of teeth.

Primitive, Oil-Painted Features
Size: 23″   Date: late 1800s
Price: $1,800
Exaggerated features, clear face in excellent condition. Old clothes.

Printed, Uncle Moose
Size: 16″
Price: $220

ANTIQUE BLACK DOLLS, VARIOUS

Dolls are in excellent condition and are unmarked, except as noted. Prices are non-Internet, except as noted.

China Doll, Black Man
Size: 12″   Date: 1890
Price: $1,000
Material: porcelain

China Doll, Dollhouse Size
Size: 5–6″   Date: 1890
Price: $225–$250
Material: porcelain

Frozen Charlotte
Size: 1.25″
Price: $15–$20
Material: metal
Birthday-cake size.

Frozen Charlotte
Size: 1.25″
Price: $20–$30
Material: porcelain
Birthday-cake size.

Frozen Charlotte, Molded Clothing
Size: 2.5″   All Markets: $210
Material: porcelain
Molded dress trimmed in blue.

Joel Ellis
Size: 15″   Date: 1873
Price: $500
Material: wood
Flaws including substantial paint loss to head. All wood, mortise and tenon joints, carved painted hair, metal hands, feet. Made by Cooperative Manufacturing Co., Springfield, Vermont. Higher price for better condition.

Leather Lady
Size: 13″   Date: 1900
Price: $110
Material: leather
Plantation costume, all leather.

Nutshell Doll, Pair
Size: 7″, 9″   Date: early 1900s
Price: $225
Material: nutshell
Mark: 44c "Tulsa" (paper label).

Papier-mâché, German, Character
Size: 7″   Date: 1891
Price: $350
Material: papier-mâché
Glass eyes, exaggerated features, 5-piece crude papier-mâché body, painted shoes and socks.

Papier-mâché, German, Child
Size: 13″
Price: $525   Date: 1880s
Material: papier-mâché

Gladdie. Designed by Helen Jensen. *Muslin toddler body, composition limbs. This bisque version is rarer. 15", c. 1925. Mark: Gladdie copyright by Helen W. Jensen, Germany. Courtesy Theriault's.*

Character, child, by Grace Cory Rockwell. *Muslin torso and upper legs, composition arms and lower legs. 18", c. 1925. Mark: Copr. By Grace C. Rockwell / Germany. $6,600, auction. Courtesy Theriault's.*

Shoulder head, cloth body with papier-mâché terra-cotta lower arms and legs, black pupil-less glass eyes, mohair wig.

Papier-mâché, German, Child, With Crier
Size: 12"   Date: 1880
Price: $200
Material: papier-mâché
Bellows mama crier. Glass eyes, cloth body, papier-mâché lower limbs, painted shoes.

Borgfeldt, George

One of the hardest things for new doll collectors to work out is which companies made doll heads and parts, which companies assembled dolls, and which companies distributed dolls. Sometimes companies did all three! George Borgfeldt assembled and distributed dolls. I could have just as easily listed these dolls under the companies that made their heads, but these dolls—such as Baby Bo Kaye and Gladdie—are included here under Borgfeldt because they are most often associated with that company. Also, the Borgfeldt company is an important one that had a huge effect on the doll market in the early part of the 20th century in the United States.

Market Report: Borgfeldt dolls are good, well-known, well-trademarked dolls and should continue to hold their own in the doll market.

Online/Offline Report: Prices from all sources are comparable.

Prices and Characteristics: All dolls are bisque in excellent condition, except as noted.

GEORGE BORGFELDT

Baby Bo Kaye
Size: 11"   Date: 1926
Price: $900
Imported to America by Borgfeldt. Designed by Joseph Kallus. Painted hair, sleep eyes, muslin body, composition lower limbs.
Mark: Copr. by J.L. Kallus Germany 1394/30

Baby Bo Kaye
Size: 15–16.5"   Date: 1926
Price: $1,775–$2,100

Baby Bo Kaye
Size: 19"   Date: 1926
Price: $2,500

Character, Baby
Size: 13"   Date: 1912
                    Internet: $225
5-piece composition baby body with bent knees.
Mark: G.B & Co / Germany / 5

Child, My Girlie
Size: 25"   Date: 1912
                    Internet: $350
Bisque socket head, open mouth with upper teeth, new clothes.
Mark: My Girlie / III / Germany

Gladdie

Size: 17″   Date: 1928–1930
Price: $900   Internet: $800
Made from biscaloid (a composition, bisque mix)
or bisque. By Helen W. Jensen.
Mark: Gladdie/Copyright By / Helen W. Jensen
/ Germany

Grace Cory Rockwell, Character, Child

Size: 18″   Date: 1925
Price: $6,600
From Borgfeldt line of bisque dolls designed by
American artists and made in Germany.
Mark: Copr. by Grace C. Rockwell, Germany

Bru Dolls

Bru Jne. & Cie began making dolls in 1866,
and it continued making dolls until 1899,
when it became part of the Société Française
de Fabrication de Bébés et Jouets (S.F.B.J.),
as did many of the other French dollmaking
companies.

Bru has made some of the most sought-after
antique bisque dolls—the dolls are considered icons of their genre, especially the Bru
Jne. bébés with their kid bodies and bisque
hands. Besides bébés, Bru also made French
fashion dolls (poupées) and a series of innovative dolls based on patented mechanisms,
such as its Nursing Bru (Bébé Teteur), its
"eating" Bébé Gourmand, Bébé Automate
(breathes and "talks"), Bébé Baiser (throws
kisses), and Bébé Marchant (a walker).

Market Report: The very high prices for
Bru bébé dolls have remained stable with
prices trending slightly up. When buying a
Bru, the individual "look" of the doll is very
important, and collectors will pay thousands
extra for a doll with the particular Bru
"look." Prices for Bru French fashion dolls
also remain strong.

Online/Offline Report: Brus rarely come up
for sale on eBay or other online auction sites.
The majority trade via dealers, shows, and
live auctions. Good Bru dolls on eBay will
sell for prices comparable to dealer and auction prices.

Prices and Characteristics: All Bru dolls
are bisque and in excellent condition, except

as noted, and all prices are for auction and
dealer sales, except as noted.

BRU

Bébé Mechanique

Size: 21.5″   Date: 1890s
Price: $4,500– $6,000
Pull-string activates right arm to raise and lower,
crier works when legs move, patented, open
mouth, paperweight eyes, cork pate, composition
patented body, 1-piece legs.
Mark: Bru Jne R 9

Bébé Modele, with Wardrobe

Size: 18″   Date: 1880
Price: $18,000
Fully articulated wood Bébé Modele body, sev-
eral outfits. At auction.

Bébé Modele, Painted Teeth

Size: 19″   Date: 1880
Price: $18,000
Rare variation Bébé Modele open/closed mouth
with painted teeth. Wood body, this doll with
hairline. At auction.

Bébé Breveté

Size: 11″   Date: 1880
Price: $11,500
Pressed-bisque swivel head, kid-edged shoulder
plate, enamel inset eyes, kid bébé body with
square-cut collarette, gusset, joints, bisque lower
arms.
Mark: 5/0 (head) and partial Bébé Breveté label
on front.

Bébé Breveté

Size: 20″   Date: 1880
Price: $18,500
Mark: 8 (head, shoulder plate)

Bébé, Bru Jne., Size 1

Size: 11″   Date: 1880
Price: $24,500
Bru Jnes have pressed bisque, swivel head with
closed mouths and paperweight eyes on kid-
edged bisque shoulder plate with modeled
bosom, slender kid bébé body with scalloped
edge collarette, hinged thighs, kid or wood lower
legs, hinged bisque arms with separately
sculpted fingers.
Mark: Bru Jne 1 (impressed)

Bébé, Bru Jne., Size 3

Size: 14″   Date: 1885
All Markets: $16,000–$18,000
Mark: Bru Jne 3 (head and shoulder plate)

Bru Jne. Bébé. *Pressed-bisque swivel head on shoulder plate, kid body, kid-over-wood upper arms, bisque forearms, Chevrot-hinged hips, wood lower legs. 17″, c. 1873. Mark: Bru Jne 5 (head, shoulder plate). Courtesy Theriault's.*

Bru Circle-Dot Bébé. *Swivel head on shoulder plate, kid bébé body, gusset-jointed hips and knees, kid upper arms with bisque forearms. 14″. $20,000, auction. Courtesy Theriault's.*

Bébé, Bru Jne.
Size: 15″   Date: 1886
Price: $11,500
Kid over metal upper arms, hinged kid over metal hips.
Mark: Bru. Jne 6

Bébé, Bru Jne.
Size: 16″   Date: 1882
Price: $16,500
Mark: Bru Jne 4 (head and shoulder plate)

Bébé, Bru Jne., Size 7
Size: 17″   Date: 1888–1889
All Markets: $12,500–$13,000
3 results for dolls with Chevrot bodies and flaws (restored hands, fingers broken off, etc.).
Mark: BRU. Jne / 7 (head), BRU Jne No. 7 (shoulder plate, side)

Bébé, Bru Jne.
Size: 19″   Date: 1880s
Price: $33,000

For exceptional doll with original Bru costume, Chevrot body with wood lower legs and bisque arms. At auction.

Bébé, Bru Jne., Size 8
Size: 22″   Date: 1882
Price: $15,000
Mark: 8 (shoulder)

Bébé, Bru Jne., Sizes 9 and 10
Size: 24–26″   Date: 1883–1885
Price: $21,000
Mark: Bru Jne No. 9 or Bru Jne 10 (head and shoulder plate) 10 (inside arms)

Bébé, Bru Jne., 12
Size: 31″   Date: 1882
Price: $18,000–$18,500
Mark: Bru Jne 12 (head) Bru Jne / 10 (shoulders)

Bébé, Bru Jne.
Size: 24″   Date: 1890
Price: $9,500

Bru Breveté. 13.5". Courtesy Kay Jensen.

Bébé Bru holding Bébé Teteur. Bébé Bru, 32", c. 1882. Swivel head on shoulder plate, kid gusset-jointed bébé body, bisque arms. Mark: 13. Holding Bébé Teteur, swivel head on shoulder plate, ivory button in head works nursing mechanism. Kid gusset-jointed body, bisque forearms. 12", c. 1879. Unmarked. Courtesy Theriault's.

Original, transitional composition body; jointed wrists; doll in transitional period between Bru Jne. and Bru Jne. R.
Mark: Bru Jne 11

Bébé, Bru Jne. R, Later Doll

Size: 22–23"   Date: 1891
All Markets: $4,000–$5,000
Later, 4th model of Bru Jne. Bébé. Poured, not pressed, bisque. Features not as fine as earlier models. Original composition, wood-jointed Bru body. Size 10.
Mark: Bru Jne / 10

Bébé, Circle Dot, Size 3

Size: 14–15"   Date: 1883
Price: $14,500 –$20,000
Circle Dot Bébé has swivel head, closed mouth, paperweight or enamel spiraled eyes on kid bébé body with scalloped upper rim, gusset-jointing at hips and knees, curved arms with bisque forearms.
Mark: circle/dot symbol (head) 3 (shoulder plate)

Bébé, Circle Dot, Size 10

Size: 24"   Date: 1879
Price: $25,000
Mark: circle dot symbol / Bru Jne 10 (head) Bru Jne (left shoulder)

Bébé, Circle Dot, Size 12

Size: 30"   Date: 1880
Price: $13,500
Mint kid body, no clothing.

Bébé, Circle Dot, Size 6

Size: 17–19"   Date: 1880
Price: $16,000–$19,500
Mark: circle/dot symbol (head) No. 6 (shoulder plate)

Bébé, Nursing (Teteur) Bru, Size 2

Size: 12"   Date: 1880
Price: $6,000
Bisque head with shoulder plate, open mouth, key turns to operate nursing mechanism in head.
Mark: 2

Bébé, Nursing (Teteur) Bru

Size: 13"   Date: 1879
Price: $9,500
Excellent doll, with bisque forearms.
Mark: 2 / 0 also "Bru" label on torso

Bébé, Nursing (Teteur) Bru

Size: 15–17"   Date: 1886
Price: $6,500
Doll in excellent condition.
Mark: Bru Jne 5 t (head) Bru Jne No. 5 t (shoulder plate)

Bébé, Nursing (Teteur) Bru

Size: 17"   Date: 1890s
Price: $3,000
For late doll with several flaws.

Double-Face Character Bébé

Size: 8"   Date: 1885
Price: $1,500
With flaws.

Bisque Bye-Lo Baby. *Frog-shaped cloth body with celluloid hands, painted hair. All original outfit with banner. 10" length, 9.5" head circumference, c. 1925. Mark: Copr. By Grace Storey Putnam . . . (body stamp). $400, eBay.*

Bisque Fly-Lo Baby. *Frog-shaped cloth body with celluloid hands, sculpted hair. All original outfit with banner and wings. 12", c. 1925. Mark: copr. By Grace S. Putnam / Germany. $2,900, auction. Courtesy Theriault's.*

Bébé, Gutta-percha, Closed Mouth

Size: 24″   Date: 1880s
Price: $900
Glass eyes, unusual to find surviving doll with a gutta-percha (hard rubber) head.
Mark: Bru 11

French Fashion

Size: 15″   Date: 1875
All Markets: $3,500
Kid leather gusseted body, for redressed doll.
For more Bru French fashion dolls, see the French Fashion section.
Mark: E, on head and left shoulder

Bye-Lo Babies

If you think that the Cabbage Patch dolls was the first baby-doll craze of the 20th century, you'd be wrong. In the early 1920s, the Bye-Lo Baby was the first official American doll craze. Supplies of the doll, manufac-tured by the George Borgfeldt Company, could not keep up with demand.

The doll was created by Grace Storey Putnam and was designed to represent a three-day old baby. The fact that this baby was designed to look like a real infant was revolutionary—most baby dolls designed up to that point were an idealized version of a baby. The Bye-Lo Baby continued the trend created by the German character dolls of dolls looking more like real children.

The heads of these bisque baby dolls were made by many famous makers, including Kestner, Alt, Beck & Gottschalck, and Her-tel, Schwab & Co. The dolls were made in several styles—the most popular style was a bisque head on a cloth body, with celluloid hands. Some were made all-bisque, and a few early models were made on fully jointed composition bodies. You can also find Bye-Los with celluloid and composition heads distributed by other companies. Even wax versions and rubber versions of the Bye-Lo were made.

Some Bye-Lo dolls were made into the early 1950s. In many ways, the Bye-Lo Baby with its emphasis on realism is the forerunner of the realistic baby dolls on the market today from such companies as Lee Middleton, Ashton Drake, and Berenguer.

Market Report: The Bye-Lo Babies were in production from 1922 to 1952, which accounts for the large numbers of Bye-Lo dolls available on the market today. Because so many Bye-Los are available, the dolls in all-original condition and rare variations such as the Fly-Lo bring the highest amounts. The all-bisque Bye-Los are also popular with collectors. Always popular, but also always available, prices for Bye-Los are somewhat stagnant, but there has been a recent up-tick in prices for all-original dolls.

Online/Offline Report: Very similar prices and availability from all venues; however, if you are looking for a fixer-upper needing cleaning and new clothing, your best prices and best availability will be found on eBay.

Prices and Characteristics: Prices are mixed, from all venues.

BYE-LO BABIES

All-Bisque
Size: 5″
Price: $450
Material: bisque

All-Bisque
Size: 7.25″
Price: $1,000
Material: bisque

All-Bisque, Wigged
Size: 6″
Price: $975
Material: bisque
Wigged model is rarer.

Bisque Head
Size: 10–11″
Price: $300+
Material: bisque
Cloth body, generally celluloid hands.
Mark: Copr. by / Grace S. Putnam / Made in Germany

Bisque Head
Size: 14″
Price: $400–$450
Material: bisque
All original outfit with banner. Sleep eyes.

Bisque Head
Size: 17″
Price: $575
Material: bisque
Cloth body, sleep eyes, celluloid hands.
Mark: Copr. by / Grace S. Putnam / Made in Germany (head); Bye-Lo-Baby / Pat.-Appl'd For / Copy. / by Grace

Bisque Head
Size: 19+″
Price: $900+
Material: bisque

Bye-Lo Baby Rattle
Price: $55
Material: celluloid
Rare celluloid baby rattle. Has pictures of Bye-Lo Baby Doll.
Mark: Bye-Lo Baby / Reg. U.S. PAT. Off.

Fly-Lo Baby
Size: 15″
Price: $2,500
Material: bisque, painted

Fly-Lo Baby
Size: 15″
Price: $2,900
Material: bisque
Fly-Lo banner, wings, original silk costume with cap.
Mark: Corp by Grace S Putnam Germany (incised, back head)

Candy Containers

Candy containers are included in this book because of their popularity with antique doll collectors. Certain types of candy containers from the late 1800s, such as furry dogs and Easter bunnies, are popular to display with antique dolls. And certain dolls are candy containers themselves, hiding a place for candy in their specially made bodies. Materials used to make the candy containers include papier-mâché, glass, and cardboard.

Market Report: Candy containers from the late 1800s from France and candy containers through the 1930s from Germany are the most popular and expensive, with themes including Christmas, Halloween, Easter, fruit, and animals being the most favored by collectors, as well as pieces that display especially well with dolls, including valises.

Online/Offline Report: Prices have definitely increased in the last few years, and should continue to increase as more collectors become aware of candy containers. Also note that it is much easier to find German than earlier French examples online—for French candy containers, you are more likely to find them through antique dealers, shops, live auctions, and shows.

Prices and Characteristics: All are in excellent condition. Prices are from dealers, auctions, and shows, except where indicated.

FRENCH CANDY CONTAINERS

Asian Lady
Size: 8″   Date: 1880
Price: $800
Material: bisque

Book-Shaped, Marbled Brown Cover
Size: 3″   Date: 1860
Price: $150
Material: carton

Checkers Game
Size: 6″   Date: 1885
Price: $650
Material: carton

Dog, Papier-mâché and Fur
Size: 16″   Date: 1890
Price: $1,350
Material: bisque

Dog, Papier-mâché and Mohair
Size: 9″   Date: 1900
Price: $550
Material: papier-mâché
Head removes for candy storage.

Dog, Papier-mâché and Fur, various poses
Size: 7–9″   Date: 1890
Price: $425–$500
Material: papier-mâché

Dog, Reclining, Papier-mâché and Fur
Size: 6″   Date: 1910
Price: $300
Material: papier-mâché

Doll Bed in Mahogany
Size: 20″
Price: $2,500
Material: wood
Drawers open for candy, silk bed linens, and pillows.

Don Quixote, Papier-mâché
Size: 10″   Date: 1890
Price: $650
Material: papier-mâché

Faux-Marble Rectangle
Size: 5″   Date: 1860
Price: $300
Material: carton

For Baptism, Taufling-Style with FG head
Size: 12″   Date: 1890
Price: $1,100–$1,300
Material: bisque
Lace-edged bib has child's name, bonnet and Täufling gown.

French Fashion, Swivel Head
Size: 15″   Date: 1875
Price: $5,750
Material: bisque
Carton torso hides candy; bisque lower arms.

French Fashion, Swivel Head
Size: 16″   Date: 1875
Price: $3,600
Material: bisque
Carton torso, hollow, papier-mâché lower legs, bisque forearms.
Mark: 2

French, Boy on Log
Size: 12″   Date: 1890
Price: $2,100
Material: bisque
Mark: P 3

Gaultier Bébé
Size: 6″   Date: 1882
Price: $3,000
Material: bisque
Hollow carton body separates at base. Bisque forearms.
Mark: 4/0

Lotto Game
Size: 12″   Date: 1890
Price: $400
Material: carton

Miniature Coach
Size: 18″   Date: 1890
Price: $2,200
Material: wood

Miniature Furniture
Size: 6″   Date: 1885
Price: $250
Material: carton
Drawers open for candy.

Musical Mandolin
Size: 14″   Date: 1880
Price: $900
Material: papier-mâché
Music box.

Père Noel
Size: 8″   Date: 1915
Price: $750
Material: bisque
With original Paris store label, "A La Place Clichy."

Toy Guitar
Size: 5″   Date: 1890
Price: $200
Material: carton

Troubadour
Size: 11″   Date: 1907
Price: $1,200
Material: bisque
Sitting on wood stump, S.F.B.J.
Mark: 1907 / 2

Wax Lady
Size: 18″   Date: 1920
Price: $475
Material: wax

Woven With Bisque Head by Adolphe Bouchet
Size: 7″   Date: 1895
Price: $600
Material: bisque
Mark: A.D. Bouchet

GERMAN CANDY CONTAINERS

Bisque Doll
Size: 7″   Date: 1900
Price: $325
Material: bisque
Mark: 422 dep

Boy on Snowball
Size: 7″
Price: $400
Material: bisque

Boy with bisque head, wound cotton body on snowball.
Mark: Made / in Germany

Papier-mâché Brown Dog
Size: 5″
Price: $450
Material: bisque

Papier-mâché St. Nicholas
Size: 17″   Date: 1890
Price: $5,800
Material: papier-mâché
Very large, unusual yellow coat color.

Rabbits Dancing
Size: 12″   Date: 1900
All Markets: $350
Material: papier-mâché
Pair in dancing pose.

Skiing Child, Bisque Head
Size: 8″   Date: 1910
Price: $700
Material: bisque
Schoenau & Hoffmeister.
Mark: S (pb) H

Skiing Child, Composition Head
Size: 6″   Date: 1910
Price: $350
Material: composition

St. Nicholas
Size: 10″   Date: 1915
All Markets: $400
Material: papier-mâché
Sitting on log that holds candy.

St. Nicholas, Papier-mâché
Size: 15″   Date: 1910
Price: $1,900
Material: bisque
Large, bright colors, mint.

Heubach, Black Bisque Boy With Piglet in Egg
Size: 7″   Date: 1915
Price: $1,400
Material: bisque
Mark: Heubach (sunburst)

Heubach, Gebrüder, Baby With Easter Egg
Size: 6″   Date: 1912
Price: $325
Material: bisque

Heubach, Gebrüder, Boy, Candy Container Egg
Size: 6″   Date: 1915
Price: $550
Material: bisque
Brown boots, naked.

German celluloid, E. Maar & Sohn child. *Swivel head, jointed arms, legs. 16", c. 1940s. Mark: (triple Ms, stacked) / 800/43. $50, eBay.*

German celluloid, Kämmer & Reinhardt 728. *Celluloid body, swivel head, jointed arms, legs. 11", c. 1915–1930. Mark: K * R / 728/0 /GERMANY / 25/27.*

Heubach, Gebrüder, Bunny Child With Egg For Candy

Size: 6"   Date: 1915
Price: $525
Material: bisque
Jointed arms.
Mark: Heubach (in square)

Kewpie, Rose O'Neill

Size: 4"
All Markets: $400
Material: bisque
Rare Kewpie candy container. Kewpie stands on wood container.

Pig, Papier-mâché

Size: 6"   Date: 1910
Price: $450
Material: papier-mâché

Celluloid Dolls

Celluloid dolls are fascinating, but always a bit of a stepsister to the more popular bisque, cloth, and composition dolls. Part of this may be attributed to the lore surrounding celluloid dolls—if you heat them up, they will explode. This is not really true, although it definitely is true that celluloid is a highly flammable substance and therefore not particularly suited to children's play. Collectors, though, have little to worry about—I cannot tell you one story of a celluloid doll spontaneously combusting in a collector's cabinet. However, you probably wouldn't want to examine, play with, or dress your celluloid dolls in front of a roaring winter fire.

Celluloid dolls have been manufactured around the world, from the end of the 1800s through the 1950s, by numerous companies. Production of celluloid dolls ranges from cheap carnival and travel dolls to dolls copying in looks and dress their bisque cousins.

German celluloid boy, unknown maker. 1-piece body/torso. 3". Mark: Edw / 2 / 8 / Germany. $20, dealer.

Italian celluloid, unknown maker. Original clothing, swivel head, jointed arms, legs. 5.5". Mark: Made in Italy (paper label on underwear). $35, dealer.

German celluloid, unknown maker, child. Original folklore costume. Swivel head, jointed arms and legs. 12". Mark: HD. $40, dealer.

Although countless celluloid dolls were made after 1920 (including many illustrated in this section), a great many were also made prior to 1920. Thus, although celluloid dolls could have equally well been listed in the Vintage Dolls chapter of this book, I've included them with the Antique Dolls as is generally done.

It's sometimes hard for a novice to identify celluloid dolls—the best indicator of celluloid is the weight. Celluloid dolls are much lighter than all other plastics. After handling a few celluloid dolls, you generally get the feel for them. Some collectors swear that you can smell camphor if you lightly scratch celluloid dolls and immediately sniff. I have not had success with this method, but you might want to try it.

Market Report: Marjory Fainges, in her book *Celluloid Dolls of the World,* has stated that "Celluloid dolls are now being spoken of in the doll world as the next 'sleeper' to awaken," and I have to agree. Prices of these dolls are very low, and bargains can be found for lovely, antique celluloid dolls in original dress. The great majority of celluloid dolls on the market can be purchased for under $200, and many choice examples can be found for under $100.

Look for dolls by famous German makers such as Kestner, Kämmer & Reinhardt, and Käthe Kruse. Don't overlook the beautifully costumed regional celluloids produced by Petitcolin and SNF from France. And celluloids of known characters such as Kewpie and Betty Boop are popular and bring strong prices.

- **Turtle Mark:** One of the best-known makers of German celluloid dolls is Rheinische Gummi und Celluloid Fabrik Co., which marked their dolls with a turtle logo. These dolls are plentiful, but desired by collectors. Bargains can still be found for these popular celluloids, especially online.

- **Petitcolin:** These French celluloids, marked with an eagle symbol, have wonderful costuming, usually of regional areas of France. Look for lovely lace and nice fabrics on these relatively inexpensive dolls.

- **Irwin:** Irwin is one of the best-known American makers of celluloid dolls, but prices for Irwin celluloids are generally low.

Other Celluloid Manufacturers: Other well-known manufacturers of celluloid dolls include Buschow & Beck, Minerva (helmet symbol); E. Maar & Sohn (3M symbol); Société Nobel Française (dragon symbol); Société Industrielle de Celluloid (Sicoine), and

German celluloid, Schoberl & Beck, child. Original folklore dress. 1-piece head/torso, jointed arms and legs. 5.5", c. 1920s. Mark: (Winged Mermaid & Cellba) / 22 _. $30, dealer.

French celluloid, Petitcolin, child. 1-piece torso/head, jointed arms and legs. Original folklore costume. Mark: (Eagle head) / FRANCE / 17 (torso) and tag on dress. $35, eBay.

Japanese celluloid, Royal Co. Ltd., pair. Purchased in Holland in 1952. Original outfits. 10.5". Mark: (Fleur-de-lis) (back). Courtesy of Geneva Wallen Collection.

the Parsons-Jackson Co. from the United States.

Online/Offline Report: Prices are similar from all sources, with a great selection of celluloids from all over the world available online. When shopping online, beware of fading or crushing that celluloids are susceptible too, which won't always show up in photos. Because celluloid dolls are so plentiful online, true bargains can be found there if you educate yourself on the various celluloid manufacturers and the rarer styles of celluloid dolls.

GERMAN CELLULOID DOLLS

Buschow & Beck, Girl, Molded Hair.
Size: 13" Internet: $175
Jointed arms and legs, glass eyes, molded hair.
Mark: Minerva / (helmet) / Germany / 4

Child, Folklore Dress
Size: 3"
Price: $20
Tourist-type celluloid doll, generally only arms jointed, sometimes legs.

German, Kewpie-Type, Turtle Mark
Size: 3" Date: 1915
Internet: $75
Molded hair.

Kämmer & Reinhardt, Baby, 700
Size: 18" Date: 1910
Price: $500
Kaiser Baby look-alike with celluloid head, composition baby body.
Mark: (turtle mark without diamond) K * R 700 / 36

Kämmer & Reinhardt, Girl, 728
Size: 7" Date: 1915
Price: $350
Sleep eyes, real lashes, open mouth with teeth, 5-piece toddler body, mohair wig.
Mark: K * R 728 / 5/0 Germany 19

Kämmer & Reinhardt, Girl, 728
Size: 18" Date: 1915
Price: $800
With outstanding facial modeling, wobble tongue, sleep eyes, lashes, open mouth, teeth, 5-piece composition toddler body, human hair wig.
Mark: K * R 728/6 Germany 38/11

Käthe Kruse, Child
Size: 16" Date: 1950s
Internet: $130
Very good.
Mark: turtle (in diamond) / MODELL / Käthe Kruse / 40

Käthe Kruse, Child
Size: 18" Date: 1950s
Internet: $270–$355
Mint.
Mark: with turtle mark

American celluloid, Irwin & Co.,
baby. *1-piece head/torso. 11", c.
1940s. Mark: NON-INFLAM / (in
circle:) MADE IN / IRWIN / USA.
$15, eBay.*

*American celluloid, Irwin & Co.
"Kewpie." Jointed arms only. 7", c.
1950s. Mark: (in circle:) MADE IN
/ IRWIN / USA.*

Kewpie
Size: 2"   Date: 1920
Price: $45
1-piece body, painted features.
Mark: unmarked

Kewpie With Rabbit
Size: 3"   Internet: $75
Stationary figure, Kewpie wears painted vest.

Kewpie-Type, Pincushion, Novelty Doll, Wigged
Size: 6"
Price: $70
Wigged, jointed arms only, pincushion body.

König & Wernicke, Flirty-eyed
Size: 16"
Price: $100   Internet: $100
Dressed in folklore costume.
Mark: K&W 778 / 6 turtle mark / 43

Maar E. & Sohn
Size: 15"   Date: 1930s
                  Internet: $100
Mark: 43 / triple M's (stacked) / 800/43

Turtle Mark (Rheinische Gummi), Baby
Size: 20"   Internet: $250
Swivel neck, nude, 5-piece body, molded hair.
Mark: turtle (in triangle)

Turtle Mark, Black Boy or Girl
Size: 13–15"   Date: 1930s
Price: $150   Internet: $225
Molded, painted hair.
Mark: turtle (in triangle) / 34 / 35

Turtle Mark, Child
Size: 12"
Price: $30
Nude, jointed arms and legs, simple modeling.
Mark: turtle (in triangle)

Turtle Mark, Child, Molded Hair
Size: 12"   Date: 1954
                  Internet: $140
MIB, jointed arms and legs, molded hair,
painted eyes.

Turtle Mark, Dutch Boy and Girl, Molded Clothes
Size: 7"   Date: 1915–1920
                  Internet: $250
Only arms jointed, painted features and clothing.
Mark: Schultz / Markd 17 1/2 / Germany and
turtle mark

Turtle Mark, Girl, Molded Hair
Size: 19–22"   Date: 1920s
                     Internet: $140–$250
Swivel neck, glass eyes. Higher prices for better
molded hair, more defined features.
Mark: turtle in diamond

Turtle Mark, Shoulder-Head
Size: 20"   Date: 1890
Price: $225
Shoulder-head, cloth body, stitched joints, cellu-
loid arms.
Mark: (turtle mark) / Schultz mark

Character Dolls, Bisque, German, Kämmer & Reinhardt Child 115A, 2 examples. Both 16", c. 1910. Mark: K * R/Simon & Halbig/ 115/A 42. Courtesy Theriault's.

Character Dolls, Bisque, German, Kämmer & Reinhardt Toddler 116A. Composition and wood toddler body with side-hip joints. 12", c. 1912. Mark: K * R Simon & Halbig 116A 26. Courtesy Theriault's.

AMERICAN, FRENCH, JAPANESE, AND OTHER CELLULOID DOLLS

American, Irwin-Type Celluloid Baby
Size: 7"   Date: 1940s
                Internet: $20
Jointed arms and legs.

French, Petticolin, Asian Baby
Size: 13"   Date: 1920s
                 Internet: $465
Glass eyes, closed mouth, swivel neck, 5-piece baby body.
Mark: eagle head mark / 35 / FRANCE

French, Petitcolin, Boy, Molded Hair
Size: 22"   Date: 1930s
                 Internet: $160
Sleep eyes.
Mark: eagle head mark

French, Petitcolin, Regional Dress
Size: 10"   Date: 1940s
                 Internet: $20–$30
With mint complete national costume.

French, Petitcolin, Regional Dress
Size: 11"   Date: 1930
                 Internet: $60
Elaborate costume, mohair wig.
Mark: eagle head mark

Japan, Baby, Boy, Molded Hair
Size: 30"   Internet: $140
Painted eyes, molded hair, jointed baby body.
Mark: 8 / Made In Japan

Japan, Betty Boop, Wind-Up Mechanical Acrobat
Size: 7"   Date: 1930s
                Internet: $380
Doll swings around pole when wound up.
Mark: Made In Japan

Japan, Crepe Paper Box for Christmas
Size: 6"   Date: 1920s
                Internet: $35

Mark: Made In Japan

Character Doll, Bisque, French, S.F.B.J., 226. Solid-dome head, painted hair, French composition jointed body. 17″, c. 1914. Mark: SFBJ 226 Paris 6. Courtesy Theriault's.

Character Dolls, Bisque, French, S.F.B.J., Poulbot boy and girl. 5-piece composition bodies. 14″, c. 1915. Mark: SFBJ 239 Paris Poulbot. Based on drawings by famed French illustrator Poulbot, representing war orphans from Montmartre, Paris. Courtesy Theriault's.

Japan, Doll and Buggy, Mechanical

Size: 6″   Date: 1930s
             Internet: $140
Wind up and doll pushes stroller.
Mark: Made In Japan (paper label)

Japan, Royal, Baby Boy

Size: 22″   Date: 1920s
             Internet: $140
Molded hair, painted eyes.
Mark: JAPAN / ROYAL / (fleur-de-lis symbol) / 22

Japan, Royal, Skippy-Type Baby

Size: 24″   Internet: $130
Royal Company, Japan.
Mark: Fleur-de-Lis symbol

Koge, Toddler, Girl, Molded Hair

Size: 13″   Date: late 1940s
             Internet: $120
Danish company.
Mark: J.K.Koge (in triangle)

Lady Doll

Size: 17″   Date: 1880
All Markets: $1,400
Early celluloid, rare French-Fashion type lady.
Kid body, shoulder plate, swivel neck, glass eyes.
Mark: unmarked

Character Dolls

The heyday of bisque character dolls was approximately 1908 through the end of World War I. Most were made in Germany. Character dolls differed from bisque "dolly"-faced dolls, which predominated prior to 1908, in that dolly-faced dolls were idealized versions of children, babies, and toddlers, whereas character dolls were meant to be more realistic—they were modeled on real children, babies, and toddlers. Dolly-faced dolls also all had very simple expressions—open or closed mouths, not particularly happy or sad. When character dolls came along, they imparted the full range of emotions to doll faces—happy, sad, angry, and laughing. Sometimes, the character babies look cranky or otherwise upset.

Market Report: Many fewer character dolls were made than dolly-faced dolls—after all, dolly-faced dolls were produced for over 50 years, and character dolls had the majority of their production in an approximately 10 year period, after which composition dolls started to predominate. Prices generally reflect this, with character dolls by any company across the board bringing higher prices than the dolly-faced dolls by the same company. Individual price and market trends for bisque character dolls can be found in the appropriate doll company sections.

French 1840s china doll, Jacob Petit. *Muslin body, kid arms. 22", c. 1843. These dolls are rarely marked/signed. Mark: Par Brevete & J.P. (ink script) inside head. $6000+. Courtesy Theriault's*

German 1840s china doll, KPM. *Pink-tinted porcelain. Muslin body with leather arms. 17", c. 1845. Marks: KPM blue mark. Courtesy Theriault's.*

German 1860s china doll, unmarked. *Porcelain hands and lower legs with black-painted shoes. 24", c. 1860. Unmarked. $2,500+. Courtesy Theriault's.*

Online/Offline Report: The best and rarest of the character child dolls generally trade offline, at shows, shops, and online auctions. However, the more common character babies and toddlers are plentiful online, and prices for such character babies are similar to offline prices.

Prices and Characteristics: Prices and characteristics for bisque character dolls may be found in the appropriate manufacturer's section, including Kämmer & Reinhardt, Kestner, Simon & Halbig, S.F.B.J., and others.

China Dolls

China dolls—dolls made of glazed bisque (referred to as "porcelain" in this book, as opposed to unglazed bisque, which are referred to simply as "bisque"—were produced in great quantities from approximately the late 1830s through the early 1900s, with both earlier and later examples available. The heyday of china doll production was the 1840s to the 1880s, when bisque dolls took over in wide popularity. Most china dolls are unmarked, making definite identifications as to the company that produced the dolls often difficult. Most china dolls were made in Germany.

Market Report: For many years, china dolls were considered an "unsexy" area of collecting. You could scoop up china dolls for much, much less than the prices of their bisque counterparts, and far fewer collectors actively pursued collections of china dolls. This has changed in the last few years, as more research has been released helping collectors sort through the history of these dolls and their identification, and as more collectors become educated as to what makes a desirable china doll.

When collecting china dolls, look for dolls with unusual hairstyles and decoration. More elaborate hairstyles are always more desirable than more common ones, and individual details such as deep curls, combs, or floral accents can add much to the value of a doll. Early china dolls from the 1840s are scarce, artistically done, and very desirable. Prices reflect this, with 1840s chinas from KPM and Royal Copenhagen being some of the most expensive china dolls.

Most china dolls have black hair, so other hair colors are desirable (except for late-production blondes), and almost all china dolls have blue eyes, with brown eyes being rare. Pink-tinted china dolls are also rare, since most china dolls have no tint. Marked, early

German 1860s "Biedermeier" china doll, unmarked. *Solid dome, muslin fashion body with porcelain arms above elbows, c. 1865. Courtesy Theriault's.*

German 1860s "High Brow" china doll. *Muslin body with porcelain lower arms, painted boots on porcelain lower feet. 24". $550, dealer.*

German 1860s china doll. *Muslin body, leather lower arms. 30". $700, dealer.*

dolls are also sought after, and hard to find. Stay away from dolls with extensive pitting or peppering of the porcelain, and later dolls with over-applied cheek blush.

- **American:** By far, the majority of china dolls were made by German companies, and there were no major American makers of antique china dolls. However, in 1939, an American dollmaker named Emma Clear started to reproduce the earlier German-made china dolls. Her dolls are clearly marked (so that collectors would not confuse them with the antique dolls), and these dolls have become collectible in their own right. Her dolls include both china and parian (untinted bisque) dolls. Another dollmaker, Ruth Gibbs, made china dolls starting in the mid-1940s, which were called "Godey's Little Lady Dolls" which are also sought by collectors today.

- **Dollhouse:** An often overlooked area of china doll collecting are the littlest china dolls—china dolls intended to be inhabitants of dollhouses. Not all small china dolls qualify to be dollhouse dolls—some were made in a heavy, crude manner, and others with overly bulky bodies. However, certain small china dolls were clearly made for the dollhouse. Some of these are early, choice examples from the 1840s through 1860s (for some

excellent examples of these early china dollhouse dolls, see *Dolls in Miniature* by Evelyn Ackerman; see the Bibliography). Bodies for the early china dollhouse dolls could be jointed wood, kid leather, or the more common cloth. Later china dollhouse dolls made in the very late 1800s into the early 1900s have cruder features and tend to have simpler molded hairstyles.

- **French:** French china dolls are rare and were produced early. Many were made to be French fashion (or poupée) dolls by companies such as Huret and Rohmer. For other china dolls, there are a few very early choice examples that have been documented from France, but many experts feel that the majority of the china dolls, even those originally thought to be from France, were actually produced by German firms.

- **German:** German china dolls were made for many, many years, from the 1830s through the early 1900s. They vary as widely as can possibly be imagined in style and artistry. The very early dolls from the 1830s to the 1840s are most highly sought after, and very expensive when they can be found at all. Made by firms such as Royal Copenhagen and KPM, these early dolls can easily bring between $5,000 and $10,000. The middle of the china doll period, from the 1860s through the 1870s featured

German 1870s sculpted-bonnet china doll, unmarked. Muslin body, porcelain lower limbs. 13". Courtesy Theriault's.

German 1865 china doll, unmarked. Brown eyes, muslin body, porcelain lower limbs. 17". Courtesy Theriault's.

German 1860s "Flat Top" china doll. Muslin body. 29". $700, dealer.

fancy, decorated hairdos that are highly sought by collectors today. These dolls, such as "Morning Glory," can bring several thousand dollars. Even more plentiful common hairdos from this period usually have lovely painting and sell in the several-hundred-dollar range. At the very end of the china doll period, the "low brow" dolls, such as the "Pet Name" chinas, were made from the late 1890s all the way until the 1930s. These dolls have much cruder porcelain and painting, and often can be found on eBay and through dealers for $100 to $200 or even less.

Online/Offline Report: Most early and rare china dolls don't make it to online auctions—they are traded by dealers and at live auctions and shows. More common china dolls are easy to find online, where you will find prices slightly below those of other sources.

Prices and Characteristics, German China (Porcelain) Head Dolls: All dolls are porcelain, with sculpted and painted black hair (or often blonde hair, 1880s through 1890s) and painted blue eyes, on muslin or cloth bodies with arms and legs of china, leather, or bisque (legs can often be cloth), except as noted. Nearly all are unmarked as to maker, with exceptions noted. All are in excellent condition. Prices are similar from all venues,

with more results from dealers, shows and auction houses, and Internet results noted.

1840S CHINA HEAD DOLLS
The 1840s China Dolls tended to have slender faces, sloping shoulders, and simple hair styles, often with exposed ears. Often found with pink-tinted complexion. The dolls are often pressed.

Brown-Haired Man
Size: 23"
Price: $4,500
Fully exposed ears, short hair, unmarked.

Coiled Bun, Exposed Ears
Size: 11"
Price: $1,500
Hair over ears and pulled to coiled bun, nicely modeled.

Coiled Bun, Exposed Ears, Wooden Articulated Body
Size: 7"   Internet: $2,200

Center Part, Hair Looped Over Ears, Coiled Braids
Size: 14"
Price: $900
Coiled braids on back of head.

Center Part, Hair Looped to Bun at Back
Size: 5–10"
Price: $700–$800
Also for other basic 1840s hairstyles on cloth body.

German 1870s china doll. Muslin body, porcelain lower arms, original costume. 22". Mark: VI. Courtesy Theriault's.

German 1865 china doll, pink tint. Rarer pink tint and rarer brown eyes. Muslin body, leather arms. 14". $1,050, auction. Courtesy Theriault's.

KPM Brown-Haired Man
Size: 18"
Price: $4,600
Mark: K.P.M. red stamp and K.P.M. eagle symbol, blue stamp. K.P.M. is Königliche Porzellan Manufaktur.

KPM, Brown Hair, Pulled Into Bun
Size: 29"
Price: $6,200
Slight smile, pink tint.

KPM, Man
Size: 17"
Price: $2,300

KPM, Bun, Exposed Ears
Size: 16–18"
Price: $2,100–$2,600

Molded Bonnet, Pink Tinted
Size: 11.5"
Price: $8,000

Center-part black hair, pink bonnet, indicated white lace around bonnet, painted ribbon, molded ears.

Pink Tint, Wooden Articulated Body
Size: 8.5"
Price: $2,200
Black center-part hair falls above ears, bun in back.

Pink Tint, Bun and Coiled Braid
Size: 18"
Price: $3,700

Pink Tint, Peg-Wooden Body, Various Hairstyles
Size: 5–6.5"
Price: $1,400–$1,700
For various 1840s hairstyles including short hair and brushstrokes, looped hair, on mortise and tenon-jointed body, painted orange slippers.

Slender Face, Exposed Ears, Snood
Size: 15"
Price: $3,000

German 1870s china doll with elaborate hairdo, unmarked. Hair in braided coronet with stippling details around face. Muslin body, porcelain arms and legs with painted rose ankle boots. 20". $2,200, auction. Courtesy Theriault's.

1890s (or later) "Low Brow" china doll. Cloth body with porcelain lower arms and legs. 12". $100, dealer sale.

Hair brush strokes around face; pressed china head.

1850S CHINA HEAD DOLLS

These include the Biedermeier-type which has a solid dome, a painted black top of head instead of a molded hairstyle, and is wigged. Also found are the very common Covered Wagon styles, which have a center part with loose, short spiral curls that conform closely to the head.

Biedermeier-type, Huret look
Size: 26"
Price: $2,600

Biedermeier
Size: 18"
Price: $400
So-called Biedermeier-type has wigged solid dome, and head with painted, unglazed black spot on top to indicate placement of wig.

Biedermeier
Size: 12–15"
Price: $1,200

Biedermeier
Size: 17–22"
All Markets: $1,000–$1,500

Covered Wagon
Size: 5–7"
Price: $300

Covered Wagon
Size: 9–11"
Price: $300–$400

Covered Wagon
Size: 15–19"
Price: $375–$450

Covered Wagon
Size: 22–24"
Price: $450–$600

Covered Wagon, Bottom Painted Lashes
Size: 19–22"
Price: $1,900–$2,500
Early Covered Wagon.

Covered Wagon, Brown Eyes
Size: 22–28"
Price: $800+

Lydia
Size: 12"
Price: $1,300
12 long curls, undercut, sloping shoulders.

Morning Glory Lady, Attributed Schlaggenwald
Size: 24"
Price: $5,100
Sculpted morning glories in hair.

Pink Tint, Boy
Size: 21"
Price: $2,200
Brushstrokes around face.

Pink Tint, Deep Sausage Curls

Size: 23″
Price: $1,750
Deeply undercut curls, part Sophia Smith and
part Lydia.

Sophia Smith

Size: 24″
Price: $6,300
Kestner.

1860S CHINA HEAD DOLLS

Flat Tops and High Brows (really just a Flat
Top doll with a very high forehead!) are similar to the Covered Wagons, since both have
short curls closely around the head, but
whereas the Covered Wagon is completely
smooth on the top, the Flat Top and High
Brow dolls have some waves at the forehead.
The Flat Top and High Brow dolls also tend
to have chubbier modeled faces. These simple
dolls gave way to very elaborate hairdos including extravagant curls on late 1860s–1870s
China Dolls.

Boy, Boyish Sculpted Hair

Size: 22″
Price: $2,000

Brown Hair, Center-Part Style

Size: 13″
Price: $1,300
Golden brown hair.

Brown Eyes, Center-Part Hair With Short Curls

Size: 19–26″
Price: $2,500–$2,700

Brown Eyes, Center Part With Waves

Size: 22″
Price: $1,600

Brown Eyes, Painted Lashes

Size: 17″
Price: $1,600
Rare painted lower lashes.

Brown Eyes, Simple Center Part

Size: 15–24″
Price: $400–$550
Brown eyes on simple 1860s center-part style,
such as Flat Top/High Brow.

Character Expression

Size: 18″
Price: $1,750
Unusual expression, brown eyes.

Flat Top/ High Brow

Size: 11″
Price: $200–$275
Flat Top and High Brow hairstyles feature a
simple style with center part, with a high showing forehead.

Flat Top/ High Brow

Size: 14–18″
Price: $300–$400

Flat Top/ High Brow

Size: 20–22″
Price: $400–$450

Flat Top/ High Brow

Size: 22–24″
Price: $400–$500
Slightly more with brown eyes.

Flat Top/ High Brow

Size: 26–30″
Price: $600–$750

Flat Top/ High Brow

Size: 30+″
Price: $800+

Flat Top/ High Brow, Brown Eyes

Size: 32″
All Markets: $1,225

Flat Top / High Brow, Pink Tinted Porcelain, Brown Eyes

Size: 14″
Price: $1,000

Glass Eyes, Sloping Shoulders

Size: 17″
Price: $2,100
Dark eyeliner and upper lashes.

Grape Lady, Molded Hat

Size: 23″
All Markets: $1,650
Pink grapes, detailed hat.

Hair in Wings on Side, Coiled Braids

Size: 26″
Price: $2,000

Jenny Lind

Size: 8.5″
Price: $225
Hair pulled back into bun.

Jenny Lind

Size: 20–24″
Price: $700–$1,000

Jenny Lind, Fancier Bun, or Known Maker
Size: 15–24″
Price: $1,500–$2,200
Fancier bun or coronet, earlier sloping shoulders, or known maker such as A. Kister.

Long Finger Curls, Wooden Articulated Body
Size: 5″
Price: $1,600

Mary Todd Lincoln
Size: 16″
Price: $850
Molded snood (painted black) with bows on side.

Ringlet Curls, Wooden Articulated Body, Pink Tint
Size: 5″
Price: $1,500
Orange painted shoes.

Snood, Modeled
Size: 8–10″
Price: $650–$750

Sausage Curls, Deep, Pink Tint
Size: 26″
Price: $1,600

Snood, Modeled, Blonde Hair
Size: 12″
Price: $1,000
Molded blue scarf with tassels and gold accents.

Täufling Baby, Alice-Type, Rare Brown Hair and Headband
Size: 12″
Price: $5,900
"Alice"-type doll, original costume including straw cap täufling crier body, mama crier.

Täufling Baby, Boyish Hair
Size: 11″
Price: $1,500
Stippling detail around face, bellows mama crier, täufling crier body.

Vertical Finger Curls, Center Part
Size: 18″
Price: $2,500

1870S CHINA HEAD DOLLS

Many late 1860s styles were made into the early 1870s, and some of the fancy, curly styles and snoods could be listed as 1860s or 1870s dolls; flat tops were also made into the 1870s.

Adelina Patti
Size: 11.5″
Price: $600

Boyish Short Hair, Stippled
Size: 24″
Price: $1,000

Braided Coronet at Crown, Pierced ears
Size: 20″
Price: $2,200

Center Part, 9 Curls, Deep Dimples
Size: 20″
Price: $2,350

Center Part, Vertical Curls
Size: 13″
Price: $325

Center Part, Short Vertical Curls
Size: 18″
Price: $500

Center Part, Deeply Modeled Curls
Size: 29″
Price: $1,000+

Coronet at Crown, Molded Hairband
Size: 23″
Price: $3,700
Pierced ears, brushstrokes around face.

Curly Top (Blonde)
Size: 20.5″
Price: $700
Dark blonde curls covering head.

Curly Top
Size: 15–19″
All Markets: $500

Currier & Ives, 1870s, Long Spill Curls on Shoulders, Bangs
Size: 15.5″
Price: $325

Decorated Snood
Size: 5″
Price: $325

Dolley Madison
Size: 16–24″
Price: $450–$700
Curly blonde hair with bow.

Dolley Madison
Size: 30″
Price: $1,400
Unusual large size.

Empress Eugénie
Size: 11″
Price: $1,400
Conta & Boehme, green molded snood with
plumes.

Fancy Hair, Waves and Snood
Size: 22″
Price: $800

Fancy Hair, Pierced Ears, Cluster Curls on Forehead
Size: 22″
Price: $900

Finger Curls
Size: 18″
Price: $850
Finger curls around head.

Kling, 203
Size: 21″
Price: $500
Mark: 203.

Pageboy Curls, Modeled Bodice
Size: 13″
Price: $1,800

Sculpted Bonnet
Size: 13″
Price: $2,900
Detailed sculpted bonnet.

Spill Curls
Size: 19″
All Markets: $500

Spill Curls, Café Au Lait
Size: 20″
Price: $2,000
Rare café-au-lait-colored hair, black hair band,
curls spill down back over shoulders.

1880S CHINA HEAD DOLLS

Many china dolls from this period resemble
children, not adults. Makers such as Alt, Beck
& Gottschalck and Kling produced large
numbers of these. Blonde china heads became
more popular, and remained so through the
1890s.

Alt, Beck & Gottschalck, Blonde Sculpted Hair
Size: 22″
Price: $700
Mark: 1046 #10.

Alt, Beck & Gottschalck, Blonde With Bangs
Size: 11″
Price: $300

Blonde Sculpted Hair, Curls
Size: 12″
Price: $1,050
Horizontal curls at forehead and vertical curls
around. Unusual bare porcelain feet.

Center Part, Curls Behind Ears
Size: 12″
Price: $525

Fashion Lady, Swivel Head, Painted Eyes
Size: 16″
Price: $850

Kling, Pink Tint, Bawo & Dotter Corset Body
Size: 20″
Price: $775
Childlike modeling, soft curls with bangs shown
on forehead.
Mark: B.D. Patented Dec 1 1880 (body stamp).

Kling, Dark Blonde Sculpted Hair
Size: 20″
Price: $725
Mark: 189 7

Light Brown Curls
Size: 17″
Price: $375
Curls over top of head.

Soft Waves and Overall Curls, No Part, Childlike
Size: 13–16″
Price: $250–$350
Very common style, often blonde.

Soft Waves and Overall Curls, No Part, Childlike
Size: 18–22″
Price: $350–$450

Soft Waves and Overall Curls, No Part, Childlike
Size: 24+″
Price: $475–$600

1890S–1900S CHINA HEAD DOLLS

With the heyday of the china doll long over,
common, generously produced Low-Brow
dolls were mostly made in the 1890s. These
dolls have bangs, so the hair is low right over
the eyes. In the early 1900s, Dressel, Kister &

Co. made some elaborate and sought-after china dolls.

Black Man
Size: 12"
Price: $1,050

Dressel, Kister, Man
Size: 15"
Price: $1,400
Middle-aged man, detailed wavy grayish hair and brows.

Dressel, Kister, Lady, Gray Hair
Size: 15.5"
Price: $1,250
Gray hair piled on head, aqua hairband.

Fortune-Teller, Low Brow
Size: 13"
Price: $825
With fortunes, original costume.

Hertwig, Pet Name Marion
Size: 19–23"
Price: $250–$300
Other pet names include Agnes, Daisy, Mabel, and others.
Mark: MARION (front shoulder plate) Patent Applied For / Germany (back shoulder plate).

Hertwig, Pet Name Dorothy, Bertha, etc.
Size: 24+"
Price: $300–$400
Pet Name china dolls have the name of the doll in gold on the front shoulder plate, plus modeled bodices with bows.

Highland Mary
Size: 13–14"
Price: $300–$400
Highland Marys have low bangs with comb marks or brushstrokes around face.

Highland Mary
Size: 22–24"
Price: $500–$600
Some by Alt, Beck & Gottschalck, mold 1000.
Mark: 1000. Others unmarked.

Jester, Blue-Trimmed Molded Cap
Size: 14–17"
Price: $750
Brown sculpted hair, modeled mustache and goatee.

Kister, Flat Top
Size: 21"
Price: $350
With Dressel, Kister mark.

Low Brow
Size: 6–8"
All Markets: $40–$90
Mark: Germany or unmarked.

Low Brow
Size: 10–14"
Price: $120–$160

Low Brow
Size: 16–22"
Price: $175–$275
More for well-modeled, unusual curls and very well painted.

Low Brow
Size: 25–27"
Price: $300+
Blonde or black hair.

EMMA CLEAR (AMERICAN) CHINA DOLLS

All Emma Clear dolls listed here are from 1939 through the 1940s. Emma Clear was an early reproduction doll artist. All dolls have cloth bodies with china or parian limbs.

Flat Top
Size: 12"
All Markets: $260

Molded Blonde Curls
Size: 18"
All Markets: $400
Mark: Clear / 39 (inside the C).

Center Part, Bun
Size: 16"
Price: $500
Mark: Clear / 49 (inside the C).

Blonde, 1880s-Type
Size: 16"
Price: $350
Body with corset.

Spill Curls
Size: 23"
Price: $550
Original cloth body.

Grape Lady
Size: 18"
Price: $300
Pierced ears, bonnet with snood.

Curly Hair with Bow
Size: 18"
Price: $275
Pierced ears, parian limbs.

Columbian doll by Emma Adams. Oil-painted features, yellow painted hair bow in back of head, cloth body. Made by the Adams sisters of Oswego Center, NY. 20", c. 1893. Mark: Columbian Doll Emma Adams. Courtesy Theriault's.

Lithograph dolls. One doll with printed outfit (left), other doll with original clothing (sewn-on face on muslin form). Both 15", c. 1900, unmarked. Courtesy Theriault's.

Cloth Dolls

Cloth Dolls, Cottage Industry: The antique cloth dolls covered in this section were generally made by female entrepreneurs who were truly ahead of their time (Izannah Walker, Emma Adams, Ella Smith, Martha Chase). These dolls were made starting in the late 1840s, but were mostly made from the 1880s through the early 1900s. Sometimes the dolls were produced by church groups raising funds for their churches or various causes.

This section also covers printed dolls, homemade primitive dolls, and prices for certain European cloth dolls (some manufactured). The later European cloth dolls often copy the looks of more popular cloth dollmakers such as Lenci.

Market Report: Compared to antique bisque dolls, not many antique cloth dolls from cottage industries have survived, and those that have survived are often well-loved and worn. Additionally, because these dolls were made in cottage industries, their production was far below the production numbers of mass-produced dolls. These factors have contributed to high prices for the most popular dolls, including Izannah Walker dolls, Columbian dolls, and Philadelphia Babies.

Online/Offline Report: These dolls are rarely seen at online auctions, and mostly trade via dealers, shows, live auctions, and collector to collector. Collector interest and prices for these dolls are very strong and continue to rise.

Cloth Dolls, Homemade and Printed: From the end of the 1800s to the early 1900s, many patterns were made for dolls for mothers and daughters to make at home.

Martha Chase child. *Oil-painted features, bobbed molded hair, muslin body stocking body, oil-painted limbs. 13", c. 1900. Mark: (Dutch girl logo) upper leg. Courtesy Theriault's.*

Babyland Rag dolls, unmarked. *Lithograph faces stitched to muslin egg-shaped heads, muslin bodies. Both 14", c. 1900. Courtesy Theriault's.*

Bing character child. *Pressed and oil-painted features, muslin 5-piece body. Attributed to John Bing. 12", c. 1920. Courtesy Theriault's.*

Additionally, companies started to produce print-and-cut dolls that could also be made at home. Although many more of these dolls were made than the cottage industry cloth dolls discussed above, it can still be hard to find these dolls in excellent or mint condition.

Market Report: Prices for homemade and printed dolls are far lower than for cottage-industry cloth dolls. Popular printed themes include Palmer Cox Brownies and advertising characters such as Buster Brown and the Cream of Wheat Chef. When looking for homemade rag dolls from patterns, charm is everything—these dolls are truly one-of-a-kinds. Look also for old clothes, original faces (embroidered, painted) and less primitive body construction.

Online/Offline Report: These dolls are plentiful at online auctions. When selling or buying on eBay, consider the Folk Art and Antiques > Primitives categories.

Prices and Characteristics: Prices from all venues were similar and were averaged to determine the price results listed. Prices are for generally worn dolls, as indicated, with examples of prices for excellent dolls given where available. Dolls are all-cloth unless otherwise noted.

ALABAMA BABIES

Alabama Babies by Ella Smith have molded cloth faces with oil-painted features, jointed shoulders and hips, circular seams on their heads, flat bottoms, applied ears, and painted shoes.

Alabama Baby
Size: 12" Date: 1910
Price: $800
For molded ear, later doll.

Alabama Baby
Size: 18–22" Date: 1910
Price: $800
Molded ear doll.

Alabama Baby, Early
Size: various Date: 1900
Price: $1,600–$2,000
For worn dolls with applied ears.

BABYLAND RAG

Distributed by Horsman. Hand-painted or later printed faces (cloth mask faces by Bruckner), mohair wigs, stitch-jointed at shoulders and hips. Unmarked.

Babyland Rag, Baby
Size: 17" Date: 1893–1912
Price: $725
Hand-painted features.

Kamkins character children. Cloth swivel heads, pressed and painted facial features. Muslin bodies, stitch-jointed limbs. All 18″, c. 1930. Mark: Kamkins, a Dolly Made to Love, Patented from L.R. Kampes Studios, Atlantic City, J.J. (red heart label). Courtesy Theriault's.

Moravian child, unmarked. All-muslin doll, painted facial features. Body stitch-jointed, mitten hands. 17″, c. 1920. $1,600, auction. Courtesy Theriault's.

Buttercup lithographed doll. Arms stitch-jointed, legs disk-jointed. Character from Toots and Casper comic strip. 19″, c. 1920. Courtesy Theriault's.

Babyland Rag, Child
Size: 14″   Date: 1893–1912
Price: $550
For worn doll with hand-painted features.

Babyland Rag, Child
Size: 15″   Date: 1890s
Price: $1,200
For mint doll with early hand-painted face.

Babyland Rag, Mammy
Size: 20″   Date: 1893–1912
Price: $700
All original, white polka dot dress, kerchief.

Babyland Rag, Printed Features
Size: 15″   Date: 1907–1912
Price: $325
Printed features, later doll.

Babyland Rag
Size: 30″   Date: 1890s
Price: $1,000+
Hand-painted features.

Brückner, Child
Size: 12″   Date: 1901
Price: $275–$375
Cloth mask face.

Brückner, Child, "Dollypop"
                   Date: 1901
Price: $175–$225

Brückner, Lady
Size: 12″   Date: 1901
Price: $250

Printed cloth face, horsehair wig, jointed cloth body.

MARTHA CHASE
These Stockinet dolls have oil-painted features, textured painted hair, sateen covered torsos, oil-painted limbs, stitch-jointed shoulders, elbows, hips, and knees, and stitched fingers and toes. They were produced from the 1890s until the early 1900s.

Martha Chase Baby
Size: 12– 13″   Date: 1900
Price: $250–$275
For dolls in average condition.
Mark: Chase / Stockinet Doll / Trade Mark.

Martha Chase Baby
Size: 13″
Price: $920
Exceptionally mint with nearly no paint crazing.

Martha Chase Baby
Size: 16–20″   Date: 1900
Price: $400–$650
$200 more for dolls with earlier face. For dolls in average condition.

Martha Chase Baby
Size: 22–24″
Price: $550–$750

Martha Chase Baby

Size: 26+"
Price: $1,000
For mint doll.

Martha Chase Baby

Size: 27"   Date: 1889
Price: $700+

Martha Chase Child

Size: 14"
Price: $450

Martha Chase Child

Size: 17"
Price: $1,300
Mint. Pressed and oil-painted cloth shoulder-head, cotton sateen body.
Mark: Chase Stockinette Doll Trade Mark (stamp, hip).

Martha Chase Child

Size: 26–28"
Price: $900–$1,000

Martha Chase Child

Size: 8.75"   Date: early 1900s
Price: $8,000
Very rare.

Martha Chase Hospital Doll

Size: 40"
Price: $800–$1,000

Martha Chase Mammy, Black Doll

Size: 24–26"
Price: $6,000–$8,000

IZANNAH WALKER

Pressed head of stockinette with molded features, oil-painted features and hair, applied ears, cloth body. Patent Date: 1872.

Izannah Walker, Child

Size: 27"   Date: 1860s
Price: $8,800
Corkscrew curls in front of ear; price with damage.

Izannah Walker, Boy

Size: 15"   Date: 1870s
Price: $11,700
With wear; red paper label on back. At auction.
Mark: I.F. Walker Patent Nov 4th 1873.

Izannah Walker, Child

Size: 17–18"   Date: 1860s
Price: $6,400–$6,600+

Price for worn doll. Bare feet, ringlets in front of ears, going around head, painted features.

Izannah Walker, Girl, Pre-Patent

Size: 16"
Price: $17,600
Pre-patent doll. Made in Central Falls, Rhode Island. 2 curls in front of each ear. At auction.

LITHOGRAPHED (PRINTED) DOLLS

Printed fabric sold to make cutout dolls. Dolls are unjointed, face/body/clothing printed on one side. Stuffed. Late 1800s–early 1900s.

Lithographed (Printed Doll), Art Fabric Mills, Girl

Size: 24"   Date: 1900
Price: $100
Printed clothing.

Lithographed Child, No Joints

Size: 6.5–8.5"   Date: early 1900s
Price: $65–$100
In excellent condition.

Lithographed Girl

Size: 24–28"   Date: early 1900s
Price: $75–$125
Generally worn or darkened material. Flat stuffed unjointed body.

PHILADELPHIA BABY

Also known as Sheppard Baby. Dolls by J.B. Sheppard, Philadelphia. Stockinette dolls with molded and painted features, stitched fingers, toes.

Philadelphia Baby, Child

Size: 18–22"   Date: 1890–1900
Price: $1,800–$2,400
For worn dolls; higher prices for less worn, all-original paint. Hand-painted hair and eyes.

Philadelphia Baby

Size: 18–22"   Date: 1890–1900
Price: $3,600–$4,200
For excellent doll.

Philadelphia Baby, Child

Size: 20"   Date: 1890–1900
Price: $5,600
With trunk and extensive trousseau of home-made clothing. Doll with flaws. At auction.

AMERICAN PRIMITIVE CLOTH DOLLS

Handmade dolls, made noncommercially. Very hard to price because of individuality of dolls and great range of dates the dolls were made, from mid-1800s through 1920s+. Most dolls have sewn, embroidered, or oil-painted features.

Primitive, Oil-Painted or Embroidered Features, Child

Size: 18–24″　　　Date: late 1800s to early 1900s
Price: $500–$900
Played-with dolls. Painted or embroidered features, handmade, usually stitch jointing. Price depends on size, condition, and artistry of doll.

Primitive, Embroidered Features, Black

Size: 25″　　　Date: late 1800s to early 1900s
Price: $1,100
Exaggerated features, lots of teeth.

Primitive, Oil-Painted Features, Child

Size: 17–23″　　　Date: late 1800s to early 1900s
Price: $1,400
Unusual open mouth, teeth painted. Original clothing. Water stains.

Primitive, Oil-Painted Features, Child

Size: 24″　　　Date: late 1800s to early 1900s
Price: $2,500
For exceptional child.

Primitive, Sewn Features, Black

Size: 17″　　　Date: late 1800s
Price: $450

AMERICAN CLOTH DOLLS

Beecher Baby, Child

Size: 20–22″　　　Date: 1893–1910
Price: $1,800–$2,200
For worn dolls.

Columbian Doll

Size: 19–20″　　　Date: 1891–1900
Price: $3,000–$4,000
Doll is marked with stamp on torso.
Mark: Columbian Doll / Emma E. Adams / Oswego Centre / NY.

Columbian-Type

Size: 23″　　　Date: 1890s
Price: $2,200
Mint. Oil-painted features.

Columbian-Type

Size: 31″　　　Date: 1900
Price: $800
Worn.

Kamkins

Size: 18–20″　　　Date: 1920s
Price: $2,400+
For mint dolls. Oil-painted cloth, swivel head, painted eyes, mohair wig.

Kamkins

Size: 18″　　　Date: 1920s
Price: $900–$950
For played-with, worn condition.

Mammy Doll, Handmade

Size: 10″　　　Date: 1930s–1940s
Price: $30–$60
Handmade, wool yarn hair, often with earrings, head scarf, embroidered features.

Moravian, Girl

Size: 17″　　　Date: 1920
Price: $1,600
All-muslin doll with flat face, sewn-on bonnet, mitten hands.

Native American Play Doll

Size: 14″　　　Date: 1880
Price: $450
For worn dolls.

Presbyterian Rag

Size: 16″　　　Date: 1890s
Price: $1,800
Dolls have separate thumbs and black lower legs.

Rollinson, Child

Size: 18–19″　　　Date: 1920s
Price: $600–$800
For worn dolls. Molded, oil-painted shoulder-head, lower limbs, hand-painted features, human hair wig, cloth body.
Mark: Rollinson Doll / Holyoke / Mass (diamond w/doll in middle, stamped back) 2318.

Rollinson, Child

Size: 28″　　　Date: 1916
Price: $1,350
For excellent condition, all-original paint.

EUROPEAN CLOTH DOLLS

English, Dean's Patent Tru-To-Life Rag Doll

Size: 14″　　　Date: 1920s
Price: $325–$350
Molded stockinette face, painted eyes, mohair wig, stuffed body, may have paper label: "I am

British from the top of my head to the tip of my toes."

English, Dean's Patent Tru-To-Life Rag Doll
Size: 16″   Date: 1920s
Price: $500
Tagged on foot.
Mark: Made in England / By Deans Rag Book / Co. Ltd. / London.

English, Farnell, King George
Size: 16″   Date: 1930s
Price: $275
Felt swivel head, painted features, 5-piece jointed felt body, uniform. Original wrist tag.
Mark: H.H. The King, made in England by J.K. Farnell & Co. Ltd

English, Grecon, Bobby
Price: $90
Mint from England. Metal feet.

French, Character Girl, "Sans Rival"
Size: 20″   Date: 1925
Price: $575
MIB.

French, Character Girl, Winter Costume
Size: 21″   Date: 1925
Price: $900
Resembles Lenci.

French, Character, Girl
Size: 21″   Date: 1930
Price: $750
Resembles Lenci. Bright colored costume, painted eyes, mohair wig, 5-piece cloth body.
Mark: P.F. France (medallion)

French, Character, Pouty Girl
Size: 21″   Date: 1930
Price: $500
Resembles Lenci. Bright colored costume, painted eyes, mohair wig, 5-piece muslin body.

French, Ecco France, Girl
Size: 10″
Price: $175
Cloth mask face.

French, Eugénie Poir, Girl
Size: 15″
Price: $200
Organdy costume.

French, Leather Baby Doll
Size: 4.5″   Date: 1920
Price: $1,300
Firmly stuffed leather, pressed facial features, swivel head, painted blonde hair.

French, Ravca, tiny
Size: 7–12″   Date: 1920s–1930s
Price: $80–$120
Stockinette characters.
Mark: Original Ravca / Fabrication Francaise

French, Ravca
Size: 18″   Date: 1920s–1930s
Price: $300–$400
Various characters including men, old ladies.

French, Raynal, Lady
Size: 18″   Date: 1930
Price: $1,900
MIB French, felt swivel head, pressed, painted eyes, closed mouth, white mohair wig, 18th-century dress, muslin body with jointing at shoulders, hips, celluloid hands.
Mark: Poupée Raynal (shoe) Raynal (back of brooch)

French, Venus Boy
Size: 16″   Date: 1930s
Price: $475
Pressed felt, Lenci-type, navy blue felt uniform.
Mark: Venus / Paris / Deposé (soles shoes)

German, Bing
Size: 10″   Date: 1920
Price: $350–$400
Cloth molded face.

Norwegian, Ronnaug Petterssen, Child
Size: 15″   Date: 1950s
Price: $550
Mohair wig, Sedestal Norway dress style. Felt.

Norwegian, Ronnaug Petterssen, Skier, Girl
Size: 8″   Date: 1965
Price: $350
MIB hang tag on sweater, marked box (date of gift on bottom). Felt.

Norwegian, Ronnaug Petterssen, Child
Size: 16.5″   Date: 1940
Price: $1,500
Lenci-type.

Norwegian, Ronnaug Petterssen, Child
Size: 18″   Date: 1930s
Price: $2,375
Lenci-type. Felt. eBay auction.
Mark: Blue paper label on skirt, Ronnaug Petterssen.

Petzold, Dora, Child
Size: 20″   Date: 1920
Price: $700
Art doll, made in Germany, cloth swivel head, painted features and finish, mohair or human

Character of man. Composition and wood jointed body. 13″, c. 1893. Attributed to Cuno & Otto Dressel. Mark: (Holz-masse stamp) torso. $9,000, auction. Courtesy Theriault's.

Fashion Lady 1469. Composition and wood flapper body. 15″, c. 1920. Mark: 1469 C & O. D. / Germany / 2. Courtesy Theriault's.

hair wig, stockinette, disk-jointed shoulders and hips, stitched fingers and separate thumbs.

Petzold, Dora, Child

Size: 26″   Date: 1920
Price: $850

COD (Cuno & Otto Dressel)

A long-standing German firm dealing in toys and dolls from the early 1700s, Cuno & Otto Dressel (originally just Dressel) made bisque dolls from the heads of other famous German suppliers, and also manufactured heads used by other companies. The majority of the dolls made by the firm were produced from the early 1870s through the early 1920s.

Market Report: The basic dolly-faced dolls of this firm are a wonderful doll for the beginning doll collector—attractively priced, and usually of good quality. The character

dolls from Cuno & Otto Dressel are also reasonably priced vis-à-vis many others in the market. Prices for the more common child, baby, and shoulder-head dolls have declined somewhat in the past few years.

Online/Offline Report: Bargains can definitely be found online in this category. Look for finer examples and the character dolls from dealers and at doll shows.

Prices and Characteristics: Many dolls are marked only Cuno & Otto Dressel, with no mold number. Dolls have bisque heads, open mouths, glass eyes, wigged with mohair or human hair, and fully jointed composition bodies, all in excellent condition, except as noted. Cuno & Otto Dressel made dolls from at least the 1870s on, but the majority of dolls priced here are from the 1890s to the early 1920s.

Jutta toddler. Composition and wood toddler body with side-hip joints. 14″, c. 1914. Mark: 3/0 / Jutta 1914 3 _. Courtesy Theriault's.

CUNO & OTTO DRESSEL

Baby, No Mold
Size: 27″   Internet: $650
Mark: Cuno & Otto Dressel

Baby/Toddler, Jutta
Size: 12–14″   Internet: $600–$650
Named in honor of Countess Jutta von Henneberg who issued the town charter of Sonneberg circa 1348.
Mark: 1920/8 / Jutta Baby / Dressel / 3

Baby/Toddler, Jutta
Size: 14–18″   Internet: $600–$700
Jutta babies have glass eyes (sometimes flirty), composition bent-limb baby bodies.
Mark: Jutta 1914 8 1/2 DRGM 856346

Baby/Toddler, Jutta
Size: 20–22″
Price: $700   Internet: $700–$800
Mark: Jutta 1914 11.5

Baby/Toddler, Jutta
Size: 22–24″
Price: $900   Internet: $900–$1,000
Sleep eyes, open mouth, sometimes wobble tongue, 2 upper teeth, bent-limb composition baby body.
Mark: Jutta 1914 14.5

Character, Baby, 1428
Size: 12″
Price: $2,600
5-piece bent-limb baby body.
Mark: 1428

Character, Child
Size: 14″
Price: $2,300

Character, Child
Size: 40″   Internet: $2,300
Mark: Cuno & Otto Dressel / Germany

Character, Farmer
Size: 11″
Price: $1,300
All original from series of historical American figures; same mold used for Uncle Sam.
Mark: S 1 Germany

Character, Gentleman With Molded Mustache
Size: 13″
Price: $9,000
To commemorate American hero in Spanish-American War.
Mark: unmarked

Character, Uncle Sam
Size: 13″
Price: $1,400
Caricature, gray eyebrows, big nose, white mohair wig and beard, all-original red, white, blue costume.
Mark: S 1

Child, No Mold
Size: 16″
Price: $300   Internet: $350
Open mouth, jointed composition body.
Mark: Cuno & Otto Dressel

Bébé DEP, open mouth. *French wood and composition jointed body. 16", c. 1900. Mark: DEP 6. Courtesy Theriault's.*

Bébé DEP, closed mouth. *French wood and composition jointed body. 15", c. 1900. Mark: DEP 6. Courtesy Theriault's.*

Child, No Mold
Size: 18"
Price: $500   Internet: $400

Child, No Mold
Size: 20"
Price: $600   Internet: $620

Child, No Mold
Size: 25"
Price: $650   Internet: $600

Child, Jutta, 1349
Size: 16"
Price: $550   Internet: $500
Mark: 1349 Dressel S & H

Child, Jutta, 1349
Size: 25"
Price: $625   Internet: $650
Mark: 1349 Jutta S & H 1/2

Child, Shoulder-Head, 1896, others
Size: 12"
Price: $225   Internet: $200
On kid body.
Mark: 1896 COD 7/0 DEP

Child, Shoulder-Head, 1896, Others
Size: 15–18"
Price: $275–$325   Internet: $200–$300

Lady, 1469
Size: 14"
Price: $2,000–$2,500   Internet: $2,000+

Generally dressed as flapper. Closed mouth, glass eyes, elongated lady body, feet posed for high heels.
Mark: 1469 C & O Dressel Germany 2

DEP Dolls

There has been a lot of confusion over the years about what constitutes a doll marked "DEP." For purposes of this book, DEP dolls are only those marked "DEP" with a size number—not dolls that have "DEP" in addition to other marks and mold numbers. According to the Colemans' *The Collector's Encyclopedia of Dolls,* "DEP" stands for either Deponirt in German or Déposé in French, both meaning registration, and both often found on doll heads with other markings. For instance, a doll marked: "S & H 1249 DEP Germany Santa 11" is not classified as a DEP doll, but is instead classified as a Simon & Halbig 1249 "Santa" doll.

DEP dolls solely marked DEP are believed by some experts to generally have been made by Simon & Halbig in Germany from approximately 1898–1910, specifically and primarily for S.F.B.J. The doll heads were given French doll bodies and costumes, and then sold as French dolls. DEP dolls are found with both open and closed mouths.

Market Report: DEP dolls can vary greatly in condition and quality, but generally

German dollhouse doll, molded hair. *Cloth body, bisque lower arms and legs. 5.5". Mark: 4115 / Germany (shoulder plate). $200, dealer.*

German dollhouse doll, molded hair. *Painted black boots, bisque lower arms and legs. 5". Mark: 9 (shoulder plate, arm rims). $120, dealer.*

All-bisque dollhouse boy and girl. *Girl 3", boy 2.5". Girl: Mark: 3 (head inner legs). Boy unmarked. $100 each, dealer.*

speaking, the dolls are well-made with lovely bisque and well-painted features. As with many categories of antique dolls that are not "hot" right now, prices are generally stable or trending slightly downward.

Online/Offline Report: DEP dolls can be found from all sources. Dolls online generally sell for less due to the difficulty in assessing their bisque.

Prices and Characteristics: All with bisque socket heads, in excellent condition, made from approximately the late 1890s to the early 1900s (most circa 1900). All with fully jointed composition and wood bodies, glass eyes (sometimes paperweights), wigged with mohair or human hair, sometimes in Jumeau/S.F.B.J. chemise. Price results are mixed and similar from all venues.

DEP DOLLS

Closed Mouth
Size: 15"
Price: $2,000
Mark: DEP / 4

Closed Mouth
Size: 20"
Price: $2,600
Mark: DEP / 6

Closed Mouth
Size: 24"
Price: $2,400
Paperweight eyes, straight-wrist French composition body.
Mark: DEP / 11

Open Mouth
Size: 13–15"
Price: $600–$750
Often found in Jumeau chemise; from S.F.B.J.
Mark: DEP / 3

Open Mouth
Size: 17–20"
Price: $750–$850
Mark: DEP / 6

Open Mouth
Size: 22–26"
Price: $800–$950
Body may have mama/papa pull strings.
Mark: DEP/ 9

Open Mouth
Size: 28–30"
Price: $900+
Mark: DEP / 12

Open Mouth, Jumeau Body
Size: 16–20"
Price: $1,300–$1,400
For doll with Jumeau stamped body.
Mark: DEP 6

German dollhouse man, woman.
Cloth bodies, bisque lower limbs.
Man in original suit (woman's
dress may be original). Man 5.5",
woman 6". Unknown marks. $200
man, $150 woman, dealer.

German dollhouse bride and groom. *Original outfits, groom wearing*
tails, molded mustache. Shoulder-heads, cloth bodies, and lower
limbs, bisque. Groom 5.75", bride 5", c. 1890s. Marks (if any) not ac-
cessible. $300 each, dealer.

Open Mouth, Original French Presentation
Box
Size: 10″
Price: $2,100
Box with trousseau in lace-edged original box.
Mark: DEP 0

Dollhouse Dolls

Dollhouses are a definite companion collectible to dolls—many doll collectors have either a latent or active interest in dollhouses and miniatures. These two areas of collecting—dolls and dollhouses—intersect with dollhouse dolls, the small dolls produced to be the inhabitants of dollhouses. Dollhouses have been a fixture of Western culture since the 1500s. Called "baby houses," they were originally made for the pleasure and play of grown-ups. The first

dolls made for the early baby houses were mostly made of wood and wax.

In the 1800s, dolls' houses became children's toys, and their inhabitants became made of many things—porcelain and bisque dollhouse dolls joined their wood and wax counterparts, and eventually became the preferred material from which dollhouse dolls were made. Some early cloth-head dollhouse dolls also exist. By the end of the 1800s into the early 1900s, an entire cast of characters was available to live in dollhouses—ladies, gentlemen, children, babies, maids, chauffeurs, chefs, and others. The majority of dollhouse dolls were made in Germany.

Most dollhouse dolls that are found today have bisque or porcelain (china) shoulder-

German dollhouse doll, bobbed hair. 6", c. 1920. Mark: Z 4010 / Germany (shoulder plate). $150, dealer.

German dollhouse maid. *Fine dollhouses in the late 1800s and early 1900s would have a full complement of servants. Shoulderhead, cloth bodies, bisque lower limbs, painted 2-strap black shoes with heels. 6.25". Marks (if any) not accessible. Each, $300, dealer.*

German dollhouse doll. *Shoulderhead, cloth body, bisque lower limbs. 7.5". Marks (if any) not accessible. $250, dealer.*

heads, with bisque or china hands and feet, with cloth bodes. Additionally, some all-bisque dolls were made for dollhouses. It is difficult to find the early wax and wood dollhouse dolls that have survived to this day.

The current standard for dollhouse scale is one inch equals one foot. This was not the standard for antique dollhouses, and so today we find many antique dollhouse dolls that are small but not really in scale for today's dollhouses.

Market Report: Unfortunately, the incredible scope and variety of antique dollhouse dolls cannot be properly conveyed by this book. The only book that I have seen that has done justice to this under-appreciated category of dolls is the landmark *Dolls in Miniature* by Evelyn Ackerman, which is unfortunately out of print (see Bibliography). Dollhouse dolls are actually hard to find, and choice examples—older dolls, those in original clothing, dolls with unusual modeling or molding—are quickly scooped up by collectors. For such choice examples, prices are strong and rising. For more common examples, such as china dollhouse dolls with common hairdos, common redressed dolls, and later dolls from

the 1920s and after, prices are weak and even declining.

Online/Offline Report: You can find dollhouse dolls at online auctions, but it isn't easy—many small all-bisque dolls are frequently mislabeled as dollhouse dolls, and many dollhouse dolls aren't labeled as such at all. So bargains are possible. Dealers have the best selection of dollhouse dolls—in fact, the national UFDC Convention sales showroom has consistently had the widest variety of dollhouse dolls available at any one venue. Sometimes groups of dollhouse dolls or early examples do come up at live auctions, but not in great numbers or variety, although those that do come up are often choice.

Prices and Characteristics: All dolls are in excellent condition. The bisque dollhouse dolls listed here have bisque shoulder-heads and bisque lower limbs with cloth bodies, except as noted; china dolls have the same bodies except with bisque or porcelain lower limbs.

Marks: Dolls are unmarked, with a number, or marked "Made in Germany" or "Germany" (sometimes with a number) except as noted.

DOLLHOUSE DOLLS

Man or Woman, Painted Eyes, Various: Bisque, China, Parian
Size: 5–7″   Date: 1860s–1920s
Price: $170–$220
Material: various
The majority of painted-eye dollhouse dolls are priced in this range, more for mint examples in original clothing, better quality painting, unusual molded hairstyles. Less for nude, replaced clothing, crude painting, common small china/parian dolls (see examples below).

Man or Woman, Glass Eyes
Size: 5–7″   Date: 1890s–1920s
Price: $200–$400   Internet: $200+
Material: bisque
Generally wigged. Higher values for mint examples in outstanding original clothing.

Child, Painted Eyes, Molded Hair
Size: 2–5″   Date: 1860s–1920s
Price: $150+
Material: bisque
More for unusual hair modeling. Sometimes parian.

Child, Glass Eyes
Size: 3–5″   Date: 1890s–1920s
Price: $200+   Internet: $250+
Material: bisque
Wigged or molded hair; more for unusual hair modeling, unusually painted shoes.

China Doll, Black
Size: 5–6″
Price: $225–$250
Material: porcelain

China Doll, Common Hair
Size: 6″   Date: 1860s–1890s
Price: $125–$165
Material: porcelain

China Doll, Rarer Hair
Size: 6–7″
Price: $225–$250   Internet: $355
Material: porcelain
Internet price for covered wagon hair, pink tint.

Bride or Groom
Size: 5–6″   Date: 1910–1920s
Price: $300,00+
Material: bisque
Original clothing, painted or glass eyes.

Maid
Size: 6″   Date: 1920s
Price: $200
Material: parian
In original maid's outfit. Painted eyes.

Flapper, Molded Pageboy
Size: 4″   Date: 1920s
Price: $200–$250
Material: bisque

Golfer
Size: 4″   Date: 1920s
Price: $275
Material: bisque
Original outfit.

Grecon, Grandpa
Size: 3″   Internet: $35
Material: cloth
Lead feet.
Mark: Grecon, Made in England (on tag).

Servant
Size: 5″   Date: 1920s
                    Internet: $200–$300
Material: bisque
In original servant's outfit (such as maid or chef).

Man in Military Uniform
Size: 7″   Date: 1890
Price: $1,500
Material: bisque
Rare modeling.

Servants, Domestic, Set of 7
Size: 6–7″   Date: 1890
Price: $2,100
Material: bisque
Original outfits—butler, parlor maid, chef, kitchen maid, additional.

Simon & Halbig, "Little Woman"
Size: 6″
Price: $300–$400
Material: bisque
Desirable glass-eye model often found in dollhouse size.
Mark: 1160 (mold number).

Soldier
Size: 6–7″   Date: 1895
Price: $1,400
Material: bisque
Original military costume, painted and sculpted hair and mustache.

Door of Hope

Door of Hope dolls were made by poverty-stricken and rescued slave girls in a missionary school in Shanghai, China, from approximately 1901 until approximately the late 1940s. The dolls have detailed handmade clothing with hand-done embroidery.

Door of Hope dolls. *Carved wood heads, painted and carved hair, cloth bodies, legs, upper arms, wood hands. 7–12", c. 1925. Courtesy Theriault's.*

The dolls themselves were made from finely carved pear wood, and each doll was individually carved by Chinese wood carvers outside the mission. Through their clothing they represent various classes of people in the multilayered Chinese society of that time, from working class people to nobility.

Earlier dolls are slightly taller than later dolls, with eyes slanted just a bit more and sometimes with bound feet. Later dolls do not have bound feet and their eyes can be larger.

Market Report: Prices for Door of Hope dolls have increased significantly in the last few years as collectors have come to appreciate their fine workmanship and detailed, realistic costuming. Since each doll is individually carved, pay attention to the facial details when buying a Door of Hope doll, since quality can vary. Also look for elaborately dressed brides and harder-to-find professions and themes such as policemen.

Online/Offline Report: You will find very few Door of Hope dolls at online auctions, and those that you do find will rarely meet reserves and actually sell. Most Door of Hope dolls trade from dealers, live auction houses, and at shows.

Prices and Characteristics: All dolls are in excellent condition, were made from 1901 to the 1930s, and are made of wood except as noted. The highest prices are for dolls with fancier silk outfits and deeper, more elaborate carving. Some of the higher prices presented here were from an auction with exceptionally mint dolls. Prices are for dolls with original outfits; prices are much lower for dolls with replaced outfits or wear. The dolls are generally unmarked.

DOOR OF HOPE

Various, Man, Woman, or Child
Size: 6–11"
Price: $500–$800   Internet: $500–$800
For dolls with wear, simple carving and simple cotton costumes, sometimes with soiling.

Amah (Nursemaid)
Size: 11–12"
Price: $850   Internet: $2,100
With child on back, comb and bun in nursemaid's hair. Lower price for soiled clothing and very simple outfit.

Baby
Size: 5"   Internet: $600
Baby, normally found with mother or nursemaid.

Bride
Size: 11.5"
Price: $1,300–$1,500

Bridegroom
Size: 11.5″
Price: $1,300   Internet: $1,500

Child
Size: 6.5″
Price: $1,000   Internet: $900
Hand-carved wood head and limbs, painted features, painted hair.

Children, Pair
Size: 6″
Price: $5,175
Rare, fancy silk outfit and elaborate headpieces.

Female Mourner
Size: 11.5″
Price: $1,350

Grandfather or Grandmother
Size: 11″
Price: $1,700–$2,000

Kindergarten Kid
Size: 6″
Price: $2,900

Male Farmer
Size: 11″
Price: $2,750

Male Mourner
Size: 11.5″
Price: $1,300–$1,400

Man, Cloth Outfit
Size: 11″
Price: $700
Hand-carved wood head and limbs, painted features, painted hair, original outfit.

Man, Straw Outfit
Size: 12″
Price: $1,000
Hand-carved wood head and limbs, painted features, painted hair, original straw outfit.

Manchu Woman
Size: 11″
Price: $8,000
Rare, intricately carved wood with elaborately carved headpiece.

Mother
Size: 9″
Price: $500
Simple cotton outfit, soiling of cloth and some wear.

Policeman
Size: 12″
Price: $3,100

Priest
Size: 11.5″
Price: $3,150

Schoolgirl or Schoolboy
Size: 8–9″
Price: $1,100–$1,300

Small Girl
Size: 7.25″
Price: $3,450
Fancy silk outfit and elaborate carving.

Table Boy
Size: 11.5″
Price: $1,300

Widow
Size: 11″
Price: $1,400

Woman
Size: 8″
Price: $1,200   Internet: $900
Lower price for doll with some wear.

Young Boy
Size: 8″
Price: $1,000

Young Girl
Size: 9″
Price: $1,400

Young Man
Size: 11–12″
Price: $1,000–$1,800   Internet: $1,000–$1,200
Highest price for very mint doll in rarer outfit.

Young Woman
Size: 11–12″
Price: $1,100–$2,275
Price varies depending on outfit and wear.

French Fashions (a.k.a. Poupées)

French fashion dolls are the forerunners to the modern fashion dolls of today—Barbie, Cissy, Gene, and Tyler. These first ladies of fashion were produced in France in the 1850s by Adelaide Huret, Leontine Rohmer, and others.

The first French fashion dolls made in the 1850s and early 1860s were mostly childlike or young ladies—as were most dolls manufactured until that time. They had wardrobes and accessories associated with French fash-

Huret, French Fashion, painted eyes. On bisque shoulder plate, original gutta-percha body replaced with wood body in 1870 and replaced by Maison Huret. Exceptional face. 17", c. 1860 (head). Mark: Medaille D'Argent Huret, 22 Boulevard Montmartre Paris, Exposition Universelle 1867 (stamp on kid collarette). This doll, $30,000 at auction in 2000. Courtesy Theriault's.

French fashion, unmarked. Gusseted kid body, swivel head on shoulder plate. $3,200, dealer.

ion dolls, but the clothing was mostly fashionable clothing for a child or young woman—they were not yet truly women dolls, and they did not yet truly have a woman's wardrobe. In the 1870s these dolls became clearly adult in form and wardrobe.

The dolls were played with by children primarily six to thirteen years old, and were intended to teach little girls how to live in the grown-up world as a woman. However, the dolls were also admired and collected by grown women. Critics at the World Exposition in 1867 and again in 1878 complained that the dolls were really created for grown women and were too fancy for child's imaginative play. This explains to me, in part, why so many of these dolls have reached us in amazing condition (although even little girls were careful with their dolls then, since most girls were lucky to have even one).

An entire industry arose in Paris surrounding the French fashion doll. Companies made heads, bodies, eyes, wigs, and trousseaus, with innumerable accessories sold separately—everything a lady would need to live the life of a lady at that time: sewing kits, parlor games, furniture, toilette items, nightgowns, furs, hats, shoes, purses, jewelry, stationery. There were literally hundreds of retail shops in Paris that catered to the fashion doll trade, and popular journals such as *La Poupée Modele* focused on the dolls and provided sewing patterns for them.

The earliest dolls had stationary china heads, painted eyes and wood or gutta-percha bodies. Eventually, many varieties of the French fashion dolls were created—dolls were made with glass eyes, swivel heads, kid bodies, cloth bodies, bisque arms and hands, blown leather bodies, and many other variations. The vast

Rohmer French fashion. *Swivel head, glass eyes, kid body with wood upper arms, bisque lower arms. 16", c. 1860s. Mark: (Rohmer blue stamp) on torso. $3,800, dealer.*

French fashion, unmarked. *Gusseted kid body, swivel head on shoulder plate. Original outfit. c. 1875. Private collection.*

Jumeau French fashion. *Portrait-like, fully jointed wood body. Swivel head on shoulder plate. 22", c. 1875. Mark: 9 (head and shoulder plate). $6,500, auction.*

majority of dolls had bisque heads, glass eyes, and kid leather bodies. French fashion dolls almost always have closed mouths. Almost all dolls made were of Caucasian women, although a few rare dolls were clearly modeled to be men (with molded mustaches) and a few Asian and Black dolls exist. Most French fashion dolls were between 16 and 22 inches in height.

The heyday of the French fashion doll was from 1850 to 1880, at which time the doll began to be supplanted by the newly fashionable bébés—dolls in the form of children, meant for mothering by their owners.

Certain information in this section is from *A Fully Perfected Grace—The World of the French Fashion Doll, 1850–1880* by Florence Theriault (see Bibliography).

Market Report: Collectors of today are still fascinated by the French fashion dolls and their intricate, miniature world.

For collectors of French fashion dolls, clothing and accessories are as important as the dolls. An early French fashion dress can cost well over $1,000, a pair of shoes several hundred dollars, and little accessories like sewing kits or well-made hats also several hundred dollars each. When assessing a French fashion doll, a nude doll or a doll in

modern clothing is worth considerably less than a doll appropriately dressed in French fashion clothing of the appropriate period.

For collectors on a budget, a nude doll can be obtained, and then appropriate clothing and accessories for the doll obtained slowly over time. Some ambitious collectors over time create trousseaus for their dolls. Also, many collectors of French fashion dolls enjoy sewing for their dolls using original patterns from *La Poupée Modele* or authentic patterns from commercial sources.

When buying French fashion dolls, be aware that forgeries and fakes exist, so it is best to purchase from a reputable dealer or auction house. Look for dolls with beautiful features and fine bisque or china heads. Also, the body of a French fashion doll is all-important. If you have a doll on a cloth or kid body, make sure the body is appropriate and sturdy with as little damage as possible. More elaborate bodies increase the desirability and price of the doll—articulated wood bodies are the most sought-after bodies, and any body that allows posing of the doll is desired. Also, swivel necks are generally more sought after than shoulder-head dolls, and glass-eye dolls are more sought after than painted-eye dolls, although not necessarily so for the earliest dolls from the late 1850s. Since most French

Barrois French fashion. *Wood body, glass eyes, flat-cut swivel neck, shoulder plate. 18", c. 1865. Unmarked; doll identified by neck articulation. Courtesy Theriault's.*

Simone French fashion. *Gusseted kid body, swivel head on shoulder plate. 14". Mark: (Simone stamp on front torso). $3,800, dealer. Courtesy Janet Lawrence.*

F.G. French fashion. *Gusseted kid body, swivel head on shoulder plate. 17", c. 1870s. Mark: 5. $1,700, eBay.*

fashion dolls are unmarked, a marked doll generally sells for more than an unmarked doll.

Online/Offline Report: You can find French fashion dolls online—in fact, I have even seen $17,000 Huret dolls trade at on-line auctions. However, the best selection can be found with dealers and at live auctions, as well as at large doll shows focusing on antiques. Prices from all sources are comparable, except that the most common unmarked dolls on kid or cloth bodies with newer clothing can be found at bargain prices on eBay. As with any expensive purchase made via eBay or other online auction houses, it is helpful to personally know the dealer or source and have a money-back guarantee if you are not satisfied with the doll.

Prices and Characteristics: All dolls are bisque, in excellent condition. Dolls have bisque heads and are wigged, with stationary glass eyes and swivel necks on shoulder plates, except as noted. Kid bodies denote bodies with gusset jointing except as noted. The vast majority of French fashion dolls are unmarked. Prices are for dolls in old clothing except as noted.

A Note on Prices: Within each category, generally the least expensive French fashion

dolls are shoulder-heads (one-piece head/shoulders, head does not swivel) on a cloth or kid leather gusset-jointed body. Next are swivel heads on shoulder plates with cloth or kid bodies, and the most expensive dolls tend to have bodies with bisque limbs and wood or other articulated bodies. Exceptional portrait-like faces are sought after. Original outfits, wigs, boots, and accessories can add considerable value to any doll—nearly any original French fashion outfit can cost several hundred dollars, with magnificent original couture outfits often costing thousands. Shoes, boots, and original accessories can be several hundred dollars.

BARROIS FRENCH FASHION

Shoulder-Head, Kid Body, Painted Eyes
Size: 14"   Date: 1880s
Price: $2,200
Mark on shoulderplate.
Mark: E. Deposé 1 B

Shoulder-Head, Kid Body
Size: 13"   Date: 1870
All Markets: $2,600
Glass eyes.
Mark: E 1 Deposé B

Shoulder-Head, Kid Body
Size: 28"   Date: 1860
Price: $3,500
Glass eyes.

German fashion doll, Simon & Halbig. Twill-over-wood body. Swivel head, glass eyes. 11", c. 1885. Unmarked. Courtesy Theriault's.

Kid or Cloth Body

Size: 15"   Date: 1880
Price: $2,400–$3,000
Kid or sturdy original commercial muslin body.
Mark: E.B. or E 2 B

Kid Body

Size: 18"   Date: 1870s
Price: $5,900
In original clothing and wig. At auction.

Kid Body

Size: 23"   Date: 1870
Price: $3,000–$4,000
Swivel head, glass eyes.
Mark: E. 3 B.

Kid Body, Wooden Upper Arms

Size: 15"   Date: 1878
Price: $3,800
Bisque forearms.
Mark: 2 (head, shoulder plate)

Barrois Manner, Kid Body

Size: 12"   Date: 1865
All Markets: $1,600
Has Barrois look, pale bisque, chubby cheeks.
Unmarked.

Barrois Manner, Kid Body

Size: 15"   Date: 1865
All Markets: $1,800–$2,000
More with original clothing, wig.

Barrois Manner, Kid-over-Wood Body

Size: 18"   Date: 1860s–1870s
Price: $3,500
Bisque forearms.

Barrois Manner, Fortune-Teller

Size: 15"   Date: 1860s–1870s
Price: $3,150
Likely Barrois.

BRU FRENCH FASHION

Asian

Size: 15"
Price: $9,500
Fully articulated wood body. Attributed to Bru.

Black

Size: 14"   Date: 1875
Price: $19,000
Open mouth, swivel head. Attributed to Bru.
Mark: 2

Kid Body

Size: 13"   Date: late 1860s
Price: $3,000–$3,500
Pale bisque.
Mark: E (impressed)

Wood Body

Size: 15"   Date: 1870s
Price: $4,000–$4,700
Jointed only at shoulders, hips.

Poupée Criant

Size: 21"   Date: 1870
Price: $6,400–$7,500
Rare doll patented by Casimir Bru in 1867; kid-covered carton torso has a pull string mechanism to make doll talk.

Smiler, Cloth Body

Size: 15″   Date: 1870
Price: $2,700
Early muslin-stitched body, leather arms.
Mark: D

Smiler, Kid Body

Size: 13″   Date: 1868–1873
Price: $5,000
All original.

Smiler, Kid Body

Size: 15–16″   Date: 1868–1873
Price: $3,000–$4,000
Lower end of range for attributed dolls.
Mark: E (head, shoulder plate) or number

Smiler, Kid Body

Size: 28″   Date: 1868–1873
Price: $7,500
Mark: M (head) Deposé M (forehead)

Smiler, Kid Body, Wood Arms

Size: 17″   Date: 1870
Price: $4,250
Mark: E

Smiler, Wood Body

Size: 12″   Date: 1870
Price: $4,400
Body jointed at shoulders, elbows, hips, knees
only.
Mark: Deposé (forehead) 0

Smiler, Wood Body

Size: 15″   Date: 1870
Price: $5,200
Patented wood articulated body includes waist
and wrist joints. Fingers separately carved.
Mark: E (head, shoulder plate)

Smiler, Wood Body

Size: 16″   Date: 1870
Price: $4,500
Joints only at shoulders, hips, knees.
Mark: F Deposé (near front crown)

Smiler, Wood Body

Size: 17–20″   Date: 1870
Price: $5,000–$7,000
Patented fully jointed articulated body.
Mark: E (head, shoulder plate) or G (head) H
(shoulder plate)

FRANÇOIS GAULTIER FRENCH FASHION

Gesland Body

Size: 17–19″   Date: 1875
Price: $3,400–$4,500

Gesland bodies are made of cloth with inner
wire jointing, bisque lower arms and legs, bare
feet.

Gesland Body

Size: 20–24″   Date: 1875
Price: $3,600–$4,800
Mark: 5 or 7 (head) F.G. (shoulder plate) or un-
marked.

Kid Body

Size: 10–12″   Date: 1875–1880s
All Markets: $1,500–$2,000
Less for budget models with crude painting or
peppery bisque, simple cloth stitch-jointed bodies.
Mark: F.G (shoulder plate) 10/0 (top arms) or FG
in scroll

Kid Body

Size: 13–15″   Date: 1875–1880s
Price: $2,300–$2,800
Less for budget models with crude painting or
peppery bisque, simple cloth bodies or unjointed
kid.
Mark: F 1 G (back shoulder plate)

Kid Body

Size: 16–18″   Date: 1875–1880s
All Markets: $2,500–$3,000
Mark: F.G. (block letters, shoulder), or F.G. (in
scroll) 4.

Kid Body

Size: 24–28″   Date: 1875+
Price: $2,800–$3,600
Mark: F.G. 6 (head, shoulder plate)

Shoulder-Head, Kid Body

Size: 15–17″   Date: 1875+
Price: $1,200–$1,800
With minor flaws.
Mark: F 1 G (bottom shoulder plate)

Shoulder-Head, Kid Body

Size: 25″   Date: 1875+
Price: $3,200
For doll with great expression and outfit, pale
bisque.
Mark: F.G.

Shoulder-Head, Painted Eyes

Size: 8–12″   Date: 1870
Price: $1,000–$1,500
Kid or cloth body, mitten hands; less if crudely
painted.

Wood Body

Size: various   Date: 1870s
Price: $3,500–$4,500

HURET FRENCH FASHION DOLLS

Early Huret fashion dolls are also made of porcelain (china heads); prices are slightly lower for models with porcelain heads.

Blown Kid Body, Painted Eyes, Swivel Neck
Size: 17″　　　　　Date: 1860s
Price: $22,500

Gutta-percha Body, Painted Eyes, Shoulder-Head
Size: 17″　　　　　Date: 1860s
Price: $17,500
Gutta-percha is hardened rubber; very few bodies have survived. Often found with body flaws.
Mark: Huret Blvd Haussman mark (stamp)

Gutta-percha Body, Painted Eyes, Swivel Neck
Size: 17″　　　　　Date: 1860
Price: $25,000

Wood Body, Shoulder-Head, Painted Eyes
Size: 17″　　　　　Date: 1865
Price: $12,500

Wood Body, Shoulder-Head, Glass Eyes
Size: 18″　　　　　Date: 1865
Price: $9,000–$10,000
Original.
Mark: Huret 2 (head) Huret 88 Rue de al Boite (body)

Wood Body, Swivel Neck, Painted Eyes
Size: 18″　　　　　Date: 1866
Price: $11,000–$15,000
Body age often differs from head; bodies often replaced by Huret firm as they were damaged.
Mark: Medaille D'Argent Huret (body label)

Wood Body, Swivel Neck, Glass Eyes
Size: 17″　　　　　Date: 1867
All Markets: $17,000
Huret stamp on kid portion of chest.
Mark: Medaille D'Argent Huret (body label)

Kid Body, Painted Eyes, Swivel Neck
Size: 17″　　　　　Date: 1860s
Price: $9,500–$12,500
Later face, replaced body, later clothing.

Kid Body, Shoulder-Head, Painted Eyes
Size: 17″　　　　　Date: 1860s
Price: $11,000

JUMEAU FRENCH FASHION DOLLS

Cloth Body
Size: 19″　　　　　Date: 1868–1870s
Price: $2,000–$2,400

Sometimes with kid arms.
Mark: 4 (neck, bottom) 4 (right shoulder)

Kid Body
Size: 11–13″　　　　Date: 1868–1870s
Price: $2,200–$2,800

Kid Body
Size: 16–18″　　　　Date: 1875
Price: $2,600–$3,400
Later models with almond-cut eyes.
Mark: 3 (head and shoulder plate)

Kid Body
Size: 16–18″　　　　Date: 1860s
Price: $3,900+
For earlier desirable face, model.

Kid Body
Size: 19–22″　　　　Date: 1878
Price: $3,400–$4,000+
Varies greatly depending on face, sturdiness of body, outfit.
Body Mark: Jumeau Medaille d'Or Paris.
Mark: 7 (artist's checkmarks) or 9

Kid Body, Portrait Face
Size: 17–19″　　　　Date: 1875
Price: $4,000+
Mauve eye shadow.

Kid Body, Portrait Face
Size: 32″　　　　　Date: 1875
Price: $5,750
Exceptional size, mauve eye shadow.

Wood Body, Portrait Face
Size: 17″　　　　　Date: 1878
Price: $17,500
Exceptional. At auction.

Wood Body, Portrait Face
Size: 33″　　　　　Date: 1875
Price: $20,000
Exceptional. At auction.
Mark: 12

UNMARKED/UNKNOWN MAKER FRENCH FASHION DOLLS

Black, Kid Body, Open Mouth
Size: 17″　　　　　Date: 1870s
Price: $4,500
Open mouth with teeth.

Cup and Saucer Neck
Size: 14″　　　　　Date: 1865
Price: $5,000
Early doll, pale bisque, original.

Cup and Saucer Neck, Bisque Arms, Wardrobe

Size: 18″   Date: 1870
Price: $9,400

Kid Body, Exceptional Face

Size: 22″   Date: 1875
Price: $4,500
Exceptional face.
Mark: 6

Kid Body

Size: 12″   Date: 1868–1880s
Price: $1,500–$2,000
Less for kid with no gussets, painted eyes, crude painting, cloth bodies, new clothing; more for exceptional face or original couture outfit.

Kid Body

Size: 14–15″   Date: 1868–1880s
Price: $2,800–$3,200
Same as above listing.
Mark: 1 or 2 or unmarked.

Kid Body

Size: 16–18″   Date: 1868–1880s
Price: $2,800–$3,600
Same as above listing.
Mark: 4 or 6 or similar or unmarked.

Kid Body

Size: 20–24″   Date: 1868–1880s
Price: $3,000+

Kid-Over-Wood Body

Size: 15–18″   Date: 1870s
Price: $3,500–$4,200

Man, Kid Body

Size: 17–21″   Date: 1870s
Price: $4,600–$8,800
Sculpted to be man (not just dressed as man), sometimes with molded mustache and goatee or sculpted hair.

Shoulder Head

Size: 10–12″   Date: 1865–1875
Price: $800–$1,200
Generally less with painted eyes, cloth bodies, crude painting.
Mark: unmarked

Shoulder Head, Kid Body

Size: 16–18″   Date: 1865–1875
Price: $1,400–$2,200
Generally less with painted eyes, cloth bodies, crude painting.
Mark: unmarked

2-Faced, Shoulder Head

Size: 18″   Date: 1865
Price: $2,000
Possibly for display, identical double faces. Short wig.

Wood Body, Early, Pale Bisque

Size: 18″   Date: 1865
Price: $7,500
Pale bisque, unpierced ears, dowel-jointed articulated wood body, pivot joints at waist and thighs.
Mark: Sch (shield mark) (head and backside)

Wood Body

Size: 18″   Date: 1870
Price: $6,250
Fully articulated.
Mark: 4

Wood Body, Wardrobe

Size: 17.5″   Date: 1870
Price: $9,975
Elaborate wardrobe and provence.

Wood Mannequin

Size: 22″   Date: 1865
Price: $3,000
Joints include ankles and wrists, ball-jointed waist, inspiration for the wood fashion doll bodies of Bru and others.

FRENCH FASHION DOLLS, PORCELAIN (CHINA HEAD)

Porcelain French fashion dolls tend to be from the 1860s and are unmarked.

Shoulder Head, Kid Body, Glass Eyes

Size: 15–17″
Price: $2,500–$3,000+

Shoulder Head, Kid Body, Painted Eyes

Size: 13″
Price: $1,800+

Man, Kid Body

Price: $6,000
Painted black head, suit. Kid body.

Rohmer, Kid Body

Size: 14″
Price: $3,500+

Rohmer, Kid Body, Kid Over Wood Upper Arms

Size: 15″
Price: $4,500+

FRENCH FASHION DOLLS, BISQUE, OTHER KNOWN MAKERS

Blampoix

Size: 14″   Date: 1860
Price: $3,100
Kid body.

Clement, Blown Kid Body

Size: 17″   Date: 1866–1870
Price: $6,200–$6,400
Body based on Clement's 1869 patent.

Dehors, Portrait Face

Size: 18″   Date: 1870s
Price: $15,000
Bisque hands, exceptional portrait face.

Dehors, Trunk and Trousseau

Size: 15″   Date: 1861
Price: $7,000
Kid body, bisque arms, 5 exceptional original outfits.

Leverd, Alexandre

Size: 19″   Date: 1870
Price: $10,500
Price for doll with great damage, at auction; very rare. Kid over gutta-percha body.
Mark: E. Leverd Cie PARIS Brevete S.G.D.G (body) SGDG (head)

Lily from Lavalle-Peronne Shop

Size: 17″   Date: 1867
Price: $12,000
Wood body, original paper label. At auction.

Radiguet & Cordonnier

Size: 17″   Date: 1880
Price: $8,500
Bisque limbs; lower legs with hole modeled in bisque shoes for stand. At auction.
Mark: R.C. Deposé 2 (shoulder plate)

Rohmer, Swivel Neck

Size: 16″   Date: 1860
Price: $3,800–$4,500
Swivel neck, kid-over-wood upper arms, bisque lower arms.

Rohmer or Rohmer-Type, Shoulder Head

Size: 16″   Date: 1860
Price: $3,000+
Shoulder head, kid-over-wood upper arms, bisque lower arms.

Rohmer, Kid Body

Size: 18″   Date: 1860
Price: $4,000+
Cup and saucer neck, kid body, bisque arms, pale bisque.

FRENCH FASHION DOLL ACCESSORIES

Huret Pedestal Table (Gilded, Twisted Metal)

Size: 1865
Price: $1,600–$2,800
Miniature gilt cast-iron furniture identical to human-sized furniture produced by the Huret family.
Mark: Maison Huret stamp, table underside

Huret-Marked Shoes

Size: 1860s
Price: $1,200
Ankle strap flat-rosette square toe glazed brown kid shoes.
Mark: HURET a PARIS (stamp)

Ermine Tippet and Fur Muff

Size: 1870
Price: $265

Fur Muff in Original Box

Size: 1870
Price: $470
Green box labeled "A L'Hermine, Marseille" (furrier).

Fur-Covered White Dog

Size: late 1800s
Price: $450–$650
Sometimes candy container, spitz-type or Borosi white dog. Glass eyes.

Glove Case and 3 Pair Wrist-Length Gloves

Size: 1870
Price: $1,200
Case of Moroccan leather.

Gloves

Size: 1870
Price: $200–$300
White kid gauntlet-length.

Huret-Marked Boots

Size: 1865
Price: $1,900
Ice blue, high-laced, no tongues, scalloped top.
Mark: HURET a PARIS (stamp)

Shoes or Boots

Size: 1865–1880s
Price: $250
More for early or marked shoes or boots.

Tennis Racquet

Size: 1885
Price: $85

Turquoise Beaded Bracelet, Necklace, Earrings

Size: late 1800s
Price: $265

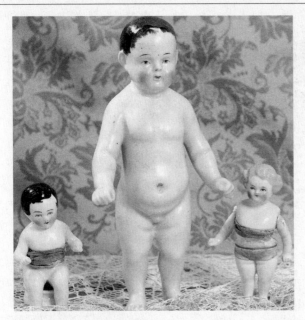

Frozen Charlotte with gold shoes. 3.5". Mark: 200 (back). $100, dealer.

Pink-tinted frozen Charlotte boy with 2 bellows dolls. Boy 8", c. 1875. Bellows 4.5", c. 1870. One bellows doll on potty, seated. Unmarked. Boy, $800 auction; Bellows dolls, $1,200 together, auction. Courtesy Theriault's.

Frozen Charlottes

There is something intrinsically charming about a Frozen Charlotte, with its simple, one-piece, unjointed body. However, it could be said that there is nothing very charming about how the doll received its name. The name of the doll is said to come from a folktale from the 1840s and a poem in the 1860s about a young socialite girl named Charlotte who froze to death, quite solid, on her way to a ball, wearing a gossamer gown.

Most Frozen Charlottes are made of china, but some are parian or crude bisque. Most were sold nude, some had molded clothing, some were sold dressed. Other tales and interesting uses surround the dolls. Some people called the dolls "teacup" dolls, and used the dolls at tea parties to help cool the tea by placing them in teacups—the doll was then a party favor for the guest to take home. Older ladies have told me that in the early part of the twentieth century, the tiny-size Frozen Charlottes were tied onto ribbons, baked into birthday cakes or puddings, and little girls would pull the ribbons out before the cake or pudding was eaten, keeping the dolls as favors. The dolls were made from the late 1800s through the 1920s.

Market Report: Frozen Charlottes are generally not expensive dolls, although some early dolls with "Alice"-type hair (short bob with a molded ribbon), and certain dolls with unusual modeling or hairstyles, or unusually colored painted boots can be valuable. Simple Frozen Charlottes can be inex-

"Birthday cake" or "pudding" frozen Charlottes. *These dolls would be baked inside cakes or puddings, with a ribbon attached that allowed a child to pull out the doll before eating; used as a birthday party favor. 1.5", c. early 1900s. $12–$30 (depends on quality, decoration), dealers & eBay.*

Frozen Charlotte as pincushion. *Original box and presentation. 4". $200, dealer.*

Frozen Charlotte penny bank. *Doll has slit in head for coins. 6", c. 1880. Courtesy Theriault's.*

pensive but delightful to display with other antique dolls. The market for these dolls is always steady, neither hot nor cold. Look for unusually large Frozen Charlottes with finely painted and modeled hair, pink-tinted Charlottes, and those with unusual molded clothes or other special painted or molded features.

Online/Offline Report: Frozen Charlottes can be found in ample supply on eBay and through dealers; prices for the very smallest Frozen Charlottes (under one inch) can be as little as $20 or less. Very crude, simple painted Frozen Charlottes of average size (say three to five inches) with simple hairstyles can sell for a fraction of the price that a Charlotte which is well-painted and with more intricate hair sells for.

Prices and Characteristics: Frozen Charlottes are porcelain (china doll-type) except as noted. Most Frozen Charlottes and Charlies are one piece, with painted black hair and features, with clenched fists and bare feet. Frozen Charlottes are generally unmarked, but sometimes marked "Germany" or with a number. Prices are for dolls in excellent condition, traditionally sold unclothed. Frozen Charlottes were made over a long period of time, from the 1850s through approximately

1920 and can be very difficult to individually date.

FROZEN CHARLOTTE

Classic, "Birthday Cake" or "Pudding" Size

Size: 1.25– 2"   Date: early 1900s
Price: $10–$20   Internet: $15–$25
These used to be baked into birthday cakes or puddings with strings attached, and children pulled out the dolls as favors before eating.

Classic, Black, "Birthday Cake" Size, Porcelain or Metal

Size: 1.25–2"   Date: early 1900s
Price: $10–$20   Internet: $10–$25
Lower part of range for metal black Frozen Charlottes.

Classic, Black Hair

Size: 2–3"
Price: $75–$100   Internet: $50–$75
High-color cheeks, bare feet, basic "flat top"-type hair, simple painting. More for dolls with painted shoes and socks, pink tint, better than average modeling or painting, etc.

Classic, Black Hair

Size: 4–5"
Price: $100–$145   Internet: $65–$100

Classic, Black Hair

Size: 6–7"
Price: $150+   Internet: $150+
Much more for larger sizes.

Classic, Gold Shoes and Blue-Rimmed Stockings
Size: 1.5″   Internet: $105

FROZEN CHARLOTTE, VARIATIONS

Bank
Size: 5.5″   Internet: $600
Very rare! Frozen Charlotte with shoulder-length hair, money slot in back. Most were broken by original owners to get their money out.

Blonde Hair, Gold Shoes
Size: 5″
Price: $75
Parian type with painted gold shoes.

Blonde, Gold Boots, With Mohair Ponytail
Size: 4.5″   Date: 1890s
                                    Internet: $245
Original hole in back of head with mohair ponytail lock of hair.

Charlie, Pink Tint
Size: 5″   Date: 1860
Price: $1,000
Entire body and face pink-tinted, hair, with brushstrokes, well painted.

Charlie, Pink Tint, Ears Exposed
Size: 7.5″   Date: 1860
Price: $645

Chubby Baby-Type Body
Size: 4.5″
Price: $375
Dressed.

Frozen Alice
Size: 4.5″   Date: 1865
Price: $825
Blonde molded hair with black Alice headband.

Frozen Charlie, Dressed in Tuxedo
Size: 4.25″   Date: 1850
Price: $525

Frozen Charlie, Pink-Tint Face, Blonde Hair
Size: 15″
Price: $800

Frozen Charlie, Pink Tint, Whole Body
Size: 16″
Price: $1,100
Entire doll pink tinted.

Frozen Charlie, Pink-Tinted Face
Size: 9.5″
Price: $300   Internet: $175–$225
White body, pink-tinted face only.

Frozen Charlie, Pink-Tinted Face
Size: 12–15″
Price: $525–$625+

Light Brown Hair, Plump Face
Size: 5″
Price: $350
Dressed.

Molded Bonnet, Tinted
Size: 3.75″   Date: mid-1800s
Price: $530
Attributed to Kister.

Molded Bonnet, Tinted
Size: 5″   Date: late 1800s
Price: $880
Attributed to Kister, bonnet has molded ribbon tied under chin.

Molded Boxer Shorts
Size: 6.5″   Internet: $160
With flaws; more if perfect porcelain.

Molded Clothing
Size: 4.5″   Internet: $225
Molded dress trimmed in blue.

Molded Clothing, Black
Size: 2.5″   Internet: $210
Molded dress trimmed in blue.

Pink Luster, Painted Light Brown Hair
Size: 12″
Price: $400

Pink Luster, Light Brown Hair
Size: 9″   Date: 1850s
Price: $550

Pink-Tinted, Arms Down at Sides
Size: 4.5″   Date: late 1800s
Price: $950
Hair with comb marks, pulled behind ears.

Stone Bisque, Painted Hat and Painted Boots
Size: 2.5″
Price: $45
Stone bisque type. Blue hat, red hat.

Googlies

Googlies, googly dolls, or googly-eyed dolls are a phenomenon of the early 20th century, from about 1912 on. There was never a particular doll sold as a "googly doll," but many dolls from the early 1900s had the popular googly-eyes. Googly-eyes are large, exaggerated, round side-glancing eyes. Googly dolls often, but not always,

Borgfeldt googly, "Oh You Flirt" (also known as "Hug Me Kiddie"). Composition mask face. 9″, c. 1910–1915. $400, eBay.

Armand Marseille googly 323. 7″, c. 1920. Mark: Germany / 323/A 10/0 M. $800, eBay.

Our Fairy and googly in blue pajamas. Our Fairy, jointed arms, sleep eyes. 8.5″, c. 1915. Mark: 222 / 22. Blue pajamas: 1-piece, 6″, c. 1920, unmarked. Courtesy Theriault's.

had a small, watermelon-shaped smiling mouth. Googly dolls became popular, and certainly were influenced, by the popularity of the Kewpie doll, a doll, with its exaggerated side-glancing eyes and watermelon smile, that can certainly be considered a googly in its own right. Googlies were made by many doll firms, mostly German, including Kestner, Armand Marseille and a host of others. Although you occasionally find large googlies, googlies tend to be small dolls, often under 12″ in height. Some were done in all-bisque, others had (sometimes crude) composition bodies. Besides the popular bisque googlies, you can find googlies made in almost any material—celluloid, painted bisque, composition, stone bisque and more.

Market Report: Googlies truly charm the socks off collectors today, and they seem to be a perenially hot category of dolls. There are googlies for every price range, from the rarest of the German molds which run several thousand dollars, to the simplest bisque carnival googly for under $20. Googlies are an often-reproduced doll, so be especially careful to examine googlies before purchase.

Online/Offline Report: The finest, rarest googlies tend to sell through doll dealers and auction houses, but you can find googlies at all price ranges through eBay and at doll shows, although the selection of googlies on

eBay is a bit more sparse than you might think. Beware of reproduction googlies that aren't sold as such.

Prices and Characteristics: All googlies are bisque socket heads, except as noted. Googlies can have glass or painted eyes, but always in an exaggerated round manner and generally side-glancing, with a closed, smiling mouth (assume glass eyes unless painted eyes are noted). They have molded and painted or wigged hair (mohair or human hair), with stationary or sleep eyes, all as individually noted. Most googlies come on chubby five-piece toddler composition or composition/papier-mâché bodies, and some can be very crude. Prices are similar from all venues. Most googlies were made from 1915 to 1925.

ALL-BISQUE GOOGLIES

With Original Box, Outfits
Size: 6.5″
Price: $1,000
Crude body, store box and wardrobe.
Mark: S. W. & Co. / 405 / 16

189, Glass Eyes
Size: 7″
Price: $1,250
Swivel head, jointed arms and legs, painted socks and black 1-strap shoes.
Mark: 189 0

Limbach googly. Socket head, 5-piece composition chubby body, in Becassine costume. 8″, c. 1920. Mark: SK / 8/0 / (crown and cloverleaf symbols). Courtesy Theriault's.

Kestner 221 googlies. Larger, 15″, smaller, 11″, c. 1912. Mark: (larger) F made in Germany / 10 / JDK 221 / Ges. Gesch. Larger doll, $6,500, smaller, $5,000. Courtesy Theriault's.

217, Glass Eyes
Size: 6–7″
Price: $1,000
1 piece head/torso, glass eyes, wigged, loop-jointed, painted socks, 1-strap shoes.
Mark: 217 18

218, Baby
Size: 6.5″
Price: $700
1 piece bisque head/torso, jointed arms, legs, loop-jointed, wigged, bare feet.
Mark: 218 16

111, Jointed Knees
Size: 7″
Price: $750
1-piece head/torso.
Mark: 111 (head and legs)

179, Painted Eyes
Size: 5″
Price: $600

Wigged, loop-jointed, painted socks, 1-strap black shoes.
Mark: 179 (inside limbs)

292, Glass Eyes
Size: 5″
Price: $725
Swivel head.
Mark: 292 Germany

ARMAND MARSEILLE GOOGLIES

Marseille, 200
Size: 9″
Price: $1,000–$1,400
Sleep eyes, wigged.
Mark: 200 A 10/0 M Germany

Marseille, 200
Size: 9″
Price: $1,600
Flirty eyes.

Kämmer & Reinhardt, 131 googlies. 15" and 16", c. 1915. Mark: K * R / Simon & Halbig / 131. $13,000 (boy), $12,000 (girl) auction. Courtesy Theriault's.

Marseille, 200
Size: 10"
Price: $3,000
Slant-hip toddler body. Wigged.

Marseille, 210
Size: 7"
Price: $250
Painted eyes, molded hair.
Mark: 210 A 10 M Germany

Marseille, 240, Topknot Googly
Size: 11–12"
Price: $2,500–$3,000
Molded topknot, glass eyes, 5-piece composition toddler body.
Mark: 240 / 7

Marseille, 252, Topknot Googly
Size: 8"
Price: $575
Molded topknot, 5-piece composition baby body, painted eyes/hair. For Borgfeldt.

Marseille, 252, Topknot Googly
Size: 11"
Price: $1,100
Mark: G.B. 252 Germany A 0 M

Marseille, 253
Size: 6–7"
Price: $700–$1,000
Crude 5-piece composition body. For Borgfeldt.
Mark: G 253 B / Germany A. 11/0 M

Marseille, 253
Size: 11–12"

Price: $2,400–$2,600
Mark: 253 G.B. Germany A 0 M DRMR

Marseille, 253
Size: 13.5"
Price: $3,600+
Sleep eyes, wigged.

Marseille, 255
Size: 8"
Price: $800–$900
Sleep eyes, open mouth with 2 teeth.

Marseille, 322
Size: 7"
Price: $200–$300
Painted hair and eyes.

Marseille, 323
Size: 7"
Price: $800–$900
Mohair wig, crude 5-piece composition toddler body, painted socks and shoes.
Mark: 323 Germany A 11/0 M

Marseille, 323
Size: 9"
Price: $900–$1,000
Mark: Armand Marseille Germany 323 A.6/0 M.

Marseille, 323
Size: 10"
Price: $1,300–$1,400

Marseille, Nobbi Kid
Size: 7"
Price: $1,000–$1,200

Wigged, 5-piece papier-mâché body with painted shoes, socks, Original paper label "Nobbi Kid Germany."
Mark: A 253 M Nobbi Kid Reg. U.S. Pat Off. Germany 11/0

GERMAN GOOGLIES—VARIOUS

Oscar Hitt, Black, Snowflake
Size: 3"
Price: $300
Moving eyes, 1-piece doll.
Mark: Snowflake copr. Oscar Hitt Germany

Demalcol
Size: 9–10"
Price: $650–$850
Sleep eyes, composition 5-piece baby or toddler body, wigged, body can be crude.
Mark: Demalcol / 5/0 / Germany

Demalcol
Size: 12"
Price: $1,100
Fully jointed composition body.
Mark: Demalcol / 5/0 / Germany

German, 455
Size: 8.5"
Price: $1,000
Sleep eyes, wigged.

Goebel
Size: 6.5"
Price: $400–$600
Painted eyes and hair.
Mark: Crown (over W) P 12/0 Germany

Handwerck, Helmet
Size: 12"
Price: $2,100
Sculpted helmet, glass eyes.
Mark: Dep Elite D 1

Handwerck, Military
Size: 11"
Price: $1,550
Original Uncle Sam outfit.
Mark: Dep Elite 1 USA

Steiner, Hermann, 133
Size: 9–10"
Price: $750
Flirty sleep eyes, wigged.
Mark: 133 H S Germany 3

Wislizenus
Size: 5.5"
Price: $3,600
Mark: AW

GEBRÜDER HEUBACH GOOGLIES

Heubach, Elizabeth
Size: 7"
Price: $2,500
Crude 5-piece body with painted socks and shoes, glass eyes.
Mark: Elizabeth 6/0 /Heubach (square)

Heubach, Various
Size: 7"
Price: $650
Very crude 5-piece body with unfinished torso.
Mark: 3/0/D / 90 Heubach (in square) 58

Heubach, Original Cossack Costume
Size: 7–9"
Price: $2,000–$2,800
All-original Cossack festival costume with elaborate jeweled headdress.
Mark: Heubach (square) Germany

"Einco" Googly
Size: 18"
Price: $13,500
Exhibition size, all-original. At auction.
Mark: 8723 Einco S Heubach (in square) Germany

Heubach, 10542
Size: 7–8"
Price: $700–$800
Composition 5-piece body with painted shoes and socks.
Mark: 10542 Heubach (square)

Heubach, 8556
Size: 16"
Price: $23,000
At auction. Painted eyes, looks aghast, sculpted hair.
Mark: 8556 Heubach (in square) Germany

Heubach, 8590
Size: 16"
Price: $12,000
Painted eyes.
Mark: 8590 Heubach (square)

Heubach, 9573
Size: 7–8"
Price: $850–$1,000
Sleep eyes, wigged, more for elaborate original costumes.
Mark: 9573 Heubach (square) Germany

Heubach, All-Bisque, 9542
Size: 4.5"
All Markets: $1,630
Pouty

Heubach, Googly-Type, Worried
Size: 10″
Price: $1,800
5-piece papier-mâché body.

Heubach, Topknot Googly
Size: 9″
Price: $1,700
Painted eyes, modeled and painted hair with topknot, pouty, 5-piece papier-mâché body with painted socks, shoes.
Mark: Heubach (square)

HERTEL, SCHWAB & CO. GOOGLIES

Hertel, Schwab
Size: 13″
Price: $1,775
Painted eyes.

Hertel, Schwab, 172, "Jubilee"
Size: 15″
Price: $6,750
Fully jointed side-hip toddler body.
Mark: 172 - 6

Hertel, Schwab, 165, "Jubilee"
Size: 10–12″
Price: $2,500–$3,000
Bent-limb baby body.
Mark: 165-1 or 165-2

Hertel, Schwab, 165, "Jubilee"
Size: 14″
Price: $4,300–$5,000
Fully jointed side-hip toddler body.
Mark: 165/4

Hertel, Schwab, 163, "Jubilee"
Size: 16″
Price: $5,500–$7,000
Sculpted hair, side-hip toddler body.
Mark: 163/6

Hertel, Schwab, 163, "Jubilee"
Size: 20–21″
Price: $25,000–$27,000
Wooden ball-jointed toddler body. Very large exhibition size, wigged hair.
Mark: 165-12 or 163-13

KÄMMER & REINHARDT, KESTNER GOOGLIES

Kämmer & Reinhardt, 131
Size: 9″
Price: $5,800
5-piece composition toddler body, side-hip jointing, watermelon smile and pug nose, mohair wig, starfish hands.
Mark: K * R Simon & Halbig 131

Kämmer & Reinhardt, 131
Size: 15–16″
Price: $10,000–$13,000
Mark: K * R Simon & Halbig 131

Kestner, 221
Size: 10–11″
Price: $3,700–$4,800
5-piece toddler body, side-hip joints, watermelon smile, pug nose, mohair wig.
Mark: A made in Germany 5 JDK 221 Ges Gesch.

Kestner, 221
Size: 13″
Price: $6,000+
Mark: C 7 JDK 221 Ges Gesch

Kestner, 221
Size: 15″
Price: $6,500+
Mark: F made in Germany 10 JDK 221 Ges Gesch.

RECKNAGEL GOOGLIES

Recknagel, 45
Size: 6–8″
Price: $250–$300
Painted eyes and hair, 5-piece crude body.
Mark: R 45 A

Recknagel, 46, Headband
Size: 7″
Price: $600
Painted eyes and hair, headband, 5-piece papier-mâché body with painted white socks and green 1-strap shoes.
Mark: R 46 A 11/0

S.F.B.J. GOOGLIES

S.F.B.J. Model 245
Size: 8″
Price: $1,800–$2,600
Mark: 0

GOOGLY DOLLS, OTHER MATERIALS

Cloth Mask Face
Size: 9″
Price: $500
Cloth and composition mask face googlies are from the 1920s.
Mark: unmarked

German half doll. *Porcelain, arms away, molded flowers in hair, original base and costume. 3.5". Private collection. Courtesy Ellen Johnson.*

Dressel, Kister half doll from Medieval series. *Cloth lower torso and porcelain legs attached to porcelain chair. Porcelain, 8.5" seated, c. 1910. Unmarked. $3,700, auction. Courtesy Theriault's.*

German wigged half dolls. *Arms away. 4.5–6", c. 1920s. Courtesy Theriault's.*

Composition, Mask Face, Oh My Flirt

Size: 10–12"
Price: $450–$550
Oh My Flirt or similar type. Pink cloth felt body jointed at shoulders and hips. Mohair fabric wig.
Mark: unmarked

Composition, Mask Face

Size: 14–15"
Price: $1,100

Composition, Mask Face

Size: 10"
Price: $850
5-piece felt body with working crier, pristine mint.
Mark: unmarked

Half Dolls

Half dolls have a fascinating place in doll history. Half dolls were not playthings for children, as were most dolls created before the advent of the modern collectible doll, but dolls made to decorate useful items that were mostly used by ladies. The dolls were generally unjointed, molded from the waist up, and with sew-holes or another means of securing the dolls to their useful item, be it a pincushion, powder puff, tea cozy, or lamp. The majority of half dolls decorated items used on ladies' dressing tables from the late 1900s through the 1920s. Almost all represented ladies, from Victorian through Flapper styles.

Half dolls were made overwhelmingly by German firms, although lesser-quality Japanese half dolls from the early 1900s abound, and there have been half dolls found by American and French makers as well. Half dolls can be done in china or bisque. Most half dolls are unmarked except for the country of origin and perhaps a mold number, but certain firms such as Goebel (crown mark) and Dressel, Kister & Co. sometimes did mark their half dolls.

Market Report: Prices and quality on these dolls vary wildly. Certain rare Dressel, Kister & Co. figures, Ernst Bohne & Söhne figures, figures with unusual modeling and painting of clothing, and figures holding unusual items can bring four figures; common, arms-molded-to-sides, and crudely painted examples from Japan can be worth only $20 to $30. When buying half dolls, look for exceptional decoration and painting. Half dolls holding interesting items are sought after, as are dolls with arms away from the body—these dolls were more intricate to make, and because of their delicacy, many have broken over time. One "arm away" is good, two "arms away" is better. And an arm away holding something like a parrot or a doll is fantastic.

Online/Offline Report: There is a good supply of these dolls on Internet auction sites;

Half doll. *Painted bisque. 9″, including base. Private collection. Courtesy Ellen Johnson.*

Hertwig half dolls as powder boxes. *Porcelain from waist up, porcelain lower legs. 5″, c. 1920s. Courtesy Theriault's.*

you can even find very rare models. Prices are comparable for dealers, shows, and the Internet except for the most common, simple models which can be found in abundance on eBay, and at very low prices. Dealers tend to handle better examples overall.

Prices and Characteristics: It is very difficult to price half dolls because there is such a huge variety. Small differences in modeling and painting, arm position, and extras such as items held, modeled clothing and hats, etc., can mean large differences in prices.

All half dolls listed here are made of porcelain (china doll glazed type) and are in excellent condition, except as noted. Nearly all are from 1910 to the 1920s with a few earlier and a few from the early 1930s, when their popularity declined. The half dolls with prices listed here are made in Germany, except as

noted. Generally examples of lesser quality are made in Japan, although German factories also produced lesser quality models with crude painting and simple modeling. "ORA" means "open and returning arm."

Marks: Half dolls are often unmarked. If marked, they may be marked "Made In Germany" or "Germany." Sometimes they are marked with a four-digit number (with or without the "Germany" mark). Certain companies such as Dressel, Kister & Co. or Goebel have the half dolls marked with their mark, sometimes on the inner rim of the piece.

PORCELAIN HALF DOLL, ARMS CLOSE

Germany, Arms Close, Simple Decoration, Various

Size: 2–4″
Price: $40–$70   Internet: $40–$70

German half dolls, porcelain.
Later; common quality. Arms
close. 3". Mark: Germany (back).
$30, dealer.

Prices for the most simply painted and simply modeled half dolls, sometimes holding rose, fan, or simple object. Slightly more for larger.

Japan, Arms Close, Simple Decoration, Various

Size: 2–6"
Price: $15–$30   Internet: $15–$30
Made in Japan. Common, simple painting and style, sometimes holding rose or other simple object.

Dutch Girl

Size: 4.5"   Internet: $145
Chunky girl.

Flapper, Holding Fan

Size: 4.5"   Internet: $195

Garden Party Girl

Size: 6.5"   Internet: $210
Red molded hat and red and white molded outfit, light green trim.

Holding Puppy

Size: 4"
Price: $1,100
7590.

Holding Rose, Fancy Ruffled Blouse

Size: 4.75"
Price: $150
Hat with plume.

PORCELAIN HALF DOLL, OPEN AND RETURNING ARMS (ORAS)

Germany, ORAs, Various

Size: 2–4"
Price: $50–$125   Internet: $50–$125
For nicely painted but common styles. Higher prices in range for molded clothing, hat, holding common object. Much more for better examples, rarer, or marked half dolls; see examples.

Germany, ORAs, Various

Size: 4–6"
Price: $100–$150   Internet: $100–$150
For nicely painted but common styles. Higher prices in range for molded clothing, hat, holding common object.

Japan, ORAs, Various

Size: 2–6"
Price: $25–$40   Internet: $25–$40
Made in Japan. Common, simple painting and styles.

Chocolate Lady

Size: 5.25"
Price: $275

Ernst Bohne & Söhne, Elaborate Blouse and Hat With Painted, Applied Flowers

Size: 6.5"
Price: $5,000
At auction.

Flower Basket, Fancy Blouse, Hat, 9196

Size: 5.5"
Price: $5,000
At auction.

Galluba & Hoffmann, Chocolate Girl

Size: 5"   Internet: $465
Holds cup of hot chocolate; price for piece with
flaws.

Goebel Chocolate Lady, Holding Tray With Pot, Cups

Size: 3.75"
Price: $2,250
Painted roses on clothing.

Large Cape, Muff, Floral-Painted Blouse, Hand-Stroke Hair

Size: 5.5"
Price: $4,000
At auction.

Lavinia, 9331, Tray of Fruit, Fancy Hair Piece

Size: 5.5"
Price: $4,500
At auction.

Large Hat, Plumes, 3319

Size: 4.5"
Price: $2,500

Pincushion, 22409, Holding Book, With Legs

Size: 4.25"
Price: $300
Separate legs attached to pincushion.

Pincushion, Flapper, With Legs

Size: 3.75"
Price: $200
Separate legs attached to pincushion.

Pincushion, Shawl and Hair Bow

Size: 7.75"
Price: $400

Tennis Player, Art Deco

Size: 4.5"   Internet: $270

PORCELAIN HALF DOLL, ARMS AWAY

Germany, Arms Away, Various

Size: 3–5"
Price: $175–$300   Internet: $175–$300
For most common styles, well painted, may have
modeled features or holding objects. Less for
dolls with crude painting. Much more for better
examples, rarer, or marked; see examples.

Dresden, Holding Rose

Size: 4.75"
Price: $3,250
Hand-stroke painted hair with plume, ruffled
blouse. At auction.

Ernst Bohne & Söhne, Holding Flowers, Applied Hair Flowers

Size: 3.75"
Price: $1,000

Ernst Bohne & Söhne, Fingers Folded

Size: 4.25"
Price: $2,500
Flowers applied to blouse and hair.

Fancy Floral Painted Blouse

Size: 6"
Price: $4,250
Number 9310.

Goebel, Flowers in Hair

Size: 4.75"   Internet: $310

Holding Fan With Fancy Hat.

Size: 6.25"
Price: $1,100

Holding/Reading Letter

Size: 4.5"   Internet: $365
Nude, hair piled on head in curls.

Karl Schneider, 14972, Nude With Necklace

Size: 4"
Price: $600

Pincushion, Holding Rose, Nude, Bonnet With Bow

Size: 6.25"
Price: $1,750
Hand-stroke painted hair.

Pincushion, Necklace, Nude

Size: 6.5"
Price: $1,100

Volkstedt-Rudolstadt, Fancy Ruffled Blouse, Hair Bows

Size: 5.5"
Price: $3,250

With Legs, Cloth Body, Fancy Gray Hair

Size: 14"
Price: $900
In original clothing.

With Legs, Cloth Body, Fancy Gray Hair

Size: 15"
Price: $1,000
In original clothing.

PORCELAIN HALF DOLL, ARMS MIXED

Germany, 1 arm close, 1 arm ORA, or Other Arm Mix; Simple Decoration, Various
Size: 2–4"
Price: $50–$125   Internet: $40–$125
Arms: mixed
For common styles, simple painting and modeling. Sometimes with modeled bodice or hat, simply painted and decorated. Much more for better, rarer, or marked half dolls; see examples.

Japan, Common Styles, Various
Price: $20–$50   Internet: $20–$50
Arms: mixed
For common styles, simple painting and modeling.

Ernst Bohne & Söhne, Holding Flowers
Size: 3.5"
Price: $1,750
Arms: 1 arm away, 1 ORA
Fancy blouse.

Ernst Bohne & Söhne, Holding Pen and Tablet, Elaborate Blouse
Size: 5.75"
Price: $3,500
Arms: 1 arm away, 1 ORA
Elaborate floral painted blouse and large hat with bow. At auction.

Fancy Blouse, Hat With Bows, Plume, Hand-Stroke Painted Hair
Size: 6.25"
Price: $5,000
Arms: 1 arm away, 1 arm close
At auction.

Fur and Beads, Roses, 6717
Size: 4"
Price: $350
Arms: 1 ORA, 1 arm close

Gibson Girl, Holding Yellow Roses
Size: 4.5"   Internet: $525
Arms: 1 away arm, 1 arm close
Hands hold yellow roses, molded clothes and hat, molded flowers.

Holding Doll
Size: 4.25"   Internet: $1,100
Arms: 1 arm away, 1 ORA. Holding porcelain clown doll.

Pincushion, Fancy Hat
Size: 7.25"
Price:$600
Arms: 1 arm away, 1 ORA

Pincushion, Holding Fan, Tall Hair with Hat, Nude
Size: 6.25"
Price: $1,100
Arms: 1 arm away, 1 ORA

Wigged, Molded Clothes, Art Deco
Size: 4"   Internet: $300
Arms: 1 arm away, 1 ORA

PORCELAIN HALF DOLLS—DRESSEL, KISTER

The Dressel, Kister & Co. mark looks like a blue "9" with a swirly top and some small spikes, with a small blue mark beside it. Not all Dressel, Kister half dolls are marked—identifying features include a tapered and not flared waist/base and beautifully detailed palms of hands—you can often see the palm lines in the modeled hands (although this is not enough to identify a Dressel, Kister, as other fine German half dolls also had this feature).

Dressel, Kister, Various
Size: 4–7"
Price: $250–$500   Internet: $200–$400
Arms: various
For most common styles, much more for examples with exquisite modeling, unusual dolls, unusual accessories or clothing. See examples.

Hand-Stroke Hair, Nude
Size: 5"
Price: $4,500
Arms: arms away
At auction.

Hand-Stroke Hair, Nude
Size: 6"
Price: $3,250
Arms: arms away
At auction.

Hand-Stroke Hair, Mme. Mole Raymond
Size: 8.5"
Price: $5,000
Arms: arms away
Large hat with bow, long flowing hair, nude, china legs, with base.

Hand-Stroke Hair, Pincushion, Holding Letter, Nude
Size: 7.5"
Price: $2,500

Arms: arms away
Hat with plume.

Holding Hands, Art Deco
Size: 3″   Internet: $250
Arms: close
Black painted hair, not molded, simple face painting.

Holding Parrot
Size: 4.5″   Internet: $1,500
Arms: away
In pointed hat, parrot perched on arm.

Holding Rose, Applied Hair Flowers, Nude
Size: 5.5″
Price: $1,600
Arms: away
Exceptional modeling.

Holding Rose, Applied Roses In Hair
Size: 2″
Price: $275   Internet: $250
Arms: away

Holding Rose, Molded Hat
Size: 3.5″   Internet: $325
Arms: away

Holding Yellow Flower
Size: 4″   Internet: $350
1 arm ORA, 1 arm away
Mark: 4767/7.

Medieval Male
Size: 5.5″   Internet: $5,385
Mint; 12.5″ long. Magnificent piece including original chair, outfit, velvet pants, porcelain falcon on hand. eBay auction.

Pierrot, Folded Hands, Nude
Size: 5″
Price: $2,250
Arms: ORAs

Pierrot, With Mandolin, Nude
Size: 4.5″
Price: $4,500
Arms: ORAs
At auction.

GERMAN HALF DOLLS, OTHER MATERIALS

Arms Away, Molded Brown Hair and Comb
Size: 5″
Price: $200
Material: bisque

Dressel, Kister, Jointed Arms
Size: 8.5″
Price: $3,700
Material: bisque
Adult lady with modeled bosom, jointed arms, cloth lower torso and porcelain legs, attached in seated position on porcelain chair, elaborate medieval headdress. One of rarest half dolls.

German, Medieval Lady
Size: 6″
Price: $475
Material: bisque
Crudely painted, downcast eyes, simple costume.

Goebel, Lamp Pair, Arms Away Holding Ring
Size: 15″
Price: $4,250
Material: bisque
Mohair wigs, ceramic base with molded legs, wire frame. At auction.

Jointed Arms, Nude, Wigged
Size: 6.5″   Internet: $250
Material: bisque

With Legs, Cloth Body, Arms Away, Fancy Gray Hair
Size: 14″
Price: $1,200
Material: bisque
Original clothing.

Wire Frame
Size: 16″
Price: $75
Material: composition
Attached arms.

Powder Box, Wigged, Attached Arms
Size: 7.5″
Price: $100   Internet: $75–$100
Material: composition

Wax-Over-Composition, Wire Frame
Size: 16″
Price: $20–$30   Internet: $20–$30
Material: composition
Very good, attached arms.

Handwerck, Heinrich

Heinrich Handwerck was one of the most prolific of the German bisque dollmakers, making countless dolly-faced dolls. Their dolls were produced from 1876 through the

Heinrich Handwerck, Child 109.
Jointed composition body. 18", c. 1900. Mark: 109-10 _ / Germany / Handwerck / 2/12. $650, auction.

Heinrich Handwerck, Child 99.
Jointed composition body. 22", c. 1900. Mark: 11 _ / 99 / DEP / Germany / Handwerck / Halbig.

Heinrich Handwerck, Child 99.
Jointed composition body. 24", c. 1900. Mark: 14 / 99 dep. Courtesy Theriault's.

1920s. Many of the dolls were made using Simon & Halbig bisque heads.

Market Report: Just like with Armand Marseille and Cuno & Otto Dressel dolls, many antique doll collections begin with a Handwerck doll. Therefore, although these dolls are very common, the best examples are still sought after.

A few of the closed-mouth and largest size of the Handwerck dolls bring over $1,000, but the vast majority of these dolls can be purchased for a few hundred dollars. Prices for Heinrich Handwerck dolls have declined somewhat in recent years, but now appear to be holding steady.

Online/Offline Report: Many bargains can be found for the most common of these dolls on eBay and at other internet auction sites. At auction houses and from doll dealers, look for all-original dolls with original wigs, clothing, and body finish, which will bring premium prices.

Prices and Characteristics: All prices are for Heinrich Handwerck dolls from molds 69, 79, 89, 99, 109, or 119 or dolls marked with no mold number, generally marked: Germany / Heinrich Handwerck / Simon & Halbig / 6 or Handwerck Germany 3 or something similar; further examples are given below. Bodies may be stamped "Heinrich Handwerck" in red on back of torso. Dolls have open mouths, fully jointed composition bodies, sleep or set glass eyes, wigs with mohair or human hair. The vast majority of dolls listed here are from the 1890s through 1910. Prices are from all venues.

HEINRICH HANDWERCK

Child
Size: 11–12″
Price: $400–$500
Mark: 79 / 3x / HH / Germany

Child (harder to find size)
Size: 14–16″
Price: $550–$700

Child
Size: 17–18″
Price: $450–$650
Mark: Germany / Heinrich Handwerck / Simon & Halbig / I

Child
Size: 20–23″
Price: $450–$600
Mark: 79 10 Germany or 119 - 10 1/4 x / Handwerck / Germany

Child
Size: 24–27″
Price: $500–$700

Hertel, Schwab & Co., Character Baby 142. Painted hair, composition bent-limb baby body. 10", c. 1915. Mark: 142 / 1. Courtesy Theriault's.

Googly 165. Composition bent-limb baby body. 14", c. 1915. Mark: 165 – 5. Courtesy Theriault's.

Mark: Germany / Heinrich Handwerck / Simon & Halbig / 4 or 69 12.X Germany Handwerck 4

Child, Shoulder Head
Size: 28"
Price: $350

Child, 99, DEP
Size: 28"
Price: $775
Mark: 99/15 / DEP

Child
Size: 28–29"
Price: $600–$800
Mark: 109 / 15 1/2 Handwerck Germany 6 1/2 or Germany / Heinrich Handwerck / Simon & Halbig / 5

Child
Size: 30–31"
Price: $650–$850
Mark: Germany / Heinrich Handwerck / Simon & Halbig/6 1/2

Child
Size: 32"
Price: $850–$1,300

Child
Size: 41–42"
Price: $3,500–$4,500
Mark: Germany Handwerck

Hertel, Schwab & Co.

Hertel, Schwab & Co. was a later-to-the scene German bisque dollmaker specializing in character children and babies. Its characterized baby dolls are easily recognizable, even by beginning collectors. The company produced dolls from 1910 through the early 1930s.

Market Report: Beginning doll collectors especially enjoy the reasonably priced Hertel, Schwab & Co. character baby dolls, although more advanced collectors enjoy their well-modeled features as well. Prices on these dolls are generally holding steady, with prices on the most popular baby molds and character children increasing slightly.

Online/Offline Report: Lesser-quality Hertel, Schwab & Co. dolls abound on eBay, often at prices less than found in most price guides, but the best examples and rarer character children can be found via dealers and auction houses.

Prices and Characteristics: Hertel, Schwab & Co. dolls have bisque heads and glass eyes. Character babies have five-piece bent-limb composition baby bodies and open/closed mouths generally with a modeled tongue. Most of the dolls listed here were made from

1912 to 1915 and into the 1920s. For googlies, see the "Googlies" section.

HERTEL, SCHWAB & CO.

All-Bisque, 208, Prize Baby
Size: 7"
Price: $400
Sleep eyes, wigged.

Character Baby, 125
Size: 12–13"
Price: $450–$650
Solid-dome head with painted hair.
Mark: 125/2

Character Baby, 142
Size: 10"
Price: $600
Solid-dome head with painted hair.
Mark: 142 1

Character Baby, 142
Size: 12–13"
Price: $450–$550

Character Baby, 142
Size: 18"
All Markets: $650
On side-hip jointed toddler body.

Character Baby, 150
Size: 12"
Price: $350
Wigged.
Mark: made in Germany / 150

Character Baby, 151
Size: 10"
Price: $250–$300
Solid-dome head with painted hair.

Character Baby, 151
Size: 18–22"
Price: $400–$550
Mark: Made in Germany / 151 /11

Character Baby, 151
Size: 24+"
Price: $1,000
On side-hip jointed toddler body, all original.

Character Baby, 152
Size: 10"
Price: $250–$350
Wigged.
Mark: Made in Germany / 152 / 0

Character Baby, 152
Size: 14–16"
Price: $400–$500
Mark: Made in Germany / 152 / 10

Character Baby, 152
Size: 18–22"
Price: $500–$700
Mark: Made in Germany / 152 / 14

Character Baby, 152
Size: 33"
Price: $1,000
Solid-dome head with painted hair.

Child, 136
Size: 13"
Price: $225
Wigged, sleep eyes, open mouth with teeth, fully jointed composition body.

Child, 136
Size: 22–23"
Price: $275–$375
Mark: Made in Germany 136/9

Child, Character, 149
Size: 19"
Price: $8,000
Wigged, fully jointed composition body. At auction.

Child, Character, 149
Size: 28"
Price: $10,250
At auction.
Mark: 149

Hertwig

Much has come to light in the last few years about the production of dolls from Hertwig & Co. An auction in 2000 by the Theriault's auction house, which auctioned original factory samples from the Hertwig family, helped collectors attribute many unmarked bisque dolls and bisque novelties to the Hertwig company. Further research is taking place in Germany by researchers such as Mary Gorham Krombholz. The prolific production from this firm includes many all-bisque dolls, bonnet-head dolls, china dolls, miniature dolls, half dolls, Snow Babies, bathing beauties, nodders, and much more. Dolls and other bisque items were produced by Hertwig from the early 1860s through the late 1930s, with the majority of the items priced here produced from 1890 on.

Market Report: Collectors really enjoy these dolls, and many of their bisque items which are not dolls nevertheless fit in well with a display of antique dolls from the same time

Hertwig all-bisque babies. 1-piece head/torsos; original costumes. 4.5", c. 1935. Unmarked, from Hertwig factory. Courtesy Theriault's.

Original Hertwig factory sample card of all-bisque dolls. Shows Kewpie-type carnival dolls and all-bisque babies produced by factory, c. 1920.

Hertwig all-bisque children. All 1-piece, the pairs are joined. Original costumes. 2–3", c. 1920. Unmarked, from Hertwig factory. Courtesy Theriault's.

period. It's a rare general antique doll collection that doesn't have a few items from Hertwig hiding somewhere.

Dolls from this company range from exquisite bonnet-head dolls and bathing beauties to very common and low-quality all-bisques. Prices for better-quality and newly identified items are increasing, while prices for the crudest all-bisque babies and other lower-quality items are stagnant. Some of the lowest-quality dolls were originally thought to be unmarked all-bisques from Japan (marked on the box originally but not on the doll) but are actually from Hertwig.

Online/Offline Report: Many items from this company are unmarked and if you educate yourself, you can find unmarked gems at online auctions for low prices. Almost every dealer has a small selection of smaller

bisque items from this company, and you can find many Hertwig items on eBay (not always identified as Hertwig) at any one time.

Prices and Characteristics; Marks: Most dolls are unmarked, marked "Germany," or marked with a number. All dolls are in excellent condition except as noted. Most items priced here are from 1890 to 1930. These prices represent only a fraction of the items produced by Hertwig.

HERTWIG

Bonnet Head Doll
Size: 9"
Price: $225
Material: bisque
Butterfly molded bonnet, crudely painted features, shoulder head on cloth body.
Mark: 203.

Ernst Heubach child, 275. Kid
body, bisque lower arms. 11".
Mark: 275 / (illegible)/ (horseshoe
mark). $125, eBay.

Ernst Heubach Black child.
Painted hair, composition bent-
limb baby body. 13". Mark:
Heubach Koppelsdorf / 399 12/0 /
Germany. $450, dealer.

Bonnet Head Doll
Size: 16.5"
Price: $210
Material: parian
Molded red hat, painted features, shoulder head
on muslin body, porcelain lower limbs, molded
necklace.
Mark: 205.

Figure, Boy With Bunny
Size: 9.5"
Price: $1,100
Material: bisque

Hertwig, "Swimming" Doll
Size: 3"
Price: $75
Material: all-bisque
Comes as male or female in painted swim wear.
Arms jointed.
Mark: Germany.

Hertwig, 1-Piece Head/Torso, Painted Eyes
Price: $50–$65
Material: all-bisque
Crude bisque, brown paint on shoes often rubs
off, white socks.
Mark: 20-11-made in Germany.

Hertwig, Boy, Molded Hair
Size: 7.5"
Price: $100
Material: all-bisque
Pink-tinted bisque, painted black shoes with
blue socks, 1-piece head/torso.

Hertwig, Character-Type Face, Painted Eyes, Molded Hair
Size: 8"
Price: $120
Material: all-bisque
1-piece head/torso, side-glancing eyes.

Hertwig, Molded Hair and Clothes
Size: 4"
Price: $100
Material: all-bisque
Pin-jointed arms, painted side-glancing eyes,
pouty expression, molded and painted uniform.

Hertwig, Native American, Molded Clothing
Size: 7.5"
Price: $120
Material: all-bisque
Jointed arms only, lesser quality, painted hair,
headdress, and clothing.

Heubach, Ernst
(Koppelsdorf Mark)

Maker of mostly lower-quality bisque dolls
in Germany from the late 1880s through the
early 1930s. Production included shoulder-
head bisque dolls and simple character children.

Market Report: Ernst Heubachs are definitely good dolls for the beginning antique
doll collector on a budget! Sweet dolly-faced
shoulder-head dolls, baby dolls, and small
toddler dolls can be purchased for under

$300. Prices for these dolls have declined slightly in the last few years.

Online/Offline Report: You can find definite eBay bargains here, and dealers will often have one or two Ernst Heubachs available for their beginning collectors. Individual sellers will often list the dolls by their mark and not their name, as a "Heubach Koppelsdorf" doll.

Prices and Characteristics: Dolls have bisque heads and fully jointed composition bodies (babies have five-piece composition bent-limb bodies, toddlers have side-hip jointed five-piece composition bodies). All dolls have glass eyes and mohair or human hair wigs, and open mouths. Prices are similar from all venues. Most dolls listed here were produced from the 1890s to 1920 (character dolls starting in approximately 1915).

ERNST HEUBACH, CHARACTER BABY DOLLS

Baby, 267
Size: 14"
Price: $500
Open mouth with teeth, wigged.

Baby, 300
Size: 8–9"
Price: $125–$150
Open mouth with teeth, wigged.

Baby, 300
Size: 13–15"
All Markets: $300–$400
Baby body.
Mark: Heubach / 300 3/0 / Koppelsdorf / Thuringia

Baby, 300
Size: 17–19"
Price: $400–$500

Baby, 300
Size: 22"
Price: $500+

Baby, 320
Size: 15"
Price: $375
Baby body.

Baby, 321
Size: 16"
Price: $400

Can be "breather" with open nostrils (nostril holes pierced in bisque).

Baby, 342
Size: 24"
Price: $400

Baby, 342
Size: 27"
Price: $750
Very large size of this baby, baby body.
Mark: 342-11 / Germany

Baby, 399, Black
Size: 9–10"
Price: $275–$325
South Seas Series. Closed mouth, solid dome, painted hair, pierced ears.
Mark: Original paper label: "South Sea Baby-Made in Germany." Heubach / Koppelsdorf / 399 / 13/0 / DRGM / Germany

Baby, 399, Black
Size: 12"
Price: $550
South Sea Series. Closed mouth, solid dome, painted hair.
Mark: Heubach Koppelsdorf 399 6/0 Germany DRGM

Baby, 452
Size: 12.5"
Price: $500
South Seas Series. Closed mouth, solid dome, painted hair.
Mark: Heubach Koppseldorf 452 10/0 Germany

Baby, 463, Black
Size: 9"
Price: $575
South Seas Series. Open mouth, solid dome, painted hair.
Mark: Heubach Koppelsdorf 463 15/0 Germany DRGM

ERNST HEUBACH, CHILD DOLLS

Child, 1900, Shoulder Head
Size: 20"
Price: $275–$325
Gusset-jointed kid body, bisque lower limbs.
Mark: (horseshoe mark)

Child, 1902, Shoulder Head
Size: 19"
Price: $275–$325
Gusset-jointed kid body, bisque lower limbs.
Mark: 1902.8 made in Germany/ (horseshoe)

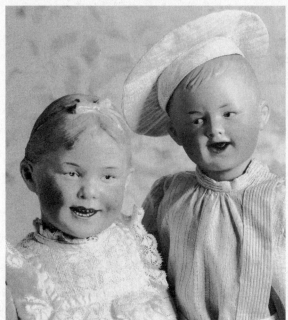

Gebrüder Heubach Dolly Dimple and Laughing Character. Dolly Dimple (on left): 12″, c. 1910. Laughing Character, 14″, c.1912. Both, jointed composition and wood body. Marks: Dep Dolly Dimple H Germany Heubach (in sunburst); illegible model # on other. Laughing Character, $700; Dolly Dimple $2,200, auction. Courtesy Theriaults.

Gebrüder Heubach Laughing Character Girl 8050 and 1911 Character. Both, composition and wood jointed body. Both 16″, 1912. Mark (girl): Heubach (square). Mark (boy): 7911 / Heubach (square) / Germany. Courtesy Theriault's.

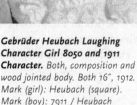

Child, 250
Size: 9″
Price: $175–$250
5-piece composition body.

Child, 250
Size: 16–20″
Price: $300–$350
Sleep eyes, 4 teeth.
Mark: Heubach / 250-1 /Koppseldorf

Child, 250
Size: 24–28″
Price: $300–$450
Fully jointed composition body.

Child, 251
Size: 22″
Price: $500
Mark: Heubach Koppelsdorf / 251

Child, 275
Size: 11″
All Markets: $150–$175
Shoulder head on kid body.

Child, Character, 312
Size: 14–15″
All Markets: $400–$450
Ernst Heubach for Seyfarth & Reinhardt.
Mark: Heubach Koppelsdorf / 312 / SuR / 50x / Germany

ERNST HEUBACH, TODDLER CHARACTER DOLLS

Toddler, 267
Size: 28″
Price: $600
Flirty eyes, open mouth, toddler body.
Mark: Heubach / 267 * 11/Koppelsdorf / D.R.G.M / Thuringia

Toddler, 320
Size: 9″
Price: $200–$275
On 5-piece toddler body, also made in painted bisque (lower prices).
Mark: Heubach * Koppelsdorf / 320 * 4/0 / Germany

"Action" babies. 1-piece bisque. 5–6". Mark: (impressed Heubach square). $1,200, pair, at auction. Courtesy Theriault's.

Baby Stuart, character with glass eyes. Composition and wood jointed body. 13", c. 1915. Mark: 7975 / Heubach (sunburst mark) / Germany. Courtesy Theriault's.

Heubach Coquette all-bisque. 1-piece head/torso. 8", c. 1920. Mark: 10499. $650, auction. Courtesy Theriault's.

Toddler, 320
Size: 12–15"
Price: $300–$375
Dolls can be "breathers" with open nostrils. Wig, sleep eyes, 5-piece composition toddler body. Mark: Heubach Koppelsdorf / 320-12/0 / Germany

Toddler, 342
Size: 8–9"
Price: $125
Painted bisque, 5-piece composition toddler body, wigged.

Toddler, 342
Size: 13"
Price: $270

Heubach, Gebrüder

Another late-comer to bisque dollmaking in Germany, Gebrüder Heubach is well-known for its distinctive character children, mostly with painted and molded hair and often with painted eyes. The company also made all-bisque and baby dolls, and was active from about 1910 through the early 1920s.

Market Report: Prices for the more common Gebrüder Heubach dolls have definitely decreased in the past few years—these dolls are simply out of fashion. Overall, this perplexes me, since Gebrüder Heubach dolls have a distinctive look which makes them less common than the usual dolly-faced an-

tique dolls, and, generally, their quality is very good. Since dolls do come in and out of fashion, if you like Gebrüder Heubach dolls, now is a good time to purchase some of the more common examples, since they have definite potential for price increases in the future.

The rarer Heubach character dolls, however, have definitely increased in value in the past few years. Look for some rarer glass-eyed characters and some of the characters with more unusual facial expressions—surprised, laughing—in this category.

Online/Offline Report: Overall, there are not great quantities of these dolls available on eBay. Some bargains can be found there, but the rarer Heubach character dolls are especially scarce on the Internet, and they will command high prices whether on eBay or from dealers or auction houses. For the more common dolls, bargains can be found from most outlets at this time.

Prices and Characteristics: The vast majority of these dolls were made between 1910–1920. Prices are for bisque dolls in excellent condition, and prices are similar from all venues, but slightly lower on the Internet. All are character dolls with bisque heads, with painted intaglio eyes and closed mouths (often modeled as if open with modeled tongue and teeth) except as noted. Dolls have fully jointed composition bodies unless a cruder composition or papier-mâché, cloth or kid body is indicated. Dolls with painted hair have the hair sculpted in bisque. Heubach is also known for its detailed bisque figurines which are beyond the scope of this book.

Marks: See the "Marks" listings for specific examples, where "sunburst" denotes the typical Heubach mark of a sunburst (looks like a sunflower) on top of a semicircle with "H" and "G" intertwined and "dep" in an oval shape beneath. "Square" denotes "HEU / BACH" in block letters in a square.

GEBRÜDER HEUBACH CHARACTER DOLLS, BY MOLD NUMBER

5636, Laughing Child, Glass Eyes
Size: 18"
Price: $2,300
Mark: 5636 (sunburst) / Germany

5686, Laughing Girl, Glass Eyes
Size: 21"
Price: $2,750
Sleep eyes, molded tongue and teeth.
Mark: 5686 8 (sunburst) mark

5730, Santa
Size: 20–22"
Price: $1,450
Wigged, mohair lashes, open mouth, 4 teeth, sleep eyes.
Mark: SANTA 7-1/2 (sunburst)

6894, Pouty Baby
Size: 13"
Price: $800
On better-quality baby body, painted hair.

6969, Pouty Child, Glass Eyes
Size: 16"
Price: $1,500–$1,800
Mark: 6969 5 Germany Heubach (sunburst)

6969, Pouty Child, Glass Eyes
Size: 12"
Price: $1,200–$1,300
As boy or girl. Fully jointed composition body, wigged.
Mark: 6969 3 Germany

6969, Pouty Child, Painted Eyes
Size: 14"
Price: $500

Painted eyes and hair, fully jointed composition body.
Mark: 4 6996 Germany

6970, Child
Size: 20"
Price: $2,500–$4,400+
Painted eyes (rarer on this model).
Mark: 6970 8 Germany

6970, Child, Glass Eyes
Size: 18–19"
Price: $2,300–$2,600
Wigged.
Mark: 6970 Germany 7

6970, Child, Glass Eyes
Size: 11"
Price: $1,300
Sleep eyes.
Mark: 6970 Germany 1

6971, Laughing Child, Glass Eyes
Size: 17"
Price: $1,500–$1,800
Mark: 6971 7 Germany

7054, Child, Dimpled
Size: 21"
Price: $700
Painted hair.

7072, Pouty Boy, Shoulder-Head
Size: 12"
All Markets: $650–$700
Kid body, painted eyes.
Mark: 3 / 126 / Germany / 7072

7109, Boy
Size: 15–20"
Price: $500–$700
Painted hair, 5-piece body.

7187, Boy, Shoulder-Head
Size: 17"
Price: $500
Kid body, bisque arms, painted eyes and hair.

7246, Pouty Boy, Glass Eyes
Size: 11–13"
Price: $2,000–$2,200
Wigged, sleep eyes.
Mark: 7246 3 Germany Heubach (sunburst or square)

7246, Pouty Boy, Glass Eyes
Size: 20–21"
Price: $2,200+
Mark: 7246I Germany sunburst mark

7247, Baby
Size: 8″
Price: $3,000
Wigged, sleep eyes, crude 5-piece baby body.
Mark: 7247 (sunburst) 3 Germany

7247, Child, Glass Eyes
Size: 17″
Price: $2,000

7307, Child, Glass Eyes
Size: 16″
Price: $3,400
Painted teeth.
Mark: 7307 Germany Heubach (sunburst)

7347, Pouty Child
Size: 20″
Price: $2,250

7407, Child
Size: 16″
Price: $2,900
Painted eyes, hair.
Mark: 7407 Germany Heubach (sunburst)

7580, Boy, Shoulder Head
Size: 19″
Price: $1,400
Painted eyes, sculpted hair. Kid body, composition jointed arms.

7602, Pouty Baby
Size: 18–19″
Price: $500–$600
Solid dome, painted hair, bent-limb baby body.
Mark: Heubach (sunburst) 7602 Germany

7602, Pouty Boy
Size: 15″
Price: $1,100

7603, Boy
Size: 17″
Price: $1,000
Painted eyes, sculpted hair.

7622, Boy
Size: 19″
Price: $2,300
Mark: 7622 Heubach (sunburst) Germany

7628, Boy
Size: 18″
Price: $1,500
Painted eyes, sculpted hair.
Mark: 7828 Heubach (sunburst)

7644, Dimpled Laughing Boy
Size: 20″
Price: $1,700

Shoulder head on kid body with bisque forearms, painted eyes and hair.

7647, Smiling Boy
Size: 27″
Price: $1,800
Painted eyes and hair, unusually large size.
Mark: Heubach (sunburst) 7647 Germany

7663, Boy
Size: 18″
Price: $1,000
Painted eyes and hair.
Mark: 7663 Heubach (sunburst) Germany

7711, Child, Glass Eyes, Open Mouth
Size: 18″
Price: $10,500
Mark: 7711 Germany 7 Heubach (sunburst)

7744, Boy
Size: 17″
Price: $6,600
Painted eyes and hair.
Mark: 7744 Heubach (sunburst) Germany

7759, Boy
Size: 15″
Price: $900
Painted eyes, hair, crude 5-piece toddler body.

7759, Pouty Child
Size: 16″
Price: $2,900+
Mint and all-original at auction, fully jointed composition body.
Mark: Heubach (sunburst) 7759 Germany

7760, Baby
Size: 10″
Price: $700
Painted eyes and hair, crude bent-limb baby body.

7760, Baby
Size: 14″
Price: $4,500+
Painted eyes and hair, bent-limb baby body.
Mark: 7760 Heubach (sunburst)

7761, Boy, Fretting
Size: 14″
Price: $4,350+
Painted eyes and hair.

7764, Singing Heubach
Size: 12–14″
Price: $5,600–$6,300
Sculpted, painted hair with bow, painted eyes, closed mouth with molded teeth.
Mark: Heubach (square) 7760 Germany

7764, Singing Heubach
Size: 16″
Price: $13,000+
Mark: 7764 Heubach (sunburst) Germany

7788, Child, Coquette
Size: 14″
Price: $950–$1,100
Painted eyes, sculpted hair with sculpted blue ribbon and bow. Also mold 7850 and all-bisque.

7788, Child, Coquette
Size: 17″
Price: $1,700–$2,300

7804, Pouty Child
Size: 10″
Price: $750
Wigged, painted eyes.

7849, Child, Shoulder Head
Size: 9″
Price: $700
Painted hair and eyes, cloth body with composition lower arms and legs.
Mark: 5/0 / 7849 Heubach (square)

7852, Smiling Girl, Shoulder Head
Size: 18″
Price: $1,900
Painted eyes and hair, kid body, bisque forearms.

7865, Child, Molded Blue Ribbon/Bow In Hair
Size: 12″
Price: $3,800
Painted eyes and hair.

7911, Boy
Size: 16″
Price: $2,100
Painted eyes and hair.
Mark: 7911 Heubach (square)

7925, Lady, Smiling, Turned Shoulder Head
Size: 18″
Price: $2,000–$2,300
Wigged, cloth body, bisque or composition lower arms/legs (sometimes cloth legs), open mouth, teeth, glass eyes.

7975, Baby Stuart, Glass Eyes
Size: 11″
Price: $1,600
Molded, painted bonnet.
Mark: 7975 Heubach (sunburst) Germany

7977, Baby Stuart
Size: 16″
Price: $1,250
Molded, painted bonnet, painted eyes.
Mark: 7977 Heubach (sunburst) Germany

8050, Laughing Girl
Size: 15–16″
Price: $4,500
Sculpted hair with blue bow and ribbon, molded teeth/tongue, jointed composition body.
Mark: 8050 Heubach (square) Germany

8191, Laughing Boy
Size: 11″
All Markets: $800
5-piece crude composition body, painted hair, teeth.

8191, Laughing Boy
Size: 7–8″
Price: $300–$400
5-piece crude composition body, painted hair, teeth.

8191, Laughing Boy
Size: 16″
Price: $3,000
Sculpted hair, fully jointed composition body.

8192, Child, Glass Eyes, Open Mouth
Size: 9–10″
All Markets: $250–$300
5-piece crude flapper body, painted socks and boots, sleep eyes.
Mark: 8192 / Germany / Gebr. Heubach

8192, Child, Glass Eyes, Open Mouth
Size: 16–22″
Price: $600–$800

8244, Child, Glass Eyes
Size: 13″
Price: $2,200
Mark: 8244 Heubach (square) Germany

8381, Princess Juliana
Size: 19″
Price: $16,000+
Painted eyes and hair. Princess Juliana of the Netherlands.
Mark: 8381

8413, Child, Glass Eyes
Size: 16–19″
Price: $1,600–$2,200
Wigged, modeled tongue and 2 modeled teeth.
Mark: 8413 Heubach (square) Germany

8413, Child, Glass Eyes
Size: 24″
Price: $7,000+

8420, Baby, Painted Eyes
Size: 13″
Price: $1,200
Bent-limb baby body.

Mark: 8420 (crown) 5 / Heubach (square) / 41 / Germany

8420, Pouty Girl, Glass Eyes
Size: 16″
Price: $2,400

8545, Grumpy Baby
Size: 18″
Price: $500
Glass sleep eyes, pouty mouth.
Mark: 8545 Germany

8587, Pouty Child
Size: 18″
Price: $13,000+
Glass eyes, wigged, chubby face, fully jointed toddler body.
Mark: 8587 Heubach (square) Germany

8636, Laughing Boy, Glass Eyes
Size: 13″
Price: $2,700
Wigged, sleep eyes, modeled tongue and 2 teeth.
Mark: 8638 3 _ Heubach (sunburst) Germany

8649, Baby, Molded Bonnet
Size: 12″
Price: $900–$1,200
Bent-limb baby body, open/closed mouth with molded teeth and tongue, molded bonnet with holes for ribbon tie.

8729, Baby
Size: 8″
Price: $200
Painted eyes, hair, crude body.

8733, Child
Size: 9″
Price: $325
Painted eyes and hair, crude body.
Mark: 5/0 D / 87 Heubach (square) 33 / Germany

8771, Whistling Jim
Size: 11″
Price: $650
Whistling mouth, swivel head on cotton twill body with working whistle mechanism.

9487, Native American
Size: 13″
Price: $3,400
Native American costume, brown bisque.
Body Mark: Hand Stuffed Made in Germany.
Mark: Heubach (square) 9487 Germany

9908, Action Baby
Size: 5″
Price: $600
1-piece figure, resting on open bisque egg.
Mark: 9908

10532, Girl, Glass Eyes
Size: 15″
Price: $3,400

10532, Girl, Painted Eyes
Size: 22″
Price: $800
Open mouth, wigged, sleep eyes.
Mark: 10532 / Heubach Germany

10532, Girl, Painted Eyes
Size: 28″
Price: $1,800
Mark: 10532 / 12 Heubach (square)

10663, Girl, Painted Eyes, Open Mouth
Size: 27″
Price: $500
Wigged, 4 teeth.

GEBRÜDER HEUBACH CHARACTER DOLLS, NO MOLD NUMBER

All-Bisque, Coquette-Type
Size: 9.5″
Price: $1,150
Molded 3 blue bows, ribbon and hair, 1-piece head/torso, painted eyes.

All-Bisque, Molded, Bobbed Hair
Size: 9″
Price: $500
Molded hair bobbed with bangs, painted eyes, ankle-strap molded shoes and socks.

Baby, Crying
Size: 11″
Price: $1,550

Baby, Painted Eyes and Hair
Size: 7–10″
Price: $250–$400
Crude 5-piece baby body, may be pouty or smiling. May have flocked hair.

Boy, Painted Eyes and Hair
Size: 16–19″
Price: $800–$850
Toddler or child body.
Mark: 7 / Germany

Child, Shoulder Head
Size: 10″
Price: $400–$500
Cloth or kid body with composition limbs.
Mark: Heubach (square) / 2/0D / Germany

Child, Sculpted Pink Bow in Hair
Size: 12″
Price: $800–$900

Child, Shoulder Head, Painted Eyes, Hair
Size: 15–18″
Price: $500–$650
Cloth or kid body, composition arms, legs.

Child, Startled
Size: 8″
Price: $4,200

Dolly Dimple, Child
Size: 12″
Price: $2,200
Holz-masse symbol on body, glass eyes, wigged, open mouth.
Mark: Dep Dolly Dimple H Germany Heubach (sunburst)

Dolly Dimple, Child
Size: 19″
Price: $1,700
Glass eyes, wigged, open mouth.
Mark: Dep Dolly Dimple Germany 7 1/2

Key-Wind Mechanical Walker
Size: 8″
Price: $500
5-piece composition body, painted eyes, hair.

Laughing Child
Size: 14–15″
Price: $1,300–$1,700
Painted hair and eyes, sculpted forelock, painted teeth.
Mark: Heubach (in square) Germany

Laughing Child, Glass Eyes
Size: 12″
Price: $900
Mark: Heubach (sunburst) Germany

Skier, Cotton, Bisque Head
Size: 5″
All Markets: $290
On skis, original clothes.

Japanese Dolls (From Japan)

This category includes a wide range of dolls, from the exquisite antique Ichimatsu dolls made from gofun (oyster paste) to the cheap knockoffs of German dolls made during and after World War I for export to the United States. This section focuses on the Ichimatsu dolls and also some better knockoffs of German dolls, including dolls by Morimura Brothers, which were imported to the United States in great numbers once German dolls became unavailable during World War I. Inexpensive Japanese all-bisque and similar dolls are covered in the appropriate sections.

Traditional Japanese Dolls, Ichimatsu: The dolls can be of exquisite quality, or simply made, especially in the later eras. Most have glass eyes and are wigged. Antique dolls from Japan have their own unique beauty and are vastly under-appreciated by Western collectors. Japanese dolls from the late 1800s were made from entirely different processes than German and French dolls from that period, and they have intricate histories and places in Japanese society. The dolls were made for use on specific days such as the Girl's Day and Boy's Day festivals, and were ceremonial dolls—not play dolls in the sense that most German and French bisque dolls were, although later 20th century dolls made of gofun often were made for play. These dolls have increased slowly in value over the last few years as more Western collectors have come to appreciate their history and art.

Morimura Brothers: One of the best-known manufacturers of Japanese dolls, Morimura, produced many bisque-head dolls similar to their German counterparts, as well as all-bisque dolls, and they also imported many other dolls from Japan of many types. Their bisque-head dolls vary in quality, but some can rival that of the German manufacturers. The best Morimura Brothers dolls are highly sought after by collectors and are valued at several hundred dollars.

German Knockoffs Marked "Japan": After the Nippon era (see the "Nippon Dolls" section) through the 1930s, many bisque dolls were made in Japan that were direct knockoffs of German dolls. These dolls tend to be of lesser quality, and are easily found today. Many can be easily found for under $30 both on eBay and at doll shows. See the "All Bisque," "Half Dolls," and other appropriate sections for these dolls.

Online/Offline Report: The oldest and best-quality of the Ichimatsu dolls are, for the most part, found from specialty dealers in-

Japanese family. *Gofun/oyster shell composition (Ichimatsu). Family purchased in Japan in 1937 from Mission School. Original costumes, box with original price list from mission. Largest doll 6.75". Private collection.*

Japanese pair. *Gofun/oyster shell composition (Ichimatsu). In original wicker basket. 4", c. 1940s. Brought to the United States during World War II. Courtesy Ellen Johnson.*

cluding specialty dealers of Asian art. Inexpensive and later examples can be found on eBay, but not in great quantities. Morimura Brother dolls can be found easily from both antique doll dealers and on the Internet, for similar prices.

ICHIMATSU DOLLS / TRADITIONAL JAPANESE DOLLS

This is a very small sampling of prices for these dolls. For further pricing and information, contact J.A.D.E., the Japanese American Doll Enthusiasts, www.jadejapandolls.com, and browse Asian art dealers on the Internet that have wide selections of traditional antique Japanese dolls. Prices are for dolls in excellent condition, and all traditional Japanese dolls listed here are made of gofun, a mixture of glue and oyster shells to make oyster paste, generally over carved wood, and they have glass eyes.

Geisha Girl
Size: 19″   Date: 1950s
                     Internet: $300
Signed by artist, made in Kyoto.

Girl With Wigs
Size: 5″   Date: 1911
                     Internet: $130
For early doll with wigs, in wood box. Much less for later dolls.

Girl With Wigs
Size: 6″   Date: 1950s
                     Internet: $30
In wood box.

Empress Doll, Kokin Bina
Size: 16″   Date: mid-1800s
                     Internet: $900
Late Edo period. For Hina (Girl's Day).

Ichimatsu, Boy, Jointed
Size: 14″   Date: 1950s
                     Internet: $445
In silk clothing.

Ichimatsu, Girl
Size: 7–17″   Date: 1912–1926
                     Internet: $400
Taisho period. In silk kimono.

Ichimatsu, Girl
Size: 13″   Date: 1930s
                     Internet: $200
Early Showa period. In silk kimono.

Samurai Warrior Doll (Musha)
Size: 10″   Date: late 1800s–early
                     1900s
                     Internet: $365
Meiji period. Hemp and silk garment.

Musha Doll Pair
Size: 18″   Date: late 1800s–early
                     1900s
                     Internet: $350
Meiji period. Male dolls displayed on Boy's Day. Silk hair, silk clothing.

MORIMURA BROTHERS, BISQUE DOLLS

All dolls are bisque in excellent condition. Dolls are generally from 1914 to 1926. Dolls have glass eyes and are wigged. Prices are nearly identical on and off the Internet.

Baby Darling, All-Bisque
Size: 6"
Price: $35–$65
"Baby Darling" sticker on tummy. Jointed arms only, molded hair ribbon.

Character Baby
Size: 7–10"
Price: $150–$200
All Morimura character babies have socket heads and 5-piece bent-limb composition bodies. Prices lower for very crude body.

Character Baby
Size: 13"
Price: $300
Mark: 2 / M.B (in circle with mark) / Japan / 4

Character Baby
Size: 16"
Price: $350
Mark: 2 / M.B (in circle with mark) / Japan / 10

Character Baby
Size: 20+"
Price: $400+

Child
Size: 12"
Price: $150
All Morimura child dolls have fully jointed composition bodies, open mouths, and teeth.

Child
Size: 15"
Price: $200

Child
Size: 17"
Price: $275

Child
Size: 22+"
Price: $350

Ella
Size: 18"
Price: $300
5-piece bent-limb composition body.
Mark: 2 / MB (in circle with mark) / Japan / 11

Jumeau

It is very hard to give a brief summary of Jumeau dolls. Jumeau dolls are known worldwide as the ultimate in antique dolls. The fascinating history of the firm, and the firm's place in the history of French doll-making are fascinating, the dolls' styles are distinctive, and Jumeau dolls are known even to the most casual of doll collectors.

The Jumeau firm began dollmaking in the 1840s, founded by Pierre François Jumeau. The first dolls were papier-mâché, but by the very end of the 1850s they started selling porcelain dolls. Throughout the 1860s, they made mainly French fashion dolls with bisque heads (poupées), with heads supplied by companies including François Gaultier. In approximately 1873, the company started its own porcelain doll factory.

In the 1874s, the second generation of Jumeaus became involved in the family business. Emile Louis Jumeau took over running the business, and his wife, Ernestine Stephanie Ducruix took over the costuming of the poupées and the bébés.

By the 1870s, Jumeau started production of its bébé dolls. Although the Jumeau poupées are highly sought after by French fashion doll collectors, it is the bébé dolls, with their exaggerated eyebrows, for which Jumeau is world-famous today.

The company won numerous awards and produced dolls until about 1899 when the cost pressures and changing doll styles brought about by the German dollmakers caused Jumeau to be subsumed into S.F.B.J.

Market Report: Almost all antique doll collectors I know crave at least one Jumeau for their collection. Jumeau dolls are the centerpiece of most French antique doll collections, and German antique doll collectors often admire and seek them as well. Because Jumeau dolls are so admired and sought after, demand remains high even with an ample supply of Jumeau dolls from dealers and auction houses, and even on eBay (although you won't find the same range of

Jumeau Portrait Bébé. *French composition and wood 8 loose-ball jointed body, straight wrists. 26″, c. 1877. Mark: 10. $20,000, auction. Courtesy Theriault's.*

Jumeau Depose Bébé. *French composition and wood jointed body, straight wrists. 27″, c. 1886. Mark: Depose Jumeau 13 (incised). Courtesy Theriault's.*

Jumeau dolls on eBay). The market for more common and later Jumeau dolls (such as Tête Jumeaus) is relatively stable, maybe slightly down from highs just two or three years ago, with prices for the rarest and earliest dolls continuing to increase.

Online/Offline Report: Prices are comparable from all sources—expect to pay a bit less at online auctions but you have the great disadvantage of not being able to personally inspect your doll prior to purchase.

Prices and Characteristics: All dolls have bisque, wigged socket heads, glass eyes, and fully jointed French composition and wood bodies, except as noted. For prices for Jumeau French fashion (lady) dolls, see the section on French Fashion Dolls. Prices for earlier dolls are generally from non-Internet sources.

Marks: Marks are given for bisque heads only; most Jumeaus also have Jumeau-stamped bodies: "Jumeau Medaille d'Or Paris" or "Jumeau Bte SGDG Deposé." Also, many artists have left checkmarks after their marks on the dolls' heads.

PORTRAIT JUMEAU

Each doll is marked with the size number, generally with a body stamp. These dolls have closed mouths, paperweight eyes, pierced ears, and straight-wrist loose ball-jointed bodies. First Series dolls are from 1877 to 1878, and Second Series dolls are from 1880 to 1883.

Bébé, Portrait
Size: 11″
Price: $14,000
Rare small size.
Mark: 1

EJ Bébé, Size 11. French composition and wood jointed body, straight wrists. 24″, c. 1885. Mark: Depose E. 11 J (and artist checkmarks). Courtesy Theriault's.

Jumeau Bébé, Tête Jumeau. French composition and wood jointed body. All-original chemise, socks, shoes. 14″, c. 1890. Mark: Depose Tete Jumeau Bte SGDG 5 (head) and signed body. $5,500. Private collection.

Bébé Marcheur. Walking mechanism in torso of doll still operates. When strings are pulled, doll's legs move and head goes side-to-side. From Jumeau/S.F.B.J. transitional period. 22″, c. 1900. Private collection.

Bébé, Portrait, 1st Series
Size: 15″
Price: $12,000–$13,500
Mark: Only body marked.

Bébé, Portrait, 1st Series
Size: 15″
Price: $12,750

Bébé, Portrait, 1st Series
Size: 15″
Price: $14,250
Mark: 0

Bébé, Portrait, 1st Series
Size: 18″
Price: $11,000
Mark: 2

Bébé, Portrait, 1st Series
Size: 22″
Price: $21,000
Mark: 4

Bébé, Portrait, 1st Series
Size: 24″
Price: $34,000
Mark: 5

Bébé, Portrait, 2nd Series
Size: 13″
Price: $2,800–$3,800
Later 2nd Series.

Bébé, Portrait, 2nd Series
Size: 14–15″

Price: $6,000–$8,500
Mark: 6

Bébé, Portrait, 2nd Series
Size: 18″
Price: $7,000+

Bébé, Portrait, 2nd Series
Size: 21–23″
Price: $9,000–$11,000
Applied ears.
Mark: 10

Bébé, Portrait, 2nd Series
Size: 26″
Price: $20,000
Mark: 10

PREMIERE JUMEAU
Premiere Bébés have closed mouths, paperweight eyes, pierced ears, straight-wrist loose ball-jointed bodies. They are from approximately 1878.

Bébé, Premiere (Smiling Face)
Size: 8″
Price: $5,200
With flaw.
Mark: N 1

Bébé, Premiere, Size 4
Size: 11–12″
Price: $4,000 –$5,000
Mark: 4

Bébé, Premiere
Size: 13″
Price: $3,500
Mark: Only body marked.

Bébé, Premiere, Size 5
Size: 14–15″
Price: $5,250–$6,500
Mark: 5

Bébé, Premiere, Size 8
Size: 18″
Price: $7,000
Mark: 8

JUMEAU, E.J. BÉBÉS

These dolls have paperweight eyes, closed mouths, pierced ears, and straight-wrists (early models have loose-ball joints). The earliest dolls are from 1880; later dolls are from 1885.

Bébé, E.J., Size 1
Size: 9″
Price: $7,000–$9,000
Size 1 is rarer size.
Mark: Deposé EJ 1

Bébé, E.J., Size 3
Size: 11″
Price: $5,000–$7,000
Mark: "E. 3 J." or "Deposé E. 3 J."

Bébé, E.J., Size 5
Size: 13–14″
Price: $4,500–$6,000
Mark: "E. 5 J." or "Deposé E.5 J"

Bébé, E.J., Size 7
Size: 16″
Price: $5,000–$6,000
Mark: E. 7 J.

Bébé, E.J., Size 8
Size: 18–19″
Price: $7,000–$8,000
Mark: "E 8 J" or "E. 8 J. Deposé"

Bébé, E.J., Size 8, Early
Size: 19″
Price: $8,000–$9,000
Note early mark, with size number over "EJ."
Mark: 8 / EJ

Bébé, E.J., Size 9 or 10
Size: 23–24″
Price: $8,000

Bébé, E.J., Size 9, Early
Size: 24″
Price: $13,500–$16,500
Early mark very rare in this size.
Mark: 9 / E.J.

Bébé, E.J., Size 12
Size: 25″
Price: $8,000–$10,000
Mark: Deposé E. 12 J.

Bébé, E.J., Size 15
Size: 32″
Price: $13,500
Mark: Deposé E. 15 J.

Bébé, E.J.A., Size 10
Size: 24″
Price: $19,500
Mark: E.J.A 10

TÊTE JUMEAU BÉBÉS, CLOSED MOUTH

Tête Jumeaus have glass eyes and fully jointed composition bodies with jointed or straight wrists. Their heads have red-stamped marks; their bodies are usually stamped. They were produced from 1885 through the 1890s.

Bébé, Tête
Size: 9″
Price: $2,500–$3,800
Simpler, 5-piece composition.

Bébé, Tête, Size 1
Size: 9–10″
All Markets: $5,000–$7,000
Small size with rarer fully jointed composition body.
Mark: Deposé Tete Jumeau Bte SGDG 1

Bébé, Tête, Size 2
Size: 11–12″
Price: $2,500–$3,500
Mark: Deposé Tete Jumeau Bte SGDG 2

Bébé, Tête, Size 3
Size: 12–13″
Price: $3,400–$4,000
Mark: Deposé Tete Jumeau Bte SGDG 4

Bébé, Tête, Size 6
Size: 14–15″
Price: $3,000–$4,000
Mark: Deposé / Tete Jumeau / Bte. S.G.D.G. / 6

Bébé, Tête, Size 7

Size: 17–18″
All Markets: $3,500–$5,000
Mark: Deposé Tete Jumeau / Bte S.G.D.G / 7

Bébé, Tête, Size 8

Size: 19–20″
Price: $3,500–$5,000
Mark: Tete Jumeau Deposé Bte SGDG 8

Bébé, Tête, Size 11

Size: 24″
Price: $4,000–$6,000
Mark: Deposé Tete Jumeau Bte SGDG 11 or
Deposé Tete Jumeau

Bébé, Tête, Size 12

Size: 26–27″
Price: $4,000–$5,000
Mark: Deposé / Tete Jumeau / 12

Bébé, Tête, Size 13

Size: 29″
Price: $2,500
One result, doll with flaws, at auction.
Mark: Deposé / Tete Jumeau / 13

Bébé, Tête

Size: 35″
Price: $3,100
One result, doll with flaws, at auction.

TÊTE JUMEAU, OPEN MOUTH

Bébé, Tête

Size: 15″
All Markets: $1,200–$2,200
Sleep eyes.
Mark: Only body marked.

Bébé, Tête

Size: 19–20″
Price: $1,600–$2,500
Sleep eyes.

Bébé, Tête

Size: 22″
Price: $4,400
For all-original doll.
Mark: Deposé Tete Jumeau 9

Bébé, Tête

Size: 24″
All Markets: $2,475

Tête, Adult Female Body

Size: 24″
Price: $3,800
Dressed as Spanish dancer.
Mark: Deposé Tete Jumeau Bte SGDG

Bébé, Tête

Size: 30″
Price: $1,100
Very late S.F.B.J. "Tête" Jumeau, dressed in
factory-original outfit from 1930s.
Mark: "Tete Jumeau" label on back of head.

JUMEAU BÉBÉS, VARIOUS

Bébé, 1907

Size: 14–16″   Date: 1907
Price: $1,800
1907 bébés have open mouths, jointed composition bodies with jointed wrists, glass eyes. Price
for doll with some flaws.

Bébé, 1907

Size: 19–22″   Date: 1907
Price: $2,300
All original.
Mark: 1907 / 10

Bébé, 1907

Size: 29″   Date: 1907
All Markets: $1,900
With newer clothing.
Mark: 1907 / 14

Bébé, 1907

Size: 32–35″   Date: 1907
Price: $1,200–$1,600
For dolls with minor flaws (repainted bodies, re-
placed newer clothing).
Mark: 1907 / 15

Bébé, 1907, Black

Size: 14″   Date: 1907
Price: $1,300–$1,800

Bébé, Block Letter, Size 1

Size: 11″   Date: 1878
Price: $4,200
First signature bébé made by Jumeau.
Mark: Jumeau (incised block letters in banner) 1

Bébé, C EJ

Size: 16″   Date: 1882
Price: $4,750
Early model bébé, straight-wrist body.
Mark: C EJ

Bébé, Closed Mouth

Size: 12″   Date: 1870s
Price: $3,600

Bébé, Closed Mouth

Size: 22″   Date: 1880s
Price: $3,335

Bébé, Closed Mouth

Size: 24″   Date: 1885
Price: $4,500
All original.

Bébé, Déposé

Size: 17–20″   Date: 1885
Price: $5,000–$7,000
Mark: "Deposé Jumeau 7" or "Deposé Jumeau"

Bébé, Déposé, Size 9

Size: 22″   Date: 1885
Price: $6,000–$7,000
Straight-wrist body.
Mark: Deposé Jumeau 9

Bébé, Open Mouth

Size: 13″
Price: $1,500
Mark: Dep 2

Bébé, Open Mouth

Size: 18″   Internet: $2,650
With original outfit, but flaws.
Mark: JUMEAU / Medaille D'Or / PARIS

Bébé, Open Mouth

Size: 22″
Price: $1,300
Mark: 9

Bébé, Open Mouth

Size: 24″   Date: 1892
Price: $4,300
All original, in original box.
Mark: Only body marked.

Bébé, Open Mouth

Size: 32″
Price: $2,200
Mark: 14

Bébé, Phonographe

Size: 24″   Date: 1892–1893
Price: $5,000–$6,000
Open mouth, phonograph mechanism in torso
that plays music cylinders from key-wind.
Mark: Deposé Tete Jumeau 11 (sometimes only
body mark)

Bébé, Phonographe

Size: 25″
All Markets: $2,400
For doll with noticeable firing faults, badly re-
dressed, no cylinders.

Bébé, Française

Size: 14″   Date: 1892
Price: $3,300
Mark: B. 5 F

Bébé, Louvre

Size: 11″   Date: 1890
Price: $4,600
For Au Louvre department store in Paris; this
doll with flaws, at auction.
Mark: B. 2 L.

Bébé, Scrub Mark

Size: 10.5″
Price: $1,700
Area on back where mark "scrubbed off" at fac-
tory; closed mouth. For doll with flaw (hairline).

Bébé, Triste

Size: 20–24″   Date: 1884
Price: $13,500–$18,000
Sad-faced Bébé, straight-wrist loose-ball jointed
body. Plus one result, $24,500 at auction.
Mark: 11

Bébé, Triste

Size: 25–26″   Date: 1885
Price: $16,000–$19,000
Mark: 12

Bluette, Premiere

Size: 10.5″   Date: 1905
Price: $3,250
Cork pate, paperweight eyes, fully jointed
French composition body, 4 teeth, pierced ears.
For more Bluettes, see the SFBJ /UNIS France
Section.
Mark: 2

Flowered Chemise

                        Date: 1900
Price: $940
Clothing for Jumeau doll.

Paris Bébé

Size: 26″   Date: 1892
Price: $4,000
Mark: Paris Bébé Tete Deposé 11 (head) Paris
Bébé Deposé (and Eiffel Tower symbol torso)

Kämmer & Reinhardt (K ❋ R)

The bisque dolls of Kämmer & Reinhardt
are some of the most sought after of the German-made dolls, and with good reason—
from its dolly-faced dolls to its later
character babies and children, its dolls were
generally beautifully made. Commencing in
1886 and ending with the general end of the
German bisque period in the early 1930s,
Kämmer & Reinhardt was a prolific doll
manufacturer and designer of dolls, generally using heads made by Simon & Halbig (a

Kämmer & Reinhardt child, Simon & Halbig head. *Jointed composition body. 24", c. 1890. Mark: SIMON 8 HALBIG / K * R. $900, dealer.*

Kämmer & Reinhardt, Character Baby 126. *Flirty eyes, bent-limb composition baby body. 20". Mark: K * R / SIMON & HALBIG / 126 / Germany. $649, dealer.*

Kämmer & Reinhardt, Toddler 121. *Composition toddler body, side-hip jointing. 24", c. 1920. Mark: K * R / Simon & Halbig / 121. Courtesy Theriault's.*

firm which they combined with in 1920), but also using heads from other companies.

One of the most significant things Kämmer & Reinhardt did was popularize the character doll, the forerunner of today's artist dolls. Kämmer & Reinhardt character dolls were modeled after real children, which was a huge innovation circa 1909. Until that time, most dolls had stylized "dolly" faces which lacked emotion and realism.

Market Report: Kämmer & Reinhardt dolls are always desirable. Prices for most of the dolly-face dolls and common character dolls have been relatively stable in the past few years, with prices on some of the more sought-after character baby and child dolls increasing.

Online/Offline Report: The rarest Kämmer & Reinhardt character dolls rarely turn up online—they are found with dealers and at auction houses. Many common Kämmer & Reinhardt bisque dolls can be found online, however, and if you're careful about condition and quality, prices can be lower than at doll shows and from dealers due to the difficulty of assessing bisque online.

Prices and Characteristics: Dolls are bisque, except as noted. Prices are for dolls in

excellent condition; Internet prices are included and noted in the results.

KÄMMER & REINHARDT CHILD DOLLS

These dolls have fully jointed composition bodies, open mouths, glass eyes, wigs, except as noted. The child dolls were made from the 1890s–1930s.

Child, 191
Size: 28"
All Markets: $600–$800

Child, 192
Size: 7–10"
Price: $350–$450
Open mouth. 5-piece composition body, sleep eyes, open mouth, upper teeth, painted shoes and socks.
Mark: 192

Child, 192
Size: 16–18"
Price: $350
Fully jointed composition body. More if completely original.
Mark: 192 / 8 or 192 / 10 1/2

Child, 192
Size: 21–24"
All Markets: $700+

Child, 192, Closed Mouth
Size: 29"
Price: $1,400

Gretchen 114 character children.
*Composition and wood jointed
bodies. 22.5" and 18", c. 1910.
Mark: larger: K * R 114 57; Smaller:
K * R 114 46. Larger, $5,750,
smaller, $3,600. Courtesy
Theriault's.*

**Mein Liebling Character Child
117.** *Composition and wood jointed
body. 18", c. 1912. Mark: K * R /
Simon & Halbig / 117 46. Courtesy
Theriault's.*

Marie Character 201. *Shoulder
head model of popular 101 Marie.
16.5", c. 1915. Mark: 201 / K * R
(on shoulder plate). $1,400, dealer.*

Child, 192

Size: 31"
Price: $650

Child, 192, Closed Mouth

Size: 17–18"
Price: $1,500–$1,900
White space between lips, sleep eyes, straight-
wrist K * R body.
Mark: 192 10

Child, 403

Size: 18"
Price: $650–$850
Mark: K * R / Simon & Halbig / 403 / Germany /
46

Child, 403

Size: 19–20"
Price: $850+
Mark: K * R Simon & Halbig 403 Germany 50

Child, No Mold Number

Size: 6"
Price: $200
Crude, 5-piece composition body, painted shoes
and socks.

Child, No Mold Number

Size: 8"
Price: $500
1920s bob, 5-piece composition body, molded
shoes with 2 straps.
Mark: Halbig K * R Germany 21

Child, No Mold Number

Size: 9–10"
Price: $300–$400

5-piece composition body; more for fully jointed.
Mark: Halbig / K * R / 23

Child, No Mold Number

Size: 12"
Price: $400–$500
Child dolls with no mold number are marked K
* R and a size number. They have open mouths,
glass eyes, fully jointed composition bodies, and
are wigged.
Mark: L / Simon & Halbig / K * R / Germany /
30

Child, No Mold Number

Size: 14–15"
Price: $550–$650
Mark: Simon & Halbig K * R 43

Child, No Mold Number

Size: 18–19"
All Markets: $650–$775
Sometimes flirty eyes.
Mark: K * R / Simon & Halbig / 29

Child, No Mold Number

Size: 22–24"
All Markets: $725–$850
Mark: Halbig / K * R / 55

Child, No Mold Number

Size: 28–29"
Price: $800–$1,000
Mark: Simon & Halbig / K * R / Germany / 73
(or 76)

Child, No Mold Number

Size: 32–33"
Price: $1,100–$1,400
Mark: K * R / Simon & Halbig /80 (or 85)

Peter and Marie 101 character children. *Composition and wood jointed bodies. 17˝ and 18˝, c. 1909. Mark, Peter: K * R 101 46 Mark, Marie: 101 K * R 43. Courtesy Theriault's.*

Kämmer & Reinhardt Flapper Child. *Composition and wood jointed body with slender legs and torso. 16˝, c. 1915. Mark: Simon & Halbig K * R Germany 36. Courtesy Theriault's.*

Child, No Mold Number
Size: 36˝
Price: $1,600
Mark: K * R Simon & Halbig 90

Lady, 191
Size: 19˝
Price: $500
Lady body, composition, jointed.
Mark: 1 / 191 / C

KÄMMER & REINHARDT CHARACTER BABY AND TODDLER DOLLS

Character babies have five-piece bent-limb composition baby bodies. They are wigged or have solid domes with painted hair, as indicated. Toddler dolls generally have five-piece toddler bodies with side-hip jointing. Character baby and toddler dolls were made from 1909–1920s.

Baby, 100, Kaiser
Size: 11–12˝
Price: $300–$400
Solid dome, painted hair, open/closed mouth.

Baby, 100, Kaiser
Size: 14–15˝
Price: $400–$500
Mark: 36 / K * R / 100

Baby, 100, Kaiser
Size: 18–20˝
Price: $750+
Often called the "Kaiser Baby."
Mark: K * R 100 50

Baby, 116, Laughing
Size: 11˝
Price: $1,200
Mold more often found as child. Sleep eyes, closed/open mouth.
Mark: K * R 116 28

Baby, 115A

Size: 11″
Price: $1,200
Male version is known as Phillip; see below for
toddler version.
Mark: K * R / S & H / 115A/A/30

Baby, 116A

Size: 25″
Price: $2,500
On bent-limb baby body, wigged. Closed mouth.
Mark: K * R / Simon & Halbig / 116A / 62

Baby, 121, 122

Size: 10″
Price: $250–$350

Baby, 121, 122

Size: 14–15″
Price: $450–$550
Wigged, open mouth, sleep eyes.
Mark: K * R Simon & Halbig 121

Baby, 121, 122

Size: 18″
All Markets: $550+
Also called "My Little Darling."
Mark: K * R / Simon & Halbig / 121-42

Baby, 121, 122

Size: 20–22″
Price: $700+

Baby, 121, 122

Size: 23+″
Price: $800–$1,000
Mark: K * R / Simon & Halbig / 121 / 62

Baby, 126, 127, All-Bisque

Size: 10–12″
Price: $1,300–$1,600
126 is wigged, 127 is solid dome with painted
hair.
Mark: "K * R 126 23" or "K * R 127 / 32"

Baby, 126

Size: 14–15″
Price: $400+

Baby, 126

Size: 20–22″
All Markets: $500–$700
May have wobble tongue. Wigged.

Baby, 126

Size: 22–24″
All Markets: $550–$650
Mark: K * R / Simon & Halbig / 126 / 56

Baby, 126, With Wardrobe

Size: 10″
Price: $1,500

Composition bent-limb baby body, with trunk
and wardrobe.
Mark: K * R Simon & Halbig 126 21 / Germany

Baby, 127

Size: 20″
Price: $900
Painted hair, open mouth.

Baby, 136

Size: 23″
Price: $2,300

Baby, 200

Size: 20″
Price: $600
Open/closed mouth, painted hair, cloth body
with compositon hands and lower limbs.
Mark: 200 50 K * R 50

Baby, No Mold Number

Size: 16″
Price: $400
Open mouth, wigged.

Baby, No Mold Number

Size: 23″
Price: $500
Mark: X / K * R / 22 /Germany / 62

Baby, Puz, Composition

Size: 22″
Price: $500
Composition head, molded hair, cloth body.

Baby, Puz, Composition

Size: 34″   Internet: $1,500
Very rare largest size.
Mark: GERMANY / 30328

Toddler, 126

Size: 6.5″
Price: $600
5-piece composition body with painted shoes.

Toddler, 115, Painted Hair

Size: 15″
Price: $3,000+
Painted hair rarer on this model, closed mouth.

Toddler, 115A

Size: 12–13″
Price: $3,000
Toddler body. Male version is known as Phillip.
Closed mouth, glass eyes, wigged.
Mark: K * R Simon & Halbig 114/A 30.

Toddler, 115A

Size: 15–16″
Price: $3,200–$3,700
Mark: K * R / S&H / 115/A / 38

Toddler, 115A
Size: 17–19″
Price: $3,900–$4,900
Mark: K * R Simon & Halbig 115/A 48

Toddler, 115A
Size: 23–24″
Price: $3,700–$4,000+
Mark: K * R / S & H / 115A / 68

Toddler, 115A
Size: 38″
Price: $4,500
Mark: K * R Simon & Halbig 115A 38

Toddler, 116
Size: 17″
Price: $2,600
Mark: K * R S&H 116 36

Toddler, 116, Painted Hair
Size: 20″
Price: $2,300
Painted hair rarer on this model.

Toddler, 116A
Size: 15″
Price: $1,500
Laughing expression, open/closed mouth.
Mark: K * R Simon & Halbig 116/A 36

Toddler, 116A
Size: 20″
Price: $2,900

Toddler, 122
Size: 11″
Price: $900
Mark: K * R Simon & Halbig 122 26

Toddler, 122, 121
Size: 16–18″
Price: $1,200–$1,700
5-piece toddler body with side-hip jointing.
Mark: K * R / Simon & Halbig / 122 / 42

Toddler, 126
Size: 7–10″
Price: $900–$1,100+
Composition 5-piece toddler body with side-hip jointing, starfish hands, open mouth, wig.
Mark: K * R Simon & Halbig Germany 126-19 (or 21, 22)

Toddler, 126
Size: 18–20″
Price: $600
Can have flirty eyes. Prices for 5-piece bodies; more if fully jointed.
Mark: K * R / Simon & Halbig / 126 / Germany / 45

Toddler, 126
Size: 32″
Price: $1,200+

Toddler, 127
Size: 21″
Price: $1,700
Mark: Germany Simon & Halbig K * R 127 46

Toddler, 135
Size: 16″
Price: $1,400
Mark: K * R Simon & Halbig, 135 32

Toddler, 728, Composition
Size: 12″
Price: $450
Composition head, kid body, open mouth, wigged.
Mark: K * R 728/2 Germany 29/31

Toddler, 728, Celluloid
Size: 14″
Price: $250–$350
Celluloid head and body. See "Celluloid Dolls" section for other K * R celluloid dolls.

Toddler, 926, Composition
Size: 14″
Price: $400
Open mouth, wig, cloth and kid body.
Mark: K * R 926 Germany 3

KÄMMER & REINHARDT CHARACTER CHILD DOLLS

Character child dolls have fully jointed composition bodies except as noted, generally with closed mouths and with painted or glass eyes, as noted. Hair is wigged or painted, as noted. The character child dolls were made from 1909 to the 1920s.

Child, 101, Marie/ Peter
Size: 8–11″
Price: $1,300–$1,600
Fully jointed composition body, painted eyes, wigged.
Mark: K * R / 101 / 21 or K * R Simon & Halbig 29 101

Child, 101, Marie/Peter
Size: 12″
Price: $2000–$2200
Peters generally sell slightly under Maries.
Mark: K * R 30 101

Child, 101, Marie/ Peter
Size: 15″
Price: $4,000
Mark: K * R 101 39

Child, 101, Marie/ Peter
Size: 18–19″
Price: $3,500–$3,800
Mark: K * R 101 46

Child, 101, Marie/ Peter
Size: 20″
Price: $4,000–$5,000
Completely factory original and mint.
Mark: K * R 101 50

Child, 101X
Size: 15″
Price: $2,700
Has flocked hair.
Mark: K * R 101X 39

Child, 102
Size: 12″
Price: $11,500
Closed mouth, painted eyes, hair.

Child, 107, Karl
Size: 12″
Price: $8,600–$10,000
Wigged, painted eyes, somber look.
Mark: K * R 107 30

Child, 109
Size: 14″
Price: $5,175
Wigged, painted eyes, from the art character series.

Child, 109
Size: 17″
Price: $5,750
Mark: K * R 109 43

Child, 112
Size: 14″
Price: $5,200
From character art series.
Mark: K * R 112 34

Child, 114, Gretchen or Hans
Size: 9″
Price: $1,800
K * R 114 23

Child, 114, Gretchen or Hans
Size: 12″
Price: $2,400–$2,800
Painted eyes, pouty closed mouth, wigged.

Child, 114, Gretchen or Hans
Size: 16–18″
Price: $3,000–$3,800
Mark: K * R 114 46

Child, 114, Gretchen or Hans
Size: 22–25″
Price: $5,750–$6,250
Mark: K * R 114 57

Child, 114, Gretchen, Glass Eyes
Size: 12″
Price: $6,000
Sleep eyes.
Mark: K * R 114 30

Child, 114, Gretchen, Glass Eyes
Size: 25″
Price: $10,000
Sleep eyes.
Mark: K * R 114 64

Child, 116A, Laughing
Size: 20″
Price: $2,300
Mark: K * R S & H 116/A 42

Child, 117, Mein Liebling
Size: 22″
Price: $4,300
Closed mouth, wigged, glass eyes.

Child, 117, Mein Liebling
Size: 23–24″
Price: $4,500–$4,800
Mark: K * R Simon & Halbig 117 62

Child, 117, Mein Liebling
Size: 27″
Price: $3,100
Body repainted.
Mark: 117

Child, 117A, Mein Liebling
Size: 8″
Price: $2,000–$2,800
Wigged, closed mouth, 5-piece flapper body with painted shoes.
Mark: K * R Simon & Halbig 117/A 21

Child, 117A, Mein Liebling
Size: 16–17″
Price: $3,900–$4,500
Closed mouth, wigged, glass eyes.
Mark: K * R Simon & Halbig 117/A 39

Child, 117A, Mein Liebling
Size: 29–30″
Price: $6,000
Mark: K*R / Simon & Halbig / 117/A / 68

Child, 117N

Size: 11"
Price: $1,550
Open mouth. Known as "My New Darling."
Rare in this size.

Child, 117N

Size: 17–19"
Price: $800–$1,000
May have flirty eyes.
Mark: K & R Simon & Halbig 117n

Child, 117N

Size: 22+"
Price: $1,100+
Mark: K * R / Simon & Halbig / Germany / 117n
/ 80

Character, 124, Moritz

Size: 16"
Price: $13,000–$17,000
Impish, flirty eyes.

Character, 123, Max

Size: 16"
Price: $13,000–$17,000
Composition body modeled solely for this doll
with painted socks and sculpted shoes. Based on
stories of Wilhelm Busch. Flirty, "roguish" eyes.

Child, 127

Size: 16"
Price: $2,400
Original Boy Scout outfit.
Mark: K * R / Simon & Halbig / 127 36

Child, 127

Size: 23"
Price: $1,300
Mark: K * R 127n 50

Child, 135

Size: 13"
Price: $550
Teenage-style composition body.
Mark: K * R / Simon & Halbig / 135 / 26 / Germany

Child, 201

Size: 13"
Price: $1,800
Mark: 201 K * R

Child, 817, Rubber

Size: 21"
Price: $375
Head made of rubber. Very rare; most have disintegrated.

Kestner

The great popularity of Kestner bisque dolls can be attributed to many things, including the long-term production of the dolls, the many types of dolls they produced (everything from early china and shoulder-head bisque dolls to later all-bisques and character dolls) and the general high quality of the dolls. Although the quality of Kestner dolls can vary widely (just as with all other producers of antique bisque) the quality of Kestner dolls can sometimes even rival the quality of the best French bisque dolls.

The J.D. Kestner firm made dolls in the Waltershausen, Thuringia, region of Germany. The company made dolls starting as early as the 1820s (wood and papier-mâché), and continued until the early 1930s. The dolls mostly discussed in this section are generally the bisque dolls produced from the late 1860s onward. Kestner continuously produced dolls for one of the longest periods of any of the German bisque doll firms.

Market Report: Collectors truly love Kestner dolls and many antique doll collectors have based entire collections on them. Demand for Kestner dolls has always been high, and prices reflect this, with only the most common molds and certain shoulder-head dolls decreasing in value in the past few years.

The most desirable Kestner dolls include its earliest bisque dolls on composition bodies, the rarer mold numbers from the dolly-face era, the character children and babies, and its all-bisques, of which the better examples have increased exponentially in value in the past few years.

Online/Offline Report: The majority of the best Kestner dolls will not be found at online auction sites. For the great all-bisque Kestner dolls, the character dolls, and the choice early bisque child dolls, your best bet is auction houses and dealers. Also, be careful when buying "Kestner all-bisques" on eBay—many of the dolls described as "Kestner all-bisques" on eBay are only "Kestners" due to the wishful thinking of their sellers.

Kestner child, shoulder head. Kid body, bisque lower arms. 16″. Mark: 7. $700, dealer.

Kestner JDK baby. Composition bent-limb baby body. 11″. Mark: J.D.K./ 7 / made in Germany. $450, auction.

Kestner, Child 171. Composition jointed body. Although this is the "Daisy" mold, Daisy dolls will be 18″ with blonde hair. 20″. Mark: Made In / Germany / 171.

KESTNER, CHARACTER BABIES AND TODDLERS

These have glass sleep eyes, open mouths, composition five-piece baby bodies (if babies) or composition fully jointed toddler bodies with side-hip jointing (if toddlers). They are wigged with mohair or human hair, or have painted hair as indicated. The Babies and Toddlers are generally from 1912 to the 1920s. Prices are similar from all venues.

Baby Jean
Size: 16–18″
Price: $1,000–$1,400
Molded, painted hair; highest price on toddler body.
Mark: J.D.K. / made in Germany / 12

Baby, 211
Size: 11″
Price: $600–$700
Wigged, open/closed mouth with molded tongue.
Mark: C. made in / Germany 7/211/J.D.K. or 7 JDK 211

Baby, 211
Size: 14–16″
Price: $500–$600
Mark: G Made in Germany 11 211 J.D.K

Baby, 211
Size: 22–25″
Price: $800+
Wigged, open mouth, molded tongue.
Mark: G Made in Germany 20 211 J.D.K 20

Baby, 220
Size: 24″
Price: $1,700
Mark: 16 JDK 220

Baby, 226
Size: 15″
Price: $500
Mark: H made in / Germany 12 / J.D.K. / 226

Baby, 234
Size: 13″
Price: $800
On original rarer kid baby body.
Body Mark: Crown and streamer.
Mark: JDK 234 C Made in Germany

Baby, 238
Size: 13″
Price: $800+
Baby on rarer kid baby body.

Baby, 243, Asian
Size: 13″
Price: $4,400
In silk costume. See "Asian Dolls" section for more Asian Kestner babies.
Mark: J made in Germany 10 JDK 243

Baby, 247
Size: 16″
Price: $850
Sleep eyes, composition baby body.
Mark: H. made in / Germany / 12 / 247 / J.D.K.

Kestner, Child 146. *Composition and wood jointed body. 22", c. 1900. Mark: K made in Germany 14 / 146. Courtesy Theriault's.*

Kestner Child 168. *Composition jointed body. 19", c. 1890. Mark: made in Germany / E 168 9. $525, dealer.*

Kestner toddler 260. *5-piece composition toddler body, chubby tummy. 9.5", c. 1920. Mark: made in Germany / JDK / 260. Courtesy Theriault's.*

Baby, 257
Size: 9"
All Markets: $500–$650
Mark: made in / Germany / JDK / 257

Baby, 257
Size: 15"
All Markets: $500+

Baby, Character, No Mold Number
Size: 20–23"
Price: $750–$850
Open mouth with wobble tongue, molded, painted hair.

Baby, No Mold Number, Painted Hair
Size: 8.5"
Price: $300

Century Baby
Size: 11"
Price: $500

Century Baby
Size: 16"   Date: 1925
Price: $600–$700
Cloth body, composition hands.
Mark: Century Doll Co/ Kestner / Germany

Century Baby
Size: 21"
Price: $600+
Dome head, cloth body, composition limbs.

Hilda, 237, 245, 1070
Size: 10–12"
Price: $1,800–$2,400

Hildas are molds 237, 245 and 1070 (solid dome); 247 and 245 are wigged, sometimes with skin wig. Dolls have molded or wobble tongues and 2 teeth. Less for the painted-hair version.
Mark: 5 245 J.D.K. Jr. 1914© Hilda

Hilda
Size: 16–18"
Price: $2,300–$2,600
Wigged or solid dome.
Mark: Germany JDK N. 1070 Ges. Gesch. or JDK #237

Hilda
Size: 19–20"
Price: $2,800–$3,000+
Mark: M / made in Germany / 16 / 245 / J.D.K. Jr / 1914 / c / Hilda

Hilda, Painted Hair
Size: 19"
All Markets: $1,600
1070 model.

Hilda
Size: 24–27"
Price: $5,200–$5,700

JDK Baby
Size: 14"
Price: $400–$500
Dome head, molded, painted hair.
Mark: JDK

JDK Baby
Size: 20"
Price: $550–$800
Mark: J.D.K. / made in 16 Germany

Kestner character baby 211. Composition bent-limb baby body. 11.5″. Mark: B Made in Germany G / Germany / J.D.K. / 211. $550, dealer.

Pair of Hilda character babies. Composition bent-limb baby bodies. 15″ and 10″, c. 1915. Mark (large): Hilda c. JDK Jr. 1914 Ges Gesch N. 1070 Made in Germany. Mark (small): C made in Germany 7 237 JDK Jr. 1914 c. Hilda.

O.I.C. Baby
Size: 13″
Price: $1,300
Dome head, cloth body, 1921.
Mark: OIC 2

Toddler, 211
Size: 19″
Price: $1,300
Mark: K made in Germany 14 211 JDK

Toddler, 211
Size: 24″
Price: $1,400–$1,700
Mark: G made in Germany 211 JDK 20

Toddler, 247
Size: 10″
Price: $1,800
Side-hip toddler body.
Mark: A made in Germany 5 247 JDK 5

Toddler, 247
Size: 16″
All Markets: $1,850
Original basket presentation.

Toddler, 247
Size: 21″
Price: $2,000
Mark: K made in Germany 14 247 JDK

Toddler, 257
Size: 12″
Price: $1,000

Toddler, 257
Size: 14–16″
Price: $850–$1,000
Fully jointed composition toddler body, wigged, 2 teeth, may have flirty eyes.

Toddler, 257
Size: 27″
Price: $1,100
Mark: JDK 257 57

Gibson Girl, Fashion Lady. *Kid lady body with slender torso, pin-jointed limbs, bisque forearms. 21", c. 1900. Mark: 172 7. $1,600, auction. Courtesy Theriault's.*

Toddler, 260
Size: 7"
Price: $1,300
Fully jointed composition toddler body.
Mark: JDK 260 Made in Germany

Toddler, 260
Size: 11"
Price: $700+
Mark: Made in Germany J.D.K. 260

Toddler, Hilda, 237
Size: 27"
Price: $5,200
Mark: Q made in Germany 20 237 JDK Jr. 1914
c. Hilda Ges Gesch N1070

Toddler, Hilda, 245
Size: 18"
Price: $4,300
Mark: K made in Germany 14 245 JDK Jr. c.
1914 Hilda Ges Gesch.

Toddler, Hilda, 245
Size: 23"
Price: $4,800

KESTNER, CHARACTER DOLLS

The character dolls have fully jointed composition bodies, glass eyes, and wigs, except as noted, and were produced from approximately 1910 to 1920. Prices are similar from all venues, and Internet prices are noted.

Child, 177
Size: 11"
Price: $5,000
Painted eyes.

Child, 180
Size: 15"
Price: $2,600
Painted eyes, closed mouth.

Child, 180, Glass Eyes
Size: 19"
Price: $6,000

Child, 185
Size: 12"
Price: $2,600
Smiling, painted eyes, spring-jointed composition body.

Child, 249
Size: 19"   Internet: $1,050
Glass eyes.

Child, 249
Size: 24"   Internet: $1,200
Mark: K 1/2 made in Germany 13 1/2 J.D.K. 249

Child, 249
Size: 30"   Internet: $1,200
Mark: M made in Germany 16 / JDK / 249

Child, 260
Size: 6.5"
Price: $575

Child, 260

Size: 17–26″
Price: $500–$700
Mohair lashes, sometimes on flapper-style body with elongated limbs.
Mark: JDK 260

Child, 260

Size: 32″
All Markets: $900–$1,000+
Mohair upper lashes.
Mark: Made in Germany / J.D.K. / 260

Child, 260

Size: 35″
Price: $1,700–$1,900
Mark: made in / Germany / J.D.K. / 260 / Germany / 92

Character, Wunderkind, 3 heads

Size: 15″
Price: $7,000–$9,000
Very rare set, doll with 4 interchangeable heads, painted eyes. 183 doll, 179 and 208 heads included.
Mark (mold marks): "182," "179," "171," "183" for heads

EARLY KESTNER CHILD DOLLS, SOCKET HEAD

Dolls have socket heads, glass set or sleep eyes, open mouth, teeth, fully jointed composition and wood bodies. Prices are similar from all venues, but most results are from dealers, auctions and shows. These early dolls were produced from approximately 1880–1890 with a few after.

Child, 102

Size: 30″
Price: $4,400
Closed mouth, very plump body.
Mark: 18 / 102

Child, 102

Size: 8.5″
Price: $3,800
Mark: 102

Child, 128, Closed Mouth

Size: 10″
All Markets: $1,700

Child, 169, Closed Mouth

Size: 20″
Price: $2,000

Child, A.T. Kestner

Size: 12″
Price: $2,300
Mark: 7

Child, A.T. Kestner

Size: 27″
Price: $11,500
Resembles the French A.T. doll. Closed mouth.
Mark: 16X

Child, Bru-Type

Size: 15–17″
Price: $3,000+
Open/closed mouth, molded teeth, swivel head on shoulder plate, kid body, bisque lower arms.

Child, Bru-Type

Size: 17″
Price: $2,400
Resembles Circle-Dot Bru, called "Kestner Bru."
Mark: 10

Child, Closed Mouth

Size: 8″
Price: $2,000+
On fully jointed composition body.
Mark: 2 1/2

Child, Closed Mouth

Size: 10–11″
Price: $1,100–$1,600
Jointed composition body with straight wrists.
Mark: unmarked or "5"

Child, Closed Mouth

Size: 12–13″
Price: $2,000–$2,200
Straight-wrist body.
Mark: 6 or 7

Child, Closed Mouth

Size: 14–15″
Price: $2,400–$2,600
Early chunky straight-wrist Kestner body.
Mark: 10

Child, Closed Mouth

Size: 20–22″
All Markets: $2,200–$2,400
Straight-wrist body.
Mark: 14

Child, Closed Mouth

Size: 24–28″
Price: $2,500+

Child, Closed Mouth

Size: 31″
Price: $2,700+

Child, Open Mouth
Size: 12–15"
Price: $1,000+
Square-cut teeth, early Kestner body.

Child, Open Mouth
Size: 17–22"
Price: $1,000–$1,200+
Square-cut teeth, early Kestner body.

Child, Pouty
Size: 7–9"
Price: $1,700

Child, Pouty
Size: 12–14"
All Markets: $2,350–$2,500
Closed mouth, early style Kestner bodies with straight wrists, flat bottom.

Child, XI
Size: 16"
Price: $4,000–$5,000
Closed mouth.
Mark: XI

LATER KESTNER CHILD DOLL, SOCKET HEAD

Dolls have socket bisque heads with open mouths, glass sleep or set eyes, fully jointed composition bodies, and wigs, except as noted. The later dolls are generally from the 1890s to 1910.

Child, 129
Size: 16–17"
Price: $950–$1,200
Mark: E. Made in Germany 9 129

Child, 142
Size: 36"
Price: $1,500–$1,700
Mark: 0 1/2 made in Germany 18 1/2 142

Child, 143
Size: 7–9"
All Markets: $525–$650
Mark: E made in Germany O 143 (or "For G")

Child, 143
Size: 10–12"
Price: $900–$950
Mark: H made in Germany 3 143

Child, 143
Size: 16–19"
Price: $750–$850
Mark: H made in / Germany 12 / 143

Child, 143
Size: 20–22"
All Markets: $1,000–$1,300
Mark: J made in Germany 12 143

Child, 143
Size: 27"
Price: $1,500+
Mark: G made in / Germany 11. / 143 (back of head)

Child, 146
Size: 8"   Internet: $950

Child, 146
Size: 24"
Price: $600

Child, 146
Size: 29"   Internet: $850

Child, 149
Size: 20"
Price: $1,700
Mark: F 1/2 made in Germany 149 10 1/2 (head) Germany (body)

Child, 152
Size: 12–15"
All Markets: $500–$750
Mark: A Made in Germany 4 / 152

Child, 152
Size: 17–20"
All Markets: $700–$1,000
Mark: Made in Germany / 8/0 / 152

Child, 155
Size: 7"
Price: $2,000–$3,000
For fully jointed composition body.
Mark: K made in Germany 155 2/0

Child, 155
Size: 11"   Internet: $1,600
Mark: C made in 7 / Germany / 155.

Child, 160
Size: 16–18"
Price: $550–$700
Mark: Made in Germany C 1/2 DEP 7 1/2 160

Child, 161
Size: 14"
Price: $500+
Mark: B made in / Germany 6 / 161

Child, 161
Size: 18"
Price: $650+

Child, 164
Size: 24–25″
Price: $700–$900
Mark: K 1.2 made in Germany 14 1/2 164

Child, 164
Size: 27–28″
All Markets: $800–$900
Mark: L made in / Germany 15 / 164 / u

Child, 164
Size: 30″
Price: $1,400
Mark: M Made in Germany 16 164(head) Germany (body)

Child, 167
Size: 14–16″
All Markets: $500–$650
Mark: B Made in Germany 6, 167

Child, 167
Size: 18–20″
Price: $500
Mark: C 1/2 made in Germany 7 1/2 167

Child, 167
Size: 22–24″
Price: $600–$750
Body stamped Excelsior / Germany / 4 (in red on hip).
Mark: H 1/2 made in Germany / 12 1/2 167

Child, 167
Size: 32″
Price: $1,000+

Child, 168
Size: 16–18″
Price: $325–$400

Child, 168
Size: 20–22″
Price: $475–$600

Child, 171
Size: 20–21″
Price: $700–$800
Mark: E. made in / Germany 9 / 171

Child, 171
Size: 24–26″
All Markets: $500–$700

Child, 171
Size: 27–29″
Price: $900–$1,200
Mark: L made in / Germany 15 / 171

Child, 171
Size: 33″
All Markets: $1,300–$1,500
Mark: M 1/2 made in Germany 171

Child, 171, Daisy
Size: 18″
Price: $1,000–$1,200
Always with blonde mohair wig and blue eyes.
Mark: C1/2 made in / Germany 7 1/2 / 171 / 10 and Germany / 1 1/2 (red body stamp)

Child, 196
Size: 30″
Price: $450
Slits in bisque for fur brows; not preferred by collectors.

Child, 214
Size: 12″
All Markets: $675

Child, 214
Size: 18–21″
All Markets: $800–$950
Mark: D 1/4 / made in Germany / 8 1/4 / J.D.K. / 214

Child, 214
Size: 24–26″
Price: $650–$850
Mark: K made in Germany 14/ J.D.K. 214

Child, 214
Size: 32″
All Markets: $700–$950

Child, 214
Size: 35″
All Markets: $1,225
Mark: M 1/2 Made In Germany 16 1/2 JDK 214

Child, Black
Size: 16″
Price: $1,700
Mark: E made in Germany

Child, Long-Faced
Size: 21″
Price: $700
Open mouth.
Mark: Made in K Germany

Child, Long-Faced
Size: 22.5″
Price: $1,600
Open mouth, early-Kestner chunky straight-wrist body.
Mark: K 12 C (at crown)

KESTNER CHILD DOLLS, SHOULDER-HEADS

Dolls are shoulder-heads on cloth or kid bodies, generally with bisque lower arms, glass eyes, and wigged. They were produced from the late 1890s to the early 1900s.

Child, 147
Size: 32–33″
All Markets: $650–$800
Cloth or kid body jointed at shoulders, celluloid or bisque lower arms.
Mark: 17 / 147

Child, 148
Size: 13″   Internet: $300
Gusseted kid body.
Mark: 2/148

Child, 148
Size: 20″
Price: $300

Child, 154
Size: 14–16″
Price: $200–$300

Child, 154
Size: 18–19″
Price: $250+
Gusset- or rivet-jointed kid body, bisque or composition arms.

Child, 154
Size: 22″
Price: $300+
Mark: K 154 14

Child, 154
Size: 26–28″
Price: $325–$440+

Child, 161
Size: 24″
Price: $300+

Child, 166
Size: 27″
Price: $600+

Child, 195
Size: 20″
Price: $425
Original paper torso label, sleep eyes, fur brows (not in favor with collectors, although rarer than painted).
Mark: L 195 Dep. (head) Made in Germany (shoulder plate)

Child, 195
Size: 36″
Price: $500+
Fur brows.

Child, Closed Mouth
Size: 15″
Price: $500–$600
Kid body, bisque forearms.
Mark: 1

Child, Closed Mouth
Size: 17–19″
All Markets: $400–$650
Gusseted kid body, bisque lower arms.
Mark: 8 or C (bottom shoulder)

Child, Closed Mouth
Size: 21–23″
Price: $500+
Mark: 1 / Made in Germany (back shoulder plate) or 6

Child, Turned Shoulder-Head, Closed Mouth
Size: 16″
Price: $650–$750

Child, Turned Shoulder-Head, Closed Mouth
Size: 22″
Price: $700+

Child, Turned Shoulder-Head, Open Mouth
Size: 15–16″
Price: $350+
Gusseted or rivet-jointed kid body with bisque lower arms.
Mark: F

Child, Turned Shoulder-Head, Open Mouth
Size: 22″
Price: $350

Child, Turned Shoulder-Head, Open Mouth
Size: 26–27″
Price: $400–$550

KESTNER LADY DOLLS

The Kestner lady dolls are generally from the early 1900s, except for the shoulder-head fashion ladies from the 1880s to 1890s period.

Fashion Lady, Shoulder-Head
Size: 18″
All Markets: $450–$500
Kid body with gusset jointing, bisque forearms, dressed as lady.
Mark: 7 or 8

*Rose O'Neill bisque Kewpie. 6",
c. 1915. Mark: O'Neill, foot (see
next photo). $200, dealer.*

*O'Neill mark on foot of Rose
O'Neill Kewpie in previous
photo.*

*Blunderboo laughing baby Kew-
pie. Bisque. 3.5", c. 1915. Mark:
O'Neill on base, original red label.
Courtesy Theriault's.*

Fashion Lady, Shoulder-Head, Closed Mouth

Size: 25"
Price: $550
Similar to shoulder-head child dolls but dressed
as lady.
Mark: 13 Made in Germany

Gibson Girl, 172

Size: 15"
Price: $1,000–$1,400
Swivel head on shoulder plate, sleep eyes, closed
mouth, kid body with bisque lower arms, pin
joints.
Mark: 2/0 / 172 / 4

Gibson Girl, 172

Size: 20"
Price: $2,600–$3,200
Kid body.
Mark: 172 7 Germany C

Lady, 162, Open Mouth

Size: 17"
Price: $1,200
Redressed, stamped body.
Mark: D made in / Germany 8 / 162

Lady, 162, Open Mouth

Size: 19"
Price: $1,400
Mark: Made in Germany 10 162

Kewpie Dolls

Kewpies were quite the craze in their day—
the Cabbage Patch dolls of their time. Created by noted illustrator, artist, author, and
sculptor Rose O'Neill, the Kewpie is an
iconic doll that has stood the test of time.
Kewpies are still in production today, and
many people who don't know the first thing
about dolls can still identify a Kewpie doll on
sight.

Rose O'Neill was a bit of a childhood prodigy
in art. By the age of 19 she was already a
known illustrator, and her work appeared in
magazines including *Harpers, Colliers,* and
Ladies' Home Journal, in novels, and in well-
known advertisements of her time.

In 1909, Rose O'Neill's first published images of Kewpies appeared in *Ladies' Home
Journal* as illustrations for a poem. The illustrations were so popular that plans quickly
formed to create a doll based on the illustrations, and in 1912 the first Kewpie dolls were
produced, based on sculpting by Joseph
Kallus. They were an instant hit, and Kewpie became one of the first doll merchandis-
ing icons—she was the star of books, talcum
powder boxes, postcards, soap, china, picture
frames, and even a comic strip. Kewpie dolls
were produced by many firms—bisque
Kewpies mostly in Germany by firms such
as Kestner; compositon Kewpies by the
Cameo Doll Co. and others in America. Celluloid Kewpies were also made in Germany,
and later vinyl Kewpies were made by many

Kewpie with elephant. *Bisque, attached with Kewpie's arm around back of elephant . 3.25", c. 1915. Mark: 9378. Very rare. $6,750 at auction in 2000. Courtesy Theriault's.*

Kewpie wearing brown hat. *Bisque. 6", c. 1915. Mark: O'Neill (foot) and red-heart label on back. $4,200, auction. Courtesy Theriault's.*

Kewpie, composition. *On blue molded base. 13", c. late 1920s–early 1930s. Unmarked. $35, eBay (with damage to blue base). Courtesy Geneva Wallen Collection.*

firms including Cameo and Effanbee. Many other companies in Japan and elsewhere produced "unofficial" versions of Kewpie.

Market Report: There is always a strong market for Kewpies! Look especially for rare larger-size bisque dolls, bisque dolls with jointed legs (most Kewpies have stationary legs), bisque dolls with glass eyes (most are painted), and Kewpies in unusual poses or holding unusual molded items. Also look for bisque Kewpies in original boxes. All of these variations of Kewpie are rarer than the standard jointed-arms, painted-eye Kewpies. When buying a "classic" Kewpie, look for Kewpies with feet signed O'Neill and/or Kewpies with their original red heart label.

Online/Offline Report: Prices are weakest for the classic bisque Kewpies and for inexpensive, crudely "made in Japan" versions. Prices for common models on eBay are relatively low, but anything rare has strong competition, which brings prices in line with dealer and show prices. Dealers who are familiar with the rarity of various Kewpie variations are invaluable when buying Kewpies.

Prices and Characteristics: All dolls are in excellent condition, except as noted. "Classic" Kewpie denotes the traditional, standing, straight, all-bisque Kewpie with only jointed arms; many other types of Kewpies in intricate poses (Action, Blunderboo) are one-piece dolls with no jointing. The majority of the Rose O'Neill bisque Kewpies were produced from 1912 through the 1920s.

Marks: For Rose O'Neill bisque Kewpies, a red-heart Kewpie label may be found on the front of the doll (often missing) and "O'Neill" may be incised on the bottom of the feet. Sometimes a doll has no marks at all; and sometimes the back will have "Made In Germany" on a label.

ROSE O'NEILL ALL-BISQUE KEWPIES

Action Kewpie, Holding Basket
Size: 4"   Internet: $800
Sitting.

Action Kewpie, Holding Sack
Size: 4.5"   Internet: $700–$1,000
Holding open bisque sack.

Action Kewpie, Lying on Floor, Arms Away
Size: 3.5"   Internet: $300
Action Kewpies are unjointed.

Action Kewpie, Waving
Size: 6"   Internet: $650

Blunderboo, Crawling
Size: 3"
Price: $650

Carnival Kewpie, celluloid. *Jointed arms only. Original decoration. 11.5". Mark: Japan. $50, dealer.*

Kuddle Kewpie by Cameo / Knickerbocker. *Vinyl head, cloth stuffed body. 13" sitting. Mark: CAMEO © (front neck). $125, dealer.*

Lefton Kewpie. *Bisque. 3.75", c. late 1950s–early 1960s. Mark: Label (bottom): Lefton® / TRADEMARK / EXCLUSIVES /TAIWAN. $15-$30, eBay.*

Blunderboo, Crawling
Size: 3"
Price: $700

Bride
Size: 8"
Price: $850
Dressed as bride, original clothes.

Bride
Size: 12"
Price: $2,900
Very large, original bride clothes.

Card Holder
Price: $550

Classic Kewpie
Size: 4.5"
Price: $75–$100   Internet: $75–$100
Average, no label or mark.

Classic Kewpie, With Label
Size: 4.5"
Price: $100–$175   Internet: $130–$175
Mint, with label or mark.

Classic Kewpie
Size: 5–6"
Price: $100–$175   Internet: $100–$150
Average, no label or mark.

Classic Kewpie, With Label
Size: 5–6"
Price: $225+   Internet: $210–$300
Mint, with label or mark.

Classic Kewpie
Size: 6–6.5"
Price: $100–$175   Internet: $100–$150
Average, no label or mark.

Classic Kewpie
Size: 6–6.5"
Price: $155–$300   Internet: $250–$350
Mint, with label or mark.

Classic Kewpie
Size: 8–10"   Internet: $475–$510
Mint, classic Kewpie in large size.

Classic Kewpie, With Box
Size: 5"
Price: $500–$700
MIB.

Doodle Dog
Size: 1.5"
Price: $250+
Rare companion dog for Kewpie; little wings.

Doodle Dog
Size: 3"
Price: $475
For damaged Doodle Dog with hairline.

Doodle Dog
Size: 4.5"   Internet: $1,650

Doodle Dog
Size: 6"   Internet: $1,525
Largest size Doodle Dog.

Vinyl Kewpies. All jointed only at arms. 3–8″, c. late 1960s–1970s. Marks: Either "Japan" or "Hong Kong." $5–$10, eBay. Courtesy Clara Robbins and Martha Robbins.

Doodle Dog With Kewpie
Size: 5″
Price: $900
Molded together.

Drumming Kewpie, Drum on Stool
Size: 3.5″   Internet: $3,050
Mint.

Farmer
Size: 6″   Internet: $425
Holding rake, with molded bisque hat.

Huggers
Size: 2.5–3″
Price: $135–$175   Internet: $125–$75

Huggers
Size: 3.5–4.5″
Price: $175–$225   Internet: $145–$200

Jasperware Kewpie Clock
Size: 5.75″
Price: $350
Blue, marked Germany and Rose O'Neill.

Jasperware Kewpie Vase
Size: 6.5″
Price: $275
Green.
Mark: Germany and Rose O'Neill.

Jasperware Kewpie Wall Plaque
Size: 4.5″
                         Internet: $280
Blue, 3 Kewpie images.

Jointed Arms and Legs
Size: 8″   Internet: $900

Jointed Arms and Legs
Size: 5–6.5″
Price: $600–$750   Internet: $500–$840
Higher prices for larger, also with original clothing.

Kewpie Fireman
Size: 4.5″   Internet: $1,800
Molded red fireman's hat.

Kewpie Head
Size: 2.5″
Price: $200
Shoulder-head.

Kewpie Holding a Pen
Size: 3–4″
Price: $400   Internet: $640

Kewpie Holding a Pen on a Tray
Size: 3″
Price: $400
China tray reads "With Kewpish Love from Rose O Neill."

Mayor
Size: 4″
Price: $275
Sits with arms crossed in bisque "wicker chair" with curved back.

Pincushion
Size: 6.5″
Price: $150
With original pincushion base.

Place Card Holder, Vase, Playing Mandolin
Size: 3″   Internet: $415
Card goes between doll and vase.

Reclining
Size: 2.5″
Price: $300

Salt and Pepper Shakers (1 With Bunny, 1 With Chick)
Size: 3″
Price: $750

Scootles, All-Bisque
Size: 6.5″
Price: $900
Mark: Rose O'Neill Scootles (feet).

Thinker
Size: 2.5″
Price: $175

Traveler
Size: 3.5–4″
Price: $175–$225

Traveler
Size: 4″   Internet: $500
Holding suitcase and umbrella.

With Black Cat, Sitting
Size: 3.5″   Internet: $250

OTHER BISQUE KEWPIES

German, Pudgy-Type, Jointed Arms
Size: 4″
Price: $50   Internet: $30–$50
Not Rose O'Neill; a knockoff.

Japanese, Pudgy-Type, Jointed Arms
Size: 4″
Price: $40   Internet: $20–$40
Knockoff Kewpie-type.

Enesco, Kewpie Trick or Treat
Size: 4.5″   Internet: $95
MIB, also known as Jesco Kewpie.

Enesco, Riding in Blue Car
Size: 4.5″   Internet: $100
MIB.

Enesco, Sitting With Rainbow
Size: 4.5″   Internet: $150
MIB.

Kewpie-Type, Poor Quality
Size: 4″
Price: $25   Internet: $10–$30
Made in Japan.

Reproduction, Glass Eyes
Size: 12″
Price: $175
Late 20th-century reproduction, well done.

KEWPIE, OTHER MATERIALS

Black
Size: 2–3″   Date: 1920s
     Internet: $50–$100
Material: celluloid

Wedding Party
Size: 4″   Date: 1920s
Price: $140
Material: celluloid
Bride, bridegroom, 2 bridesmaids in original crepe paper costumes.

Japan, Asian Kewpie Thinker
Size: 6.5″   Date: 1913
Price: $55–$85
Material: chalk
1-piece chalk, painted, label on base with date 1913.

Cuddle Kewpie, Richard Krueger
Size: 8″   Date: 1930
     Internet: $165
Material: cloth
Red satin cloth body with shaped wings.

R. John Wright
Size: 7.5″   Date: 1999
     Internet: $325
Material: cloth, felt
MIB.
Mark: R. JOHN WRIGHT DOLLS / JESCO 1999 / 0414 (paper label attached by metal button) LE 1,000.

Black
Size: 10″   Date: 1920s
Price: $150
Material: composition

Cameo, Scootles
Size: 12–13″
Price: $375   Internet: $335
Material: composition
Also see Cameo section. Unmarked, all original.

Cameo, Scootles

Size: 13"   Internet: $210
Material: composition
Average condition.

Cameo, Scootles

Size: 15–16"
Price: $250   Internet: $315
Material: composition
Unmarked, all original.

Classic Kewpie

Size: 13–14"   Date: late 1930s
Price: $100   Internet: $100
Material: composition
Average, crazing.

Classic Kewpie, Swivel Head

Size: 12"
Price: $165
Material: composition

Kewpie

Size: 7–13"   Date: 1913
Price: $115   Internet: $100
Material: composition
Original 1913 Rose O'Neill sticker; jointed arms, on blue base; several sizes.

Kewpie Talcum Powder Holder, Rose O'Neill

Size: 7"   Date: 1917
Price: $205   Internet: $265
Material: composition
Original labeled box.

Kewpie Talcum Powder Holder, Rose O'Neill

Size: 7"   Date: 1917
                            Internet: $555
Material: composition
MIB; exceptional example. Metal talcum-powder dispenser on head. Original label on box: "Kewpie Talcum Makes Me Rosy, Bright and Cheery, Cool and Cozy."

Christmas Bulb

Size: 3.5"
Price: $55
Material: glass
Painted glass.

Kewpie Bank

Size: 3"
Price: $75
Material: glass
Made by George Borgfeldt.

Kewpie Mold

Size: 11"
Price: $175
Material: metal
2 pieces hinged; all metal.

Paperweight

Size: 4"
Price: $65
Material: nickel
Kewpie Thinker on Pillow, cast pewter.

Kewpie China Sugar Bowl

Size: 3.5"
Price: $135
Material: porcelain

Kewpie Coasters, 2

Size: 3"
Price: $145
Material: porcelain

Strombecker Kewpie/Scootles

Size: 27"   Internet: $125
Material: vinyl

Kley & Hahn

Kley & Hahn was one of the latecomers to the German porcelain dollmaking scene. Starting in business in 1902, it produced bisque dolls using the heads of many famous bisque firms, including Kestner. Most of the dolls produced by Kley & Hahn were character babies or children, although it also produced simple dolly-faced dolls like the Walküres.

Market Report: As with dolls from most German bisque companies, the most common Kley & Hahns have decreased in value during the last few years, while the prices for the rarest items have held steady or increased.

Online/Offline Report: You will mostly see the lesser-quality dolly-faced dolls, including Walküres, on eBay, and very few of the rarer character children. For the desirable character children, look to dealers and auction houses. A beginning collector can pick up very nice (if not in original clothing or wigs, etc.) Walküres and character babies for reasonable prices on eBay—just the type of doll that is affordable and fun for a beginning antique doll collection.

Kley & Hahn, Character Toddler
525. Composition and wood jointed toddler body with side-hip jointing. 18″, c. 1912. Mark: Germany K & H (in banner) 525 9. $1,700, auction. Courtesy Theriault's.

Kley & Hahn, Character Child
546. Composition and wood jointed body. 19″, c. 1915. Mark: K & H (in banner) 546 8 Germany.

Prices and Characteristics: Dolls are bisque, with glass eyes and open mouths, wigged, except as noted, in excellent condition. Dolls are on fully jointed composition bodies, and generally were produced from 1910 to 1915 and later, with some child dolls also produced earlier. Prices are similar from all venues.

KLEY & HAHN CHARACTER DOLLS

Baby, 154
Size: 12″
All Markets: $425
Bent-limb baby body.
Mark: II / 154/4

Baby, 160
Size: 24″
Price: $700

Baby, 525
Size: 12–14″
Price: $500–$550
Painted dome head, painted eyes, open mouth.

Baby, 531
Size: 17″
Price: $600
Painted eyes and hair.

Child, 157
Size: 20″
Price: $850
Glass eyes, painted dome.

Child, 526
Size: 15″
Price: $3,300–$3,500
Closed mouth.
Mark: K & H (in banner) 526 3 1/2 Germany

Child, 526
Size: 20″
Price: $3,500+
Mark: K & B H (in banner) / 526 / 7

Kley & Hahn, Character Toddler 548. *Composition and wood jointed toddler body with side-hip jointing. 25″, c. 1912. Mark: K & H (in banner) 548 15 Germany. Courtesy Theriault's.*

Child, 549, Glass Eyes
Size: 20″
Price: $18,000
Rarer with glass eyes. At auction.

Toddler, 158
Size: 17–19″
All Markets: $700–$900
Painted hair, glass eyes.
Mark: K & H 158 12

Toddler, 160
Size: 18″
Price: $2,100
Pouty expression.
Mark: K & H (in banner) 169 – 9

Toddler, 166, "Tommy Tucker"
Size: 24″
Price: $2,000+
Painted hair, glass eyes, side-hip jointed toddler body.
Mark: K 8 H (banner) / 166-13

Toddler, 167
Size: 12″
Price: $350
Fully jointed toddler body.

Toddler, 169
Size: 17–21″
Price: $2,000+
Closed mouth.
Mark: K & H (in banner) / Germany 169-9

Toddler, 525
Size: 18″
Price: $1,700

Toddler body with side-hip jointing, chubby tummy.
Mark: Germany K&H (in banner) 525 9

Double-Faced Character Baby
Size: 11″
Price: $9004
Mark: #4

KLEY & HAHN CHILD DOLLS

Child, 250, 282
Size: 19″
All Markets: $350–$400

Child, 250, 282
Size: 24–26″
Price: $500+

Child, Walküre
Size: 17–19″
Price: $500+
Can be on mechanical body.
Mark: 6 / Walkure/ Germany

Child, Walküre
Size: 22 –25″
Price: $650+

Child, Walküre
Size: 35″
Price: $1,100
Mark: 19 / Walkure / Germany

Child, Walküre
Size: 40–42″
Price: $2,200–$2,600

Kling, Child 190, Sonneberg (shown with smaller Sonneberg child). Solid flattened dome bisque head, composition and wood jointed body with straight wrists. 15" c. 1890. Mark: 190 / 7. Courtesy Theriault's.

Open mouth, fully jointed compositon body.
Mark: Walkure Germany

Kling

Kling is another long-standing German doll firm, making china and bisque dolls from the 1830s through the 1930s. Kling is best known for its shoulder-head bisque dolls with molded hair, although it also made beautiful china dolls, untinted bisque dolls commonly referred to as "parians," and even all-bisques.

Market Report: Although German shoulder-head bisque dolls are somewhat out of fashion with collectors, some of the Kling shoulder-heads, especially those with fancier decorations like molded collars and decorated bodices, are highly sought-after. Some of the more common Kling dolls with molded hair can have lovely bisque and painting, while others were clearly "budget models" so, as with most German bisque, each piece must be individually assessed. Those dolls with finer bisque and decoration than the majority of dolls from a mold will bring higher than "book" prices. Although prices have trended downward on the more common Kling shoulder-heads (as with most antique shoulder-heads), prices seem to be stabilizing. Prices on the better Kling china dolls and decorated shoulder-heads

are rising, although some of the simple dolls with deeply molded hair and glass eyes are charming and should not be overlooked.

Online/Offline Report: You can definitely find the more common china and bisque Kling shoulder-heads on the Internet, often with bargain prices. If you have a sharp eye and can educate yourself about Kling dolls and bisque quality, you can also find bargains from dealers on the prettier and rarer (although not decorated) Kling shoulder-heads.

Prices and Characteristics: Prices are for bisque dolls, in excellent condition, and prices are mixed from all venues. Except as noted, dolls are shoulder-heads, with cloth or kid bodies and bisque or china lower limbs and closed mouths. Most dolls are from the 1870s–1890s. Some dolls are marked with a bell symbol which has a "K" inside the bell; others just have a mold number and size number.

KLING

103, Child
Size: 12"
Price: $300
Wigged, painted eyes.

123, Child
Size: 11"
Price: $450

Glass eyes, may have celluloid lower arms.
Mark: 123 K (in bell)

123, Child
Size: 14–16″
Price: $500+
Glass eyes.

123, Marotte
Size: 12″
Price: $500
Jester costume, musical mechanism, glass eyes.
Mark: 123 / 3

128, Lady
Size: 18–19″
Price: $500–$600
Blonde molded hair, pierced ears.

131, Child, Boy
Size: 20″
Price: $750
Blonde molded hair, glass eyes.

131, China Doll
Size: 14″
Price: $250
Blonde molded hair, painted eyes.

167, Child
Size: 16″
Price: $1,300
Wigged, solid dome.
Mark: 167 K (in bell) 5

186, Lady, Parian-Type
Size: 21″
Price: $825
Blonde molded hair, glass eyes.
Mark: 186 / 7

193, Lady With Molded Headband
Size: 18″
Price: $1,500
Molded black headband, pierced ears, glass eyes, molded blonde hair.
Mark: 193 / 5

203, China Doll
Size: 21″
Price: $500
Pink-tinted china doll, painted eyes.
Mark: 203

300, Gentleman
Size: 18″
Price: $400
Detailed molded blonde hair, glass eyes, closed mouth, rivet-jointed leather body with original compositon arms and legs.
Mark: 300 and the bell symbol

Child, No Mold Number, Painted Eyes
Size: 15–18″
Price: $350–$500
Painted eyes, wigged or molded hair marked with bell. More with glass eyes.
Mark: Bell mark

Child, Various Mold Numbers, Glass Eyes
Size: 14–18″
Price: $450–$600
The majority of the bisque child shoulder heads with glass eyes trade in this range. Less for painted eyes and less for china dolls. Most mold numbers are in the 100s and 200s series, a few in the 300s.

Lady, Parian or China, Well-Decorated
Size: 16–21″
Price: $1,500
Dolls with extra fancy hair or bodice decorations.

Lanternier

Lanternier was seriously late to the French dollmaking world, with its first dolls produced in 1915 in Limoges, France. Lanternier made mostly late bébé dolls as well as lady dolls, often dressed in provincial costumes of France. Production continued until 1924.

Market Report: Sure it's French, but don't confuse Lanternier dolls with the much earlier Brus, Jumeaus, and Steiners. By the time Lanternier hit the doll scene in 1915, most other French dollmakers had long since closed up shop or folded into S.F.B.J. That said, a collector who cannot afford a Bru or a Jumeau can get a lovely, very French-looking Lanternier at a more affordable price. Be careful when buying a Lanternier bisque doll—it does help to see them in person, since the bisque for these dolls can sometimes be a bit ruddy or muddy in complexion.

Online/Offline Report: You don't see these dolls very often on eBay or online. Actually, since doll production at this company lasted barely ten years, you hardly see Lanternier dolls at all. That doesn't mean that they bring high prices, however, since demand is not huge and the quality isn't often fantastic. Look for pretty open-mouth Lanternier

Lanternier, character child "Toto." Composition and wood jointed body. 16", c. 1918. Mark: Depose Toto N5 A.L. & C. Limoges. Courtesy Theriault's.

Lanternier, character child "Caprice." Composition and wood jointed body. 29", c. 1915. Mark: Depose Fabrication Francaise Caprice No. 12 S. L. & Co Limoges. Courtesy Theriault's.

dolls from dealers and at doll shows, and ladies in their original costumes.

Prices and Characteristics: All dolls are bisque with fully jointed French composition bodies and glass eyes. Prices are for dolls in excellent condition.

LANTERNIER

Cherie
Size: 11"
Price: $260
Open mouth.

Cherie
Size: 25"
Price: $400
Mohair upper lashes.
Mark: Fabrication Francaise A L & Cie Limoges Cherie 10

Favorite
Size: 18"
Price: $550
Open mouth with molded teeth.
Mark: Deposé Fabrication Francaise Favorite No. 2 Ed. Tasoon AL & Cie Limoges

Favorite
Size: 29"
Price: $575

Lorraine (Lady)
Size: 22"
All Markets: $400

In regional dress, cloth stuffed body, bisque lower legs, compositon hands.
Mark: Lorraine

Bébé, Open Mouth
Size: 18"
Price: $300–$500
Mark: Limoges France

Bébé, Open Mouth
Size: 27"
Price: $600–$800
Mark: Mon Cheri L F Paris 23

Character, Boy
Size: 20"
Price: $1,125
Open/closed mouth with molded teeth.

Armand Marseille

Countless antique doll collectors started their doll collections with either an Armand Marseille doll passed down in their family, or an Armand Marseille 370 or 390 found at an antique mall or shop. Armand Marseille has been hailed by many doll experts as one of the most prolific of all the German bisque dollmakers (if not the most prolific), and given the number of their dolly-face dolls available on eBay at any given time, and the number that most dealers see from original family collections, this certainly seems to be true. By some estimates, the factory of Ar-

Queen Louise, child. *Composition jointed body. 22". Mark: 29 / Queen Louise / 100 / Germany. $300, dealer.*

Armand Marseille, 345 Character. *Composition and wood jointed body. 12", c. 1912. Mark: Made in Germany A 2 M 345. Courtesy Theriault's.*

Armand Marseille, 590 Toddler. *Composition and wood toddler body with side-hip jointing. 17", c. 1916. Mark: 590 1 5 M Germany DRGM. Courtesy Theriault's.*

mand Marseille was producing over 1,000 doll heads a day at the height of their production!

Armand Marseille, however, produced many more types of dolls than just the common 370 and 390 bisque head dolls. Although not in the business of dolls for as long as German firms such as Kestner or Hertwig, their production spanned from 1885 through the early 1930s. Besides their ubiquitous dolly-face dolls, they produced character baby and toddler dolls, a highly sought after (and now very expensive) line of character children, and lovely lady and flapper dolls. Later production included more infant and baby dolls, googlies, and the ever-popular Just Me.

Market Report: Although you rarely find a devoted collector of Armand Marseille dolls the way you find devoted collectors of Kestner or Simon & Halbig dolls, there is a good, healthy market for them. The lower-priced dolls find their way into the collections of eager new antique doll collectors, and character doll collectors can't get enough of their character children series.

Overall, prices for Armand Marseille dolls have declined with the advent of eBay, with a few exceptions, including for prices of googlies and the rarest character children.

As mentioned frequently in this book, you need to individually inspect any antique bisque doll that you are considering buying for bisque quality and painting quality, but this can be especially true with Armand Marseille dolls—I've seen 390s with ugly one-stroke eyebrows and chalky bisque, and also 390s with bisque rivaling that of a Kestner and with intricate, multistroke brows.

Online/Offline Report: Prices are very similar for the more common dolls, baby dolls, googlies and Just Mes on eBay and at shops and shows. Dealers and auction houses will tend to have more dolls with all-original bodies, wigs, and clothing, as well as the rarer character children.

Prices and Characteristics: All dolls are bisque, in excellent condition, appropriately dressed with clothing of the appropriate period. Prices are similar and mixed at all venues although some specific Internet results have been noted. Please also note that for the most common Armand Marseille dolls (390, 370, 1894, 341), the prices are much lower for dolls that are not in excellent condition—you can sometimes find such dolls naked or poorly presented for approximately $100.

Armand Marseille, Child 390.
*Jointed composition body. One of
the most common German bisque
dolls, made for over 40 years in
many sizes and styles. 16", c.
1890s–1930. Mark: Armand Marseille / Germany / 390 / A 2 M.
$200 dealer.*

Just Me. *5-piece composition body
with slender limbs, bent right arm.
9.5", c. 1928. Mark: Just Me Registered Germany A 310/7/0 M. Courtesy Theriault's.*

Our Pet, baby. *5-piece composition baby body. 12". Mark: Germany / 0 / R 127 A (very rubbed;
hard to read) and red "Our Pet"
label.*

ARMAND MARSEILLE BABY AND TODDLER DOLLS

Babies are on five-piece composition bent-limb baby bodies and toddlers are on five-piece side (or slant) hip baby bodies, except as indicated. All baby and toddler dolls are considered character dolls, including the infant-type dolls, 341, 351 (Dream Baby) and Our Pet. The dolls have glass eyes and are wigged, except as noted. Baby dolls were made starting in 1910, with later babies including Dream Baby and Rock-A-Bye Baby circa 1925.

Baby, 251
Size: 10"
Price: $550
Wigged, for Borgfeldt, closed mouth.
Mark: 251 G.B. Germany A 4/0 M 248/1

Baby, 328
Size: 15"
Price: $230
For Borgfeldt.
Mark: G 328 B A 4 M

Baby, 329
Size: 15"
Price: $290
Open mouth, sleep eyes.

Baby, Ellar, 335
Size: 14"
Price: $400–$500

Closed mouth, painted hair with tuft of hair through opening on top, sleep eyes.
Mark: A. Ellar M. / Germany / 355./3 1/2 K

Dream Baby, 341
Size: 7.5–8"
All Markets: $125–$225
Set eyes, painted hair (socket head), set or sleep eyes, cloth body with composition or celluloid hands, sometimes crier.
Mark: A.M. Germany 341/2

Dream Baby, 341
Size: 9–11"
All Markets: $175–$300

Dream Baby, 341
Size: 13"
All Markets: $195–$250
Mark: AM / Germany / 351/3

Dream Baby, 341
Size: 15–16"
All Markets: $250–$300
Mark: AM Germany 341/4 A

Dream Baby, 341
Size: 18"
Price: $300+

Rock-A-Bye Baby, 351
Size: 8"
Price: $125
Painted, molded hair, set eyes, cloth body with celluloid or composition hands.

Armand Marseille Native American child. *12″. Mark: made in Germany / AM / 3/0. $375, dealer.*

Rock-A-Bye Baby, 351
Size: 14–16″
Price: $225–$275

Rock-A-Bye Baby, 351
Size: 18″
Price: $300+

Rock-A-Bye Baby, 352
Size: 10″
Price: $500
MIB factory presentation, clothing, pacifier, painted hair, sleep eyes, cloth body.
Box Mark: Rock-A-Bye Baby / Name Registered / 1/12...Germany.
Mark: A.M. / Germany / 352 12/0

Baby, 352
Size: 20″
Price: $175
Solid dome, painted hair, sleep eyes, cloth body with celluloid hands.

Baby, 371
Size: 8″
Price: $150
Solid dome, painted hair.

Baby, 410
Size: 12.5″
Price: $500
Mark: Made in Germany / Armand Marseille / 410 / A.O.M. / D.R.G.M.

Baby, 542
Size: 15″
Price: $375
Painted hair, cloth body, composition limbs. Open mouth.

Baby, 560a
Size: 9″
Price: $385
Wigged.

Baby, 590
Size: 13–15″
All Markets: $500–$600
Mark: 590 / A.3.M. / Germany / D.R.G.M.

Baby, 971
Size: 8″
Price: $125
Wigged, sleep eyes.

Baby, 985
Size: 12″
Price: $275
Mark: 985 A. 1 M.

Baby, 985
Size: 19″
Price: $375
Wigged, sleep eyes.
Mark: A.M. 985 Germany 9

Baby, 990
Size: 7.5″
Price: $250

Baby, 996
Size: 15″
Price: $400

Baby, Gloria
Size: 17"
Price: $400
Painted hair, open mouth.

Baby, Our Pet
Size: 14"
Price: $350
With label. Glass eyes, painted hair.

Toddler, 971
Size: 12"
Price: $300
Mark: 971 DRGM 267 A 5/0 M

Toddler, 975
Size: 9.5"
Price: $350
Mark: Armand Marseille / A. 975 M / Germany / 6/0

Toddler, 980
Size: 12"
Price: $350
Mark: 980 A 6/0 M

Toddler, 990
Size: 19"
All Markets: $425
Mark: Armand Marseille / Germany / 990 / A.8.M

Toddler, No Mold Number
Size: 10"
Price: $500
Painted eyes and hair.
Mark: Made in Germany A M 0 DRGM

ARMAND MARSEILLE CHARACTER CHILD DOLLS

These dolls have fully jointed compositon bodies with wigs and glass eyes, except as noted. Character children were made starting in 1910.

231, Fany
Size: 15"
All Markets: $4,000–$5,000+
Glass eyes, closed mouth, wigged, straight-wrist compositon body.

233, Boy, Attributed
Size: 17.5"
Price: $1,500
Attributed to Marseille. Wigged, open mouth.
Mark: 223 / 3

345, Child
Size: 10"
Price: $850
Glass eyes.
Mark: A 2/0 M 345

345, Painted Eyes
Size: 11"
Price: $2,900
Sonneberg compositon body, straight wrists.
Mark: A 0 M 345

345, Painted Eyes
Size: 14"
Price: $24,000
Solemn expression, fully jointed composition body. At auction.
Mark: Made in Germany A 3 M 345

353, Child
Size: 12"
Price: $1,000
Mark: AM Germany 353/1/K

449, Child, Painted Bisque
Size: 19"
All Markets: $250
Shoulder-head, kid body.
Mark: A 49 Germany 1/2

500, Child
Size: 13"
Price: $600
Painted eyes, hair.

500, Child
Size: 17"
Price: $525
Mark: 500 / Germany / A.1.M. / D.R.G.M.

550, Child
Size: 13"
Price: $1,950
Sleep eyes, bob mohair wig.
Mark: 550 A. 1 M

560a, Child
Size: 22"
Price: $1,250
Sleep eyes, open mouth, cheek and eye dimples.
Mark: Made in Germany Armand Marseille 560a A 7h M

590, Child
Size: 18"
Price: $400
Open mouth.
Mark: 590 / .5.M. / Germany / D.R.G.M.

590, Laughing Child
Size: 20″
Price: $950
Open/closed mouth.
Mark: 590 / A. 5 M. / Germany / D.R.G.M.

590, Laughing Child
Size: 20″
Price: $650
Open mouth, sleep eyes.

996, Child
Size: 16″
Price: $450
May be "breather" with open nostrils. Fully
jointed compositon body.

Character Girl, No Mold Number, A. M. mark
Size: 21–24″
Price: $23,000–$27,000
Very rare characters in large sizes. Painted eyes,
closed mouths, wigged, fully jointed composition
bodies, c. 1910.
Mark: Germany A. 6 M. or Germany A. 7 M.

Character, Child, No Mold Number, Pouty
Size: 14″
Price: $7,200
Painted eyes, dome head with molded painted
hair, closed mouth.
Mark: Made in Germany A 2 M

Just Me, 310
Size: 7– 8″
Price: $1,000–$1,200
Wigged, closed mouth, 5-piece composition body
with chubby torso, modeled bent right arm,
elongated limbs. Paper label: I'm Just Me, Your
Dolly.
Mark: A 310 / 7/0 M

Just Me, 310
Size: 9– 10″
Price: $1,600–$2,200
Paper label: Just Me Registered Your Dolly, Ger-
many.
Mark: Just Me Germany Registered 310 7/0 AM

Just Me, 310
Size: 11″
Price: $2,200
Mark: Just Me, Registered Germany A 310 M
3/0

Just Me, 310, Painted Bisque
Size: 7″
Price: $800

ARMAND MARSEILLE CHILD DOLLS

Child dolls are on fully jointed composition
bodies, except as noted. Shoulder-head dolls
have kid or cloth bodies, except as noted,
generally with bisque or composition lower
arms. (If no body type is noted, the body is
fully jointed composition.) The dolls have
glass eyes and are wigged, except as noted.
Child dolls were made from approximately
1890 to 1930.

Child, 390, No Mold Number
Size: 41″
Price: $950
Applied upper lashes.

Child, 1894, 1897
Size: 9– 12″
Price: $175–$200
Prices for fully jointed composition bodies. All
prices less for 1894s with crude 5-piece or card-
board bodies.
Mark: 1894 A.M. Dep

Child, 1894, 1897
Size: 14– 16″
Price: $175–$300
Compositon body.
Mark: 1894 A M 3 DEP

Child, 1894, 1897
Size: 14–17″
Price: $250
Shoulder-head with kid body.

Child, 1894, 1897
Size: 20+″
Price: $300–$500+
Higher prices for all-original dolls.

Child, 1894, Factory Presentation
Size: 18″
Price: $425
Completely original.
Mark: 1894 / A.M. 8 DEP / Made in Germany

Child, 370
Size: 11– 12″
Price: $90–$125
Shoulder-head with kid or cloth body, composi-
tion or bisque lower arms, gusset or kid jointed.

Child, 370
Size: 14– 16″
Price: $150–$200

Child, 370
Size: 23–26+″
Price: $250+

Child, 390

Size: 9– 10″
Price: $225+
On fully jointed composition body. For all 390s, less for 5-piece crude composition body or painted bisque.

Child, 390

Size: 12– 14″
Price: $200+
On fully jointed composition body. Less for 5-piece crude composition body.

Child, 390

Size: 16– 18″
All Markets: $150–$200
390 prices include prices for 390N dolls.
Mark: Made in Germany 390 A. 2 M.

Child, 390

Size: 20– 22″
Price: $200–$300

Child, 390

Size: 23– 25″
Price: $250–$350

Child, 390

Size: 26– 28″
All Markets: $375–$475
Sometimes without mold number.
Mark: Armand Marseille Germany 390 A. 5 M.

Child, 390

Size: 32″
All Markets: $600+
No mold number.
Mark: A. 15 M.

Child, 390

Size: 40– 42″
All Markets: $1,675–$2,000
No mold number.
Mark: A. 17. M

Child, 390, Bébé Dormeur

Size: 9″
Price: $1,000
Original box and presentation.
Mark: 390 Made in Germany

Child, 390, Flapper

Size: 12″
Price: $350
5-piece elongated composition flapper body with painted shoes, socks.
Mark: Armand Marseille/Germany 390 A 6/0 M

Child, 390N

Size: 24″
Price: $600

For MIB original box and outfit, very mint; generally, follow 390 prices for 390N dolls.
Mark: Armand Marseille / 390n / Germany / A.7 1/2. M.

Child, Baby Betty

Size: 16″
Price: $350
Wigged, fully jointed composition body.

Child, 2000

Size: 13″
Price: $1,000
Swivel head on shoulder plate, kid body.

Child, 3200

Size: 13″
Price: $250
Shoulder-head, cloth body, bisque arms.

Child, 3300

Size: 18″
All Markets: $1,000
Shoulder-head, kid body, unique carved wood lower arms and legs with good detail.

Child, Darling Dolly

Size: 9″
Price: $150
Shoulder-head, kid body, bisque arms.

Child, Darling Dolly

Size: 18– 20″
Price: $225–$250
Shoulder-head, kid body, bisque arms.

Child, Duchess

Size: 13″
Price: $200
Shoulder-head, kid body, bisque arms.
Mark: Duchess A 0 _ M

Child, Duchess

Size: 20″
Price: $400
Fully jointed composition body.
Mark: A 10 M Duchess Made In Germany

Child, Florodora

Size: 11– 12″
Price: $175–$200
Fully jointed composition body. Clothing sometimes sewn on.
Mark: Made in Germany / Florodora / A. 5/0. M.

Child, Florodora

Size: 16– 18″
Price: $175–$225
Prices for Florodoras with fully jointed composition bodies; less for dolls with crude 5-piece bodies.
Mark: Made in Germany Florodora / A 0 1/2 M

Child, Florodora
Size: 22– 23″
All Markets: $150–$250
Mark: Florodora A.2 M. D.R.P. Made in Germany

Child, Florodora
Size: 25″
Price: $250

Child, Lilly, Mabel
Size: 12–14″
Price: $225

Child, Lilly, Mabel
Size: 20– 22″
Price: $275–$300
Shoulder-head, kid or cloth body, bisque arms.

Child, Queen Louise
Size: 18″
Price: $250–$300

Child, Queen Louise
Size: 22– 24″
Price: $300–$400
Composition body.
Mark: Queen Louise / Germany

Child, Queen Louise
Size: 28– 30″
All Markets: $475–$500

ARMAND MARSEILLE LADY DOLLS & OTHER

Lady, 401, Flapper
Size: 14″
Price: $1,600–$2,000
For articulated composition lady body with straight wrists and feet arched for high heels. More for rarer body types. Sleep eyes, closed pursed mouth.
Mark: Armand Marseille Germany 401 A 5/0 M

Native American, Painted Bisque
Size: 9″
Price: $125
Open mouth, 5-piece composition body.

Native American, Painted Bisque
Size: 11″
Price: $200

Pillow Puppet
Size: 8″
Price: $200
Solid dome, painted hair, sleep eyes, closed mouth, celluloid hands on cloth puppet torso, on pillow.
Mark: Tag: "Tee-Wee Hand Babe, Atlantic City"

Topsy Turvy
Size: 9″
All Markets: $500
Black head worn. Black head papier-mâché, white head bisque.
Mark: 3200 / AM 10 / OX DEP / Germany

Googly Dolls
For Armand Marseille googly dolls, see the Googly section.

Metal Head Dolls

It was sensible (sort of) for companies to make metal head dolls. After all, metal was unbreakable, unlike bisque. However, doll companies didn't balance the unbreakable nature of metal with the fact that the material was cold, uncuddly, and that the paint used for flesh tones would easily chip.

Metal doll heads were produced, mainly in Germany although also in the United States, for approximately 40 years from 1890 to approximately 1930. The heads were mostly made from tin sheet metal. The faces of most metal head dolls look nearly identical to the bisque-head dolly-faced dolls and molded-hair parian-type dolls produced during the same time period. The dolls made by Buschow & Beck, carrying the Minerva trademark, are the best-known of these dolls.

Market Report: I think it is safe to say that the market for metal head dolls is not a hot one. Many collectors have trouble warming up to these dolls, and many of these dolls have come to us with great damage over time—primarily with heavily chipped and cracked paint. Even perfect dolls can often have trouble finding a buyer for $100 on eBay.

Online/Offline Report: Metal head dolls have similar price and availability from all venues.

Prices and Characteristics: All dolls have metal shoulder-heads (stamped from sheet metal) with molded hair, generally with cloth bodies (sometimes leather) and glass eyes. Prices are lower for painted eyes. Dolls generally show some wear to the paint on the metal, and prices are for dolls with such typ-

Minerva child. Tin head, cloth body with lower bisque arms and legs (replaced). 22". Mark: MINERVA / (helmet symbol) on front shoulder plate and GERMANY / 7 (back shoulder plate).

ical wear. The dolls marked MINERVA are by Buschow & Beck. All dolls priced here are from Germany except as noted.

Marks: Minerva dolls are generally marked: MINERVA (front shoulder plate), DEPONIERT or GERMANY (back shoulder plate), or some variation thereof, sometimes with a number following GERMANY. Other metal head dolls from Germany can be marked only Germany, unmarked, or marked Juno.

METAL HEAD

Metal Molded Head, Braided Bun
Size: 15.5"
Price: $2,200
Early, rare metal head, from mid-1800s. Metal shoulder-head looking like papier-mâché dolls of mid-1800s, with milliner's model body. At auction.

Minerva
Size: 18– 24"
Price: $40–$100   Internet: $40–$60
Dolls in average condition, generally replaced clothing, usually composition or bisque lower arms.

Minerva
Size: 12– 14"
Price: $125   Internet: $100
Doll with well-molded hairstyle, old clothing, minimal face wear.

Minerva
Size: 24"   Internet: $125
Original cloth body; hands are leather, well dressed in antique clothing.

Nippon Dolls

By law, dolls manufactured in Japan which were sold in the United States had to be marked "Nippon" (the Japanese word for "Japan") from 1891 through 1921. After 1921, by law the items had to be marked "Japan" or "Made in Japan." The dolls were not always marked on the bisque (sometimes they were marked only on a box which was discarded) but collectors of Nippon dolls look for the Nippon mark. Most of the Nippon dolls were sold in the United States after World War I, since that was when German doll exporting to the United States essentially stopped for a number of years.

Market Report and Online/Offline Report: You can find dolls marked Nippon on eBay, but not as many as you might think. Dolls marked "Japan" are much more plentiful than dolls marked "Nippon." Prices are similar from all venues. The Nippon dolls are very popular with collectors—some collectors specialize in them. For general information on collecting Nippon items, visit www.nipponcollectorsclub.com.

Bisque boy with hat, jointed arms. *5.25". Mark: 99 / NIPPON (back). $100, dealer.*

Best Baby by Haber Bros., celluloid. *Company was successfully sued by Borgfeldt and O'Neill for infringing their Kewpie patents. 5.75", c. 1917. Mark: (Upside-down top) / MADE IN NIPPON; also BEST / BABY / JAPAN (red label, front). $35–$40, eBay.*

Prices and Characteristics: Although Morimura bisque dolls are certainly from the Nippon era, they were an anomaly, all marked "Japan" instead of "Nippon," and they are included in the Japanese Dolls section. This section focuses exclusively on dolls marked "Nippon." Nippon dolls tend to be bisque-head knockoffs of German dolls, all-bisque, celluloid, and porcelain dolls. All dolls listed here are in excellent condition. All prices are for bisque dolls from 1890–1921, and prices are mixed from all venues. For celluloid Nippon dolls, see the Celluloid section.

NIPPON DOLLS

All-Bisque Kewpie-Type
Size: 4– 6"
Price: $20–$40
Less for very crude models.
Mark: NIPPON (back)

All-Bisque, German Knockoff
Size: 4– 6"
Price: $20–$40
Knockoff of all-bisque "penny dolls," painted eyes, wigged, less for very crude.
Mark: NIPPON (back)

All-Bisque, Betty Boop-Type
Size: 4– 8"
Price: $8–$15

Generally crude stone-bisque quality.
Mark: NIPPON

Character Baby, BE or RE Mark
Size: 12–22"
Price: $150–$250
Composition bent-limb baby body.
Mark: BHS-30 /RE or BE in diagonal box / Nippon (or similar)

Character Baby
Size: 15"
Price: $300
Mark: NIPPON / M-15

Child, Yamato Importing
Size: 11–24"
Price: $250
Nippon version of German dolly-faced doll, composition body.
Mark: Yamato Importing Co.-No. 70018-Nippon-+06 or Nippon /405 / FY in scroll mark.

Child
Size: 17"
Price: $175–$200
Nippon dolly face.
Mark: NIPPON (back)

Child, Teenage Body
Size: 16"
Price: $150
Elongated teenage composition body, Yamato Importing.
Mark: FY / NIPPON / 402

German 1840s papier-mâché lady, flirty eyes. *Shoulder-head, muslin body, wood lower limbs, orange painted shoes. 22", c. 1840. $3,600, auction. Courtesy Theriault's.*

German papier-mâché milliner's model. *Slender kid body with wooden lower arms and legs, painted flat shoes. 12", c. 1850. Unmarked. $1,500, auction. Courtesy Theriault's.*

German papier-mâché lady with Apollo's knot. *Slender kid body, wood lower arms and legs, painted flat shoes. 18", c. 1840. Unmarked. Courtesy Theriault's.*

German papier-mâché doll with ringlet curls. *Muslin body. 21", c. 1860. Unmarked. $1,000, auction. Courtesy Theriault's.*

German papier-mâché child. *Shoulder-head, muslin body, composition lower arms and legs, bare feet. Probably Schilling. 21", c. 1880. Unmarked. Courtesy Theriault's.*

French papier-mâché child fashion doll. *Solid dome papier-mâché head with painted and stippled hair. Kid fashion body with gusseted hips, knees. 21", c. 1850. Unmarked. Courtesy Theriault's.*

French papier-mâché, pair. *Carton bodies, wire-spring attached head and arms, carved wood hands. In original costumes of L'Auvergne. 10", early 1800s. Private collection.*

Papier-Mâché Dolls

The early German papier-mâché dolls are, in some sense, the parents of the later bisque dolls to follow. The German doll industry really began with the production of papier-mâché dolls from pressure molds in the very early 1800s. The majority of the papier-mâché dolls represented ladies, although some (especially later dolls) represented children. These dolls are frail and prone to crazing and cracking like the later compositon dolls of the early 20th century.

The vast majority of papier-mâché dolls are not marked, and although we know many German companies that made these dolls, we can rarely assign a maker to a particular doll.

- **German:** The earliest German papier-mâchés include milliner's models, made as early as 1810, with black molded hair (in an infinite variety of hairdos), painted eyes, and kid bodies with wood lower limbs. Shoulder-head dolls with cloth or kid bodies became popular in the mid-1800s, and remained popular until the ascendancy of the bisque dolls. The later papier-mâché dolls, including the "Patent Washables," were simply copies of the prevalent china dolls and dolly-face dolls, on shoulder-heads, wigged, with glass eyes.

- **French:** The early "French-type" papier-mâchés, made in the 1830s through the 1850s, have glass eyes and a black-painted spot on the top of the pate, with a wig—these dolls are also favorites of collectors. Most experts concur that these dolls were made not in France, but in Germany. But they continue to be referred to as "French-type." Most are dressed and presented as ladies.

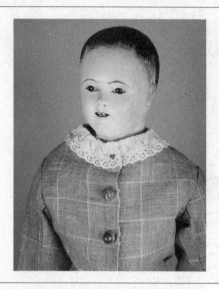

French papier-mâché fashion lady. Shoulder-head, pupil-less glass eyes, kid body only gusseted at hips. 18", c. 1850. Unmarked. $700, auction (some face damage).

- **American, Including Greiner Papier-Mâchés:** Several companies made papier-mâché dolls in America in the 1800s. The company best known for these dolls, and the one with the earliest American patent for papier-mâché dolls, is the Greiner company run by Ludwig Greiner. These dolls often come with their original label. Most of the other early American papier-mâché dolls have come to us unmarked.

Market Report: When you realize that many of the early German papier-mâché dolls are close to 200 years old, it is amazing that so many have survived. On the older dolls, a certain amount of crazing, paint rubs, etc., is tolerated by collectors and will not bring the value down greatly unless the damage is in an extremely prominent area (a badly rubbed nose, for example).

Also because of their age, dolls in original condition and especially those in original clothing receive a premium from collectors. As with china dolls, dolls with rarer and more elaborate hairstyles sell for much more than their common-haired sisters.

The most desirable of the German papier-mâché dolls are the dolls made prior to the bisque dollmaking era, including the early shoulder-heads, the French-types and the milliner's models. Later dolls made out of papier-mâché which simply ape the look of the dolly-faced bisque dolls are more available and not as popular, and prices reflect this.

Online/Offline Report: You certainly will find German papier-mâché dolls on eBay, including some milliner's models and later examples, but even for those you will find at best a handful at any one given time, making comparisons nearly impossible. Also, be wary online, since some repaintings and certain types of papier-mâché damage won't show up in low-resolution Internet photos. Prices for quality and early dolls are similar at all venues, with occasional bargains to be found for later German papier-mâchés on eBay.

Prices and Characteristics: All dolls are shoulder-heads on cloth or kid leather bodies, with cloth, kid, wood, or papier-mâché limbs as noted. Dolls have painted features, including eyes, except as noted. Early American, German, and milliner's models have closed mouths; later German dolls may have open or closed mouths. French papier-mâchés may have closed or open mouths. Most dolls are unmarked and prices are generally from non-Internet sources, except as noted.

Grenier papier-mâché child.
Shoulder-head, muslin body,
leather arms. 23", c. 1865. Mark:
Greiner's Improved Patent Heads,
Mar. 30 '58 (paper label). $1,300,
auction. Courtesy Theriault's.

Grenier papier-mâché child.
Shoulder-head, muslin body,
carved wood lower arms. 30", c.
1972. Mark: 1872 paper Grenier
label on back. Private collection.

PAPIER-MÂCHÉ—AMERICAN

Judge & Early
Size: 24"   Date: 1870s
Price: $590
Alice hairdo with molded band, long curls.
Worn.
Mark: Judge & Early No. 5 Patented July 27,
1875 (label, back).

Greiner, 1858, Child
Size: 11.5"   Date: 1858
Price: $1,900
Rare tiny size, center-part hairstyle with curls
above temples, 10 vertical curls, exposed ears.
Mark: '58 Grenier label (back shoulder plate).

Greiner, 1858, Child
Size: 15– 20"   Date: 1858
Price: $1,000+
Black center-part hair with exposed ears; much
less for worn dolls.

Greiner, 1858, Child
Size: 22– 26"   Date: 1858
Price: $1,500–$1,800
Black center-part hair with exposed ears; much
less for worn dolls.

Greiner, 1858, Molded Teeth
Size: 25"   Date: 1850s
Price: $1,000
Rare model, with damage.

Grenier, 1872
Size: 20– 24"   Date: 1872
Price: $500+

Grenier, 1872
Size: 27– 29"   Date: 1872
Price: $600+
Mark: Greiner's Patent Doll Heads, No. 8 Pat.
March 30.'58 Ext. '72 (label).

Grenier, 1872
Size: 30"   Date: 1872
Price: $700–$900
Black hair.

Greiner, 1872, Blonde Hair
Size: 32– 34"   Date: 1872
Price: $800–$1,000

Lerch and Klag, Philadelphia
Size: 16– 18"   Date: 1860s
Price: $2,000+
Blonde hair, Alice-style molded hair band.
Phillip Lerch made papier-mâché doll heads
from 1866 into the 1870s.
Mark: Lerch and Klag (label).

Long Molded Curls, Robinson
Size: 17"   Date: mid-1800s
Price: $2,700
Painted eyes, 9 long molded curls, exposed ears.
Sarah Robinson 1883 patented body with kid
arms and articulation.

Pre-Greiner, Glass Eyes
Size: 20"   Date: 1850
Price: $450
Worn. Glass eyes, large leather arms, simple
hairdo.

PAPIER-MÂCHÉ—FRENCH

Bébé-Type, Open Mouth
Size: 16″
Price: $450
Head resembles typical bébé doll, socket head, 5-piece French composition body. Worn.

Lady, Bride, Wigged
Size: 20″
Price: $1,800
Exceptional French-type papier-mâché, pale-pink kid body with gussets, stitched fingers, hair painted black under wig, enamel eyes.

Lady, Fashion
Size: 18″   Date: 1850
Price: $800–$900
Early French fashion-type, enamel eyes, solid dome, painted black hair (short), kid body with straight limbs. Price for wear, redressed, much more for excellent, all original.

Lady, Fashion
Size: 14– 18″   Date: 1840s
Price: $2,100–$2,600
Original costume, dome shoulder-head, black painted pate under human hair wig, enamel eyes, kid body.

Lady, Fashion
Size: 23″
Price: $2,200
Original folklore costume. Human hair wig in braid down back, with painted short black hair with brush marks toward face, inset dark eyes, cloth body with stitched joints, leather arms with stitched fingers.

Lady, Painted Eyes
Size: 8– 10″
Price: $500
Painted eyes, painted pate with human hair wig, kid body, replaced clothing.

Lady, Painted Eyes
Size: 14– 18″
Price: $600–$700

Schmitt et Fils, Bébé
Size: 17″   Date: 1875
Price: $2,500
1st model of firm's Bébé series, prior to pressed bisque models. Original outfit.
Mark: Sch (shield mark, on bottom).

Shell Costume
Size: 9″   Date: 1840
Price: $300
Wax-dipped shells form most of original costume.

PAPIER-MÂCHÉ GERMAN, 1820–1860S ("EARLY")

It can be difficult to classify the pre-1870s German papier-mâché dolls. Generally, for purposes of this book, dolls with painted eyes, slender bodies, wood lower limbs and painted slippers are classified as Milliner's Model types. Dolls with painted eyes but slightly chubbier bodies, mimicking China Dolls of the period, and those with glass eyes, have been classified as "Early" German Papier-mâchés. These dolls may have all-leather or cloth bodies, but sometimes do have wood lower arms. Early German Dolls are circa 1810 to 1860s. "Late" dolls were made from 1870s on. All unmarked.

Early, Glass Eyes, Blonde Ringlet Curls
Size: 21–22″   Date: 1860–1865
Price: $1,000–$1,500
Short hair with deeply waved curls at forehead, glass enamel eyes, muslin stitch-jointed body.

Early, Glass Eyes, Brown Hair, Glass Eyes
Size: 14″   Date: 1840s
Price: $1,100
Glass pupil-less eyes, hair looping behind ears to bun on head, milliner's-model body.

Early, Glass Eyes, Lady
Size: 14″   Date: 1840
Price: $1,300–$1,500
Average prices for nice but not overly elaborate hairstyles.

Early, Glass Eyes, Lady, Narrow Face
Size: 18″   Date: 1840s–1860s
Price: $900+
Narrow face with high forehead, eyes without pupils, center-part hair with curls starting in front of ears, cloth body, mitt hands.

Early, Painted Eyes, Simple Hair Style
Size: 7.5″   Date: 1840
Price: $500
Simple hairstyle.

Early, Painted Eyes, Bun
Size: 11″   Date: 1840
Price: $1,800
Exposed ears.

Early, Painted Eyes, Simple Hair Style
Size: 17″   Date: 1850s
Price: $500
Center-part covered wagon-style hair. Cloth body with kid lower arms.

Early, Painted Eyes, Elaborate Hair

Size: 19″   Date: 1830s
Price: $2,000
Cloth body, hair pulled up in front, molded comb, braid in back.

Early, Painted Eyes, Man

Size: 18″   Date: 1840s–1860s
Price: $900+
Man with black painted hair.

Sonneberg Täufling Baby

Size: 6″   Date: 1850s
Price: $500
Prices for Täufling Babies are for dolls with some wear.

Sonneberg Täufling Baby

Size: 12″   Date: 1850s
Price: $1,000+

Sonneberg Täufling Baby

Size: 16–18″   Date: 1850s
Price: $1,600
Also called "Motschmann's Baby." Inspired by Japanese Ichimatsu baby at 1850 London Exhibition. Painted hair, pupil-less glass eyes, composition/wood body with cloth-covered midsection with crier, cloth-covered upper arms and legs. Heads are also made of porcelain and wax.

Sonneberg Täufling Baby

Size: 22+″   Date: 1850s
Price: $2,500+

PAPIER-MÂCHÉ GERMAN, 1870S–1900 ("LATE")

Late, Black, With Bellows, Crier

Size: 12″   Date: 1880
Price: $200
Bellows and mama crier, original clothes. Glass eyes, cloth body with papier mâché lower limbs; painted shoes.

Late, Child, Glass Eyes, Molded Curls

Size: 14–16″   Date: 1870s–1900s
Price: $150–$250
Cloth body, glass eyes, composition limbs and molded boots. Sometimes called "Patent Washable"-type.

Late, Child, Glass Eyes, Wigged

Size: 18–21″   Date: 1885
Price: $350–$450
Common looking, glass eyes, closed mouth, wigged, cloth body, composition lower limbs or legs of cloth or leather with sewn boots.

Late, Lady, Glass Eyes, Wigged

Size: 11″   Date: 1880
Price: $450
Closed mouth, cloth body with composition lower limbs, painted shoes and socks, wigged.

Late, Lady, Glass Eyes, Wigged

Size: 22″   Date: 1890
Price: $300
Closed mouth, cloth body, leather arms, sewn-on striped stockings. Wigged.

Late, Painted Eyes, Child

Size: 14″   Date: 1920
Price: $175
Later papier-mâché, original peasant outfit, braided mohair wig.

Late, Painted Eyes, Curls

Size: 30″
Price: $475
Short finger curls, linen body with kid forearms.

Late, Glass Eyes, Lady

Size: 12″   Date: 1885
Price: $900
Turned shoulder-head. Attributed to Schilling. Closed mouth.

MILLINER'S MODEL-TYPE PAPIER-MÂCHÉS, GERMAN, 1820S–1860S

The so-called "Milliner's Model" Papier-Mâchés were never used as Milliner's Models in the 1800s—this is just the name that collectors use for them.

Milliner's Model, Desirable Hairstyle

Size: 9–12″   Date: 1820s–1860s
Price: $700–$900
For buns, braids, looped hair, curls, etc. Much less for covered wagon simple hairstyles and worn dolls. Carved, painted black hair, painted eyes and features, kid body, wood lower limbs, painted flat slippers.

Milliner's Model, Desirable Hairstyle

Size: 14–17″   Date: 1830s
Price: $800–$1,000
Same as above listing.

Milliner's Model, Desirable Hairstyle

Size: 18–22″   Date: 1850
Price: $1,200–$1,400+
Same as above listing.

Milliner's Model, Molded Blue Bonnet

Size: 15″
Price: $3,000

German parian lady. Kid body. 15". Unmarked. Courtesy Janet Lawrence.

Parian-type bisque doll with Alice-type headband. Muslin body, bisque lower limbs, painted boots. 12", c. 1885. Unmarked. $525, auction. Courtesy Theriault's

Molded, painted curls under bonnet, painted ribbon, milliner's model body.

Milliner's Model, Apollo's Knot
Size: 9– 12"
Price: $1,200–$1,600

Milliner's Model Type, Very Early
Size: 33"   Date: 1810
Price: $4,400
3 tufted curls in front of exposed ears, braided bun, milliners model body type.

Milliner's Model, Long Finger Curls
Size: 12"   Date: 1850
Price: $1,500
Elongated face and long finger curls onto shoulders.

Parians

There have been all sorts of arguments over whether or not there should even be a category of dolls called parian, and whether or not the term "parian" has any real meaning in the world of doll collecting.

Whatever the debate, it seems that the term "parian" has stuck to a certain group of dolls and has come to refer to dolls with pale, untinted bisque and molded hair and decoration, usually with painted eyes, and sometimes with glass eyes. The dolls are shoulder-heads on cloth or kid bodies, and almost always unmarked. Parian dolls have been reported as early as the 1850s and as late as the 1890s, but the majority were made in the 1860s and 1870s.

Market Report: The same collectors who love china dolls tend to love parian dolls, since the parians are often unglazed examples of the same molds. Just as with china dolls, rarer hairdos and extra decorations molded in the bisque add greatly to value.

Parian-type bisque doll. *Purple hair bow, glass eyes, pierced ears. Swivel head on shoulder plate, muslin body, bisque lower arms, painted boots. 11″, c. 1875. Courtesy Theriault's.*

Parian-type lady. *Brown hair, glass eyes, blue painted comb in hair, muslin body with bisque forearms. 17″, c. 1870. $1,450, auction. Courtesy Theriault's.*

Parian type lady. *Ruffled bodice and fancy hair, kid body, ungusseted limbs. 22″, c. 1870. $1,700, auction. Courtesy Theriault's.*

Look for elaborate hairdos, parians with glass eyes, and parians with molded accents such as jewels, fancy collars, molded hats and bonnets, flowers, and pierced ears. Some rare parians will have swivel necks, and a very few parians may have wigged solid domed heads.

Online/Offline Report: Prices are generally steady, but for rare styles with only a few examples known, the sky can be the limit, especially at auction. Basic, simple hairstyle, painted eye parian dolls can be found on eBay for a few hundred dollars or less, but remember that not every doll described as a parian on eBay actually is one!

Prices and Characteristics: All dolls are untinted bisque shoulder heads, unmarked, with painted eyes, closed mouths, molded painted hair (generally blonde), and muslin stitch-jointed or kid stitch- or gusset-jointed bodies, generally with bisque lower limbs, all except as noted. Dolls are made in Germany, and all dolls represent a lady unless "child" is indicated. Lady dolls with fancier hairstyles tend to have pierced ears.

PARIAN-TYPE, FANCIER HAIRSTYLES

Black Hairband, Simple Hair
Size: 12″   Date: 1885
Price: $525
Painted black boots.

Black Hairband, Fancy Upswept Curls, Decorated Necklace
Size: 17″   Date: 1870s
Price: $2,000+

Blue Hairband, Simple Hair
Size: 16″   Date: 1880
Price: $750

Blue Hairband, Fancy Upswept Hair
Size: 24″   Date: 1870s
Price: $1,600

Black Hair, Hat With Feather
Size: 7″   Date: mid-1800s
Price: $1,750
Early, with squeaker torso, hat with lustre purple feather.

Bonnet Head, Butterfly Bonnet
Size: 14″
Price: $850
Inexpensive, rough stone-bisque type often made by Hertwig.

Bonnet-Head Doll, Common Bonnets
Size: 14″   Date: 1890s
Price: $140–$200
Inexpensive, rough stone-bisque type often made by Hertwig.

Brown Hair
Size: 7″   Date: 1870
Price: $1,050

Brown Hair With Widow's Peak, Bun
Size: 16"   Date: 1850
Price: $5,275
Defined widow's peak with wispy tendrils.

Child, Alice In Wonderland
Size: 18"   Date: 1880s
Price: $675
With headband, ears not pierced.

Child, Alice In Wonderland, Exposed Ears
Size: 16"   Date: 1880s
Price: $1,000
Price for exceptionally sculpted hair.

Decorated Bodice, Blue Bow in Hair
Size: 18"
Price: $800
Ruching (Dresden-type) on bodice.

Decorated Bodice, Feathers in Hair
Size: 16"
Price: $650

Decorated Bodice, Simple Hair
Size: 14"
Price: $600

Decorated Bodice (Ruffled), Brown Hair
Size: 16"   Date: 1870
Price: $1,100

Decorated Bodice, Upswept Hair
Size: 17"
Price: $1,200

Decorated Bodice (Ruffled), Fancy Braided Hair With Applied Flowers
Size: 20"
Price: $2,750
Molded, painted boots.

Fancy Curled Upswept Hair With Molded Beads and Flowers
Size: 15"
Price: $800

Glass Eyes
Size: 10"   Date: 1885
Price: $600
Simpler hairstyle.

Glass Eyes, Curls
Size: 14"   Date: 1870s
Price: $1,000

Glass Eyes, Braid and Ringlets
Size: 17"
Price: $800

Glass Eyes, Fancy Hairstyle
Size: 17"   Date: 1870s
Price: $1,500
Painted yellow-heeled boots.

Glass Eyes, Ruffled Bodice
Size: 16"   Date: 1880s
Price: $1,000

Glass Eyes, Sculpted Collar and Necklace
Size: 22"   Date: 1875
Price: $2,300

Luster Coronet
Size: 22"   Date: 1870
Price: $2,200

Man, Decorated Shoulder Plate
Size: 17– 21"   Date: 1875
Price: $600–$700
Brown hair, molded, painted tie on shoulder plate, often with collar.

Man, Decorated Shoulder Plate, Glass Eyes, Fancier Hair
Size: 23"   Date: 1875
Price: $1,750
Fancy, well-sculpted hair.

Slender Face, Elongated Throat, Brown Hair
Size: 22"
Price: $1,050
Early.

Swivel Neck, Curls, Bow
Size: 22"   Date: 1860s
Price: $1,300

Tiny Marcelled Curls
Size: 9"   Date: 1870
Price: $950

Upswept Hair, Molded Black Ribbon and Bow
Size: 18"
Price: $375
Print lower legs for stockings, leather boots for feet.
Mark: 137-7.

Waterfall Hairstyle
Size: 21"
Price: $900
Hair piled high, curls fall onto neck in back.

PARIAN-TYPE, SIMPLE HAIRSTYLES

Boy, Short Hair
Size: 17– 19"
Price: $300
Blonde.

Pair of piano babies. Large with sculpted white smocks. 12″, c. 1910. Mark: Heubach (sunburst). $1,550 for pair. Courtesy Theriault's.

Piano baby in sculpted bonnet, outfit. Deep sculpting. 12″, c. 1910. Unmarked. $1,900, auction. Courtesy Theriault's.

Piano baby. Typical size and style. 3″ tall, 5″ length, c. 1910. Mark: Heubach (sunburst mark) / MADE IN GERMANY (red stamp). $100, eBay.

Child, Common Hair (Flat Top or Covered Wagon-Type)
Size: 12– 14″
Price: $200–$275
Center part.

Child, Common Hair (Flat Top or Covered Wagon-Type)
Size: 18– 24″
All Markets: $250–$350
Center part.

Child, Common Hair (Flat Top or Covered Wagon-Type)
Size: 33″
Price: $400
Center part.

Hair Piled Simply on Head
Size: 14″
Price: $275–$375

Low Brow
Size: 16″
Price: $150–$200

Short Hair, Cluster of Curls at Center Forehead
Size: 17″
Price: $250
Ears not pierced.

Piano Babies

Piano babies are another one of those interesting categories of antique dolls—never meant as a plaything for children, these dolls are sometimes not included in doll price or guide books. However, piano babies are collected by many antique doll collectors and sold by antique doll dealers, and are therefore included here.

Piano babies were indeed created to sit atop pianos! Sizes varied from a small 4″ up to about 16″. These babies generally are posed in a frolicking position, and it is easy to imagine them delighting their owners in Victorian, Edwardian, and later homes. Piano babies were made from the late 1880s through the 1930s, mostly by German firms including Heubach, Hertwig, Kestner, Dressel, Kister & Co., and others.

Market Report: Piano babies enjoy a pretty steady market, neither declining nor advancing, except for the most common examples which have had a price decline. Look for intricate poses, unusual molded clothing and larger-size piano babies, which are rarer.

Online/Offline Report: Be careful on Internet auction sites—reproductions of piano babies abound. The finest examples are more frequently found through dealers; prices on low and mid-range piano babies are slightly cheaper via Internet auctions. Prices vary greatly depending on the rarity of the design and quality of painting.

Revalo Child. *5-piece composition and wood body, all-original outfit. 12″, c. 1900. Mark: Revalo. $800, dealer. Courtesy Theriault's.*

Revalo character baby. *Bent-limb baby body. 10″. Mark: Germany / Revalo / 22 2/0.*

Prices and Characteristics: All are all-bisque, made in Germany, in excellent condition, with painted eyes and features, and no jointing. Most were produced between 1910 and 1920.

Marks: Piano Babies are either unmarked, marked "Germany," or marked with the Heubach mark, which includes a sunburst and sometimes a four-digit number.

PIANO BABIES

Common Poses (Lying Down Playing With Toes or Lying Down Perched on Arms, Common Molded Clothing)
Size: 4– 6″
Price: $100–$200   Internet: $80–$145
Generally marked Heubach, Germany, or unmarked.

Common Poses (Lying Down Playing With Toes or Lying Down Perched on Arms, Common Molded Clothing)
Size: 6– 8″
Price: $150+   Internet: $125+
Generally marked Heubach, Germany, or unmarked.

Hertwig, Fancy Molded Smock and Bonnet
Size: 10″
Price: $450

Heubach, Lying Down, Playing With Toes
Size: 7.5″
All Markets: $500
Mark: sunburst mark. Uncommon clothing.

Heubach, Perched on Arms on Log
Size: 9″   Internet: $800

Heubach, Seated With Legs Drawn Up, Modeled Bathing Cap, Nude
Size: 11″
Price: $7,600
At auction.

Heubach, Sitting, Arms Raised
Size: 11″
Price: $700

Heubach, Sitting, Unusual Size
Size: 11.5″   Internet: $2,250
Mark: sunburst mark

Heubach, Standing in Chemise and Brother's Boots
Internet: $350

Heubach, Wearing Dutch Cap, Lying on Back, Molded Baby Smock
Size: 6″
Price: $375

Holding Rattle
Size: 6″   Internet: $230
Marked Germany with shield.

On Back, Molded Cap, Playing With Toes
Size: 12″
Price: $1,900

On Potty

Size: 9″
Price: $2,000
Composition body; unusual sculpted hair, wearing molded ruffled-collar nightshirt.

Unusual Reclining Position, Molded Smock and Sleep Cap

Size: 4″   Internet: $175
Unmarked

Revalo (Gebrüder Ohlhaver)

Revalo (Ohlhaver spelled backward, sans the "h"s) is the trademark of the dolls made by the Gebrüder Ohlhaver firm in Germany. Its dolls were made in the early 1910s through the 1920s.

Market Report: These dolls, especially when found in original clothing, can be quite charming. Collectors tend to overlook these dolls because they are often on cheaper composition bodies, but real gems can be found at reasonable prices, and some of the painting of the features is quite lovely on certain models. Look for Revalo's character children and the dolls in original factory clothing.

Online/Offline Report: Prices for these dolls are trending downward but stabilizing, with prices similar from all venues. Very few are available on eBay or on similar sites.

Prices and Characteristics: All dolls have bisque heads, and prices are for dolls in excellent condition.

REVALO (OHLHAVER, GEBRÜDER)

Child

Size: 13–17″
Price: $500   Internet: $450
Fully jointed composition body, set eyes, open mouth, teeth.
Mark: Germany / Revalo / 4 (or similar)

Child

Size: 18–25″
Price: $600–$650
Fully jointed composition body, set eyes, open mouth, teeth.
Mark: Germany Revalo 8 1/2 64
(or similar).

Child

Size: 8– 14″
Price: $400–$600
5-piece composition body; sometimes in original folklore outfit. More for exceptional painting or costume.

Coquette

Size: 13″
Price: $1,000   Internet: $700
Solid dome, painted, molded hair with ribbon, painted eyes.

German Character Baby

Size: 14″   Internet: $320–$350
Original 5-piece composition baby body with bent knees.
Mark: Revalo / Germany / 22-5

Children, Pair, Boy and Girl

Size: 24″
Price: $525
Jointed composition bodies, sleep eyes.
Mark: Germany / Revalo / 7 1/4

Schoenau & Hoffmeister

Another latecomer to the German bisque dollmaking scene, Schoenau & Hoffmeister was founded in 1901, and continued to make bisque doll heads until 1953! Its dolls include dolly-faced dolls, character babies, Black dolls, and characters such as Princess Elizabeth.

Market Report: The dolls from Schoenau & Hoffmeister tend to be well made and are liked by collectors. However, the market for its dolls is relatively quiet at this time. New collectors can pick up sweet character babies and nice dolly faced dolls at reasonable prices.

Online/Offline Report: Prices for these dolls are currently stagnant, and are similar through all venues. A handful of these dolls can be found on eBay at any given time.

Prices and Characteristics: All dolls have bisque heads with open mouths, glass eyes and fully jointed composition bodies except as noted. Prices are similar from all venues, and are for dolls in excellent condition.

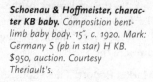

Schoenau & Hoffmeister, character KB baby. Composition bent-limb baby body. 15″, c. 1920. Mark: Germany S (pb in star) H KB. $950, auction. Courtesy Theriault's.

Schoenau & Hoffmeister, character baby. Composition bent-limb baby body. 13″, c. 1920. Mark: S (pb in star) H 2 Germany. Courtesy Theriault's.

SCHOENAU & HOFFMEISTER

Baby, Character, Burggrub
Size: 12″
Price: $275
Burggrub babies have sleep eyes, open mouths with teeth, wigged, 5-piece bent-limb baby body.

Baby, Character, Burggrub
Size: 15″
Price: $400
Mark: Porzellanfabrik Burggrub 169

Baby, Character, Burggrub
Size: 19″
Price: $540

Baby, Character, Hanna
Size: 14″
Price: $450–$550
Sleep eyes, open mouth, 5-piece bent-limb baby body.

Baby, Character, Hanna
Size: 20″
Price: $650–$750
Mark: S PB (in star) H. / Hanna / 5 Germany

Baby, Character, K.B.
Size: 15″
Price: $950
Composition bent-limb baby body.
Mark: S(PB in star) H KB

Baby, Hanna, Black
Size: 6– 7″
Price: $200–$300
Sleep eyes, open mouth, brown 5-piece baby body.
Mark: S PB (in star) H / Hanna

Child, 1906, 1909
Size: 11″
Price: $225
Mark: S (PB in 5-pooints star) H / 1909 / Germany

Schoenau & Hoffmeister, character baby. *Composition bent-limb baby body. 22", c. 1915. Mark: S pb (in star) H B 7 Germany. Courtesy Theriault's.*

Princess Elizabeth character. *5-piece composition toddler body. 20", c. 1931. Mark: Porzellanfabrick Burggrub / Princess Elizabeth / 5 / Made in Germany. Courtesy Theriault's.*

Child, 1906, 1909
Size: 16–17"
Price: $250–$300
Sleep eyes.

Child, 1906, 1909
Size: 24–26"
Price: $475–$575
Mark: 6 / S / PB (in star) H / 1906/10 / Germany

Child, 1906, 1909
Size: 30"
Price: $550–$700

Child, 1906, 1909
Size: 40"
Price: $2,000

Child, 5700, 5800
Size: 24"
Price: $250–$325

Child, Character, 914
Size: 28"
Price: $675
Mark: S (PB in star) H / 914

Child, Character, Princess Elizabeth
Size: 17–20"
Price: $2,000+
Smiling face, toddler body.

Child, Shoulder-Head, 1000, 1800
Size: 20–24"
Price: $250–$300
Kid body, bisque arms.
Mark: Germany / S PB (in star) H / 1800

Child, Shoulder-Head, 4000
Size: 14"
Price: $150.
Set eyes, kid body, bisque arms.

Child, Shoulder-Head, No Mold Number
Size: 16"
Price: $200

Child, Shoulder-Head, No Mold Number
Size: 23"
Price: $250
Sleep eyes.

Schoenhut

Schoenhut dolls are unique—manufactured dolls made of all wood. Made in the United States, Schoenhuts are rarely confused with any other dolls. Made by a company specializing in wood toys of all types (including the well-known Schoenhut pianos) since the start of the 1870s, typical Schoenhut dolls were made with spring-metal joints, and were finished with oil painting. They nearly always represented children and babies. Schoenhut also produced some small all-wood dolls as part of its circus set, as well as some cartoon and character dolls.

Most of the Schoenhut dolls were made between 1911 and 1930, and the vast majority have painted eyes, and are either wigged or have molded hair.

Schoenhut character girl. *Pressed and carved wooden socket head, all-wood spring-jointed body. 17″, c. 1912. Mark: Schoenhut Doll Pat. Jan 17 '11 USA. $1,000, auction. Courtesy Theriault's.*

Schoenhut character girl. *Pressed and carved wood socket head, all-wood spring-jointed body. 16″, c. 1912. Mark: Schoenhut Doll Pat. Jan 17 '11 USA & Foreign Countries. Courtesy Theriault's.*

Market Report: Collectors love the character dolls from Schoenhut, and also the rarer dolls with glass eyes or pouty faces. Carved hair is very desirable as well. Many Schoenhut dolls have well-worn paint, so dolls with original paint and no paint retouches are large pluses for value. It seems that many Schoenhut dolls have paint rubs right on the tips of their noses.

Online/Offline Report: Prices have been generally stable, with slight trending upward for dolls in excellent or better condition. Schoenhuts are plentiful on eBay and the Internet, but it can be hard to tell the quality of the paint finish and whether or not there are any paint retouches in Internet photos. Therefore, prices for Schoenhuts on eBay tend to be lower than prices for dolls from dealers and shows.

Prices and Characteristics: Dolls are all wood (except where noted), with painted intaglio eyes and wigged with mohair, except where carved hair is indicated. The child dolls are character dolls, with spring-jointed wood bodies that have holes in feet to fit for stands. All in excellent condition (some scuffing acceptable) and appropriate old clothing. Wear and restored painting greatly affects prices; prices are much less with wear or restoration. Prices are generally from dealers, shows and auctions; adjust accordingly for eBay. Dolls were made from 1911 through the early 1920s.

Marks: Dolls are incised on the head or back with: Schoenhut Doll / Pat. Jan. 17, '11 U.S.A. / & Foreign Countries; some dolls have a paper oval label: "Schoenhut Doll / Pat. Jan/17, '11 USA" on torso.

Schoenhut girl, carved hair.
Carved wood socket head, all-wood spring-jointed body. 16", c. 1912. Unmarked. $1,700, auction. Courtesy Theriault's.

SCHOENHUT

Carved Hair, Girl or Boy
Size: 14"
Price: $1,700–$2,500
Wood spring-joint body with holes in feet for positioning, painted eyes. More for mint.

Carved Hair, 201, Boy
Size: 16"
Price: $2,100
Pouty mouth.

Carved Hair, Girl or Boy
Size: 16– 17"
Price: $2,000–$2,800
Varies greatly depending on condition; much less for dolls with repainting, wear.

Carved Hair, Girl, 105, Pouty
Size: 16"
Price: $3,300
With trunk and trousseau.

Carved Hair, Boy, 206
Size: 19"
Price: $1,400
Very good with carved hair. Nose repaired, repainting in various places, spring-jointed wood body.

Child, Painted Eyes and Wigged
Size: 15"
Price: $2,100
Mint.

Child, Painted Eyes and Wigged
Size: 15"
Price: $1,400
Excellent. More for dolls with pouty expressions.

Child, Painted Eyes and Wigged
Size: 16– 18"
Price: $600–$750
Average condition with some wear.

Child, Painted Eyes and Wigged
Size: 19– 22"
Price: $1,400–$1,600
Excellent.

Child, Painted Eyes and Wigged
Size: 19– 22"
Price: $900
Average condition with some wear.

Girl, 308
Size: 19"
Price: $3,100
MIB, pristine.

Girl, 301
Size: 16"
All Markets: $2,200

Girl, 313
Size: 16"
All Markets: $2,550
Mint.

Miss Dolly
Size: 17– 19"
Price: $575–$855

Lower prices for more wear. Painted eyes, wigged, c. 1920s.

Miss Dolly, Sleep Eyes
Size: 17″
Price: $1,000

Boy, 401
Size: 16″
All Markets: $2,500
Looks like K * R 114.

Toddler
Size: 11– 12″
Price: $500–$600
Wigged, painted eyes, jointed wood toddler body (shorter legs) or bent-limb baby body.

Toddler
Size: 14– 17″
Price: $600–$700
Wigged, painted eyes, jointed wood toddler body (shorter legs) or bent-limb baby body.

Toddler, 110
Size: 19″
Price: $900
Mint, less for average condition.

Circus Performer, Ringmaster
Size: 8″
Price: $275
Bisque swivel head, molded/painted black hair and mustache, goatee, carved wood painted body.

Circus Performer, Acrobat
Size: 8″
Price: $250
Bisque swivel head, molded and painted hair in waves and curls with top bun.

Circus Performer, Bare Back Rider and Horse
Size: 8″
Price: $425
Same as above listing.

Circus Performer, Lion Tamer
Size: 8″
Price: $600
Bisque swivel head, molded/painted black hair and mustache, goatee, carved wood painted body.

Pinn Family
Size: 5–12″
Price: $125
c.1930, simple all-wood dolls, heads not carved, mother, father, children (price per doll).

Native
Size: 8″
Price: $3,000–$4,200
Part of Safari Set. Wood socket head, painted features, molded ears, hole in top of head with curved wire for stringing, wood body.

Walker
Size: 17.5″
Price: $950
Wigged mohair wig, original wedge-soled shoes.

S.F.B.J.

S.F.B.J. was formed at the end of the heyday of French dollmaking, right at the end of the 19th century, when the great French dollmaking companies could no longer individually fend off the German dollmakers and their large production of much cheaper bisque dolls. Formed in 1899, original members included what was left of Jumeau, Bru, Rabery & Delphieu, Gaultier, and others, with additional French dollmaking companies joining after that.

At the height of their production, S.F.B.J. made many millions of dolls each year. Quality of the dolls varied widely, since the heads used to make the dolls were made in many factories. S.F.B.J. made a wide variety of dolls, including bébés, dolls in folklore costumes for the tourist trade, Bleuettes, and character dolls. S.F.B.J. dolls were made in one form or another until the early 1960s.

* **Bleuette:** Bleuette is so popular with collectors today that some collectors, especially those who enjoy sewing wardrobes for their dolls, will base an entire collection around her. In 1905, the first Bleuette dolls (a small bisque child doll, approximately 11″ tall with a fully jointed composition body) were offered as a premium (for a one-year subscription) to a weekly magazine for little French girls, *La Semaine de Suzette*. Included in most issues of the magazine were patterns for clothing for Bleuette, as well as stories, advice columns, games, and crafts. The magazine, intended for girls aged 8–14, was published until 1960.

Over 1,000 patterns were printed in the magazine for Bleuette in the 55-year period of

S.F.B.J., Character Boy, 226.
*French composition and wood
jointed body. 17", c. 1912. Mark:
SFBJ 226 Paris 6. Courtesy
Theriault's.*

S.F.B.J., Character Girl, 238.
*French composition and wood
jointed body. 18", c. 1912. Mark:
SFBJ 238 Paris 6. Courtesy
Theriault's.*

her production. The first Bleuettes (referred to by collectors as the "Premiere" Bleuette) used a Jumeau mold, and the second production of Bleuettes used a German mold from Fleischmann and Bloedel (part of S.F.B.J.; neither doll was marked with a mold number; see below). The next two molds used were the well-known S.F.B.J. 60 and 301. Bleuettes made until 1933 were 10 5/8" tall; after 1933, Bleuettes were 11 3/8" tall. Some Bleuettes carry the UNIS, France mark (see below).

Today's collector is just as passionate about Bleuette as little girls were in the first half of the 20th century. A magazine about Bleuette, *Bleuette's World,* is published bimonthly, in English, and Bleuette collectors often have their own get-togethers at doll conventions.

• **Unis, France:** Unis, France is simply one of the marks used by S.F.B.J. on some of its dolls. The Unis France dolls were made from approximately 1916 into the 1930s.

Market Report: The most popular S.F.B.J. dolls are the Jumeau-type S.F.B.J. bébé dolls, the sought-after character dolls, and the Bleuettes. The Bleuette dolls have increased greatly in value in the last few years; the character dolls are also increasing in value, although slower than the Bleuettes.

A note of caution to the collector: Many S.F.B.J. dolls, including character dolls and the Bleuettes, have been reproduced in great numbers by modern dollmakers. Although usually not made with the intent to deceive, the fact that these dolls are popular for reproduction, and this should be kept in mind when buying from unknown sources, espe-

S.F.B.J. Bébé. *Jointed composition and wood body, original folklore costume of Brittany. 12", c. 1910. Mark: 1907 / 2. $700, eBay.*

Unis France Bleuette with trunk, clothes. *French composition and wood jointed body, with trunk, original Gautier-Langereau clothes. 11", c. 1940. Mark: Unis France 149 301 1 _ (head) 2 (torso). Courtesy Theriault's.*

cially on the Internet where you cannot examine the doll in person.

Online/Offline Report: S.F.B.J. character dolls and Bleuettes in excellent condition bring premium prices on the Internet and from dealers and auction houses, since competition is fierce for the best examples of these dolls. For lower-quality, later Bleuettes, you can sometimes find a bargain.

Bleuettes have become so popular (and expensive—a world record of $9,800 was set in 2004 for a "Premiere" Bleuette with a trousseau of original clothing) that well-made artist reproductions of Bleuette, sold as such, can bring $200 to $300 or more on eBay.

Prices and Characteristics: Dolls have bisque heads, open mouths, sleep or set eyes, mohair or human hair wigs, fully jointed composition bodies (except as noted). Bébés are from the early 1900s to approximately 1915, Bleuettes were produced from 1905 to the early 1960s, and character dolls from 1912 to approximately 1920.

S.F.B.J. BÉBÉS

Bébé
Size: 9– 10"
Price: $400–$600

For doll with no mold number and fully jointed composition body; much more for outstanding examples.
Mark: SFBJ Paris 0

Bébé
Size: 12"
Price: $450–$650
Same as above listing.
Mark: Deposé / S.F.B.J. / 2

Bébé, 1907
Size: 12"   Internet: $700
Regional costume of Brittany.
Mark: 1907 / 2

Bébé, 1907, Black
Size: 12"
Price: $1,900
Mark: 1907 2

Bébé, 1907
Size: 32"
Price: $3,500
Mint, with Jumeau labeled body.
Mark: 1907 15

Bébé, 301
Size: 9"
Price: $500
On fully jointed composition body.
Mark: S.F.B.J. / 301 / Paris/ 2/0

Bébé, 301
Size: 12"   Internet: $900

UNIS France Bleuette, 1930 period, with trunk and clothes.
French composition and wood jointed body, wearing original Gautier-Langereau dress. 11", c. 1930. Mark: 71 Unis France (oval 149 301 1-1/4.

Unis France Bleuettes, 1940 (sitting in trunk) and 1935 periods. *12" (1940) and 11" (1935). Both French composition and wood jointed bodies. 1940 doll Mark: Unis France 71 149 301. 1935 doll Mark: Unis France 71 149 301 1 _ (head) 2 (torso). 1940 doll with trunk, clothes, $1,600, auction. 1935 doll, $1,300, auction. Courtesy Theriault's.*

Bébé, 301
Size: 15–16"
Price: $400–$500

Bébé, 301
Size: 21–22"
Price: $550   Internet: $550–$650
Mark: 25 France SFBJ 301 Paris 9

Bébé, 301
Size: 27–28"
Price: $900–$1,100   Internet: $785–$900
Mark: SFBJ 301 Paris

Bébé, 301, Harlequin
Size: 16"
Price: $2,000
Original outfit.
Mark: SFBJ 301 Paris 5

Bébé, 301, Kiss-Throwing
Size: 21"
Price: $1,600
Mint, walks, cries, and throws kiss.
Mark: SFBJ 301 Paris 8

Bébé, 301, Kiss-Throwing, Walks
Size: 22"
Price: $950
For doll with kiss mechanism not working.
Mark: S.F.B.J. / 301 / Paris / -9-

Bébé, 60
Size: 7"
Price: $400
Mint.

Bébé, 60
Size: 13–14"
Price: $350–$450
With 5-piece composition body.
Mark: SFBJ 60 Paris 4/0

Bébé, Le Petit Cherubin, Marcheuer
Size: 15"
Price: $950
In original marked box. 5-piece composition body.
Mark: Deposé SFBJ 2

S.F.B.J. BLEUETTES

Bleuette, Premiere
Size: 10.5″   Date: 1905
Price: $3,500–$5,000+   Internet: $6,300
Jumeau, 27 cm.
Mark: 2 (head) 2 (body) 1 (feet)
Mark: 2/1

Bleuette, 301
Size: 10.5–11″
Price: $2,200+   Internet: $2,800
27 cm (the proper size of early Bluettes).
Mark: SFBJ 301 Paris 1

Bleuette, 301, Composition Head
Size: 10.5–11″   Date: 1945
Price: $400
Probably a wartime doll or wartime repair.
Mark: SFBJ/301/PARIS

Bleuette, 60
Size: 10.5–11″
Price: $1,400–$1,600   Internet: $1,200+
27 cm.
Body Mark: Torso with 2 between shoulder
blades, 1 on soles of feet. 1-stroke brows, painted
upper and lower lashes.
Mark: SFBJ 60 Paris 8/0 or 60 8/0

Bleuette, Gautier Languereau dress
Price: $250–$350
More for ultra-mint, rarer outfits.

Bleuette, La Semaine de Suzette, 1920s
                    Internet: $125–$150
For 1 year of the magazine containing Bleuette
patterns.

S.F.B.J. CHARACTER DOLLS

Character, 226, Black
Size: 17″
Price: $1,100
Paperweights, open/closed mouth.

Character, 226, Boy
Size: 17″
Price: $1,200+
Painted hair, open/closed mouth.

Character, 227, Boy
Size: 19″
Price: $1,400+

Character, 230
Size: 22″
Price: $1,000+
Mark: SFBJ 230 Paris 10

Character, 233, Child, Crying
Size: 15″
Price: $2,000
Dome head, modeled hair, toddler body, side-hip
jointing.
Mark: SFBJ 233 Paris 6

Character, 233, Child Crying
Size: 18– 21″
Price: $4,500+
Mark: SFBJ 233 Paris 6

Character, 234, Child
Size: 15″
Price: $5,400
Mark: SFBJ 234 Paris 4

Character, 235, Boy
Size: 14– 17″
Price: $1,000–$1,400
Flocked or painted hair.
Mark: SFBJ 235 Paris

Character, 236, Baby
Size: 12″
Price: $500+

Character, 236, Baby
Size: 16″
Price: $600+
Wigged.

Character, 236, Baby
Size: 19″
Price: $800+
Mark: S.F.B.J. / 236 / Paris / -10-

Character, 236, Toddler
Size: 15″
Price: $1,200
"Laughing Jumeau," toddler body.
Mark: S.F.B.J. / 236 / Paris / -6-

Character, 236, Toddler
Size: 24–26″
Price: $1,000–$1,300   Internet: $1,000–$1,100
Mark: S.F.B.J. / 236 / Paris / 11

Character, 237, Child
Size: 16″
Price: $3,100–$3,400
Smiling child.
Mark: SFBJ 237 Paris

Character, 242, Baby
Size: 14″
Price: $900+
Can have flocked hair.

Character, 247, Toddler
Size: 13– 14″

Price: $1,700   Internet: $1,400
Higher price for mint factory costume. Composition fully jointed toddler body, side-hip jointing.
Mark: SFBJ 247 Paris 4

Character, 247, Toddler
Size: 20″
Price: $1,800–$2,000
Composition toddler body with side-hip jointing.
Mark: 21 SFBJ 247 Paris 10

Character, 247, Toddler
Size: 27″
Price: $1,700
Mark: 22 / S.F.B.J. / 247 / Paris / 12 Fabrication Francaise Paris / S.F.B.J.

Character, 251, Toddler
Size: 8″
Price: $1,600
Composition fully jointed toddler body, side-hip jointing.
Mark: SFBJ 251 Paris 0

Character, 251, Toddler
Size: 23″   Internet: $1,600
Mark: SFBJ 251 Paris

Character, 252, Toddler
Size: 8–9″
Price: $2,800–$3,700
Pouty, on fully jointed composition toddler body.
Mark: 23 SFBJ 252 Paris 0

Character, 252, Toddler
Size: 12–13″
Price: $3,200
Mark: 22 SFBJ 252 Paris 4

Character, 252, Toddler
Size: 20″
Price: $5,000+

Character, Doll, Interchangeable Heads, 200 Series
Size: 13– 15″
Price: $4,000–$4,200
Faces pivot on turn-screw at top of head. Heads can include 237, 235, 233. In original box.
Mark: 7

Poulbot, Character Doll
Size: 14″
Price: $7,000
Designed by Paris illustrator Poulbot; represents Paris street urchin.
Mark: SFBJ Paris (incised) Poulbot (signature)

UNIS FRANCE BÉBÉS

All dolls have bisque heads, open mouths, sleep or set eyes, mohair or human hair wigs, and fully jointed composition bodies (except as noted). Dates for Unis France dolls track those of similar S.F.B.J. marked dolls.

Bébé, 301
Size: 12– 14″
Price: $400   Internet: $300–$400
Often in regional dress.
Mark: Unis France (in football shape) / 301

Bébé, 301
Size: 18– 20″
Price: $260–$450   Internet: $300–$450
Mark: Unis France (in football shape) / 301

Bébé, 301
Size: 22– 26″   Internet: $450–$550

Bébé, 301
Size: 29– 31″
Price: $800–$1,000   Internet: $600–$800

Bébé, 60
Size: 7– 9″
Price: $450
For mint doll with fully jointed composition body, often in regional dress.

Bébé, Black, Small
Size: 6″
Price: $120

UNIS FRANCE BLEUETTES

Bluette, 60, Model 4, With Trunk and Trousseau
Size: 10.5″   Date: 1925
Price: $2,800
8 original costumes, underwear, trunk
Mark: Unis France 71 60 149 8/0 (head) 2 (torso) 1 (foot)

Bluette, 302, Model 4
Size: 10.5″   Date: 1925
Price: $1,900
1925.
Mark: Unis France 71 149 302 8/0 (head) 2 (torso) 1 (foot)

Bleuette, 301, Model 5
Size: 11.5″   Date: 1935
Price: $1,300–$1,500   Internet: $1,500
Number 5 Bleuette (29 cm) French composition and wood fully jointed body; also marked 2 (torso) 1 (foot).
Mark: UNIS / FRANCE / 71 149 / 301 1 _

Simon & Halbig, 929 Child.
French composition and wood jointed body; look of doll modeled after Triste Jumeau; for French trade; rare in this large size. 27˝, c. 1886. Mark: 929 S 14 H. $7,250 at auction in 2000. Courtesy Theriault's.

Simon & Halbig, 949 Child. *Sonneberg composition and wood jointed body with straight wrists. 25˝, c. 1885. Mark: S 15 H / 949. $3,200, auction. Courtesy Theriault's.*

Simon & Halbig, 1079 Child for French market. *Jointed composition/wood body. 22˝, c. 1900. Mark: SH 1079/5 1/2/Dep Germany (head); blue stamp: (blue triangle) Article Francaise / Marque Depose / No. 84 (body). Private collection.*

Bleuette, 301

Size: 11.5˝　　　　Date: 1935–1940
Price: $1,000–$1,300　Internet: $1,500
Fully jointed composition body.
Mark: Unis France 301 71/149

Bleuette, 301

Size: 11.5˝　　　　Internet: $2,850
Wearing original Gautier-Languereau outfit, mint.

UNIS FRANCE, CHARACTER DOLLS

Character, Toddler, 247, "Twerp"

Size: 18˝
Price: $775
Mark: 71 Unis France 149 247

Character, Toddler, 251

Size: 22˝
Price: $1,000+
Wobble tongue, fully jointed composition toddler body.
Mark: 71 Unis France 149 / 251 / 19

Simon & Halbig

Simon & Halbig is almost synonymous with German bisque dolls. It was one of the largest factories producing bisque heads, and the companies that used its heads for their dolls form a virtual "Who's Who" in the German dollmaking world: C.M. Bergmann, Cuno & Otto Dressel, Handwerck, Kämmer & Reinhardt, Kley & Hahn, and many others, and even French firms such as Jumeau and S.F.B.J.

Simon & Halbig started production of bisque dolls in 1869. It produced not only bisque heads for dolly-face dolls, but also shoulderheads, lady dolls, parians, dollhouse dolls, all-bisque dolls, character children and babies, Black and Asian dolls, and nearly every other type of doll of its time period. The only type of doll that I've never seen attributed to Simon & Halbig is a china doll.

Simon & Halbig, like most of its German counterparts, made dolls into the 1930s.

Market Report: Always strong dolls with collectors, Simon & Halbig dolls continue to enjoy great popularity. The dolls are usually of excellent quality, and whether you're an all-bisque collector looking for a black-stocking girl for your collection, or a lady doll collector seeking out one of its fashion dolls, collectors of all types of antique dolls tend to have some Simon & Halbigs.

The market is especially strong for the Simon & Halbig all-bisques, lady dolls and early closed-mouth dolls. The prices for the

Simon & Halbig, 1249 Child.
Composition and wood jointed body. 26", c. 1900. Mark: SH 1249 dep Germany 12. Courtesy Theriault's.

Simon & Halbig, 1279 Child.
Composition body. 28", c. 1912. Mark: S & H 1279 dep Germany 14. Courtesy Theriault's.

Simon & Halbig, 1299 Character Child. *Composition and wood jointed body. 10", c. 1912. Mark: S & H 1299 8/5". Courtesy Theriault's.*

700 and 900 series of molds have increased substantially, as have later mold numbers with closed mouths.

Online/Offline Report: The rarest dolls and best selection of Simon & Halbig dolls will be found through dealers and auction houses, although dolly-faced Simon & Halbig dolls abound online, often at lower prices than from dealers or terra-firma auctions.

Prices and Characteristics: All dolls have bisque heads with fully jointed composition bodies, glass eyes (set or sleep), human hair or composition wigs, in excellent condition, except as noted. French or Sonneberg body denotes a fully jointed composition and wood body with straight wrists. If no body style is stated, the doll has a fully jointed composition body with jointed wrists. The child dolls are from 1885–1900 (some dolls, such as the 1249s, were made as late as the 1910s).

SIMON & HALBIG CHILD DOLLS

Asian Child (or Lady)
See section on Asian Dolls.

Black Child
See section on Antique Black Dolls.

Child, 719, Open Mouth
Size: 21"
Price: $2,200

Child, 719, Closed Mouth
Size: 26"
Price: $6,900

Child, 740
Size: 11"
Price: $1,500
Muslin stitch-jointed body with bisque lower arms and legs, bare feet.

Child, 769
Size: 17"
Price: $900
Open mouth, French body.
Mark: S 8 H 769 DEP

Child, 905
Size: 13"
Price: $2,300
Mark: SH 6 905

Child, 908
Size: 18"
Price: $1,650–$2,400
Open mouth.
Mark: S 9 H 908

Child, 929
Size: 14"
Price: $1,850
Closed mouth, French body.

Child, 939, Closed Mouth
Size: 9"
Price: $1,450
This small size is rare.

Simon & Halbig, 1488 Character Baby. Composition bent-limb baby body. 19″, c. 1912. Mark: 1488 Simon & Halbig 12. Courtesy Theriault's.

Simon & Halbig, 1159 Fashion Lady (on left, shown with Kestner 162 lady). Composition and wood jointed body with woman's shape. 19″, c. 1910. Mark: 1159 S & H dep 7. Courtesy Theriault's.

Child, 939, Closed Mouth
Size: 12″
Price: $1,700
Sonneberg body.
Mark: S 5 H 939

Child, 939, Closed Mouth
Size: 18–23″
All Markets: $1,700–$2,600
Solid dome head, Sonneberg body.
Mark: S 12 H 939

Child, 939, Closed Mouth
Size: 26–29″
Price: $2,800–$3,200
Mark: SH 939

Child, 939, Closed Mouth
Size: 34″
Price: $2,460

Child, 939, Open Mouth
Size: 17″
Price: $900

Sleep eyes, inset upper teeth, French body.
Mark: S 7 H 939

Child, 939, Open Mouth
Size: 34″
Price: $2,100–$2,200
French body.
Mark: S 17 1/2 H 939

Child, 949, Closed Mouth
Size: 15–16″
Price: $1,600–$2,200
Composition fully jointed body or kid gusset-jointed body, bisque forearms (lower prices for kid body).
Mark: S 8 H 949

Child, 949, Closed mouth
Size: 25– 26″
Price: $3,000–$3,200
Sonneberg body.
Mark: S 15 H 949

Child, 949, Open Mouth
Size: 18– 30″

Simon & Halbig, 1469 Fashion Lady. *Composition and wood jointed body with woman's shape. 14", c. 1910. Mark: 1469 Simon & Halbig 2. $6,800, auction. Courtesy Theriault's.*

Price: $1,700–$2,000+
French body or composition body with jointed wrists.

Child, 950

Size: 8"   Internet: $250
Very good; more for better condition. Cloth body with bisque arms, in Folklore Costume.
Mark: SH / 950 / 2/0

Child, 969

Size: 14– 15"
Price: $5,700–$6,250
Open mouth, teeth, dimples.

Child, 979

Size: 21"
Price: $3,200
Open mouth, square-cut teeth, French body.

Child, 1009

Size: 11"
Price: $325
Model 1009 has open mouth.
Mark: S 3 H 1009 / DEP / St.

Child, 1009

Size: 12.5"
Price: $1,100
Original Folklore Costume.

Child, 1009

Size: 17– 20"
Price: $500–$800
Kid body. Swivel head on shoulder plate.

Child, 1009

Size: 22– 25"
Price: $700–$900

Child, 1039

Size: 22"
Price: $600–$800
Model 1039 has open mouth.
Mark: Simon & Halbig 1039 / DEP

Child, 1039

Size: 24"
Price: $450
Very good.

Child, 1039 Walking, Kiss-Throwing

Size: 22"   Internet: $750
Composition French-type body with walking and kiss-throwing mechanisms.
Mark: 1039 / Germany / Simon & Halbig / S & H / 10 1/2

Child, 1040

Size: 26"
Price: $600
Open mouth, kid body, original military costume.
Mark: Germany / S.H. 1040 / 12 (bottom edge shoulder plate)

Child, 1078

Size: 7"
Price: $225
For dolls with crude 5-piece composition body.
Mark: 1078 / Simon & Halbig / 4/0

Child, 1078

Size: 8"
Price: $400
Model 1078 has open mouth. This size, 5-piece jointed composition body.

Child, 1078
Size: 17–19″
Price: $375–$435
Sleep eyes.

Child, 1078
Size: 22– 25″
Price: $500–$550
Mark: 1078-Germany-Simon&Halbig-S&H-11

Child, 1078
Size: 33–35″
Price: $750–$1,200
Mark: 1078 / Germany / Simon & Halbig / S & H / 15 _ (or 17)

Child, 1078
Size: 42″
Price: $3,700

Child, 1079
Size: 10″
Price: $275
Model 1079 has open mouth.
Mark: 1079-2 / DEP / SH / Germany

Child, 1079
Size: 17– 19″
Price: $350–$450
Mark: S H 1079 Dep 7 Germany

Child, 1079
Size: 22– 24″
Price: $450–$550
Standard doll, replaced clothing.
Mark: S H 1079 DEP 9

Child, 1079
Size: 25″
Price: $1,400
With deluxe antique clothing, mint.
Mark: SH 1079 13 Dep

Child, 1079
Size: 27– 30″
Price: $550–$700
Standard doll, replaced clothing.
Mark: S & H 1079 DEP Germany 14

Child, 1079
Size: 30″
All Markets: $900–$1,000
For French trade or otherwise deluxe.

Child, 1079
Size: 33–34″
Price: $1,000–$1,550
More for excellent antique clothing.

Child, 1079
Size: 37″
Price: $2,300
Mark: 1070 S & H dep Germany

Child, 1078 or 1079, Walking
Size: 13–14″
All Markets: $725–$800
Wind key and doll "walks." Composition body with jointing at hips, shoulders, wrists only.

Child, 1080
Size: 20″
Price: $450
Model with kid body (pin or rivet jointing), open mouth, sleep eyes.
Mark: Germany Simon & Halbig 1080 S&H 10

Child, 1080
Size: 27″
Price: $550

Child, 1248
Size: 12″
Price: $775
1248s, although less common than 1249s, are priced similarly.

Child, 1249
Size: 18″
All Markets: $950–$1,400
Model known as Santa. Model has open mouth, sleep eyes. 1910.
Mark: S&H 1249 dep Germany 6 1/2 (head)
Santa, Germany (red body stamp)

Child, 1249
Size: 20″
Price: $1,000–$1,100
Sometimes with mohair upper lashes, not painted.
Mark: Simon & Halbig / 1249 / DEP / Germany / Santa / 9

Child, 1249
Size: 23– 25″
All Markets: $1,300–$2,000
Mark: S & H 1249 / DEP / Germany / 11 (head)
Santa / Germany (stamped back)

Child, 1249
Size: 31″
Price: $1,500+
Mark: 1249 Germany Santa Halbig S & H 14

Child, 2-Faced, 900 Series, White and Black Faces
Size: 11″
Price: $3,000

Head revolves from cardboard cap with metal pivot ring, using Carl Bergner multi-faced system.
Mark: 902 dep 3 (forehead, white face).

Mechanical Swimmer
Price: $1,700

SIMON & HALBIG LADY DOLLS

Fashion Lady
Size: 12"   Date: 1875
Price: $3,000–$4,000
Twill over wood body, bisque limbs, swivel head.
Mark: unmarked

Fashion Lady
Size: 15–18"   Date: 1875
Price: $1,900–$2,500
Swivel head, kid gusset-jointed body, pale bisque, to compete in French Fashion doll market. Allow more for original clothing.
Mark: unmarked

Lady, 908
Size: 12"
All Markets: $2,000
To compete in French market; swivel head, pale-pink kid body, lower bisque arms, sleep eyes.
Mark: SH3 / 908

Lady, 908
Size: 16"   Date: 1880
Price: $1,000–$1,200
Open mouth, socket head, kid body, bisque forearms.
Mark: SH 6 908

Lady, 939, Folklore Outfit
Size: 13"   Date: 1890
Price: $1,100
Muslin body, bisque arms, original folklore outfit, closed mouth.

Lady, 949, Folklore Outfit
Size: 12"   Date: 1890
Price: $1,200
Same as above listing.

Lady, 1050
Size: 13"
Price: $1,200
Open mouth, 4 upper teeth, jointed flapper body with high knee joints.
Mark: Germany / S & H / 1158 / 3

Lady, 1159
Size: 19–21"
Price: $1,500
Open mouth, mohair upper lashes, sleep eyes, composition jointed shapely lady body.

Mark: 1159 S & H Dep 8 Germany (incised) plus red Wimpern stamp (head) or 1159 Halbig / Germany / S & H / 6.

Lady, 1159
Size: 23"
Price: $2,400
Composition and wood body with adult female shape (tiny waist, bosom, long limbs).
Mark: Germany 1159 Simon & Halbig dep 9 1/2

Lady, 1159
Size: 25"
Price: $2,300
Factory original outfit, open mouth, sleep eyes, signed Handwerck lady body, Edwardian dress.
Mark: 1159 Germany Halbig S & H 10

Lady, 1469, Flapper
Size: 14"
Price: $3,100
Original wedding dress, wigged, closed mouth, elongated flapper body.

Lady, 1469
Size: 14"   Date: 1912
Price: $4,600
Exceptional, all-original Edwardian dress.
Mark: 1469 Simon & Halbig 2

Little Woman, 1160
Size: 5–7"
All Markets: $250–$350
Glass eyes, wigged, cloth body with bisque lower limbs, painted stockings and boots.

Little Woman, 1160
Size: 8–10"
Price: $300–$400
Same as above listing.

SIMON & HALBIG CHARACTER DOLLS

Character babies have five-piece bent-limb baby bodies made of composition. Toddler bodies have side-hip jointing. These dolls were generally produced from 1910–1915 with exceptions noted.

Baby Blanche
Size: 23"
Price: $500
Mark: Baby Blanche / Halbig / S&H / 8

Character, Baby, 121
Size: 8"
Price: $650
Bent-limb baby body, sleep eyes.

Character, Baby, 121
Size: 12″
Price: $500
Bent-limb baby body, sleep eyes.

Character, Child, 120
Size: 18–21″
Price: $2,800–$3,200
Open mouth, sleep eyes.
Mark: Simon & Halbig 120 62

Character, Baby, 1428
Size: 10–13″
Price: $1,100
Bent-limb baby body, open/closed mouth,
wigged, sleep eyes.
Mark: 1428 4

Character, Child, 1279
Size: 21″
Price: $2,000
Mark: S & H 1279 / DEP / Germany / 9

Character, Child, 1279
Size: 23–27″
Price: $2,200–$2,900
Chin and mouth dimples, open mouth, sleep eyes.
Mark: S& H 1279 Dep Germany 11 (or 13)

Character, Child, 1279
Size: 31″
Price: $2,800
Early plump body with straight wrists.
Mark: S & H 1279 Dep Germany

Character, Child, 1299
Size: 16–17″
Price: $1,300
Open mouth.
Mark: 1299 Simon & Halbig / S & H 6

Character, Child, 1303
Size: 15″   Date: 1900
Price: $6,750–$10,000+
Mark: 1303 Dep S&H Germany

Character, Child, 1418
Size: 13″
Price: $11,500
Extremely rare. At auction.
Mark: 1418 4

Character, Child, 1488
Size: 20″
Price: $3,000
Mark: 1488 Simon & Halbig 12

Character, Child, Marked "IV"
Size: 19″
Price: $11,500
Handwerck stamped body, closed mouth.
Mark: IV

Character, Lady, 1307
Size: 19–23″   Date: 1902
Price: $9,700–$19,000
Extremely rare, lower price for 19″ doll with
hairline
Mark: 1307 11

Character, Man with Molded Mustache
Size: 13″
Price: $20,000
Attributed to Simon & Halbig. Solid-dome head,
closed mouth, molded mustache, wigged.
Mark: unmarked

Character, Toddler, 1294
Size: 8″
Price: $750
Crude 5-piece composition toddler body with
straight legs, painted torso.
Mark: 1294 / Simon & Halbig / Made in / Ger-
many / 22

Character, Toddler, 1428
Size: 11–15″
Price: $1,500–$2,000
Jointed toddler body.

Character, Toddler, 1428
Size: 18–24″
Price: $2,000–$3,300

Character, Toddler, 1488
Size: 16″
Price: $3,500
Mark: 1488 Simon & Halbig 8 1/2

Character, Toddler, 1488
Size: 22″
Price: $5,000
Closed mouth, toddler body.
Mark: 1488 / Simon & Halbig / 12

Character, Toddler, 1498
Size: 26″
Price: $2,600
Open/closed mouth, toddler body.

Character, Toddler
Size: 26″
Price: $4,000
Molded hair, toddler body.

Figure A Steiner Bébé. *French composition jointed body, straight wrists. 18", c. 1889. Mark: J. Steiner Bte SGDG Paris Fred A 11. Courtesy Theriault's.*

Bébé Gigoteur. *Carton moule torso with clockwork mechanism, kid-over-wood upper legs, composition lower arms and legs. When wound, dolls turns head side to side, kicks feet, waves arms, cries "mama." 17", c. 1879. Unmarked. Courtesy Theriault's.*

Steiner, Jules Nicholas

The Steiner dollmaking firm was founded in 1855 in Paris, France. The original owner, Jules Nicholas Steiner, was at the helm until 1891; after that, various successors kept the firm alive until 1908. Besides producing lovely standard bébé dolls, including the "Figure" series, the company also produced very innovative dolls such as the Bébé Gigoteur (a bébé that kicks and cries with key-winding) and the lever-eye sleep doll.

Market Report: For some collectors, Steiner dolls, with their heavy brows and distinctive look, are an acquired taste. The open-mouth dolls, especially, with their very toothy grins (sometimes with two rows of multiple teeth), have a look quite different from the dolls of other French dollmakers of the same time period. However, almost all Steiner dolls are

highly valued because of their outstanding quality and unique look.

Prices for Steiner dolls are generally steady, with some of the rarer Series and Figure models increasing, and prices for some of the lower-quality Gigoteur dolls decreasing.

Online/Offline Report: Most fine Steiner dolls are obtained from dealers and auction houses, with the occasional gem on eBay. Prices for Steiner dolls are similar at all venues.

Prices and Characteristics: All dolls are bisque, in excellent condition. Except as noted, dolls have fully jointed French wood and composition bodies with straight wrists, paperweight eyes or sleep eyes operated with wire lever, closed mouth, and mohair or human hair wigs. Prices are generally from

Figure C Steiner Bébé. *French composition jointed body, straight wrists. 16", c. 1885. Mark: J. Steiner SGDG Sie C 1 (incised) Bougouin (script). Courtesy Theriault's.*

Bébé Phénix. *French composition body with shoulder and hip jointing only. 22", c. 1895. Mark: Phenix *23. Courtesy Theriault's.*

Black Steiner Bébé. *French jointed composition body. 11", c. 1890. Mark: A. I. Private Collection.*

non-Internet sources, although Internet prices are mixed in for later dolls.

Body Marks: Bodies are usually stamped, with Bébé Le Parisien Medaille d'Or Paris or Le Petit Parisien (body stamp) or Le Petit Parisien Bébé Steiner.

STEINER

Bébé, Early
Size: 10"   Date: 1870s
Price: $6,200
Two rows of teeth
Mark: 3/0

Bébé, Gigoteur
Size: 18– 22"
Price: $2,000–$2,400
When wound and lever released, bébé waves arms, kicks legs, turns heads, says "Mama." Open mouth, 2 rows tiny teeth.
Mark: Unmarked, sometimes with paper body label.

Bébé, Gigoteur With Trousseau
Size: 20"   Date: 1875
Price: $6,250

STEINER SERIES DOLLS, SERIES A & C

Steiner Series dolls are from the 1880s. Their marks have an additional red script stamp such as J Steiner Bte SGDG Bourgoin, Succ. (red script). Other Series include E and G which are very rare.

Bébé, Series A
Size: 24"
Price: $4,000–$6,000
Mark: Steiner Bte SGDG Bougouin (tiny ink script) Sie A 5 (incised)

Bébé, Series A, Black, Open Mouth
Size: 10"
Price: $3,800

Bébé, Series C
Size: 12"
Price: $4,000
Wire-lever sleep eyes.
Mark: Sie C 9/0 J. Steiner SGDG Bougouin, Succ

Bébé, Series C
Size: 15– 17"
Price: $5,000–$6,000
Mark: Sie. C 0 (incised)

Bébé, Series C
Size: 20"
Price: $7,000
Mark: Sie C 3

Bébé, Series C
Size: 23– 24"
Price: $6,000–$7,000
Mark: Sie C 5

Bébé, Series C, Open Mouth
Size: 18"
Price: $4,000
2 rows tiny teeth, Wire-lever sleep eyes.
Mark: Sie C 2 (incised) Bte SGDG Bougouin (red ink script)

STEINER FIGURE DOLLS (FIGURES A, B, & C)

Figure dolls are from 1887 through the early 1890s. They have straight or jointed wrists.

Bébé, Figure A, Size 3
Size: 10– 11″
Price: $2,800–$3,600
Mark: J. Steiner / Bte. S.G.D.G. Paris / Fre A 3 or J. Steiner Paris Fre. A 3

Bébé, Figure A, Size 7
Size: 13– 14″
Price: $3,000–$4,200
Mark: J Steiner Bte SGDG Paris Fre A 7

Bébé, Figure A, Size 9
Size: 16″
Price: $4,200–$4,500
Mark: J Steiner Bte SGDG Fre A 9

Bébé, Figure A, Size 11
Size: 18″
Price: $4,500–$5,100
Mark: J Steiner / Bte SGDG / Paris / Fre A-11 or Figure A No 2 J. Steiner Bte SGDG Paris

Bébé, Figure A, Size 13
Size: 21″
Price: $5,000–$6,000
Mark: Steiner / Paris / Fre A 13

Bébé, Figure A, Size 17
Size: 24″
Price: $5,000–$6,000
Mark: J Steiner Bte SGDG Paris Fre A 17

Bébé, Figure A
Size: 28″
Price: $7,000

Bébé, Figure A, Open Mouth
Size: 12″
Price: $2,600

Bébé, Figure B, Open Mouth
Size: 17″
Price: $5,200–$5,500
Open mouth, 2 rows teeth.
Mark: Figure B No. 1 / J Steiner Bte SGDG Paris

Bébé, Figure C, Size 1
Size: 16″
Price: $6,000
Mark: Figure C No. 1 Steiner Bte SGFG Paris

Bébé, Figure C, Size 6
Size: 25″
Price: $7,400

Lever sleep eyes.
Mark: Figure C No. 6 Steiner Bte SGDG Paris

STEINER BÉBÉ PARISIEN DOLLS

Parisien bébé dolls are from the early 1890s. They have straight or jointed wrists.

Bébé, Parisien
Size: 9–12″
Price: $3,200–$4,300
Original chemise.
Mark: J. Steiner Bte SGDG Paris A 2 or A 2 Paris

Bébé, Parisien
Size: 10″
Price: $3,200–$3,800
All original.

Bébé, Parisien
Size: 18– 20″
Price: $3,600–$4,000
Mark: A 9 Le Parisien Bte SGDG

Bébé, Parisien
Size: 24– 29″
Price: $4,000–$5,000+
Lever sleep eyes.
Mark: A 19 Paris

Bébé, Parisien
Size: 35″
Price: $7,250
Mark: J Steiner Bte SGDG Paris Fre 20

Bébé, Parisien, Black
Size: 10″
Price: $6,000
Mark: A3

Bébé, Parisien, Black, Open Mouth
Size: 14– 15″
Price: $2,500–$3,000
Mark: A7 Le Parisien SGDG A7

Bébé, Parisien, Open Mouth
Size: 14″
Price: $3,500

Bébé, Parisien, Trunk and Trousseau
Size: 8″
Price: $3,500
5-piece composition body, various clothing.

Bébé, Parisien, Trunk and Trousseau
Size: 25″
Price: $6,750
Mark: A 17 Paris (head) and Steiner stamp

Poured wax man. *Poured beeswax head with bead eyes. Wood body wrapped with cloth, wearing original Turkish costume which was fashionable in late 18th century. 8″, c. 1795. Private collection.*

Wax-over-papier-mâché Täufling baby. *Solid-dome shoulder-head, muslin midriff with bellows "mama" crier, muslin upper arms and legs, wood lower arms, legs, papier-mâché lower torso. 18″, c. 1860. Courtesy Theriault's.*

English poured-wax lady. *18″. Courtesy Margaret Kincaid.*

Bébé, Petit Pas

Size: 23– 25″
Price: $4,250–$5,000
French composition body with kid-over-metal hinging at hips; walks. Patented model.
Mark: A 17 Paris or A 15 Paris

BÉBÉ, PHÉNIX STAR DOLLS

Phénix Star dolls were made by the successors to Steiner. They were made from 1892–1900. They have straight or jointed wrists.

Bébé, Phénix Star

Size: 17″
Price: $3,000
Mark: *90 / Le Petit Parisien Bébé Steiner (body)

Bébé, Phénix Star

Size: 19– 21″
Price: $2,600–$3,400
Mark: *93 ((head) Le Petit Parisien Bébé Steiner (paper label, body)

Bébé, Phénix Star

Size: 23″
Price: $3,200
Mark: *94

Bébé, Phénix Star, Bisque Hands

Size: 24″
Price: $6,000
Rare body model.
Mark: *96

UNIS France

See S.F.B.J.

Wax

Wax is known to be one of the earliest substances known for the making of dolls; wax dolls are even documented in ancient Greek and Roman times. The earliest surviving wax dolls that have been documented by collectors date to the late 1700s, although they are quite rare. Although it is in poor condition, one set of wax dolls pictured above is from 1795, although the majority of wax dolls that the collectors can find today are from the 1850s–1860s and later.

- **Poured Wax:** The first wax dolls mass-produced in England were poured into molds, and are hence referred to as "poured wax" dolls. These dolls were mostly made in the 1850s–1870s and later. These dolls tend to be very fragile and prone to melting, although the skin tones can be quite lovely and translucent. Many collectors favor the poured wax dolls because of the beauty of the faces; the highest-priced dolls can have extremely well-modeled portrait-type faces.

- **Wax-Over-Composition:** Later wax dolls were mostly wax-over-composition (or pa-

English poured wax baby by Pierotti. *Poured wax shoulder head, muslin body, poured wax arms and legs, bare feet. 19", c. 1870. Unmarked. $1,050, auction. Courtesy Theriault's.*

English poured wax child. *Poured wax shoulder head, muslin body, poured wax lower limbs. 22", c. 1880. Unmarked. Courtesy Theriault's.*

pier-mâché) dolls, made both in England and Germany, but mostly in Germany. The wax-over dolls were made by applying a thin coat of wax over composition or papier-mâché heads and limbs. These dolls were hailed as an improvement over the poured dolls because they were more durable, but the dolls had a serious problem that became evident only over time: the wax and the composition material expand and contract at different temperatures, and thus the wax surface is very prone to crazing and cracking.

- **Reinforced Wax:** Another variation of the wax doll is called a "reinforced-wax" doll. This type of doll also has a composition or papier-mâché interior, but the wax head is first poured and then reinforced on the inside with plaster of paris or strips of cloth soaked in composition. These were made mostly in Germany.

Market Report: It is simply fascinating that so many of the early wax dolls still exist today, when you consider how fragile they are. Of course, not many have reached us in good condition, and so a large premium is placed on early wax dolls with their original finish or otherwise in excellent, unretouched condition. Therefore, when buying wax dolls, realize that more damage is tolerated than would be tolerated in a bisque or china doll of the same period.

It can be very difficult for a beginner to tell the difference between a wax-over (or wax reinforced) doll and a poured wax doll. The best way to learn to do this is to visit a doll show and compare many examples of both types of dolls. Soon the difference in the look and construction of the dolls and their complexions will become evident. You can also learn the difference by viewing many photo-

German Wax-over-papier-mâché child. Socket head, composition and wood loose-ball jointed body, straight wrists. 11", c. 1880. Unmarked, possibly Kestner. Courtesy Theriault's.

German poured wax child. Wax shoulder head, kid body, wax arms, original costume. 11", c. 1880. Mark: C.L. Petson Berlin (oval stamp, torso). $800, auction.

French wax fashion lady. On base, signed by artist. Wrapped body. 12", c. 1920s. $300, auction.

graphs of both types of dolls, although it is harder to learn the difference in this manner.

Wax dolls require special preservation techniques, and should never be stored in areas without climate control (this is, of course, true with many types of dolls, but one summer in a hot attic can be the end of a wax doll).

When collecting wax dolls, look for better modeling of features, torsos stamped with the original maker, dolls that have not been restored with additional wax, popular molded bonnet dolls and original outfits. English dolls are most popular at this time.

Online/Offline Report: Collecting wax dolls is very popular in certain areas right now, including England, where many of the early wax dolls were made. Many sales of wax dolls made on eBay and from other online auction sites in the United States right now end up with buyers in England and other parts of Europe.

Especially in Internet auctions, older examples of wax dolls, even in fair condition, can bring surprising prices. However, wax is just as difficult to assess with online pictures as bisque is, and skin tones and subtle retouching or damage to the wax may not show up in a low-resolution Internet photo at all.

Prices are all over the map in all venues as this area of collecting matures and gains popularity.

Prices and Characteristics: All dolls are in excellent condition, with some wear acceptable, and in original clothing from the period, except as noted. Dolls are generally shoulder-heads with stuffed cloth bodies (mostly stitch-jointed), with lower limbs of wax, papier-mâché, or compositon, glass eyes, and mohair or human hair wigs, except as noted. Dolls are generally unmarked, but some dolls have body stamps on the front torso that indicate the maker of the doll or the store it was sold at.

ENGLISH POURED WAX DOLLS

Dolls have inset hair (hair set into the wax) and wax lower limbs except as noted, often with bare feet, plus cloth bodies, generally stitch-jointed, sometimes stamped with maker on front torso, glass or enamel eyes.

Baby
Size: 20"   Date: 1870s
Price: $750
Open mouth, teeth.

Baby
Size: 18– 29"   Date: 1865–1880
Price: $1,200–$1,500

French wax fashion ladies by Lafitte-Desirat. Painted features, mohair wigs. 11″ and 14″, c. 1917. Mark: Lafitte-Desirat (signed on base bottom, doll with dog) and La Jarretelle (gold label, other). $2,400 for pair, at auction. Courtesy Theriault's.

Elaborate baby outfit, well-defined features, closed mouth, bare feet.
Marks: Sometimes with body stamp, such as Hamley's, sometimes made by Pierotti.

Baby With Trousseau
Size: 17″   Date: 1860
Price: $4,500
Elaborate trousseau, for French market, in blue French store box.

Baby, Lucy Peck
Size: 20″   Date: 1890s
Price: $315
Very good. Simple features.
Mark: Lucy Peck (torso).

Baby, Morrell
Size: 20″   Date: 1875
Price: $1,600
Very good.
Mark: 164 Oxford Street, Morrell, Burlington Arcade (body stamp).

Child
Size: 14–20″   Date: 1890s
Price: $250–$350
Very good, for later doll.

Child
Size: 21″   Date: 1865–1880
All Markets: $1,125–$1,500
Exceptional wig, bare feet, well-defined features.

Child
Size: 24–26″   Date: 1875–1880
Price: $2,000–$2,100

Well-defined features, closed mouth, sometimes plump.

Child
Size: 27″   Date: 1860
Price: $3,800
Exceptional features, inset lashes and brows.

Child
Size: 38″   Date: 1880s–1890s
Price: $800
Very good. Original clothing, later doll.

Child as "The Doll Fairy"
Size: 15″   Date: 1890
Price: $600
Original outfit, from ballet *The Doll Fairy,* from a London doll boutique, bare feet.
Mark: Hamley's of Regent Street.

Child, Fashion Doll
Size: 14–16″   Date: 1865–1875
Price: $525–$600
Bare feet. For most common faces.

Child, Mrs. Peck's London
Size: 25″   Date: 1870
Price: $2,350
Closed mouth.
Mark: Mrs. Peck's London (body stamp)

Child, Portrait
Size: 30″
Price: $2,150
Closed mouth, plump wax limbs, molded lower lids.

Hamley's, Child, Original Box
Size: 18″   Date: 1880
Price: $2,500–$3,400
Near mint in original Hamley's box.

Lady
Size: 17″   Date: 1910
Price: $425
Very good, standard features, redressed.

Lady, Fashion
Size: 18″   Date: 1875
Price: $900–$950
Very good, original clothing, molded shoes.

Lady, Portrait
Size: 22 –24″   Date: 1860+
All Markets: $2,600–$2,900
Closed mouth, lifelike features, original clothing, most by Pierotti.

Lady, Turned-Shoulder Head
Size: 29″
Price: $420
Good. Molded high heels.

Marsh, Charles, Child
Size: 20″   Date: 1875
Price: $850
Closed mouth, inset eyes.
Mark: From C. Gooch Soho Bazaar / Chas.
Marsh Sole Manufacturer, London, Dolls
cleaned and repaired (body stamp).

Montanari, Poured Wax
Size: 28″   Date: 1860
Price: $3,000
Good, but exceptional features.

Peddler
Size: 13″   Date: 1840
Price: $2,200
All original with original wares.

Pierotti, Child
Size: 17–19″   Date: 1870
Price: $1,000–$1,600
More for better molded features retaining some
original coloring.
Mark: Pierotti.

Wax-Over, Mad-Alice-Type
Size: 14″   Date: 1834
All Markets: $650
Very good.

Wax-Over, Child
Size: 16″   Date: 1860s
Price: $585
Very good. Closed mouth, wigged.

Wax-Over, Child
Size: 18″   Date: 1860
Price: $400
Very good. Beeswax over thin papier-mâché,
sleep eyes, open mouth, 4 teeth, nailed-on wig,
wax-over arms and legs.

GERMAN WAX-OVER-COMPOSITION DOLLS

Wax-over dolls are generally wax over papier-mâché or composition with glass inset or sleep eyes, wigged with mohair or human hair, and sometimes with molded hair or bonnet. Bodies are cloth, generally with composition or papier-mâché lower limbs.

Baby, 2 Faces, Bartenstein
Size: 15″   Date: 1880s
Price: $300
Fair. 1 face smiles, 1 cries with open mouth.
Motschmann-type body with 2 pull cords, 1
turns head, 1 for crier.

Baby, 2 Faces, Mechanical
Size: 15″   Date: late 1800s
Price: $500
3 pull strings rotate solid dome head, moves
arms, makes crying sound. Smiling and weeping
faces, cloth-over-cardboard body, cardboard bonnet, attached mohair bangs.
Mark: Deutches Reiche / Patent U.S.P. No.
243762 (body).

Baby, Wire-Eyed
Size: 11.5″   Date: 1850
Price: $825
Motschmann-type body with cloth segments and
composition limbs, factory outfit.

Poured, Child, Shoulder-Head
Size: 11.5″
Price: $835
MIB.

Wax-Over, Baby
Size: 20– 25″   Date: late 1800s
Price: $225–$300
Inset or sleep eyes.

Wax-Over, Child
Size: 12– 15″   Date: late 1800s
Price: $230–$400
Very good; higher prices for better condition,
swivel head, unusual body.

Wax-Over, Child
Size: 19– 20″   Date: 1880s
Price: $400–$500
Sleep eyes, fancy painted boots.

Wax-Over, Child
Size: 26–27″   Date: late 1800s
All Markets: $400–750
Very good; lower price for faces with much crazing/cracking.

Wax-Over, Lady
Size: 19″   Date: 1870s
Price: $250
Molded, painted hair, carved wood limbs.

Wax-Over, Lady
Size: 28″   Date: 1870s
Price: $325
Very good. Wig over molded hair, molded orange boots.

Wax-Over, Lady
Size: 32″   Date: 1870
Price: $2,100
Exceptional face, open/closed mouth, molded teeth, pierced ears, straw-stuffed muslin body with wax-over lower limbs, molded fancy black boots, original fashion outfit.

Wax-Over, Molded Bonnet
Size: 14″   Date: mid-1800s
                     Internet: $835
Very good. Wear, but desirable bonnet, well dressed. Wood lower limbs, crier.

Wax-Over, Molded Bonnet
Size: 14– 32″   Date: 1850s–1860s
All Markets: $200–$300
For doll with much wear, simple bonnet. Pupilless glass eyes.

Wax-Over, Molded Bonnet, Lady
Size: 17″   Date: 1860s
Price: $1,200
Little mohair tufts under molded hat, feather plumes, carved wood hands and feet, crier, French fashion-type costume.

VARIOUS AND REINFORCED WAX DOLLS

Reinforced wax dolls are poured wax shoulder-heads with the inside of the heads reinforced with composition or papier-mâché. They have mohair wigs with set or sleep eyes and composition or papier-mâché limbs, except as noted.

Crèche Figure, Child or Man
Size: 8– 18″   Date: late 1800s
All Markets: $450–$550
Very good, with flaws.

French, Lafitte-Desirat, Fashion Lady
Size: 11″   Date: 1917
Price: $1,200
Woman in velvet checkered walking suit with dog on leash.
Mark: Lafitte-Desirat (ink signed on base, gold label).

French, Wax-Over, Schmitt, Bébé
Size: 17″
Price: $2,700
Paperweight eyes, Schmitt fully jointed composition body.

Lady, Bride
Size: 11″
Price: $1,500

Lady, Lever-Operated Sleep Eyes
Size: 22″
Price: $2,150
Seam-jointed cloth body with kid forearms and hands, separate fingers, original fashion outfit.

Peddler Doll With Wares
Size: 10″
Price: $2,900
Very good. Table full of merchandise, most pieces original.

Peddler, Pincushion
Size: 7″
Price: $600

Reinforced Wax, Lady
Size: 30″   Date: late 1800s
Price: $825
Original clothes, leather body.

Reinforced Wax, Baby or Child
Size: 24–25″   Date: late 1800s
Price: $300–$450
Very good, for doll with wax flaws and redressed or worn costume.

Reinforced Wax, Lady
Size: 18″
Price: $300
Very good.

Reinforced Wax, Lady
Size: 22″   Date: 1870s
Price: $225
Good. Open/closed mouth, molded painted boots.

Shell Doll, Holding Dog
Size: 7″   Date: early 1800s
Price: $1,500
Painted eyes, wool wig.

Wood Dolls

Wood is another material from which dolls have been made since ancient times. Many of the wood dolls which collectors covet today were made in England, and wood dolls are some of the earliest dolls which still exist today, with some surviving early English examples from the 1600s and 1700s.

Market Report: Because of rarity, very few collectors can specialize in early English wood dolls of the William and Mary and Queen Anne periods. However, many collectors who specialize in early dolls do try to have an example or two of later English or German Grodner Tal peg wood and tuck comb dolls from the 1800s in their collections if they can afford them. Even collectors who do not specialize in wood or early dolls often cannot pass up the charm of early wood dolls, and such collectors also tend to have one or two tucked away in the doll cabinet with their bisque and china antique dolls.

Most early wood dolls have experienced wear, and it is rare to find the dolls in undamaged condition today, so more damage is tolerated for wood dolls than for the later bisque dolls.

Prices are relatively stable for wood dolls, mostly, I think, because of the difficulty in dating these dolls and how impossible it usually is to know anything about their history or makers. Prices remain very high for the very early 1600s and 1700s dolls.

Online/Offline Report: Very early wood dolls are not found on eBay. The few examples that exist usually trade hands via dealers, private sales, or auction houses. Later peg woodens can easily be found online, as can Swiss dolls. Joel Ellis and early American wood dolls are also rarely found for sale on eBay, though the occasional early peg wood or tuck comb does turn up.

Prices and Characteristics: All dolls are wood. Dolls are generally unmarked except for an occasional paper label on later wood dolls. Dolls are in very good condition with wear and some paint loss acceptable in early dolls. Prices are similar from all venues with most price results found from non-Internet sources.

AMERICAN WOOD DOLLS

Joel Ellis, Lady
Size: 12″   Date: 1873
All Markets: $450–$600
Usually with substantial paint loss, pewter hands and feet (boots), sometimes a paper label, carved features and hair, mortise and tenon joints.

Joel Ellis, Black
Size: 15″   Date: 1873
Price: $500
Made by Cooperative Manufacturing Co., Springfield, Vermont. Very worn; much more for dolls with less wear.

Mason, Taylor (Springfield, VT)
Size: 11– 12″   Date: 1880s
All Markets: $300–$500
For dolls with much wear; considerably more for dolls in better condition.

Black Man, Carved, Primitive
Size: 11″
Price: $875
Carved wood, cotton hair, button pupils, mortise and tenon joints, original clothing.

ENGLISH WOOD DOLLS

William and Mary, Female
Size: 17″   Date: late 1600s
Price: $46,000
Very early and exceedingly rare. Carved ears, painted eyes, eyebrows and eyelashes with dots, defined fingers, wood legs. At auction.

Queen Anne
Size: 14– 24″   Date: early 1700s
Price: $10,000–$20,000
Very rare, no sales during research period for this book, prices from earlier sales.

Georgian Period, Excellent Condition
Size: 17– 19″   Date: 1780
Price: $4,000–$6,000
Black pupil-less glass eyes, line and dot eyebrows, dots for lashes, carved ears, nailed-on wig.

Georgian Period, Fair Condition
Size: 14–18″   Date: late 1700s
Price: $1,700–$2,200
Glass eyes, dotted eyebrows and lashes, peg- and pin-jointed hips and arms, sometimes linen upper arms with wood forearms. For dolls with

Two Grodner Tal wood dolls with tuck combs. Dowel jointed wood bodies at shoulders, elbows, hips, knees, painted flat shoes. Decorative "tuck comb" at top of head. 8" and 15", c. 1830 (larger) and c. 1840 (smaller). Unmarked. $2,400, larger; $600, smaller. Courtesy Theriault's.

English wood dolls. Carved wood heads. Homespun bodies. 8.5", c. late 1700s. Unmarked. Courtesy Theriault's.

much wear; considerably more for dolls in better condition.

English Wood Dolls, Sometimes Sold as "Queen Anne" Dolls, Excellent Condition

Size: 13– 23"   Date: late 1700s–early 1800s
Price: $2,000–$3,000
These dolls are not from the Queen Anne period but are generally sold as such by collectors and some dealers and auction houses. True Queen Anne dolls are from the early 1700s and are exceedingly rare.

English Wood Dolls, Sometimes Sold as "Queen Anne" Dolls, Fair Condition

Size: 13– 23"   Date: late 1700s–early 1800s
Price: $800–$1,000
Dolls in fair condition, much wear, sometimes replaced parts or repainting. See above listing for description. Generally these dolls are either late Georgian period or early 1800s.

Turner's Doll

Size: 8"   Date: 1820s
Price: $1,250
Black painted domed head, torso to waist, rolled cloth arms and legs.

FRENCH WOOD DOLLS

French Court Doll, Hermaphrodite, Elaborate Hair

Size: 17"   Date: late 1700s
Price: $5,400
Male/female sexed, wood torso with legs, painted socks, shoes, carved bust, hands connected at elbow. At auction.

French Court Doll, Pair

Size: 14"   Date: late 1700s
Price: $18,000
Carved wood shoulder-heads with features and hair of aristocracy, male is anatomically correct. Dolls used in theater and play presentations of

Wood hand puppet from Punch and Judy, boy in checkered suit. *Chip-carved wood head, hands, hollow cloth body. 12", c. late 1800s. Private collection.*

Swiss wood carved dolls. *Larger, wooden shoulder-head on wood body; smaller, 1-piece head/torso, wood limbs. 11" and 14", c. 1920. Unmarked. Courtesy Theriault's.*

French court scandals and happenings. Very rare, at auction.

GERMAN WOOD DOLLS

Grodner Tal, Peg Wood
Size: 4– 5"   Date: 1830s
Price: $325–$500
Painted black hair and features, dowel-jointed body, painted wood lower arms and legs, painted shoes.

Grodner Tal, Peg Wood
Size: 4.5"   Date: 1840
Price: $850
Original outfit, dressed as dandy.

Grodner Tal, Peg Wood
Size: 13"   Date: 1840
Price: $2,500
Original central Asian attire.

Grodner Tal, Peg Wood, Early, Articulated Body
Size: 11.5"   Date: 1820
Price: $2,200
Painted features, black tendrils around face, articulated body at shoulder, elbow, hips, knees, painted shoes.

Grodner Tal, Shell Doll
Size: 4–5"   Date: 1830–1835
Price: $1,300–$1,650
Peg wood doll with painted features and carved ringlets, shell outfit.

Grodner Tal, Tuck Comb Dolls, Pair
Size: 1– 3"   Date: early 1800s
Price: $300–$400

Grodner Tal, Tuck Comb
Size: 4– 5"   Date: 1820s–1840s
Price: $400–$500
Spit curls, carved tuck comb, painted facial features, mortise and tenon peg joints.

Grodner Tal, Tuck Comb
Size: 12–13"   Date: 1820s–1840s
Price: $550–$850
Spit curls, carved tuck comb, painted facial features, mortise and tenon peg joints. Good condition, sold nude.

Grodner Tal, Tuck Comb
Size: 12–13"   Date: 1820s–1840s
Price: $1,000–$1,200
For exceptional examples, excellent condition and dressed.

Grodner Tal, Tuck Comb
Size: 18"   Date: 1820s–1830s
Price: $3,750
Early and unusually large. Carved head, painted eyes and features, tiny lashes, hair with curls around face, painted comb, wood body with ball joints, carved fingers, painted shoes. At auction.

Peg Wood, Late 19th Century
Size: 11–12"   Date: late 1800s
Price: $150–$250
Less elaborate carving, generally sold nude.

Peg Wood, 20th Century
Size: 11–12″   Date: 20th century
Price: $40–$60
Advertised in magazines in the mid-20th century into the early 1970s. Newer paint and look.

Wood, Carved, Folklore Attire
Size: 13″   Date: 1870s
Price: $1,200–$1,300
All-wood body, separately carved fingers, body jointed like mannequin figure, original costume. Possibly French.

SWISS WOOD DOLLS

Carved Lady or Man
Size: 9– 12″   Date: early 1900s
Price: $300–$400
All carved, jointed body, nude or regional attire, sometimes with paper label.

Carved, Lady
Size: 29″   Date: 1920
Price: $1,500

Very large size, swivel head, carved hair in bun, painted eyes, dowel joints.

WOOD DOLLS, MISCELLANEOUS

Wood Walking Body With 7 Legs, Carved Hair
Size: 20″   Date: early 1800s
Price: $5,800
Rare, flat swivel-neck on dowel, elongated face, jointed arms (shoulders and elbows), when costumed, appears doll has 2 legs and walks on them

Wood Walking Body With 8 Legs, Wigged
Size: 17″   Date: early 1800s
Price: $5,200
When costumed, appears doll walks. Carved face, human hair wig, jointed arms, 1-piece torso with leg cut out for walking legs.

5 VINTAGE DOLLS

Advertising Dolls

Advertising dolls are a fascinating specialty collecting area. The dolls run the gamut from the well-known Toni and Miss Revlon dolls from the 1950s to the multitudes of "premium" dolls that children could order with box tops and a small shipping fee in the mid-20th century. Most of these dolls, but not all, were small plastic dolls or printed cloth dolls. Advertising dolls were first mass-produced starting about 1900 and are still being made today.

Market Report: Advertising dolls are a strong crossover collectible, with advertising as well as doll collectors seeking them out, although the market, overall, is somewhat soft. Because of the soft market, now is a good time to jump into advertising dolls, since many popular dolls such as cloth Mr. Peanut dolls are available for under $20. When collecting advertising dolls, pay special attention to condition—cloth dolls in mint condition with no soiling of the cloth are especially desirable.

Online/Offline Report: Online auction prices are under dealer/show prices at this time, since it is often difficult to assess the condition of advertising dolls, especially cloth dolls, via photos. When buying or selling advertising dolls at online auction sites, it is very important to look for or list them in the Collectibles/Advertising category and not just the Dolls area—there is a better selection of the dolls in the Collectibles/Advertising area and the prices are usually stronger. For instance, a plush Planters Mr. Peanut doll can sell for $15.99 in the Advertising category, but the same doll, listed only in the Dolls area, will often not even get one bid for $5.99.

ADVERTISING DOLLS

Blue Bonnet Margarine Sue, Dakin
Size: 11.5″   Date: 1972
Price: $25
Material: cloth

Brown Uniroyal Nauga Advertising Doll
Size: 14″   Date: 1967
Price: $200
Material: vinyl
Mark: Naugahyde Vinyl Fabric Uniroyal Inc 196 (foot)

Buddy Lee
Size: 12–13″   Date: 1922
Price: $250–$415
Material: composition
Price can depend on outfit. By H.D Buddy Lee Mercantile Co.

Buddy Lee, Train Conductor
Size: 14″
Price: $465
Material: composition

Buddy Lee
Size: 13″   Date: 1948–1950s
Price: $250–$350
Material: hard plastic
Buddy Lees made by H.D. Lee Company, Inc.

Campbell Kid, American Character
Size: 12.5″   Date: 1928
Price: $210
Material: composition
Mark: A PETITE DOLL

Campbell Kid, Horsman
Size: 12″   Date: 1910–1914
Price: $350
Material: composition
Mark: Campbell's Kid / A Horsman Doll / Permission of Campbell Soup Company (paper tag)

Palmer Cox Brownie. *Arnold Printworks. Cloth lithographed, 1 piece. 6", c. 1892. Unmarked.*

Miss Curity, Ideal. *Hard plastic head; 5-piece hard plastic body. 14", c. 1953. Mark: P-90 / Ideal Doll / Made in USA (head) Ideal Doll, P-90 (back). Courtesy Theriault's.*

Campbell Soup Kid as Martha Washington. *Vinyl. 10.5", c. 1976. Unmarked. $60 if MIB, eBay. Courtesy Geneva Wallen Collection.*

Campbell Kid, Horsman
Size: 12"   Date: 1930s
Price: $390
Material: composition
Mark: paper label: Campbell's' Kid—A Horsman Doll

Campbell Kid, Horsman
Size: 12"   Date: 1948
Price: $150
Material: composition
Mark: unmarked

Campbell Kids, George and Martha Washington
Size: 10"   Date: 1976
Price: $125 for pair MIB
Material: vinyl
For the Bicentennial.

Campbell Kid
Size: 10.5"   Date: 1988
Price: $30
Material: vinyl

Campbell Kid, Chef, Black
Size: 4.25"   Date: 1993
Price: $20
Material: bisque

Campbell Soup Doll, Boy and Girl, by Eugene
Size: 17"   Date: 1985
Price: $75
Material: vinyl

Campbell Soup Doll, by Francine Cee
Size: 16"   Date: 1993
Price: $170
Material: bisque

Coca-Cola Doll, Rushton
Size: 15"   Date: 1940s
Price: $75
Material: vinyl/ cloth
Mark: The Rushton Co. (tag)

Eskimo Pie, Boy, by Chase Bag Company
                              Date: 1964
Price: $35
Material: cloth
Premium doll, from Eskimo Pie wrapper.

General Mills, Sippin Sam, Kenner
Size: 6.5"   Date: 1972
Price: $10
Material: vinyl
Cereal premium.
Mark: 1972 / GENERAL MILLS FUN GROUP, INC. (back) ©1972 / G.M.F.G.I. (boots)

General Mills, Sippin Sue, Kenner
Size: 6.5"   Date: 1972
Price: $12
Material: vinyl
Cereal premium.

Gerber Baby Doll, 50th Anniversary, Atlanta Novelty Co.
Size: 17"   Date: 1979
Price: $50
Material: vinyl

Snap, Crackle, Pop (Rice Krispies), Princess Soft Toys, Inc. 8″, c. 1997. Set, $15, dealer.

Fig Newton Cookies Doll, Talbot Toys. Vinyl. 4.25″, c. 1983. $10, eBay.

Sippin Sam, General Mills. Vinyl. 6.5″, c. 1972. Mark: 1972 / GENERAL MILLS / FUN GROUP, INC. (back) and ©1972 / G.M.F.G.I. (boots bottom). $10, eBay.

Gerber Baby Doll, Atlanta Novelty Co.
Size: 12″ Date: 1980s
Price: $60
Material: vinyl
Black.

Golden Crisp Sugar Bear
Size: 4.25″
Price: $10
Material: cloth
Post Golden Crisp cereal premium.

Harry Hood, Milk Advertising Doll
Size: 8.5″ Date: 1980s
Price: $45
Material: vinyl

Jordache Fashion Doll, Mego
Size: 11.5″ Date: 1971
Price: $10–$30
Material: vinyl

Levi's Denim Doll, Knickerbocker
Size: 17″ Date: 1974
Price: $10
Material: vinyl

Little Miss Just Rite, Dakin
Size: 8″ Date: 1969
Price: $25
Material: vinyl
Just Rite Denim Jeans, printed on jeans.

Miss Curity, Kendall Company
Size: 18″ Date: 1955
Price: $185
Material: hard plastic

Miss Sunbeam, Eegee
Size: 18″ Date: 1950s
Price: $55
Material: vinyl
Sunbeam bread.

Mountain Dew Hillbilly (Canadian Market), Takara
Size: 9.25″ Date: 1960s
Price: $60
Material: vinyl
Mountain Dew banner on overalls.

Pillsbury Dough Boy, Store Display
Size: 48″ Date: 1970s
Price: $75–$110
Material: vinyl

Pillsbury Dough Girl, 1st Issue
Size: 6″ Date: 1972
Price: $20
Material: vinyl
1st edition has smooth, not grainy vinyl.
Mark: ©The Pillsbury Co. 1972

Pillsbury Dough Grandma
Size: 4.75″ Date: 1970s
Price: $85
Material: vinyl

Planters, Mr. Peanut
Size: 25″ Date: 1991
Price: $20
Material: cloth

Planters, Mr. Peanut
Size: 8.75″
Price: $80
Material: wood

Planters, Mr. Peanut, by Schoenhut
Size: 8″
Price: $250
Material: wood

Post Health Products, Clown, Lithographed Cloth
Size: 13.5″   Date: 1925
Price: $100
Material: cloth
POST HEALTH PRODUCTS in red circle on doll.
Mark: 1925 P.C.CO (back)

Puffy Quaker Puffed Wheat and Rice
Size: 16.5″   Date: 1930s
Price: $100
Material: cloth

Pure Oil, Lion Uniform Company, Boy
Size: 12.75″
Price: $65
Material: hard plastic
Mark: LION (back)

Smokey the Bear
Size: 12.25″   Date: 1960s
Price: $25
Material: cloth
Mark: Three Bears, Inc. Newport, R.I. 02840 (tag)

Smokey the Bear
Size: 16″   Date: 1960s
Price: $90
Material: cloth
Made 1950s through the 1960s. Price for doll with badge, belt, and hat.

Tintair, Effanbee
Size: 14″   Date: 1952
Price: $350
Material: hard plastic
Doll came with hair tinting and setting accessories. Honey doll used.

Tony the Tiger
Size: 7.5″   Date: 1974
Price: $55
Material: vinyl
Kellogg's.

Uneeda Kid, Uneeda
                            Date: 1910
Price: $700
Material: composition
Advertising Uneeda Biscuits, Nabisco.

Western Union Dolly Gram
Size: 6.5″
Price: $15
Material: vinyl

White Stag, Klumpe, Skier
Size: 10″
Price: $180
Material: cloth
White Stag featured prominently on skis and zipper.

Woodsy Owl, Dress-Me Doll
Size: 14″   Date: 1960s–1970s
Price: $35
Material: cloth

American Character

American Character produced composition, hard plastic, and vinyl dolls for 60 years. A quintessential American doll company based in New York City, American Character was founded in 1918 and specialized in composition dolls until the early 1950s.

Many of their early composition dolls were sold under the "Petite" trademark. Popular molds from their composition era included the Campbell Kids and Toodles, and they produced many Mama Dolls. When the hard plastic era dawned, American Character found great success with Sweet Sue, Tiny Tears, and Betsy McCall.

The advent of the fashion doll found American Character adding teenage dolls to their inventory. They turned their successful Sweet Sue into a teenager and also produced vinyl-head Toni dolls after they were granted the license to make Toni dolls from the Gillette Corporation in 1958.

The 1960s brought difficult times for American Character (also known in the 1960s as the American Doll and Toy Corporation) thanks to the overwhelming popularity of Mattel's Barbie doll. American Character tried to compete with Barbie by introducing its own 11.5″ fashion dolls including Tressy (with growing hair) and Mary Make-Up, as well as innovative, original dolls such as the Whimsies, but ultimately Barbie proved too tough a competitor, and American Character closed its doors in 1968.

American Character Toni. *Vinyl head, 5-piece body, in original box, wearing Dinner Date #1402. 13", c. 1958. Unmarked. Courtesy Theriault's.*

Market Report: American Character is one of the stars of the mid-20th-century doll scene. The dolls produced by this company were "better quality" dolls—the type of dolls that companies such as Eegee and Deluxe Reading tried to knock off. Their dolls bring a premium price compared to many of the dolls produced by their contemporaries, and they are eagerly sought after by collectors.

Just like most mid-20th-century manufactured dolls, mint and all-original American Character dolls continue to increase in price, while played-with, common examples in replaced clothing continue to decline in price. This has been caused directly by eBay, which, through the sheer volume of auctions for played-with, redressed dolls, has educated collectors on how abundant these manufactured dolls really are. At the same time, eBay has also illustrated to doll collectors how rare pristine, unplayed-with examples of those same dolls truly are. For more on this eBay effect, read the "Online/Offline Report" in this section.

Online/Offline Report: If you've been reading this book straight through, you'll notice a significant change at this point in the book. Whereas many of the antique dolls are somewhat scarce on eBay and other online auction sites, the number of mid-20th-century dolls generally available on eBay is huge. There is a giant split in prices between prices for mint-quality, mint-in-box, all-original and complete vintage dolls and the played-with, not-original vintage dolls. Most of the dolls available on eBay and other online auction sites fall into the played-with, not-original, and therefore lower-priced category. Most of the mid-20th-century dolls that well-known dealers and auction houses offer collectors fall into the first category of dolls, which are at least all-original and generally in excellent or better condition.

American Character is a good example of this. At any given time, you'll find pages and pages of American Character merchandise for sale on eBay. On the final day I was researching this section of this book, there were 360+ recently completed auctions for American Character dolls. All but the first page of those dolls—about 50 dolls in all—sold for less than $50. Most of these were in played-with condition. Some of the auctions showing a final price of under $50 were for dolls that didn't meet their reserve (the effect of reserve prices on final selling prices for dolls is discussed in the "Doll Collecting and the Internet" chapter).

So the online/offline report for American Character dolls (and for many of the other

Two "Petite" American Character dolls; one George Washington, one "Sally". Composition socket heads, composition bodies (except George has original rubber arms). Both 19", c. 1932. Mark: Petite. Courtesy Theriault's.

American Character composition baby. Composition head, lower arms, cloth body. 15". Mark: AM. CHAR DOLL. Courtesy Ellen Johnson.

American Character Toni. Vinyl. 10.5", c. 1958. mark: AMERICAN © CHARACTER (in circle) / 1956 (in box). $50, this condition, eBay. More for mint dolls.

---

vintage dolls in this section) is that American Character dolls are abundant from all venues, with an overabundance of lesser-quality dolls available on eBay. Percentage-wise, you'll find more excellent and mint American Character dolls from dealers and auction houses, and often for prices comparable to eBay prices. However, eBay prices for lesser-quality dolls tend to be lower than the prices for similar quality dolls from dealers or auction houses.

Prices and Characteristics; Marks: Prices are for dolls in excellent condition unless otherwise noted; dolls generally have 5-piece bodies. Early American Character composition dolls will be marked "PETITE" or "A PETITE DOLL"; later dolls can be marked "AM CHAR" or "AMER CHAR DOLL." Most hard plastic and vinyl dolls are marked "American Character" (in circle, on back or back of head), sometimes with the copyright date, or "American Character Doll Corp." Tiny Tears are occasionally just marked with the patent number.

AMERICAN CHARACTER, COMPOSITION

Campbell Kid
Size: 12"   Date: 1928
                             Internet: $150–$210

5-piece composition body, painted eyes.
Mark: A PETITE DOLL.

Chubby
                             Date: 1920s
                             Internet: $200
Mark: PETITE.

Little Love
Size: 16"   Date: 1940s
                             Internet: $120

Mama Doll, Petite
Size: 28"   Date: late 1920s
                             Internet: $175
Composition shoulder plate, composition arms, legs, cloth body, sleep eyes.
Mark: PETITE / AM CHAR DOLL CO.

Puggy
Size: 12"   Date: 1920s
                             Internet: $125
5-piece composition body, PETITE mark.

Sally Joy
Size: 12"   Date: 1930s
                             Internet: $300

AMERICAN CHARACTER, HARD PLASTIC

I Love Lucy Baby
Size: 16"   Date: 1952
                             Internet: $210–$285
Soft rubber body. Produced for a few months while Lucy was pregnant on TV show until real-life Ricky Jr. was born.

Sweet Sue

Size: 14″   Date: 1950s
Price: $615
Pristine MIB with tags.

Sweet Sue

Size: 18″   Date: 1950s
Price: $240   Internet: $200–$295
Excellent condition.

Sweet Sue

Size: 24″   Date: 1950s
Price: $350
Mint, original outfit, tag, box (plaid coat).

Sweet Sue Bride

Size: 15″   Date: 1950s
Price: $625
MIB.

Sweet Sue Bride, Unmarked

Size: 17″   Date: 1950s
Price: $125
Average condition.

Sweet Sue Sophisticate

Size: 14″   Date: 1957–1958
                       Internet: $125

Sweet Sue Sophisticate

Size: 18″   Date: 1957–1958
                       Internet: $150
Average.

Sweet Sue Sophisticate

Size: 18″   Date: 1950s
                       Internet: $430
Mint.

Sweet Sue Sophisticate

Size: 20″   Date: 1950s
                       Internet: $80
Average; redressed.

Sweet Sue Walker

Size: 14″   Date: 1950s
Price: $60
Redressed.

Sweet Sue Walker

Size: 17″   Date: 1950s
Price: $80
Redressed

Sweet Sue Walker

Size: 18″   Date: 1950s
Price: $180

Sweet Sue Walker

Size: 20″   Date: 1950s
Price: $130
In original gown.

Sweet Sue Walker

Size: 23″   Date: 1950s
Price: $80
Average.

Tiny Tears

Size: 12–13″   Date: 1950s
                       Internet: $100–$135
More with clothes or trunk.

Tiny Tears

Size: 12″   Date: 1950s
                       Internet: $190
Molded hair, soft rubber body.

Tiny Tears

Size: 12″   Date: 1950s
Price: $475
With layette in case; mint.

Tiny Tears, Molded Hair

Size: 12″   Date: 1950s
                       Internet: $1,250
With full layette attached in original box, perfect
rubber body.

**Tiny Tears, Molded Hair "Rock-a-Bye Baby,"
Layette**

Size: 12″   Date: 1950s
                       Internet: $350
Rock gently in cradle and doll SLOWLY closes
eyes—lie down without rocking and eyes stay
open.

Tiny Tears

Size: 15–16″   Date: 1950s
Price: $110 –$220   Internet: $145–$170
For VG to excellent dolls.

Tiny Tears in Rocking Crib

Size: 16″   Date: 1950s
Price: $150
Excellent. Rock-a-bye eyes, Tiny Tears crib.

Tiny Tears, Rubber Body

Size: 17″   Date: 1950s
Price: $500
Mint, earlier model.

Tiny Tears

Size: 19″   Date: 1950s
                       Internet: $100
For doll with original outfit, pamphlet, and
small trousseau.

Tiny Tears, 1st Edition, Molded Hair

Size: 20″   Date: 1950s
                       Internet: $250
With layette.

Tiny Tears, Original Dress
Date: 1950s
Internet: $45
Dress sized for 16″ doll.

AMERICAN CHARACTER, VINYL

Campbell Kid
Size: 10″ Date: 1950
Price: $65
5-piece vinyl body, painted eyes.

Cricket, Tressy's Sister
Date: 1960s
Internet: $110
Known as "Snooks" in Great Britain.

Hedda Get-Bedda
Size: 20″ Date: 1960–1961
Internet: $300
MIB with tags. 3-faced doll, 1-piece stuffed body.
Comes with thermometer.

Hedda Get-Bedda
Size: 22″ Date: 1960–1961
Internet: $60
Doll in good condition with flaws.

Little Love
Size: 17″ Date: 1950s
Internet: $80
Later version.

Mary Make-Up (Friend of Tressy)
Size: 12″ Date: 1960s
Internet: $35
Good condition, flaws.

Mary Make-Up
Size: 12″ Date: 1960s
Internet: $290
MIB with all accessories.

Ricky Jr.
Size: 21″ Date: 1954
Internet: $120
"Ricky Jr." embroidered on shirt.

Ricky Jr.
Size: 21″ Date: 1954
Internet: $220
With original box.

Sandy McCall, Betsy McCall's Brother
Size: 38″ Date: 1958
Internet: $255

Sweet Sue
Size: 19″ Date: 1950s
Price: $275
Vinyl head on rigid vinyl jointed body.

Sweet Sue Bride
Size: 20″ Date: 1950s
Internet: $395

Sweet Sue Bride
Size: 31″ Date: 1950s
Price: $250

Sweet Sue Bride, Peek-A-Boo Eyes
Size: 24″ Date: 1950s
Price: $500
Plastic and vinyl walker body.

Sweet Sue Bridesmaid, Peek-A-Boo Eyes
Size: 24″ Date: 1950s
Price: $600
Plastic and vinyl walker body.

Sweet Sue Sophisticate
Size: 20″ Date: 1957
Price: $120 –$190 Internet: $100
Lower prices are for redressed dolls.

Sweet Sue Sophisticate
Size: 25″ Date: 1957
Price: $280

Teeny Tiny Tears
Size: 12″ Date: 1963
Internet: $65

Teeny Weeny Tiny Tears
Size: 9″ Date: 1963
Internet: $175

Toni
Size: 10″ Date: 1950s
Price: $220 Internet: $130–$265
Varies greatly depending on condition.

Toni
Size: 14″ Date: 1950s
Internet: $390

Toni
Size: 24″ Date: 1958
Internet: $250
Uses Sweet Sue Sophisticate doll with minor
makeup changes.

Toodles
Size: 18″ Date: 1950s
Internet: $350
With hang tag, mint; toddler-type.

Toodles
Size: 28″ Date: 1950s
Internet: $300–$330

Toodles Baby
Size: 21″ Date: 1950s
Internet: $85

Toodles Baby With Peek–A-Boo Eyes
Size: 26″–28″   Date: 1960
Price: $110   Internet: $125
All original, hang tags.

Tressy
Size: 11″   Date: 1964–1966
          Internet: $40–$60
Hair grows. With original key. For more Tressy information and prices, see Tressy section.

Whimsie, Fanny the Fallen Angel
Size: 19″   Date: 1960
          Internet: $115
Fanny has pink hair.
Mark: Whimsie / Amer. Doll & Toy Corp./ 1960.

Whimsie, Fanny the Fallen Angel
Size: 19″   Date: 1960
          Internet: $75

Whimsie, Hilda the Hillbilly
Size: 19″   Date: 1960
          Internet: $125–$175

Whimsie, Lena the Cleaner
Size: 19″   Date: 1960
          Internet: $55

Whimsie, Samson the Strong Man
Size: 19″   Date: 1960
          Internet: $225
Leopard-skin outfit, hair on chest!

Whimsie, Simon the Degree
Size: 19″   Date: 1960
          Internet: $200
Mint, including diploma, hat, and medallion.

Whimsie, Simon the Degree
Size: 19″   Date: 1960
          Internet: $55
Average condition, no diploma or medallion.

Whimsie, Suzie the Snoozie
Size: 19″   Date: 1960
          Internet: $80

Whimsie, Tillie the Talker
Size: 19″   Date: 1960
          Internet: $300
With phone, very hard to find.

Whimsie, Zack the Sack
Size: 19″   Date: 1960
          Internet: $55
More if in mint condition.

Whimsie, Zero the Hero
Size: 19″   Date: 1960
          Internet: $80
Should have ICU pennant.

Arranbee

Arranbee produced quality composition, hard plastic, and vinyl dolls from 1922 to 1958, as well as some bisque dolls (e.g., My Dream Baby) at the very end of the bisque doll era. The quality and inventiveness of Arranbee dolls could sometimes equal that of its rival, Madame Alexander, although Arranbee would also produce look-alikes of popular dolls such as Patsy and several of the Madame Alexander dolls.

The American dollmaking scene in the 20th century was as incestuous as the German dollmaking scene of the late 19th century, and indeed, Ruby Hopf, the sister of Georgene Averill, was the main designer for Arranbee for many years, while Virgil Kirby, Georgene Averill's brother-in-law, was the plant manager.

Popular Arranbee dolls included the composition Debu'Teen and Nancy Lee, and later the hard plastic Nancy Lee and Nanette. The company was acquired by Vogue in 1958.

Market Report: Arranbee dolls were high-quality dolls with a known brand name when they were made, and collectors today still seek them out. However, prices for mint Arranbee composition and hard plastic dolls don't meet the heights that prices for mint vintage Madame Alexander dolls bring today.

Online/Offline Report: Prices are generally lower on eBay except for mint dolls, and there is a great availability of played-with examples on eBay.

Prices and Characteristics; Marks: The majority of dolls are marked "R & B" on the head or back and a few are marked "AR-RANBEE" except where noted. Prices are for dolls in excellent condition. Dolls generally have 5-piece bodies (except where noted), and all dolls have sleep eyes.

Arranbee Nancy Lees. *Hard plastic heads, 5-piece bodies. 20" and 17.5", c. early 1950s. Unmarked with original tags. Courtesy Theriault's.*

Arranbee Nancy Twins. *Composition. All original, from original owner. 12.5", c. 1946. Mark: 13 (back). $400 each, dealer (this condition).*

ARRANBEE, BISQUE

Baby, Character
Size: 16"   Date: 1920s
Price: $115
13" circumference, closed mouth, cloth body.

My Dream Baby
Size: 16"   Date: 1920s
Price: $270   Internet: $120
Lower price for doll with flaws.
Mark: AM GERMANY 341.14
See also Armand Marseille.

ARRANBEE, COMPOSITION

Child
Size: 14"
Price: $200–$250   Internet: $75–$200
5-piece composition body, original outfit.

Debu'Teen
Size: 14"   Date: 1930s–1940s
        Internet: $140–$200

Can be unmarked, with 5-piece teen composition bodies.

Debu'Teen
Size: 17"   Date: 1930s–1940s
        Internet: $225
Excellent condition.

Debu'Teen
Size: 17"   Date: 1930s–1940s
Price: $500
MIB, blue plaid jumper and beret.

Drink'N Babe, Original Case and Presentation
Size: 10"
Price: $775
Original diaper, pink bunting, label, extra clothing, bottle with disappearing milk, rattle.
Mark: Dream Baby (head) Drink 'N Babe, etc. (box lid).

Little Angel Baby
Size: 16"   Date: 1940s
Price: $225

Arranbee Littlest Angel. Hard plastic. 10.5″, c. 1950s. Mark: R & B (head and back). $125, eBay.

Composition lower limbs, cloth body, molded hair.

My Dream Baby
Size: 10″   Date: 1930s
                             Internet: $100–175
Higher price for MIB; all-composition bent-limb baby body, molded hair.

Nancy
Size: 12″   Date: 1930s
                             Internet: $250
Doll in marked trunk with outfits, VG condition.

Nancy
Size: 12″   Date: 1930s
Price: $700
MIB, with mohair wig—Nancy dolls can have molded hair or be wigged.

Nancy
Size: 16–17″   Date: 1930s
Price: $200–$315   Internet: $325–$375
For excellent to mint dolls in original outfits. Mark: Unmarked, Nancy (head), or R & B.

Nancy
Size: 19″   Date: 1930s
Price: $250 to $400
Celluloid over tin sleep eyes, human hair wig. Dolls in gowns are desirable.

Nancy Lee
Size: 12″   Date: 1940s
                             Internet: $600
Exceptional, mint example in floral gown and straw hat. Unmarked.

Nancy Lee
Size: 14″   Date: 1940s
Price: $200–$300   Internet: $100–$200
Bride, skating costume or taffeta dress, excellent condition.

Nancy Lee
Size: 17″   Date: 1940s
                             Internet: $685
Exceptional mint example with hang tags, taffeta dress, parasol.

Nancy Lee
Size: 21″   Date: 1940s
Price: $270–$400   Internet: $250–$300

Nancy Lee
Size: 27″   Date: 1940s
Price: $400
In trunk with homemade vintage outfits.

ARRANBEE, HARD PLASTIC

Beautiful Bride
Size: 21″   Date: 1950s
                             Internet: $275
Ivory satin gown with ruffled hems, veil with satin crown, flowers at wrist.

Child, Marked R & B
Size: 14″   Date: 1950s
                             Internet: $275
Walker, sleep eyes, braided blonde hair, blue and white striped dress with organdy apron.

Nancy Lee

Size: 14–15″   Date: 1952
Price: $325   Internet: $475
MIB dolls or very mint dolls. Can be unmarked.
Dolls in gowns, taffeta, skating outfits often
found.

Nancy Lee

Size: 18″   Date: 1950s
Price: $300

Nancy Lee

Size: 21″   Date: 1950s
              Internet: $650–$725
Exceptional dolls in elaborate gowns.

Nanette

Size: 14″   Date: early 1950s
              Internet: $125–$185

Nanette

Size: 14″   Date: early 1950s
Price: $500   Internet: $500
MIB, or in trunk with outfits.

Nannette

Size: 18″   Date: early 1950s
Price: $250–$300   Internet: $150–$250
For mint dolls.

Littlest Angel, Straight Leg

Size: 10.5″   Date: 1954
                Internet: $125–$150
Mint, original outfit.

Littlest Angel, Straight Leg

Size: 10.5″   Date: 1954
                Internet: $175–$250
MIB. See also Vogue section for Littlest Angels;
the rights to the doll were sold to Vogue.

Nannette Bride #7718

Size: 14″   Date: 1955
              Internet: $115

ARRANBEE, VINYL

Littlest Angel, Straight Leg

Size: 11″   Date: 1956
              Internet: $40–$100
Mint, original dress. Littlest Angels have hard
plastic bodies jointed at neck, shoulders, hips,
and knees.

Littlest Angel, Straight Leg

Size: 11″   Date: 1956
              Internet: $175–$250
MIB.

Littlest Angel, Tiny Belle Trunk

Size: 11″   Date: 1956
Price: $240
In trunk with wardrobe.

Wee Imp

Size: 10″   Date: 1960
Price: $150
Red hair and freckles, hard plastic body, knees
jointed, original sailor outfit. See also Vogue.

Averill, Georgene

The Averill Manufacturing Company was
one of the first American companies that seriously challenged the stranglehold that German firms had on the doll market. The
popularity of its mama dolls eventually
helped bring the German dollmaking industry to its demise.

Some dolls that are considered mama dolls
were produced as early as 1915. (Georgene
Averill was granted a patent for a mama doll
in 1918, and made some of the first ones.) By
1922 to 1923, the mama doll's popularity took
off, and American companies such as Averill,
Effanbee, Horsman, Ideal, and others were
producing mama dolls by the truckload.
Their popularity was due to the fact that they
were "unbreakable" (well, at least they were
far less breakable than their bisque forerunners) and seemed very lifelike in feel, especially compared to bisque dolls. Children also
loved the fact that the dolls could "talk" and
"walk." And, all the features of this doll allowed for inventive advertising by the doll
companies that produced them. The dolls
seemed very new and exciting compared to
the bisque dolls that had been on the market
for so many years.

Of course, the Averill Manufacturing Company produced much more than just the
mama dolls. They produced some of the last
popular bisque dolls, including the Bonnie
Babe, and many other composition dolls.
Their mask-faced cloth dolls are well
known and include popular characters such
as Little LuLu, Dolly Dingle, and Becassine.
And, of course, Averill is probably best-
known as one of the longtime producers of
the Raggedy Ann dolls.

Averill's Bonnie Babe. Solid domed bisque head, flanged neck, muslin body, composition limbs. Original tagged romper. 15", c. 1925. $1,900, auction. Courtesy Theriault's.

Averill Brownie. Cloth, 14". Courtesy Lorie Roller.

Nancy by Averill (comic strip character). Cloth mask face, muslin body. 14", c. 1945. Unmarked except for Georgene paper label. Courtesy Theriault's.

The Averill Manufacturing Company also did business as Madame Georgene Dolls, Georgene Novelties, and Madame Hendren.

Market Report: The mama dolls and cloth mask-face dolls of Georgene Averill and the Averill Manufacturing Company are somewhat underappreciated. In fact, I think all the Averill dolls are underappreciated and undercollected, with the exception of Raggedy Ann and Andy (which are covered in the Raggedy Ann and Andy section). These dolls—some of which are now nearly 100 years old—have the potential to appreciate in the future.

Online/Offline Report: Look for the occasional bargain on these dolls, which sometimes get lost in the shuffle of dolls with bigger "names," both online and off. Also look for dolls on eBay which are not identified as Georgene Averill dolls by their sellers (especially some of the cloth mask-face dolls). Prices for the best dolls are similar from all venues.

Prices and Characteristics: Most of the cloth mask-face dolls are unmarked except for tags. Cloth mask-face dolls have painted features and firmly stuffed cloth bodies. For Raggedy Ann and Andy dolls, see the Raggedy Ann and Andy section.

GEORGENE AVERILL, BISQUE OR CELLULOID

Bonnie Babe
Size: 15"   Date: 1925
Price: $1,900
Material: bisque
At auction.

Bonnie Babe
Size: 17"   Date: 1920s
Price: $435   Internet: $300–$500
Material: bisque
George Borgfeldt for Averill. Cloth body, composition limbs; higher value for original clothes or mint doll.
Mark: Copr. By / Georgene Averill / 1005/3652 / 4 Germany

Bonnie Babe
Size: 21–22"   Date: 1920s
                            Internet: $800–$900
Material: bisque
Cloth body, composition lower limbs, crier.
Mark: Copr. by Georgene Averill / 1005/3652/5-Germany (sometimes additional numbers).

Bonnie Babe
Size: 15"   Date: 1920
                            Internet: $450
Material: celluloid

Bonnie Babe, All-Bisque
Size: 4.5–5"   Date: 1925
Price: $750–$1,000
Material: bisque

Averill Scout and Girl. All-muslin dolls, cloth bodies. 15" and 19" (Scout), c. 1940. Unmarked. Courtesy Theriault's.

Hawaiian girl. Cloth mask face, cloth body. 13", c. 1941. Possibly Averill. Unmarked. $100, eBay. Courtesy Dana Probert.

5-piece body, painted socks and shoes, painted hair, open mouth.
Mark: 847 / 11; can be unmarked

Sunny Boy
Size: 14"   Date: 1927
Price: $300
Material: celluloid
Cloth and composition body.
Mark: turtle mark

Sunny Girl
Size: 14"   Date: 1927
Price: $300
Material: celluloid
Cloth and composition body.
Mark: turtle mark

GEORGENE AVERILL, CLOTH

Becassine
                   Date: 1953
Price: $695
Price for mint with tag.

Beloved Belindy
Size: 15"   Date: 1940s
                   Internet: $1,000
For more information, see Raggedy Ann and Andy section.

Brownie
                   Date: 1930s
Price: $450
MIB. Mask face.

Child, Girl
Size: 13"   Date: 1930s
                   Internet: $160
With wrist tag, mask face.
Mark: A Genuine Georgene Doll. / A product of / Georgene Novelties, Inc., / New York, NY. / Made in the USA (wrist tag)

Dutch Doll
Size: 11"   Date: early 1950s
                   Internet: $65
Painted face, original tag.
Mark: A Genuine Georgene Doll / A PRODUCT OF / Georgene Novelties, Inc. / NEW YORK, N.Y. / Made In U.S.A (tag)

Girl
Size: 21"   Date: 1930s
Price: $80–$100
Yellow yarn hair.

Girl Scout
Size: 13"   Date: 1930s
Price: $450
MIB, mask face.

Hawaiian
Size: 10"   Date: 1930s–1940s
Price: $120–$160
Mint. Mask face.

Hawaiian
Size: 14"   Date: 1930s–1940s
Price: $175–$250
Mint, higher price for MIB. Mask face.

Ireland
Size: 10″   Date: 1930s
Price: $160
Mint. Mask face.

Little Lulu
Size: 14″   Date: 1944–1965
                            Internet: $70–$100
For dolls with dents in face, worn. Mask face.

Little Lulu
Size: 14″   Date: 1944–1965
Price: $375   Internet: $350+
For excellent or better, with original purse (came in 3 colors). Mask face.

Martha Washington
Size: 14″   Date: 1930s
Price: $315
With hang tag. Mask face.

Nancy
Size: 14″   Date: 1940s
                            Internet: $80–$100
Worn, average condition. Mask face.

Nancy
Size: 14″   Date: 1940s
Price: $900   Internet: $400
Higher price for MIB, with tags; from cartoon strip. Mask face.

Sluggo
Size: 14″   Date: 1940s
                            Internet: $200
VG. Mask face.

Uncle Wiggly
Size: 20″   Date: 1930s
Price: $110
Price for Average dolls.

GEORGENE AVERILL, COMPOSITION

Body Twist Dimmie and Jimmie
Size: 14″   Date: 1920s
                            Internet: $300+
Ball joint at waist; for excellent or better condition.

Bonnie Babe, Trunk, Wardrobe
Size: 16″   Date: 1920s
                            Internet: $1,125
With extensive wardrobe and old trunk. Composition head.
Mark: Copr. By / Georgene Averill / 1005/3552

Dolly Reckord, Madame Hendren
Size: 26″   Date: 1920s
                            Internet: $350
For doll with flaws; phonograph in stomach, crank on right side.

Mark: Genuine Madame Hendren Doll (blue ink, back)

Girl, Jointed Waist, Molded Hair
Size: 13″   Date: 1920s
                            Internet: $150
Doll with flaws; painted eyes, muslin undies.
Mark: Stamped Madame Hendren Dolls / Patent Pending

Little Brother
Size: 14″   Date: 1927
                            Internet: $400
Shoulder head, cloth body, painted eyes.
Mark: Grace Cory

Little Cherub
Size: 13″   Date: 1937
Price: $450
Designed by M. Harriet Flanders.

Little Cherub
Size: 17″   Date: 1937
                            Internet: $300
Painted blonde hair.
Mark: Harriet Flanders 1937

Polly Peaches
Size: 17″
Price: $140
Tin sleep eyes, molded brown hair.

BAPS

There has been an upswing in interest in small metal-footed cloth dolls in the past few years, particularly the dolls of Tiny Town from California and BAPS from Germany. BAPS dolls were made in a short period of time during World War II in Germany by Baroness Edith von Arps. The production of BAPS dolls was a small cottage industry, and the dolls were frequently sold to soldiers during the war. The dolls are made on wire armature with painted metal shoes.

The dolls portray children and storybook characters, among other themes, and with their tiny hand-painted faces and sweet felt costuming, they have captured the hearts of today's collectors.

Market Report: Prices are trending up as more and more collectors become aware of this genre of dolls. Look for further price increases if a planned book on these dolls hits the market. Price increases in a genre of dolls often follow publication of a new book on that particular genre of dolls, especially

BAPS boy and girl. *Cloth face and cloth wire-armature body, metal feet. 4". Unmarked. $75, dealer.*

BAPS Puss in Boots. *Cloth face and cloth wire-armature body, metal feet. 3.5". Unmarked. $95, dealer.*

where there has been scant collector information previously.

Online/Offline Report: BAPS dolls are hard to find both online and at doll shows. Your best sources are knowledgeable dealers. Educate yourself as to what BAPS dolls look like, and you can find them improperly marked or unmarked, and also sometimes misidentified at online auctions.

Prices and Characteristics: All dolls are cloth, with wire-wrapped frames and black metal shoes. Clothing is felt, and hair tends to be heavy thread. Faces have painted features. All dolls are from the 1940s–1950s. Dolls are unmarked unless they are found with their original box.

BAPS DOLLS

Alice in Wonderland
Internet: $50
Average, no rabbit.

Alice in Wonderland and White Rabbit
Size: 7"   Internet: $330
Mint.

Boy
Size: 4"
Price: $40–$50   Internet: $40–$60

Christmas Elf
Size: 3"   Internet: $25
1950s, no metal feet.

Girl
Size: 3.5–4"
Price: $40–$50   Internet: $40–$90

Goldilocks and Three Bears
Size: 7"   Internet: $120

Hansel, Gretel, and Witch
Size: 4", 6"   Internet: $120
4" Hansel, 6" Witch, 4.5" Gretel.

Little Red Riding Hood and Wolf
Size: 6", 3.5"   Internet: $160

Mary, Mary Quite Contrary
Size: 4"   Internet: $55
With rake.

Puss in Boots
Size: 3.5"
Price: $85

Snow White and Seven Dwarfs
Price: $645
Rare set.

Barbie, Vintage (1959 through the 1970s)

See the Barbie section in the Modern Dolls chapter for Barbies from the 1980s to today.

Barbie, Barbie, Barbie! She is the queen of dolls to many, and the star of many hours of delightful play to nearly three generations of children. Barbie hit the doll scene in 1959

#1 Ponytail Barbie. *Vinyl (all Barbies in this section are vinyl). 11.5", c. 1959. Mark: See Text. Courtesy Theriault's. Note: Marks for dolls in this section appear on the lower behind except where noted.*

#3 Ponytail Barbie, blonde. *11.5", c. 1960. Mark: Barbie T. M. / Pats. Pend. / ©MCMLVIII / by / Mattel / Inc. $800, MIB, dealer.*

when she was created by Ruth Handler, who loosely based her on the Bild Lilli doll from Germany. Bild Lilli was a doll based on a comic strip and created for adults in Germany, with an overexaggerated woman's body.

Barbie Takes the Doll World By Storm: Barbie may have had an adult body, but she was a doll clearly made for children. With her amazing wardrobe, elegant accessories, and entire world, Barbie enveloped the children of the 1960s in a world of fantasy and possibilities. Barbie's fashion doll predecessors, Cissy, Miss Revlon, and the other ladies of the 1950s, only hinted at what Barbie would be. The earlier 1950s dolls had wardrobes and high fashion, but what they didn't have were the brilliant commercials aimed at children during children's television programs. They also didn't have Bar-

bie's perfect handheld, miniaturized size, and her attractive price. The combination of television commercials, a perfect-size world, and price helped Barbie take the doll world by storm, and it has never been the same.

Early Vintage Barbie: The earliest "ponytail" Barbies came in six versions—please see below for identification help. These were the only dolls issued until 1961, when the Bubble Cut Barbie was introduced. Bubble Cut Barbies were made from 1962 to 1967. There were several other types of vintage Barbies in the early and mid-1960s, including the Fashion Queen Barbie with molded hair and wigs, the Swirl Ponytail Barbie (no bangs, hair pulled-to-side from front ponytail) and the Miss Barbie with sleep eyes.

900 Series Clothing: The earliest vintage Barbie clothing through the 1960s was

#4 Ponytail Barbie, brunette, wearing Career Girl #954. *11.5", c. 1963. Doll, $300–$375, eBay; outfit, $50 mint, complete, eBay,*

#4 Ponytail Barbie, blonde, wearing Suburban Shopper. *Doll $250–$300 this condition, eBay, outfit, $200 if mint and complete.*

Bubble Cut Barbie. *11.5", c. 1961. Mark: Barbie ®. / Pats. Pend / ©MCMLVIII / by / Mattel / Inc. $100, dealer.*

numbered in series—the 900 series is the classic early outfit series designed in the era of the Ponytail and Bubble Cut Barbie dolls. The clothing was all made in Japan, and featured fine fabrics, tiny buttons, and wonderful, detailed accessories. The 900 series of clothing had Barbie ready for nearly every type of outing or career—skating, picnicking and fishing, nursing, evenings out, even barbecuing and winter holidays. There was also an 800 series of clothing which focused on international and drama outfits. Today, many vintage Barbie collectors focus as much on collecting the complete clothing outfits as on collecting the early Barbie dolls.

American Girl and 1600 Series Clothing:

In 1965, the ultra-sophisticated American Girl Barbie debuted. She had a short pageboy haircut and was tailor-made to wear Jackie Kennedy-style mid-1960s clothing—luncheon suits, glamorous formals, outfits for cruising, and tea. Some collectors consider the mid-1960s clothing (the 1600 series of outfits) to be the ultimate in Barbie glamour and design. Because of this, and because these outfits were generally issued in smaller numbers than the 900 series outfits, these outfits NRFB and mint and complete tend to be more expensive than all but the rarest 900 outfits. The American Girl Bar-

bie was made for only two years, from 1965 to 1966.

Mod Barbie Hits the Scene:

With the social revolution that hit in the mid-1960s, Barbie started to look outdated. To address this, Barbie got a new mod look and little girls were allowed to trade in their older Barbies for a new, hip "Twist 'N Turn" Barbie. This doll marked the beginning of a whole new era for Barbie in 1966. Barbie got a twist waist, real eyelashes, and long, more youthfully styled hair. Along with Twist 'N Turn Barbie came a whole host of new friends and characters. Early Barbie had Midge, her best friend, Skipper, her little sister, and Ken. Now Barbie had Francie, Stacey, Casey, and a host of other "groovy" friends and relations. This was also the era that Barbie continually started to reinvent herself with little tricks and gimmicks. Talking Barbie, Color Magic Barbie, Dramatic Living Barbie, Barbie With Growing Pretty Hair, Hair Fair Barbie, and others were released in the mod era.

Mod-Era Clothing:

In the later 1960s, the clothing also changes style to go along with Barbie's new mod look. Gone were the glamorous formal gowns and designer suits. In came flowered rainwear, minidresses, sil-

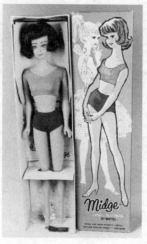

Straight-Leg Midge (Barbie's friend). *11.5", c. 1963. Mark: Midge T.M. / © 1962 / Barbie ® / © 1958 / by / Mattel, Inc. ("Midge/Barbie Mark")*

Bubble Cut Barbie, White Ginger. *11.5", c. 1961. Mark: Barbie ®. / Pats. Pend / ©MCMLVIII / by / Mattel / Inc. $500 MIB, dealer.*

ver lamé, bell-bottom pants, and psychedelic pantsuits. The clothing was still very detailed and well-made in the mod era. Mod era clothing included the 1400, 1700, 1800, and 3400 series of clothing.

End of an Era: Most collectors consider the vintage Barbie era to have ended in 1972. At this point, Mattel hit financial trouble and began to cut corners in the production of the dolls and clothing. Quality went down considerably, detail was gone, and the vintage Barbie era ended. Many collectors believe that Mattel didn't produce Barbies of any quality again until the 1990s, but the quality 1990s dolls were produced for collectors and not children.

How to Identify Ponytail Barbies: There are 6 versions of the earliest ponytail Barbie dolls. There is a great difference in value among these dolls, with the #1 and #2 ponytail Barbies often worth several thousand dollars, but with the #5 and #6 ponytail Barbies worth only $200 to $400, even if in mint condition.

Here is how to tell which Ponytail Barbie you have:

Examine your ponytail Barbie. Note her facial features, skin color, feet, the feel of her torso and hair, and the markings on her behind (a.k.a. "butt markings").

#1 Ponytail Barbie: Does your doll have white irises, severely arched eyebrows, and holes in her feet/copper tubing in legs? Is the original swimsuit black-and-white zebra? Is her skin faded white? Does her torso feel solid? If all this is true, and if your doll's markings are Barbie™ / Pats.Pend. / ©MCMLVIII / by Mattel / Inc, then you

Straight-Leg Skipper. *9″, c. 1965. Mark: Skipper / © 1963 / Mattel, Inc. $145, eBay.*

Painted-hair Ken, dressed doll in Switzerland #0776. *In original dressed-doll box. 12″, c. 1964. Mark: Ken T.M. / Pats. Pend / © MCCCCCCMLX / by / Mattel / Inc. $500, dealer.*

Fashion Queen Barbie. *Doll has molded hair, came with 3 wigs on a wig stand. Wearing original swimsuit and turban. Midge/Barbie Mark. $260 with original swimsuit, turban, wigs, stand, eBay.*

have a #1 ponytail Barbie. This doll can be worth several thousand dollars.

#2 Ponytail Barbie: If your Barbie meets all of the criteria for a #1 ponytail Barbie except that she does not have holes in her feet/copper tubing, then you have a #2 ponytail Barbie doll, which also can be worth several thousand dollars.

#3 Ponytail Barbie: If your Barbie meets all of the criteria for a #2 Barbie (skin faded white, solid torso, black-and-white bathing suit, markings, etc.) except that the doll has blue irises (not white) and the eyebrows are curved (not arched), then you have a #3 ponytail Barbie doll. Number 3s can have blue or brown eyeliner and they sometimes smell like Crayola crayons. This doll is worth several hundred dollars.

#4 Ponytail Barbie: If your Barbie meets the criteria for a #3 Barbie except that her skin tone is tan and not pale white, then you have a #4 ponytail Barbie. Number 4s and above only have blue eyeliner, never brown. See below for values.

#5 Ponytail Barbie: If your Barbie meets the criteria for a #4 Barbie except that the body is hollow (not solid) and the doll is marked

Barbie® and not Barbie™, then you have a #5 ponytail Barbie. Number 5s were also the first to come as a redhead, so if you have a redhead, it's a #5 or #6.

#6 Ponytail Barbie: Finally, if your Barbie meets all of the criteria for a #5 but it wears an original red jersey swimsuit and it has a slightly chubbier face, you most likely have a #6 ponytail Barbie and not a #5. Some experts do not differentiate between a #5 or a #6, and there is little difference in value. You know for sure you have a #6 ponytail if the markings read "Midge™ / © 1962 / Barbie® / © 1958/by/Mattel, Inc" (only #6s produced in 1963 and 1964 had this marking). By the way, this "Midge/Barbie" mark confuses many new collectors who think they have a Midge doll when the doll has this mark, a mark which graces the behind of millions of 1960s Barbie dolls.

Mattel Reproduction Ponytail Barbies: If you are a new collector, and you could find no markings on the doll's behind, but the doll looks like an early ponytail Barbie, you may be looking at a 1990s-or-later reproduction Barbie. These dolls are not marked on their behinds; they are marked on their backs, and the markings say: Barbie / ©1958, 1993 / Mattel, Inc. / Malaysia.

Swirl Ponytail Barbie, Lemon Blonde. 11.5", c. 1964. Midge/Barbie Mark. $785 MIB, eBay.

Barbie/Scooter Case. Vinyl. c. 1965. $10, eBay

Midge Case. Vinyl. c. 1963. $10, eBay.

Market Report: Vintage Barbies were sold by the millions, and so were her outfits. Because of this, vintage Barbie has suffered a price decline due to the easy, open market of eBay—anyone could go into his or her attic, find an old Barbie trunk, and sell directly to the collectors. That said, there are signs of a renaissance in the Barbie market, and truly mint and NRFB dolls and outfits are still hard to find and command premium prices. Look for mint dolls with their original hairstyles and originally painted features. As more and more collectors touch up the paint on their dolls or redo the hairdos, these all-original dolls become harder to find. Also look for rarer outfits, NRFB outfits, and un-played-with mint outfits from the early and mod series. Try to stay away from "greasy"-faced dolls which leak plasticizer, giving the dolls a greasy look. There is no way to permanently fix the greasy appearance, and over time it ruins the doll's painted features.

Online/Offline Report: For a truly mint doll or a mint, complete desirable outfit, prices can be higher on eBay than from a dealer or show, because of instant, worldwide collector competition. For common outfits, especially bits and pieces of those outfits, bargains can be found on eBay but expect the condition to often be played with and not collection-worthy. People selling out

of attics do not understand vintage Barbie collector sensitivity to small differences in the condition of outfits, and defects are generally not sufficiently described.

Prices and Characteristics: All Barbie dolls are 11.5 inches tall. All dolls are vinyl, with rooted hair, except as noted. All marks are on the upper right-hand buttock of the doll, and only those marks are given, as those are the marks that are followed by vintage Barbie collectors, not the head marks. Prices are for dolls in excellent condition, except as stated.

PONYTAIL BARBIE DOLLS

Pedestal Stand for #1 Barbie:
                              Date: 1959
Price: $1,000 –$1,300
#1 stand (2 metal prongs) is so valuable, it is often sold separately.

Ponytail, #1
                              Date: 1959
Price: $3,000 –$4,000
For dolls with flaws, sometimes with flawed box.
Mark: Barbie™ / Pats.Pend. / ©MCMLVIII / by / Mattel / Inc.

Ponytail, #1
                              Date: 1959
Price: $7,000 –$8,000
Near mint with box.

Allan (Ken's friend). *12", c. 1964. Mark: ©1960 / by /Mattel, Inc. / Hawthorne / Calif. U.S.A. $110 MIB with tag, eBay.*

Color Magic Barbie, Ruby Red. *In plastic closet box (also comes cello-cardboard wrapped). 11.5", c. 1966. Mark: ©1958 / MATTEL, INC. / U.S. PATENTED / U.S. PAT PEND / MADE IN JAPAN. $1,100 MIB, auction.*

Ponytail, #1, Blonde

Date: 1959
Price: $25,500
Pristine, mint, a record price for a vintage Barbie doll at auction.

Ponytail, #1, Brunette

Date: 1959
Internet: $12,000
For mint doll in mint box ("MIB").

Ponytail, #2

Date: 1959
Price: $2,500
With serious flaws.
Mark: Barbie™ / Pats.Pend. / ©MCMLVIII / by / Mattel / Inc.

Ponytail, #2

Date: 1959
Price: $3,200
Very good ("VG") or excellent condition.

Ponytail, #2

Date: 1959
Price: $6,550
MIB.

Ponytail, #3, Blonde

Date: 1960
Price: $500
With flaws.
Mark: Barbie™ / Pats.Pend. / ©MCMLVIII / by / Mattel / Inc.

Ponytail, #3, Blonde

Date: 1960
Price: $625   Internet: $700
Excellent, in box.

Ponytail, #3, Blonde

Date: 1960
Price: $500– $650
Mint, no box.

American Girl Barbie, Pale Blonde. *Bendable legs. 11.5″, c. 1966. Mark: ©1958 / MATTEL, INC. / U.S. PATENTED / U.S. PAT PEND / MADE IN JAPAN. $700 MIB, eBay.*

American Girl Barbie in Formal Occasion #1697. *Bendable legs. 11.5″, 1965 doll, 1967 outfit. Mark: (indented): ©1958 / MATTEL, INC. / U.S. PATENTED / U.S. PAT PEND. Doll, $300+ mint, eBay. Outfit: $175, eBay (with white pumps).*

American Girl Barbie in Reception line #1654. *Bendable legs. 11.5″,c. 1966 (doll); outfit, 1966–1967. $400 doll, outfit $250 mint, complete, dealer.*

Ponytail, #3, Blonde

Date: 1960
Price: $1,050   Internet: $1,500
For pristine, MIB.

Ponytail, #3, Brunette

Date: 1960
Price: $600–$650
Excellent, no box.

Ponytail, #3, Brunette

Date: 1960
Price: $800   Internet: $750
MIB.

Ponytail, #3, Brunette

Date: 1960
Price: $1,575
Pristine, mint doll.

Ponytail, #4, Blonde or Brunette

Date: 1960
Price: $275–$350   Internet: $200–$300
VG.
Mark: Barbie™ / Pats.Pend. / ©MCMLVIII / by / Mattel / Inc.

Ponytail, #4

Date: 1960
Price: $300–$350
VG, in box.

Ponytail, #4

Date: 1960
Price: $495   Internet: $320
Minor flaws, in box.

Ponytail, #4

Date: 1960
Price: $500   Internet: $640
MIB.

Ponytail, #5, Blonde or Brunette, Greasy

Date: 1961
Price: $160–$200   Internet: $150–$175
VG; for greasy face dolls, all hair colors, with flaws.
Mark: Barbie® / Pats.Pend. / ©MCMLVIII / by / Mattel / Inc.

Ponytail, #5, Blonde

Date: 1961
Price: $270   Internet: $325–$355
MIB.

Ponytail, #5, Brunette

Date: 1961
Price: $200+   Internet: $200+
Excellent condition.

Ponytail, #5, Brunette

Date: 1961
Price: $350   Internet: $315
MIB.

Ponytail, #5, Titian

Price: $200–$300   Date: 1961
VG; sometimes with greasy face.

Bendable-Leg Midge. *Original swimsuit. 11.5″, c. 1965. Mark: ©1958 / MATTEL, INC. / U.S. PATENTED / U.S. PAT PEND / MADE IN / JAPAN. $265, auction.*

Twist 'N Turn Barbie, Flip "Marlo Thomas" hairstyle. *Waist twists, legs bend. 11.5″, c. 1969. Mark: © 1966 / Mattel Inc / U.S. Patented / U.S. Pat. Pend / Made in / Japan. $350, auction.*

Twist 'N Turn Stacey, blonde. *Waist twists, legs bend. 11.5″, c. 1969. Mark: ©1966 / Mattel Inc. / U.S. Patented / U.S. Pat Pend / Made in Japan. $450, auction.*

Ponytail, #5, Titian
Date: 1961
Price: $400   Internet: $400
MIB.

Ponytail, #6, Ash Blonde
Date: 1962–1965
Price: $230   Internet: $175
Excellent condition.
Mark: Midge ™ / © 1962 / Barbie ®/ © 1958 / by / Mattel, Inc.

Ponytail, #6, Brunette
Date: 1962–1965
Price: $200   Internet: $245
Excellent condition.

Ponytail, #6, Titian
Date: 1962–1965
Price: $220   Internet: $240
VG.

Ponytail, #6, Titian
Date: 1962—1965
Price: $350   Internet: $400
MIB.

Ponytail, Swirl, Blonde
Date: 1964
Price: $225
VG, flaws.
Mark: Midge ™ / © 1962 / Barbie ®/ © 1958 / by / Mattel, Inc.

Ponytail, Swirl, Blonde
Date: 1964
Price: $350–$380
Near mint.

Ponytail, Swirl, Blonde
Date: 1964
Price: $480–$600
MIB.

Ponytail, Swirl, Brunette
Date: 1964
Price: $300
Excellent, no box.

Ponytail, Swirl, Brunette
Date: 1964
Price: $400–$500
Excellent, in box.

Ponytail, Swirl, Brunette
Date: 1964
Price: $600
In the rarer gold and white Fashion Queen swimsuit, MIB.

Ponytail, Swirl, Carnation Promo, Ash Blonde
Date: 1964
Internet: $2,125
With original shipper, pristine mint.

Ponytail, Swirl, Platinum
Date: 1964
Internet: $250–$300
For dolls with flaws, ear or face discoloration.

Ponytail, Swirl, Platinum
Date: 1964
Price: $500+   Internet: $400+
VG or better in box or mint, no box. White lips.

Twist 'N Turn Casey, wearing It's a Date #1251. *11.5", c. 1967. Mark: ©1966 / Mattel Inc. / U.S. Patented / U.S. Pat Pend / Made in Japan. $100 doll, $65–$70 complete mint outfit, eBay.*

Talking Barbie. *Pull string at back of neck, doll talks. Most mechanisms have broken with time. 11.5", c. 1970. $300 NRFB, auction.*

Ponytail, Swirl, Platinum
Date: 1964
Internet: $1,175
NRFB and pristine mint.

Ponytail, Swirl, Platinum
Date: 1964
Internet: $1,400
Exceptionally MIB, white lips, tag.

Ponytail, Swirl, Redhead
Date: 1964
Internet: $400
MIB.

Ponytail, Swirl, Wheat Blonde
Date: 1964
Price: $265
VG.

Ponytail, Barbie, Montgomery Ward
Date: 1972
Price: $200–$225

VG; reproduction of earlier 1960s ponytail Barbie. Painted features and hair texture is different than earlier ponytails.
Mark: Midge ™ / © 1962 / Barbie ®/ © 1958 / by / Mattel, Inc.

Bubble Cut Barbies

Bubble Cut Barbies were produced from 1961 to 1966.

BUBBLE CUT BARBIE DOLLS

Bubble Cut
Price: $100–$175   Internet: $75–$120
For VG dolls; blonde, ash blonde, titian, brunette, with flaws.
Mark: 1961 Bubble Cuts have this mark: Barbie® / Pats.Pend. / ©MCMLVIII / by / Mattel / Inc.

Bubble Cut
Price: $200   Internet: $150+
Excellent for blonde, ash blonde, titian, brunette.

Talking Barbie, Sun-kissed blonde. 11.5", c. 1968. $425 NRFB, auction.

Twist 'N Turn Christie. 11.5", c. 1969. $300 NRFB, auction.

Talking Julia. 11.5", c. 1969–1970. Mark: ©1967 / Mattel, Inc. / U.S. & Foreign / Pats Pend / Mexico. $225, dealer.

Prices slightly higher for 1961 Bubble Cuts.
Mark: 1960s and later Bubble Cuts have this mark: Midge ™ / © 1962 / Barbie ®/ © 1958 / by / Mattel, Inc.

Bubble Cut

Price: $255–$500   Internet: $225–$350
MIB. For blonde, ash blonde, titian, brunette. Higher prices for pristine mint dolls.

Bubble Cut, Black Hair

Internet: $250
For VG doll, in darker, desirable raven hair color.

Bubble Cut, Brownette

Price: $3,200
Rarest Bubble Cut hair color; true brown.

Bubble Cut, Brunette, Fashion Queen Swimsuit

Price: $2,625
Pristine MIB or NRFB, in its original rarer swimsuit.

Bubble Cut, Dressed Doll, in Guinevere

Price: $250
With flaws; without flaws, $500.

Bubble Cut, Green Ear

Internet: $70 and under
With green ear caused by original metal post earrings.

Bubble Cut, Platinum

Price: $300–$400
Also known as White Ginger, very pale lips. MIB.

American Girl Barbie Dolls

American Girl dolls all have bendable legs and are from 1965 to 1966, with prices generally higher for 1966 dolls.

AMERICAN GIRL BARBIE DOLLS

American Girl

Price: $270–$400   Internet: $250–$400
Mint. Original striped turquoise swimsuit and turquoise open-toed shoes.
Mark: 1965 dolls: (indented)
© 1958 / Mattel, Inc. / U.S. Patented / U.S. Pat. Pend.

American Girl

Price: $600–$900   Internet: $500–$800+
MIB. For hair colors blonde, ash blonde, brunette, pale blonde, and titian.

American Girl, Long Hair, 1966

Price: $1,100–$1,300   Internet: $950
American Girls with very long hair near shoulder have higher values. 1966.
Mark: 1966 dolls: (indented) © 1958 / Mattel, Inc. / U.S. Patented / U.S. Pat. Pend. / (raised letters) Made in / Japan (later dolls, all raised letters)

American Girl, Long Hair, High Color

Price: $1,500
MIB. High color makeup, 1966.

American Girl, Platinum

Price: $600–$750
Near mint.

Francie with Growin' Pretty Hair.
10.5", c. 1970. Mark: ©1966 /
Mattel, Inc. / U.S. Pat & other /
Pats Pend. / Pat. Canada / 1967 /
Japan. $70, eBay.

Dream Date Ken. 12", c. 1982.
$40 NRFB, eBay.

American Girl, Side Part
Price: $1,200–$2,500   Internet: $3,400–$3,500
MIB. With wrist tag and correctly marked box,
1966.

Twist 'N Turn Barbie Dolls

Mark for most Twist 'N Turn ("TNT")
dolls: © 1966 / Mattel Inc. / US Patented /
U.S. Pat Pend / Made in / Japan. All TNT
dolls have bendable legs, twist waist, and
"real" eyelashes. Twist 'N Turn dolls were
made from 1966 to 1971.

TWIST 'N TURN BARBIE DOLLS

TNT Barbie
Price: $125–$200   Internet: $125+
VG. Dolls have orange ribbon tie in long hair,
and 2-piece orange swimsuit with mesh cover-
up.

TNT Barbie
                         Internet: $600–$700
NRFB, brunette.

TNT Barbie
                         Internet: $900
NRFB. High color, cello still on, mint.

TNT Barbie, Brunette
Price: $200–$285
Excellent.

TNT Barbie, Platinum
Price: $200   Internet: $150
Excellent.

TNT Barbie, Platinum
Price: $480
NMIB.

TNT Barbie, Titian
Price: $500   Internet: $335
Titian, excellent to near mint.

TNT Barbie, Trade-In
Price: $325
In original box, with flaws.

TNT Barbie, Flip
Price: $145–$200   Internet: $100–$175
Excellent condition, brunette or blonde.

TNT Barbie, Flip
Price: $300–$350   Internet: $400–$600
NRFB. Marlo Thomas flip hair, brunette or
blonde.

TNT Barbie, Flip, Brownette, Centered Eyes
Price: $350
Near mint, centered eyes, brownette.

OTHER VINTAGE BARBIE DOLLS AND GIFT SETS

Ballerina
                         Date: 1975
                         Internet: $60
NRFB.

Barbie, Supersize
                         Date: 1976
                         Internet: $70
NRFB.

Barbie, Sweet 16
Date: 1973
Internet: $105
NRFB.

Bild Lilli
Date: 1955
Price: $550+
Near mint. Precursor to Mattel's Barbie. Produced by Greiner and Hauser GmbH. $1,000+ mint in original tube.

Busy Barbie
Date: 1971
Internet: $120
Excellent.

Busy Talking Barbie
Date: 1971
Internet: $175
NRFB.

Color Magic
Date: 1966
Price: $400
VG, with flaws.

Color Magic
Date: 1966
Price: $550
Near mint.

Color Magic
Date: 1966
Price: $1,600
MIB, in plastic closet with accessories. Hair changed color.
Mark: 1966 doll: (indented) © 1958 / Mattel, Inc. / U.S. Patented / U.S. Pat. Pend. / (raised letters) Made in / Japan

Color Magic, Platinum
Date: 1966
Internet: $975
Rarer hair color, mint.

Deluxe Quick Curl Barbie
Date: mid-1970s
Internet: $80
NRFB, box worn.

Dramatic New Living Barbie
Date: 1969
Internet: $300
NRFB, all joints work, crispy mint.
Mark: © 1968 Mattel, Inc. / U.S. & For. Pat'd / Other Pats. Pend / Taiwan.

Fashion Photo Barbie
Date: 1977
Internet: $50
NRFB.

Fashion Queen
Date: 1963–1964
Price: $65
Internet: $50+
Average doll, 1 wig.

Fashion Queen
Date: 1963–1964
Price: $190–$210
Internet: $140–$170
Excellent, with 3 wigs, stand, gold and white swimsuit and turban.

Fashion Queen
Date: 1963–1964
Price: $650
Internet: $700–$750
NRFB.

Fashion Queen Gift Set
Date: 1964
Internet: $1,575
MIB.

Free-Moving Barbie
Date: 1974
Internet: $55
NRFB.

Gift Set, Barbie and Ken
Price: $575
VG in box; flaws.

Gift Set, Barbie Trousseau
Date: 1960
Internet: $2,900
NRFB.

Gift Set, On Parade, Ken and Midge
Date: 1964
Price: $920

Gift Set, Wedding Party
Date: 1964
Price: $2,600
NRFB.

Growin' Pretty Hair, Barbie
Date: 1971
Internet: $75
Excellent.

Hair Happenin's Barbie
Date: 1971
Internet: $225
Excellent.

Kissing Barbie
Date: 1978
Internet: $50–$60
NRFB.

Live Action Barbie
Date: 1970
Internet: $60
Mint.

Living Barbie, Redhead or Brunette

Date: 1970
Price: $75–$80   Internet: $75–$120
VG.

Living Barbie Action Accents Gift Set

Date: 1970
Internet: $900
Pristine mint rare gift set; Sears Exclusive. Titian Dramatic Living Barbie, 15 pieces of clothing, accessories for skiing, skating, scuba diving, and dance.

Malibu Barbie

Date: 1971
Internet: $25–$45
Excellent to mint.

Malibu Barbie

Date: 1971
Internet: $60–$75
MOC, average.

Malibu Barbie

Date: 1971
Internet: $155
MOC, very mint; light blue swimsuit.

Miss Barbie

Date: 1964
Internet: $100–$140
Excellent.

Miss Barbie, Swing and Planter

Date: 1964
Price: $275   Internet: $600
Internet price for very mint NRFB doll; lower price for mint doll in flawed box.

Newport Barbie

Date: 1973
Internet: $30
Excellent.

Pink 'N Pretty Barbie

Date: 1974
Internet: $75
NRFB.

Quick Curl Barbie

Date: 1960s
Price: $75–$95   Internet: $30–$50
VG; common nose fading.

Standard Barbie

Date: 1969
Price: $180–$245
Excellent.

Standard Barbie

Date: 1966
Price: $425   Internet: $600–$900
MIB. $900 for center-eyed doll, $600 for 2-piece rose swimsuit boxed doll (rarer), $425 for standard doll, some flaws.
Mark: Midge ™ / © 1962 / Barbie ®/ © 1958 / by / Mattel, Inc.

Switzerland Barbie, Dressed Doll

Date: 1964
Internet: $900
Pristine mint, possibly NRFB.

Talking Barbie

Date: 1967
Price: $300   Internet: $250–$350
MIB. Many swimsuits and 2 hairstyle variations.
Mark: ©1967 / Mattel, Inc. / U.S. & Foreign / Pats. Pend / Mexico

Talking Barbie, Brunette

Date: 1967
Price: $120–$180   Internet: $100–$170
Most dolls mute with age and have had their hips "freeze" over time; many have broken legs. For excellent, mute doll.

Twirly Curls Barbie

Date: 1982
Internet: $30
NRFB.

Walk Lively Barbie

Date: 1972
Internet: $100
Excellent.
Mark: 1967 Mattel Inc, U.S. Pat. Pend. Taiwan

Western Barbie

Date: 1980
Internet: $75
NRFB.

Ken

Ken, Barbie's boyfriend, is 12 inches tall. The first, flocked Ken is marked (on the behind): Ken™ / Pats. Pend. / ©MCMLX / By / Mattel / Inc.

KEN

Ken, Flocked

Date: 1961
Price: $70   Internet: $70
For excellent dolls. First Ken ever issued. Available in blonde or brunette. Flocked hair normally flaked off.

Ken, Flocked
Date: 1961
Price: $100–$120   Internet: $125
Mint, with all flocking, mint face paint, original outfit or MIB. With red swim trunks, cork sandals, towel.

Ken, Flocked
Date: 1961
Price: $70   Internet: $70
For excellent dolls.

Ken, Painted Hair, Straight Leg
Date: 1961
Price: $50–$65   Internet: $40–$50
Excellent.

Ken, Painted Hair, Straight Leg
Date: 1961
Price: $100–$140   Internet: $175
No hair rubs, with original outfit and accessories.

Ken, Painted Hair, Straight Leg
Date: 1963
Price: $40   Internet: $20–$30
VG; hair rubs.

Ken, Bendable Leg
Date: 1965
Internet: $125
Mint doll with tag.

Ken, Bendable Leg
Date: 1965
Price: $125–$280   Internet: $155
MIB. Lower prices with minor flaws, higher price for mint.

Ken, Talking
Date: 1969
Internet: $100
NRFB.

Ken, Live Action
Date: 1970
Price: $20   Internet: $25
Excellent.

Ken, Busy Talking
Date: 1971
Internet: $75
NRFB.

Ken, Mod Hair
Date: 1972
Price: $15   Internet: $5–$15
Flaws, not original clothing.

Ken, Mod Hair
Date: 1972
Price: $30   Internet: $30–$50
Near mint.

Ken, Mod Hair
Date: 1972
Internet: $65
NRFB.

Midge

Midge, Barbie's best friend, is 11.5 inches tall.

MIDGE

Midge, Straight Leg ("SL")
Date: 1963– 1966
Price: $55–$90   Internet: $50–$75
Slightly more for brunette dolls. Original swimsuit is 2-piece.
Mark: Midge ™ / © 1962 / Barbie ®/ © 1958 / by / Mattel, Inc. / Patented (later dolls have Patented added)

Midge, SL
Date: 1963–1966
Price: $135–$220   Internet: $150–$200
MIB, higher prices for brunette dolls, dolls with tag and liner. Also comes in blonde and titian.

Midge, Bendable Leg ("BL")
Date: 1964
Price: $230–$265   Internet: $150+
Excellent.

Midge, BL
Date: 1964
Price: $550
MIB.
Mark: (indented) © 1958 / Mattel, Inc. / U.S. Patented / U.S. Pat. Pend./ (raised letters) Made in / Japan (later dolls, all raised letters)

Midge, Japanese Market, Molded Hair
Price: $850
VG.

Midge, Wig Wardrobe, Molded Hair
Date: 1964
Internet: $50
For excellent, head only; molded heads were sold in package with wigs.

Skipper and Friends

Skipper, Barbie's sister, and her friends are 9 inches tall.

SKIPPER AND FRIENDS

Skipper, SL

Date: 1964–1966
Price: $40–$105   Internet: $25–$50
Excellent; lower prices for nude dolls, flaws.
Mark: Skipper / © 1963 / Mattel, Inc. (later dolls,
no Skipper name)

Skipper, SL

Date: 1964–1966
Price: $150–$250   Internet: $170–250
MIB; higher prices with tag and liner, dolls with
lighter skin tones.

Skipper, BL

Date: 1960s
Price: $125   Internet: $150
MIB.
Mark: © 1963 / Mattel, Inc.

Skipper, Dramatic Living

Date: 1969
Internet: $60–$90
MIB.
Mark: © 1969 / Mattel, Inc / Taiwan / U.S. & for.
Pat / other Pats. Pend / Pat. in Canada 1967

Skipper, TNT, Sausage Curls

Date: 1969
Price: $135   Internet: $50–$75
Near mint.

Skipper, TNT, Sausage Curls

Date: 1969
Internet: $300
NRFB, Java brown hair/marked box.

Skipper, Living

Date: 1970
Internet: $25–$40
Excellent.

Skipper, Living

Date: 1970
Internet: $60–$70
MIB.

Skipper, Reissue

Date: 1970
Internet: $80–$120
Excellent.

Skipper, Malibu

Date: 1971
Price: $60   Internet: $60–$80
MOC / MIB, most varieties.

Skipper, Quick Curl

Date: 1972
Price: $20   Internet: $10–$20
Excellent.

Skipper, Quick Curl

Date: 1972
Price: $75–$100   Internet: $135
MOC.

Ricky

Date: 1965
Internet: $25–$50
Excellent.

Ricky

Date: 1965
Internet: $75–$135
MIB; higher prices with tag and liner.
Mark: © 1963 / Mattel, Inc.

Skooter

Date: 1965
Price: $145   Internet: $160–$180
MIB.
Mark: © 1963 / Mattel, Inc.

Skooter, BL

Date: 1966
Internet: $225
MIB.
Mark: © 1963 / Mattel, Inc.

Living Fluff

Date: 1970
Internet: $150
NRFB; box flaws.

Francie

Francie, Barbie's cousin, is 11 inches tall.

FRANCIE

Francie, SL

Date: 1965
Price: $110   Internet: $50–$90
VG.

Francie, SL

Date: 1965
Price: $175   Internet: $260
MIB, original 2-piece polka-dot swimsuit.
Mark: same as above listing

Francie, BL

Date: 1965
Price: $95–$140   Internet: $275
VG to excellent; Internet price for mint doll.
Mark: © 1965 / Mattel, Inc. / U.S. Patented /
U.S. Pat. Pend / Made in / Japan

Francie, Black

Date: 1965
Internet: $765–$900

Excellent dolls, hair generally oxidized to red.
Mark: same as above listing

Francie, Black
Date: 1965
Price: $1,900   Internet: $1,300
NRFB.

Francie, TNT
Date: 1965
Price: $300–$500   Internet: $300–$400
NRFB, for first TNT doll in pink and white
striped swimsuit.
Mark: © 1966 / Mattel, Inc. / U.S. Patented /
U.S. Pat. Pend / Made in / Japan

Francie, TNT
Date: 1969–1970
Price: $500+   Internet: $700–$800
NRFB. Later, harder to find swimsuits, dolls.

Francie, TNT, Flip
Date: 1969
Price: $100   Internet: $80
VG; often with face fading.

Francie, TNT, Short Flip
Date: 1969
Price: $150   Internet: $310
Mint.

Francie, No Bangs
Date: 1969
Price: $1,200   Internet: $1,600
NRFB.

Francie, Growin' Pretty Hair
Date: 1970
Internet: $35–$65
Excellent.
Mark: © 1969 / Mattel, Inc / U.S. Pat. other /
Pats. Pend / Pat. Canada / 1967 / Japan

Francie, Growin' Pretty Hair
Date: 1970
Price: $175   Internet: $200–$350
NRFB, with some flaws.

Francie, Hair Happenin's
Date: 1970
Internet: $150–$230
Mint, higher price with mint wigs.
Mark: © 1966 / Mattel, Inc. / U.S. Patented /
U.S. Pat. Pend / Made in / Japan

Francie, Rise & Shine Gift Set
Price: $1,450
NRFB.

OTHER FRIENDS AND FAMILY OF BARBIE

Allan, SL
Date: 1964
Price: $30   Internet: $30–$40
Excellent or better. Midge's boyfriend, 12".
Mark: © 1960 / by / Mattel, Inc. / Hawthorne /
Calif U.S.A.

Allan, SL
Date: 1964
Price: $85–$100   Internet: $75–$100
For MIB.

Allan, BL
Date: 1965
Price: $145
Mint, with accessories.

Allan, BL
Date: 1965
Price: $325–$450
For MIB.
Mark: © 1960 / by / Mattel, Inc. / Hawthorne /
Calif U.S.A.

Brad, Talking or BL
Date: 1969
Internet: $30–$60
Excellent. Black doll, Christie's boyfriend, 12".
Mark: © 1968 Mattel, Inc. / U.S. & For. Patd /
Other Pats / Pending / Hong Kong

Brad, BL
Date: 1969
Internet: $140
NRFB.
Mark: © 1968 Mattel, Inc. / U.S. & For. Patd /
Other Pats / Pending / Hong Kong

Buffy and Mrs. Beasley
Date: 1967
Internet: $40–$65
Excellent, includes hard to find Granny glasses;
3.75" size.

Buffy and Mrs. Beasley
Date: 1967
Internet: $130–$150
NRFB, with tag, cello. Mrs. Beasley is 3.75", the
same size as Tutti.
Mark: ©1965 / Mattel, Inc. / Japan / 26 on Buffy,
no marks on Mrs. Beasley.

Casey
Date: 1966
Internet: $140–$200
Mint; gold and white swimsuit and earring.
Comes with brunette, blonde, and oxidized
brunette (red) hair.

Mark: © 1966 / Mattel Inc. / U.S. Patented / U.S.
Pat Pend / Made in / Japan

Casey
Date: 1966
Internet: $245–$300
MIB. Casey is 11″ and fits Francie's clothing.

Chris
Date: 1966
Price: $155   Internet: $130
NRFB. Tutti-size.
Mark: ©1965 / Mattel, Inc. / Japan

Chris, Fun-Timers Set
Date: 1967
Price: $385
MIB.

Christie, Talking
Date: 1969
Price: $270   Internet: $200
NRFB.
Mark: ©1967 / Mattel, Inc. /U.S. & Foreign /
Pats.Pend / Mexico

Christie, TNT
Date: 1969
Price: $275   Internet: $300+
NRFB. Hair oxidation to red is common—some
collectors like it.

Christie, Malibu
Date: 1973–1977
Internet: $100–$160
MOC. Christie is a black doll.
Mark: © 1966 / Mattel, Inc / U.S. Patented / U.S.
Pat Pend / Made in / Korea

Christie, Malibu
Date: 1973–1977
Internet: $30–$60
Excellent.

Julia
Date: 1968
Price: $200   Internet: $140–$160
NRFB.
Mark: ©1967 / Mattel, Inc. /U.S. & Foreign /
Pats.Pend / Mexico

Living Fluff
Date: 1970
Internet: $30–$40
Excellent.

Living Fluff
Date: 1970
Price: $75
NRFB, with wear.
Mark: © 1969 Mattel, Inc. / Taiwan / U.S. & for.
Patd / other Pats. Pend / Patd. in Canada 1967

P.J., Live Action
Date: 1971–1972
Price: $80   Internet: $20–$40
Excellent, prices similar for most P.J.s.
Mark: © 1968 Mattel, Inc. / U.S. & Foreign
Patented / Patented in Canada 1967 /Other
Patents pending/Taiwan

P.J., Twist and Turn
Date: 1970–1971
Internet: $90
Original swimsuit, glasses; hair beads.
Mark: © 1966 / Mattel Inc. / U.S. Patented / U.S.
Pat Pend / Made in / Japan

Pretty Pairs Lori and Rori
Date: 1969
Price: $150   Internet: $140–$200
NRFC. Tutti-size. Rori is a bear.

Pretty Pairs, Nan 'n' Fran
Date: 1969
Price: $140   Internet: $120
MOC.

Stacey, Talking
Date: 1968–1970
Price: $325   Internet: $225
NRFB, Barbie's mod British friend.
Mark: ©1967 / Mattel, Inc. /U.S. & Foreign /
Pats.Pend / Mexico

Stacey, TNT
Date: 1968–1971
Price: $145–$200   Internet: $250–$300
VG; platinum or copper penny.
Mark: © 1966 / Mattel Inc. / U.S. Patented / U.S.
Pat Pend / Made in / Japan

Stacey, TNT, Flip, Copper Penny
Date: 1968–1971
Internet: $300
Mint; multicolored swimsuit; titian hair.

Steffie, Busy, Talking
Date: 1972
Internet: $320–$360
MOC.

Steffie, Walk Lively
Date: 1972–1973
Internet: $225
NRFB.
Mark: © 1967 Mattel, Inc. / U.S. Pat. Pend. /Tai-
wan

Truly Scrumptious
Date: 1969
Internet: $90–$110
Excellent.

Truly Scrumptious

Date: 1969
Price: $325–$400
NRFB.
Mark: ©1967 / Mattel, Inc. /U.S. & Foreign / Pats.Pend / Mexico

Tutti

Date: 1965
Price: $30   Internet: $40–$60
Excellent. Tutti is 6″ tall.
Mark: ©1965 / Mattel, Inc. / Japan

Tutti

Date: 1965
Price: $100   Internet: $200
MIB.

Twiggy

Date: 1964
Price: $185   Internet: $100
VG.

Twiggy, TNT

Date: 1966
Internet: $220–$255
Excellent.

Twiggy, TNT

Date: 1964
Price: $270
NRFB.
Mark: ©1966 / Mattel, Inc. / U.S. Patented / U.S. Pat. Pend / Made in / Japan

Walking Jamie

Date: 1970
Internet: $130–$160
Excellent.

Walking Jamie

Date: 1970
Price: $305
MIB.
Mark: © 1967 Mattel, Inc. / U.S. Patented / Patd. Canada 1967 /other Pats. Pend. / Japan

Walking Jamie Furry Friends Set

Date: 1971
Price: $575
NRFB.

Barbie Clothing

The following is only a small selection of the outfits available for vintage Barbie and friends. "C" stands for "complete," so "MC" is "mint, complete," and "VGC" is "very good, complete." Outfits still in their original boxes are designated as such, with "MIB" or "NRFB."

CLOTHING, 800, 900 SERIES BARBIE

Barbie, American Airline Stewardess

Date: 1961–1964
Price: $90
Outfit: #984   Condition: VGC.

Barbie, Bride's Dream

Date: 1963–1965
Price: $265
Outfit: #947   Condition: VGC.

Barbie, Candy Striper

Date: 1964
Price: $130
Outfit: #889   Condition: NMC.

Barbie, Career Girl

Date: 1963–1964
Price: $80
Outfit: #954   Condition: VGC.

Barbie, Enchanted Evening

Date: 1960–1963
Price: $200
Outfit: #983   Condition: NRFB, VG.

Barbie, Evening Splendor

Date: 1959–1964
Price: $105
Outfit: #961   Condition: VGC.

Barbie, Fancy Free

Date: 1963–1964
Price: $20
Outfit: #943   Condition: MC.

Barbie, Gay Parisienne

Date: 1959
Price: $525
Outfit: #964   Condition: MC.

Barbie, Gay Parisienne

Date: 1959
Internet: $3,000
Outfit: #964   Condition: NRFB.

Barbie, Golden Elegance

Date: 1963
Price: $115
Outfit: #992   Condition: VGC.

Barbie, Knitting Pretty

Date: 1963
Price: $90
Outfit: #957   Condition: VGC.

Barbie, Let's Dance

Date: 1960–1962
Price: $55
Outfit: #978   Condition: VGC.

Barbie, Mood For Music

Date: 1962–1963
Internet: $375
Outfit: #940   Condition: MIB.

Barbie, Orange Blossom

Date: 1961–1964
Price: $50
Outfit: #987   Condition: VGC.

Barbie, Plantation Belle

Date: 1959–1961
Price: $145   Internet: $280
Outfit: #966   Condition: MC.

Barbie, Red Flare

Date: 1962–1965
Price: $140
Outfit: #939
Condition: NRFB, box flaws.

Barbie, Registered Nurse

Date: 1961–1964
Price: $85
Outfit: #991   Condition: VGC.

Barbie, Roman Holiday

Date: 1959
Internet: $1,875
Outfit: #968
Condition: EC; includes compact.

Barbie, Roman Holiday, Compact

Date: 1959
Price: $230
Outfit: #968
Condition: Rare compact, most were vacuumed up, price for compact with many flaws.

Barbie, Theatre Date

Date: 1963
Price: $75
Outfit: #959
Condition: VGC; with pillbox hat.

CLOTHING, 1600 SERIES, BARBIE

Barbie, Campus Sweetheart

Date: 1965
Price: $255
Outfit: #1616   Condition: NMC.

Barbie, Crisp 'n Cool

Date: 1964–1965
Price: $165
Outfit: #1604   Condition: NRFB, VG.

Barbie, Dog 'n Duds

Date: 1964–1965
Price: $70
Outfit: #1613   Condition: VGC.

Barbie, Evening Gala

Date: 1966–1967
Internet: $125
Outfit: #1660   Condition: MC.

Barbie, Fashion Editor

Date: 1965
Internet: $225
Outfit: #1635   Condition: MC.

Barbie, Floating Gardens

Date: 1967
Price: $195
Outfit: #1696   Condition: VGC.

Barbie, Gold 'n Glamour

Date: 1965
Price: $465
Outfit: #1647   Condition: VGC.

Barbie, Knit Separates

Date: 1960s
Price: $50
Outfit: #1602   Condition: VGC.

Barbie, Midnight Blue

Date: 1965
Price: $210   Internet: $205
Outfit: #1617   Condition: NMC.

Barbie, On The Avenue

Date: 1965
Internet: $200
Outfit: #1644   Condition: Ex.

Barbie, Shimmering Magic

Date: 1966–1967
Internet: $260
Outfit: #1664   Condition: VGC.

Barbie, Student Teacher

Date: 1965–1966
Internet: $370
Outfit: #1622   Condition: NRFB.

MOD CLOTHING

Barbie, Hair Originals

Date: 1969
Internet: $13
Condition: NRFC.

Barbie, Happy Go Pink
Date: 1969
Price: $135
Outfit: #1868   Condition: NRFB, VG.

Barbie, Plush Pony
Date: 1969
Internet: $60
Outfit: #1873   Condition: MC.

Barbie, Poncho Put-On
Date: 1971–1972
Price: $125
Outfit: #3411   Condition: NRFB, box
                       flaws.

Barbie, Sparkle Squares
Date: 1968–1969
Internet: $430
Outfit: #1814   Condition: MC.

Barbie, The Color Kick
Date: 1971–1972
Price: $155
Outfit: #3422   Condition: NRFB, box
                       flaws.

Barbie, Tropicana
Date: 1967–1968
Price: $125
Outfit: #1460   Condition: NRFB, VG.

Barbie, Wedding Whirl
Date: 1970–1971
Internet: $175
Outfit: #1244   Condition: MC.

CLOTHING, KEN

Ken, Army & Air Force
Date: 1963–1965
Internet: $170
Outfit: #797   Condition: NRFB.

Ken, Business Appointment
Date: 1966–1967
Price: $125
Outfit: #1424   Condition: NRFB, VG.

Ken, College Student
Date: 1965
Price: $295
Outfit: #1416   Condition: NRFB, VG.

Ken, Drum Major
Date: 1964–1965
Price: $155
Outfit: #775   Condition: NRFB, box
                      flaws.

Ken, Going Huntin'
Date: 1964
Price: $115
Outfit: #1409   Condition: VGC.

Ken, Holiday
Date: 1965
Price: $185
Outfit: #1414   Condition: NRFB, VG.

Ken, Ken in Switzerland
Date: 1964
Price: $155
Outfit: #776   Condition: VGC.

Ken, Mr. Astronaut
Date: 1965
Price: $285
Outfit: #1415   Condition: NRFB, box
                       flaws.

Ken, Roving Reporter
Date: 1965
Price: $270
Outfit: #1417   Condition: NRFB, VG.

Ken, Special Date
Date: 1964–1965
Price: $120
Outfit: #1401   Condition: NRFB, VG.

Ken, The Prince
Date: 1964–1965
Price: $215
Outfit: #772   Condition: NRFB, VG.

Ken, Time For Tennis
Date: 1961–1963
Price: $115
Outfit: #790   Condition: VGC.

Ken, Victory Dance
Date: 1964
Price: $125
Outfit: #1411   Condition: NRFB, flaws.

CLOTHING, FRANCIE

Francie, The Combination
Date: 1969–1970
Price: $125
Outfit: #1234   Condition: NRFB, box
                       flaws.

Francie, Long on Looks
Date: 1969
Internet: $30
Outfit: #1227   Condition: MOC.

Francie, Satin Happenin' Francie
                    Date: 1969
Price: $105
Outfit: #1237   Condition: NRFB, VG.

Francie, Tennis Tunic
                    Date: 1969
Price: $95
Outfit: #1221   Condition: VGC.

CLOTHING, SKIPPER AND TUTTI

Skipper, Land & Sea
                    Date: 1965–1966
Price: $125
Outfit: #1917   Condition: VGC.

Skipper, Learning To Ride
                    Date: 1966
Price: $155
Outfit: #1935   Condition: VGC.

Skipper, Sweet Orange
                    Date: 1971
                    Internet: $50
Outfit: #3465   Condition: NRFB.

Skipper, Town Togs
                    Date: 1965–1966
Price: $125
Outfit: #1922   Condition: VG.

Skipper Clone, Outfit, Clone Red Dress Outfit
                    Date: 1966
                    Internet: $9
Condition: MOC.

Tutti, Sea Shore Shorties
                    Date: 1968–1969
Price: $115
Outfit: #3614   Condition: NRFB.

Tutti, Skippin Rope
                    Date: 1966
Price: $60
Outfit: #3604   Condition: MIB.

FURNITURE, STRUCTURES, LICENSED PRODUCTS

Barbie Dream House
                    Internet: $180
1962, in box, unassembled.

Barbie Fashion Grooming Set
Price : $465
Barbie foaming bath oil, Barbie cologne, 2 bars soap.

Barbie Ge-Tar
Price : $110

Barbie Goes to College
                    Internet: $150
Cardboard set scenes and furniture; some furniture missing.

Barbie's Around the World Trip, GAF Talking View-Master Reels
Price : $75

Fashion Shop
Price : $220

Irwin Boat
Price : $95

Irwin Car
Price : $100

Karosel Kitchen
Price : $75

Knitting for Barbie
Price : $60
In purple canister.

Paper Dolls, Barbie and Ken Stand-Up Dolls
Price : $175
MIB, uncut with plastic stands. For more Barbie paper dolls, see the Paper Dolls section.

Product, Barbie Thermos
Price : $55

Skipper Coin Change Purse
                    Internet: $80
Pink.

Skipper Nurse Bag
Price: $250
For little girl to play nurse.

Suzy Goose Barbie 4-Poster Bed and Hope Chest
Price : $60
MIB.

Suzy Goose, Music Box Piano
Price : $85

Webster's Dictionary
Price : $60

Betsy McCall

Betsy McCall is one of those rare dolls that nearly every girl in a generation remembers

American Character Betsy Mc-Call in "Sunday Best" outfit with original box. Hard plastic. 8", c. 1958. Mark: McCall © Corp (in circle) on back. Courtesy Theriault's.

Ideal Betsy McCall. Vinyl. 14", c. 1952–1953. Mark: McCALL CORP ™ IDEAL DOLLS / P-90 (back). $100, eBay.

American Character Betsy Mc-Call in original box, vintage dress by Joanie Kay / Glendale / CA (tag). Hard plastic. 8", c. 1858. Mark: McCall © Corp (in circle) on back.

fondly—either she had one, her best friend had one and she wanted one, or she always longed to have one but had to settle for the paper dolls in *McCall's* magazine. I carry the modern Betsy McCalls by the Tonner Doll Company in my shop, and almost on a weekly basis, women who played with dolls in the 1950s will do a dead stop in front of the Betsy McCall display and be transported back to their childhood.

Betsy McCall started out as a paper doll in *McCall's* magazine in 1951. She was an instant hit, and a doll was planned nearly immediately. The 14-inch Ideal Betsy McCall doll debuted in 1952. In 1957, the 8-inch hard plastic Betsy McCall by American Character was released, and was an immediate hit. She had a wide range of outfits available for her. In the early 1960s, American Character produced a large vinyl Betsy McCall ranging from 14 inches to Playpal (36 inches) size (Ideal also produced a Playpal-size Betsy in 1959). Other companies that produced vintage versions of Betsy McCall include Horsman and Uneeda.

In 1997, Robert Tonner reintroduced the 14-inch Betsy McCall to collectors (and children) and he followed her with the 8-inch Betsy thereafter. Both dolls are still being produced by the Tonner Doll Company today.

Market Report: Nostalgia is a strong drive for the collectors market, and Betsy McCall is definitely a baby-boomer-driven market. Mint examples of American Character Betsys can sometimes bring $400 to $600 online, which is far above where the prices were just a few short years ago. Dolls in elaborate gowns bring the highest prices, as do certain rare variations (like flirty eyes on the 1959 American Character 20-inch doll). The American Character dolls bring higher prices than the Ideal dolls, except for the Ideal Playpal-size Betsy.

Online/Offline Report: Prices for mint examples tend to be higher on eBay due to intense competition. Prices for all other dolls tend to be similar at all venues.

Prices and Characteristics: All 8-inch hard plastic Betsy McCall dolls are made of vinyl, with jointed vinyl bodies, including jointing at knees. First year (1957) dolls have wigs and peg joints, and prices are slightly higher for these dolls; later dolls have rooted hair and metal pin joints. Dolls are marked McCall © Corp (in circle) on the back, and all dolls and outfits are from 1957 to 1963.

Betsy McCall Pretty Pac tote for Betsy, by Amsco. $15, eBay.

AMERICAN CHARACTER, HARD PLASTIC BETSY MCCALL

Betsy McCall
Size: 8″   Internet: $150–$175
In played-with condition, original outfit.

Betsy McCall
Size: 8″
Price: $300 +   Internet: $250–$300
Mint in desirable outfit.

Betsy McCall
Size: 8″
Price: $300   Internet: $255–$310
NMIB. In original onesie and shoes, but with minor flaws.

Betsy McCall
Size: 8″   Internet: $375–$485
MIB in desirable outfit.

Betsy McCall, in Sugar & Spice Outfit
Size: 8″
Price: $500+   Internet: $500–$565
MIB, formal dress.

Betsy McCall, in Sunday's Best
Size: 8″
Price: $375   Internet: $325
Higher price includes box.

Betsy McCall, Outfit, Bon Voyage
          Internet: $225
MIP.

Betsy McCall, Outfit, Bar-b-Que
Size: 8″   Internet: $140
MOC, flawed box.

Betsy McCall, Outfit, TV Time
          Internet: $170
MIP.

Betsy McCall Designer Studio Gift Set
Size: 8″   Internet: $1,875
MIB.

American Character, Vinyl Betsy McCall

Vinyl American Character Betsy McCall dolls are from 1958–1961 and other dolls are dated as noted.

AMERICAN CHARACTER, VINYL BETSY MCCALL

Betsy McCall
Size: 14″
Price: $250 –$300   Internet: $255–$280
For dolls in excellent condition and original outfit.
Mark: McCALL 19 (C) 58 CORP (in circle)

Betsy McCall, in Town & Country
Size: 14″   Internet: $700
MIB, pristine mint.

Betsy McCall, Bride

Size: 20"
Price: $500   Internet: $620
Mint.

Betsy McCall, Flirty Eyes

Size: 20"   Internet: $600

Betsy McCall, Flirty Eyes, in Sugar & Spice

Size: 20"   Internet: $455
Mint, formal outfit.

Betsy McCall

Size: 22"   Internet: $125
VG, nude with flaws. Joints include waist,
wrists, ankles.

Betsy McCall

Size: 30"   Internet: $120
VG. Joints include wrists, ankles, waist.
Mark: McCall Corp.1961 (in circle)

Linda McCall

Size: 36"   Internet: $1,400
NRFB, with tags.

OTHER BETSY MCCALL

Ideal Betsy McCall

Size: 14"   Date: 1952–1953
Price: $90   Internet: $65–$100
VG; original outfit.

Ideal Betsy McCall

Size: 14"   Date: 1952–1953
Price: $170 –$210
Mint dolls with hang tags and curlers. Soft vinyl
head with Toni hard plastic body.
Mark: © / McCALL CORP. (head) IDEAL
DOLL / P-90 (back)

Horsman Betsy McCall

Size: 29"   Date: 1974
                   Internet: $180
MIB

Tonner Betsy McCall

See the Tonner section in the Modern Dolls
chapter.

Uneeda Betsy McCall

Size: 12"   Date: 1963
                   Internet: $120–$150
MIB

Black Dolls, Composition, Hard Plastic, and Vinyl

Many of these dolls are included in their appropriate sections, but it is also appropriate
to have an additional section on Black dolls,
since few books have been written about
20th-century Black dolls and identification
can be difficult. This section doesn't try to
include all Black dolls, but it does have a
representative sample. Hopefully, future
editions of this book will add additional
dolls.

Market Report: Every year, more and more
collectors become interested in the Black
dolls of the 20th century. Although some
Black dolls in this period are simply the
same dolls as the Caucasian dolls but with
darker skin tones, as the 20th century pro-
gressed, more and more dolls were made
with appropriate features and original
sculpting.

Look for dolls from known firms, as well as
dolls in all-original clothing. Skin tones are
also important, and look for dolls with even
skin tones and not overdone blushing.

Prices for Black dolls continue to rise. Black
dolls, overall, were produced in much
smaller numbers than their Caucasian counterparts, and this coupled with the burgeoning interest in Black dolls may lead to
additional price increases in the future.

Online/Offline Report: Many black composition, hard plastic, and vinyl dolls can be
added to collections relatively inexpensively
on eBay, especially the latest vinyl dolls.
Finer, older examples in original clothing
are hard to find from any venue, and prices
tend to be similar at all venues.

Prices and Characteristics: This is just a
small selection of the thousands of Black
dolls available in composition, hard plastic,
and vinyl. Dolls are in excellent condition,
except as noted. Due to space limitations, if
the doll is covered in another section, see that
section for body types and other doll characteristics as well as marks. Prices are predominantly from the Internet, but dealer and
auction prices are similar and some examples
are noted. The composition dolls are generally from the 1920s to 1930s.

Composition Child, Effanbee.
Composition shoulder head,
muslin torso and upper limbs,
lower composition limbs. 14", c.
1925. Mark: Effanbee Dolls Walk,
Talk and Sleep. Courtesy
Theriault's.

Aunt Dinah Grumpy, and Black Baby Patsy
by Effanbee. Aunt Dinah: composition head,
lower limbs with cloth body. 17", c. 1923. Baby
Patsy: all-composition (5-piece baby body).
11", c. 1936. Marks: Effanbee Baby Grumpy
Copr. 1923 (back) and Effanbee Patsy Baby
(head & back). Courtesy Theriault's.

COMPOSITION BLACK DOLLS

Anne Shirley by Effanbee
Size: 22"   Internet: $365
VG.
Mark: EFFANBEE / ANNE SHIRLEY (back)

Grace Drayton, Chocolate Drop
Size: 14"
All Markets: $1,050
For Madame Hendren and Georgene.
Mark: g.g. Drayton (head) Genuine Madame
Hendren Doll 814C, made in USA (torso, front)

Kewpie
Size: 10"
All Markets: $150

Noma, Walking Mammy With Carriage
Size: 10"
All Markets: $550
MIB, molded hair and boots, painted features,
wheeled carriage with composition baby, pull-
string.

Our Gang Character
Size: 8"
All Markets: $140
Heavy composition, molded hair, painted eyes.

Patsykins by Effanbee
Size: 11"   Internet: $600
Mark: Effanbee Patsy Jr. Doll.

Topsy
Size: 11"   Internet: $130
3 braids with red ties, with original clothing,
often with hoop earrings.
Mark: unmarked

Hard Plastic Black Dolls, Company

The hard plastic Black dolls are generally
from the 1950s.

Composition Child. Molded hair, 5-piece composition body. 12", c. 1930s. Unmarked. $100, eBay. Courtesy Karen Cvitkovich.

Composition Child, "Topsy" type. Molded hair with 3 inserted hair "tufts." 5-piece composition baby body. 9.5". $75, eBay.

Composition doll, "mammy" type. All-composition, 5-piece body. 12", purchased in 1937 in South Carolina. $75, eBay. Courtesy Dana Probert.

HARD PLASTIC BLACK DOLLS, COMPANY

Madame Alexander, Cynthia
Size: 14" or 20"   Internet: $700–$850
Made from Maggie mold.

Pedigree, Child
Size: 22"   Internet: $240
Mint child, all original.

Pedigree, Various
Size: 14–22"   Internet: $140–$185
For babies or hard plastic, including walkers.

Terri Lee Company, Terri Lee
Size: 16"   Internet: $1,125
Mint.

Vogue, Ginny, Hawaiian, Strung
Size: 10"   Internet: $940
VG with flaws.

Vogue, Ginny, PLW
Size: 8"   Internet: $1,100
MIB, painted lash walker.

VINYL BLACK DOLLS, COMPANY

Effanbee, Kewpie
Size: 16"   Date: 1990
                   Internet: $160
MIB.

Hasbro, Jem, Shana
Size: Date: 1985
               Internet: $300
NRFB.

Hasbro, Talking
Size: 12"   Date: 1960s
                   Internet: $165
VG.

Hasbro, GI Joe, Action Soldier, #7900
Size: 12"   Date: 1960s
                   Internet: $900
Mint.

Hasbro, GI Joe, GI Joe
Size: 12"   Date: 1960s
                   Internet: $380

Ideal, Many Happy Returns
Size: 14"   Date: 1983–1984
                   Internet: $30
Battery operated, moves and walks.

Ideal, Newborn Thumbelina
                   Internet: $220
NRFB.

Ideal, Crissy Family, Baby Crissy
Size: 24"   Date: 1973
                   Internet: $45
For average doll.

Ideal, Crissy Family, Baby Crissy
Size: 24"   Date: 1973
                   Internet: $85–$115
For mint doll.

Ideal, Crissy Family, Cinnamon, Velvet's Little Sister
Size: Date: 1971–1972
               Internet: $100–$165
Mint.

Rogark hard-plastic boy. All hard-plastic, 5-piece body. From England, military boy. 6″, c. 1950s. Mark: Rogark (back). $20, dealer.

Mattel Dancerella. All vinyl; twirls when you push crown in and out. Also available in white version. 18″, c. 1972. Mark: 1972 MATTEL INC. $40, eBay. Courtesy Geneva Wallen Collection.

EG Softina skin toddler. Vinyl head, Softina soft vinyl body. 15″, c. late 1970s. Mark: Dukon (script in circle) / Pat Nos. 3.432. 501 / 3856.046 / OTHER PAT's PENDING / EG Softina (in circle). (back; plus mark on head). $20, dealer.

Ideal, Crissy Family, Crissy
Size: 17″   Date: 1970–1971
              Internet: $30–$50
Average, naked dolls or dolls in original clothing with flaws.

Ideal, Crissy Family, Crissy
Size: 17″   Date: 1971
              Internet: $50–$80
Excellent to mint, all original.

Ideal, Crissy Family, Crissy, 1st Issue
Size: 18″   Date: 1969
              Internet: $520
MIB, hair to floor.

Ideal, Crissy Family, Crissy, Twirly Beads
Size: 17″   Date: 1974
              Internet: $250
MIB, all accessories.

Ideal, Crissy Family, Tara
Size: 16″   Date: 1969–1974
              Internet: $235
MIB.

Ideal, Crissy Family, Tressy
Size: 17″   Date: 1971
              Internet: $300
Mint.

Knickerbocker, Daisy
              Date: 2001
              Internet: $30–$100
NRFB; for different dressed dolls.

Mattel, Chatty Baby
Size: 20″   Date: 1960s
              Internet: $235

Mattel, Chatty Cathy
Size: 20″   Date: 1963
              Internet: $950
Longer hair, some flaws.

Mattel, Chatty Cathy
Size: 20″   Date: early 1960s
              Internet: $990
Near mint in rare "Sunday Visit" dress.

Mattel, Chatty Cathy
Size: 20″   Date: 1960
              Internet: $1,500
MIB.

Mattel, Dancerella
Size: 18″   Date: 1972
              Internet: $40
Average.

Mattel, Dancerina
Size: 24″   Date: 1968
              Internet: $95
Average, flaws.

Mattel, Happy Family
              Date: 1975
              Internet: $20
Mom (Hattie), dad (Hal), and Baby Hon.

Mattel, Honey Hill Bunch, Solo
Size: 4″   Date: 1975
              Internet: $35
NRFB, with guitar.

Mego Corp., Diana Ross
Size: 13″   Date: 1977
              Internet: $100
NRFB, authorized by Motown.

Mego Corp., Nubia, from Wonder Woman
              Date: 1976
              Internet: $150
NRFB.

Pedigree, Sindy
Size: 12″   Date: 1970s
              Internet: $140–$170

Sasha Dolls, Baby
Size: 11″
              Internet: $115

Sasha Dolls, Cora or Caleb
Size: 16″   Date: 1965–1986
              Internet: $115
Made by Trendon.

Vinyl Dolls, Judith, The Mommy to Be Doll
Judith Corporation
              Date: 1991
              Internet: $20
MIB. Baby inside the "mommy's" tummy.

Vogue, Ginnette
Size: 8.5″   Date: late 1950s-early
              1960s
              Internet: $540
Mint, tagged.

VINTAGE BLACK DOLLS, OTHER

Magic Skin and Rubber Dolls, Sun Rubber Company, AmoSandra
Size: 10″   Internet: $200–$230
Soft rubber. From Amos and Andy series.
Mark: AMOSANDRA...COLUMBIA BROAD-CASTING SYSTEM, INC...,MFD. BY THE SUN RUBBER CO...

Nancy Ann Storybook, Mammy
Size: 5″   Internet: $485
Bisque

Nancy Ann Storybook, Topsy and Eva Pair
Size: 5″   Internet: $1,800–$1,900
Bisque
MIB, pudgy. Black Topsy has painted black boots with buttons, shorter arms.

Wellings, Norah, Mammy
Size: 9–13″
All Markets: $150–$170
Cloth
VG, exaggerated, painted features.

Blythe

Blythe was produced by Kenner (see Kenner section). With her huge, oversize head, large eyes, and somewhat futuristic look, Blythe was not popular with little girls and was produced for one year only, in 1972.

Blythe is 11.5 inches tall, with rooted hair. She has a hard-plastic head and torso with twistable waist, and vinyl arms and legs. The legs click at the knees for posing, just like a bendable-leg Barbie doll. Her eyes are her most interesting feature. If you pull a string attached to the back of her head, Blythe's eyes close, and when they open, they change color! There are four eye colors (according to Kenner)—"Groovy Green," "Bouncy Brown," "Beautiful Blue," and "Pretty Purple." The eyes not only change color, but they change position as well, giving Blythe many looks. Blythe also has very long hair to the knees, in four different hair colors—brunette, blonde, redhead, and black. Dolls came with bangs or no bangs in a side part, and all wore very mod-looking peasant-style midi dresses.

Market Report: Fast forward to today, and Blythe is one of the hottest dolls around. Fueled more by a new appreciation for her distinct, mod look than by nostalgia, Blythe's newfound popularity can be attributed to websites and photos on those sites beautifully showcasing Blythe, as well as a book about Blythe with exceptional photography. Blythe is as popular in Japan as she is in the United States.

Prices for Blythes have skyrocketed, and for rarer examples of Blythe such as a mint, red long-haired Blythe, you can pay several thousand dollars—as much as for a closed-mouth Tête Jumeau from the late 1890s! With Blythe's popularity, Hasbro (who now owns the rights to Blythe) has licensed her to Takara in Japan for the past few years, and, finally, to Ashton Drake in 2004.

Online/Offline Report: Vintage Blythe is more readily available from the Internet than from dealers or auction houses. Prices for mint and rare examples of the original

Takara Velvet Minuet Blythe. *Korean exclusive. 12", c. 2004. $100 NRFB, eBay.*

Takara Mini "Pow Wow Poncho" Blythe. *5", c. 2004. $25 NRFB, eBay.*

Kenner Blythe can be well over book value because of intense competition for these dolls.

Prices and Characteristics: All vintage Blythe dolls are made of hard vinyl and are either 11.5 or 12 inches. On all Blythes, when you pull the string at the doll's back, the eyes change color (4 colors). All prices are Internet prices. Differences in condition have a huge effect on prices for Blythes.

Mark (Vintage Dolls): Blythe TM / Kenner Products / Cincinnati, Ohio / ©1972 General Mills Fun Group Inc / Patents Pending / Made in Hong Kong.

Vintage Blythes are from 1972; modern Blythes listed here are from 2001 to 2003.

Blythe

Internet: $355–$600

Condition: Fair
Fair to good dolls, with flaws such as hair cut, foot off, chew marks, stomach crack, knee not bending, replaced clothing.

Blythe

Internet: $700–$1,000

Condition: VG
VG to nearly excellent condition, rubbed makeup, other flaws such as knee defects, hair very frizzy.

Blythe

Internet: $1,200–$1,500

Condition: Ex
Excellent dolls, with minor flaws, with blonde or brunette hair. Flaws such as frizzy hair, legs not holding pose, but all original and eyes work.

Blythe

Internet: $2,225

Condition: MIB
MIB, box wear. Brunette.

Blythe

Internet: $3,200

Condition: NRFB
NRFB, blonde.

Blythe, Black Hair

Internet: $1,600–$1,900

Condition: Ex
Excellent but with flaws. Black hair is sought after.

Blythe, Red Hair

Internet: $1,500–$2,000

Condition: Ex
Desirable red hair, excellent, minor flaws.

Blythe, Red Hair

Internet: $2,000–$2,550

Condition: Mint
Mint, all original.

Blythe, Red Hair, Extra Long

Internet: $2,750

Condition: Gd
Eye mechanism works, sold nude, face melts, but very rare hair.

a. **Bébé Triste by Emile Jumeau,
c. 1884. 28".** *Courtesy Theriault's.*

b. **French fashion doll with early
F.G. mark and French fashion
doll by Louis Dalloz,
c. 1867–1870. 15" and 18".**
Courtesy Theriault's.

c. **French fashion dolls (also called
poupées) by Adelaide Huret,
c. 1862–1865. 17".** *Courtesy
Theriault's.*

a. **All-bisque French mignonettes, c. 1880. 5"–6".** *Courtesy Theriault's.*

b. **Kestner all-bisque doll with yellow boots, c. 1885. 9".** *Courtesy Theriault's.*

c. **German wood "Tuck Comb" doll, c. 1840. 6.5".** *Courtesy Theriault's.*

a. **Two French Bébé Bru Jne,
c. 1883–1884. 15" and 18".**
Courtesy Theriault's.

b. **French papier-mâché fashion doll,
c. 1840.** *Courtesy Theriault's.*

c. **Three Tête Jumeau Bébés
(12"–14") and one Jumeau Bébé
Louvre (32"), c. 1890–1895.**
Courtesy Theriault's.

a. **Frozen Charlotte dolls, c. 1870. 3"–7".** *Courtesy Theriault's.*

b. **German papier-mâché doll with beehive coiffure, c. 1840. 6.5".** *Courtesy Theriault's.*

c. **English poured wax dolls, c. 1865–1885. 14"–29".** *Courtesy Theriault's.*

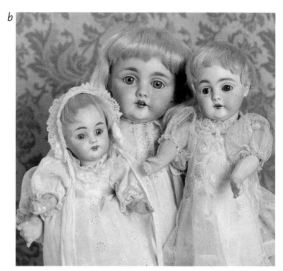

a. **Child doll by Heinrich Handwerck holding German candy container, c. 1900. 24" and 9".**
Courtesy Theriault's.

b. **Group of Kestner 143 child dolls, c. 1910. 9"–16".**
Courtesy Theriault's.

c. **Half dolls by Hertwig, c. 1925. 4"–5".** *Courtesy Theriault's.*

a. **Character child doll, Mein Liebling by Kämmer & Reinhardt, c. 1912. 24".** *Courtesy Theriault's.*

b. **Jubilee googly dolls by Hertel, Schwab, c. 1914. 11" and 17".** *Courtesy Theriault's.*

c. **Bleuette dolls by Unis France (c. 1935, center) and S.F.B.J., c. 1921. 11".** *Courtesy Theriault's.*

c

a. **Character babies by Kestner: Hilda, 247 and 211, c. 1912–1915. 11"–20".** *Courtesy Theriault's.*

b. **Character babies: two Kestner 211s (11" and 17") and a Kämmer & Reinhardt 136 (largest doll, 23"), c. 1912.** *Courtesy Theriault's.*

c. **Piano babies by Heubach, c. 1910. Up to 9".** *Courtesy Theriault's.*

b

a

c

a. *Kewpies by Hertwig, c. 1915.*
    3.5"–4". Courtesy Theriault's.

b. *Character Asian children: two*
    Simon & Halbig 1199s (standing,
    12" and 16"), c. 1895 and a
    Kestner 243 Baby (12", 1915).
    Courtesy Theriault's.

c. *Kewpie by Rose O'Neill with*
    original box, c. 1912. 5.5".
    Courtesy Theriault's.

a. **Schoenhut children,
c. 1915–1917. 16"–19".**
Courtesy Theriault's.

b. **Lenci 109 Pouty Girl with additional Lenci child, c. 1928–1930.
22"–23".** *Courtesy Theriault's.*

c. **Group of composition dolls: Dolly
Record by Averill, Rosemary by
Effanbee, and an early Patsy by
Effanbee, c. 1920s. 24"–30".**
Courtesy Theriault's.

a. **Kamkins cloth dolls, c. 1930. 18".**
   Courtesy Theriault's.

b. **Käthe Kruse dolls, c. 1940.**
   13"–20". Courtesy Theriault's.

c. **Skookum dolls, c. 1920. 13"–21".**
   Courtesy Theriault's.

a. **Sweet Sue Bride, Shirley Temple, Ideal Toni, and Effanbee Honey Walker. All hard plastic, with vinyl Shirley, c. 1950s. 14"–19".** Courtesy Theriault's.

b. **Shirley Temple dolls by Ideal, c. 1936. 18"–22".** Courtesy Theriault's.

c. **Beloved Belindy by Georgene, Raggedy Ann by Molly-'es, and The Strawman by Ideal, c. 1935–1940. 16"–30".** Courtesy Theriault's.

a

b

c

d

a. **Sasha dolls by Götz,
c. early 1960s. 17".**
Courtesy Theriault's.

b. **Blonde #1 Barbie by Mattel,
c. 1959. 11.5".** *Courtesy
Theriault's.*

c. **Strung, painted lash ginny dolls
by Vogue, c. 1951. 8".** *Courtesy
Theriault's.*

d. **Cissy by Madame Alexander,
c. 1957. 21".** *Courtesy Denise
Van Patten.*

a. **Mayor of Munchkinland by Madame Alexander, c. 1993–1995. 8".** *Courtesy Denise Van Patten.*

b. **McGuffey Ana by Madame Alexander, c. 1965. 14".** *Courtesy Denise Van Patten.*

c. **Elizabeth Taylor Cut-Out Dolls by Whitman Publishing, c. 1957. 12.5".** *Courtesy Theriault's.*

d. **Kewpie paper dolls from Woman's Home Companion magazine, c. 1912. 16".** *Courtesy Theriault's.*

a. **Christian Dior Barbie II by Mattel. Commemorating the 50th anniversary of Christian Dior, 1997. 11.5".** *Courtesy Denise Van Patten.*

b. **Color Magic Barbie doll, by Mattel, c. 1966. 11.5".** *Courtesy Denise Van Patten.*

c. **American Girl Barbie doll by Mattel, c. 1965. 11.5".** *Courtesy Denise Van Patten.*

d. **Delphine Silkstone Barbie doll by Mattel, c. 2000. 11.5".** *Courtesy Denise Van Patten.*

a. **Gene, Crème de Cassis by Ashton Drake, c. 1999. 15.5".** *Courtesy Denise Van Patten.*

b. **Sydney Chase, Black and White Ball, c. 2002, 16".** *Courtesy Tonner Doll Company, Inc.; photograph supplied by Storm Photo, Kingston, NY.*

c. **Tyler Wentworth, Hope by Tonner Doll, c. 2002. 16".** *Courtesy Tonner Doll Company, Inc.; photograph supplied by Storm Photo, Kingston, NY.*

d. **Urban Geisha Kyori Sato by Integrity Toys, c. 2004.** *Courtesy Integrity Toys, Inc. and Jason Wu; photograph supplied by Alain Tremblay.*

a

b

c

d

a. **The Little Prince by R. John Wright, c. 1984. 17".** *Courtesy R. John Wright Dolls, Inc.*

b. **Pinocchio by R. John Wright., c. 1992. 9".** *Courtesy R. John Wright Dolls, Inc. © DISNEY.*

c. **Rosalind from the Lifetime Award Collection by Hildegard Günzel, c. 2004. 27".** *Courtesy Porzellanpuppenmanufaktur Hildegard Günzel.*

d. **French Floozies by Jan McLean Designs, c. 1998–2000. 12" seated, 21" standing.** *Courtesy Jan McLean Designs.*

BLYTHE, MODERN

Hasbro, Asian Butterfly
Internet: $210
Condition: NRFB
Limited edition full-size collector's Blythe. Japan only.

Takara, Bohemian Beat
Internet: $100
Condition: NRFB
In white peasant skirt.

Takara, Fancy Pansy
Internet: $155
Condition: NRFB
Limited edition of 3000, produced exclusively for Toys "R" Us in Japan only.

Takara, FAO Schwarz, Exclusive
Internet: $100
Condition: NRFB
In tan coat and fur collar, blonde.

Takara, Nike 2nd Anniversary
Internet: $500–$700
Condition: NRFB
Reproduction of vintage Blythe. Sold in Japan.

Takara, Picadilly Dolly
Internet: $400
Condition: NRFB
Sold in Japan only.

Takara, Rosey Red
Internet: $250
Condition: NRFB
Reproduction of vintage Blythe. Sold in Japan.

Boudoir Dolls

Boudoir dolls "break the mold" for vintage dolls, in the sense that they were not dolls made for children, but dolls made for grown women. However, the dolls were made not for collection or play as today's modern collector's dolls are made, but for decoration—mostly, as the name implies, in the bedroom, where they more often than not graced a bed or dresser.

Dolls were made by many firms in many countries, generally from the 1920s through the 1940s. Early dolls were often done in an art-deco style. Later dolls from the 1940s sometimes had war themes. Makers of boudoir dolls included Lenci (Italy), The Anita Doll Company and Blossom Company (United States), Cubeb (known for their smokers), and Chad Valley and Nora Wellings (England). French companies also made the dolls, and, in fact, were the first known makers of them, with some experts believing boudoir dolls were made as early as 1910 in France.

Market Report: The early French boudoir dolls with silk faces are very desirable, as are the silk-faced dolls by The Blossom Company. Composition-faced dolls are more common. Look for well-painted or sculpted faces, deluxe and original clothing in silks, velvets, and metallic laces, great shoes, and dolls with particularly art-deco looks. Large dolls (30 inches plus) are harder to find.

Collecting boudoir dolls is something of a "hot" trend—in fact, collecting boudoir dolls, with their art-deco sensibility, is very popular with certain Hollywood celebrities.

Online/Offline Report: The best sources for boudoir dolls are specialty dealers and online sources—besides eBay, there are several dealers with comprehensive selections of boudoir dolls on the Internet. Prices can skyrocket on eBay for mint, rare boudoir dolls by desirable makers because of the international competition for them.

Prices and Characteristics: Boudoir dolls tend to be unmarked, and all dolls listed here are unmarked unless otherwise indicated. All dolls listed are from the 1920s and 1930s and are in excellent condition unless otherwise noted. Most have painted eyes and elongated limbs, and were produced to sit on a bed or in a bedroom setting.

BOUDOIR DOLLS

Cloth, Blossom
Size: 29″   Internet: $255
VG; all cloth; original dress, painted eyes, real lashes, sewn-on black slippers, some flaws.

Cloth Mask Face
Size: 29–30″
Price: $260–$280   Internet: $280
Excellent condition, mohair wig, original costume, high heels.

Boudoir doll. Composition shoulder head, celluloid limbs, cloth stuffed body. 30″, c. 1920s. $40 eBay, some crazing and cracking on shoulder plate.

Boudoir doll, patriotic dress. Composition shoulder head, arms, feet with painted shoes, stuffed cloth body. 27″, c. 1945. Courtesy Dana Probert.

Cloth Mask Face, Feathered Outfit
Size: 23″   Internet: $375

Cloth Mask Face, French
Size: 36″
Price: $150
Good condition; cloth face.

Cloth Mask Face, Swivel Head, French
Size: 25″   Internet: $270
Rarer swivel head, cloth body, with hard-to-find metallic-thread hair.

Cloth Mask Face, Swivel Head, French
Size: 29″   Internet: $275
Rarer swivel head, cloth body, partial original costume.

Cloth, Pierrot Man, Molded Mask Face
Size: 31″
Price: $350
Painted weeping features; cloth body, composition lower limbs, silk costume.

Composition, Big-Faced Boudoir Doll
Size: 22″   Internet: $300
Big face, composition, minor crazing, original outfit. Cloth body.

Composition, French
Size: 22″   Internet: $175
Cloth body, composition hands, original outfit.

Composition, Glass Eyes
Size: 28″
Price: $230
Cloth body.

Composition, Glass Eyes
Size: 30″
Price: $180
Lashed tin sleep eyes, taffeta gown, mohair wig.

Composition, Keeneye
Size: 20″   Internet: $60
Long legged cloth Anita-type body, replaced outfit. Keeneye label on back shoulder plate.

Composition, Keeneye, Bride

Size: 32″   Internet: $500
Tagged KEENEYE, molded pink shoes, elaborate original silk gown.

Composition Lady

Size: 27″   Internet: $200
Elaborate ecru and yellow gown.

Composition, Miss America

Size: 28–30″   Date: 1940s
Price: $150   Internet: $75–$125
In patriotic red, white, blue outfit, American. Composition shoulder head, composition lower arms and legs with painted shoes. Higher prices for dolls with less crazing, better costumes.

Composition Shoulder Head

Size: 26″
Price: $60–$100   Internet: $40–$70
VG, composition shoulder head and cloth body; composition with flaws such as crazing, minor cracking; some wear, with old appropriate dress.

Composition Shoulder Head

Size: 28–30″
Price: $130–$150   Internet: $100+
Excellent or better, with nice original dress or gown.

Cubeb Smoking Doll

Size: 22–25″   Date: 1924
Price: $700   Internet: $450 –$600
Excellent condition; first patented boudoir doll. Completely composition, jointed body. Cubebs are considered by some to be the first 20th-century lady doll.

Lenci / Lenci-Type

Size: 28″   Internet: $785
Molded felt face. Spanish Flamenco elaborate costume.

Lenci, Smoking Doll

Size: 27″   Internet: $600
Molded felt face. Fanny Brice-type smoker. In wool smoking suit.

Lenci-Type, Egyptian Costume

Size: 27″   Internet: $3,000
Very rare.

Cabbage Patch Dolls

An entire generation of moms stood in line at a Toys "R" Us for several hours in the 1980s, hoping to get one of these dolls for their child's Christmas or birthday present. Competition for these dolls was so tough that sometimes a fight would break out as a crate of Cabbage Patch dolls got pulled out onto the selling floor. If you didn't live during this time period, it is hard to imagine the craze that these soft, cuddly dolls created.

In 1979, Babyland General Hospital in Cleveland, Georgia, began producing Cabbage Patch dolls. The dolls were designed by Xavier Roberts, a sculptor residing in Georgia. The dolls were very different than anything that had been produced before, and quite strange-looking at first glance. They had very round, lumpy faces and tiny, soft, pudgy arms. The eyes were close set, and they had hair made of yarn. Each doll was just a bit different than the next doll, making each original "Cabbage Patch Kid" a unique individual. Babyland was also a unique place—the Cabbage Patch dolls were displayed in what looked like a real maternity ward, with the sales personnel dressed in maternity-ward outfits. The dolls were put "up for adoption" instead of just being "for sale" (of course, they were for sale, but the adoption gimmick really struck a chord with collectors and children). Roberts and his dolls made several television appearances, which helped the dolls become instantly well known.

Roberts sold mass-production rights to his Kids to the Coleco toy company in 1982. The Coleco dolls had vinyl heads, but were otherwise very similar to the originals. Each Cabbage Patch Kid came with its own unique name and birthday, adoption papers, and a birth certificate. And due to random computer generation, each doll had some small variation, so it was a "one of a kind." Children loved the process of "adoption" for the dolls, where they would send the adoption papers to Coleco to adopt the dolls once purchased.

For the first few years, Coleco couldn't produce the dolls fast enough. The marketing gimmick and television coverage combined to make sales explode starting in 1983. The doll was in short supply, and Christmases in the early 1980s saw parents scrambling to find dolls for gifts, as they fought scalpers

Cabbage Patch Kid. *Porcelain head and hands, cloth body. 15", 1984. $100 MIB, eBay.*

Cabbage Patch Kid, Coleco. *Vinyl head, cloth body; "Arnold Vernon," sandy-hair boy. 16", c. 1984. $35 MIB, eBay.*

Cabbage Patch Kid, Coleco, Mold #9. *Lemon-Loop hair boy. Vinyl head, cloth body. 16", c. 1985. Mark: 9 / ©1978, 1983. P.A.A., INC / 89. $12, eBay (played-with condition).*

and other profiteers who also were scooping the dolls up and reselling them for large profits through newspaper and magazine ads. Coleco posted record sales of $600 million in 1985, thanks to their Cabbage Patch Kids. Many people believe that Cabbage Patch dolls were the fad of the 1980s.

Most fads and crazes are short-lived, and the Cabbage Patch doll mania was no exception. From $600 million in sales in 1985, sales of Cabbage Patch dolls fell to $250 million in 1986. Some scalpers and profiteers were caught with closets full of unsold dolls that, suddenly, no one wanted to buy, even at retail. Coleco tried many things to revive the Cabbage Patch market, including dolls that "did" things, such as talk. But, things went downhill from there, and in 1988, Coleco filed for bankruptcy. Hasbro took over the rights to produce Cabbage Patch dolls in 1989, and Hasbro continued to make dolls with gimmicks, such as dolls that played kazoos. The Hasbro dolls never recaptured the glory of the Coleco dolls, and in 1994 Mattel purchased the rights to the dolls, which they made in an all-vinyl version until 2003, when the rights to the dolls were sold yet again. As of publication time for this book, the latest version of the Cabbage Patch dolls were in production and on their way to retailers.

Market Report: It's the craze and the resulting overstock at the end of the craze that keeps Cabbage Patch doll prices very low for collectors today. You can find hundreds, nay, thousands of Cabbage Patch dolls on eBay at any given moment. Some estimates say that over 80 million Cabbage Patch dolls have been produced, so they are by no means rare. You can find naked and dirty, very forlorn Cabbage Patch dolls, near-mint-in-box Cabbage Patch dolls, Cabbage Patch clothing, and Cabbage Patch licensed merchandise in droves. However, certain rare varieties (black, freckled Cabbage Patch dolls) and very early mint-in-box dolls can fetch over $100. Cloth collector Cabbage Patch Kids from Babyland General can also bring high prices. Most Cabbage Patch dolls, however, bring prices in the $5 to $50 range, with the majority selling for under $30.

Prices on mint examples of these dolls may rise as the children who coveted them in the early 1980s move into their thirties, which is prime collecting time for toys of youth. Only time will tell, however, if nostalgia for these dolls can overcome the high quantities produced. Even though millions and millions of vintage Barbie dolls were produced in the 1960s, high prices are paid by collectors for them today, but the dolls were produced in a pre-eBay era when old toys were discarded and not sold for pin money on eBay, as many of the Cabbage Patch dolls have been sold from the late 1990s to now.

Online/Offline Report: You will find far more Cabbage Patch dolls on eBay and online than from dealers or auction houses. Prices are similar at all venues, except for very low prices for common, played-with dolls on eBay.

Prices and Characteristics: All vintage Cabbage Patch dolls have cloth bodies (later dolls produced by Mattel can have all-vinyl bodies). Most have painted/decaled features and yarn hair. Prices are Internet prices. Dolls were made as playthings for children, not as collectibles, and as the Little People were started in the 1970s, they are included in the Vintage Dolls chapter.

CABBAGE PATCH DOLL

Coleco, Baldie, Black
Size: 12″   Internet: $230
Material: vinyl
Condition: Good
#14, Kentucky factory

Coleco, Baldie, Black, with Freckles
                    Date: 1983
                    Internet: $130
Material: vinyl
Condition: Mint
Black Stamp, #2 mold.

Coleco, Baldie, Freckles
Size: 12″   Date: 1984
                    Internet: $40
Material: vinyl
Condition: MIB

Coleco, Baldie, Pacifier
                    Date: 1983
                    Internet: $160
Material: vinyl
Condition: MIB

Coleco, Cabbage Patch, Various
                    Date: 1983–1985
                    Internet: $10–$30
Material: vinyl
Condition: Mint
Depends on rarity; more for rare varieties, see below.

Coleco, Cabbage Patch, Various
                    Date: 1983–1985
                    Internet: $30–$60
Material: vinyl
Condition: MIB
Most dolls in this price range, more for rarer varieties, see examples below.

Coleco, Girl, Tan Lion-Mane bangs
                    Date: 1986
                    Internet: $255
Material: vinyl
Condition: NMIB
#4 head mold. 1986 box.

Coleco, Italian Girl
                    Date: 1994
                    Internet: $100
Material: vinyl
Condition: MIB
In blue and pink jogger.

Coleco, Red Fuzzy, Large Eyes
                    Date: 1983
                    Internet: $175–$255
Material: vinyl
Condition: Mint or MIB
Rare variation, red yarn-like fuzzy hair with large eyes.

Coleco, Red Poodle, Spanish Jesmar
                    Date: 1983
                    Internet: $175
Material: vinyl
Condition: MIB
#4 mold, made in Spain; girl in "red poodle" ponytails.

Coleco, Twins
                    Internet: $355
Material: vinyl
Condition: MIB
Jillie and Shana, pigtails and pacifiers.

Coleco, World Traveler
                    Date: 1985
                    Internet: $25–$50
Material: vinyl
Condition: MIB

Porcelain, Della Frances
Size: 16″   Date: 1985
                    Internet: $100
Material: porcelain
Condition: MIB
"Genuine Shader" doll made at the Shader factory in Newark, Delaware

Roberts, Xavier, Little People Doll (pre-Cabbage Patch)

Date: 1978
Internet: $1,800

Material: cloth
Condition: Ex
Pre-Cabbage Patch, signed 1978 on bottom, 1979 on certificate.

Soft Sculpture, Twins

Size: 22"   Date: 1992–1994
Internet: $230

Material: cloth
Condition: Ex
With papers, tags. For various sets.

Soft Sculpture, American Indian Set, Tar-Ka-BaKee and Canoe Buster

Date: 1983
Internet: $375, pair

Material: cloth
Condition: Ex
With papers, tags.

Celebrity Dolls

See also the Celebrity Dolls section in the Modern Dolls chapter.

Although a few dolls representing famous people were released in the 19th century, celebrity dolls are a true product of the 20th century, with media and popular mass culture creating large demands for these dolls. A celebrity doll is a doll that portrays a real person who is famous. The Shirley Temple doll is a celebrity doll, a doll of Vivian Leigh as Scarlett O'Hara is a celebrity doll, but a doll portraying the fictional Scarlett O'Hara from the book *Gone With the Wind* is not.

One of the first runaway successes of a celebrity doll was the Baby Peggy doll produced by the Louis Amberg & Sons Company in 1923. Shirley Temple is the doll that really put celebrity dolls on the map in the 1930s, produced by Ideal. Ideal was one of the first manufacturers to popularize celebrity dolls in the United States, with their Shirley Temple and later Judy Garland dolls. Soon many companies including Madame Alexander were producing celebrity dolls, including Sonja Henie, Jane Withers, and Deanna Durbin. Celebrity dolls picked up further steam in the 1960s

and 1970s when multitudes of dolls were produced of stars and characters from the most popular baby-boomer TV shows.

Market Report: People collect celebrity dolls for a variety of reasons. Some collectors are drawn to the dolls because they are fans of the celebrity the doll portrays or of the television show or movie that featured the person. For instance, some collectors of *Wizard of Oz* memorabilia collect Judy Garland dolls (although they do not collect any other type of doll). Some doll collectors specialize in the many versions of the Shirley Temple doll throughout the years (often because they were a fan of Shirley and her movies as a child). Other collectors of celebrity dolls aren't doll collectors at all, but collectors of movie memorabilia including movie-related celebrity dolls. Finally, doll collectors may simply like a doll, and collect the doll although they are not particularly drawn to the celebrity that the doll represents (for instance, a collector of composition dolls from the 1930s would most likely have some Shirley Temple dolls in his or her collection, even if he or she was not a "fan" of Shirley Temple).

Celebrity dolls are especially popular today, given the cult of celebrity that has developed starting in the 1980s. Because of the wide collecting audience for these dolls and their appeal as a crossover collectible in many instances, some collectors also believe that the dolls have the possibility of appreciating in value in the future, although the great numbers of celebrity dolls released by some collectibles manufacturers may prevent those dolls from rising significantly in value.

Online/Offline Report: There is a very wide selection of vintage celebrity dolls online, especially on eBay. Dealers that specialize in celebrity dolls are also a good source; prices are similar from all venues.

Prices and Characteristics: The prices listed are for just a small percentage of the celebrity dolls available—there are literally hundreds. We have, for instance, listed some Mego dolls here, but Mego released count-

Two Jane Withers dolls by Madame Alexander. *Composition socket head, 5-piece composition body. 19" and 17", c. 1935. Marks: Alexander Doll (head) and Jane Withers tagged costumes. Courtesy Theriault's.*

Judy Garland, by Ideal. *Composition socket head, 5-piece composition body. 15", c. 1938. Mark: Ideal Doll Made in USA (head) USA 16 (body). Courtesy Theriault's.*

less other similar celebrity vinyl dolls in the 1970s, mostly themed to popular television shows. For celebrity dolls released after 1980, see Celebrity Dolls in the Modern Dolls chapter. For other celebrity dolls, see the appropriate manufacturer (Madame Alexander for Sonje Henie dolls and Ideal for Judy Garland, etc.). All prices are for dolls in excellent condition, except as noted.

CELEBRITY DOLLS, VINTAGE

Angie Dickinson

Size: 9"   Date: 1976
                           Internet: $15
Material: vinyl
Manufacturer: Horsman
MIB.

Ann Francis, *Honey West*

Size: 12"   Date: 1965
                           Internet: $50
Material: vinyl
Manufacturer: Gilbert
Much more if MIB with leopard.

Baby Sandy

Size: 13–14"   Date: 1939
                           Internet: $250
Material: composition
Manufacturer: Freundlich, Inc.
Mint.

Barbara Eden, *I Dream of Jeannie*

Size: 20"   Date: 1966
                           Internet: $150
Material: vinyl
Manufacturer: Libby

Betty Boop

Size: 12"   Date: 1930s
                           Internet: $800

Barbara Ann Scott by Reliable.
Canadian child skating star. Com-
position socket head, 5-piece com-
position body. 15", c. 1940s. Mark:
Reliable (head) and paper label on
skate. Courtesy Theriault's.

Material: wood
Manufacturer: Fleischer Studio
MIB. Available in red, black, and green dresses;
green is the rarest.
Mark: Betty Boop Des. Copyright by Fleischer
Studios (paper label)

Charlie Chaplin

Size: 13"   Date: 1915–1920s
                             Internet: $200
Material: composition
Manufacturer: Louis Amberg
Cloth body, lower arms composition. Unmarked,
sometimes tagged on sleeve.

Charlie Chaplin

Size: 9"   Date: 1920s
                             Internet: $150
Material: wood
Manufacturer: Bucherer
Naked, worn.
Mark: MADE IN / SWITZERLAND /
PATENTS / APPLIED FOR

Cher, Baggie

                             Date: 1977
                             Internet: $30
Material: vinyl
Manufacturer: Mego Corp.
Hollow, non-bending body.

Cher, Black Travel Trunk

                             Date: 1976
                             Internet: $45
Material: vinyl
Manufacturer: Mego Corp.

Cher, Brocade Caper Outfit

                             Date: 1976
                             Internet: $150
Manufacturer: Mego Corp.
Boutique Collection. Mackie outfit.

Cher, Outfit, Charisma

                             Date: 1977
                             Internet: $95
Manufacturer: Mego Corp.
Mint.

Cher, Outfit, Electric Feathers

                             Date: 1976
                             Internet: $55
Manufacturer: Mego Corp.
MOC.

Cher, Outfit, Green Good Earth

                             Date: 1977
                             Internet: $500
Manufacturer: Mego Corp.
MOC.

Cher, Outfit, Hanky Panky

                             Date: 1976
                             Internet: $500
Manufacturer: Mego Corp.
MOC.

Cher, Outfit, Radiant

                             Date: 1976
                             Internet: $40

Manufacturer: Mego Corp.
Mint. Complete.

Cher, Outfit, White Out
Date: 1976
Internet: $40
Manufacturer: Mego Corp.

Cher, With Trunk of Clothes and Accessories
Date: 1976–1977
Internet: $415
Material: vinyl
Manufacturer: Mego Corp.
For doll with trunk and outfits including several
of the desirable Mackie outfits.

Cheryl Ladd, *Charlie's Angels*
Size: 11.5″   Date: 1978
Internet: $60–$80
Material: vinyl
Manufacturer: Mattel
NRFB.

Cheryl Ladd, *Charlie's Angels*
Size: 11.5″   Date: 1978
Internet: $30
Material: vinyl
Manufacturer: Mattel
Mint, loose.

David McCallum, Illya Kuryakin, *Man from U.N.C.L.E.*
Size: 12″   Date: 1965
Internet: $100+
Material: vinyl
Manufacturer: Gilbert
MIB.

Debbie Boone
Size: 11.5″   Date: 1970s
Internet: $50
Material: vinyl
Manufacturer: Mattel

Diana Ross
Size: 13″   Date: 1977
Internet: $100
Material: vinyl
Manufacturer: Mego Corp.
NRFB, box wear, authorized by Motown.

Dick Clark
Size: 26″   Date: 1958–1959
Internet: $250–$300
Material: vinyl
Manufacturer: Juro
"Dick Clark" written on jacket.

Dolly Parton
Size: 11.5″   Date: 1978
Internet: $30
Material: vinyl
Manufacturer: Goldberger
MIB.

Dracula
Size: 7.5″   Internet: $70
Material: vinyl
Manufacturer: Mego Corp.

Elvis Presley
Size: 18″   Date: 1957
Internet: $725
Material: magic skin
Manufacturer: EPE
Very rare because most of these dolls, made of
Magic Skin (rubber), seriously disintegrated.

Farrah Fawcett
Size: 12″   Date: 1977
Internet: $130
Material: vinyl
Manufacturer: Mego Corp.
NRFB.

Flying Nun
Size: 4.5″   Date: 1960s
Internet: $45
Material: vinyl
Manufacturer: Hasbro
MIB.

Gene Autry
Size: 16″   Date: 1950
Internet: $1,000
Material: hard plastic
Manufacturer: Terri Lee
With flaws; more if perfect and outfit complete.
Tagged "Gene Autry."

Jackie Coogan
Size: 5.5″   Internet: $100
Material: celluloid
Manufacturer: Viscoloid Co.

Jaclyn Smith, *Charlie's Angels*
Size: 11.5″   Date: 1978
Internet: $100
Material: vinyl
Manufacturer: Mego Corp.

Jerry Mahoney Ventriloquist Doll
Size: 23″   Internet: $260
Material: vinyl

Jimmie "J.J." Walker
Size: 21″   Date: 1975
Internet: $50
Material: cloth

Manufacturer: Shindana
Talking doll.

John Lennon

Size: 5″   Date: 1960s
                            Internet: $90–$120
Material: vinyl
Manufacturer: Remco
With guitar.
Mark: NEMS.

Kiss

Size: 13″   Date: 1977
                            Internet: $250–$320
Material: vinyl
Manufacturer: Mego Corp.
Including original instruments, set of 4.

Laverne and Shirley

Size: 11.5″   Date: 1977
                            Internet: $150
Material: vinyl
Manufacturer: Mego Corp.
MIB, Penny Marshall and Cindy Williams.

Lenny and Squiggy

Size: 11.5″   Date: 1977
                            Internet: $80
Material: vinyl
Manufacturer: Mego Corp.
MIB.

Mama Cass, Show Biz Babies

                            Date: 1967
                            Internet: $380
Material: vinyl
Manufacturer: Hasbro
MIP, with record.

Nubia, from *Wonder Woman* (black)

                            Date: 1976
                            Internet: $150
Material: vinyl
Manufacturer: Mego Corp.
NRFB.

Robert Vaughn, Napoleon Solo, *Man from U.N.C.L.E.*

Size: 12″   Date: 1965
                            Internet: $100+
Material: vinyl
Manufacturer: Gilbert
MIB.

Sonny and Cher

Size: 12″   Date: 1976
                            Internet: $120
Material: vinyl
Manufacturer: Mego Corp.
For pair, MIB. For more Cher, see above.

Steve Trevor, *Wonder Woman*

Size: 12″   Date: 1976
                            Internet: $150
Material: vinyl
Manufacturer: Mego Corp.
MIB, Wonder Woman's best friend.

Susan Dey, *Partridge Family*

Size: 19″   Date: 1973
                            Internet: $140
Material: vinyl
Manufacturer: Remco
MIB.

Vince Edwards, *Ben Casey*

Size: 11.5″   Date: 1960s
                            Internet: $40
Material: vinyl
Manufacturer: Unknown

Waltons, Various

Size: 8″   Date: 1974
                            Internet: $20–$30
Material: vinyl
Manufacturer: Mego Corp.
For various characters MIB (2 in each box).

Wizard of Oz

Size: 10″   Internet: $10
Material: vinyl
Manufacturer: Mego Corp.

Chad Valley

Chad Valley was an English company that produced cloth dolls from 1917 into the 1940s and later. Its early dolls had stockinette cloth faces; later it also produced hand-painted felt-faced dolls. Its cheapest dolls had printed clothing, while better dolls had removable clothing, molded faces, and glass eyes. Norah Wellings (who produced her own line of dolls concurrent with these dolls; see the section on Norah Wellings) was one of several designers used by Chad Valley, as was Mabel Lucie Atwell. Many hundreds of designs of dolls were produced by this firm, mostly representations of children.

Market Report: The glass-eyed dolls from Chad Valley are less plentiful and considered more desirable by collectors than the painted-eye dolls, and prices and demand reflect this. In spite of a general uptick in interest in cloth dolls, the prices of Chad Valley dolls, although stable, have not risen much in the past few years, and may have declined a bit.

Snow White and the Seven Dwarves, Chad Valley. *Snow White felt-swivel head, all-muslin body. Dwarfs all muslin with applied mask-felt faces. Snow White 116″, Dwarfs 6″, c. 1935. Mark: Hygienic Toys, Made in England Chad Valley Co. Ltd.*

Online/Offline Report: The choice Chad Valley dolls will normally be found from dealers, shows, and auction houses. Despite the large output of this company, very few Chad Valley dolls are available on eBay (or even eBay UK) at any given time. Prices are similar from all venues.

Prices and Characteristics: All dolls are made of felt cloth and prices are for dolls in excellent condition, except as noted. Dolls with obvious moth holes, nude, or with serious flaws will sell for much less. Dolls are generally from the 1920s to 1940s; the earliest dolls had stockinette faces, later dolls, felt.

Marks: Many dolls are found unmarked; dolls that are marked are found with a tag on their feet or a celluloid button: HYGIENIC TOYS / MADE IN ENGLAND BY / CHAD VALLEY CO. LTD. or Chad Valley / Hygenic Toys / Made in England / The Seal of Purity, or something similar. Clothes are sometimes tagged, and the dolls can have hang tags. Clothes are sometimes tagged "Made In England."

CHAD VALLEY

Child, Glass Eyes
Size: 12–18″
Price: $500+   Internet: $500+

Child, Painted Eyes
Size: 13–16″
Price: $200–$230   Internet: $200–$285
Painted eyes, usually mohair wig, jointed shoulders and hips.

Mabel Lucie Atwell
Size: 14″   Internet: $1,000
Desirable character, mint. Hang tag, feet tagged, original celluloid identifying button.

Norah Wellings, Sailor
Size: 9″   Internet: $50–$70
Very common, also done by the Norah Wellings Company.

Prince Edward
Size: 15″   Internet: $750

Princess Alexandra
Size: 14″   Internet: $750
Labeled on feet and dress, hang tag.

Princess Elizabeth
Size: 16.5″   Internet: $750

Royal Guard, Glass Eyes
Size: 17″
Price: $550

Royal Guardsman, Painted Eyes
Size: 9″   Internet: $50–$100

Snow White
Size: 16″
Price: $1,400

Snow White and the Seven Dwarfs, Set
Size: 17″, 9.5″   Internet: $3,000+

Chatty Cathy

The gimmick of a talking doll has been long-standing in the doll industry, from Jumeau's Bébé Phonographe to the composition Dolly Reckord and beyond. However, Chatty Cathy was the talking doll for the baby-boomer generation. She was sculpted to look like a real little girl (including freckles) and she was introduced in 1960. When you pulled her string, she could clearly say 11 things, including "I love you" and "Please brush my hair." Her pull-string mechanism, which could make the doll say any one of her phrases at random, was a true innovation and Mattel based many of its future talking dolls, including the talking Barbie, on it. Chatty Cathy was a huge hit for Mattel, and although she lasted only four years on the market, she made a big impact on toys that followed, with many gimmicky baby and child dolls produced from the early 1960s through to today (dolls that eat, move, dance, and yes, continue to talk, like the Amazing Ally, which is nothing more than a Chatty Cathy-type doll with a computer chip).

Chatty Cathy had an entire family—a Chatty Baby, a Tiny Chatty Brother, and others. The doll has been reissued twice by Mattel, the first time in 1969 (with the voice of Maureen McCormick from The Brady Bunch) and again in the late 1990s for collectors.

Market Report: The pull-string talking mechanism, a revolution for its era, unfortunately doesn't hold up well over time with the inner-elastic parts of the mechanisms breaking. Therefore, most Chatty Cathys and other Mattel talking dolls come to us mute today, although there are many doll hospitals that can fix the talk boxes.

Chatty and her friends and family are very popular with collectors. Prices for rarer dolls (and even complete dolls that are not mint) have increased greatly in the last few years. Look for "piggy" dolls (dolls with original pigtail hairstyle), brown eyes, and Canadian models. Soft-faced, earlier Chattys are generally preferred by collectors over the later hard-faced models.

Online/Offline Report: You can find pages and pages of Chatty Cathy and related dolls, clothing, and accessories for auction on eBay at any one time. Prices for rare Chatty items are sky-high on eBay right now. Although you may find a wider selection of rare Chatty items on eBay than from a general doll dealer, if you find a rarer Chatty from a dealer your price may well be a bargain compared to eBay.

Prices and Characteristics: All dolls are vinyl and in excellent condition except as noted. All dolls are from 1960 to 1964, except for Chatty Cathy reissues, which are from 1998 to 1999. For all dolls, brown eyes skew prices toward the higher end of the range.

Marks: All dolls, except the number 1 Chatty Cathy, are clearly marked with a several-line Mattel mark on the back. Typical Chatty Cathy mark: CHATTY CATHY® / ©1960 / CHATTY BABY ™/ ©1961 / BY MATTEL, INC. / U.S. PAT. 3.017.187. / OTHER U.S. & / FOREIGN PATS PEND. Here is an example of a Tiny Chatty mark: Singin' Chatty" ... "Tiny Chatty Baby" ... "Tiny Chatty Brother" ... C. 1962 MATTEL INC. HAWTHORNE CALIF USA. US pat 3017 187. For marks on Canadian dolls, see below.

CHATTY CATHY

Charmin' Chatty
Size: 24″   Internet: $200
Doll has slot to insert records to make her talk. Records include Scary-Animal Noises, Mother-Ridiculous, Proverbs-Poems, Get Acquainted. Values higher with original records and if not mute.

Charmin' Chatty, Canadian
Size: 25″   Internet: $490
MIB, rarer Canadian version; still talks.
Mark: MADE IN CANADA / BY DEE & CEE TOY COMPANY LIMITED / A DIVISION OF MATTEL INC

Tiny Chatty baby. *Vinyl, 5-piece body, talks when you pull string at back of neck. 15", c. mid-1960s. Mark: Square mark (see Chatty Cathy, above) on back. $30, eBay.*

Chatty Cathy by Mattel with soft vinyl "piggy" face. *Vinyl, 5-piece body. Talks when you pull string. 20", c. early 1960s. Mark (lower back): CHATTY CATHY / PATENTS PENDING / © MCMLX / BY MATTEL, INC. / HAWTHORNE CALIF (in box) and underneath, in circle: MATTEL, INC. (symbol) TOYMAKERS. $200, more in mint condition and rarer varieties. Courtesy Ellen Johnson.*

Chatty Baby
Size: 18"   Internet: $40–$100
Dolls in average, played-with condition.

Chatty Baby, Black
Size: 18"   Internet: $175–$230

Chatty Cathy, #1
Size: 20"   Internet: $610
MIB, no marks (determining factor for a #1), cloth-covered speaker. Cartoon box.

Chatty Cathy, Black
Size: 20"   Internet: $900–$1,200
For dolls that are excellent or better, with or without fixed talker.

Chatty Cathy, Black
Size: 20"   Internet: $1,500
MIB doll, talks.

Chatty Cathy, Canadian
Size: 20"   Internet: $400–$650
Canadian Chatty Cathys are rarer. 11 phrases; higher price for blue pinwheel eyes.
Mark: Chatty Cathy © 1960 / Chatty Baby 1961 / by Mattel, Inc / U.S. Pat 3017187 / Pat'd In Canada 1962.

Chatty Cathy, Canadian, Piggy
Size: 20"   Internet: $1,500
Pristine MIB, auburn hair, Dee & Cee tagged dress.

Chatty Cathy, Hard Face
Internet: $175–$300
For excellent or better dolls in original clothing; higher prices for Piggy hairstyles.

Chatty Cathy, Piggy
Size: 20"   Internet: $350+
For excellent or better doll, soft face.

Chatty Cathy, Piggy
Size: 20"   Internet: $230–$350
"Piggy" Chatty refers to original hairstyle in pigtails. For average doll, usually mute or repaired, clothing replaced.

Chatty Cathy, Soft Face
Size: 20"   Internet: $280–$450
For excellent or better dolls in original clothing.

Chatty Cathy, Soft Face
Size: 20"   Internet: $900
MIB, window box.

Chatty Cathy, 1990s Reissue
Size: 20"   Internet: $60–$70
MIB.

Chatty Cathy, 1990s Reissue, Holiday
Size: 20"   Internet: $150–$200
NRFB. Hardest to find of the reissues, only reissue with a newly designed dress.

Chifferobe Chatty Cathy Wardrobe by Suzy Goose
Internet: $785
Rare licensed item.

Tiny Chatty brother. *Vinyl, 5-piece body, talks when you pull string at back of neck. 15", c. mid-1960s. Mark: Square mark (see Chatty Cathy, above) on back. $30, eBay.*

Singin' Chatty
Size: 18" Internet: $30–$75
More if sings.

Tiny Chatty Baby
Size: 15" Internet: $30–$60
Average dolls or redressed.

Tiny Chatty Baby
Size: 15" Internet: $80 to $100
Mint.

Tiny Chatty Brother
Size: 15" Internet: $50
Excellent or mint, much less if average.

Tiny Chatty Brother
Size: 13" Internet: $100
MIB.

Tiny Chatty Outfits
    Internet: $40–$100
MIB.

Canopy Bed, Suzy Goose
    Internet: $630
Rare licensed item.

Cochran, Dewees

Dewees Cochran was one of the first American doll artists. Her dolls captured childhood in the way few others have be-fore or since, and her work is cited by many modern doll artists as a source of inspiration.

Dewees Cochran had a classical art education and then married in 1924, residing in Europe for many years before returning to the United States. Upon her return to the United States in the 1930s, she started to sculpt and create dolls. Her portrait dolls soon followed. These dolls, based on six basic sculpts, could be customized to look like nearly any child. Effanbee hired Dewees Cochran based on her early work, and Effanbee produced four dolls known as the American Children.

After the American Children, Dewees designed the Cindy doll for the Molded Latex Company of New Jersey. Very few of these dolls were produced before the partnership dissolved.

In the early 1950s, Dewees produced a new series of dolls, the Grow-Up dolls. These dolls, including Angela Appleseed and Susan Stormalong, were created at various ages of development (5, 7, 11, 16, and 20) so that children could have a doll that mirrored them in each stage of their lives.

Peter Ponsett at Five by Dewees Cochran. Latex composition head, 5-piece latex composition toddler body, from the Grow-Up Series. 12", c. 1955. Mark: Dewees Cochran (head and torso). $1,400, auction. Courtesy Theriault's.

Portrait of child by Dewees Cochran. Latex composition head and 5-piece body. 16", c. 1955. Mark: Dewees Cochran. $1,400, auction. Courtesy Theriault's.

Dewees Cochran died in 1991. Some of her designs were reproduced in hard plastic by the Effanbee doll company in the late 1990s, including Angela Appleseed, Susan Stormalong, and Cindy.

Market Report: In spite of the growing appreciation of the dolls of Dewees Cochran, prices have evened out and dropped slightly after heights reached in the late 1990s.

Online/Offline Report: Other than an occasional American Child and the later Effanbee reproductions, Dewees Cochran dolls rarely make their way to eBay or other online auction sites. Look to specialty doll dealers and auction houses especially to obtain the artist portrait dolls and the Grow-Up dolls.

Prices and Characteristics: For dolls in excellent condition. Most dolls are made of latex composition, with swivel necks, 5-piece bodies, and painted eyes, except as noted.

DEWEES COCHRAN

American Children, Effanbee
Size: 16–17"   Date: 1937
All Markets: $450–$700
Higher price for mint doll.
Mark: Effanbee / Anne Shirley (body) or Effanbee USA

American Children, Effanbee, Girl
Size: 20"   Date: late 1930s
Price: $675

American Children, Effanbee, Reproductions
Size: various   Date: late 1990s
Price: $40–$70
In hard vinyl; reproductions from the late 1990s; also Cindy. For MIB.

American Children, Effanbee, Boy
Size: 17.5"   Date: late 1930s
Price: $750

American Children, Effanbee, Gloria Ann
Size: 20"   Date: 1936–1940
Price: $1,900

Angela
Size: 15"
Price: $1,600

Angela (Older Child)
Size: 15"
Price: $1,200

Angela, Age 20
All Markets: $1,250
Mark: Signed, D & C intertwined / AA-58 / 5

Artist Doll
Size: 15"   Date: 1955
Price: $1,200
Average price for various characters.
Mark: Dewees Cochran

Dewees Cochran American Children by Effanbee. *Composition heads, 5-piece composition bodies. Mark: Effanbee American Children (head) Effanbee Anne Shirley (back). Each 20", c. 1937–1939. Courtesy Theriault's.*

Belinda, Girl
Size: 14"
Price: $650

Belinda, Lady
Size: 18"
Price: $450

Cindy
Size: 14.5"
Price: $1,000

Girl, Model #10
Size: 18"   Date: 1935
Price: $1,100
Stuffed stockinette body, dress labeled "This is Model 10."
Mark: Deewees Cochran Doll (cloth tag on body)

Jeff
Size: 12"
Price: $1,200

Jeff
Size: 16.5"
Price: $1,150

Peter Ponsett
Size: 16"
Price: $1,150

Peter Ponsett at Five
Size: 12"   Date: 1955
Price: $1,400
Mark: Dewees Cochran

Portrait Doll
Size: 16"   Date: 1955
Price: $1,400
Mark: Dewees Cochran (head and torso)

Portrait Doll, Boy
Size: 14"
Price: $2,100
Boy with reddish hair, teeth.
Mark: Dewees Cochran (ink signed, raised symbol)

Stormie at Five
Size: 10"   Date: 1955
Price: $1,100
Mark: Dewees Cochran (head and body)

Susan Stormalong
Size: 11"
Price: $1,100

Susan Stormalong
Size: 15–16"
Price: $800–$1,150

Tiny Tim
Size: 12"   Date: 1955
Price: $3,600
Mark: Dewees Cochran

Composition, Unmarked and Smaller Companies

Composition was hailed as a great innovation for doll heads when it overtook the bisque doll head market at the beginning of the 20th century. American doll makers pointed out how "unbreakable" composition was compared to the (mostly) German-produced bisque doll heads. Of course, composition was never truly "unbreakable" (as anyone with an old composition doll whose hand has a few fingers missing can tell you) and, in fact, composition was quite frail over time and much less durable than bisque. Most composition dolls which still exist have quite a bit of crazing, and many have lifting and other damage to the composition, since composition is a material that doesn't mix well with humidity, water, or extreme temperature changes.

Nevertheless, most of the dolls produced during the first half of the 20th century in the United States were made of composition. Of those dolls, a great many of them were unmarked as to their maker, or made by small, lesser-known companies. Those are the dolls that are covered in this section, along with some of their German and Japanese counterparts.

Market Report: The market is weak for unmarked composition because of the great number of dolls that exist, and because collectors prefer marked dolls by known makers.

The good news about the soft market for unmarked composition (and dolls by lesser-known companies) is that a collector drawn to vintage dolls can build a good collection without breaking the bank. All-original, unmarked composition dolls with minimal crazing can be found at prices much lower than those of their marked contemporaries of similar quality. And collectors with a talent for refurbishing composition can create beautiful dolls with a minimal outlay (although, of course, such dolls should be resold as refurbished).

Price Report: When buying unmarked or other composition dolls on eBay, take great care that the dolls are fairly described—many composition dolls on eBay have had some refurbishing work, including application of Compo Craze concealer (a product that makes crazing less visible), something sellers call "resealing" the doll's skin, repainting, and other work. All such work should be disclosed, and there is nothing wrong with buying such a doll as long as the work is known.

Also beware on eBay because photos won't always clearly show the amount of crazing or other composition damage. Overall, eBay has the largest selection, but auction houses and dealers will generally have a larger percentage of dolls which are all-original or in better overall condition.

Prices and Characteristics: All dolls listed are composition and all are in excellent condition except as noted. Composition dolls were made variously by American, German, and Japanese companies, with the majority of dolls made in the United States. Dolls priced here were made in the United States, except as noted.

Australian, Vera Kent
Size: 24″   Date: 1930s
                      Internet: $295
With tag.

Baby, Unmarked
Size: 8–10″   Internet: $25–$50
All composition bent-limb body, painted eyes, often Dionne Quintuplet-type.

Baby, Unmarked
Size: 13–15″
Price: $70–$100
Cloth body, sleep eyes.

Baby, Unmarked
Size: 18–22″   Internet: $140
Original outfit, tin sleep eyes, cloth body, composition arms and lower legs.

Becassine (French Comic Character)
Size: 15″
Price: $575
Popular French comic character, usually found in cloth. Wears a Dutch outfit.
Mark: unmarked

Belgium, Character
Size: 13″
Price: $60
Sewn-on costume, wood pipe.

Goldberger Child. *Composition head and lower limbs, cloth body with mama crier. 14", c. 1917–1925. Mark: Goldberger Doll / NYC / Brooklyn. Courtesy Marsha L. Cumpton.*

Composition nun. *All composition, 1-piece head/torso. 9", c. 1930s. Unmarked. $45, dealer.*

Composition Carmen Miranda type. *All composition, 1-piece head/torso. 11". Unmarked.*

Bobbi Mae, Swing & Sway

Size: 11"
Price: $160
Separate head and 1-piece body; novelty inspired by Sammy Kaye Orchestra.

Child, Alexander-Type, X in Circle Mark

Size: 14"
Price: $150   Internet: $200
In original outfit.

Dionne Quintuplets, Freundlich

Size: 7"   Date: 1935
                  Internet: $400+
Set, in case with 9" Nurse.

Dionne Quintuplets

Size: 7"   Date: 1930s
                  Internet: $225+
For typical, unmarked set with some flaws.
Mark: unmarked

Dionne Quintuplets, Japan

Size: 8"   Date: 1930s
                  Internet: $1,500+
For quality set, similar to Madame Alexander Quints with good modeling, minimal crazing.
Mark: JAPAN

Dolly Record

Size: 26–27"   Date: 1922
                      Internet: $425+
Composition shoulder head, cloth body, composition lower limbs, tin sleep eyes. Price with 1 cylinder record; more with added cylinder records.

Dolly Record, Cylinders

                  Date: 1922
                  Internet: $40
For cylinder records for Dolly Record, Mae Starr, and similar dolls.

Dream World

Size: 10–14"   Date: 1940s
                      Internet: $25–$50
All-composition dolls, painted eyes, in either national costume or bride dress.
Mark: unmarked

Fam Lee, Doll With 14 Heads

                  Date: 1920s
Price: $400 to $420
MIB with original instructions; and at least half of original 16 heads, more for complete set. Heads include Baby, Indian Girl, Sailor Boy, Suzy Bumps, and Chinese Boy.

Fidema, Character Girl

Size: 20"
Price: $200

Freundlich, Ralph, Baby Sandy

Size: 8"   Date: 1940s
                  Internet: $160
Mark: Baby Sandy (back of neck)

Freundlich, Ralph, General MacArthur Portrait Doll

Size: 18"   Date: 1942
                   Internet: $120
Molded general hat, original costume.
Mark: unmarked

Composition baby. *Composition head and lower limbs, cloth body with mama crier. Owner has photo of herself with doll at age 4. 21", c. 1944. Courtesy Marsha L. Cumpton.*

Ming Ming baby, Quan-Quan Co. (LA and San Francisco). *All composition, 1-piece head/torso. $120, dealer. Courtesy Dana Probert.*

Campbell Kid. *Socket head, 5-piece composition body. 11". Unmarked. Courtesy Ellen Johnson.*

German, Baby

Size: 23"

Date: 1920s

Internet: $350

Cloth body, lower composition limbs, identical to bisque head models.

Mark: Germany 303 / 5

German, Child

Size: 22"

Date: 1920s

Internet: $225

Similar model to dolly-faced bisque dolls. With 5-piece toddler composition body.

Girl

Size: 16"

Price: $150

Internet: $50–$100

Typical girl with sleep eyes, mohair wig, all-composition body, minor crazing, outfit of the period.

Girl, Unmarked, All-Original

Size: 20"

Date: 1930s

Price: $190–$250

Internet: $130–$210

5-piece composition body, mohair wig, minimal crazing.

Girl, Southern Belle Costume

Size: 21"

Date: 1930s

Price: $240

Yellow Southern Belle costume.

Girl, Unmarked, Scottish Costume

Size: 13–20"

Date: 1930s

Price: $100

Braids.

Ice Skater

Size: 11–12"

Date: 1935

Internet: $250

Original outfit with skates; more if mint.

Mark: unmarked

Italian, Bugarella, Pair, Boy and Girl

Size: 17"

Date: 1925

Price: $2,400

Court costumes, painted eyes.

Composition Trudy, 3-faced doll.
Composition head with knob on top, knob turns head to reveal happy, sad, and sleeping faces. Cloth body. 14". Unmarked. Courtesy Shirley Williams.

Jane, Toddler
Size: 17"   Date: 1920s
       Internet: $160
Mark: JANE

Jeep
Size: 13"   Date: 1935
Price: $500
Jointed, original chest label.
Mark: 1935 King Features Syn.

Kämmer & Reinhardt, Marilu
Size: 16"   Date: 1932
       Internet: $400
Dolly-faced type. Body marked "Marilu."
Mark: K * R / 917

Kiddy Kelly
Size: 17"   Internet: $145
Cloth body.
Mark: KIDDY KELLY

Madame Hendren, Body Twists
Size: 14"
Price: $150
Toddler; molded hair, painted eyes, twisting waist.

Madame Hendren, Toddler
Size: 23"   Date: 1918-1920s
Price: $260
Cloth body, tin eyes, Hendren medallion.

Mae Starr
Size: 30"   Internet: $300
Phonograph inside doll plays cylinder records.
Mark: MAE / STARR / DOLL

Mama Doll
Size: 16–20"   Date: 1920s
Price: $150   Internet: $150+
Tin sleep eyes, mohair wig, crier, cloth body, composition lower limbs.

Mama Doll
Size: 24–36"   Date: 1920s
       Internet: $200+
For mint.

Marx Toy Co., Bonnie Braids
Size: 12"   Date: 1940s
       Internet: $180
MIB, had creeping action, doll in crawling position.

Ming Ming Baby
Size: 14"   Date: 1954
Price: $220
Pristine mint.

Ming Ming Baby (Chinese)
Size: 14"   Date: 1930s
       Internet: $100
Mint, by the Quan-Quan Company.

Molly'es, Sabu
Size: 15"   Date: 1940
Price: $415   Internet: $275
In turban and Arabian dress.

Molly'es, Switzerland
Size: 15"   Date: 1930s
Price: $225
MIB, all composition

Composition Trudy, 3-faced doll.
Later version of previous doll, with
composition head, cloth body, and
vinyl lower limbs. 14". Unmarked.
Courtesy Ellen Johnson.

Monica

Size: 21–22″   Date: 1940s
       Internet: $265+
Monica is the only composition doll that was
made with rooted human hair.

Nancy Ann Storybook-Type

Size: 5– 7″   Date: 1940s
       Internet: $15–$25
More with original box, Hollywood Dolls, or
similar.

Nun

Size: 8″
Price: $20   Internet: $20–$30
Painted features, cloth body.

Nun

Size: 20″
Original habit.   Internet: $50+

Paris Doll Co., Peggy, Walker

Size: 24″   Date: 1947
       Internet: $200
Company also made hard plastic dolls.

Patsy-Type, Girl, Molded Hair

Size: 18″   Date: 1930s
Price: $120

Patsy-Type, Original Trunk and Wardrobe

Size: 11″   Date: 1930s
Price: $290

Patsy-Type, Trunk

Size: 11″   Date: 1930s
Price: $90

Reliable, Hiawatha Indian Maiden

       Internet: $140
In worn box, says "Reliable, Hiawatha, A Cana-
dian Indian Doll."
Mark: Reliable, made in Canada

Reliable, Mountie

Size: 17″
Price: $110
Cloth body.

Ribbon Doll

Size: 17″   Date: 1930s
       Internet: $35
Loop in head for ribbon. Molded hair, painted
eyes, cloth body, composition limbs.

Roberta Doll Company, LuAnn Simms

       Date: 1953
Price: $350
MIB, walker, tag.

Santa Claus, Swivel Head

Size: 19″
Price: $300
Closed mouth, painted eyes, molded beard and
hat.

Sayco, Baby Coquette

Size: 24″   Date: 1940s
       Internet: $225
Flirty eyes, soft cloth body with crier.

Sewing Mannequin

       Date: 1940s
Price: $120–$145

Native American Child, Reliable of Canada. *Composition socket head, 5-piece composition body. 14". Mark: RELIABLE / MADE IN CANADA (back). Courtesy Karen Cvitkovich.*

Merilee, Effanbee. *Mama doll with composition shoulder head, cloth body with mama crier, composition arms and lower legs. 30", c. 1928. Mark: Effanbee Merilee Doll (in circle, back). Dress also tagged. Courtesy Theriault's.*

Sewing Mannequin, Susanne
Date: 1940s
Internet: $170
Latexture Sewing Mannequin Doll. Box, stand, 3 patterns, in nurse uniform from pattern.

Shirley Temple Look-Alike
Size: 12–22"   Date: 1930s
Internet: $100–$200
VG. More for exceptional condition, modeling, outfits.
Mark: unmarked

Shirley Temple Look-Alike
Size: 13"   Date: 1930s
Internet: $300+
For doll in original clothing, mint.

Three-In-One Doll Corp., Trudy, 3-Faced Doll
Date: 1940s–late 1950s
Price: $170   Internet: $200

3 faces: sleepy, weepy, smiling. Composition head, cloth body, knob on top of head to turn faces. For doll in original clothing.

Toddler, Unmarked
Size: 17"   Date: 1930s
Price: $80
Cloth body, composition lower limbs.

Topsy, Black
Size: 11"   Date: 1930s
Internet: $130
3 braids with red ties, original clothing, earrings (hoops).

Unmarked, Spanish Señorita
Size: 11"   Date: 1930s
Price: $50

Unmarked, WWII WAC or WAVE
Size: 8"   Date: 1940s
Price: $75

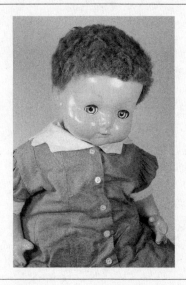

Effanbee composition mama doll. *Composition head, lower limbs. Mama crier, skin wig. 22″, c. 1920s–early 1930s. Mark: EFFAN-BEE. $75, eBay. Courtesy Ellen Johnson.*

Witch

Size: 18″   Date: 1930s
                        Internet: $360
Molded "hag"-type features, original dress.
Mark: WGP c 1922

Crissy

Crissy is a doll of the late baby boomers. The doll with "hair that grows and grows" hit the market in 1969. Crissy was all about hair play—she was a vinyl play doll of a young teenager with hair that could be any length you wanted, from just below the shoulder to nearly to her feet (first issue only; later dolls had hair that would only go to just below the waist). The hair grew thanks to a button in her tummy that could be pushed to extract a long pony tail of red hair from her head, and a knob in the back that could be used to wind the hair back into her head.

Crissy was very popular, and an entire family of dolls was produced with the same grow-hair concept—Velvet, Kerry, Baby Crissy (with a pull-string grow hair mechanism), Cinnamon, Mia, Harmony, and others. Later Crissys sometimes had an additional gimmick, such as Movin' Groovin' and Swirl-Curler Crissys.

As with most dolls based on a "gimmick," however, Crissy's time on the market was somewhat short-lived, and Crissy and friends were mostly gone by 1975, with a few attempts at reissues of the dolls through the early 1980s.

Market Report: The 1969 Crissy with hair down to her feet, dolls in rare original outfits, mint dolls in original boxes, and rarer dolls such as Black Crissy and friends bring the highest prices. Recently, some of the rarer Crissy's have sold for $500 on eBay, which is several hundred dollars above the price these dolls would have brought only two years ago.

Nevertheless, a played-with doll in not-original clothes will usually not even bring $30 on eBay due to the huge number of these dolls available. Dolls with major flaws such as cut or very messy hair won't even bring $15.

For the best examples of these dolls, expect prices to continue to rise, with prices staying the same for common played-with dolls.

Online/Offline Report: Intense competition for the rarest of these dolls on eBay means that eBay prices are top-dollar for rare Crissys. Expect a nice selection from dealers, however, and sometimes at more reasonable prices for rare examples than from eBay. Crissys rarely show up at auction houses. For fixer-upper Crissy and friends, eBay is a gold mine, and you'll find countless examples at bargain prices there.

Prices and Characteristics: All dolls are vinyl with sleep eyes and hair that "grows" when you press a button and pull it from the head; it retracts when you turn the knob on the back. All dolls have bodies jointed at shoulders and hips, some with swivel waists as indicated. Played-with dolls with very worn boxes are priced as average dolls, not as MIB.

Marks: Most dolls are marked ©1969 / IDEAL TOY CORP. / GH – 17 –H329 (head) and on upper back or buttocks, usually with copyright date and patent number, sometimes also with IDEAL TOY CORP. Baby Crissys are marked: © 1973 IDEAL TOY CORP. GHB.

CRISSY FAMILY

Baby Crissy
Size: 24″
Date: 1973–1976
Internet: $30–$65
Condition: Av
For played-with doll, clothes not original.

Baby Crissy
Size: 24″
Date: 1972
Condition: Mint
All Crissy babies have softer (than head) vinyl limbs.

Baby Crissy
Size: 24″
Date: 1972–1973
Internet: $300
Condition: MIB

Baby Crissy, Black
Size: 24″
Date: 1973
Internet: $45
Condition: Av

Baby Crissy, Black
Size: 24″
Date: 1973
Internet: $85–$115
Condition: Mint

Brandi
Size: 17.5″
Date: 1972
Internet: $30–$50
Condition: Av
Naked, redressed, or with original clothing but flaws. Brandis have "tanned" skin.

Brandi
Size: 18″
Date: 1970s
Internet: $285
Condition: MIB
Pristine mint.

Cinnamon
Size: 12″
Date: 1971
Internet: $20–$50
Condition: Ex
Velvet's little sister.

Cinnamon, Black
Size: 12″
Date: 1972
Internet: $100–$165
Condition: Mint

Cricket, Posin'
Size: 15.5″
Date: 1971
Internet: $55–$70
Condition: Ex

Cricket, Posin'
Size: 15.5″
Date: 1971
Internet: $220+
Condition: MIB

Crissy, 1st Issue
Size: 17.5″
Date: 1969
Internet: $125–$175
Condition: Ex
Hair to floor; later Crissy's hair only goes to waist. In original orange lacy outfit.

Crissy, 1st Issue, Rare Outfit
Size: 17.5″
Date: 1969
Internet: $495
Condition: Mint
In rare yellow and orange dress with boa trim.

Crissy, 2nd Issue
Size: 17.5″
Date: 1969–1972
Internet: $15–$30
Condition: Av
Played-with dolls with flaws, with partial or no original clothing.

Crissy, 2nd Issue
Size: 17.5″
Date: 1969–1972
Internet: $30–$60
Condition: Ex
In original outfit.

Crissy, 2nd Issue
Size: 17.5″
Date: 1969–1972
Internet: $100–$150
Condition: MIB

Crissy, 3rd Issue
Size: 15.5″
Date: 1972
Internet: $50–$60

Crissy. 2nd issue (knee-length hair; 1st issue has floor-length hair). Vinyl socket head and 5-piece vinyl body, in-body mechanism with button on front and knob on back to make hair grow (push in button and pull) and retract (wind knob). 18", c.1969. Mark: © 1968 / ideal Toy Corp. / GH-17-H129 (head, with similar mark on back). No box, mint $50; with box, $130. Childhood doll of author.

Condition: Ex
In light blue minidress with hard to find belt.

Crissy, 3rd Issue
Size: 17.5"   Date: 1970
                   Internet: $150
Condition: MIB

Crissy, Australian
Size: 17.5"   Date: 1970
                   Internet: $70
Condition: MIB
Unusual Crissy with Australian mark; doll mint, box wear.

Crissy, Black
Size: 17.5"   Date: 1971
                   Internet: $30–$50
Condition: Av
Dolls with flaws or no clothing.

Crissy, Black
Size: 17.5"   Date: 1971
                   Internet: $50–$80
Condition: Ex
In original dress.

Crissy, Black, 1st Issue
Size: 17.5"   Date: 1969
                   Internet: $500
Condition: MIB

Crissy, Look-Around
Size: 17.5"   Date: 1972
                   Internet: $25
Condition: Ex
Pull string and upper body moves side to side.

Crissy, Magic Hair
Size: 17.5"   Date: 1977
                   Internet: $50
Condition: MIB
MIB; later Crissy with white and pink outfit and wigs, no hair-grow device.

Crissy, Movin' Groovin'
Size: 17.5"   Date: 1971
                   Internet: $20–$30
Condition: Ex
First Crissy with twist waist; original outfit is orange knit-type dress; string pull makes upper body move.

Crissy, Twirly Beads, Black
Size: 17.5"   Date: 1974
                   Internet: $250
Condition: MIB
With all accessories and box. Pink polka-dot long dress.

Dina
Size: 15"   Date: 1972
                   Internet: $25–$40
Condition: Av
Played-with dolls and dolls without original clothing.

Dina
Size: 16"   Date: 1972
                   Internet: $180–$300
Condition: MIB
Velvet's "beautiful friend." Dinas have "tanned" skin.

Black Crissy. *18", c. 1969. See preceding photo caption for full information. $100, eBay.*

Tressy. *Crissy hair-grow mechanism and same-style body. Sears exclusive. 17.5", c. 1969. $50–$80 excellent condition, eBay; $150+ if MIB, eBay.*

Brandi, in Crissy tagged dress. *Crissy hair-grow mechanism and same-style body. 18", c. 1971. Mark very similar to Kerry doll. $50+ mint, eBay. Courtesy Marsha L. Cumpton.*

Harmony
Size: 21"   Date: 1972
                             Internet: $150
Condition: MIB
Harmony is the only member of the early 1970s Crissy family with no hair-grow device. With guitar, records, amp; runs on batteries.

Kerry
Size: 17.5"   Date: 1971
                             Internet: $15–$30
Condition: Av
Average dolls, either redressed or other flaws.

Kerry
Size: 17.5"   Date: 1971
                             Internet: $30–$60
Condition: Ex

Kerry
Size: 17.5"   Date: 1971
                             Internet: $70–$125
Condition: MIB
Original outfit is a green and yellow playsuit.

Mia
Size: 15"   Date: 1971
                             Internet: $15–$30
Condition: Av
Played-with dolls.

Mia
Size: 15"   Date: 1971
                             Internet: $40–$60
Condition: Ex

Mia
Size: 15"   Date: 1971
                             Internet: $75
Condition: MIB

Tara
Size: 16"   Date: 1969-1974
                             Internet: $235
Condition: MIB
Black doll.

Tressy
Size: 17.5"   Date: 1969–1971
                             Internet: $100
Condition: Ex

Tressy
Size: 17.5"   Date: 1969–1971
                             Internet: $155
Condition: MIB
Original outfit is white and yellow print.

Tressy, Black
Size: 17.5"   Date: 1971
                             Internet: $300
Condition: Mint

Tressy, Posin'
Size: 17.5"   Date: 1971
                             Internet: $80
Condition: Ex
Twist waist, aqua dress.

Velvet
Size: 15"   Date: 1971
                             Internet: $100
Condition: Av

Look Around Crissy. In addition to hair-grow mechanism, doll has waist-turning mechanism. Original dress. 18", c. 1972. Mark: 57 / HONG KONG / © 1958 / IDEAL TOY CORP / GH-17 / H129. $30 mint, eBay.

Kerry in Drenched Trench. Crissy's "Irish Cousin." Crissy hair-grow mechanism and same style body. 17.5", c. 1971. Mark: © 1970 / Ideal Toy Corp / HGH -18-h-172 / Hong Kong / 18 EYE (head and similar mark on back). $50–$75 excellent condition, eBay; $100+ MIB. Childhood doll of author.

First release Velvet with velvet dress with white ribbon trim.

Velvet

Size: 15"

Date: 1971

Internet: $70–$100

Condition: MIB

Crissy's little sister.

Velvet, Swirly Daisies

Size: 15"

Date: 1974

Internet: $225

Condition: MIB

Rarer Velvet with swirly daisies to style hair; lavender box.

Velvet's Little Sister

Size: 13.5"

Date: 1972

Internet: $50

Condition: Ex

With box marked "Velvet's Little Sister," but played with; same as Cinnamon, only earlier.

Dawn

Dawn is another doll familiar to later baby boomers. Dawn was about half of Barbie's size, but she was her own little fashion maven with friends, cars, furniture, clothing, and everything else that a fashion doll needs.

Dawn dolls hit the market in 1970, produced by Topper Corp. at the end of the Barbie era. The first four dolls produced included Dawn and her friends Angie (black hair), Gloria (red hair), and Dale (black doll). The small size of Dawn dolls and their shiny, glittery, pink clothing appealed to little girls, and their inexpensive price appealed to moms. The clothing was presented sewn attractively to cards (like the vintage Barbie clothing) and each outfit had a tiny pair of shoes, dress form, and hanger.

The dolls were produced for only three years, doomed by the instability of Topper Toys which went bankrupt in 1973, and by Topper's inability to "innovate" such a small doll fast enough. It was hard to change Dawn or her fashions fast enough to keep girls interested. The tiny fashions, after three years on the market, started to look suspiciously alike, and once different hair colors and "gimmick" versions of the dolls had been made (dolls with wigs, dancing dolls), Topper seemed to run out of ideas to keep the dolls new and fresh. This was quite unlike Barbie, who regained her footing in the early 1980s and has been endlessly reinvented ever since.

In the late 1990s, Checkerboard Toys reproduced Dawn and her friends, and reinvented new versions of Dawn and her outfits. The company ceased operations in 2003.

Dancing Dawn. *Vinyl, jointed at neck, shoulders, hips, and waist. Move left arm and doll "dances," waist twisting and head turning. 6″, c. 1970. $55 NRFB, eBay.*

Dawn in "Gold Glow Swirl" and Jessica in original outfit, in front of Dawn case. *Vinyl 5-piece bodies. 6″, c. 1970. Loose, common Dawn dolls, $10–$20 mint, eBay. Gold Glow Swirl $40, mint, dealer. Childhood dolls of author.*

Market Report: Dawn dolls have never been expensive, and it is possible to build a lovely collection for very little money. However, as recently as ten years ago you could find nearly any NRFB Dawn doll or outfit for $30 or under, while now only the most common dolls and outfits can be found at that price level. Also look for never-produced salesman samples from the 2003 line, which are very rare and sought after by collectors. Priced at several hundred dollars, these sample dolls and accessories are not included in the price section because no more than a dozen were made of each item.

Online/Offline Report: Prices and supply are comparable from dealers and online auctions; to build a collection of loose Dawn items very cheaply, look for large lots sold on eBay.

Prices and Characteristics: All Dawn dolls are 6 inches tall, vinyl with painted eyes and "real" eyelashes. Vinyl bodies have twist waists. Most dolls are marked: ©1970 / TOPPER CORP / HONG KONG (on buttocks, often with letter following) and numbers on head. Some early, rarer dolls are marked "Japan." Prices are from the Internet.

DAWN DOLLS

Dawn, Various Dolls, Loose, Played With
Date: 1970–1972
Internet: $5–$10
Condition: VG
Dressed.

Dawn, Various Dolls, Loose Dolls, Mint
Date: 1970–1972
Internet: $20–$40

Dawn Outfit, "Wrap In The Night" #820. c. 1970. $60 NRFB, dealer.

Dawn Outfit, "Flirty Flounce" #8112. c. 1971. $65 NRFB, dealer.

Dawn Outfit, "Tangerine Tunic" #718. c. 1970. $25 NRFB, eBay.

Condition: Mint
Mint, loose dolls in mint complete costumes.

Dawn, Various Dolls, NRFB
Date: 1970–1972
Internet: $40–$60
Condition: NRFB
The majority of NRFB Dawn dolls and friends sell for $40 to $60. More for rarer dolls and pristine mint.

Dawn, Outfits
Date: 1970–1972
Internet: $25–$60
Condition: NRFB
More for rare outfits.

Angie Head to Toe
Date: 1971
Internet: $215
Condition: MIB
Very long hair; with 3 wigs.

Dawn, Dancing, in Fringed Pink Pussycat
Date: 1970
Internet: $55
Condition: MIB

Dawn, Majorette
Internet: $130
Condition: NRFB

Dawn, Flower Fantasy
Date: 1971
Internet: $115
Condition: Ex
With original flower stand.

Dawn, Flower Fantasy
Date: 1971
Internet: $325
Condition: NMIB

Dawn, Head to Toe
Date: 1971
Internet: $150
Condition: NRFB
Pink and silver minidress, with 3 wigs.

Dawn, Majorette
Date: 1971
Internet: $100
Condition: NRFB

Dawn, Outfit, Socko Swirls #8227
Internet: $140
Condition: NRFB
Box crushing; rarer outfit.

Glori, Center Part, No Bangs
Date: 1970
Internet: $250
Condition: VG
No box, body flaws.

Glori, Center Part, No Bangs
Date: 1970
Internet: $400
Condition: NRFB
Rare, early Glori, made in Japan.

Glori, Side Part, Swing-N-Sway Dress
Date: early 1970s
Internet: $150
Condition: NRFB

Angie in "Wrap in the Night," Dale in original outfit, and Longlocks (left to right). Vinyl 5-piece bodies. 6", c. 1970. Mark: © 1970 / TOPPER CORP / HONG KONG / P. (lower back) and various numbers and letters on heads. Childhood dolls of author.

Longlocks, Dancing

Date: 1971
Internet: $100

Condition: NRFB
Hair below waist.

Longlocks, Head to Toe

Date: 1971
Internet: $185

Condition: NRFB
Long fall, ponytail, braid wigs. Topper made Head To Toe Dawn, Angie, and Longlocks.

Melanie

Date: 1970
Internet: $150

Condition: MIB

Modeling Agency, Dinah

Date: 1972
Internet: $105

Condition: Mint
Pristine mint.

Modeling Agency, Melanie

Date: 1972
Internet: $140

Condition: Ex
Modeling portfolio, stand, and instruction sheet.

Van (Black Male)

Date: 1970
Internet: $200

Condition: MIB

Dancing Dawn Store Display

Internet: $900

Condition: Ex
With all dolls, in original shipping box.

Dawn Action Car, Blue

Internet: $135

Condition: Ex
Working condition with antenna (antenna usually snapped off).

Deluxe Reading

The Deluxe Reading Corp. (also known as De Luxe Premium, DeLuxe Toy Creations, Deluxe Topper, Topper Toys, and Topper Corp.) had dolls (and many other toys) that were staples of childhood from the 1950s through the early 1970s. Founded in 1951 as the Deluxe Premium Company, it first produced dolls at the end of the 1950s.

In the 1950s, its best-known dolls were a line of "supermarket dolls." Supermarket dolls were very large dolls usually over 28 inches tall, often only with a jointed head, that were dressed up in very fancy outfits and sold cheaply at supermarkets, drugstores, and other non-toy locations. The earliest of these dolls are made of soft, stuffed vinyl, and most of these bodies are deteriorating badly. Later supermarket dolls often had hard vinyl heads on soft vinyl bodies. Names for

Sweet Rosemary. *"Supermarket doll," swivel vinyl head, 1-piece hard vinyl body. All original. 24″, c. 1950s. Mark: 194 (head). $125 mint, dealer.*

"Supermarket doll," *so-called because they were inexpensive but fancily dressed to catch the eyes of girls and their mothers, and sold as impulse buys at supermarkets and drugstores. Swivel vinyl head, 1-piece soft vinyl stuffed body. 29″, c. 1950s. Mark: 25 / A – E. $55, dealer. Some crushing of soft stuffed body.*

these dolls include Gail, Debbie, Betty the Beautiful Bride, and Rosemary. Another 1950s doll was Candy, a fashion doll of lower quality than Little Miss Revlon or Cissette, which was sold at a much lower price.

In the 1960s, Deluxe Reading produced the popular Penny Brite dolls (a child doll with a whole world of clothing and accessories) and many types of gimmicky baby and toddler dolls, including Baby Tickles, Suzy Smart, and Baby Boo, plus the Suzy Homemaker line of toy appliances.

At the end of the 1960s until its bankruptcy in 1971, De Luxe (now Topper) produced the Dawn Dolls (see the Dawn section, above).

Market Report: Most Deluxe Reading toys were inexpensive when they were initially sold, and they are still inexpensive today. However, even with the dolls from this company being the inexpensive impulse-buy supermarket toys of their time, the quality of many of the products is quite good when compared with that of the dolls sold today. For instance, the costuming on the supermarket dolls can be quite elaborate, and the quality of the outfits and accessories for Penny Brite is very nice. A good collection of mint Deluxe Reading dolls can be built very inexpensively.

Online/Offline Report: There have been slight increases for these dolls in the past few years, and you'll find comparable availability and prices from dealers and on the Internet. You rarely see Deluxe Reading items through auction houses.

Prices and Characteristics; Marks: Many of these dolls are unmarked or identified by packaging only. Deluxe Reading doll marks are usually similar to this: "Deluxe Reading Corp. 1963" on head. (Penny Brite, Baby Brite). All dolls are made of vinyl and are in excellent condition, except as indicated.

DELUXE READING

Baby Boo
Internet: $85–$125
Cries when you take pacifier out of mouth.

Baby Brite
Size: 14″   Date: 1964
Internet: $65
With nursery; head turns, closes eyes, raises arms.

Baby Magic
Date: 1960s
Internet: $90
MIB, with all accessories.

Beauty Parlor Doll
Size: 24″   Internet: $70
More with original salon.

Baby Magic. Vinyl head, 5-piece vinyl baby body. Cries, raises and lowers arms, and closes eyes when child uses magnetic wand. 18", c. 1960s. Mark: EK 40 / DELUXE READING CORP © ...illegible. $95 MIB with all accessories, eBay. Childhood doll of author.

Penny Brite in "Winter Princess," in front of original "closet" plastic box and original red and white dress. 8", c. 1964. Mark: DELUXE READING CORP. / © 1963 (head) DELUXE READING CORP. / ELIZA-BETH, N.J. /PAT. PENDING. $50 MIB, dealer. Childhood doll of author.

Candy Fashion Doll

Size: 21"   Date: 1962
                             Internet: $40–$50
Doll only.

Candy, Boxed

Size: 21"   Date: 1960s
All Markets: $155–$170
In box with trousseau, accessories, 3 dresses on mannequins.

Candy

                             Date: 1960s
                             Internet: $45
Fashion doll.

Dream Kitchen, Barbie-Size

                             Internet: $235–$265
MIB, sink, dishwasher, oven, fridge, chairs, dishes, foods. NRFB, $400+.

Little Red Riding Hood

Size: 23"   Date: 1955
                             Internet: $25
Hard plastic with Magic Skin body. VG.

Nancy Nurse

                             Date: 1963
                             Internet: $75
VG; talks.

Oven and Iron, Suzy Homemaker

                             Date: 1964
                             Internet: $85

Penny Brite

Size: 8"   Date: 1963–1970
                             Internet: $40–$65
MIB, in plastic box which converts to clothing wardrobe.

Penny Brite, Store Display

Size: 8"   Date: 1963
                             Internet: $560

Penny Brite in "Anchors Away." $25, eBay.

Penny Brite outfit "Chit Chat." c. 1964. $25 NRFB, eBay.

Penny Brite outfit "Flower Girl." c. 1964. $45 NRFB, eBay.

Has 7 Penny Brite dolls on a carousel, dressed in original outfits.

Penny Brite, Play Sets
Date: 1963–1969
Internet: $75–$90
MIB, for bedroom, school, kitchen, or beauty parlor play set; more for NRFB.

Penny Brite, Play Sets
Date: 1963–1969
Internet: $135
Ultra mint sets still retaining cardboard cutout of doll wearing outfit.

Penny Brite, Outfits MIB
Date: 1963–1969
Internet: $40–$50
For Chit Chat, Singing in the Rain, Flower Girl, Winter Princess.

Penny Brite, Outfit, Sun & Fun
Date: 1963–1969
Internet: $35
MIB.

Supermarket Doll
Size: 30″
Date: 1950s
All Markets: $50
For VG dolls with wear from weight of head on soft rubber neck area.

Suzy Cute
Size: 7″
Date: 1964
Internet: $30
VG.

Suzy Smart
Size: 22″
Date: 1962
Internet: $85–$100
For played-with doll with flaws, no desk.

Suzy Smart, With Desk
Size: 22″
Date: 1962
Internet: $300–$400
For mint, talks and sings, with desk and blackboard.

Sweet Rosemary
Size: 30″
Date: 1950s
Internet: $125
NMIB soft vinyl. Box and original pamphlets, including flyer offering little girl look-alike dresses and flyer about Sweet Rosemary's "Miracle Vinyl," how doll can sit and pose.

Tickles
Size: 20″
Date: 1966
Internet: $50–$75
Baby; laughs and cries.

Effanbee

See also Patsy section.

The Effanbee Doll Company began producing dolls in 1912 at the beginning of the composition doll period. The company, under the leadership of owners Bernard Fleischaker and Hugo Baum, first produced a popular series of composition baby dolls, including Baby Dainty, Baby Grumpy, and

Little Lady. *Composition, 5-piece body. 18", c. 1940s. Mark: EFFAN-BEE / U.S.A. (head and torso). $200, dealer.*

Talking Touselhead Lovums. *Composition shoulder head, composition limbs with sturdy cloth body. Plays "record" cylinders in mechanism in torso. Came with 6 records, shown here with "Now I Lay Me Down To Sleep," "One, Two" and "Old Mother Hubbard." 20", c. 1939. Mark: EFFANBEE / LOVUMS / © / PAT NO 1,283,558.*

others. Later well-loved composition baby dolls included Bubbles and Lovums.

The biggest early success for the company was the composition Patsy doll, designed by renowned doll designer Bernard Lipfert. First advertised in 1928, Patsy was in production for many years, and spawned an entire world of doll accessories and clothing (she was one of the first dolls to have her own wardrobe commercially produced), as well as her own family of dolls that included Patsyette, Wee Patsyette, Skippy, Patsy Lou, and many others. Patsy has been a perennial favorite with doll collectors, and she has been reproduced in vinyl and hard plastic many times by later incarnations of the Effanbee Doll Company (for more information and prices, see the Patsy and Family section). In the mid-1930s, Effanbee innovated yet again with the first drink-and-wet baby doll, made out of hard rubber, the Dy-Dee Baby. Other notable dolls produced by the Effanbee company in the vintage era include Little Lady, Anne Shirley, the American Children by Dewees Cochran, Honey, and Tintair.

The company hit financial troubles during World War II, and it has had a series of owners since then, culminating with the current owner, the Tonner Doll Company (for more information, see section on modern Effanbee dolls).

Market Report: There is a strong market for early, mint-condition composition Patsy, Skippy, and American Children dolls. The dolls from the 1970s have not fared as well, with very weak prices for mid-1970s and 1980s vinyl collectible dolls. However, the latest Effanbee dolls by the Tonner Doll Company, especially the new Brenda Starr fashion doll, have been eagerly sought after (for prices, see the section on modern Effanbee dolls). Prices for mint Honeys are also on the rise.

Online/Offline Report: Prices for mint, original Patsy family and other early Effanbee dolls are strong both on eBay and at shows and auctions. Look for some of the hard-to-find early composition baby dolls in all-original condition and Honey dolls in mint outfits via shows and dealers—many early dolls in mint condition are nearly impossible to find via eBay and other online auction sites.

EFFANBEE, COMPOSITION

Anne Shirley, American Children
Size: 20″   Date: 1930s
                         Internet: $410
Condition: Ex

Light crazing. For more American Children, see Dewees Cochran section.
Mark: Effanbee/American Children (neck) and Anne Shirley (upper back)

Anne Shirley
Size: 21″   Date: 1930s
Price: $130   Internet: $125–$200
Condition: VG
Redressed doll.

Anne Shirley, Floss Wig
Size: 22″   Date: 1930s
Price: $250
Condition: Ex
In original black nylon peignoir.

Anne Shirley, Black
Size: 22″   Date: 1930s
                            Internet: $300
Condition: VG
Mark: EFFANBEE/ANNE SHIRLEY (back)

Baby Mickey
Size: 16″   Date: 1940s
                            Internet: $90+
Condition: VG
Pouty expression, side-glancing sleep eyes, cloth torso, wig over molded hair.
Mark: Effanbee/made in USA

Bubbles
Size: 17″   Date: 1920s
                            Internet: $250
Condition: Ex
Replaced clothing, composition flaws.
Mark: Effanbee Bubbles Walk/Talk/Sleep

Bubbles
Size: 17″   Date: 1924
                            Internet: $330
Condition: Mint

Bubbles
Size: 26″   Date: 1924
                            Internet: $370
Condition: Mint

Candy Kid
Size: 11″
Price: $150
Condition: Ex

Charlie McCarthy
Size: 15–20″   Date: 1930s
                            Internet: $150–$200
Condition: Gd
Mouth often stuck, worn clothing.

Charlie McCarthy
Size: 15–20″   Date: 1930s
Price: $450   Internet: $400
Condition: Mint
Pull string at back of head to open and close mouth.

Grumpykins
Size: 12.5″   Date: late 1920s
                            Internet: $200–$300
Condition: Ex to Mint
Hang tag: This is Grumpykins™/A doll so cute you just want to hug her/An Effanbee Doll.
Mark: Effanbee Durable Dolls/Made in USA

Historical Series Dolls Portraying the Fashion History of America
Size: 14″   Date: 1939
Price: $225–$500
Condition: Ex
29 dolls auctioned separately from series of 30. Composition socket heads, painted features, 5-piece bodies.
Mark: Effanbee Anne Shirley

Howdy Doody
Size: 17″   Date: 1949
                            Internet: $150
Condition: VG
Cloth body.

Lambkins, Baby
Size: 16″   Date: 1930
Price: $700
Condition: Ex
Sleep eyes, open mouth, cloth baby body, swivel head, composition lower limbs.
Mark: Lambkins

Little Lady
Size: 18–21″   Date: 1930s–1940s
Price: $130   Internet: $160
Condition: VG
Played with, redressed.
Mark: Effanbee/Anne Shirley (back torso)

Little Lady
Size: 18–21″   Date: 1930s–1940s
Price: $200–$260   Internet: $250
Condition: VG
Played with, in desirable outfit—Carmen Miranda, bride, or gown.
Mark: Some dolls unmarked; some marked only "Effanbee"

Little Lady
Size: 27″   Date: 1930s–1940s
Internet: $300
Condition: Ex

Patsy Babyette Twins. *Courtesy of Louise Lunde.*

Pair of Skippys. *Composition socket head, 5-piece composition body (black), but cloth torso for white doll. Both 14", c. 1930. Mark: Effanbee Skippy c. P.I. Crosby (head) Effanbee Pats. Pend Doll (torso; black doll). Courtesy Theriault's.*

Little Lady

Size: 18"   Date: 1930s–1940s
Price: $1,250
Condition: MIB

Marilee

Size: 16"   Date: 1937
             Internet: $300
Condition: Ex
Mark: Marilee

Marilee

Size: 29"   Date: 1937
Price: $850
Condition: Mint
Pristine. Shoulder head, muslin torso, composition arms and legs
Mark: Effanbee Marilee

Puss in Boots

Size: 9"   Date: 1940s
             Internet: $255
Condition: Mint
Black cat, painted eyes, felt outfit.

Rosemary

Size: 18"   Date: 1926–1931
             Internet: $350
Condition: Ex
Mark: Effanbee/Rosemary

Rosemary

Size: 28"   Date: 1926–1931
Price: $375
Condition: Ex
Sleep eyes, human hair wig.

Shirley Temple Look-Alike

Size: 18"   Date: 1930s
             Internet: $450
Condition: MIB
MIB; no doll name on box; box marked "An Effanbee Durable Doll."

Sugar Baby

Size: 19"
Price: $110
Condition: Ex

Suzanne

Size: 14"
             Internet: $275
Condition: Ex
Sleep eyes.
Mark: Suzanne/Effanbee

Sweetie Pie

Size: 16–19" Date: 1940s
Price: $95–$105 Internet: $120
Condition: VG
Toddler with hair.

Sweetie Pie

Size: 19"   Date: 1940s
             Internet: $200
Condition: Ex

Sweetie Pie, Flirty Eyes

Size: 23"   Date: 1940s
Price: $210
Condition: Ex

Talking Touselhead Lovums

Size: 20"   Date: 1939
             Internet: $400+

Half Pint. Vinyl, 5-piece body. 10", c. late 1960s. Mark: EFFANBEE / 19©66 (head) EFFANBEE / 2400 (body). $15, eBay.

Honey. Hard plastic, 5-piece body. 15", c. 1950s. Mark: Effanbee. Courtesy Theriault's.

Condition: Mint
Comes with records; Mae Starr record mechanism with hand crank. Original outfit, fur wig, swivel neck on shoulder plate, cloth body, composition arms and legs, sleep eyes.

Tommy Tucker

Size: 25″   Date: 1940s
Price: $210
Condition: Ex
Cloth body, flirty eyes.

Sister

Size: 24″   Date: 1931
Price: $220
Condition: Ex
Floppy cloth body, blonde floss wig.

EFFANBEE, HARD PLASTIC

Dy-Dee Baby

Size: 11″   Date: 1934+
                             Internet: $210
Condition: MIB

Actually a hard-rubber head, with soft rubber body.
Mark: EFFANBEE/DY-DEE BABY/with lots of patent info, additional lines (back)

Dy-Dee Baby

Size: 14″   Date: 1934+
                             Internet: $530
Condition: MIB
Molded hair, green eyes.

Dy-Dee Baby

Size: 20″   Date: 1934+
Price: $400
Condition: NMIB
Caracul wig, original flannel pjs, wardrobe case with added factory costumes.

Honey

Size: 16″   Date: 1950s
                             Internet: $175–$225
Condition: Ex
In simple dress or other original outfit.
Mark: Effanbee on back of neck

Gretel. Vinyl, 5-piece body. 12″, c. 1980s. Mark: EFFANBEE / ©1976s / "76 /Effanbee. $15 MIB, eBay. Courtesy Cathy Messenger.

Honey
Size: 16″   Date: 1951
Price: $300   Internet: $300
Condition: Mint
Bridesmaid or similar outfit or desirable platinum hair.
Mark: Effanbee

Honey
Size: 16″   Date: 1950s
                      Internet: $525
Condition: MIB
High color, hang tag, box, curlers.

Honey
Size: 18″   Date: 1953
                      Internet: $170
Condition: Ex, in replaced clothing
Mark: Effanbee (head and torso)

Honey
Size: 18″   Date: 1950s
Price: $280   Internet: $300
Condition: Ex, in original dress
Mark: Effanbee

Honey
Size: 18″   Date: 1950s
Price: $625
Condition: MIB

Honey, Bridesmaid
Size: 18″   Date: 1950s
                      Internet: $430
Condition: Mint

Honey as Cinderella or Prince Charming
Size: 18″   Date: 1950s
Price: $375   Internet: $310
Condition: Ex
Mark: Effanbee (head, back)

Honey, Walker
Size: 18–20″   Date: late 1950s
Price: $300   Internet: $120–$150
Condition: Ex

Honey, Schiaparelli Dress
Size: 18″
Price: $450
Condition: Ex
Schiaparelli and Effanbee tagged.
Mark: Effanbee

Mary Jane
Size: 32″   Date: 1960
                      Internet: $360
Condition: MIB

Tintair
Size: 16″   Date: early 1950s
Price: $230   Internet: $200+
Condition: VG
Used Honey doll mold.

Tintair
Size: 16″   Date: early 1950s
                      Internet: $400+
Condition: Mint
Doll came with hair tinting and setting accessories (hair could be blonde, brunette, red).

Effanbee, Vinyl

For prices on vinyl Effanbee dolls from 1980 to the present, see the Modern Dolls chapter.

EFFANBEE, VINYL

Baby Cuddle Up

Size: 20″   Date: 1954
           Internet: $50
Condition: Ex
Some with molded hair, others rooted.

Fluffy, Girl Scout or Brownie

Size: 9″   Date: 1965
           Internet: $30–$60
Condition: Ex
Mark: EFFANBEE/FLUFFY

Fluffy, Girl Scout

Size: 11″   Date: 1960s
           Internet: $150
Condition: Ex
Green and white outfit with beret.

Fluffy, Girl Scout

Size: 11″   Date: 1960s
           Internet: $300
Condition: Mint

Mickey, All-American Boy

Size: 10.5″   Date: 1956
           Internet: $60
Condition: Ex
One black eye, freckles, wearing boxer shorts, gloves.

The Most Happy Family

Size: 19″   Date: 1958
           Internet: $275
Condition: VG
Family: mother, baby, girl, and boy; dressed in light blue.

Vinyl Doll, Various

Size: 8–24″   Date: 1970–1990
           Internet: $15–$30
Condition: Mint or MIB
For most vinyl child or lady dolls from the 1970s and 1980s, including Storybook Series, Enchanted Garden, Just Friends, fancy dressed ladies, Historical Collection, and others.

G.I. Joe

G.I. Joe is rarely included in books of this type, which is not understandable. After all, G.I. Joe is definitely a doll, he's just a male, and men insist on calling him an "action figure" instead of a doll. However, G.I. Joe is a doll, and vintage G.I. Joe is a very nicely made doll at that, with the quality of his early outfits and accessories easily rivaling that of Barbie and Ken from the same time period. G.I. Joe will be covered briefly here.

Hasbro created G.I. Joe in 1964. Joe was a poseable figure—a plaything, just like a doll, but since everyone assumed that boys would not play with a doll, Hasbro created the term "action figure" for him, and that term has stuck ever since for male figures for play by boys. G.I. Joe served in all four branches of the military, as a soldier, sailor, marine, and pilot.

One interesting fact about the line is that a female figure, the G.I. Joe Nurse, was not a success in the 1960s, so she was produced in small quantities and is highly sought after today.

Military G.I. Joe was hugely popular until the end of the 1960s, when popularity of Joe and many other classic playthings waned (G.I. Joe's demise was assisted by the unpopularity of the Vietnam war). At this point, Joe was reinvented to be an adventure doll with adventures, outfits, and accessories for exploring jungles, outer space, and under the sea. This remake for the G.I. Joe line was very popular with little boys, and kept sales going for several more years.

However, sales faltered again in the mid-1970s, so classic G.I. Joe said his final farewell in 1976, was reintroduced as a much-smaller play figure in 1982 (really much more like what doll collectors think of as an "action figure"—a small, molded plastic figure), and has been available in some form or another since, with some recent larger editions such as the Hall of Fame, Classic, and Timeless editions. The Classic releases in 1996, and even more so the Timeless edition releases after that, finally captured the look and feel of the vintage G.I. Joe dolls—I mean action figures—and were very popular with collectors.

Market Report: The market for vintage G.I. Joe, and even 1980s MOC (mint on card) rarer G.I. Joe items, is very strong, with prices steadily increasing. Some items have had price declines, including the Action Soldiers of the World.

Online/Offline Report: There is a great selection of hard-to-find G.I. Joe items online, with fierce competition meaning fierce prices. There is also a plethora of lesser items, with more than 7,000 G.I. Joe items to wade through on eBay at any given time. Prices for lesser items are therefore quite low. Specialty dealers also have many of the rarer and minter Joe items at prices comparable to those online.

Prices and Characteristics: All G.I. Joe dolls are vinyl with painted features. Only a small selection of some of the choicest items are presented here—the world of G.I. Joe rivals the world of Barbie in scope.

Mark: G.I. Joe ® Copyright 1964 / by Hasbro Pat. no. / 3277602 Made in U.S.A. or Patent Pending c1967 Hasbro R Made in Hong Kong (or similar).

G.I. JOE, 12″ FIGURES

Action Soldier, Black #7900
Internet: $900
Condition: Mint

AT Air Adventurer
Date: 1971
Internet: $550
Condition: MIB
Orange jump suit, beard.

French Resistance Fighter
Internet: $500
Condition: MIB

Joe in Tan MP Outfit with Helmet, Radio
Internet: $1,800
Condition: Ex

Joe, 1st Issue, Painted Eyes
Date: 1964
Internet: $400–$500
Condition: MIB
Painted liner around eyes.

Land Adventurer Joe, Shoulder Holster, Pistol, Dog Tags #7905
Date: 1969
Internet: $735
Condition: Ex

Marine, 1st Issue, Shoulder Stamped
Date: 1964
Internet: $2,600
Condition: MIB
Shoulder stamped © HASBRO.

Nurse
Date: 1967
Internet: $650–$700
Condition: Ex
For nude doll or doll with costume flaws; more for mint.

Nurse
Date: 1967
Internet: $2,325
Condition: MIB

Outfit, Adventure Team Karate
Date: 1971
Internet: $175
Condition: MOC

Outfit, Adventure Team Secret Courier
Internet: $675
Condition: MOC

Outfit, West Point #7537
Date: 1967
Internet: $1,025
Condition: MIB

Painted Head, Talking Astronaut #7915
Internet: $950
Condition: Mint

Russian Infantryman Soldier
Internet: $1,000
Condition: MIB

Soldiers of the World, Japanese Imperial Soldier
Internet: $2,000
Condition: MIB

Talking G.I. Joe Action Pilot #890
Internet: $1,900
Condition: MIB
In orange jumpsuit.

Talking Joe with Lifelike Hair and Beard
Date: 1970
Internet: $500
Condition: Ex

Talking Marine
Condition: MIB
Internet: $650

G.I. Joe 30th Anniversary edition.
Vinyl, for the adult collector market. 12", c. 1994.

Tan Airbourne MP #7539
> Date: 1960s
> Internet: $500–$560

Condition: Ex

G.I. JOE, ACCESSORIES AND VEHICLES

Action Marine Green Camouflaged Field Telephone
> Date: 1964
> Internet: $1,200–$1,500

Condition: Mint
Rare Joe-size accessory.

Defiant (Space Shuttle, Vehicle) With Blueprints and Figures
> Internet: $700

Condition: MIB

Defiant, MIB, No Blueprints or Figures
> Internet: $500

Condition: MIB

Engineer Transit Set
> Internet: $400–$450

Condition: Ex
Marked construction hard hat, gray engineer's gloves, grease gun, Japan tagged uniform, tall brown boots, dog tag.

Polar Explorer Set
> Internet: $570

Condition: Ex
Includes sled, husky dogs, arctic jacket, more.

Striped SP Helmet and Radio
> Date: 1967
> Internet: $475

Condition: Ex

USS Flag Aircraft Carrier
> Internet: $540

Condition: MIB

White Plastic Shore Patrol Radio
> Internet: $900

Child-size accessory.

G.I. JOE, 4" FIGURES

Blowtorch
> Date: 1985
> Internet: $530

Condition: MOC

Cobra Commander
> Date: 1983
> Internet: $560

Condition: MOC
Series 2.

Cobra Firefly #836
> Internet: $700–$900

Condition: MOC

Joe "Snake Eyes" (Smaller Figure)
> Date: 1982
> Internet: $635–$800

Condition: MOC
More for pristine mint.

Joe "Snake Eyes" (Smaller Figure)
Date: 1982
Internet: $1,400
Condition: MOC
Perfect, card hanger slot not punched.

Storm Shadow
Date: 1984
Internet: $500
Condition: MOC

Ginny

See also "Vogue".

Ginny, made by the Vogue Doll Company for most of her life, is an enduring doll, created over 50 years ago in the late 1940s. Ginny was the doll for many children growing up in the 1950s, and she is the often-copied epitome of the small toddler doll. Ginny is also notable for her fine quality in a mass-produced, affordable package, as a doll and also for her charming, detailed outfits. Although Ginny lost her way in the late 1960s through the 1980s (much like Barbie, Effanbee dolls, and many other dolls of that era), today the dolls are back in production, high quality, and again favored by little girls as well as collectors.

Ginny was created by the founder of the Vogue Doll Company, (see the Vogue section) Jennie H. Graves, from Somerville, Massachusetts. The business was originally a "cottage industry" business run out of Mrs. Graves' house. She sold a variety of bisque, composition, and hard-plastic dolls through the 1930s and 1940s, for which Mrs. Graves designed most of the clothing. In 1948, she decided to create an 8-inch plastic play doll, and Ginny was born.

One of the novel things about the new Ginny doll was that the clothing was available separately from the doll. The original Vogue dolls retailed for only $1.98, in underwear and shoes, ready to dress. The outfits retailed from $1 to $2.98. Mrs. Graves designed most of the clothing, and the wonderful detailed outfits—including hats, purses, and snap shoes—added immeasurably to the doll's popularity.

A succession of models were produced in the 1950s, starting with a painted-eye doll, followed by a strung sleep-eye doll. Next, a straight-leg walker was produced, followed by a straight-leg walker with molded (not painted) lashes. The final design before the head became vinyl was a bent-knee walker. In 1960, Ginny was produced with a vinyl (not hard-plastic) head, and many believe that was the beginning of the end for Ginny.

Mrs. Graves daughter, Virginia Graves Carlson, took over the company in 1960 and ran it until 1966. The vinyl head on the doll wasn't the only problem for Ginny dolls in the early 1960s. The Vogue Doll Company would not advertise on TV, which put Ginny at a great disadvantage against Barbie, who was capturing the hearts and playtime of little girls everywhere (naturally, on TV). So Ginny's profile with little girls became smaller, and it became harder for the doll to compete with Barbie.

In 1972, the Vogue Company (along with Ginny) was sold to Tonka Company, which produced Ginny in Hong Kong (the first time the doll wasn't produced in the United States). Several more management changes ensued, including a sale to Dakin in 1986. The quality of the doll design and costuming suffered during this period. Finally, in 1995, well-known doll artist Wendy Lawton and several associates bought the rights to Ginny and the Vogue Dolls name, and Ginny as a quality doll was back. The dolls again became all hard plastic, and the costuming was inspired by the original Graves designs of the 1950s. Ginny dolls are still being produced today by the new Vogue Company, including a line of Ginny dolls which are reproductions of the 1950s dolls and outfits.

Market Report: Ginny is still a hot doll, although not as blazing hot as she was just a few years back. That said, truly exceptional Ginnys can bring astronomical prices, such as a recent sale on eBay of a MIB strung Ginny in a rare Vogue special outfit for $2,100, and other sales on eBay of strung and transitional Ginnys MIB for between $800 to $1,200. However, an excellent strung doll in

Ginny strung, painted lash.
"High color." Edie #52. All 1950s
Ginny's are hard plastic with
swivel heads and 5-piece toddler
bodies. 8", c. 1952. Mark: VOGUE
DOLL (back). $600 MIB, dealer.

Ginny strung, painted lash.
"High color." Iva #53. 8", c. 1952.
Mark: VOGUE DOLL (back).
$600 MIB, dealer.

Two strung, painted lash Ginnys.
Left, "TV Ginny," right, "Away We
Go" Ginny. Both 8", c. 1953 (TV
Ginny) and 1955. $500+ each,
dealers. Courtesy Theriault's.

a common outfit has declined in value since the late 1990s, as have all walking dolls.

The Ginny dolls which are most sought after by collectors are the 1950s hard-plastic Ginnys, and the most sought after of those are the strung dolls (the dolls before Ginny became a walker) and the "transitional" dolls with their heavy, earlier hard-plastic and transitional skin tones. All 1950s Ginnys are highly collectible, however, especially those in their original, tagged outfits.

The later vinyl Ginnys produced by Lesney, Dakin, and others, even MIB, will usually sell for less than $20 online. The latest 1990s and early 2000 Vogues have a nice following, and time will tell what they will bring on the secondary market.

Online/Offline Report: Ginny is widely available online, with more than 3,000 Ginny items on eBay at any given time. Competition for the rarest 1950s Ginnys online is very fierce, so expect to pay top dollar (often above prices from dealers or auction houses) for rare items. Also expect a glut of played-with, non-original Ginnys from all other time periods on eBay, with prices accordingly depressed for these items. Otherwise, availability and prices are comparable for all venues for most excellent-to-mint 1950s items.

Prices and Characteristics: All 1950s and 1960s Ginnys are hard plastic and 8 inches in size. Prices are for dolls in original clothing, in condition as noted with prices from all markets unless Internet price is noted.

Painted-Eye Ginny Dolls

Painted-eye Ginny dolls were made from 1948 to 1950. The dolls have heavy hard plastic with mohair wigs, and painted eyes, and are marked "VOGUE" on their heads and "VOGUE DOLL" on their backs. Transitional dolls have this earlier, heavy hard plastic, pale coloring, and mohair wigs, but sleep eyes. Some outfits were untagged, others tagged "Vogue Dolls" or "Vogue Dolls, Inc., Medford, Mass."

GINNY, EARLY AND PAINTED EYES

Toddles
See Vogue.

Painted Eyes, Crib Crowd
Price: $600
Condition: VG
Painted eyes, bent-leg baby body; represent babies.

Painted Eyes, Strung
Price: $200–$300
Condition: Av
For dolls in average condition but original dress.

"My Tiny Miss" painted-lash walker Ginny. #44. Walker toddler body. 8″, c. 1954. Mark: Ginny / Vogue Dolls Inc. /Pat. Pend / Made in USA (back). $200, dealer. Courtesy Theriault's.

Playpal-size walking Ginny. Vinyl head, hard-plastic body. 36″, c. 1960. Courtesy Theriault's.

Black Ginny painted-lash walker, outfit #54. 8″, c. 1954. Mark: Ginny / Vogue Dolls Inc / Pat Pend / made in USA (back). $2,000+, dealer. Courtesy Theriault's.

Painted Eyes, Strung
Price: $400–$500
Condition: Mint

Strung, Transitional, Wee Willie Winkie
Price: $800
Condition: MIB
Poodle wig.

Transitional
Price: $500+
Condition: Mint
Transitional dolls generally are priced above their strung Ginny counterparts for dolls of like condition.

Transitional, Holly Boy
                              Date: 1950
Price: $1,000
Condition: MIB

Strung Ginny Dolls

Strung Ginny dolls were made from 1950 to 1953. They have glass sleep eyes and painted lashes. Dolls are marked "VOGUE" on their heads and "VOGUE DOLL" on their backs; some costumes are tagged "Vogue" or "Original Vogue Dolls, Inc" in blue script on white.

GINNY, STRUNG

Strung Ginny
Price: $200 to $300
Condition: VG

Brows faded off or very green, outfit and other doll flaws, messy wigs, but original outfit.

Strung Ginny
Price: $300–$400
Condition: Ex
For most dolls.

Strung Ginny
Price: $400–$500
Condition: Mint
Mint, in most outfits.

Strung Ginny
Price: $600–$800
Condition: MIB
For most dressed dolls, more for rarer dolls.

Strung Ginny, Basic
Price: $350–$500
Condition: MIB
For basic dolls in underwear.

Strung Ginny, Desirable Outfit or Hair
Price: $500–$600
Condition: Mint

Strung Ginny, Ballet
Price: $1,000
Condition: Mint
With wrist tag.

Strung Ginny, Black, Hawaiian
Price: $950
Condition: VG
More if mint; black early Ginnys are rare.

*Lesney Ginny. Vinyl. 8", c. 1978.
$10 MIB, eBay.*

*Molded lash walker Ginny. 8", c.
1955. Mark: GINNY / VOGUE
DOLLS / INC. / PAT NO. 2687594
/ MADE IN U.S.A. (back) and
"Medford" tag, clothes.*

For desirable dolls such as platinum blondes,
Tiny Miss, Gadabouts, Debutante #64, "Ginger,"
and others.

Strung Ginny, Glad
Price: $600
Condition: Ex

Strung Ginny, Poodle Wig
Price: $425–$550
Condition: Ex
Tagged dress.

Strung Ginny, "Special" Vogue Outfit
Price: $2,100
Condition: MIB
Very rare.

Strung Ginny, Talon Zipper, Tosca Wig
Price: $565
Condition: Ex
Dynel wig, party dress from Talon Zipper series.

Strung, Margie, Kindergarten Series
Price: $350
Condition: Ex
No dress tag.

Strung, Merrilee, Christmas
Price: $1,250
Condition: MIB
Rare Christmas doll.

Painted-Lash Walker Ginnys (PLW)

Painted-Lash Walker Ginnys (PLW) were
made in 1954. They had straight-leg walking bodies and sleep eyes with painted
lashes. They are marked "VOGUE" on the
head and "GINNY / VOGUE DOLLS /
INC. / PAT. PEND / MADE IN U.S.A." on
the back. Clothing is tagged "Vogue Dolls,
Inc., Medford, Mass. U.S.A., Reg. U.S. Pat
Off." This is called the "Medford" tag.

GINNY, PLW

PLW Ginny
Price: $150+
Condition: VG or Av
Played with, mussy hair, clothes with flaws,
green/faded eyebrows.

PLW Ginny
Price: $200–$250
Condition: Ex

PLW Ginny
Price: $250–$300
Condition: Mint

PLW Ginny
Price: $300–$400
Condition: MIB

PLW Ginny, Black
Price: $1,100
Condition: MIB

PLW Ginny, Hawaiian
Price: $2,100
Condition: Ex
At auction.

PLW, Nan, Kindergarten Series
Price: $725
Condition: MIB
#32; pristine mint.

PLW, with Trunk, Wardrobe
Price: $350
Condition: Ex

Straight-Leg, Molded-Lash Walker Ginnys (MLW)

Straight-leg, molded-lash walker Ginnys
(MLW) were made from 1955 to 1956. They
have sleep eyes with plastic molded lashes
and walking bodies with straight legs. They
are marked "Vogue" on the head and
"Ginny / Vogue Dolls Inc / Pat No.2687594 /
Made In USA" on the back. The clothing
also has the "Medford" tag.

GINNY, MLW

MLW Ginny
Price: $100–$140
Condition: Av
Dolls with messy hair, clothes not mint, other
flaws.

MLW Ginny
Price: $150–$175
Condition: Ex

MLW Ginny
Price: $200+
Condition: Mint

MLW Ginny
Price: $250–$350
Condition: MIB

Ginny Outfits, 1955–1959
Price: $50–$100
Condition: Ex
General price for boxed outfit, box without out-
fit designation; more for rare or early outfits.

Bent-Knee Walker Ginnys (BKW)

Bent-knee walker Ginnys (BKW) were
made from 1957 to 1962. They have sleep
eyes with plastic molded lashes and walking
bodies with jointed, or "bend" knees. They
are marked "Vogue" on the head and
"Ginny / Vogue Dolls Inc / Pat No.2687594 /
Made In USA" on the back. The clothing is
tagged "Vogue Dolls, Inc" in blue print on a
white tag.

GINNY, BKW

BKW Ginny
Price: $75+
Condition: VG/Av

BKW Ginny
Price: $120–$125
Condition: Ex

BKW Ginny
Price: $150–$175+
Condition: Mint

BKW Ginny
Price: $200+
Condition: MIB

BKW, Cowgirl
Price: $180
Condition: VG+

LATER GINNY DOLLS

Dakin Ginny
Date: 1986–1995
Internet: $10–$20

Condition: MIB
Vinyl.

Lesney Ginny

Date: 1970s
Internet: $10 to $20

Condition: MIB
Vinyl.

Ginny, Crib Crowd, Bunny

Date: 2003
Internet: $230–$270

Condition: NRFB
LE 275 from the Vogue UFDC 22003 convention luncheon. Reproduction of 1950s doll.

Hard Plastics, Unmarked and Smaller Companies

The advent of hard plastic dolls in the late 1940s and early 1950s was an important innovation—finally, dolls that were truly unbreakable! Sure, there were celluloid dolls first, but celluloid dolls were much more fragile, and, of course, had the serious downside that they sometimes exploded when exposed to high temperatures.

It's hard to pin down who made the very first hard plastic doll, although some experts attribute that doll to an Ideal baby doll in 1940. Others report small hard plastic dolls being sold in the early 1940s as well. But World War II and material shortages intervened, and so it wasn't until the late 1940s that hard plastic dolls started to be mass-produced. The first hard plastic dolls were advertised in the Sears catalog in 1946, and then the entire hard plastic doll industry exploded. Hard plastic dolls reigned until vinyl dolls took over in the late 1950s and early 1960s, although some collector dolls today are still made from hard vinyl plastic. (Some information in this paragraph is taken from *Hard Plastic Dolls, II* by Polly and Pam Judd, © 1989).

Just as with composition dolls, many hard plastic dolls were made by companies that didn't mark the doll heads, because the doll heads were then distributed to other companies to be put together, dressed, and sold. This was a common practice that drives doll collectors absolutely crazy today.

- **A Note on The Artisan Novelty Company:** Artisan made hard plastic dolls in Gardenia, California, and is best known for its Raving Beauty doll. For many years, the unmarked Raving Beauty couldn't be identified by collectors. Then several dolls were found in original packaging. Raving Beauty was made from 1950 to 1956. Some clothing for Raving Beauty is tagged "California Originals by Michele." Raving Beauties were generally walkers, although some strung dolls have been found, and her hair was made from a distinctive fiber called Ravon, a type of dynel fiber. Raving Beauty was a deluxe doll and sold at a high price for the time—from $12.95 to $25. (Some information in this paragraph is taken from an article by Nancy Sanderson in the June/July 2003 issue of *Doll Reader*.)

Market Report: As with most other unmarked dolls and dolls from smaller companies, the market is somewhat soft right now. Collectors with a sharp eye can find unmarked but all-original hard plastic dolls of excellent quality for prices below those of comparable-quality marked dolls. Also, mint and complete dolls from smaller companies may also be good buys, with their quality sometimes rivaling that of dolls made by the larger, better-known companies.

Online/Offline Report: Prices for unmarked hard plastic dolls are relatively low on eBay. Dolls from smaller companies, such as Raving Beauty from Artisan and Sandra Sue from Richwood, are also relatively low, and beware of sellers on eBay who sell their doll as a "Raving Beauty" when it clearly is not that doll. Dealers and auction houses try to seek out the best mint and complete hard plastic dolls for their customers when possible.

Prices and Characteristics: All dolls are in excellent condition and from the late 1940s or 1950s, except as noted.

HARD PLASTIC DOLLS

Amanda Jane, Jinx
Size: 7.5″   Date: 1958
                    Internet: $70

Ginny clone.

Hard plastic child. *5-piece body. Unmarked, possibly a Nancy Lee with floss hair. c. late 1940s–early 1950s. $100, eBay.*

Roberta, Lu Ann Simms walker. *Hard plastic head, 5-piece walker body. 15", c. 1953. Mark: 170 (head) Made in USA (back); original tag. Courtesy Theriault's.*

Sandra Sue, Richwood Toys. *Hard plastic head, 5-piece high-heeled body. 8", c. 1956. Mark: 3 (inside upper arms). Courtesy Theriault's.*

Artisan Novelty Company, Raving Beauty
Size: 19″   Date: 1950s
     Internet: $75–$100
In 1950s clothing.

Artisan Novelty Company, Raving Beauty
Size: 19″   Date: 1950–1956
Price: $210   Internet: $130
Cowgirl or desirable original outfit.

Artisan Novelty Company, Raving Beauty
Size: 19″   Date: 1950–1956
     Internet: $250
Mint.

Child, Cowgirl
Size: 19″   Internet: $145
Mark: unmarked

Child, Jointed Knees
Size: 27″   Internet: $160
Original dress.

Cosmopolitan, Ginger
Size: 8″   Internet: $135
In Ginger Visits Mickey Mouse original cowgirl outfit or other desirable outfit. Holster has Mickey Mouse logo.

Duchess Dolls
Size: 7″   Internet: $10–$15
Mint. Sometimes referred to as "Gas Station" dolls. Stapled costumes, 1-piece torso/legs, sometimes swivel neck, jointed arms.

Eegee, Susan Stroller
Size: 17″   Internet: $100
With hang tag. Mama crier.

England, Rosebud
Size: 14″   Internet: $95
Baby.
Mark: ROSEBUD (head) MADE IN ENGLAND PAT#667906 (body)

Eugenia Doll Company, Lady
Size: 18″   Internet: $270
Green-apple gown trimmed with rose and ribbon; attributed to Eugenia.
Mark: unmarked

Eugenia Doll Company, Playmate
Size: 16″   Date: Late 1940s
     Internet: $210
Mark: unmarked

Eugenia Doll Company, Girl
Size: 21″   Internet: $500
Rarer mold size (most are 18″), all original.

Fryeburg, Mary Jane, Terri Lee Look-Alike
Size: 16″   Date: 1953
Price: $60   Internet: $60–$80
VG. The Terri Lee Company sued Fryeburg and won; doll produced in 1953 only.

Fryeburg, Mary Jane, Terri Lee Look-Alike
Size: 16″   Date: 1953
Price: $225
Mint.

Girl, Made In USA Mark
Size: 14″
Price: $90

Queen For A Day. *Swivel head, 1-piece torso/legs, jointed arms. Manufactured for Mutual Broadcasting. 8", c. 1950s. $20, eBay. Courtesy Ellen Johnson.*

A & H Christmas doll. *Swivel head, 1-piece torso/legs, jointed arms, swivel head. Sold in a plastic bell with handle. 8", c. 1963. Mark: A & H Doll, Woodside, NY (on bell bottom). $25, dealer.*

A & H Aquamarine Birthstone doll. *Swivel head, 1-piece torso/legs, jointed arms, swivel head. Sold in plastic bell with handle. 8", c. 1961. Mark: A & H Doll, Woodside NY (on bell bottom). $25, dealer.*

Golfer, "Made in the USA"
Size: 14.5"   Internet: $160
Original golfing outfit.

Hollywood Dolls, Queen for a Day
Size: 6"   Internet: $20
MIB. Also see "Nancy Ann" section.

Impco, Girl
Size: 21"   Internet: $130
NRFB.

Girl, Margaret-Type Face, "Made in the USA"
Size: 14"   Internet: $150
Madame Alexander Margaret-type face.
Mark: 14/Made in USA (back)

Marx, Miss Seventeen
Size: 14"   Date: 1960s
                   Internet: $95
VG. Barbie clone.

Mary-Lu Walker
Size: 17"
Price: $60
MIB.

Nun Doll, Marshall Field's
Size: 13"   Internet: $230
MIB, wool habit, rosary, cross, Marshall Field's box.

Paris Doll Company, Rita
Size: 27"   Internet: $100–$150
Excellent.

Paris Doll Company, Rita
Size: 27"   Internet: $185
With box and extra clothing.

Paris Doll Company, Rita
Size: 27"   Internet: $580
Pristine mint. Walker.

Plastic Molded Arts
Size: 8"   Internet: $100
MIB, Joanie Walker, a Ginny clone.

Richwood Toy Company, Sandra Sue
                   Internet: $70–$80
For nude doll or doll in original costume with flaws.

Richwood Toy Company, Sandra Sue
Size: 8"   Internet: $130–$180
Mint doll in original outfit; higher price for MIB. More for rarer outfits.
Mark: Generally unmarked, sometimes a number under arms, legs.

Richwood Toy Company, Twins
Size: 8"   Internet: $230
MIB.

Roberta Doll Company
Size: 18"
Price: $70   Internet: $75

Schilling, Talking Baby Doll
Size: 22"   Date: 1949
                   Internet: $325

Corrine's Brides of All Nations, Sweden. *1-piece torso/legs, jointed arms, swivel neck. With original box and pamphlet. 80 countries available. Doll unmarked. $25, dealer.*

Hard plastic, unmarked. *These dolls are sometimes referred to as "gas station" dolls because they were often given away as gas premiums in the mid-20th century. Only arms jointed. 7". $3–$10 on eBay (depends on outfit and condition).*

MIB. Cloth body, vinyl arms; legs, molded hair, voiced by J.J. Warner Recording Studios of California.
Mark: on tag: Schilling Talking Doll. She Talks! Laughs! Cries! Gurgles! Sobs! With a real human voice.

Sutton, A.D., DeDo Doll
Size: 11.5"   Internet: $195
VG; for dolls with stuck eyes.

Sutton, A.D., DeDo Doll
Size: 11.5"   Internet: $465
Mint. Eyes change like Blythe. Cult following.

Unmarked, Annie Oakley
Size: 20"   Internet: $475
VG. Walker with sleep eyes, Annie Oakley cowgirl outfit.

Unmarked, Child, Walker
Size: 19"   Internet: $140
Burgundy velvet winter outfit with hat, white muffs.

Unmarked, Lady, Formal Gown, Fur Stole
Size: 14"   Internet: $170
Formal tulle skirt attached to red felt top, red flowers.

Unmarked, United Airlines Doll
Size: 14"   Internet: $300
Comes with her large United Airlines Utility Bag and a vinyl handbag; in uniform.

Unmarked, Girl, Floss Wig
Size: 14"
Price: $220

Unmarked, Girl, Original Blue Felt Suit
Size: 20"
Price: $130

Unmarked, Toni Look-Alike, Skating Costume
Size: 15"   Internet: $260
All original.
Mark: Made in USA (back)

Unmarked, Meg from *Little Women*-Type
Size: 15"   Internet: $300
All original.
Mark: Made in USA (back)

Valentine, Roxanne Walker
Size: 21"   Internet: $190
MIB, with red camera.
Mark: 210

Virga, Lolly-Pop
Size: 8"   Internet: $70
Mint, lilac hair.

Walker, "Made in the USA"
Size: 14"   Internet: $160
Possible Raving Beauty.

Walker Doll, Unmarked
Size: 20"
Price: $130

Wanda the Walking Wonder Doll
Internet: $80
Walks with key-wind mechanism in back. Wearing original banner. Late 1940s.

Winnie the Walking and Talking Doll
Size: 24"
Price: $110
MIB.

Hasbro

Hasbro, one of the great 20th-century toy companies, was founded in 1923 by two brothers, Henry and Helal Hassenfeld. At first the company produced mainly school supplies, but by the 1940s, the company was making toys. Over the years, Hasbro has survived many other contemporary toy companies and has come to include other companies such as Parker Brothers, Playskool, and Tonka.

Hasbro started to make dolls in the 1960s. Besides the venerable G.I. Joe (see the G.I. Joe section), Hasbro is known for the 1980s Jem dolls, Little Miss No Name, and several other mass-produced vinyl dolls of the 1960s to today, including the very unusual Peteena Poodle doll, Charlie's Angels, Storykins (A Liddle Kiddles-type doll), and a host of others. Hasbro is still producing toys and dolls today.

Market Report: The market for most Hasbro play dolls is slowly increasing. For instance, the Jem dolls have only been considered collectible for the last few years, and Storykins and other Kiddle-like dolls are starting to be collected, whereas a few years back, you could pick up a Storykin for $1 from a bin at a flea market.

Online/Offline Report: Availability for vintage Hasbro dolls is greatest on the Internet; other than G.I. Joes and an occasional Little Miss No Name, the dolls are not heavily sold by dealers or auction houses. When found at all venues, prices are comparable.

Prices and Characteristics: All Hasbro dolls are vinyl, most with 5-piece bodies.

HASBRO DOLLS

ABBA, Bjorn and Benny
Internet: $200
Condition: MIB

Charlie's Angels, Set
Internet: $125–$175
Condition: MIB
Sabrina, Jill, and Kelly.

Dolly Darlings
Size: 4"   Date: 1968
                           Internet: $50
Condition: MOC

Dolly Darlings, Boy Trap
Size: 4"   Date: 1968
                           Internet: $130
Condition: MOC

Dolly Darlings, Flying Nun
Size: 4"   Date: 1968
                           Internet: $35
Condition: Ex

Dolly Darlings, John and His Pets
Size: 4"   Date: 1968
                           Internet: $90
Condition: MIB
In plastic case.

Dolly Darlings, Slumber Party
Size: 4"   Date: 1968
                           Internet: $30
Condition: MIB

Dolly Darlings, Susie Goes to School
Size: 4"   Date: 1968
                           Internet: $50
Condition: MOC

Elvis Presley Doll
                           Internet: $35
Condition: Ex

Jem Dolls, Various, Loose
Size: 12.5"   Date: 1985–1986
                           Internet: $15–$30
Condition: Ex
All Jems belonged to rock bands and came with music tapes; the original band is the Holograms.

Jem, Aja, 1st Edition
Size: 12.5"   Date: 1986
                           Internet: $290
Condition: NRFB

Jem, Aja, 2nd Edition
Size: 12.5"   Date: 1986
                           Internet: $150–$180
Condition: NRFB

Jem, Jerrica, 1st Edition
Size: 12.5"   Date: 1985
                           Internet: $100
Condition: NRFB

Jem, Jerrica, 2nd Edition

Size: 12.5″   Date: 1985
                       Internet: $40
Condition: NRFB

Jem, Jetta

Size: 12.5″   Date: 1986
                       Internet: $60
Condition: NRFB
From the fictional rock band the Misfits.

Jem, Kimber, 1st Edition

Size: 12.5″   Date: 1986
                       Internet: $180
Condition: NRFB

Jem, Kimber, 2nd Edition

Size: 12.5″   Date: 1986
                       Internet: $125
Condition: NRFB
From the Holograms.

Jem, Raya, 2nd Edition

Size: 12.5″   Date: 1985
                       Internet: $125
Condition: NRFB

Jem, Rio

Size: 12.5″   Date: 1986
                       Internet: $25
Condition: NRFB
Male.

Jem, Roxy

Size: 12.5″   Date: 1986
                       Internet: $60–$80
Condition: NRFB

Jem, Roxy

Size: 12.5″   Date: 1986
                       Internet: $150
Condition: NRFB
With box and cassette; Misfits.

Jem, Shana

Size: 12.5″   Internet: $200–$300
Condition: NRFB
Black doll.

Jem, Shana, 1st or 2nd Edition

Size: 12.5″   Date: 1985
                       Internet: $200–$250
Condition: NRFB

Jem, Stormer, 2nd Edition

Size: 12.5″   Date: 1986
                       Internet: $40–$50
Condition: NRFB
Misfits.

Jem, Synergy

Size: 12.5″   Date: 1986
                       Internet: $60–$80
Condition: NRFB

Jem, Outfits, Various

                       Date: 1986
                       Internet: $40–$60
Condition: NRFB
For most common outfits.

Jem, Outfit, We Can Change It

                       Date: 1986
                       Internet: $600
Condition: NRFB
Flip-Side Fashion.

Jem, Outfit, Puttin' It All Together

                       Date: 1986
                       Internet: $500
Condition: NRFB
Flip-Side Fashion.

Jem, Outfit, Gold Rush

                       Date: 1986
                       Internet: $175
Condition: NRFB
Glitter & Gold Fashion.

Jem, Outfit, 24 Carat Sound

                       Date: 1986
                       Internet: $175
Condition: NRFB
Music Is Magic Fashion.

Jem, Rock 'N' Roll Gold Roadster Car

                       Date: 1986
                       Internet: $130
Condition: MIB

Leggy, With Outfits

                       Internet: $80
Condition: MOC

Little Miss No Name

                       Date: 1965
                       Internet: $165
Condition: NM
With tear, knit outfit.

Little Miss No Name

                       Date: 1965
                       Internet: $310–$360
Condition: NRFB
"The doll with the tear"; also on box: "please love me."

My Buddy

Size: 23″   Date: 1985
                       Internet: $190

Ultimate Hair Queen Amidala,
Star Wars Episode I. *Vinyl. 11.5",*
c. 1998. $5 NRFB, eBay.

Condition: NRFB
Can be dressed in 3–6 month old clothing.

My Real Baby Doll

Date: 2000
Internet: $50

Condition: Ex
Loose, working.

My Real Baby Doll

Date: 2000
Internet: $75

Condition: MIB

Peteena Poodle

Size: 9"   Date: 1966
Internet: $50–$80

Condition: VG
Price for average Peteena, frequently with tail
missing.

Peteena Poodle

Size: 9"   Date: 1966
Internet: $150–$175

Condition: Ex
Fashion doll with dog's head, poodle-like hair
and retractable tail. Separate outfits available.
Price for Peteena in original outfit with tail.

Peteena Poodle, in "Surf's Up" Bikini

Size: 9"   Date: 1966
Internet: $155

Condition: Ex

Peteena Poodle, Outfits, Various

Size: 9"   Date: 1966
Internet: $80–$150

Condition: MIB

Peteena Poodle, Twinkletoes Outfit

Size: 9"   Date: 1966
Internet: $165

Condition: NRFB
Ballerina outfit.

Sindy

Size: 12"   Date: 1987–1990s
Internet: $10

Condition: Mint

Storykins, Various, Loose

Size: 2–3"   Date: 1968
Internet: $7–$20

Condition: Ex

Storykins, Rumpelstiltskin

Size: 2–3"   Date: 1968
Internet: $40

Condition: MOC

Storykins, Mother Hubbard

Size: 2–3"   Date: 1968
Internet: $70

Condition: Ex
With accessories.

Storykins, Snow White and Dwarf

Size: 2–3"   Date: 1968
Internet: $130

Condition: MOC
On record package; dwarf Doc.

Storykins, Snow White Play Set

Size: 2–3"   Date: 1968
Internet: $135

Condition: Ex

Bright Star. *Composition socket head, 5-piece body. 17", c. 1938. Unmarked, has original paper label. Courtesy Theriault's.*

Horsman composition baby. *Composition head, cloth body, original box and presentation. 13", c. 1915. Unmarked, box marked Horsman Dolls, Inc. / America's best-loved dolls. $300, dealer.*

World of Love, Peace Gift Set
Size: 10″   Date: 1970s
                    Internet: $100
Condition: MIB
Fashion doll; T-shirt says "Peace," comes with midi dress.

Horsman, E.I.

The E.I. Horsman Co., founded in 1865, sold imported German dolls during the end of the 19th century. By the end of the 1890s, Horsman started producing dolls, first with the cloth Babyland rag dolls. In 1909, Horsman introduced the composition head semi-plush Billiken doll, and from that point on Horsman began to manufacture great and varied numbers of composition dolls—Mama Dolls, Campbell Kids, HEbee-SHEbees, and a notable list of others.

Horsman changed and adapted with the times, and went from composition to hard plastic production (although most of its dolls from the hard plastic era are not considered classics today). Horsman again found its stride in the vinyl doll era starting in the early 1960s, and it produced countless baby and other play dolls. Baby boomers fondly remember many of the Horsman dolls, in-

cluding Mary Poppins, Poor Pitiful Pearl, and Patty Duke.

Horsman was one of the last large United States companies that manufactured dolls in the United States, which it did until 1986. The company, under various owners, has continued to produce some vinyl dolls, including vinyl reproductions of well-known Horsman composition dolls, in Asia ever since.

Market Report: The market for Horsman dolls is relatively soft right now, except for mint and all-original composition dolls, which are increasing in value. The later vinyl Horsman dolls, including MIB Mary Poppins, Patty Duke, and others, have declined in value in the past few years due to the eBay effect.

Online/Offline Report: Prices for better composition Horsman dolls are comparable at all venues, with excellent examples available via eBay, dealers, and auction houses. Later Horsman vinyl play dolls are widely available on eBay.

Prices and Characteristics: All dolls listed are in excellent condition; Horsman bisque dolls are from the early 1920s, and prices are from non-Internet sources.

Horsman's Campbell Kid. Composition socket head, 5-piece body. Unmarked, has original paper label. Courtesy Theriault's.

Patty Cake. All cloth, for FAO Schwarz. Courtesy Grace L. Steer.

HORSMAN, BISQUE

Baby Grumpy
Size: 24″   Date: 1924
Price: $700
Cloth body, composition hands.

Dolly Rosebud
Size: 16.5″
Price: $550
All original, including banner on front of dress, composition swivel head, cloth body with composition limbs, mohair wig, sleep eyes.
Mark: Copr. E.I.H.Co.

Horsman, Character Baby
Size: 10″
Price: $275
Molded and painted hair, sleep eyes, celluloid hands, cloth body.

Tynie Baby, All-Bisque
Size: 8″
Price: $525

Horsman, Composition

All dolls are in excellent condition, except as noted, with prices mixed from all sources.

HORSMAN, COMPOSITION

Baby
Size: 19″   Date: 1911
Price: $200–$320
All original, cloth body, limbs composition, molded hair.
Mark: E.I.H.CO. INC; Horsman doll-MFD in USA (tag)

Baby
Size: 22″   Date: 1940s
Price: $160
Molded hair. Later baby with Magic Skin lower limbs.

Baby
Size: 24″
Price: $305

Dolly Dreamland. Hard plastic, mother-made bridal gown. All composition, swivel head, 5-piece body. 15", c. 1953. Mark: 170 (head) MADE IN U..S.A. / 170 (back).

Baby Precious. Composition head, lower limbs, cloth body. 16.5". Un-marked, tag marked "Horsman's / Baby Precious / A Horsman /Super Quality / Doll." $400, dealer.

Mint.
Mark: E.I.H.C

Baby Brother
Size: 21"   Date: 1930s
Price: $275

Baby Bumps
Size: 16"   Date: 1910–1914
Price: $250
First successful Can't Break 'Em character doll. Face similar to Kämmer & Reinhardt 100 baby.

Baby Dainty
Size: 20"   Date: 1930s
Price: $205
Mark: HORSMAN

Baby Dimples
Size: 13"   Date: 1920s
Price: $190
Cloth body, composition lower limbs, molded hair.
Mark: E.I.H. CO.INC

Baby Dimples
Size: 18"   Date: 1920s
Price: $300
Mint.
Mark: E.I.H. CO.INC

Baby Dimples
Size: 22"   Date: 1920s
Price: $180
VG; largest model made.
Mark: E.I.H. CO. INC

Baby, Twins
Size: 15"
Price: $600
Pristine mint, all-original baby set.

Billiken
Size: 12"   Date: 1909
Price: $300
Mint. Composition head, molded hair, plush body.

Mary Poppins. Vinyl. Earlier doll has real umbrella; later 1973 version comes with cardboard umbrella. Earlier doll has sticker for Horsman's 100th anniversary, c. 1965. Both 12″. $100+ NRFB, dealer (1965 doll) and $30 NRFB, dealer (1973 doll).

Poor Pitiful Pearl. Vinyl. 11.75″. Mark: Horsman Dolls Inc. / J11. Courtesy Marsha L. Cumpton.

Bride
Size: 18″
Price: $75–$100
Original outfit.

Bright Star
Size: 18″   Date: 1940
Price: $250
Shirley Temple look-alike.
Mark: unmarked.

Campbell Kid
Size: 12″   Date: 1910–1914
Price: $350
MIB; original shorts outfit with knit top.
Mark: Campbell's Kid/A Horsman Doll/Permission of Campbell Soup Company (paper tag)

Campbell Kid
Size: 12″   Date: 1910–1914
Price: $450
MIB; original chef's hat outfit.
Mark: same as above

Campbell Kid
Size: 12″   Date: 1930s
Price: $390
Original muslin chef's hat outfit, painted socks and shoes.
Mark: Campbell's' Kid-A Horsman Doll (paper label)

Campbell Kid
Size: 12″   Date: 1948
Price: $160–$175

VG.
Mark: unmarked

Ella Cinders
Size: 18″   Date: 1925
Price: $500
Mint; painted surprise eyes.
Mark: ©/1925/M.N.S. (head) Horsman/Doll/ Mf'd U.S.A. (jacket), Ella Cinders (tag)

Girl, Unmarked
Size: 15″
Price: $200

Mama Baby
Size: 18″
Price: $80
Cloth body, composition lower limbs.

Mama Doll
Size: 22–25″   Date: 1930s
Price: $200–$250
Mark: E.I.H. © A.D.C. or similar

Tynie Baby
Size: 14″   Date: 1924
Price: $175
Mark: 1924/E I Horsman/Co Inc.

Horsman, Vinyl

Excellent condition except as noted; prices for vinyl Horsman dolls are predominantly from the Internet, with non-Internet pricing noted.

Ruthie. Vinyl head, 5-piece hard plastic body. 16.5", c. 1960s. Mark: HORSMAN / T16. $30, eBay.

Pitty Patty. Vinyl head and lower limbs, cloth body with "tick tock" mechanism; doll makes "tick tock" sound when you turn her over. 13", c. 1969. Mark: 50 / (c) HORS-MAN DOLLS / 67514l. Courtesy Geneva Wallen Collection.

HORSMAN, VINYL

Cindy
Size: 10"   Date: 1957
All Markets: $60
In undies.

Cindy
Size: 10"   Date: 1950s
                         Internet: $100–$140
MIB; Little Miss Revlon look-alike.

Cindy, With Wardrobe
Size: 10"   Date: 1957
All Markets: $250
MIB, with extensive trousseau.

Cindy (Hard Plastic)
Size: 16"   Date: 1950s
All Markets: $90
Hard plastic, earliest model.

Cindy, Black
Size: 18"   Date: 1950s
                         Internet: $300
VG.

Happy Baby
                         Date: late 1970s
                         Internet: $25–$30
MIB; laughs and giggles when tossed and bounced.

Little Debbie
                         Date: 1984
                         Internet: $15

Mint; made for McKee Baking Company; Snack Cakes doll.
Mark: HORSMAN DOLLS INC 1972

Love Me Baby
Size: 14"   Date: 1969
                         Internet: $50
Mark: HORSMAN DOLLS, INC./19 (c) 69 (head) HORSMAN DOLLS INC. (back)

Lu Ann Sims
Size: 17"   Date: 1953
                         Internet: $150+
Hard plastic Lu Ann.
Mark: 170

Mary Poppins
Size: 12"   Date: 1965
All Markets: $75–$100
MIB, more for pristine mint.

Mary Poppins
Size: 12"   Date: 1973
All Markets: $30–$40
MIB; cardboard umbrella.

Mary Poppins, Gift Set
Size: 12"   Date: 1965
All Markets: $200
With extra outfits, original cello.

Mary Poppins, Jane and Michael
                         Date: 1964
                         Internet: $75
VG, loose. Sold as set.

Mary Hoyer. All hard plastic, 5-piece body, original dress. 14". Same mark as above. This condition, $300 eBay. Mark: Original / Mary Hoyer / Doll (circle, back). Courtesy Ellen Johnson.

Mary Hoyer. All hard plastic, 5-piece body, original dress, molded hair under wig. Outfit from vintage Mary Hoyer pattern. 14". Same mark as in photo at left. $250, eBay. Courtesy of Nancy Jo French and Ms. Laura.

Mary Hoyer. All hard plastic, 5-piece body. 14". Same mark as in photo, far left. Courtesy Ellen Johnson.

Mary Poppins, Jane and Michael
Date: 1964
Internet: $275
MIB.

Mary Poppins, Walker
Size: 36"
Date: 1966
Internet: $255

Patty Duke
Date: 1965
Internet: $190
MIB.

Peggy Pen Pal
Date: 1970
Internet: $75
MIB.

Pippi Longstocking
Size: 11"
Date: 1972
Internet: $30

Pippi Longstocking
Size: 17.5"
Date: 1972
Internet: $75
Montgomery Ward exclusive, foam body, vinyl limbs.

Pippi Longstocking
Size: 19"
Date: 1972
Internet: $55

Poor Pitiful Pearl
Size: 11"
Date: 1963
Internet: $50
Loose.

Poor Pitiful Pearl
Size: 11"
Date: 1963
Internet: $100–$150
MIB in kerchief and poor dress, with rich outfit.

Poor Pitiful Pearl
Size: 18"
Date: 1963
Internet: $200–$250
MIB or pristine mint.

Princess Peggy
Size: 36"
Date: 1959
Internet: $135–$175
VG; Playpal-type doll.
Mark: HORSMAN 1959

Princess Peggy
Size: 36"
Date: 1959
Internet: $350
Mint: platinum hair.

Thirsty Walker
Size: 27"
Date: 1964
Internet: $165
MIB.

Walker
Size: 24"
Date: 1950s
Internet: $125
Mint.

Winnie the Pooh and Christopher Robin
Date: 1964
Internet: $350
MIB.

Hoyer, Mary

The Mary Hoyer doll introduced many little girls in the 1940s to knitting and crocheting. Mary Hoyer was born in 1901 in Lancaster County, Pennsylvania, and she was initially a designer of knit and crocheted fashions for infants and children. While designing such outfits in the 1930s, Mary Hoyer decided to create a doll that would have instruction booklets for making knitted and crocheted outfits for that doll. After an initial foray with the Ideal doll company that didn't pan out, Ideal sold dolls directly to the Hoyers so that they could market the doll themselves, and about 2,000 of this very first doll were sold.

Later in 1937, Mary had a doll designed for her by Bernard Lipfert, a well-known doll sculptor. This doll was 14 inches tall and composition, with jointing at the neck, shoulders, and hips, and with painted eyes. Soon after, the doll was given sleep eyes.

In 1946, production switched to hard plastic, and a 14-inch walking doll was produced. The walking doll was short lived due to production problems, and thereafter the doll became a non-walker. Also in the 1950s, an 18-inch doll called Gigi was made which was never as popular as the 14-inch doll and which is much harder to find today. At the end of the 1950s into the early 1960s, several vinyl dolls were produced, including a vinyl version of the original doll called Becky, and the high-heeled Vicky and several infant and toddler dolls.

Most Mary Hoyer dolls were sold through mail order. The majority were sold nude, ready to dress, with an accompanying booklet of knitting and crochet patterns for the doll. Some dolls were sold with kits that included all materials necessary to make a featured costume. However, the company also made well-constructed garments for the dolls which carried the "Mary Hoyer" label.

Mary Hoyer died in 2003. Her daughter revived the Mary Hoyer company in the 1990s and the company still exists today producing small, limited editions of dolls.

Market Report: Mary Hoyer doll prices hit a high a few years ago and prices have come down somewhat except for the very mint dolls. Keep your eyes out for the 18-inch Gigi, who is prized by collectors and much harder to find than the 14-inch dolls, and also for tagged Mary Hoyer clothing.

Online/Offline Report: Availability and prices for Mary Hoyer dolls are similar from most venues. Beware of unmarked items being sold as "Mary Hoyer" on eBay—most, although not all, Mary Hoyer dolls are clearly marked.

Prices, Characteristics, and Mark: Original / Mary Hoyer / Doll (circle, back); some dolls are unmarked. Most dolls are from the 1940s and 1950s, with exceptions noted.

MARY HOYER

Mary Hoyer, Composition
Size: 14″   Internet: $200–$220
Condition: VG

Mary Hoyer, Composition
Size: 14″   Internet: $300+
Condition: Ex

Mary Hoyer, Hard Plastic
Size: 14″
All Markets: $200–$300
Condition: VG

Mary Hoyer, Hard Plastic
Size: 14″   Internet: $335–$400
Condition: Ex
For dolls with great coloring, dressed in outfit from Mary Hoyer patterns.

Mary Hoyer, Hard Plastic
Size: 14″   Internet: $500+
Condition: MIB

Mary Hoyer, Hard Plastic
Size: 14″   Internet: $900
Condition: Mint
Rare hairstyle, red hair with braid at top of head, chignon, long cascading curl in back.

Mary Hoyer, Nun, Hard Plastic
Size: 14″   Internet: $500
Condition: MIB

Mary Hoyer, Sailor, Hard Plastic
Size: 14″
All Markets: $475

Ideal composition baby. Composition head, cloth body. 12", c. 1910s–1920s. $100, eBay.

Bonny Braids. Soft Magic Skin swivel head, all-Magic Skin body mama crier, with original box and accessories. Character from Dick Tracy comic strip. c. 1940s. Mark: CHICAGO TRIBUNE / IDEAL DOLL / U.S.A. MIB. This condition, $400 dealer.

Condition: Ex
With original box and extra outfits, all hand-made from Mary Hoyer patterns.

Mary Hoyer, Southern Belle, Hard Plastic
Size: 14"   Internet: $600
Condition: MIB

Gigi, Hard Plastic
Size: 18"   Date: 1950
                            Internet: $1,100
Condition: MIB

Outfit, Cocktail Dress
                            Internet: $130
Condition: Ex
Tagged.

Outfit, Ice Skates
                            Internet: $65
Condition: Ex

Mary Hoyer, Vicki or Becky, Vinyl
Size: 10–14"   Internet: $50–$100
Condition: Ex
Later vinyl versions of Mary Hoyer.

Mary Hoyer, Play Dolls, Vinyl
Size: 8–14"   Date: late 1950s on
                            Internet: $50–$100
Condition: Ex
Various toddler, infant, and baby dolls for play.

1999 UFDC Luncheon, Pair, Hard Plastic
Size: 14"   Date: 1999
                            Internet: $150
Condition: Mint
For male or female. Limited edition of 200. Female named Maryanna. In pink gown.

Book, *Mary Hoyer & Her Dolls*
                            Internet: $110–$140
Condition: Ex
By Mary Hoyer.

Ideal

Ideal dolls were the American play dolls for generations of little girls. The names of Ideal dolls are familiar to even non-collectors: Shirley Temple, Betsy Wetsy, Toni, Mary Hartline, Betsy McCall, Saucy Walker, Miss Revlon, Patti Playpal, Tammy, and Crissy, among others. Maybe Ideal was not always the first company to implement a new idea for dolls, but its dolls were always good quality and available at an affordable price and widely known and loved by children.

The Ideal Toy Corporation was started in 1907 by Morris Michtom and Aaron Cone as a manufacturer of dolls and teddy bears. The company's first doll was The Yellow Kid, a doll based on a comic strip. Throughout its history, Ideal understood and used licensed characters and the media to promote its dolls and make them desirable to children. By 1911, there were several composition dolls in its line.

During the composition doll era, Ideal hired Bernard Lipfert, one of the premier doll de-

Ideal Toni, tagged dress. *14", c. 1950s. Mark: P-90 / IDEAL DOLL / MADE IN USA and dress tag. $300, dealer; $225, eBay. Courtesy Marsha L. Cumpton.*

Ideal Toni with box, play wave set. *Hard plastic head and 5-piece body. 14", c. 1952. Mark: Ideal Doll / Made in USA (head) Ideal Doll / P-90 (back). Courtesy Theriault's.*

signers in America. He designed many classic dolls for Ideal and other companies, including Shirley Temple, Betsy Wetsy, Betsy McCall, and Toni.

Ideal made dolls out of nearly every material—composition, cloth, rubber, hard plastic, and finally vinyl. It was very savvy about the children's market, and always looked for new ways to make dolls interesting and affordable. It developed the "Magic Skin" dolls in the 1940s (which delighted children with their soft, realistic skin, but which have not held up well for collectors over time) and it also developed the blow-mold technology that created the first very large, affordable plastic dolls, the Patti Playpal line in the early 1960s. Ideal was also a genius in marketing, and in the 1960s it heavily advertised its dolls directly to children.

However, Ideal was not above seeing someone else's great idea in the market and changing and improving it for its own dolls. Cissy from Madame Alexander was one of the first adult-body fashion dolls, but it was a very expensive doll. Ideal took the idea and made its much-more affordable Miss Revlon line. Although American Character was the first company to come out with a grow-hair doll with Tressy, Ideal changed and improved the idea and had a runaway hit with Crissy.

The general shift to cheaper dolls and cheaper foreign labor on dolls spelled the end of Ideal (as it did for many American doll companies). By the early 1970s, Ideal was only a shadow of its former self. Dolls were produced into the early 1980s, but by then Ideal had been sold to CBS and the doll division was little more than an after-

Little Miss Revlon in original dress, box. Vinyl, original hairdo, box marked "Upsweep Bob, Blonde." 10.5″, c. 1958–1960. Mark: IDEAL DOLL / VT – 10 _. $250 MIB with original underwear and outfit, eBay.

Tiny Thumbelina in case. Vinyl head and hands, cloth body, turn knob in back and doll moves. Case also made in pink. 14″, c. 1962–1968. $125 working mint doll in case, eBay.

Pebbles Flintstone. Vinyl. 10″, c. 1965. Mark: © HANNA BAR- BARA PRODS. INC. / IDEAL TOY CORP. / F9-8 _ / 1965. $60, eBay.

thought. Ideal finally closed its doors in 1986, although rights to various dolls and trademarks are owned by several companies now, including Mattel.

Market Report: It is hard to give a general market report on Ideal dolls, since its output spans such a long time period and it made such a great variety of dolls. Look for specific market reports in the sections on Shirley Temple, Crissy, Patti Playpal, Tammy, and others.

Overall, however, the market for Ideal dolls is exceedingly healthy, due to the strong name recognition its dolls have with collectors today. Prices for mint, all-original dolls continue to rise, and look for later vinyl dolls with their original boxes. As with any 20th-century play dolls, there is an overabundance of seriously-played-with dolls on the market, and their prices have suffered in the last few years.

Online/Offline Report: Ideal dolls are abundant everywhere, with thousands of Ideal dolls for sale on eBay at any given time. However, fantastic mint dolls can be found from dealers, auction houses, and eBay, with prices for those dolls comparable from all sources. Look especially for bargains on fixer-upper Ideal dolls on eBay.

Prices and Characteristics: All Ideal dolls are in excellent condition, except as noted. For Shirley Temple dolls, please see the separate Shirley Temple section.

IDEAL, COMPOSITION

Baby

Size: 18–24″	Date: 1930s–1940s
Price: $150	Internet: $190

Cloth body, composition limbs.

Baby, Flirty-Eyes

Size: 20″	Date: 1930s
	Internet: $325

Buster Brown

Size: 17″	Date: 1929
	Internet: $430

"Buster Brown Shoes" metal buttons. Cloth body, composition lower limbs, tin sleep eyes.

Charlie McCarthy, Hand Puppet

Size: 10.5″	
Price: $100	Internet: $60

Printed cloth body, monocle.
Mark: Edger Bergens Charlie McCarthy Inc
Made in USA

Child

Size: 14″
Price: $110
Tin sleep eyes, braids.

Child's Muff
Price: $675
Mint; head turns.

Deanna Durbin
Size: 20″   Date: 1935
            Internet: $320–$400
VG; flaws. Deanna Durbins have 5-piece composition bodies, sleep eyes.
Mark: Deanna Durbin/Ideal

Deanna Durbin
Size: 21″   Date: 1940s
Price: $550
Mint.
Mark: Deanna Durbin/Ideal Doll (head) Ideal Doll (body)

Deanna Durbin
Size: 21″   Date: 1940s
Price: $810   Internet: $1,000
MIB.

Flexy, Baby Snooks (Fanny Brice)
            Date: late 1930s
Price: $240   Internet: $120
Mint. "Flexy" dolls have extra posability—arms, legs with wire.

Flexy, Boy
Size: 13″   Date: late 1930s
Price: $100
VG.

Flexy, Mortimer Snerd
Size: 12.5″   Date: late 1930s
Price: $100   Internet: $60
Good. The ventriloquist dummy sidekick of Charlie McCarthy.

Flossie Flirt
Size: 14–24″   Date: 1925
Price: $300+   Internet: $200–$300+
Cloth body, composition limbs, flirty eyes, mohair wig. For all sizes.

Judy Garland
Size: 16″   Date: 1939
Price: $1,000   Internet: $800
Near mint.
Mark: IDEAL DOLL/MADE IN USA (head) U.S.A./16 (back)

Judy Garland
Size: 21″   Date: 1940
Price: $600   Internet: $400
VG: for dolls with crazing and cloudy eyes, replaced clothing.

Judy Garland
Size: 21″   Date: 1940
Price: $1,000   Internet: $700

Near mint.
Mark: Ideal Doll/18 (back)

Princess Beatrix
Size: 22″   Date: 1938
            Internet: $270
Flirty eyes, original clothes.
Mark: unmarked

Snow White
Size: 16″   Date: 1937
Price: $335   Internet: $400
VG; see Shirley Temple section for more prices.
Mark: SHIRLEY TEMPLE

Ideal, Wood/Composition

All in excellent condition. The wood/composition Ideal dolls were produced from approximately 1935 to 1940.

IDEAL, WOOD/COMPOSITION

Jiminy Cricket
Size: 9″   Internet: $170
VG.

Jiminy Cricket
Size: 9″   Internet: $450
Mint.

Jiminy Cricket
Size: 9″
Price: $750
MIB; original, unplayed with.

Pinocchio
Size: 8–10″
Price: $225–$275

Superman
Size: 13″   Internet: $1,400
Rare, jointed at head, shoulders, elbows, hips, waist, knees, ankles, and hands.

Ideal, Hard Plastic

All dolls listed are in excellent condition, except as noted. The Ideal hard plastic dolls were produced from approximately 1947 through the 1950s.

IDEAL, HARD PLASTIC

Baby
Size: 15″
Price: $60
Condition: Ex

Betsy Wetsy, Various Sizes
Size: 11–16″   Internet: $60–$80
Condition: Av
Often redressed.

Betsy Wetsy
Size: 11″   Internet: $80
Condition: VG

Betsy Wetsy
Size: 14″   Internet: $200–$250
Condition: Ex
Molded hair, Betsy Wetsys have soft vinyl bodies.
Mark: 14 IDEAL (head) IDEAL (back)

Betsy Wetsy
Size: 16″   Internet: $110–$125
Condition: VG

Betsy Wetsy With Trunk
Size: 14″   Internet: $155
Condition: VG
With trunk, some accessories.
Mark: 14 IDEAL DOLL/MADE IN USA

Bonnie Braids, Walker
Size: 13″   Internet: $100
Condition: Ex

Dy-Dee Baby, With Layette Case
Size: 15″
Price: $300
Condition: NMIB
Rubber body, applied ears, original labeled case,
layette.

Howdy Doody
Size: 13″   Internet: $500
Condition: Mint
Wood body.

Howdy Doody
Size: 20″   Internet: $215
Condition: Ex
1st edition (rubber gloved hands; 1951 and later,
stuffed hands).

Mary Hartline, P-91
Size: 16″
Price: $210   Internet: $150
Condition: VG
Mussy hair, flaws, original outfit.

Mary Hartline, P-91
Size: 16″   Internet: $350
Condition: Ex
Original red dress, white boots.
Mark: Ideal Doll-P-91

Mary Hartline, P-91, Walker
Size: 16″   Internet: $535
Condition: Mint
With baton.

Miss Curity
Size: 21″   Internet: $1,000
Condition: Mint
Made with Toni head and body. Nurse outfit,
first-aid booklet, Curity care kit with cotton
balls, gauze, bandages.

Penny Walker
Size: 12″
Price: $200
Condition: MIB
With tag.

Plassie
Size: 22″   Internet: $125
Condition: Ex
Baby, cloth body, composition limbs.

Posie, Walker
Size: 23″   Internet: $215
Condition: VG

Saucy Walker
Size: 14″
Price: $230
Condition: VG
In box.

Saucy Walker
Size: 16″
Price: $80
Condition: VG

Saucy Walker
Size: 16″
Price: $200

Saucy Walker
Size: 16″   Internet: $295
Condition: MIB
All original.

Saucy Walker
Size: 22″
Price: $130
Condition: VG

Saucy Walker
Size: 22″
Price: $140–$250   Internet: $165–$180
Condition: Ex
In original outfit.
Mark: Ideal Doll (head and body) Pat. Pending.
(legs)

Saucy Walker

Size: 22"
Price: $230–$280   Internet: $270–$325
Condition: MIB
Higher prices for "high color" dolls.

Saucy Walker

Size: 28"   Internet: $300
Condition: VG

Sparkle Plenty

Size: 14"   Internet: $225
Condition: Ex
For excellent but nude dolls. Sparkle Plentys
have bodies of Magic Skin, yellow yarn hair.

Sparkle Plenty

Size: 14"   Internet: $1,200
Condition: Mint
Pristine mint in rare jumpsuit. Magic Skin body.
Mark: IDEAL DOLL/MADE IN USA

Toni, P-90

Size: 14"
Price: $190   Internet: $120–$150
Condition: VG

Toni, P-90

Size: 14"
Price: $225   Internet: $175–$190
Condition: Ex

Toni, P-90

Size: 14"
Price: $500   Internet: $450
Condition: MIB
With wave kit and all accessories.
Mark: P-90 (head) Ideal Doll Made in USA
(body)

Toni, P-90, Bride, Walker

Size: 14"   Internet: $580
Condition: Ex
All original bride.

Toni, P-90, Black Hair

Size: 14"   Internet: $325
Condition: VG
Flaws, rarer hair color.

Toni, P-91

Size: 16"   Internet: $200
Condition: Ex

Toni, P-91

Size: 16"
Price: $500–$700   Internet: $350–$475
Condition: MIB
With all accessories.
Mark: P-91/Ideal Doll/Made in U.S.A.

Toni, P-92

Size: 20"
Price: $210–$240   Internet: $170–$190
Condition: Ex

Toni, P-93

Size: 21"   Internet: $180–$265
Condition: VG
Clothing not original or other flaws.

Toni, P-93

Size: 21"   Internet: $300–$325
Condition: Ex

Toni, P-93

Size: 21"   Internet: $635
Condition: MIB
For platinum hair.

Toni, P-93

Size: 21"   Internet: $450
Condition: Mint
For redhead.

Ideal, Vinyl

For Crissy, Patti Playpal, and Tammy family
dolls, please see the separate sections on those
dolls. Prices are mixed, but are predominantly from the Internet with some non-Internet pricing noted.

IDEAL, VINYL

Baby Coos

Size: 24"   Date: 1958
        Internet: $75
Condition: Ex
Nude.
Mark: Ideal Doll B-25

Betsy Wetsy

Size: 11–16"   Date: late 1950s–1960s
        Internet: $30–$60
Condition: Av
Average, often redressed. The later Betsy in all
vinyl.

Betsy Wetsy

Size: 16"   Date: late 1950s–1960s
        Internet: $110
Condition: Ex
Mark: IDEAL DOLL VW3

Betsy Wetsy, With Trunk, Layette

Size: 14"   Date: late 1950s–1960s
        Internet: $330
Condition: Mint
Mint with trunk and layette.

Bewitched, Samantha

Size: 12″   Date: 1965
           Internet: $325
Condition: Ex
In red original outfit with broom and hat.
Mark: M-12 E-2 (1965) IDEAL TOY CO

Bewitched, Samantha

Size: 12″   Date: 1965
           Internet: $1,600
Condition: MIB
Pristine mint; 1 eBay auction.
Mark: M-12 E-2 (1965) IDEAL TOY CO

Bonny Braids

Size: 14″   Date: 1951
           Internet: $125
Condition: Ex
Magic Skin body usually is deteriorated. In original christening dress, diaper, booties.
Mark: Chicago Tribune Ideal Doll made in U.S.A.

Bonny Braids

Size: 11″   Date: 1951
           Internet: $250
Condition: MIB
More with all accessories.

Bonny Braids

Size: 14″   Date: 1951
All Markets: $385–$500
Condition: MIB
Soft vinyl, Magic Skin body, Ipana toothpaste, toothbrush, letters, banner. Molded yellow hair with 2 synthetic braids. Often spelled "Bonnie Braids," "Bonny" on box.
Mark: COPR 1951/CHICAGO TRIBUNE/IDEAL DOLL/USA

Bonny Braids, Walker

Size: 14″   Date: 1953
All Markets: $200
Condition: Ex
Hard-to-find model with plastic walking body.

Bouncing Baby Coos

Size: 20″   Date: 1962–1963
           Internet: $200
Condition: Ex
Cloth torso.
Mark: Ideal Toy Corp./YTT-19-L-5

Captain Action

           Date: 1966
           Internet: $210
Condition: Ex
With extra outfits and accessories.

Crown Princess

Size: 10″   Date: 1957
All Markets: $130
Condition: MIB
Similar to Little Miss Revlon.

Diana Ross

Size: 18″   Date: 1969
All Markets: $600
Condition: MIB
Pristine mint.

Flatsy

Size: 5″   Date: 1969
           Internet: $10–$20
Condition: Ex
Ideal Flatsys from 1960s, all-original, prices not for later versions.
Mark: IDEAL (oval)/1969/Pat. Pending/HONG KONG

Flatsy

Size: 5″   Date: 1969
           Internet: $20–$40
Condition: Mint
With original frame and accessories.

Flatsy

Size: 5″   Date: 1969
           Internet: $40–$60
Condition: NRFB
Original packaging and frame.

Flatsy, Judy

Size: 5″   Date: 1968
           Internet: $60–$85
Condition: NRFB
With tub and slippers.

Giggles

           Date: 1967
           Internet: $160
Condition: MIB
Move arm, eyes flirt, head moves, doll giggles.

Harriet Hubbard Ayer Makeup Doll

Size: 14–21″   Date: 1953–1954
           Internet: $200
Condition: Ex
For all sizes; uses Toni body.
Mark: Ideal Doll P-90 (or similar)

J. Fred Muggs

Size: 15″   Date: 1950s
           Internet: $150
Condition: Ex
With name tag: "MY NAME IS J. FRED MUGGS WHAT'S YOURS" from 1950s NBC *Today Show* with Dave Garroway.

Joey Stivic (*All in the Family*)
Size: 15″   Date: 1976
    Internet: $20–$25
Condition: Ex
Produced for a few months only. Anatomically correct and controversial. Box states "Archie Bunker's Grandson."

Kissy
Size: 22.5″   Date: 1961
    Internet: $200
Condition: NMIB
Press hands together and it puckers; kissing sound.
Mark: Ideal Toy Corp.

Little Lost Baby
Size: 22″   Date: 1968
    Internet: $110
Condition: MIB
3 faces: crying, smiling, sleeping. Cloth body, vinyl hands, pink fur-trimmed suit.

Little Miss Revlon
Size: 10.5″   Date: 1958–1960
All Markets: $40–$60
Condition: Av
Average dolls, naked or redressed, some flaws.
Mark: IDEAL VT-10 1/2

Little Miss Revlon
Size: 10.5″   Date: 1958–1960
All Markets: $70–$100
Condition: Ex
In Little Miss Revlon outfit.

Little Miss Revlon
Size: 10.5″   Date: 1958–1960
    Internet: $150–$175
Condition: Mint
Box relatively common.

Little Miss Revlon
Size: 10.5″   Date: 1958–1960
All Markets: $150–$300
Condition: MIB
Bra, hose, girdle, heels, earrings and outfit; most mint dolls priced at $200+.

Lori Martin
Size: 30″   Date: 1960s
    Internet: $350–$400
Condition: Ex
National Velvet character.
Mark: METRO-GOLDWYN-MAYER INC MFG BY IDEAL TOY CORP 30

Lori Martin, Playpal
Size: 38″   Date: 1961
    Internet: $550
Condition: VG

With banner.
Mark: Metro Goldwyn Mayer MFG BY IDEAL TOY CORP

Lori Martin, Playpal
Size: 38″   Date: 1961
    Internet: $1,250
Condition: Mint

Many Happy Returns
Size: 14″   Date: 1983–1984
    Internet: $20
Condition: Gd
Battery operated, moves and walks.

Many Happy Returns, Black
Size: 14″   Date: 1983–1984
    Internet: $30
Condition: Ex

Miss Ideal
Size: 25″   Date: 1961
    Internet: $100–$125
Condition: Ex
Jointed ankles, wrists, arms, legs, and waist.

Miss Ideal
Size: 30″   Date: 1961
    Internet: $165–$185
Condition: Ex

Miss Revlon
Size: 15″   Date: 1956–1959
    Internet: $160
Condition: VG
Played with.

Miss Revlon
Size: 15″   Date: 1956–1959
All Markets: $250–$365
Condition: Ex
Original tag and banner.

Miss Revlon
Size: 18–20″   Date: 1956–1959
All Markets: $40–$60
Condition: Av
Naked, redressed dolls or doll with flaws.

Miss Revlon
Size: 18″   Date: 1956–1959
All Markets: $70–$100
Condition: VG
Dolls with flaws, original clothing; sometimes missing outfit parts.

Miss Revlon
Size: 18″   Date: 1956–1959
All Markets: $150–$240
Condition: Ex

Miss Revlon

Size: 18″   Date: 1956–1959
                    Internet: $250–$300
Condition: Mint
Cherries a la Mode dress (light pink).
Mark: VT-18/IDEAL DOLL

Miss Revlon

Size: 18″   Date: 1956–1959
All Markets: $400–$525
Condition: MIB
MIB; pristine mint in white and red Cherries Jubilee or similar desirable outfit.

Miss Revlon

Size: 20″   Date: 1956–1959
All Markets: $150–$175
Condition: Ex

Miss Revlon

Size: 22″   Date: 1956–1959
                    Internet: $125–$175
Condition: VG
Harder to find size.

Miss Revlon

Size: 22″   Date: 1956–1959
All Markets: $285–$390
Condition: Ex
In rarer outfits.

Miss Revlon

Size: 22″   Date: 1956–1959
                    Internet: $570
Condition: Mint
Pristine mint, rare outfit.
Mark: VT-22/IDEAL DOLL

Miss Revlon, Bride

Size: 20″   Date: 1956–1959
                    Internet: $250–$285
Condition: Mint

Pebbles Flintstone

Size: 12″   Date: 1960s
                    Internet: $185
Condition: Ex
In box, with hang tag, great box graphics.

Pebbles Flintstone

Size: 12″   Date: 1960s
                    Internet: $255
Condition: MIB
With hang tag, great box graphics.

Pebbles Flintstone

Size: 16″   Date: 1963–1964
                    Internet: $125–$150
Condition: Ex

Pebbles Flintstone

Size: 16″   Date: 1963–1964
                    Internet: $230–$255
Condition: Mint
Pristine mint or MIB, with bone in hair.

Sara Ann

Size: 19″
                    Internet: $90
Condition: Ex
Hard plastic body.

Saucy Walker

Size: 28″   Date: late 1950s
All Markets: $250–$275
Condition: Mint
Later vinyl version of doll.
Mark: Ideal Toy Corp. T28X-60

Smokey the Bear

Size: 17″   Date: 1950s–1960s
                    Internet: $120
Condition: MIB
Vinyl face, cloth body, with badge, belt, and hat.

Suzie Playpal

Size: 28″   Date: early 1960s
                    Internet: $130
Condition: VG
Mark: IDEAL DOLL OB 28-5

Tabitha

Size: 13″   Date: 1966
                    Internet: $200
Condition: VG
Tabitha Stevens, baby from *Bewitched* TV show.

Terry Twist

Size: 30″   Date: 1962
                    Internet: $125
Condition: Ex
Same doll as Miss Ideal, but in Ideal cheerleader's outfit and megaphone.

Thumbelina

Size: 16″   Date: 1961
                    Internet: $80
Condition: Ex

Thumbelina

Size: 16″   Date: 1961
                    Internet: $200
Condition: Mint
Wooden knob. Thumbelinas wriggle when you wind knob. Cloth body, vinyl limbs, painted eyes, rooted hair.
Mark: Ideal Toy Corp. OTT-16

Thumbelina

Size: 19–20″   Date: 1961
                    Internet: $180–$240

Condition: Ex
Wooden knob, crier.

Thumbelina
Size: 19–20″   Date: 1961
                                    Internet: $405
Condition: Mint
Pristine mint. Original 2-piece pink and white
knit outfit, "Thumbelina" ribbon.

Thumbelina
Size: 19–20″   Date: 1960s
                                    Internet: $300–$375
Condition: MIB

Thumbelina, Newborn
Size: 10″   Date: 1967
                                    Internet: $140
Condition: Mint
ID bracelet, cloth body, pull-string mechanism.
Mark: 1967 IDEAL TT-9-H108/JAPAN

Thumbelina, Newborn, Black
                                    Date: 1967
                                    Internet: $220
Condition: NRFB

Thumbelina, Tiny
Size: 14″   Date: 1962–1968
                                    Internet: $400
Condition: Mint
Pristine mint, moves, has dress banner.

Thumbelina, Tiny
Size: 14″   Date: 1962–1968
                                    Internet: $250–$315
Condition: MIB
Mark: IDEAL TOY CORP/OTT-14

Thumbelina, Tiny
Size: 14″   Date: 1962–1968
                                    Internet: $600
Condition: NRFB

Thumbelina, Tiny
Size: 14″   Date: 1962–1968
                                    Internet: $40–$60
Condition: Av
Played with, redressed.

Thumbelina, Tiny, Outfits
                                    Date: 1962–1968
                                    Internet: $200–$250
Condition: NRFB
Per outfit.

Tiffany Taylor
Size: 19″   Date: 1975
                                    Internet: $15
Condition: Av
Loose.

Tiffany Taylor
Size: 19″   Date: 1975
                                    Internet: $60
Condition: MIB
Twist wig around to change doll from blonde to
brunette.

Tuesday Taylor
Size: 11.5″   Date: 1977
                                    Internet: $10
Condition: Av
Loose doll, original clothing.

Tuesday Taylor
Size: 11.5″   Date: 1977
                                    Internet: $75
Condition: MIB
Twist wig around to change doll from blonde to
brunette.

Tuesday Taylor, Suntan
Size: 11.5″   Date: 1977
                                    Internet: $50–$75
Condition: MIB
Doll "tans" in light.

Velvet Skin Baby Dreams
                                    Date: 1975
                                    Internet: $300
Condition: MIB

Kenner

Kenner Products was formed by Albert, Philip, and Joseph Steiner in Cincinnati, Ohio, in 1947. The company is named after its original office location on Kenner Street. In the early years, Kenner mostly produced toys, including the revolutionary Play-Doh in 1946. Along with Ideal and Mattel, it was an early adopter of television advertising and advertised toys nationally as early as 1958 on the *Captain Kangaroo* show. In 1963, it created the Easy-Bake toy oven.

Dolls from Kenner didn't really show up until the 1970s, by which time the company was owned by the international conglomerate General Mills. Most of the dolls produced by Kenner were inexpensive affairs, suffering from the 1970s "disease" of cheap product at cheap prices. Notable exceptions include the Blythe doll, which was produced for only a year and is a virtual craze with collectors today, and the Strawberry Shortcake dolls in the 1980s (see the separate Blythe and Strawberry Shortcake sections).

In 1973, it produced Baby Alive, a doll that would eat and then, ahem, expel the "food" in a natural way. Baby Alive was the number-one selling baby doll of that year. It had a foray into the fashion doll market with Darci in 1978, and produced dolls with tie-ins with such TV shows as *The Six-Million-Dollar Man* and *The Bionic Woman*. It produced the hugely popular Strawberry Shortcake dolls starting in 1980, and it also had the lucrative license for *Star Wars* action figures starting in 1977. Also produced at the end of the 1970s were the See Wees.

Various dolls continued to be produced in the 1980s and 1990s, including a remake of Baby Alive, Baby Go Bye-Bye in 1996, and the Classic Collection of G.I. Joe.

Unfortunately, Kenner became the victim of cheaper overseas jobs, and Kenner shut the doors to its Cincinnati operations in 2000. (Several historical facts presented in this section are from www.kennertoys.com.)

Market Report: Except for the hot Blythe dolls, the market for Kenner dolls is really just developing, since Kenner was one of the latecomers to the doll scene in America. However, don't discount other Kenner products—See Wees have a growing following, and a first-issue Baby Alive doll MIB can easily sell for over $300. Plus Strawberry Shortcake dolls are all the rage with the Gen-X crowd, with the rarer MIB examples easily bringing $200 to $300 on eBay.

Online/Offline Report: The online market for Blythe and Strawberry Shortcake is hot, and in fact, online seems to be the place to find these later dolls which many dealers and auction houses are just starting to notice. Prices can actually be higher online for mint Kenner items because of bidding competition.

Prices and Characteristics: All dolls are vinyl. For Blythe and Strawberry Shortcake prices, see their separate sections.

KENNER DOLLS

Baby Alive, 1st Issue
Size: 16″
Date: 1973
Internet: $250–$300

Condition: MIB
Pristine mint, with food, bottle, dish, spoon.

Baby Alive
Size: 16″
Date: 1980s
Internet: $20

Condition: Av
Loose, with some accessories. Later issues.

Baby Alive
Size: 16″
Date: 1980s
Internet: $100

Condition: MIB
Later issues.

Baby Angel Cake
Size: 14″
Date: 1983
Internet: $70

Condition: MIB

Beetlejuice, Talking
Size: 16″
Date: 1989
Internet: $35

Condition: MIB
Says many phrases: "I'm the ghost with the most"; "Show time!" etc.

Bionic Woman
Size: 12″
Date: 1972
Internet: $10–$15

Condition: Ex
For loose dolls.

Bionic Woman, Jamie Sommers
Size: 12.5″
Date: 1976
Internet: $100–$110

Condition: NRFB

Care Bear, Birthday Poseable
Date: 1984
Internet: $50

Condition: MIB

Crumpet
Size: 18″
Date: 1971
Internet: $50

Condition: MIB

Darci, Loose With Accessories
Size: 12″
Date: late 1970s
Internet: $45

Condition: Ex
With portfolio, bracelets, 3 magazine covers.

Darci
Size: 12″
Date: 1979
Internet: $40–$50

Condition: MIB
Darci and friends, the "Cover Girls."

Darci, Friend, Dana

Size: 12″   Date: 1979

Internet: $70

Condition: MIB

Darci, Friend, Erica

Size: 12″   Date: 1979

Internet: $125

Condition: NRFB

Darci, Disco

Date: 1979

Internet: $50

Condition: Ex

Play environment.

Darci, Outfits, Various

Date: 1979

Internet: $30–$40

Condition: NRFB

More for rarer outfits.

Dusty

Size: 11″   Date: 1974

Internet: $15–$25

Condition: MIB

Gabbigale, Talking Doll

Size: 14″   Date: 1970s

Internet: $30

Condition: Ex

Hardy Boys, Joe Hardy, Shaun Cassidy

Size: 12″   Date: late 1970s

Internet: $30–$60

Condition: MIB

Indiana Jones

Size: 12″   Date: 1981

Internet: $40

Condition: Ex

Indiana Jones

Size: 12″   Date: 1981

Internet: $145

Condition: NRFB

Photos from *Raiders of the Lost Ark* on box.

International Velvet

Size: 11″   Date: 1978

Internet: $15–20

Condition: Ex

Tatum O'Neal.

Oscar Goldman, *Six Million Dollar Man*

Size: 13″   Date: 1970s

Internet: $110

Condition: NRFB

Rose Petal Place Dolls

Size: 7″   Date: 1984

Internet: $25–$45

Condition: MIB

Rosebud, Daffodil, Orchid, Lilly, Iris.

Rose Petal Place, Daffodil

Date: 1984

Internet: $40

Condition: MIB

See Wees, Bubble Ballet, Satin & Baby Swirl

Size: 4″   Date: 1983

Internet: $100

Condition: MOC

Tiny, like Liddle Kiddles.

See Wees, Loose

Size: 4″   Date: 1979–1983

Internet: $5–$15

Condition: Ex

Loose, higher range with accessories.

See Wees, Sandy, Mermaid

Size: 4″   Date: 1979

Internet: $15

Condition: Ex

Mark: C.P.G./1979 (back)

See Wees, Sandy, Mermaid

Size: 4″   Date: 1979

Internet: $50

Condition: MOC

With baby star.

See Wees Lagoon

Size: 4″   Date: 1983

Internet: $100

Condition: MIB

A play environment for the See Wees.

***Star Wars*, Boba Fett**

Size: 4″   Date: 1983

Internet: $280

Condition: MOC

Return of the Jedi.

***Star Wars*, C3PO**

Size: 4″   Date: 1977

Internet: $150

Condition: MOC

Star Wars.

***Star Wars*, Chewbacca**

Size: 15″   Date: 1977

Internet: $380

Condition: MOC

The Empire Strikes Back.

***Star Wars*, Luke Skywalker Doll**

Size: 11.5″   Date: 1977

Internet: $340

Condition: MIB

Star Wars.

Group of Klumpe dolls. *Muslin and felt, wire-armature-shaped bodies, exaggerated poses and facial features. Each approximately 10", c. 1930s and later. Marks: Gold or white paper labels with "Klumpe Made in Spain." Courtesy Theriault's.*

Klumpe Spanish dancer. *Felt, wire-armature body. 11". Un-marked doll, Klumpe tags. $30, eBay.*

Star Wars, Luke Skywalker, Bespin Fatigues
Size: 4"   Date: 1980
                             Internet: $430
Condition: MOC
The Empire Strikes Back.

Star Wars, Princess Leia Doll
Size: 11.5"   Date: 1977
                             Internet: $155
Condition: MIB
Star Wars.

Star Wars, Tri-Logo Yoda
                             Date: 1983
                             Internet: $400
Condition: MOC
Return of the Jedi.

Steve Scout
Size: 9"   Date: 1974
                             Internet: $30
Condition: MIB
Salutes when you raise left arm.

Terminator
Size: 13"   Date: 1991
                             Internet: $15
Condition: MIB
Arnold Schwarzenegger.

Klumpe and Roldan Dolls

Very little is actually known about Klumpe dolls or Roldan dolls. The dolls are very similar, both made in Barcelona, Spain, from the early 1950s to the early 1970s. The dolls were often sold to the tourist trade, and several companies imported them for sale in the United States as well. It is often difficult to tell if you have a Klumpe or a Roldan doll if the original cardboard tags have been removed. The dolls are all made of felt with painted faces and armature wire inside for posing. In some ways, these dolls are cousins of the American Annalee dolls. The dolls portray everything from Spanish dancers and ballerinas to mothers with children and skiers.

Market Report: The market is very soft for these dolls right now. If you like vintage cloth dolls, it would be easy to build a collection of these dolls at bargain prices. Many of the common dolls can be found for under $100.

Online/Offline Report: You can find a handful of Klumpe and Roldan dolls on eBay at any given time, and dealers who carry vintage dolls from the 1950s through the 1970s and dealers who specialize in cloth dolls will often have a few in stock. On eBay, dolls without tags will often be listed as "Klumpe Roldan" dolls.

Prices and Characteristics: All Klumpe and Roldan dolls are made of cloth felt bodies, with a wire armature for posing. The face is a cloth mask, and all facial features are painted. All dolls are from the 1950s to the 1970s, with the earlier 1950 Klumpe dolls favored by collectors. All prices are for dolls in excellent condition. Prices for Klumpe and Roldan dolls are very specific to the character and the intricacy of the clothing and accessories. Dolls are unmarked, but did come with tags. Prices will be much lower if there is extensive moth damage.

KLUMPE

Lady, Man, or Spanish Dancer
Size: 7–10″   Internet: $40–$80
For common lady or man in Spanish costume or Spanish dancer.

Artist, Abstract
Size: 10″   Internet: $140
With abstract painting and paint box.

Bathing Beauty
Size: 10.5″   Internet: $125
Holding beach bag and towel; straw hat.

Clown
Size: 12″   Internet: $160

Clown, Playing Guitar
Size: 14″   Internet: $460

Gardener, Lady or Girl
Size: 10″   Internet: $160–$200

Lady, With Fruit Basket
Size: 11″   Internet: $50

Persian Flute Player
Size: 8″   Internet: $220

Scientist
Size: 8″   Internet: $160
With test tubes, microscope, and mice in cage.

ROLDAN

Lady, Man, or Spanish Dancer
Size: 7–10″   Internet: $40–$80
For common lady or man in Spanish costume or Spanish dancer.

Bellhop, With Poodle
Size: 8″   Internet: $150
Mark: Original Roldan trademark Made in Spain (tag)

Bellhop, Holding Luggage, Bird Cage, Golf Clubs
Size: 9.5″   Internet: $115

Doctor, Nurse, or Dentist
Size: 8–10″   Internet: $40–$60
More for mint with outfit completely white.

Lady, Holding Flowers
Size: 9″   Internet: $65

Lady, Pushing Baby in Carriage
Size: 8″   Internet: $400
Mark: Roldan Original, Made In Spain (tag)

Santa Claus
Size: 9″   Internet: $160

Scuba-Diving Fisherman
Size: 9″   Internet: $165
Face mask, tanks, spear, and fish.

Skier
Size: 10″   Internet: $150–$175
With skis.

Knickerbocker

Formed in 1925 in New York by Leo L. Weiss, the Knickerbocker company licensed and manufactured a wide variety of dolls until it went out of business in 2002 (with certain assets of the company purchased by Marian, owned by Marie and Brian Osmond).

Little LuLu. Cloth-mask pressed face, cloth body. 17″, c. 1930s. Unmarked, paper label only. Courtesy Theriault's.

Snow White and the Seven Dwarfs, Knickerbocker. Dwarfs have 1-piece composition head/torso/legs. Snow White has cloth mask pressed face, muslin stitch-jointed, oil-painted body. 15″ and 9″, c. 1940. Mark: Walt Disney Co. Knickerbocker Toy Co. (body, dwarves). $3,600, auction. Courtesy Theriault's.

The company produced dolls with many instantly recognizable names: Disney characters, Little Orphan Annie, Holly Hobbie, Marie Osmond dolls, and, of course, Raggedy Ann and Andy from 1962 to 1983 (see the separate section on Raggedy Ann and Andy for further information). At the end of the life of Knickerbocker, in the late 1990s and early 2000s, the company was best-known for collectible dolls—not only for its Marie Osmond dolls, but also for Terri Lee reproductions and the Somers and Field fashion dolls (a greatly underappreciated line of 16-inch fashion dolls with a 1960s/1970s sensibility—also known as the Willow and Daisy dolls). Knickerbocker also briefly produced the Collection of the Masters for Richard Simmons before the collection went to Goebel. For information and prices on Knickerbocker's modern collectible doll lines, see the Knickerbocker section in the Modern Dolls chapter.

Market Report: Unlike Madame Alexander, Ideal, or Horsman dolls, very few people collect only Knickerbocker dolls. I think this is because the dolls are so eclectic, without a unifying style or theme. Also many of the 1960s and 1970s dolls are not particularly well made.

Prices for vintage Knickerbocker dolls are generally soft, without much upward momentum at this time, except for Raggedy Ann and Andy dolls, and certain Disney dolls.

Online/Offline Report: Similar prices and availability from all venues.

KNICKERBOCKER

Annie, Punjab, Molly, Daddy Warbucks, or Miss Hannigan

Size: 5–6″   Date: 1982
                          Internet: $5–$10

Material: vinyl
Condition: MIB
From *Annie* movie.

Annie

Size: 15″   Date: 1982
                          Internet: $15

Material: cloth
Condition: Ex
Little Orphan Annie, from movie.

Astro Puppet

Size: 12″   Date: 1960s
                          Internet: $40

Material: vinyl
Condition: Ex
Cloth body, from *Jetsons* cartoon.

Baba Looey

                          Date: 1959
                          Internet: $50

Material: vinyl
Condition: Mint

Little Orphan Annie. *Vinyl. 6″, c. 1982. $7 MIB, eBay.*

From *Quick Draw McGraw.* Cloth body, price with hat and original tag.

Campbell Kid
Size: 10.5″   Internet: $30
Material: cloth
Condition: Ex

Captain Kirk or Mr. Spock
Size: 12″   Date: 1979
                                     Internet: $10
Material: vinyl
Condition: Ex
Cloth body.

Carnival Doll
Size: 4″   Internet: $8
Material: celluloid
Condition: Ex

Dolly Pops, Dolls
                                     Date: 1980s
                                     Internet: $5–$10
Material: vinyl
Condition: MOC
Pigtails grow, plastic clothing "snaps" on.

Dolly Pops, House
                                     Date: 1982
                                     Internet: $60
Material: plastic
Condition: Ex

Dolly Pops, Poptown Set
                                     Internet: $30
Material: vinyl
Condition: MIB

Dwarf
Size: 9″   Date: 1940s
All Markets: $200
Material: cloth
Condition: Ex
From *Snow White and Seven Dwarfs* set.

Holly Hobbie
Size: 9–16″   Date: 1975–1980
                                     Internet: $10–$20
Material: cloth
Condition: Ex
Any size.

Huckleberry Hound, Puppet
                                     Date: 1961
                                     Internet: $10
Material: vinyl
Condition: Ex
Cloth body.

Kuddle Kewpie
Size: 16″   Internet: $70
Material: vinyl
Condition: Ex
Cloth body.

Laurel and Hardy
Size: 11″   Date: 1966
                                     Internet: $15
Material: vinyl
Condition: Ex
Per doll; cloth body.

Little Lulu
Size: 18″   Date: 1939
                                     Internet: $500

Material: cloth mask
Condition: VG
Curtis Publishing, as premium for magazine subscriptions.
Mark: (dress tag) A SANITARY TOY, makers, Knickerbocker Toy Co., New York.

Little Lulu
Size: 18"   Internet: $850
Condition: Mint
With hang tag, purse.

Mickey Mouse Cowboy
Size: 11"   Date: 1930s
                  Internet: $600
Condition: VG+

Nancy and Sluggo
Size: 6"   Date: 1973
                  Internet: $35
Material: cloth
Condition: MIB

Raggedy Ann or Andy, Hand Puppet
Size: 10"   Date: 1973
                  Internet: $10–$15
Material: cloth
Condition: MIP

Sleepy-Hand Indian Doll
Size: 15"   Date: 1930s
                  Internet: $50
Material: composition
Condition: Ex

Smokey the Bear
Size: 15"   Date: 1970s
                  Internet: $55
Material: cloth
Condition: Ex
Mark: KTC Knickerbocker tag.

Snow White and the Seven Dwarfs (also Ideal)
Size: 9"–15.5"   Date: 1930s
All Markets: $1,600
Material: cloth and composition
Condition: VG
Snow White in stockinette by Ideal; Dwarfs by Knickerbocker; crazing, some wear, all hats with names.

Snow White and the Seven Dwarfs
Size: 9–15"   Date: 1940
All Markets: $2,800–$3,600
Material: cloth
Condition: Mint
All original, set of 8, wrist tags, box.
Mark: Walt Disney Co. Knickerbocker Toy Co (on dwarfs).

Kruse, Käthe

Käthe Kruse was one of the original bohemians, and one of the first doll artists. She led an unconventional life, and through her own search for a proper doll for her children she created a truly innovative doll for its time. When Käthe's soft painted dolls came on the scene in 1910, bisque dolls reigned in the doll market, and Käthe's dolls were amazingly different. What started out as a small cottage industry from her home became a large company that continues to produce dolls today.

Born in 1883 in Germany, Käthe and her husband, Max, had 8 children. She disliked bisque dolls because she thought them cold and unrealistic, and when she couldn't find the type of baby doll she wanted for her children, she created her own made of cloth. This doll led, eventually, to the Käthe Kruse doll company, which Käthe led until 1953, when her children became the owners. Käthe died in 1968, and the company has survived under various owners until today.

Market Report: Prices have been stable, with some decrease in later collectible market dolls (dolls produced as collectibles, not as playthings for children).

Online/Offline Report: You don't see early Käthe Kruse dolls in great numbers on eBay—maybe a handful, at most, at any given time. For the best availability, find older Käthe Kruse dolls from dealers, shows, and auctions. Newer Käthe Kruse dolls are widely available on eBay, and at good prices. There are also unmarked dolls sold as "Käthe Kruse" on eBay when they clearly are not.

Prices and Characteristics: Hard-pressed cloth socket heads, painted eyes and features, painted or wigged hair as indicated, closed mouth, all-cloth body with jointing at shoulders and hips. Dolls are marked on their feet.

KÄTHE KRUSE

Series I, Child
Size: 17"   Date: 1915
Price: $3,500–$4,000+

Käthe Kruse Character, Series 1.
All-cloth, pressed and oil-painted face, muslin body with stitch-jointed shoulders, hip-jointed legs. 17". Mark: Käthe Kruse and illegible number (feet). Courtesy Theriault's.

Käthe Kruse Series I Pouty Child.
All-muslin doll, pressed, oil-painted features. stitch-jointed arms, hip-jointed legs. 17", c. 1915. Mark: Käthe Kruse (foot). Courtesy Theriault's.

Wide-hipped early model. Pressed and oil-painted head, painted hair.
Mark: Käthe Kruse/1322

Series I, Child
Size: 17"   Date: 1929
Price: $2,500–$3,000
Slim hips—later Series I model. Pressed and oil-painted head, painted hair, modeled forelock.

Series II, Schlenkerchen, Baby
Size: 13"   Date: 1922
Price: $5,400–$7,500
All stockinette, oil-painted, smiling expression.

Series V, VI, Traumerchen, Baby
Size: 21"   Date: 1925
Price: $3,900
Closed eyes.

Series VII
Size: 14"   Date: 1930s
Price: $2,700

Painted hair, separately sewn-on thumb.
Mark: 2171/Käthe Kruse

Series VIII, Girl
Size: 20.5"   Date: 1930s
All Markets: $2,150

Series, IX, Little German Child
Size: 14"   Date: 1945
Price: $800–$1,100
Mohair wig, swivel head. Original tag: Käthe Kruse/Macke/IX (or similar).
Mark: Käthe Kruse 36264

Series X
Size: 14"   Date: 1930
Price: $1,500
Mark: Käthe Kruse 1588

Series XII
Size: 17"   Date: 1950s
Price: $1,300
Original tag: Käthe Kruse XII 120 Nancy.
Mark: Käthe Kruse 10566

Käthe Kruse character boy. *Cloth pressed/painted swivel head, stitch-jointed arms, hip-jointed legs. 19", c. 1935. Mark: Käthe Kruse (feet). Courtesy Theriault's.*

Käthe Kruse Character Child, Type 1. *All-cloth, painted, pressed features, stitch-jointed arms, hip-jointed legs. 18", c. 1935. Mark: Käthe Kruse 112999 (foot stamp). Courtesy Theriault's.*

Character, Kämmer & Reinhardt, Pouty

Size: 18"   Date: 1910
Price: $2,900+
Rare model for Kruse. Cloth socket head, painted brown hair, closed pouty mouth, all-cloth body with hidden ball-jointing at knees and shoulders.

Celluloid, Child

Size: 16"   Date: 1955
Price: $475
All celluloid. Swivel neck, wigged.
Mark: (turtle mark)/Modell Käthe Kruse/740

Hard Plastic, Baby, Pouty

Size: 20"   Date: 1965
All Markets: $750
MIB; hard plastic; wigged.

Hard Plastic, Painted, Girl

Size: 14"   Date: 1950s
Price: $350
Painted hard plastic, some crazing typical.
Mark: 148/8

Tommy Pyjama

Size: 20"
Price: $2,100
Mint, with all tags.

Traumerchen, Reissue (Baby)

Size: 19"
Price: $435
MIB.

Lenci

The Lenci company is by far the most famous Italian maker of dolls. Elena König, a German, married an Italian, Enrico di Scavini in 1916, and the couple settled in Torino (Turin), Italy. In 1919 they applied for their first patent for making fabric doll heads. Their cottage industry business increased quickly, and by 1922, they coined the name "Lenci" after Elena's nickname.

The Lenci dolls were made from fine wool felt. The felt was molded to form the head and the facial features of the doll were painted. Both muslin bodies and molded felt bodies were used for the early dolls. Types of dolls made ranged from boudoir dolls and smokers clearly made for adults to adorable child and storybook dolls clearly made for children. The doll outfits were also of highest quality, made of felt and other fine fabrics.

These dolls were considered "art" dolls in their day and were marketed to children and adults alike. The dolls were costly, and their look was immediately known and copied by dollmakers in many countries. The dolls were hugely successful and exported around the world until difficulties caused by World War II prevented it.

Lenci Mannequin No. 1, 6-
month-old child. Felt swivel head,
all-felt baby body. 20″, c. 1930. Unmarked. Courtesy Theriault's.

**Lenci Character Boy and Girl, Se-
ries 110.** Felt swivel heads, 5-piece
felt bodies, jointed limbs. Alsatian
costumes. 19″, c. 1930. Unmarked.
Courtesy Theriault's.

Lenci Character Model 1500. Felt
swivel head, 5-piece felt body with
jointed limbs. 18″, c. 1928. Courtesy Theriault's.

After World War II, the business was sold to
the Garella family, which continued to operate the company through modern times.
After the war through the 1970s, most of the
Lenci dolls were not the cloth dolls the company was known for. In the late 1970s, the
company did start to make cloth dolls again
from old, original Lenci molds.

Market Report: The market is slightly down
from a few years ago, especially for more
common child dolls.

Online/Offline Report: Later Lenci dolls
abound at online auctions; the choicest, earliest dolls are mostly located through dealers,
doll shows, and auction houses. Be cautious
at online auctions—many dolls are sold as
"Lencis" that were actually made by other
companies.

Prices and Characteristics: Lencis have a
pressed swivel felt head, felt or cloth torso,
arms, and legs, and are jointed at shoulders
and hips. Lencis have painted features, including painted eyes (generally) and are
wigged, usually with mohair, sometimes
with yarn or other material. Dolls are often
found unmarked; marks if found are on
tags, Lenci buttons, and labels. Occasionally,
a doll is stamped on the foot. Lenci dolls
have sewn-on ears; many of their competi-
tors and imitators did not. Earlier dolls

(1920s–1930s) are more sought after as they
are considered better painted and the costumes have more details than those of the
later 1930s and 1940s dolls.

LENCI

American Indian
Size: 10″
Price: $450
Painted eyes, war paint, smiling, brown yarn
wigs, all-felt bodies.

Arabian Boy
Size: 17.5″　　　　　　　Date: 1931
Price: $600
VG; more if excellent.

Asian Child, #300
Size: 17″　　　　　　　Date: 1930s
　　　　　　　　　　　　Internet: $1,800

Autumn Googly
Size: 21″　　　　　　　Date: 1939
Price: $3,500
Mark: Lenci Turin Made in Italy (foot stamp)

Boudoir-Type, Gish Face
Size: 27″　　　　　　　Date: 1920s
Price: $1,800
VG; more if excellent.

Boxer, 300 Series, Character
Size: 17″　　　　　　　Date: 1920s
　　　　　　　　　　　　Internet: $1,800

Lenci Spanish Girl. Felt swivel
head, muslin torso, felt jointed
arms. 14″, c. 1930. Unmarked,
paper label. Courtesy Theriault's.

Lenci, The Golfer, Model 109/40.
Felt swivel head, 5-piece felt body,
jointed limbs. 22″, c. 1920s–1930s.
Mark: Unmarked, paper Lenci
label. Courtesy Theriault's.

Boy
Size: 14″
Price: $260–$500

Boy, Sailor's Uniform With Flag
Size: 17″
Price: $700

Boy, Tyrolean Costume
Size: 17″   Date: 1930
Price: $2,800

Child, Benedetta
                    Date: 1930s
Price: $925
VG; more if excellent.

Child, Ciociara
                    Date: 1940
                    Internet: $450
Mark: Bambola, Italia/Lenci, Torino/Made in
Italy/model Ninetta A/6 (tag)

Child, Diana
Size: 14″   Date: 1980s
                    Internet: $125

Child, Lucia
Size: 14″   Date: 1930s
Price: $1,100
Mint, with label.

Child, Pouty
Size: 12″   Date: 1930
Price: $475
Peach felt outfit.

Child, Pouty Face, Series 1500
Size: 17″
Price: $850
VG.

Child, Series 110
Size: 23″   Date: 1930s
Price: $1,000

Child, Val Gardena Wrist Tag
Size: 19"   Date: 1940s
Price: $850
Tall hat.

Edith, The Lonely Doll
Size: 21"   Internet: $900–$1,400
Higher prices for dolls in better condition.

Fascist Boy, Series 300
Size: 17.5"   Date: 1930s
                  Internet: $3,275
Nazi youth outfit with hat.

Flirty-Eyed, Surprised Look
Size: 20"
Price: $1,500
Spanish dress.

Girl
Size: 11"   Date: 1935
Price: $625
Impish smile.

Girl
Size: 14"
Price: $300–$500

Girl
Size: 16.5"
Price: $420
Aqua dress, green coat and hat.

Girl
Size: 20"   Date: 1930
Price: $650

Girl, Series 300
Size: 17"   Date: 1928
Price: $1,400
In Dutch costume.
Mark: Lenci (paper label)

Girl, Series 300
Size: 17"
Price: $1,400
Near mint; cape and red, beige, and black felt
dress with plaid pattern.
Mark: Lenci (bottom, feet)

Lady
Size: 24"   Date: 1928
Price: $2,000
Elaborate purple felt costume with organdy ruf-
fles. High heel feet.

Lady, Series 165
Size: 24"   Date: 1920s
                  Internet: $2,000
Swivel neck, dressed as flapper.

Lady, Series 165
Size: 24"
Price: $2,000
Organdy gown, high heel feet.

Lady, Coral Felt and Organdy Gown
Size: 18"
Price: $750
White organdy gown with orange dots, orange
jacket.

Little Drummer Boy
Size: 18"   Internet: $2,550

Marlene Dietrich
Size: 30"   Date: 1930
Price: $10,500
VG.
Mark: Lenci (box)

Mascotte, Vatican Guard
Size: 8.5"
Price: $150–$250
Round paper tag on clothing.
Mark: Lenci/Torino/Made in Italy (tag)

Mascottes, Various
Size: 8–9"   Date: 1930s
Price: $300+   Internet: $265–$300
Often in regional outfits.

Matador
Size: 14"
Price: $500
VG.

Nursery, Tom, Tom the Piper's Son
Size: 8"
Price: $525
With painted pig.

Opium Smoker
Size: 14"
Price: $2,250
With hard-to-find original pipe.

Pierrot
Size: 19"   Date: 1920s
Price: $2,250
Mint; all original.

Salon Doll
Size: 27"   Date: 1930
Price: $1,600
VG; more if excellent.

Spanish Outfit, Flirty Eyes
Size: 20"
Price: $700

Orange Blossom Kologne Kiddle.
All vinyl, jointed. 2.5″ doll, 5″ with case, c. 1969–1970. $50 with case, eBay.

Annabelle Autodiddle Kiddle.
Missing shoes and skediddle pusher. Vinyl. 4.5″, c. 1968. Mark: ©1967 / MATTEL, INC. / MEXICO / U.S. PAT PEND. $30, eBay, this condition.

Olivia Orange Kola Kiddle. *Vinyl. 2″ doll, 5.25″ with case, c. 1968–1969. $60 with case, eBay.*

Sports Boy Golfer
Size: 16.5″   Internet: $1,750
178 series.

LENCI, MODERN

Girl, Souvenir of 1991 Exposition of Dolls Regional Conference
Size: 12″   Date: 1991
Price: $200

Modern Reproductions of 1920s and 1930s Dolls
Size: various   Date: 1980s–2003
                      Internet: $75–$125
Various reproductions, all MIB with certificates. More for very large dolls, more elaborate outfits.

Liddle Kiddles

My favorite fact about Liddle Kiddles comes from the Paris Langford book, *Liddle Kiddles, an Identification and Value Guide:* "By the time the 'World of Kiddles' had completed its production run, the company had sold enough Kiddles for every young girl in the United States to own six of them."

I love this quote because I know the truth of it firsthand—as a child, I owned far more than my share of 6—I had more like 20! Kola Kiddles, Lucky Locket Kiddles (I can still sing the TV commercial jingle), Storybook Kiddles, Kologne Kiddles—you name

it, I had it, and so did every little girl growing up on my block in New York.

For the uninitiated, Liddle Kiddles were produced by Mattel from 1966 through 1971. They were tiny dolls, representing children, mostly from 2.75 inches tall to about 4 inches. This size of doll was a novelty in the world of Barbie dolls and baby dolls in the mid-1960s. The dolls were made of vinyl, with oversize heads. All Liddle Kiddles had adorable accessories to go with them, and Liddle Kiddles were made in countless varieties, with delightful, rhyming names: Tracy Trikediddle (Kiddle with a tricycle) Windy Fliddle" (Kiddle with a plane), Freezy Sliddle Liddle Kiddle (Kiddle with a sled), and so on.

Liddle Kiddles were so successful that countless companies "borrowed" the idea and made lines of similar little dolls. The official Mattel Liddle Kiddles were always marked with a Mattel mark (either "Mattel" or "MI" in most cases), but the mark can often not be seen if the doll has on original clothing; see more on marks below. The Liddle Kiddles generally are of much higher quality than the knockoff Kiddles. Kiddles had rooted hair, little shoes (except on the smallest styles), and quality vinyl, painting, and clothing.

Liddle Kiddles Cape Cod House.
Vinyl. $30, dealer.

Market Report: Liddle Kiddles were red-hot a few years ago when the baby boomers rediscovered them, but they've come back to earth somewhat since then. Rarer Kiddles NRFB or MOC with all-original accessories can still easily bring several hundred dollars, while very common, played-with, unboxed Kiddles missing their accessories can easily be found for $10 or under.

Online/Offline Report: Rarer Kiddles are easier to find via eBay than through dealers, unless you know a dealer specializing in them, and rarer, MOC or NRFB Kiddles can also be found at auction houses. MOC rare Kiddles bring comparable prices on eBay, from auction houses, and with dealers. Common Kiddles, with their original outfits but minus accessories, can generally be found easiest (and cheapest) via eBay.

Prices and Characteristics: All Liddle Kiddles are vinyl, between 1 inch and 4 inches high, and they were produced from 1966 to 1971. Many of the packages included a small brush and comb (in addition to accessories separately listed). The accessories have a great influence on price; see the prices for Sleeping Biddle below as an example. Most prices are from Internet sources, with exceptions noted.

Marks: Mattel Liddle Kiddles have some variant of the following marks (with marks on the tiniest of Kiddles often impossible to read), under clothes or right under the hairline—a magnifying glass is a must for the hairline marks: © MATTEL, INC. / JAPAN (tiny, around base of neck) and © 1965 / MATTEL, INC. / JAPAN / 7 (generally earlier marks) or HONG KONG / MATTEL, INC. / 1967 (tiny, around base of neck) and © 1967 / MATTEL, INC. / MEXICO / U.S. PAT. PEND. (body). Most Kiddle clones are unmarked as to the maker.

LIDDLE KIDDLE

Liddle Kiddles, Various, Loose
Internet: $10–$30
Condition: Av
Prices for loose Liddle Kiddles, no accessories and with wear and/or flaws; often missing shoes.

Baby Liddle Kiddle
Internet: $500
Condition: Av
Played with, surface dirt, but with blue stroller and pink hair bow. Very rare.

Baby Liddle Kiddle
Internet: $800
Condition: Mint
Exceptional price for very mint and perfect baby—includes blue stroller, pink hair bow.

Beat a Diddle
Internet: $175
Condition: Gd
Rare Sears exclusive, no accessories.

Beat a Diddle
Internet: $255–$295
Condition: Ex
Complete. With her microphone and guitar.

Biff Boodle, Rare Variety
Internet: $360
Condition: MOC
In rare yellow T-shirt.

Calamity Jiddle, Cowgirl
Internet: $120–$130
Condition: Ex
With horse, cowgirl boots, and hat.

Chitty Chitty Bang Bang Set
Internet: $170
Condition: MOC
Set of 4 Kiddles from movie.

Cinderiddle
Internet: $150
Condition: Ex
In rich outfit, with poor outfit and storybook.

Colorforms
Internet: $100
Condition: NRFB

Jewelry Kiddles Heart Bracelet
All Markets: $85
Condition: MOC

Kampy Kiddle
Internet: $230
Condition: MOC
With sleeping bag, fishing pole, pan. Box wear.

Kiddle Kologne
All Markets: $125–$175
Condition: MIP
For MIP, with tag, cardboard base. Series includes Lilly of the Valley. Rosebud, Violet Kiddle, Orange Blossom, others.

Kiddle Kolognes Sweet Three Boutique
All Markets: $250–$350
Condition: NRFB
3 Kiddle Kolognes sold in 1 box.

Kola Kiddle, Laffy Lemon
All Markets: $75
Condition: MOC
Kiddle in soda pop bottle.

Kosmic Kiddle
Internet: $90
Condition: VG
With spaceship, no rock. Kosmic Kiddles are little space aliens.

Kosmic Kiddle, Purple Gurple
Internet: $225–$300
Condition: Mint
Spaceship spins around when pushed. With space rock, hang tag. Series includes Purple Gurple and Yelloe Felloe.

Liddle Biddle Peep
Internet: $280
Condition: MOC

Lola Liddle
Internet: $185
Condition: Ex
With sailboat, booklet.

Lucky Locket, Various
Internet: $20–$35
Condition: Ex
Prices for dolls with original lockets. Varies on condition, rarity, and date of doll. With locket.

Lucky Locket, Various
All Markets: $50–$75
Condition: MOC
Prices for dolls on original cards; more for pristine mint.

Lucky Lockets, Wee Three Set
Internet: $500
Condition: MOC
Lorna, Lou, and Larky Lockets.

Nappytime Baby Liddle Kiddle
Internet: $170
Condition: MIP
In pink plastic crib.

Playhouse Kiddles in Box With Cookin' Kiddle
Internet: $200
Condition: NRFC

Pretty Priddle
Internet: $125
Condition: Ex

Ride N' Run Action Skediddle, Harriet Helididdle
Internet: $170
Condition: MIB

Rolly Twiddle
Internet: $500–$700
Condition: MOC
With wagon, bucket, and pail.

Skediddle Kiddle, Heather Hiddlehorse
Internet: $200
Condition: Mint
With pink plastic horse, hair in original set with flowers, pusher.

Skediddle Kiddle, Swingy Skediddle
                    Internet: $195
Condition: Mint
With hard-to-find earrings and pink purse, pusher.

Skediddle Kiddle Sheila Skediddle
All Markets: $55–$75
Condition: Ex
With orange plastic pusher; higher price for MIB.

Sleeping Biddle
                    Internet: $45
Condition: Av
With chaise only, played with.

Sleeping Biddle, with Chaise Only
                    Internet: $150–$200
Condition: Ex
With chaise only.

Sleeping Biddle, With Castle
                    Internet: $300
Condition: Ex
With castle, chaise, and booklet.

Soapy Siddle
                    Internet: $215
Condition: MOC
In robe with tub, "bubbles," towel.

Storybook Kiddle, Liddle Middle Muffet
                    Internet: $150
Condition: Ex
With tuffet, bowl of whey, spoon, and spider.

Storybook Kiddle, Liddle Middle Muffet
                    Internet: $300
Condition: NRFC

Storybook Kiddles, Robin Hood and Maid Marian
                    Internet: $110
Condition: VG
Storybook: Kiddles Sweethearts.

Storybook Kiddles, Romeo and Juliet
                    Internet: $275
Condition: MIB
Storybook: Kiddles Sweethearts.

Tea Party Kiddle
                    Internet: $150+
Condition: MIP
Includes cup and saucer.

Teeter-Time Baby
                    Internet: $75
With yellow duck rocker.

Telley Viddle
                    Internet: $150
Condition: Mint
With pretzels and TV.

Trikey Triddle
All Markets: $150
Condition: MOC
With balloon, tricycle.

Windy Fiddle
All Markets: $200–$230
Condition: NRFP
Pilot with plane.

Zoolery Kiddles
                    Internet: $200
Condition: MOC
Liddle Kiddle animals (such as Chummy Chimp, Brawny Bear), in rolling zoo wagon which is a necklace.

Madame Alexander

For most of this century (since 1929), the dolls of Madame Alexander have epitomized the "better" doll—the special occasion doll that children get to play with only on Sundays, or get to admire on their bedroom shelves. Certain doll companies, such as Arranbee and American Character, would compete in this arena, but only Madame Alexander dolls had an immediate recognizable cachet to little girls and their mothers everywhere.

The dolls were made special by the incredible costume design of Madame. Beatrice (née Bertha) Alexander was born in 1895 in Brooklyn, New York. Her family and her upbringing were steeped in dolls and costuming, with her family having a long history in the doll industry, including a father who started the first doll hospital in the United States. During World War I, when there was an embargo against German goods including dolls, Beatrice and her sister created cloth Red Cross nurse dolls. Baby dolls soon followed, and in 1923, Madame's fledgling company was born.

Soon composition dolls were added to the offerings of the company. The company continued to grow steadily, even through the Great Depression. In 1930, Madame produced the Alice in Wonderland doll in pressed felt, which was a huge success. Then

Little Betty as McGuffey Ana.
Composition, 5-piece body. 9", c.
1939. Mark: Mme. Alexander
(torso) and tagged costume. Cour-
tesy Theriault's

Tiny Betty Bride. *Composition,*
stationary head, jointed arms, legs.
7.5", c. 1935. $325 MIB, eBay.

came the Little Women dolls in cloth. The Little Women dolls became a mainstay of the Madame Alexander line, and a group of the dolls have been available from the company nearly every year since.

Success after success continued to roll in for the company—the Dionne Quintuplets, Scarlett O'Hara, Princess Elizabeth, Cissy, Alexander-kins. Its place in the world of dolls grew stronger as the years went on, from composition to the elegant hard plastic dolls of the 1940s, to the revolutionary adult-figured, high-heeled hard-plastic Cissy in the 1950s and then the Wendy-faced 8-inch dolls, all the way through the 1960s. As with many companies trying to adapt to a post-Barbie, overseas-production doll world, difficulties started to crop up in the late 1970s and were compounded in the 1980s.

In 1988, Madame Alexander sold the company to private investors. The company had a difficult transition, and many collectors feel that the company's dolls lost quality at this time.

Beatrice Alexander died in 1990. In 1995, faced with management and quality problems and a changing doll market, Madame Alexander filed for chapter 11 bankruptcy protection. A Japanese firm with international financing purchased the company out

of bankruptcy. New management helped reinvigorate the company, quality improved greatly, and the dolls of Madame Alexander continue to delight new collectors and children today.

- **A Note on Cissy:** Madame Alexander's Cissy is the adult-shaped, high-heeled glamorous fashion doll that paved the way for modern fashion dolls as we know them. Without Cissy, which was first sold in 1955, Barbie, Miss Revlon, Tammy, and all of the other fashion dolls that followed might not have been. Cissy was considered quite scandalous by many in her time. Cissy was reintroduced to modern doll collectors in 1996 and this new Cissy is still available today.

Market Report: Madame Alexander dolls are responsible for starting many doll collections—often the very first doll in a personal collection is a well-preserved Madame Alexander doll from childhood.

The Madame Alexander doll market has a complete dichotomy—there is an oversupply of dolls from the 1970s to 1990s, especially on eBay, which has greatly depressed the resale prices of these dolls. Often prices for these dolls MIB on eBay will be less than their original purchase prices. These prices are down considerably from pre-eBay days,

Fairy Princess. Composition, 5-piece body. 15", c. 1938. Mark: Mme. Alexander and tagged costume. Courtesy Theriault's.

McGuffey Ana. Composition, 5-piece body. 13", c. 1938. Mark: 13 (torso) and McGuffey Ana tagged costume and box. Courtesy Theriault's.

and the modern dolls also suffered from the aftereffects of a crash in the Madame Alexander doll market which occurred in the 1990s, after a speculative Madame Alexander collecting bubble "broke."

However, the market for the early Madame Alexander dolls—composition and hard plastic—is very strong—with early, mint composition dolls, mint Alexander-kins, mint Cissys, and others bringing higher prices than just a few years ago (although, perhaps, prices not as high as at the height of the collecting bubble).

Because Madame Alexander has relied so heavily on costumes to define its dolls, with only a limited number of face molds used at any given time, and with the same face molds used for long periods of time (such as the Wendy-faced dolls, which just cele-

brated their 50th anniversary), naked or redressed Madame Alexander dolls are virtually worthless (with exceptions, of course, for the rarest and earliest dolls).

Online/Offline Report: The vast majority of fully mint-in-box 8-inch Wendy dolls from the 1970s to 1990s can often be purchased for $30 and under on eBay; most dealers are now also pricing these dolls similarly. Of course, this doesn't hold true for rarer and more sought-after dolls from this period, such as certain dolls from popular series including *Peter Pan, Gone With the Wind,* and the *Wizard of Oz* series.

Both online and off, the highly sought-after composition and hard-plastic Madame Alexander dolls can be found. The tendency of the Internet to have lower prices than dealers, shops, and shows on most items is

Babs Skater. Hard plastic, 5-piece body. 15˝. Unmarked doll, "Babs Skating" tagged outfit. Courtesy Cathy Messenger.

Sonja Henie. Composition, 5-piece body. 13˝, c. 1940. Mark: Wendy-Ann Mme. Alexander New York (doll) and Sonja Henie tagged outfit. Courtesy Theriault's.

counterbalanced by fierce competition for mint vintage and rarer items, so prices from dealers and auction houses for certain items may be more reasonable.

Prices and Characteristics: Nearly all dolls have 5-piece bodies, with certain 8-inch walking dolls having jointed "bend" knees and many lady dolls such as Cissy having additional jointing. Dolls are generally wigged with glass eyes. All prices are for dolls with original clothing, in condition as noted. Dates given for the dolls are sometimes in the middle of a range of years that the doll was produced—often, a model of Madame Alexander doll is produced for many years.

Marks: Common marks include "Alex" or "Mme. Alexander" or "Alexander" or "Madame Alexander" or similar marks, on the back of the doll's torso or on the doll's

head. However, not all early dolls are marked. Early composition dolls are sometimes marked with the name of the character on the doll: Madame Alexander / Sonja / Henie (head) or Jane Withers / Alexander Doll Co. (head).

Dresses tagged: Nearly all the Madame Alexander dresses have a cloth tag. They are tagged: Madame / Alexander / New York or similar; most tags will give the name of the doll as such: Cissette / © Madame Alexander / New York, U.S.A. (tagged dress). The model of many dolls (such as the Alexander-kins and most later dolls) are nearly impossible to identify without their original clothing.

MADAME ALEXANDER, CLOTH

Alice in Wonderland, Yarn Hair
Size: 21˝   Date: 1940
Price: $150

Dionne Quintuplets. *Composition 5-piece bodies. 7". Mark: ALEXAN-DER (head, body). Courtesy Ellen Johnson.*

Composition bridesmaid. *Composition 5-piece body. 15", c. 1940s. Mark: MME ALEXANDER (head) Madame / Alexander / New York USA (tag). $400, auction.*

John Robert Powers Model. *Hard plastic head, 5-piece body. 15", c. 1952. Mark: costume only, tagged "John Powers Model Madame Alexander." Courtesy Theriault's.*

Condition: Gd

Cloth Face Musical Doll
Size: 10"   Date: 1952
Price: $650

Little Shaver
Size: 9"   Date: 1940
Price: $500
Condition: Ex
Mark: "Little Shaver" Madame Alexander

Little Shaver
Size: 11"   Date: 1940
Price: $750
Condition: MIB

Little Shaver
Size: 20"   Date: 1940
Price: $450
Condition: Ex

Little Women
Size: 14"   Date: 1935
                  Internet: $325+
Condition: Ex

Posey Pet
Size: 17"   Date: 1940
Price: $650
Condition: MIB
Organdy dress.

Posey Pet, Striped Dress
Size: 17"   Date: 1940
Price: $200
Condition: VG
Mark: "Posey Pet" (cloth tag).

MADAME ALEXANDER, COMPOSITION

Baby McGuffey
Size: 12"   Date: 1940s
                  Internet: $340
Condition: Ex
Cloth body, composition lower limbs, sleep eyes, organdy baby dress.

Betty
Size: 12"   Date: 1936
Price: $600
Condition: MIB

Betty
Size: 14"   Date: 1930s
Price: $325
Condition: MIB

Bride, Blonde Hair
Size: 14"   Date: 1940
Price: $800
Condition: Ex

Bride, Embroidered Tulle Gown
Size: 21"   Date: 1940
Price: $800
Condition: Ex

Bridesmaid
Size: 21"   Date: 1945–1946
                  Internet: $400
Condition: Ex

Bridesmaid in Rose Gown
Size: 18"   Date: 1940
Price: $500
Condition: Ex

Nina Ballerina. Hard plastic, 5-piece body. 17.5″. Mark: MADAME ALEXANDER and tagged outfit. Courtesy Marsha L. Cumpton.

Cissy wearing outfit #2019. Hard plastic head and body. 21″, c. 1957. Mark: ALEXANDER. $800, dealer.

Cissy wearing outfit #2014. Hard plastic head, vinyl arms, jointed at neck, shoulders, elbows, hips, and knees. 21″, c. 1956. $600, dealer.

Child, Kate Greenaway
Size: 13″   Date: 1940
Price: $425
Condition: Ex

Dionne Quint, Each
Size: 14″   Date: 1930s
Price: $375
Condition: Ex

Dionne Quint, Each
Size: 17″   Date: 1937
                   Internet: $275
Condition: VG
With flaws.

Dionne Quint, Each
Size: 20″   Date: 1930s
Price: $325   Internet: $400
Condition: Ex
Glass eyes, with minor flaws.

Dionne Quintuplets, Set
Size: 8″   Date: 1934–1939
Price: $850   Internet: $675–$850
Condition: VG
Set, with major flaws.

Dionne Quintuplets, Set
Size: 8″   Date: 1930s
Price: $1,500–$1,700   Internet: $1,100–1,400
Condition: Ex
With flaws, minimal crazing. Original organdy dresses and hats, or rompers, Annette in yellow; Yvonne in pink; Cecile in green; Emilie in lavender, and Marie in blue.

Dionne Quintuplets, Set in Layette
Size: 8″   Date: 1935
Price: $3,600+
Condition: Mint
For pristine mint, or mint in unusual original outfits.

Dionne Quintuplets, Set
Size: 11″   Date: 1930s
                   Internet: $1,500
Condition: Ex

Dionne Quintuplets, Set
Size: 11″   Date: 1930s
                   Internet: $2,000–$2,500
Condition: Mint
Minimal crazing, names on bibs.

Dionne Quintuplets, Nurse
Size: 13″   Date: 1936
Price: $850   Internet: $500
Condition: VG
Sleep eyes. Nurse Louise De Kirilene.

Dionne Quintuplets, Dr. Dafoe
Size: 14″   Date: 1936
Price: $1,500
Condition: Ex
Painted eyes.

Fairy Princess
Size: 15″   Date: 1938
Price: $600
Condition: Ex
Mark: Mme. Alexander (head) "Sleeping Beauty" Madame Alexander (outfit).

Cissy in yellow formal gown.
Hard plastic head and body with jointing at neck, shoulders, elbows, hips, and knees. 20", c. 1956. Mark: Alexander and tagged dress. Courtesy Theriault's.

Cissette in tagged formal dress.
Hard plastic. 10", c. 1957. Mark: MME / ALEXANDER.

Cissette. *Hard plastic head and body, jointed at neck, shoulders, hips, and knees. 9". Mark: MME / ALEXANDER (back). This doll, in original box and underwear with this extra dress. $350, dealer.*

Flora McFlimsey

Size: 15"	Date: 1938
	Internet: $250

Condition: VG
Crazed doll, outfit flaws.

Flora McFlimsey

Size: 15"	Date: 1930s

Price: $550–$725
Condition: Mint
Minimum crazing, unplayed with. Freckles.

Flora McFlimsey

Size: 14"	Date: 1938

Price: $950
Condition: MIB
Mark: Princess Elizabeth Alexander Doll Co.
Only 14" size with this mark.

Girl

Size: 20"	Date: 1930s
	Internet: $325

Condition: Ex
Mark: Mme. Alexander (head). Original pink veil gown with pink ribbons.

Jane Withers

Size: 15"	Date: 1937

Price: $425–$500
Condition: VG

Jane Withers

Size: 13"	Date: 1937
Price: $700	Internet: $700–$900

Condition: Ex

Jeannie Walker

Size: 13–14"	Date: 1940s
	Internet: $460–$525

Condition: VG

Jeannie Walker

Size: 18"	Date: 1940
	Internet: $750

Condition: Ex
Mark: ALEXANDER DOLL CO PAT. NO.
2171281 (back) Jeannie Walker (outfit).

Kate Greenaway

Size: 13"	Date: 1940s
	Internet: $325

Condition: Ex
Original pink dress with matching bonnet.

Kate Greenaway

Size: 15"	Date: 1938
	Internet: $1,025

Pristine mint, yellow organdy dress.
Mark: Princess Elizabeth-Alexander Doll Co
and dress tagged Kate Greenaway.

Kate Greenaway

Size: 17"	Date: 1930s
Price: $400	

Condition: Ex

Little Betty

Size: 9"	Date: 1935–1939
Price: $150–$225	Internet: $225

Condition: Ex
Various outfits. Painted eyes.
Mark: Wendy-Ann-Madame Alexander-New York.

Shari Lewis. *Hard plastic head and 5-piece hard plastic body with vinyl arms. 14", c. 1958. Mark: 1958 Alexander (doll) and tagged Shari Lewis costume. Courtesy Theriault's.*

Little Betty, McGuffey Ana
Size: 9"   Date: 1939
Price: $325
Condition: Ex

Little Genius
Size: 12"   Date: late 1930s
Internet: $200
Condition: Gd

Madelaine DuBain
Size: 12"   Date: 1937
Price: $680
Condition: Mint
Wendy-Ann.

Madelaine DuBain
Size: 18"   Date: 1937–1939
                           Internet: $300
Condition: Ex
Exclusive for FAO Schwarz, 1880s late French-style costume.

Margaret Face, Bride
Size: 18"   Date: 1956
Price: $375
Condition: Ex

Margaret O'Brien
Size: 14"   Date: 1946+
Price: $950   Internet: $500–$825
Condition: Ex
Margaret O'Brien (dress tag).

Margaret O'Brien
Size: 14"   Date: 1946
                           Internet: $2,125

Condition: Mint
Pristine mint.

Margaret O'Brien
Size: 18"   Date: 1946
                           Internet: $1,000
Condition: Mint
Blue/white dress, braided hair, blue straw hat with flowers.

McGuffey Ana
Size: 9"   Date: 1930s
                           Internet: $140–$160
Condition: Gd
Painted side-glancing eyes. Dolls with crazing, replaced clothes.

McGuffey Ana
Size: 9"   Date: 1935
                           Internet: $455

McGuffey Ana
Size: 13"   Date: 1935
Price: $750   Internet: $800
Condition: Mint, MIB
No crazing, original outfit tagged: "McGuffey Ana"
Mark: 13 (torso).

McGuffey Ana
Size: 15–16"   Date: 1935
                           Internet: $425+
Condition: Ex
Pale rose organdy dress. Navy coat.
Mark: Princess Elizabeth-Alexander Doll Co. (head) McGuffy Ana—Madame Alexander—NY (dress).

McGuffey Ana
Size: 20″   Date: 1937
Price: $350–$400
Condition: Ex
Mark: Princess Elizabeth/Madame Alexander.

McGuffey Ana
Size: 23″   Date: 1930s
                     Internet: $675
Condition: VGIB
With flaws.

Miss America
Size: 14″   Date: 1939
                     Internet: $700+
Fingers of right hand in grasping position to
hold a flag.

Portrait Lady
Size: 21″   Date: 1935
Price: $2,800–$4,000+
Condition: Ex
Prices vary greatly depending on outfit.

Princess Elizabeth
Size: 13″   Date: 1937
Price: $200
Condition: Ex
Mark: 13 (doll), Princess Elizabeth Madame
Alexander (costume).

Princess Elizabeth
Size: 14–15″   Date: 1930s
Price: $350+
Condition: Mint

Princess Elizabeth
Size: 17″   Date: 1937
Price: $400   Internet: $1,200
Condition: MIB
$1,200 for pristine mint.

Princess Elizabeth
Size: 24″   Date: 1935
                     Internet: $350
Condition: Ex
Light crazing, organdy dress, coat.
Mark: Princess Elizabeth-Alexander Doll.

Sally Bride
Size: 15″   Date: 1938
Price: $325
Condition: Ex

Scarlett O'Hara
Size: 11″   Date: 1940s
                     Internet: $400
Condition: VG
With flaws.

Scarlett O'Hara
Size: 11″   Date: 1930s
                     Internet: $675
Condition: Ex
Green velvet gown; light crazing OK.

Scarlett O'Hara
Size: 11″   Date: 1930s
                     Internet: $1,500
Condition: MIB
Pristine mint, tag.

Scarlett O'Hara
Size: 14″   Date: 1939
                     Price: $500
Condition: VG
With flaws.

Scarlett O'Hara
Size: 17″   Date: 1940s
Price: $475   Internet: $360
Condition: VG
With flaws.

Sleeping Beauty
Size: 18″   Date: 1941
                     Internet: $350
Condition: VG

Snow White
Size: 13″   Date: 1937–1939
                     Internet: $550–$600
Condition: Ex
Snow White pale skin, dress tagged Snow
White-Madame Alexander . . . and Walt Disney
paper label.
Mark: Princess Elizabeth-Alexander.

Soldier in WWII Uniform
Size: 15″   Date: 1943
Price: $525
Condition: Ex

Sonja Henie
Size: 14″   Date: 1935–1940
Price: $260–$350   Internet: $460
Condition: Ex
With minor crazing, common outfit.
Mark: Sonja Henie.

Sonja Henie
Size: 14″   Date: 1935–1940
Price: $700
Condition: MIB

Sonja Henie
Size: 18″   Date: 1940
Price: $400–$600   Internet: $350
Condition: Ex
With minor crazing and flaws. Common outfit.

Sonja Henie in Ivory Skating Costume
Size: 14″ Date: 1940
Price: $1,550
Condition: MIB
Mark: Wendy-Ann Mme. Alexander New York (doll), Genuine "Sonja Henie" Doll Madame Alexander (costume).

Sonja Henie in Ski Costume
Size: 14″ Date: 1942
Price: $700
Condition: Ex

Sonja Henie in Yellow Skating Costume
Size: 15″ Date: 1940
Price: $525
Condition: Ex
Mark: Alexander Sonja Henie.

Sonja Henie in Pink Taffeta Skating Costume
Size: 20″ Date: 1940
Price: $1,250
Condition: Ex
Unplayed with.

TINY BETTY, VARIOUS
Size: 7″ Date: 1935
Price: $150–$200+ Internet: $150–$200+
Condition: VG
Various common outfits, dolls with flaws.

Tiny Betty
Size: 7″ Date: 1937
Internet: $350
Condition: MIB

Tiny Betty, Alice in Wonderland
Size: 7″ Date: 1930s
Internet: $390
Condition: Ex

Tiny Betty, Carmen Miranda
Size: 7″ Date: 1939
Price: $450
Condition: Ex

Tiny Betty, China
Size: 7″ Date: 1937
Internet: $375
Condition: Ex

Tiny Betty, Colonial
Size: 7″ Date: 1940s
Internet: $275
Condition: Ex

Tiny Betty, Polish Girl
Size: 7″ Date: 1935
Price: $125
Condition: Ex

W.A.A.C. in WWII Uniform
Size: 15″ Date: 1943
Price: $1,000
Condition: Ex

W.A.V.E. in WWII Uniform
Size: 15″ Date: 1943
Price: $1,500
Condition: Ex

Wendy
Size: 18″ Date: 1940s
Internet: $250
Condition: Ex

Wendy-Ann
Size: 12″ Date: 1935
Price: $150 Internet: $200
Condition: Ex
In common outfit.
Mark: Wendy-Ann-Mme Alexander-New York (back torso).

Wendy-Ann, Bridesmaid
Size: 14″ Date: 1940s
Price: $250 Internet: $550
Condition: Ex

Wendy-Ann, Bridesmaid
Size: 18″ Date: 1930s
Internet: $800
Condition: Mint
With tag, delicate organdy dress.

Wendy-Ann, in Riding Costume
Size: 13″ Date: 1936
Price: $625
Condition: Ex

A Note on Alexander-Kins: Alexander-kins are also known as Wendy, Wendy-kin, and Wendy-Ann. Dolls and costumes are marked as either, but they are the same doll. Wendy-kin and Wendy pricing generally follow the Alexander-kin pricing; see below for additional dolls.

MADAME ALEXANDER, HARD PLASTIC

ALEXANDER-KINS, STRUNG, VARIOUS
Size: 8″ Date: 1953
Price: $500+ Internet: $450+
Condition: Ex
1953 dolls have heavier plastic and are non-walkers.

Alexander-kins, Strung
Internet: $700–$800
Condition: MIB
Pristine mint with complete outfit and wrist tag.

Alexander-kins, Strung, Agatha

Internet: $1,500

Condition: MIB
Pristine mint; like new.

ALEXANDER-KINS, SLWS, VARIOUS

Size: 8″   Date: 1954–1955
Price: $375–$525   Internet: $400–$500
Condition: Ex
SLW means straight leg walker. For dolls in common outfits.

Alexander-kins, SLW, Blue Danube

Size: 8″   Internet: $825
Condition: Mint
#34. Rarer outfit.

Alexander-kins, SLW, Davy Crockett

Size: 8″
Price: $1,000
Condition: Ex
Rarer outfit.

Alexander-kins, SLW, Little Women, Beth

Size: 8″   Internet: $900
Condition: Ex
Red and white print dress. Fuzzy-soled shoes.

ALEXANDER-KINS, BKW, VARIOUS

Size: 8″   Date: 1956–1965
Price: $225–$325   Internet: $175–$250
Condition: Av
Dress flaws or messy hair, but all original. More for rarer outfits, mint dolls, as below. BKW means bent knee walker.

Alexander-kins, BKW, Parlor Maid

Size: 8″   Date: 1956
Price: $600
Condition: Ex
#579

Alexander-kins, BKW, Riding Costume

Size: 8″   Date: 1956
Price: $525
Condition: Ex
#571 in 1956 Alexander catalog.

Alexander-kins, BKW, Scarlett

Size: 8″   Date: 1959
Price: $525
Condition: Ex
Mark: Alex (doll), Alexander-kins (costume)

Alexander-kins, BKW, Southern Belle

Size: 8″   Date: 1956
Price: $1,000
Condition: Ex
Mark: Alex (doll), Alexander-kins (costume)

Alice in Wonderland, Maggie Face

Size: 14–15″   Date: 1951
Price: $800   Internet: $700
Condition: Ex
#1874.

Alice in Wonderland, Margaret Face

Size: 21″   Date: 1948
Internet: $325+
Condition: VG

Annabelle, Maggie Face

Size: 18″   Date: 1952
Price: $800
Condition: Ex
#1810.

Artie & Smarty, Gift Set

Size: 8″   Date: 1962
Internet: $465
Condition: MIB
Gift set; clothing unattached. FAO exclusive, presented in hat box.

Babs Skater

Size: 14–15″   Date: 1950
Price: $900–$1,300   Internet: $600
Condition: Mint

Babs Skater, Margaret Face

Size: 17–18″   Date: 1948
Price: $300–$400
Condition: Ex

Binnie Walker

Size: 14–15″   Date: 1954–1955
Price: $450   Internet: $400
Condition: Ex

Binnie Walker

Size: 14″   Date: 1955
Price: $500–$600   Internet: $1,500
Condition: MIB
$1,500, pristine mint.

Binnie Walker

Size: 22″   Date: 1954
Price: $500   Internet: $400
Condition: Ex

Blue Danube, Maggie Face

Size: 18″   Date: 1953
Internet: $800
Condition: MIB
Glamour Girl series.

Bride

Size: 14″   Date: 1950s
Price: $400–$600   Internet: $750
Condition: Mint MIB
Hard plastic Madame Alexander brides.

Cinderella, Gown

Size: 14–15″   Date: 1951
Price: $800–$900   Internet: $900
Condition: MIB Mint
Margaret face.

Cinderella, Gown

Size: 18″   Date: 1950
Price: $450
Condition: Ex
Margaret face.

Cinderella, Lissy, Gift Set

Size: 12″   Date: 1966
Price: $2,000
Condition: MIB
For rare gift set, unopened.

Cinderella, Poor

Size: 15″   Date: 1951
Price: $650
Condition: Ex

CISSETTE, DAY CLOTHES, VARIOUS

Size: 10″   Date: 1957–1963
Price: $200–$300   Internet: $150–$250
Condition: Ex
In day dresses, common outfits.

CISSETTE DAY CLOTHES, VARIOUS

Size: 10″   Date: 1957–1963
Price: $300–$400   Internet: $350–$450
Condition: MIB
Slightly less for basic dolls (in undies) MIB; more for gowns and rare outfits; see examples below.

Cissette, Bridesmaid

Size: 10″
Price: $500   Internet: $550
Condition: Mint
Long pink gown.

Cissette, Gold Gown

Size: 10″   Internet: $800
Condition: Mint
"High Color" doll, rarer long gown.

Cissette, Green Velvet Gown

Size: 10″   Date: 1958
Price: $450
Condition: Ex

Cissette, Jacqueline

Size: 10″   Date: 1962
Price: $400
Condition: Ex #895.

Cissette, Taffeta Party Dress, Gown, Bride

Size: 10″   Internet: $400–$500
Condition: Ex

Excellent; black taffeta short dress, black tulle sleeves, black straw hat.

Cissette, Taffeta Dress

Size: 10″   Internet: $1,100
Condition: Mint
Rare pink dress; pristine mint.

CISSETTE, PORTRETTES, VARIOUS

Size: 11″   Date: 1968–1973
Price: $400–$500
Condition: MIB
Original window boxes; Agatha, Godey, Melinda, Renoir, Southern Belle, others.

Cissette, Portrette, Scarlett

Size: 11″   Date: 1968
Price: $200
Condition: MIB

CISSY, DAY CLOTHES, VARIOUS

Size: 21″   Date: 1955–1959
Price: $350–$450+   Internet: $300–$350+
Condition: Av
For doll in played with condition.

CISSY, DAY CLOTHES, VARIOUS

Size: 21″   Date: 1955–1959
Price: $500–$650   Internet: $400–$600
Condition: Ex
For basic dolls in common tagged or known dresses. More for evening wear, gowns; see examples below.

CISSY, SEMIFORMAL (OFTEN TAFFETA OR TULLE DRESS), VARIOUS

Size: 21″   Date: 1955–1959
Price: $750–$900   Internet: $800–$1,000
Condition: Mint
For mint dolls with great face color.

CISSY, GOWNS, VARIOUS

Size: 21″   Date: 1955–1959
Price: $1,200–$1,700 Internet: $1,100–$1,500+
Condition: Ex-Mint

Cissy, Bridesmaid

Size: 21″   Date: 1956
Price: $700
Condition: Ex
#2030 from Cissy Fashion Parade Series of 1956.

Cissy, Formal Gowns Series

Size: 21″   Date: 1957
Price: $2,100   Internet: $2,000
Condition: Mint
Cissy Models her Formal Gowns series in 1957 catalog.

Cissy, Garden Party Dress #2120

Size: 21″   Date: 1958
                   Internet: $850–$1,000

Condition: Ex
Yellow taffeta dress with flower prints; black
straw bonnet.

Cissy, Green Party Dress
Size: 21″   Date: 1950s
                 Internet: $2,500
Condition: MIB
Pristine mint with tag.

Cissy, Lilac Taffeta Dress
Size: 21″   Date: 1958
                 Internet: $2,500
Condition: Mint
Elaborate coiffure, rare dress.

Cynthia, Black Doll
Size: 14″   Date: 1952
                 Internet: $700–$850
Condition: VG
Maggie face. Made in 1952 only. Price depends
on outfit.

Cynthia, Black Doll
Size: 18″   Date: 1952
Price: $950   Internet: $700
Condition: VG

Deborah Ballerina Portrait
Size: 21″   Date: 1951
                 Internet: $9,500
Condition: MIB
eBay auction; Fashion Academy tag. Very rare; 1
of 6 1951 Portrait dolls.

ELISE, DAY DRESS, VARIOUS
Size: 16″   Date: 1957–1964
Price: $300–$400   Internet: $300–$400
Condition: Ex
Hard plastic with vinyl, jointed arms, legs.

ELISE, BALLERINAS, VARIOUS
Size: 16″
Price: $200   Internet: $225–$300
Condition: Ex

ELISE, GOWNS, VARIOUS
Size: 16″   Internet: $600
Condition: Mint

Elise, Bride
Size: 16″
Price: $450   Internet: $500
Condition: Ex

Elise, Pink Bride Dress
Size: 16″   Internet: $1,300
Condition: MIB
Pristine mint, tag.

Fairy Queen
Size: 19″   Date: 1950
Price: $600
Condition: Ex

Fischer Quints
Size: 7″   Date: 1964
                 Internet: $295
Condition: MIB
In open-window box, babies in pink blanket.

Glamour Girl in Picnic Day Costume
Size: 18″   Date: 1953
Price: $2,000
Condition: NM

Gold Rush
Size: 10″   Date: 1963
Price: $350   Internet: $300
Condition: Mint
Tagged dress. Produced for 1 year only.

Good Fairy
Size: 14″   Date: 1948
Price: $300
Condition: Ex

Groom, Godey Series
Size: 14″   Date: 1950
Price: $1,700
Condition: VG

John Robert Powers Model
Size: 15″   Date: 1952
Price: $2,000
Condition: Ex

Kathy Skater
Size: 21″   Internet: $1,000
Condition: Mint
With Fashion Academy gold tag.

Kelly
Size: 20″   Date: 1950s
                 Internet: $355
Condition: Ex

LISSY, VARIOUS
Size: 12″   Date: 1950s
Price: $300–$400   Internet: $300–$400
Condition: Ex
Day dresses and common evening wear.

Lissy, Ballerina
Size: 12″   Date: 1957
Price: $300   Internet: $375
Condition: Ex

Lissy, Cinderella
Size: 12″   Internet: $285
Condition: Ex

Lissy, Formal Gown
Size: 12″   Date: 1956
Price: $400
Condition: Ex

Lissy, Formal Gown, #1240
Size: 12″   Date: 1956–1958
                      Internet: $775
Condition: MIB
Pink tulle formal gown.

Lissy, Little Women
Size: 12″   Date: 1966
Price: $125–$150   Internet: $150–$250
Condition: Ex

Lissy, Organdy Dress
Size: 12″   Date: 1956–1958
Price: $700
Condition: Mint
With booklet.

Lissy, Bridesmaid
Size: 12″   Date: 1957
Price: $550   Internet: $545–$575
Condition: MIB
Pink sheerest nylon gown with insert of wide
Valençion lace, matching tulle hat.

Little Genius
Size: 8″   Date: 1956–1962
                      Internet: $200+
Condition: Ex

Little Genius, #116
Size: 8″   Date: 1957
                      Internet: $400
Condition: MIB
With baby bottle. Vinyl body.

**Little Women, Jo, Meg, Amy, Beth, or Marme,
Maggie Face**
Size: 14″   Date: 1949–1950
                      Internet: $550–$625
Condition: MIB Mint

Little Women, Margaret Face
Size: 14″   Date: 1950s
Price: $300+   Internet: $300–$400
Condition: Ex

Little Women, Marme, Margaret Face
Size: 14″   Date: 1950
                      Internet: $425
Condition: MIB
Dark green taffeta dress with lace at front.

**Maggie, Strung, Blouse and Skirt or Day
Dress**
Size: 15″   Date: 1954
Price: $500+   Internet: $500+
Condition: Ex

Maggie, Walker
Size: 20″   Date: 1949–1953
Price: $500   Internet: $300–$400
Condition: Ex

Maggie, Teenager
Size: 17″   Date: 1949–1950
                      Internet: $2,100
Condition: MIB
1 eBay auction, pristine mint.

Maggie Mix-Up, Blue Angel
Size: 8″   Date: 1961
                      Internet: $450
Condition: Ex
Outfit includes wings.

Maggie Mix-Up
Size: 8″   Date: 1960
Price: $200
Condition: Ex
#578.

Maggie Mix-Up
Size: 17″   Date: 1961
Price: $425
Condition: Ex
Tagged clothing.

Margaret Face, Bride
Size: 15″   Date: 1950
Price: $700
Condition: Ex

Margaret Face, Girl
Size: 14″   Date: 1948–1956
Price: $200–$250   Internet: $200
Condition: Ex

Margot Ballerina
Size: 18″   Date: 1955
Price: $275–$400   Internet: $600
Condition: Ex
Maggie face.

Mary Ellen, Walker
Size: 31″   Date: 1950s
Price: $400   Internet: $250+
Condition: Ex
Also comes as non-walker.

Mary Martin, *South Pacific*
Size: 14″   Date: 1950
Price: $875
Condition: Ex

Mary Martin
Size: 17″   Date: 1950
Price: $425
Condition: Av
Played with.

McGuffey Ana
Size: 14″   Date: 1949–1950
                   Internet: $950+
Condition: Ex

McGuffey Ana
Size: 18″   Date: 1948–1951
                   Internet: $1,000+
Condition: Ex

Me and My Shadow Series, Cherie
Size: 18″   Date: 1954
Price: $3,300
Condition: NM
#2030B from the 1954 Alexander catalog.

Me and My Shadow Series, Mary Louise
Size: 8″   Date: 1954
                   Internet: $2,000
Condition: MIB
SLW dressed in Godey period costume; outfit
matches 18″ doll.

Me and My Shadow Series, Victoria
Size: 18″   Date: 1954
Price: $1,350   Internet: $1,500–$2,000+
Condition: Ex
#2030C from the 1954 Alexander catalog. Mag-
gie face.

My Fair Lady in Ice Capades Costume
Size: 20″   Date: 1962
Price: $3,800
Condition: Ex

Little Men Series, Stuffy, Nat, etc.
Size: 15″   Date: 1952
Price: $450+   Internet: $400
Condition: Ex
1952 catalog.

Little Men Series, Tommy Bangs
Size: 15″   Date: 1952
Price: $1,300
Condition: Mint
At auction; with wrist tag.

Nina Ballerina
Size: 14–19″   Date: 1949–1951
                   Internet: $275–$325
Condition: Ex
Floss hair; comes in several color tutus.

Nina Ballerina
Size: 14″–19″   Date: 1949–1951
                   Internet: $500+
Condition: Mint

Peter Pan, 1505
Size: 15″   Date: 1953–1954
Price: $375   Internet: $325
Condition: Mint

Polly Pigtails
Size: 14″   Date: 1949–1951
                   Internet: $825
Condition: Ex
Red sweater, short denim pants, roller skates, red
felt hat with feather.

Precious (Baby)
Size: 12″   Date: 1948–1951
                   Internet: $375
Condition: Ex

Prince Charming
Size: 15″   Date: 1950
Price: $950
Condition: Ex

**Queen Elizabeth from the Beaux Art Cre-
ations**
Size: 18″   Date: 1953
Price: $1,800   Internet: $850
Condition: Ex
#2025 from the 1953 Alexander catalog. Mar-
garet face.

Rosamund in Yellow Taffeta and Tulle
Size: 18″   Date: 1953
Price: $375
Condition: Ex
#1551 in the 1953 Alexander catalog.

Royal Evening of the Beaux Art Creations
Size: 18″   Date: 1953
Price: $3,400
Condition: NM
#2020E, named "Royal Evening" from the Beaux
Art Series of 1953.

Scarlett, BKW
Size: 8″   Date: 1965
                   Internet: $300+
Condition: Ex

Shari Lewis in Afternoon Dress
Size: 14″   Date: 1959
Price: $400
Condition: Ex
Mark: 1958 Alexander (doll), Shari, Madame
Alexander New York (costume).

Shari Lewis in Gold Lace Evening Dress
Size: 14″   Date: 1959
Price: $800
Condition: MIB

Snow White
Size: 15″   Date: 1952
Price: $475–$600
Condition: Ex

So Lite Baby
Size: 18″   Date: 1930s
Price: $400
Condition: Mint
Cloth body.

Southern Belle
Size: 21″   Date: 1965
                    Internet: $900
Condition: MIB
Produced for 1 year only.

Story Princess
Size: 15″   Date: 1954
Price: $425
Condition: Ex
Aqua taffeta gown.

Sweet Violet (or Miss Active)
Size: 18″   Date: 1954
                    Internet: $1,000
Condition: Ex
Doll has jointed elbows and knees.

Wendy-Ann, Party Dress
Size: 21″   Date: 1949
Price: $1,600
Condition: Ex

WENDY AND WENDY-KIN, VARIOUS
See pricing above for Alexander-kins.

Wendy as Amanda
Size: 8″   Date: 1961
Price: $300–$400
Condition: Ex
#489 in the 1961 Alexander catalog.

Wendy Goes to a Rodeo, SLW
Size: 8″   Date: 1955
Price: $725
Condition: Ex
#483 in the 1955 Alexander catalog.

Wendy Loves Series, SLW (Ballet Lessons, Swimming, Waltzing, etc.)
Size: 8″   Date: 1955
Price: $300–$350   Internet: $250+
Condition: Ex
SLW. 1955 catalog.

Wendy on Her Way to Beach, BKW
Size: 8″   Date: 1956
                    Internet: $325
Condition: Ex

Wendy, American Girl, BKW
                    Date: 1962–1963
Price: $200–$250   Internet: $275–$350
Condition: Ex
#388. $350 MIB.
Mark: Alex (doll), "American Girl" (costume)

Wendy, Cousin Karen, BKW
Size: 8″   Date: 1956
Price: $575
Condition: Ex
#630 in the 1956 Alexander catalog.

Wendy, Easter Girl, BKW
Size: 8″   Date: 1968
Price: $450
Condition: Ex
#719, limited edition of 200 was made for distribution on the West Coast.

Wendy, Hawaiian Girl, BKW
Size: 8″   Date: 1966
Price: $500
Condition: Ex
#722.

Wendy-kin, BKW, Basic Doll
Size: 8″   Date: 1962
Price: $275–$400   Internet: $450
Condition: MIB
With tag in undies.
Mark: Alex (doll), Wendy-kin (costume)

Wendy-kin, BKW, Cotton Dress, Hair Braid
Size: 8″   Date: 1965
Price: $675
Condition: MIB
#622 in 1965 catalog with original wrist booklet.

Wendy in Easter Egg, BKW
Size: 8″   Date: 1965
Price: $2,700
Condition: MIB
FAO Schwarz label. FAO exclusive 1965.

Winnie Walker
Size: 18″   Date: 1950s
Price: $400
Condition: VG
Untagged outfit.

Winnie Walker
Size: 25″   Date: 1953
Price: $575
Condition: Ex

Winnie Walker, #1536

Size: 15"   Date: 1950s
                   Internet: $1,725
Condition: MIB
Red taffeta dress, navy blue coat, tag, hat, Mme.
Alexander hatbox.

Madame Alexander, Vinyl, 1950s–1960s

Please see the Madame Alexander section in
the Modern Dolls chapter for most Madame
Alexander dolls from 1970 through today.

MADAME ALEXANDER, VINYL, 1950s–1960s

Farmer

Size: 10"   Date: 1951
Price: $175
Condition: MIB
#620B, soft latex doll.

Agatha, Portrait

Size: 21"   Date: 1967
                   Internet: $300
Condition: Ex
Jacqueline face, red velvet outfit.

Artie & Smartie, FAO Exclusive

Size: 12"   Date: 1962
                   Internet: $400
Condition: MIB
Includes carrying case, clothing, accessories.

Binnie Walker, Strawberry Pinafore

Size: 18"   Date: 1964
Price: $100
Condition: MIB
#1830.

Brenda Starr, Various

Size: 12"   Date: 1964
Price: $100–$150   Internet: $100
Condition: MIB Mint
Brides, gowns, daywear. Box has paintings of
Brenda in outfits on box, like a vintage ponytail
Barbie.
Mark: Alexander 1964 (doll), "Brenda Starr" by
Madame Alexander (costume).

Caroline Kennedy

Size: 15"   Date: 1961
                   Internet: $175
Condition: Ex

Country Cousin

Size: 16"   Date: 1958
Price: $300

Condition: VG
Patchwork pattern dress.

Easter Girl, Limited Edition of 300

Size: 14"   Date: 1965
                   Internet: $450–$550
Condition: Ex
Commissioned by Frank Martin, a sales rep (doll
had letter). Limited edition of 300 for West
Coast only.

Edith, The Lonely Doll

Size: 20"   Date: 1958
Price: $250
Condition: Ex

Elise, Bride

Size: 17"   Date: 1957
                   Internet: $310
Condition: Ex

Elise, Bridesmaid

Size: 17"   Date: 1966
                   Internet: $355
Condition: VG+
Long yellow gown.

Elise, Gown

Size: 17"   Date: 1957
Price: $425
Condition: Ex

Goya, Portrait

Size: 21"   Date: 1968
                   Internet: $400
Condition: MIB

Jacqueline

Size: 21"   Date: 1961
                   Internet: $700
Condition: Mint
In gown; resembles Jacqueline Kennedy.

Janie, in School Dress With Book

Size: 12"   Date: 1966
Price: $100
Condition: Ex
#1157.
Mark: Alexander 1964c.

Kathy, Baby

Size: 17"   Date: 1950s
Price: $60
Condition: Ex

Kelly

Size: 16"   Date: 1959
Price: $250   Internet: $300
Condition: Ex
#1602; there is also a 22" version.

Leslie, #1620

Date: 1966
Price: $375
Condition: MIB

Little Butch

Size: 9″   Date: 1967
Price: $100
Condition: MIB
#2720.

Little Shaver, 2933

Size: 12″   Date: 1963
Price: $50
Condition: MIB

Madelaine, Ball-Jointed Body

Size: 18″   Date: 1949–1952
Price: $1,100
Condition: Ex

Mary Ellen

Size: 17″   Date: 1965
Price: $100
Condition: Ex
Exclusive for Marshall Field's, #1715.
Mark: Alexander Doll 1965.

Marybel, "The Doll That Gets Well"

Size: 16″   Date: 1960
Price: $275
Condition: MIB
Crutches, casts, bandages, and "spots" to designate measles; #1670.

Mimi, #3010, Capris

Size: 30″   Date: 1961
                             Internet: $300
Condition: VG
For doll and outfit with flaws.

Polly

Size: 17″   Date: 1965
Price: $150–$200
Condition: Ex

Coco, Portraits

Size: 21″   Date: 1966
Price: $1,000–$1,500
Condition: Ex
Produced for 1 year only. Godey, Melanie, Scarlett, others.

Scarlett, Cotton Flowered Gown, Cameo Necklace

Size: 21″   Date: 1968
Price: $900
Condition: Ex
#2180.
Mark: Alexander 1961 © (doll), "Scarlett" Madame Alexander (costume).

Scarlett, Red Velvet Gown

Size: 21″   Date: 1962
Price: $200
Condition: MIB
#2240.
Mark: Alexander 1961©.

Sound of Music, 7 Dolls, Each

Size: 11–17″   Date: 1966–1970s
                             Internet: $100–$150
Marta, Gretl, Friedrich, Louisa, Liesl, and Brigitta, Maria.

That Girl, Mod Costume

Size: 17″   Date: 1967
Price: $200
Condition: MIB
#1789.
Mark: Alexander 1966.

Mattel

Everyone knows Mattel is the company that makes Barbie dolls. However, Mattel has made hundreds of other popular dolls as well. In the 1960s, Mattel was also known for its innovative baby dolls—dolls that danced (Swingy and Dancerina), pouted (Baby Cheerful Tearful), burped (Baby Pattaburp), talked (Drowsy and Baby Say 'N See). Of course, Mattel also produced Liddle Kiddles, Chatty Cathy, and many others. Many of these dolls were familiar even to children who didn't own them, thanks to Mattel's numerous TV commercials for its dolls. Mattel also was a prolific producer of dolls that talked.

The company was founded by Ruth Handler and Harold Mattson in 1945, and produced a variety of toys and dollhouse furniture initially, turning its attention to dolls with the introduction of Barbie in 1959. For more in-depth histories of some of Mattel's most famous dolls, see the sections on Barbie, Chatty Cathy, Honey Hill Bunch, Liddle Kiddles, and Sunshine Family.

Market Report: These dolls could be found extremely inexpensively for most of the 1990s. Prices are increasing slowly after falling in price as most later 20th-century dolls did in the early 2000s, with best results seen for MIB or NRFB dolls. Most of the Mattel dolls were heavily played with, so

Sister Belle. Hard plastic head with talker inside cloth body. Pull string, doll talks. 16″, c. 1960. Mark: Mattel, Inc. / Hawthorne / Calif. (head) and Mattel, Inc. label, body. $40, eBay.

Cheerful Tearful. Vinyl. 12″, c. 1966. Mark: ©1965 MATTEL, INC. / HAWTHORNE, CALIF. / U.S. PATENTS / PENDING / 3036-014-4. $150 with box and accessories, eBay.

NRFB examples of many dolls are rarely found.

Online/Offline Report: There are always thousands of Mattel dolls available at eBay at any given time, especially played-with examples, plus there is wide availability of Mattel dolls from dealers specializing in dolls of the 1960s and 1970s.

Prices and Characteristics: All dolls are vinyl except as otherwise noted. For prices on Barbie dolls, Chatty Cathy, and Liddle Kiddles, see the appropriate sections.

MATTEL BABIES OR TODDLER DOLLS

Baby Beans
Size: 11.5″   Date: 1972
                                Internet: $50
Condition: Ex
In orange sleeper with matching bonnet.

Baby Beans
Size: 11.5″   Date: 1972
                                Internet: $75
NRFB, in yellow box. Vinyl heads and hands and bean-filled bodies.
Mark: © 1970 Mattel Inc.

Baby Beans, Talking
Size: 12″   Date: 1970
                                Internet: $30
Condition: VG+
JC Penney exclusive.

Baby Brother Tender Love
Size: 12″   Date: 1975
                                Internet: $15–$30
Condition: Av
Also black version, similar prices.

Baby Brother Tender Love
Size: 12″   Date: 1975
                                Internet: $50
Condition: MIB
Anatomically correct, body soft vinyl.

Matty Mattel. *18", c. 1960; see Sister Belle for body and mark details. $40, eBay.*

Mattel Baby Pattaburp. *Vinyl head and limbs, cloth body. 14", c. 1964. Dress tag: BABY PATTABURP / © 1964 MATTEL INC. JAPAN.*

Storybook Small Talk, Little Bo Peep. *Vinyl, 5-piece body. When you pull string, she talks. 12", c. 1960s. Mark: © 1967 MATTEL INC JAPAN (head, and mark on back). $20 missing hat and shoes, eBay; $40 mint, eBay.*

Baby Cheerful Tearful
Size: 6.5"   Date: late 1960s
                  Internet: $10–$25
Condition: Av
Flaws, or redressed.
Mark: ©1966 MATTEL, INC./HONG KONG
(head) & back mark

Baby Cheerful Tearful
Size: 6.5"   Date: 1966
                  Internet: $35
Condition: MIB
Doll pouts and cries when tummy is pressed;
with pink plastic crib.

Baby Come Back, Caucasian
Size: 16"   Date: 1976
                  Internet: $75
Battery operated.

Baby Dancerina
Size: 11"   Date: 1969
                  Internet: $10–$25
Condition: Av
Doll with mechanism problems, flaws. Blue
tutu.

Baby First Step
Size: 18"   Date: 1964
                  Internet: $100
Condition: Mint
Walks, uses 2 D batteries.

Baby First Step
Size: 18"   Date: 1964
                  Internet: $160
Condition: MIB

Baby Go Bye-Bye
                  Date: 1960s
                  Internet: $125–$150
Condition: MIB
With buggy.

Baby Hungry
Size: 17"   Date: 1967
                  Internet: $90
Condition: MIB

Baby Pattaburp
Size: 16"   Date: 1964
                  Internet: $40
Condition: Ex

Baby Pattaburp
Size: 16"   Date: 1964
                  Internet: $75
Condition: MIB
Pat her, she burps.

Baby Secret
Size: 18"   Date: 1965
                  Internet: $30–$50
Condition: Ex
Cloth body, talks.

Baby Small Talk
Size: 9.5"   Date: 1967
                  Internet: $25
Condition: Av
Mark: 1967 Mattel Inc., US and Foreign Patents
Pend, Hong Kong

Baby Hungry. *All vinyl, battery operated, mouth sucks, eyes roll. 17", c. 1967. Mark: Mattel mark on back. $90 MIB with accessories, eBay; this doll, redressed, $25, eBay.*

Baby Come Back. *Vinyl head, hard-plastic body. Battery operated, walks, turns around and comes back, starts and stops by lifting arms for hug. 16", c. 1976. © 1976 MATTEL INC. USA (head) and Mattel lower back mark. Also available in Caucasian. This doll, in mother-made crocheted outfit, $60, eBay.*

Baby Small Talk

Size: 9.5″   Date: 1967
     Internet: $105

Condition: Mint
Talks.

Baby Tender Love

Size: 15″   Date: 1972
     Internet: $25

Condition: Ex

Baby Tender Love

Size: 15″   Date: 1972
     Internet: $125

Condition: MIB

Baby Tender Love, Bless You

Size: 15″   Date: 1974
     Internet: $65

Condition: MIB
With Kleenex tissues, baby bottle, drinking instructions. Black or Caucasian.

Baby Tender Love, Tiny

Size: 11″   Date: 1972
     Internet: $25

Condition: Ex

Cheerful Tearful

Size: 13″   Date: late 1960s
     Internet: $15–$30

Condition: Av
Redressed, or original clothes with doll flaws.

Cheerful Tearful

Size: 13″   Date: late 1960s
     Internet: $75–$155

Condition: MIB

Doll pouts when you raise and lower arms, can cry tears. In light pink or bright pink and yellow outfit.

Cheerful Tearful

Size: 13″   Date: late 1960s
     Internet: $330

Condition: NRFB
Pristine mint with wrist tag.
Mark: ©1965 MATTEL, INC./HAWTHORNE, CALIF./U.S.PATENTS/PENDING/3036-014-3 (back)

Cheerful Tearful, Feed Me Set

Size: 13″   Date: late 1960s
     Internet: $75

Condition: MIB

Dancerella

Size: 18″   Date: 1972
     Internet: $65

Condition: MIB
Smaller version of Dancerina, brunette hair; white and pink tutu.

Dancerella, Black

Size: 18″,   Date: 1972
     Internet: $40

Condition: Ex
Mark: © MATTEL, INC./1969 1978/U.S.A.

Dancerina

Size: 24″   Date: 1968
     Internet: $15–$40

Condition: Av
Nonworking mechanisms and mussy hair.

Rosebud. *All vinyl. 5.5", c. 1976. Courtesy Marsha L. Cumpton.*

Baby Grows Up. *Vinyl, pull string on back of doll and she grows. Two outfits included in two sizes. 17", c. 1978. Mattel mark on back. $30, dealer.*

Love 'N Touch Baby. *Soft vinyl head, hands, bottom, cloth body. 12", c. 1979. Black doll $70, eBay; Caucasian $30, eBay.*

Dancerina
Size: 24"   Date: 1968
                             Internet: $200–$245
Condition: Mint or MIB
Pink ballet outfit, flowers at shoulder and waist, doll works (pull crown, she hops down and spins).
Mark: ©1968 MATTEL, INC. MEXICO (head) and ©1968 MATTEL, INC./MADE IN U.S.A./U.S. PATENT PENDING (back)

Dancerina
Size: 24"   Date: 1970s
                             Internet: $350–$375
Condition: NRFB
Pristine.

Dancerina, Black
Size: 24"   Date: 1968
                             Internet: $95
Condition: Fair
Dancing, but major flaws.

Dancerina, Black
Size: 24"   Date: 1968
                             Internet: $275
Condition: MIB
With box wear.

Drowsy, Talking
Size: 15"   Date: 1965
                             Internet: $40–$60
Condition: Ex
Talks.

My Child, Hispanic
Size: 12"   Date: 1985–1988
                             Internet: $200

Condition: Mint
Cloth.

Small Shot Doll
Date: 1970
                             Internet: $155
Condition: Mint
With scooter on wheels.

Teachy Keen
Size: 16"   Date: late 1960s
                             Internet: $30
Condition: Ex
Talks. Sears exclusive; teaches dressing.

Timey Tell
Size: 16"   Date: 1965
                             Internet: $15–$25
Condition: Ex
Mute.

Tippee Toes
Size: 17"   Date: 1967
                             Internet: $60–$90
Condition: Ex
With tricycle, peddles trike. For working doll.

MATTEL, TALKING DOLLS

Beanie
Size: 11"   Date: 1961
                             Internet: $270
Condition: MIB
The kid from *Cecil & Beanie* TV show.

Donny Osmond. All vinyl. 12″, c. 1976. $40 NRFB, eBay. Courtesy Ellen Johnson.

Marie Osmond. All vinyl. 11.5″, c. 1976. $40 NRFB, eBay. Courtesy Ellen Johnson.

Bozo the Clown
Size: 18″
Date: 1964
Internet: $50
Condition: Ex

Bozo the Clown
Size: 18″
Date: 1964
Internet: $100
Condition: MIB

Casper the Ghost
Size: 14″
Date: 1963
Internet: $75–$120
Condition: Ex

Cecil
Size: 15″
Date: 1961
Internet: $275
Condition: MIB
The seasick sea serpent from the *Cecil & Beanie* TV show.

Herman Munster, Talking Doll
Date: 1964
Internet: $700
Condition: MIB
Full body, pristine. Says things like: "Meet my mummy"; "You are the ghoul of my dreams"; "A tiskit, a taskit, I lost my little casket."

Herman Munster, Talking Puppet
Date: 1964
Internet: $150
Condition: Ex
Hand puppet.

Matty Mattel
Size: 18″
Date: 1960
Internet: $25–$50
Condition: Ex
Hard plastic, talks with pull string, cloth body, yarn hair. Most are mute.

Mindy
Size: 9″
Date: 1979
Internet: $15
Condition: MIB

Mork, Talking
Size: 9″
Date: 1979
Internet: $35
Condition: MIB
Talks through space pak.
Mark: 1979 PPC Taiwan (head) 1973 Mattel Inc Taiwan (back)

Mrs. Beasley
Size: 14.5″
Date: 1960s, late
Internet: $45
Condition: MIB
Cloth Mrs. Beasley issued separately (no Buffy).

Mrs. Beasley
Size: 22″
Date: 1960s
Internet: $200–$260
Condition: NM
With original collar, apron, glasses. Says "Speak a little clearer, dear, so Mrs. Beasley can hear you," etc.

Mrs. Beasley
Size: 14.5″
Date: 1970s, early
Internet: $60

Condition: Mint
Cloth, working talker.

Patootie Clown Doll

Size: 16″   Date: 1966
                      Internet: $75
Condition: Ex

Pillsbury Dough Boy

Size: 14″   Date: 1969
                      Internet: $150
Condition: Ex
Says phrases including "Do I smell something
yummy in the oven?"

Scooba Doo

Size: 21″   Date: 1965
                      Internet: $75–$100
Condition: MIB
Beatnik doll. More for working talker or price
for working talker, no box.

Shrinkin' Violette

                      Date: 1963
                      Internet: $150
Condition: Ex

Shrinkin' Violette

                      Date: 1963
                      Internet: $300
Condition: MIB
Cloth doll. Says several phrases, eyes, lips move
when you pull cord.

Sister Belle

Size: 16″   Date: 1960
                      Internet: $25–$50
Condition: Ex
Hard plastic. Talks with pull string, cloth body,
yarn hair.

Sister Small Talk

Size: 10.5″   Date: 1967
                      Internet: $35
Condition: NRFB

Small Talk, Talking Goldilocks

Size: 11″   Date: 1969
                      Internet: $25
Condition: Ex

Talk Up, Funny Talk

Size: 4.5″   Date: 1970s, early
                      Internet: $25
Condition: Ex
Plastic doll with paper face, rubber body, vinyl
clothes. You pull head (on string) to make doll
talk. Says "That's a stretch," "I'm falling apart,"
"My feet are moving closer," etc.
Mark: © 1971 MATTEL/HONG KONG on
head; © 1971 MATTEL INC./HONG KONG

Talk Up, Funny Talk

Size: 4.5″   Date: early 1970s
                      Internet: $70
Condition: Mint

Upsy Downsy, Downsy Mother What Now

Size: 3.5″   Date: 1970
                      Internet: $100
Condition: MIB
MIB.
Mark: © 1969 MATTEL, INC./HONG KONG

MATTEL, CELEBRITY DOLLS AND OTHERS

Annette Himstedt, Barefoot Children, Bastian

Size: 26″   Date: 1987
                      Internet: $300
Condition: MIB

Annette Himstedt, Barefoot Children, Käthe

Size: 26″   Date: 1987
                      Internet: $300
Condition: MIB

Audrey Hepburn, *Breakfast at Tiffany's*

Size: 11.5″   Date: 1999
                      Internet: $100
Condition: NRFB
As Holly Golightly in *Breakfast at Tiffany's;* 1st
doll authorized by Audrey Hepburn Estate.

Buffy and Mrs. Beasley

Size: 10″   Date: 1968
                      Internet: $350–$400
Condition: NRFB

Cher (in Mackie Gown)

Size: 11.5″   Date: 2000
                      Internet: $125–$140
Condition: NRFB
Lilac gown.

Donny and Marie Osmond

Size: 11.5″   Date: 1976
                      Internet: $55
Condition: NRFB
Dolls in set together, with microphones, in
lavender outfits.

Donny Osmond

Size: 11.5″   Date: 1976
                      Internet: $25
Condition: MIB
In pink and blue outfit.

Dr. Doolittle

Size: 6″   Date: 1968
                      Internet: $30
Condition: MIB

Elizabeth Taylor as Cleopatra

Size: 11.5″   Date: 1999
                        Internet: $170
Condition: NRFB

Grizzly Adams

Size: 10″   Date: 1978
                        Internet: $25
Condition: MIB

Harry Potter

Size: 8″   Date: 2001
                        Internet: $25
Condition: Ex

Hermione (from Harry Potter)

Size: 8″   Date: 2001
                        Internet: $25
Condition: Ex

I Love Lucy, "Be a Pal" (#5 in Series)

Size: 11.5″   Date: 2002
                        Internet: $100
Condition: MIB

I Love Lucy, "Job Switching"

Size: 11.5″   Date: 1999
                        Internet: $140–$150
Condition: NRFB
Episode #39.

Jimmy Osmond

Size: 11″   Date: 1978
                        Internet: $40
Condition: MIB

Marie Osmond

Size: 11.5″   Date: 1976
                        Internet: $25
Condition: MIB
In pink and blue outfit.

Rainbow Brite, Moonglow

Size: 12″   Date: 1983
                        Internet: $200
Condition: Mint
Test market doll. Pink hair, luminescent silvery
outfit.

Rainbow Brite, Tickled Pink

Size: 11″   Date: 1983
                        Internet: $100
Condition: MIB
Tickled Pink is 1 of 3 dolls in the Dress-Up se-
ries actually distributed.

Rock Flowers

Size: 6.5″   Date: 1970s
                        Internet: $3–$8
Condition: Av

Similar to Topper's Dawn dolls, but often sold
with a record.
Mark: © MATTEL INC/1970 HONG KONG
(head); back mark

Welcome Back, Kotter

Size: 9″   Date: 1973
                        Internet: $15–$20
Condition: MIB
Any character.

Nancy Ann Storybook

Countless girls growing up in the mid-20th
century had a Nancy Ann Storybook doll,
or, more likely, a whole shelf-full! Nancy
Ann Storybook Dolls were some of the first
(maybe the first?) dolls to come out in "collectible" series. The dolls were in production
from 1936 to 1960 and the dolls are perfect
shelf-size dolls: very small, at only 3.5 to 6.5
inches. The dolls were produced in bisque
until 1948, and then were made in hard plastic, then vinyl, and were available in series
such as Dolls of the Month, Mother Goose,
Brides, etc. Just like the Madame Alexander
dolls, these dolls were all about the costume—most of the dolls looked exactly
alike, and it was the detailed costuming
using the best fabrics and trims that set each
apart.

Nancy Ann Abbott, the creator of the Storybook Dolls, was born in 1901 as Rowena
Haskin. She lived in San Francisco as a
child, and she had a fondness for dolls that
lasted her entire life. Before becoming a dollmaker, she worked as an actress in Hollywood, and also as a dress designer for
various actresses. As a dress designer, she
would often dress dolls in costumes representing the full-size costumes she made.

In 1935, Ms. Abbott returned to San Francisco where she continued to dress dolls and
sell them at a bookshop where she worked.
The dolls sold well, and in 1936 the Nancy
Ann Dressed Dolls Company was born. In
1937, Les Rowland became her partner, and
by 1945 the company's name became the familiar Nancy Ann Storybook Dolls, Inc.

The first dolls created by the fledgling company in 1936 were the Hush-a-Bye Baby

Nancy Ann Storybook Dolls, Hush-A-Bye Baby series #201. Bisque, 4″. Mark: STORY / BOOK / DOLLS / USA / 11. $125 MIB, eBay.

Jack & Jill. Bisque, pudgy tummy, jointed legs with white boots, molded socks, molded bangs. 5.5″. $1,000 pair, dealer. Courtesy Marsha L. Cumpton.

To Market To Market to Buy a Fat Hen. Bisque, jointed legs, pudgy tummy. Mark: STORY / BOOK / DOLLS / USA / 11.

dolls. The bisque bodies for the dolls were made in Japan, and the dolls were only 3.75 inches tall. Later Hush-a-Bye Babies were made in the United States, and were 3.5 or 4.5 inches tall.

Soon after, a line of "Storybook" dolls including Cinderella, Little Bo Peep, and others was started. The earliest of these dolls (between 1936 and 1939) are painted bisque and are also marked "Made in Japan" or "Judy Ann USA." Most of these dolls have molded hair under their wigs and other identifying features, such as a chubby (called "pudgy") tummy. Later dolls are more slender. All Nancy Ann Storybook dolls have marks that are incised in the back. The early Storybook Dolls sold first at the Emporium in San Francisco, plus later at Marshall Field's, Harrods of London, and many other fine department stores.

Eventually, Ms. Abbott decided that the company should create the bisque for the dolls in-house, and so in the early 1940s the company opened a plant in Berkeley, California (the first of its kind in the United States) to create bisque doll bodies and parts. The doll company thrived, and during the late 1940s, Nancy Ann Storybook dolls was the highest-volume maker of dolls in the United States.

Nancy Ann painted-bisque dolls started out with hip joints. Frozen-leg bisque dolls were introduced in 1942. Bisque dolls were produced until 1948, when the hard-plastic dolls were introduced.

The dolls came in different series, which encouraged collecting by young girls and their moms. Series included Days of the Week, Months of the Year, the Storybook series, a Sports series, a Nursery Rhymes series, a Powder and Crinoline series (princesses and their courts), an All-Time Hit Parade series (keyed to different songs, such as "Over the Rainbow"), and even an Operetta series.

The company continued to do very well until the late 1950s, when both Ms. Abbott and Mr. Roland became ill. Quality declined during Ms. Abbott's illness, and new dolls such as Barbie were becoming more popular with little girls at the same time. Ms. Abbott died on August 10, 1964, and the company went bankrupt in 1965. The dolls were produced on and off by various licensees after the 1960s, but the quality was not comparable.

- **Muffie:** Also made by the Nancy Ann Storybook company was the hard-plastic Muffie doll of the 1950s. This doll was a competitor with Vogue's Ginny, and she is highly collectible today.

Close-up of pudgy tummy on "To Market To Market" doll.

Nancy Ann Storybook baby. Bisque, jointed limbs. 4". Courtesy Dana Probert.

Little Bo Peep #153. Bisque, pudgy tummy, jointed legs. 5.5". Courtesy Marsha L. Cumpton

Market Report: If you were a little girl in the 1930s or 1940s, chances are very good that you had at least a small collection of Nancy Ann Storybook dolls. And, if you are a collector of vintage dolls (dolls from 1925 through the 1970s) today, chances are very high that you have at least one Nancy Ann Storybook doll in your collection. The dolls are also ubiquitous in antique malls throughout the United States. It is this combination of nostalgia, collector interest, and high public awareness of Nancy Ann Storybook dolls that gives them such a strong market today.

The earliest dolls go for the highest prices—mint-in-box dolls dated prior to 1940 can often sell for several hundred or thousand dollars. Later hard-plastic dolls from the 1950s usually sell for under $50, but even the later bisque dolls can sell for $100 to $150 or more if mint in box and in a desirable outfit. The hard-plastic dolls are not as sought after by collectors as are the painted-bisque dolls.

Value is influenced greatly by condition—even more so than with other dolls of this era, because many Nancy Ann Storybook dolls were purchased to be on a shelf—they were collected and not played with. Because of this, unlike, say, Shirley Temple dolls or Toni dolls, great numbers of Nancy Ann

Storybook dolls have survived in mint condition today, complete with their boxes, tags, and booklets. Therefore, Nancy Ann Storybook dolls in lesser condition sell at considerable discounts. Also affecting price is the huge number of dolls produced overall. Many, many Nancy Ann Storybook dolls have been made—at one point, over 8,000 dolls a day were being produced.

Finally affecting the price is the rarity of a particular series and rarity of the costume variation. For instance, a great number of versions of each type of doll such as Tuesday's Child Is Full of Grace were produced, but some versions are much rarer than others. Sometimes a particular costume was produced for only a short period of time because of difficulty in getting a particular fabric or trim.

Online/Offline Report: There are endless numbers of Nancy Ann Storybook dolls available at eBay and other online auctions, and because of this, you can sometimes find a bargain, and you can certainly find played-with dolls at low prices. However, when looking for mint dolls on eBay, be especially wary of condition descriptions and photos, because condition is so all-important in the price of Nancy Ann dolls. Prices for the mint and rare dolls are comparable from all

Winter #93. Bisque, jointed legs. 5". Mark: STORY / BOOK / DOLL / U.S.A. / 11. $100, dealer.

Sunday's Child #186. Bisque, pudgy tummy, jointed legs, shorter arms model. $160, dealer. Courtesy Marsha C. Cumpton.

sources, with strong Internet competition. Some dealers specialize in Nancy Ann dolls, and it helps to buy from a dealer with in-depth knowledge about how the many costume and body variations of the dolls affect prices.

Prices and Characteristics: All-bisque Nancy Ann Storybook dolls have painted bisque, with frozen or jointed legs as indicated, and they are generally 5 inches to 7 inches tall, with the vast majority between 5 inches and 6 inches. They do not have swivel necks, and all dolls have jointed arms. Eyes are painted and dolls have mohair wigs. All marks are on the back torsos of the dolls. In each category individual examples with prices are included, but be aware that rare variations in costumes can affect prices greatly. Price results are mixed and similar from all venues, with Internet prices noted.

NANCY ANN STORYBOOK DOLLS, BISQUE BABIES

Baby Pattycake
Size: 4"
Price: $125
Condition: MIB

Baby
Price: $100–$130
Condition: Ex

Hush-A-Bye-Baby, Early (Gold Sticker, Dress)
Condition: Mint
Price: $300–$350
Molded hair and bangs. Starfish hands.

Hush-A-Bye Baby, Early
Condition: MIB
All Markets: $500
Pink box, blue polka dots, long baby dress.

Hush-A-Bye Baby, Later (Wrist Tag)
Condition: MIB
Price: $200–$300

Monday's Child #180. *Bisque, frozen legs. 5.5". Mark: STORY / BOOK / DOLL / U.S.A. / 11. Courtesy Marsha L. Cumpton.*

Elsie Marley #131. *Bisque, frozen legs. 5", c. 1943–1945. Mark: STORY / BOOK / DOLL / USA. $55, dealer.*

Friday's Child. *Bisque, frozen legs. 5". Mark: STORY / BOOK / DOLL / U.S.A. / 11. $45, dealer.*

Usually in long baby dress, blue, white polka dot box, #210. Starfish hands.

NANCY ANN STORYBOOK, BISQUE JUDY ANNS, MARGIES, AND OTHERS

c. 1936–1939.

Judy Ann, Various
Price: $700
Condition: Ex
Average price for Judy Anns.
Mark: JUDY/ANN/U.S.A.

Judy Ann, Gypsy
All Markets: $3,100
Condition: Ex
1938. Masquerade series. Pudgy tummy, gold earrings, red flower-print scarf, gold sticker on skirt. At auction.
Mark: JUDY/ANN

Judy Ann, Mexico, #39
Price: $450
Condition: Ex
Mark: JUDY/ANN/U.S.A.

Judy Ann, Painted Hair, To Market, To Market
All Markets: $2,900
Condition: Mint

Judy Ann, Russia
All Markets: $3,000
Condition: MIB
Pudgy tummy, pinched face, molded socks, red box.
Mark: JUDY/ANN

Judy Ann, Sweden or Scottish
Price: $825
Condition: Mint
Mark: JUDY/ANN/USA

Judy Ann, Scottish
All Markets: $2,900
Condition: MIB
Red box.

Margie Ann, Various
Price: $400
Condition: Ex
Average price for Margie Anns.

Margie Ann, Painted Hair
All Markets: $2,150
Condition: Ex
Painted, molded hair; white boots/socks.

Margie Ann, White Coat and Hat, #82
All Markets: $3,200
Condition: MIB
White boots/socks, wigged, original white hat and coat.

Margie Ann, Red Coat and Hat
Price: $200–$300
Condition: MIB
White box, red polka dots.

Topsy and Eva, Pair (Pudgy Tummy, Painted Black Boots)
All Markets: $1,800–$1,900
Condition: MIB
Topsy has painted black boots with buttons. Shorter arms.
Mark: STORY/BOOK/DOLL/USA/11

Nancy Ann Style Show. *Wearing original dress with hoop skirt. Hard plastic, 5-piece body. 18". Courtesy Marsha L. Cumpton.*

Nancy Ann Style Show. *Wearing original outfit. Hard plastic, 5-piece body. 18". Courtesy Marsha L. Cumpton.*

K & H bisque baby. *Nancy Ann look-alike doll. The company was sued by Nancy Ann Storybook Dolls and had to stop making the look-alikes. 4", original box. Mark: K & H. / USA.*

NANCY ANN STORYBOOK, BISQUE, JOINTED LEGS, PUDGY TUMMY, MOLDED SOCKS OR PAINTED BOOTS

c. 1939–1940.

Jointed Legs, Pudgy Tummy, Molded Socks, Various

All Markets: $200–$300
Condition: Mint
Varies with costume. More for MIB or molded bangs (slightly earlier), less for played-with dolls. Molded socks.
Mark: STORY/BOOK/DOLL/U.S.A.

Black, Mammy

Price: $485
Condition: Ex
Gold "Storybook Dolls" sticker on dress. Foil wrist tags after 1940.

Cinderella

Price: $425
Condition: Mint
Molded bangs under wig and socks unpainted (early doll).

Dutch, #27

Price: $450
Condition: MIB

Irish, #34

Price: $500
Condition: MIB
Red box, white polka dots.

Pussy Cat

Price: $465
Condition: Ex
Blue dotted swiss dress with pinafore.

Scottish

Price: $425
Condition: Ex

Ring Around the Rosey, #159

All Markets: $700
Condition: MIB
Red box, white polka dots.

Molded Socks, Goldilocks and Bear, #128

Price: $700
Condition: MIB
1940.

White Painted Boots, Goldilocks and Baby Bear, #128

All Markets: $3250
Condition: VG
1941.

NANCY ANN STORYBOOK, BISQUE, JOINTED LEGS, PUDGY TUMMY, NO MOLDED SOCKS

c. 1941.

Jointed Legs, Pudgy Tummy, Various

All Markets: $150–$200
Condition: Mint
Often with shorter arms.

Hollywood Dolls bride. One of many Nancy Ann look-alikes, or clones. Composition head/torso, hard plastic limbs. 5". Mark: HOL-LYWOOD / DOLL (back) . $15, dealer.

Muffie. Hard plastic, straight-leg walker. 7.25", c. 1954. Mark: STORY BOOK / DOLLS / CALI-FORNIA / MUFFIE and tagged Muffie outfit. $200, dealer.

Jointed Legs, Pudgy Tummy, Various
All Markets: $250–$300
Condition: MIB
Mark: STORY/BOOK/DOLL/USA/11

Goldilocks
Price: $250
Condition: Ex
Painted white shoes/socks.

Little Red Riding Hood
Price: $250
Condition: MIB
Painted white shoes/socks.

NANCY ANN STORYBOOK, BISQUE, JOINTED LEGS
c. 1942.

Jointed Legs, Flat Tummy, Various
All Markets: $50–$75
Condition: Mint
For common styles. More for rare costumes. Painted black shoes.

Jointed Legs, Flat Tummy, Various
All Markets: $85–$125
Condition: MIB
Mark: STORY/BOOK/DOLL/USA/11

Quaker Maid
Price: $155
Condition: MIB

Little Red Riding Hood
Price: $135
Condition: Mint

NANCY ANN STORYBOOK, BISQUE, FROZEN LEGS
c. 1943–1945; with plastic arms from 1946–1947.

Frozen Leg Nancy Ann Storybook, Common Styles
All Markets: $30–$40
Condition: Mint
Loose dolls; painted black shoes.

Frozen Leg Nancy Ann Storybook, Common Styles
All Markets: $65–$85
Condition: MIB
Mark: STORY/BOOK/DOLL/U.S.A/11

Frozen Legs, Plastic Arms
Price: $55–$70
Condition: MIB
Painted black shoes.
Mark: NANCY/ANN/STORYBOOK/DOLL

School Days, #117
Price: $160
Condition: MIB

Ann at the Garden Gate, #129
Price: $155
Condition: Ex

Going a Milkin'
Price: $125
Condition: Mint
Red and white striped outfit.

Muffie, vinyl walker. 7.25", c. 1956. STORY BOOK / DOLLS / CALIFORNIA / MUFFIE (back). $175 MIB, dealer.

Thursday's Child
Price: $100–$150
Condition: Mint
Rarer outfit.

Monday's Child, #180
Price: $100
Condition: MIB

Over the Hills, #114
Price: $135
Condition: Ex

Hard Plastic

C. 1947–1950s. Hard plastic dolls have sleep eyes, swivel heads, and jointed legs.

NANCY ANN STORYBOOK, HARD PLASTIC

Nancy Ann Storybook Dolls, Hard Plastic
Price: $30–$40
Condition: MIB
Mark: STORY BOOK/DOLLS/U.S.A./TRADEMARK/REG.

Nancy Ann Storybook Dolls, Hard Plastic
Price: $15–$25
Condition: Ex
Loose dolls.

NANCY ANN LOOK-ALIKES

Look-Alikes, Kerr & Hinz
Price: $20–$30
Condition: MIB

For adult or baby, often sold nude. Company successfully sued by Nancy Ann Storybook Dolls for infringement.
Mark: K & H

Look-Alikes, Hollywood Dolls
Price: $20–$40
Condition: Ex

Look-Alikes, Hollywood Dolls, Libra, Lucky Star Series
Price: $30–$40
Condition: MIB
Often 6" or more.

Nancy Ann Storybook Dolls, Hard Plastic

All hard-plastic dolls, including Muffie, are from the 1950s with 5-piece jointed bodies.

HARD PLASTIC, MUFFIE AND VARIOUS

Debbie, Walker
Size: 10"
Price: $150–$200
Condition: MIB

Miss Nancy Ann
Size: 10.5"
Price: $175
Condition: Ex
Tagged and original.
Mark: Nancy Ann

Muffie, Strung

Size: 8″
All Markets: $700–$1,000
Condition: MIB
Pink and white polka dotted box, with hang tag.
For pristine mint. 1953.

Muffie, Strung, 700 series

Size: 8″
Price: $300–$400
Condition: Ex
Sunday Best or similar desirable outfit.

Muffie, Walker, Side Part, #55

Size: 8″
Price: $550
Condition: MIB
In original red taffeta panties, wrist tag, box
with red polka dots marked 500 Muffie.

Muffie, Walker, Straight Leg (SLW)

Price: $200–$250
Condition: Ex

Muffie, Bent Knee Walker

Size: 8″
Price: $150–$275
Condition: Ex
1955.
Mark: Storybook CA Muffie

Muffie, Walker, Auburn Side Part

Size: 8″
All Markets: $725
Condition: MIB

Nancy Ann Style Show

Size: 18″
Price: $300
Condition: Gd

Nancy Ann Style Show

Size: 18″
Price: $300–$400
Condition: VG
Dolls with flaws, redressed, 1953–1955.
Mark: Nancy Ann Style Show dolls are un-
marked.

Nancy Ann Style Show

Size: 18″
Price: $600–$700
Condition: Ex
Elaborate dresses, often tulle or satin, dramatic
hats.

Nancy Ann Style Show

Size: 18″
Price: $1,275–$2,000
Condition: MIB
Varies greatly depending on outfit, higher end of
range for rarer outfits, pristine mint.

Little Miss Nancy Ann

Size: 8″
Price: $75
Condition: VG

NANCY ANN STORYBOOK DOLLS, VINYL, LORI ANN

Lori Ann

Size: 8″   Internet: $95
Condition: Ex
Muffie-type and -size doll.
Mark: Lori Ann 500 (tag)

Lori Ann

Size: 8″   Internet: $200
Condition: Mint
Mark: Nancy Ann, and Lori Ann (tag)

National Costume Dolls (Foreign Travel Dolls)

It always surprises me how inexpensive national costume dolls (referred to as "foreign
travel dolls" or "ethnic dolls" by some collectors, but as "national costume dolls" in this
book) are and also how underappreciated
they are. Since the late 1800s, dolls dressed in
national costumes have been sold as tourist
souvenirs to millions and millions of people
worldwide.

The dolls that are covered in this section of
the book are the national costume dolls sold
mostly in the 20th century to tourists in
countries around the world. The dolls are
made of nearly every material imaginable—
cloth, bisque, celluloid, plastic, composition.
All are dressed in the national costume of a
country or region. Many of the costumes on
these dolls are beautifully done and detailed.
Most of the makers are unknown, although
some dolls are marked, others have their
original boxes, and some are labeled as to
maker.

Germany. Celluloid, swivel head, 5-piece body. Red leather shoes, removable clothing. 12.5", c. 1930s. Mark: HU (joined). $80, dealer.

Hungary. Composition face, cloth body. 8", c. 1937. Unmarked. Courtesy Dana Probert.

Norway. Cloth mask face, wire-armature cloth body. Similar to BAPS dolls but larger and feet not metal. 5.25", c. 1939. Unmarked. Courtesy Dana Probert.

Market Report: Prices for these dolls remain low, with exceptions starting to emerge for dolls that collectors are recognizing for fine costumes or better-than-average artistry. This is good news for collectors drawn to these dolls—a lovely collection can still be assembled for a relatively low price. Dolls in this section are only representative of the many thousands of dolls in this category, to assist collectors with some ranges for pricing. Look for dolls made with better-than-average artistry, older foreign tourist dolls from the 1940s and before, and dolls with removable or fine-quality clothing.

Online/Offline Report: The majority of these dolls can be found at online auctions, at general and doll antique shops, and at doll shows. Prices are comparable at all venues, with some bargains available online for collectors with a good eye for better-than-average costuming. The national costume dolls can be hard to hunt down on eBay. Although there is an "International/Cultural" section for dolls on eBay, most sellers tend to place the dolls for sale in a wide range of categories, including "Antique," "Other," "Cloth," "Composition"—you name it. If you have an idea as to the country of a doll you'd like to find, you can search the country, but it is hard to just browse this category.

Prices, Characteristics, and Marks: Nearly all national costume dolls of the 20th century can be found for under $100 (with the exception of some early bisque dolls), and the vast majority can be found for under $50, with thousands of choices even in the under $30 range. I've listed a few prices for these dolls and I've included some wide-ranging photos of the dolls in this category as examples. Also see Peggy Nisbet dolls, which are, in effect, tourist dolls from England, and also Klumpe/Roldan, often sold as tourist dolls in Spain. Prices for post-1970 dolls are for mint dolls, and for pre-1970 dolls, for excellent dolls, except as noted, all in original clothing. Since these dolls were not intended for play, dolls in less-than-excellent condition have very little value.

Marks: Most dolls are unmarked except for paper labels, boxes or hang tags.

NATIONAL COSTUME DOLLS

Anekona Hawaii, Inc.
Size: 6–15"   Date: 1972
                              Internet: $5–$15
Material: hard plastic
Various Hawaiian dolls for tourist trade, vinyl and hard plastic.

Anekona Hawaii, Inc. of Honolulu, Hawaii
Size: 15"   Date: 1972
                              Internet: $45

Russia. *Composition face, wire-armature cloth body, floss hair. 4.5", c. 1940. Unmarked. Courtesy Dana Probert.*

India. *Composition head and arms, all cloth . 15", c. 1946. Unmarked. Courtesy Dana Probert.*

Mennonite, Lancaster, PA. *Stone bisque. 5", c. 1937. Unmarked. Courtesy Dana Probert.*

Belgian War Doll. *Papier-mâché head, cloth body, crepe paper slip and pantaloons. 18", c. 1945. Unmarked. Courtesy Dana Probert.*

Mexico. *All felt. 8", c. 1946. Unmarked. Courtesy Dana Probert.*

Italy. *Cloth mask face, metal feet. 4". Mark: Parla / Tuscany / Firenze (box).*

Australia. *Hard Plastic. 7.5". Mark: Tom Green, Sydney, Australia (label). Courtesy Dana Probert.*

Michael Lee doll, with papoose. *All cloth, made in Hong Kong. 11" sitting, c. 1970s. Mark: Hang tag. Courtesy: Dana Probert.*

Hawaiian tourist doll, USA. *Vinyl head and 1-piece body. 8", c. 1960s. Mark: MADE IN / JAPAN (foot).*

Native American doll. *All hard plastic, jointed arms only. 8″, c. 1970s. Mark: HERITAGE DOLLS (tag). $5, eBay.*

Material: vinyl
MIB.

Children, Pair, Folklore Outfits

Size: 5″   Date: 1930s
All Markets: $250
Material: painted bisque
Set eyes, closed mouths, 5-piece composition bodies with molded shoes.

French, Celluloid

Size: 7–10″   Date: 1930s–1960s
                                        Internet: $20–$40
Material: celluloid
Companies such as SNF, Petitcollin, Poupées, similar, in national costume; more for premium fabrics/trims.

Hawaiian Hula Dolls

Size: 4–8″   Date: 1940s–1950s
                                        Internet: $15–$45
Material: hard plastic
Earliest hula dolls of hard plastic.

Hawaiian Hula Dolls, Hong Kong

Size: 4–8″   Date: 1970s
                                        Internet: $5–$10
Material: vinyl
Mark: HONG KONG or MADE IN HONG KONG.

Hawaiian Hula Dolls, Japan

Size: 4–8″   Date: 1960s
                                        Internet: $10–$20
Material: vinyl
Mark: JAPAN or MADE IN JAPAN.

Hungarian Lady or Man

Size: 10–17″   Internet: $50
Material: papier-mâché
Or terra-cotta, elaborate costume.

Israel, Kimport Woman

Size: 8″   Internet: $60
Material: cloth mask

Italy, Amelia

Size: various   Internet: $20–$40
Material: cloth mask or stockinette

Italy, Eros

Size: 7–9″   Internet: $12–$30
Material: cloth mask

Japanese Doll, With 6 Masks

Size: 7″   Internet: $75
Material: gofun
MIB; set, doll with 6 masks, boxed in wood.

Japanese, Girl

Size: 17″   Date: 1950s
                                        Internet: $200
Material: gofun (oyster paste)
VG. Later doll, with flaws. See also Japanese Dolls in the Antique Dolls chapter.

Japanese, Girl

Size: 17″   Date: 1930s
                                        Internet: $400
Material: gofun
Mint.

Michael Lee

Size: 7–14″   Date: 1940s
                                        Internet: $45–$65

King Henry VIII. *Hard plastic, only arms jointed. 8". Unmarked. $25, eBay.*

Pearly King. *Hard plastic. Only arms jointed 8". Unmarked, original tag and red-sleeved Peggy Nisbet box. $15 with box, eBay.*

H.M. Queen Elizabeth II in state robes. *Hard plastic, only arms jointed. 8". Unmarked, original tag and red Peggy Nisbet box. $20 with box, eBay.*

Material: composition
Often Chinese mother and child.

Michael Lee

Size: various

Date: 1970s–1980s
Internet: $20–$40

Material: cloth

Michael Lee

Size: various

Date: 1990s
Internet: $10–$20

Material: vinyl

Russian Doll

Size: 15"

Date: 1930s–1940s
Internet: $90–$100

Material: stockinette face
Slightly less for cloth mask face; elaborate costumes.

Russian, Lady

Size: 13"
All Markets: $70
Material: terra-cotta
Cloth body, Russian peasant costume.

South America

Size: 16"

Date: 1950s–1960s
Internet: $40–$50

Material: cloth mask

Nisbet, Peggy

Peggy Nisbet started making dolls in the early 1950s. Her dolls were all made in England, and the company made dolls well after her death through the mid-1990s.

Peggy Nisbet is best known for her dolls of historical English figures, including queens and kings of England, but her dolls included Hollywood celebrities, American presidents, and many other characters as well. The dolls were made of plastic, and usually were no more than 8 inches tall. Many dolls, especially the dolls of historical English figures, were sold to tourists in England.

Market Report: The majority of Peggy Nisbet dolls can be found for between $20 and $60 on most Internet auction sites, with older dolls, scarce dolls, and limited editions bringing more. The prices for Peggy Nisbet dolls have stayed in the same range for several years.

Online/Offline Report: These dolls are abundant on the Internet and especially from English dealers, although American dealers with a broad range of 20th-century dolls will often have several in stock.

Prices and Characteristics: Dolls are generally unmarked, so boxes and tags are used for identification. Dolls are made of hard plastic, with only arms jointed and with painted eyes. Some very early tagged Peggy Nisbet dolls have been found with composition heads, although these are relatively rare. Peggy Nisbet dolls are hard to date; they were made from the 1950s through the early

Wednesday's Girl, by Peggy Nisbet for Royal Doulton. Bisque, Days of the Week Series. 11″. Unmarked; original blue box. $20, eBay.

1990s and some dolls were made for long periods of time. All dolls are in excellent condition except as noted. Most dolls are 8 inches. Prices are from the Internet but similar from all sources.

PEGGY NISBET

Various English and Other Historical Characters
Internet: $20–$50
For loose dolls in mint condition, more for rarer characters, especially elaborate outfits.

Various English and Other Historical Characters
Internet: $30–$60
MIB. More for rarer characters, especially elaborate outfits.

Anne Boleyn
Internet: $85

Artful Dodger
Internet: $120

Joan of Arc
Internet: $65
Mint, tag.

John F. Kennedy
Internet: $95
Mint, tag.

King Henry VIII
Internet: $20–$30
Mint, very common character.

Catherine of Aragon
Internet: $50–$85
MIB.

King Henry VII
Internet: $180
MIB, limited edition of 250.

King Henry VIII
Internet: $130
MIB, earlier red box.

King James
Internet: $370
MIB.

King Richard, Limited Edition
Internet: $235
MIB, limited edition of 179.

Lady Barbara Castlemaine
Internet: $95
Green and lilac dress, feathered hat.

Mikhail Gorbachev
Internet: $125
MIB.

Mistress of the Robes
Internet: $60
For Queen Elizabeth II's 1977 Silver Jubilee.

Prince Andrew and Fergie, Wedding Set
Internet: $100
MIB.

Princess Diana
Internet: $25–$30
For mint, loose dolls, very common character.

Queen Elizabeth II
Internet: $65–$85
There are many variations; these prices for beaded white gown, higher price for MIB.

Queen Elizabeth I
Internet: $130
MIB, modeled exclusively for Heritage Theatre, Stratford-upon-Avon.

Queen Isabella
Internet: $115
MIB.

Queen Judith
Internet: $115
MIB.

Paper Dolls

Paper dolls are often not included in general books about dolls, but so many collectors of three-dimensional dolls also collect paper dolls that I feel they are properly introduced here.

Paper dolls are dolls made from paper which have accompanying paper clothing. They have existed for centuries, but they weren't manufactured until the early 1800s (approximately 1810 in both England and the United States). Earlier examples of hand-painted paper dolls are very rare—for instance a few examples are known to exist of small paintings of ladies with thin mica overlays with costumes painted on them.

In the early and mid-1800s, paper dolls were often sold in boxed sets including several dolls and outfits. In the mid-1800s, a few paper dolls of famous ballerinas and of queens were published. In the late 1800s, European companies produced lithographed boxed sets of paper dolls, and many of these sets focused on famous royalty and entertainers. These early "celebrity" paper dolls foreshadowed the craze for paper dolls of celebrities that would follow in the 20th century.

One of the largest manufacturer of paper dolls in the United States was the McLoughlin Brothers, which made paper dolls from 1828 until well into the 20th century (after 1920 as part of Milton Bradley). Another U.S. manufacturer, Dennison, started in 1880 and created charming crepe paper outfits for their paper dolls. Dolls with crepe paper outfits remained popular until the early 1920s.

In England, the best-known 19th-century maker of paper dolls was Raphael Tuck. Manufactured in Germany, the dolls were just one of the many lithographed products that Tuck specialized in, including postcards, trading cards, and greeting cards. The majority of the Raphael Tuck paper dolls were made from the 1880s to the early 1900s.

Another popular source of paper dolls in the late 19th and early 20th century was advertising material—dolls were given out along with Victorian trading cards to be used in the Victorian scrapbooks that were the rage at that time. The dolls carried the trade name of the company along with other information on the back of the doll, just as the Victorian trading cards carried the information on the back of its lithographed image.

In the 20th century, children had many choices for paper dolls. Besides the many companies now producing them, magazines started to print paper dolls as well. *Ladies Home Journal* was one of the first magazines to widely print paper dolls, including Lettie Lane, starting in 1908. In the *Pictorial Review* there was Dolly Dingle. This practice continued in the 1950s with the very popular Betsy McCall paper dolls in *McCall's* magazine, and it continues today with the Ann Estelle paper dolls in *Mary Engelbreit's Home Companion*.

By the mid-20th century, paper dolls were printed in booklets with cover art to entice the purchaser. Paper dolls became a direct reflection of the popular culture—everything that interested little girls (and their mothers). Queen Holden painted many of these paper dolls from 1929–1950, including dolls of Judy Garland, the Dionne Quintuplets, and others. Movie stars and movies were extremely popular as subjects for paper dolls all through the mid-20th century. It seemed nearly every celebrity, including Sonja Henie, Shirley

Temple, Rita Hayworth, and Betty Grable was made into a paper doll

Little girls still played with paper dolls by the millions in the 1960s. Barbie and other popular dolls such as Crissy, Tammy, and Liddle Kiddles were all also created in paper doll form. Television programs became great grounds for paper doll ideas, and characters from TV programs such as *The Patty Duke Show, The Brady Bunch,* and *The Partridge Family* became paper dolls. Of course, characters from such movies as *Chitty Chitty Bang Bang* and *Mary Poppins* continued to be made into paper dolls. Whitman and Golden Books made many of the 1960s paper dolls.

Paper dolls continue to be made today, although in much smaller numbers, by companies such as Schylling and B. F. Shackman. However, you are much more likely today to find paper dolls in a specialty toy or doll shop than in the local drugstore. Paper dolls are also often printed in doll collector magazines.

Market Report: Paper dolls are a hot area of collecting, both for rare and for more common paper dolls. Paper dolls appeal not only to doll collectors, but to collectors of 19th- and 20th-century paper ephemera as well. Another factor in their popularity is the ability to store many paper dolls in a small area, which appeals to collectors who have limited storage and display space for three-dimensional dolls.

Prices for paper dolls continue to rise steadily, especially for mid-20th-century uncut paper dolls of celebrities, 19th-century paper dolls (especially in complete sets), and even for uncut baby-boomer paper dolls from the 1960s.

However, one of the nice things about paper dolls is that there are dolls available at nearly every price point. Collectors of very early boxed sets of paper dolls can sometimes pay hundreds or thousands per set. Yet uncut magazine paper dolls can be very reasonable (often as little as $10 to $15 per sheet), as are many of the advertising paper dolls from the late 1800s to early 1900s. There are also many 1960s and 1970s paper dolls still avail-

able inexpensively, generally under $20 for an uncut book.

When buying paper dolls, creasing, soiling, pen marks, and discoloration will negatively affect the value. Look for weakness in the neck area and feet for cut dolls, since these parts of paper dolls are often the first parts to show wear. Cut dolls will sell for considerably less than uncut dolls.

Online/Offline Report: Dealers specializing in paper dolls will have the best and most varied stock. There are also many paper dolls available on eBay (usually more than 1,000 at any one time), but these are generally 20th-century advertising dolls, magazine paper dolls, or incomplete 19th-century items. The 19th-century complete boxed sets are hardly ever found on eBay. Occasionally, auction houses will sell paper dolls, especially when a large, choice collection becomes available for sale all at one time.

Patsy and Family

See also "Effanbee."

Patsy was a unique doll for her time. Patsy, designed by well-known doll designer Bernard Lipfert, was first sold by Effanbee in 1928. Designed to have the proportions of a real child, Patsy was an immediate hit. She was the first doll to have an entire manufactured wardrobe, and, in fact, Patsy was the first doll to have her own little world complete with her own friends and family— Patsy Joan, Skippy, and others. Patsy also came in a variety of sizes, from the smaller Wee Patsy and Patsyettes to the larger Patsy Ann.

Patsy had molded, bobbed hair and, because of her body design, a very distinct look. Many Patsy clones were created in composition with a look, feel, and proportions similar to Patsy. These are generally unmarked dolls.

Composition Patsy was produced until approximately 1947. In the 1970s, several collector editions of Patsy dolls were issued, and Patsy was also released in vinyl in the 1980s.

Patsy dolls. Both with molded hair (one with mohair wig over it), 5-piece composition toddler bodies. 13.5", c. 1930. Mark: Effanbee Patsy (head) Effanbee Patsy Doll (back). Courtesy Theriault's.

Patsyette Brother and Sister. Composition 5-piece bodies. 9", c. 1931. Mark: Effanbee Patsyette Doll (back). Courtesy Theriault's.

Effanbee issued more vinyl reproductions of the Patsy family starting in 1995, and these dolls were produced until Effanbee's bankruptcy in 2002. After the Tonner Doll Company purchased Effanbee's assets out of bankruptcy, Tonner updated Patsy by giving her a more matte look and also, in some versions, hair!

Market Report: Values for Patsy have remained mostly steady, with a definite decrease in value for played-with and heavily crazed dolls.

Online/Offline Report: Patsy dolls are relatively available on eBay, but dealers and auction houses will have choice examples. Except for the best examples, online sources can have cheaper prices, but it is hard to assess the state of the composition via the Internet.

Prices and Characteristics: All Patsy family dolls listed here are composition, with 5-piece bodies, painted or sleep eyes, and prices are for dolls in excellent condition, except as noted. Dolls were made from 1928 through the mid-1940s. Dolls came with a heart bracelet that reads: Effanbee / Durable / Dolls.

PATSY FAMILY

Patricia
Size: 14"   Internet: $400
Mark: Effanbee/Patricia

Patsy
Size: 14"
Price: $220–$300   Internet: $200
VG.

Patsy, Early
Size: 14"   Internet: $480
MIB. Patent Pending is early version.
Mark: EFFanBEE PATSY/Pat Pending Doll

Patsy Ann. *Composition head, 5-piece body. 19", c. 1932. Mark: EF-FANBEE / PATSY – ANN / © / PAT # 1283558 (back). $520, dealer.*

Wee Patsy. *All composition, 1-piece head and torso, jointed arms and legs. Initially marketed as a Colleen Moore Dollhouse doll (see original button on outfit). Effanbee Wee Patsy (back). 5.75", c. 1932. $250, dealer.*

Patsy Tinyettes, Dutch Twins. *Composition, 4-piece bodies. 8", c. 1936. Mark: Effanbee (heads) Effanbee Baby Tinyette (backs). Courtesy Theriault's.*

Patsy, Rarer Outfit
Size: 14"   Internet: $600
Mint.

Patsy, in Travel Trunk
Size: 14"
Price: $260

Patsy, Unmarked
Size: 14"
Price: $180
Replaced costume.

Patsy-Type, Molded Hair
Size: 11", 18"   Internet: $90–$120
Unmarked competitor from another company.

Patsy-Type, Original Trunk and Wardrobe
Size: 11"   Internet: $290
Unmarked competitor from another company.

Patsy Ann
Size: 19"
Price: $350–$425   Internet: $330–$400
Mark: Effanbee/"Patsy Ann"/©/Pat # 1283558 (back)

Patsy Ann, Trunk, Extensive Wardrobe
Size: 19"
Price: $1,500
Mint with wooden steamer trunk, 10 original outfits, accessories.

Patsy Ann, Vinyl
Size: 15"
Price: $70   Internet: $50
1959, vinyl doll.

Patsy Ann, Vinyl, Brownie
Size: 15"   Internet: $260
1959, vinyl doll in desirable Brownie uniform. Doll has freckles.
Mark: Effanbee//Patsy Ann/© 1959

Patsy Babyette
Size: 9"
Price: $150   Internet: $255
Tin eyes, minor crazing.

Patsy Baby
Size: 10"   Internet: $80
VG.
Mark: Effanbee/Patsy Baby

Patsy Baby
Size: 10"   Internet: $250

Patsy Joan
Size: 16"   Internet: $160
VG; doll with flaws, redressed.

Patsy Joan
Size: 16"
Price: $350   Internet: $430
Mint. Original organdy rose dress with matching bonnet, sleep eyes.
Mark: Effanbee/Patsy Joan (back)

Patsy Jr.
Size: 11"
Price: $170   Internet: $190
VG; crazing, paint lifting.
Mark: Effanbee/Patsy Jr/Doll

Patsy Lou. Composition, 5-piece body. 24″, c. 1933. Unmarked. Courtesy Theriault's.

Patsy Jr.
Size: 11″   Internet: $400
Mint, with sleep eyes.

Patsy Lou
Size: 22″   Internet: $275
VG.

Patsy Lou
Size: 22″   Internet: $475
Original organdy dress and bonnet. Original pin: Member Patsy Doll Club-Effanbee.
Mark: Effanbee/Patsy Lou (back)

Patsy Lou
Size: 22″
Price: $850
MIB.

Patsy Ruth
Size: 26″   Internet: $1,200+
Mint.
Mark: Effanbee/Patsy Ruth (head) & body mark.

Patsyette
Size: 9″   Internet: $185
Box and hang tag, not mint.

Patsyette
Size: 9″
Price: $120   Internet: $130
VG, crazing, paint lifting.
Mark: Effanbee/Patsyette Doll

Patsykins, Black
Size: 11″   Internet: $600
Mint. Patsykins are marked with the Patsy Jr. mark.
Mark: Effanbee/Patsy Jr. Doll.

Skippy
Size: 14″   Internet: $320–$340
Sailor outfit.
Mark: Effanbee/Skippy/PL. Crosby (head) and Effanbee Patsy/Pat Pend Doll (back)

Skippy
Size: 14″   Internet: $560
Original mint military uniform with hat.
Mark: Skippy ©/Effanbee

Tinyette
Size: 8″   Internet: $150
Mark: EFFANBEE

Wee Patsy
Size: 6″
Price: $250   Internet: $200
With Colleen Moore Fairy Princess pin.

Patti Playpal and Other Companion Dolls

Patti Playpal was the first and best-known of the companion dolls. Companion dolls are so-called because the dolls are so large, generally 36 inches in height, that the dolls were made to be companions to their small owners and to share their clothing.

Horsman Playpal. *Vinyl walker. 36", c. early 1960s. Mark: HORSMAN / © / 1959. $75, eBay.*

Playpal, unknown maker. *Vinyl walker. 36", c. 1960s. Mark: U / 36. $30, eBay.*

Uneeda Playpal. *Vinyl head, hard plastic body. Non-walker. 36", c. 1960s. Mark: UNEEDA / 4. $30, eBay.*

Patti was made by Ideal from 1959 through approximately 1962, her size made possible by a new technique for the production of blown-plastic dolls (see the Ideal section). She was a hit with children and parents, and soon she had an entire family of friends—Penny Playpal, Peter Playpal, Suzy Playpal, and Bonnie Playpal. These were all sized as children of various ages.

Of course, anything successful in the world of dolls is soon copied, and before long many companies had their own Playpal-size dolls, including Horsman, Uneeda, and Eegee.

Market Report: Playpal dolls are very hot. They are desirable to collectors not only because of the nostalgia factor, but also because many collectors like to dress the dolls in children's clothing (sometimes in the outfits of their grown children) and also because no similar-size dolls are on the market today, with the exception of Ashton Drake's Patti Playpal reproduction from 2003.

The hottest dolls which bring the highest prices are the official Ideal Playpals. Other dolls can be found more reasonably, even in mint condition.

Some of the hottest and more unusual variations of Patti include the Shirley Temple Playpal, the Carrot-Topped and Platinum Hair Playpals, Black Patti Playpals and certain Playpals produced by Reliable, Canada, the Canadian subsidiary of Ideal. These dolls can sell for hundreds or thousands of dollars in excellent or mint condition. However, many collectors enjoy purchasing fixer-upper Pattis or the copycat Playpal dolls from other companies for dressing or display.

Online/Offline Report: Online collecting of Patti is also hot, and you can expect to pay top dollar for the rare and mint examples. Prices from dealers are comparable, sometimes more reasonable for mint or rare dolls. Look to the Internet and dealers specializing in baby-boomer dolls for the widest selections of Playpal dolls from all manufacturers.

Prices and Characteristics: All dolls are vinyl and made by Ideal, except as noted, with 5-piece vinyl bodies (mostly blown molded vinyl) and sleep eyes. All dolls were produced from 1959 to 1962.

Marks: Marks for Patti: IDEAL DOLL / G-35 (head) © / IDEAL DOLL CORP. / G-35-7 (back). Similar marks for other dolls in the Patti Playpal family; for Penny Playpal: IDEAL TOY CO. / 32-E.L (head); IDEAL (in the oval) / 32 (back).

Uneeda Playpal. Vinyl head, hard plastic body. Non-walker. 31″, c. late 1960s. Mark: 22 / UNEEDA DOLL CO. INC. / 19©68 / 3268. $40, eBay.

PATTI PLAYPAL AND FAMILY

Patti Playpal
Size: 35″
All Markets: $200–$350
Condition: Ex
Gently played with, original outfit.

Patti Playpal
Size: 35″
All Markets: $400–$600
Condition: Mint
Body of blown molded vinyl; more for rarer hair colors, rarer mint outfits.

Patti Playpal, Black
All Markets: $300+
Condition: Ex

Patti Playpal, Brown Hair
Size: 36″   Internet: $500–$600
Condition: Mint

Patti Playpal, Carrot-Top
Size: 35″   Internet: $900–$1,000
Condition: Ex

Patti Playpal, Platinum Hair, Walker
Size: 36″   Internet: $1,300–$1,800
Condition: Mint
Higher price for pristine mint doll in rarer dress.

Patti Playpal, Vincent DeFilippo Face
Size: 36″   Internet: $350–$400
Condition: Ex
Late 1961–1962, instead of Neil Estern, Patti sculpted by Vincent DeFilippo. Has "baby face" and "surprise" wide-eye look—the "Angel Face" Patti.

Patti Playpal, Reissue
Size: 35″   Internet: $50–$75
Condition: Mint
From 1981.

Bonnie Playpal
Size: 24″   Internet: $255
Condition: VG

Bonnie Playpal
Size: 24″   Internet: $450
Condition: Ex
Toddler.
Mark: Ideal Doll/OEB-24-3 (head) and IDEAL/23 (back)

Johnny Playpal
Size: 24″   Internet: $400
Condition: Av
Toddler.
Mark: Ideal Doll/BB-24-3 (head) IDEAL/23 (back)

Miss Ideal
Size: 30″   Internet: $450
Condition: MIB
With Play wave lotion.
Mark: IDEAL TOY CORP./SP-30-S (head) IDEAL TOY CORP./G-30-S (back)

Penny Playpal
Size: 32″   Internet: $200–$250
Condition: Ex

Peter Playpal
Size: 38″   Internet: $450–$575
Condition: Mint

Saucy Walker

Size: 32″   Internet: $250
Condition: Ex
Gently played with.
Mark: Ideal Toy Corp/BYE32-35 (head) Ideal
Toy Corp/B-32-W/Pat. Pend (back)

Shirley Temple Playpal

Size: 36″   Internet: $950–$1,500
Condition: Mint

Raggedy Ann and Andy

Raggedy Ann and Andy are not the first mass-produced cloth dolls, but they are by far the ones with the longest staying power. Raggedy Ann and Andy have been in continuous commercial production since 1920. I played with one as a child, as did my grandmother, mother, and daughter! I cannot think of another doll in this book of which the same statement could be true.

The enduring charm of Raggedy Ann and Andy has been subject to much speculation—why are these simple dolls so popular and why have they been popular for so long? Well, sometimes, simple designs are the best, and the design of Ann and Andy is classic and clean—two button eyes, red yarn hair, that classic triangle nose. Ann in her flowered dress, Andy in his overalls. Simple dolls, made for a child to hold and love, and pleasing to the eye of a collector. Children might play all day with an American Girl doll or a Barbie doll, but they are still going to tuck into bed at night with a Raggedy Ann. And collectors, of course, still remember this emotional attachment to Ann and Andy from their childhood.

Raggedy Ann and Andy may be simple, but they aren't boring. One great thing about Raggedy Ann and Andy for collectors is that many companies have produced them, creating endless varieties of faces, clothing, identification labels, and details. Ann and Andy have been made, over the years, by the following companies (among others): Volland, Molly-'es, Georgene, Knickerbocker, and Applause. The dolls have been made in every size from miniature to gigantic. There are also interesting variations on the stan-

dard-size dolls—vertical leg stripes are rare and desirable, as are stockings done in other colors, such as blue. Some dress prints and apron designs are very rare. There are variations to the faces. There are also additional characters in the Raggedy Ann and Andy universe that are highly sought after, such as Beloved Belindy, Uncle Clem, and the Camel with the Wrinkled Knees.

There are many legends and stories surrounding the origin of Raggedy Ann, but the truth is that the exact story of her birth isn't known. What is known is that the first book, *Raggedy Ann's Stories,* was written by Johnny Gruelle (born 1880) and published by Volland in 1918.

The legend of the creation of Raggedy Ann is that Marcella Gruelle, Johnny's daughter (who died tragically at 13 years of age from an infected smallpox vaccine), found a tattered rag doll that had belonged to her grandmother, and her father, a political cartoonist by trade, drew a face on the doll for her. Another legend is that Johnny created the doll as a tribute to his daughter—however, Johnny had already applied for the patent for the doll before his daughter died. It is true, however, that Johnny kept the memory of Marcella alive through the Raggedy Ann stories, with Marcella being a recurring character in the books.

The first license for the dolls was given to Volland in 1918. In the 1930s, Molly-'es produced unauthorized Anns and Andys and was sued, eventually successfully, by Gruelle. The next company to have an official license for the dolls was Georgene (see the Georgene Averill section) after Johnny Gruelle died in 1938. Georgene had the license to produce the dolls from 1938 until 1962. In 1962, Knickerbocker (see the Knickerbocker section) took over production, and they had an exclusive license for the next 20 years. Since then, companies including Applause and Hasbro have been producing Ann and Andy, but other companies such as Playskool and Schylling (licensed Raggedy Ann music boxes, jack-in-the-boxes, paper dolls) have also had Ann and Andy licenses.

Volland Raggedy Ann with Volland Uncle Clem and Percy The Policeman. *All cloth. Last Ann by Volland. Ann 15", others 16", c. 1931–1934. All Unmarked. Courtesy Theriault's.*

Molly-'es Raggedy Ann and Andy. *All cloth. 18", c. 1934–1937. Mark: Raggedy Ann and Andy Dolls Manufactured by Molly-'es Doll Outfitters (stamp, front torso). Courtesy Theriault's.*

Market Report: The final part of the puzzle of Raggedy Ann and Andy's popularity is their value—collectors, of course, are always fascinated by valuable things, and Raggedy Ann and Andy do not disappoint in this regard. A set of Volland Raggedy Ann and Andys (c. 1920s) can set a collector back $3,000, as much as a fine French bisque antique doll. Early Georgene black-outlined nose Anns and Andys are just as expensive, as is a Georgene Beloved Belindy. And the sky is the limit for certain rare variations, such as vertically striped legs on an early doll.

However, even though some of the early Raggedy Anns and Andys are so valuable, many dolls are available for under $100 (even under $50) for collectors on a budget. Many talented artists make unauthorized Anns and Andys today at very reasonable prices. Applause produced wonderful Raggedy Anns and Andys ranging in price from $5.99 for a pocket-size Ann or Andy to $60 for a 48-inch size. Plus, if a little wear is not an issue, there are lovely late Georgene and many Knickerbocker Anns and Andys from the 1950s to the 1970s that can be added to a vintage collection, often for under $50 per doll.

Overall, the market for Ann and Andy is strong and continues to grow. Prices have increased in the past few years as collectors

from countries such as Japan have become very interested in Ann and Andy.

Online/Offline Report: Because of the international flavor of the Ann and Andy market, prices on eBay tend to be quite high for the most desirable items, and prices on eBay, through dealers, and at auctions all tend to be similar, with the usual abundance of lower-priced and more common items on eBay.

Prices and Characteristics, Volland and Molly-'es Raggedy Ann and Andy

All dolls are cloth. If Volland Raggedy Anns or Andys have any markings at all, they are: "PATENTED SEPT 7, 1915." stamped on the back of the dolls. Volland dolls are from 1915 to the early 1930s and Molly-'es dolls are from 1935 to 1938.

RAGGEDY ANN, VOLLAND AND MOLLY-'ES

Volland, Raggedy Ann or Andy
Size: 15–18"
Price: $800–$1,300   Internet: $1,000–$1,400
Condition: Ex
Printed face; 1920–1921.

Volland, Raggedy Ann
Size: 18"
Price: $3,000   Internet: $5,000

Georgene Silsby Raggedy Ann and Andy. 18", c. 1946. Each with Silsby tag. Courtesy Karen Cvitkovich.

Raggedy Ann and Andy by Georgene. All cloth, 4th version of Ann. Each 19", c. 1948, Andy c. 1946. Mark: Andy has original label on back, Ann has original box. Courtesy Theriault's.

Condition: Mint
Hand-painted face. Both quotes for Ann; similar prices for Andy.

Volland, Beloved Belindy
Size: 15"
Price: $1,500   Internet: $1,800
Condition: VG
1930.

Molly-'es, Raggedy Ann or Andy, Outlined Nose
Size: 18"   Internet: $2,400
Condition: VG
Outlined nose, "covered-up" label.

Molly-'es, Raggedy Ann
Size: 18"   Internet: $715–$950
Condition: VG
Torso signed "Raggedy Ann and Raggedy Andy Dolls, Manufactured by Molly'es Doll Outfitters, Inc."

Prices and Characteristics, Georgene Raggedy Ann and Andy

Georgene Anns and Andys have a tag with various information sewn into the side seam of the doll. Some have the following: GEORGENE NOVELTIES, INC. / NEW YORK CITY / or JOHNNY GRUELLE'S OWN / /RAGGEDY ANN & ANDY DOLLS / Copyright F. Volland Co. 1918, 1920 / Rights Reserved, Myrtle T. Gruelle, 1945, 1947 / Exclusive Licensed Manufacturers / Made in the USA. There are many variations of similar tags. For the Silsby tag, see the photo on the next page. Georgene Raggedy Anns and Andys were made from 1938 to 1963. Silsby Georgenes were only made in 1946.

Close-up of Silsby tag, previous doll. Dolls with the Silsby tag were made only in 1946.

Close-up of rare vertical-striped legs on previous doll (almost all Anns and Andys have horizontal striped legs).

Georgene Silsby Raggedy Ann with vertical-striped legs. 18", c. 1946. Mark: Silsby tag sewed into doll's side (see photo of tag). Courtesy Karen Cvitkovich.

RAGGEDY ANN, GEORGENE

Ann and Andy, Pair
Size: 15"   Internet: $120
Condition: Gd
Common outfits, very played-with condition.

Ann and Andy, Pair
Size: 18"   Internet: $600
Condition: Ex

Ann and Andy, Pair
Size: 18"
Price: $1,300
Condition: Mint

Ann and Andy, Pair, Black Outlined Noses
Size: 20"
Price: $2,200
Condition: Ex
Made from 1938–1944.

Ann, Black Outlined Nose
Size: 19"   Internet: $400–$550
Condition: VG

Beloved Belindy
Size: 15" or 19"
Price: $950   Internet: $1,000
Condition: Ex

Georgene, Awake, Asleep
Price: $500+   Internet: $500+
Condition: Ex
One side has awake face, one side has asleep face.

Raggedy Ann or Andy
Size: 15"   Internet: $80
Condition: Gd
For well-loved Ann or Andy, no tag or washed tag, soiling.

Raggedy Ann or Andy
Size: 15"
Price: $200–$400   Internet: $255–$330
Condition: VG
With wear.

Raggedy Ann or Andy
Size: 19–20"   Internet: $180–$200
Condition: Gd
Repairs, stains, no tag or washed tag.

Raggedy Ann or Andy
Size: 19–20"
Price: $300+   Internet: $300+
Condition: Ex
Original and tagged.

Raggedy Ann or Andy
Size: 19–20"   Internet: $575–$700
Condition: MIB
With hang tag; higher price for Ann.

Raggedy Ann or Andy
Size: 22–24"   Internet: $175
Condition: VG

Raggedy Ann, Silsby Tag
Size: 15–22"   Internet: $900–$1,200
Condition: Ex
The "Silsby" tag was produced for 1 year, and has copyright date of 1946; sewn in left-hand side of doll. Larger dolls at higher end of range.

Georgene Beloved Belindy. 15", c. 1940s. Courtesy Karen Cvitkovich. $1,200, eBay.

Knickerbocker Raggedy Ann. All cloth. 18", c. 1970s. Knickerbocker tag on clothes (KTC / Knickerbocker / Made in China). $30, eBay.

Knickerbocker Beloved Belindy. Identical dolls, one with box. All cloth. 15", c. 1965. Mark: Beloved Belindy c. Bobbs Merrill Co Inc 1965 Cal-T-5 All New Material (cloth tag).

Raggedy Ann, Silsby Tag, Vertical Stripes
Size: 18"   Internet: $1,100
Condition: Gd
Very rare with vertical stripes; price much
higher for better condition.

Raggedy Ann, Multicolored Striped Legs
Size: 30"   Internet: $270
Condition: Gd
This doll, no hair, clothes, or tag, rare multi-
striped legs; much higher for better condition.

Prices and Characteristics, Knickerbocker Raggedy Ann and Andy

All Knickerbocker Raggedy Ann and Andy
dolls are cloth, except as noted. Most have
tags sewn into the doll's side seam; the earlier
tags have the logo "Joy of a Toy." Overall,
the Knickerbocker dolls were made from
1962 to 1982; however, I have included dates
where possible because the earlier Knicker-
bockers generally sell for more than the later
dolls. Prices are a mix of Internet and non-
Internet prices, but predominately Internet.

RAGGEDY ANN, KNICKERBOCKER

Ann and Andy, Pair
Size: 16"   Date: 1964
                   Internet: $600
Condition: MIB
Matched set in original boxes, paper tags.

Ann and Andy, Pair
Size: 45"   Date: 1964
                   Internet: $1,045
Condition: Ex
Hard-to-find huge set.

Ann and Andy, Pair, Joy of a Toy
Size: 21"   Date: 1960s
                   Internet: $345
Condition: Ex
Joy of a Toy label.

Ann or Andy, Joy of a Toy, Each
Size: 15"   Date: early 1960s
All Markets: $130–$175
Condition: Ex
Joy of a Toy label.

Ann or Andy
Size: 15"   Date: 1970s
                   Internet: $40–$90
Condition: Mint
Mint with hang tag; for later Raggedy tag, not
Joy of a Toy tag.

Ann or Andy
Size: 15"   Date: 1971
                   Internet: $150
Condition: MIB

Ann or Andy
Size: 18–19"   Date: late 1960s
                   Internet: $90
Condition: Ex
Ann with rarer red poppy dress, no tag.

Ann or Andy

Size: 18–19″   Date: 1970s
All Markets: $50–$70
Condition: Mint

Ann or Andy

Size: 18–19″   Date: late 1960s
                     Internet: $220
Condition: MIB
Blue with cellophane Knickerbocker box.

Ann or Andy

Size: 40″   Date: 1960s
                  Internet: $170
Condition: VG

Ann or Andy, Talking

Size: 18″   Date: 1973
                  Internet: $150
Condition: Ex
Still talks.

Ann, Red Poppy Dress

Size: 18–20″   Internet: $85–$90
Condition: Ex
Also earlier wool hair; not Joy of a Toy label.

Beloved Belindy, Joy of a Toy

Size: 15″   Date: 1963–1965
All Markets: $370–$525
Condition: Ex to Mint

Beloved Belindy

Size: 15″   Date: 1970s
                  Internet: $345
Condition: Mint
Later Beloved Belindy.

Camel With The Wrinkled Knees

                  Internet: $120
Condition: VG
Played with.

Camel With The Wrinkled Knees

Size: 17″   Date: 1970s
                  Internet: $190
Condition: Mint

Dress Me, Ann or Andy

Size: 20″   Date: late 1960s
                  Internet: $85
Condition: Mint
Teaches children to dress, with various buckles,
ties, buttons.

Holly Hobbie Hat, Raggedy

Size: 15″   Internet: $315
Condition: Ex
No hair, as was produced at end of Knicker-
bocker Raggedy production.

Knickerbocker, Andy, Bend 'Em

Size: 9″   Date: 1960s
                 Internet: $100–$120
Condition: MIP
Bend 'Em's have wire armatures inside for pos-
ing.

Musical Ann and Andy

Size: 16″   Date: 1970s
                  Internet: $295
Condition: Mint
With hang tags.

Pancake Face, Ann or Andy

                  Internet: $40
Condition: MIB

Raggedy Arthur

                  Internet: $400
Condition: Ex

Teach and Play, Ann or Andy

Size: 18″   Date: 1972
All Markets: $265
Condition: MIB
Mint in original bag; teaches children to dress,
with various buckles, ties, buttons.

RAGGEDY ANN, OTHER COMPANIES

Applause, Ann

Size: 50″   Internet: $45
Condition: Mint
For this size Ann only. Other recently made Ap-
plause Raggedys sell at retail.

Applause, Ann, Rags Hair

                  Internet: $60–$100
Condition: Mint
Hair is made of red rags, not yarn.

Applause, Awake, Asleep, Pair

Size: 12″   Date: 1998
                  Internet: $50
Condition: Mint
5,000 made for Home Shopping Network.

Applause, Molly-'es Reproduction

                  Internet: $125
Condition: MIB
Multicolored legs, edition of 10,000.

Applause, Moving, Musical Ann and Andy

Size: 10″   Date: 1986
                  Internet: $155
Condition: Ex
When playing music (wind-up) they twist and
turn heads. Andy plays "Raindrops Keep Falling
on My Head"; Ann plays "I'd Like to Teach the
World to Sing."

Hasbro, Ann or Andy
Size: various   Date: 1990s
                      Internet: $5–$20
Condition: Mint
More for anniversary and holiday gift sets.

Macmillan, Ann and Andy
Size: 6.5″   Date: 1990
                      Internet: $115
Condition: MIB
Vinyl heads, cloth bodies.

Playskool, Ann or Andy
Size: various   Date: 1990s
                      Internet: $5–$20
Condition: Mint
More for some exclusives.

Playskool, Black Ann, Target Exclusive
Size: 21″   Date: 1989
                      Internet: $65
Condition: MIB

Raggedy Ann and Arthur, Lets Go Camping
Date: 1981
                      Internet: $230
Condition: MIB
Bobbs-Merrill Co. with car, camper, and dog-house on wheels.

Reliable Toy Co Ltd., Ann
Size: 16″   Date: 1950s
                      Internet: $465
Condition: Ex
Canadian company.
Mark: Made by Reliable Toy Co, LTD./Toronto, Canada (tag).

REMCO

Founded at the end of the 1940s, Remco was a direct competitor with such toy and doll giants as Ideal and Mattel. It flourished in the 1950s and 1960s, only to fail in the late 1960s as so many other giant American toy makers did. Remco was sold in the 1970s to Azrak/Hamway, and the trademark still exists today, with Remco toys being produced by Jaaks, Pacific. Remco is especially known for several dolls from the 1960s including the Littlechap dolls, Beatles dolls, and the Heidi line of dolls sold in little plastic pocketbooks. Some of the dolls that were produced by Remco in the 1960s and early 1970s focused on the favorites of the teenybopper set—a Laurie Partridge doll from *The Partridge Family,* Monkees finger puppets, an *I Dream*

of Jeannie doll, even dolls of the characters of McDonaldland.

Market Report: For the most part, Remco dolls are inexpensive, fun dolls to collect which are remembered fondly by many baby boomers who grew up in the 1960s. Prices for some items, including the Littlechap family, have recently declined.

Online/Offline Report: Your best bets for finding Remco dolls include dealers specializing in 1960s dolls, toy dealers specializing in 1960s toys (especially for the Beatles dolls), and eBay. Prices are similar for all venues.

Prices and Characteristics; Marks: Dolls are vinyl unless otherwise noted. Dolls are generally marked: REMCO, INC. / 1968 (or other date).

REMCO

Beatles, John Lennon
Size: 5″   Date: 1964
                      Internet: $90–$120
Condition: Ex
Mark: NEMS. ENT. LTD. 1964 (foot)

Beatles, Paul McCartney
Size: 5″   Date: 1964
                      Internet: $130
Condition: MIB

Fab Four Beatles (Set of 4)
Size: 5″   Date: 1964
                      Internet: $300
Condition: Ex
Two versions, rubber or plastic. Gold-trimmed instruments with Beatles' signatures.

Heidi, Winking
Size: 5.5″   Date: 1967
                      Internet: $30–$45
Condition: MIB
Press button in tummy and Heidi winks; in box.

Hi, Heidi!
Size: 5.5″   Date: 1964
                      Internet: $40–$60
Condition: MIP
In red pocketbook. Press button in tummy and Hi, Heidi! series of dolls waves.

Hi, Heidi!'s Friend, Jan
Size: 5.5″   Date: 1964
                      Internet: $55
Condition: MIP
In blue pocketbook.

Judy Littlechap's Pajamas #1106.
c. 1963. On box: REMCO INDUS-
TRIES, INC. JAPAN. $45 NRFB,
eBay.

**Hi, Heidi! Vinyl, doll raises left
hand when push button in
tummy.** c. 1964. $48 in original
pocketbook, eBay.

Lyndon B. Johnson. Vinyl head,
hard plastic body. 5″, c.1960s.
Mark: 100 / REMCO IND. INC. /
1964.

Hi, Heidi!'s Sister, Hildy

Size: 5.5″
Date: 1966
Internet: $55

Condition: MIP
In pink pocketbook.

I Dream of Jeannie

Size: 6″
Date: 1977
Internet: $40

Condition: MIB

I Dream of Jeannie, Play Set

Date: 1977
Internet: $355

Condition: MIB
Complete, includes doll.

Jumpsy

Date: 1970
Internet: $20

Condition: MIB
With jump rope.

Littlechap Family, Gift Set

Size: various
Date: 1963
Internet: $185

Condition: MIB
Entire family of 4 (1 box; gift set).

Littlechap Family, Gift Set

Size: various
Date: 1963
Internet: $285

Condition: NRFB

Littlechap Family, Judy

Date: 1963
Internet: $40–$70

Condition: Ex
Daughter, age 17.

Littlechap Family, Libby

Size: 10.5″
Date: 1963
Internet: $40–$70

Condition: MIB
Daughter, age 10.

Littlechap Family, Lisa

Date: 1963
Internet: $50–$80

Condition: Ex
Mom.

Littlechap Family, Libby, YaYa Dress

Date: 1963
Internet: $45

Condition: Ex
Outfit #1306.

Littlechap Family, Dr. John

Date: 1963
Internet: $40–$70

Condition: Ex
Dad.

Littlechap Family, Dr. John's Office

Date: 1963
Internet: $90

Condition: MIB

Little Winking Herby, Hippie

Size: 16″
Date: 1968
Internet: $40

Condition: MIB
Winks eye when push button.

McDonald's Dolls, Grimace

Date: 1976
Internet: $40

Condition: MOC

McDonald's Dolls, Set of 7

Size: 7–8″   Date: 1976
Internet: $180

Condition: Ex
Officer Big Mac, Ronald McDonald, Captain
Crook, Grimace, Hamburglar, Mayor McCheese,
and Professor.

Mimi, Singing Doll

Size: 18″   Date: 1973
Internet: $20

Condition: Ex

Monkees, Finger Puppets

Size: 5″   Date: 1970
Internet: $15

Condition: Ex

Susan Dey

Size: 19″   Date: 1973
Internet: $140

Condition: MIB
As Laurie Partridge.

Sweet April

Date: 1971
Internet: $25

Condition: Ex

Sasha Dolls

Mary Magdalena Alexandra von Sinner
(nicknamed Sasha) was born in 1893 in
Switzerland. She was a formally trained
artist, who married another artist, painter
Ernst Morgenthaler, in 1916. In the early
1940s, Sasha turned her artistic talents to
dolls, and she started to create handmade
dolls in her art studio in Zurich. All the dolls
produced in Sasha's studio were one-of-a-
kind dolls made out of molded gypsum or
synthetic plastics. Dolls were made in Sasha's
studio until her death in 1975.

The artist dolls produced in Sasha's studio
were very expensive, and Sasha wanted her
dolls to be available to many more children.
So in 1964, she licensed her doll designs to
Götz to make 16-inch play dolls. These dolls,
which were marked "Sasha Serie," were
produced by Götz until 1970.

Nearly simultaneously with the Götz production of the dolls, Frido / Trendon Ltd. in
England also licensed production of the
Sasha dolls. It produced Sasha from 1965
through 1986. The majority of the English
production dolls are not marked and are
identified by a wrist tag.

Finally, in 1995, Götz again began to make
Sasha dolls, and it continued until 2001 (production of Sasha ceased before the Götz
bankruptcy in 2003, over creative differences
with the Morgenthaler family). These dolls
can be easily distinguished from the earlier
Götz dolls. Although they are also marked
"Sasha Serie" on the back, on the neck of the
doll the dolls are additionally marked "Sasha
/ Götz" with numbers.

Market Report: Sasha dolls are some of the
earliest art dolls, and thanks to their original
design, they are greatly appreciated by collectors. The early studio-made dolls can
bring several thousand dollars. Even the
early manufactured 1960s dolls can bring
several hundred dollars, although the latest
manufactured dolls by Götz can often be
found for under $150. The market for Sasha
dolls is definitely hot, and still growing.

Online/Offline Report: Although you will
find several hundred auctions for Sasha dolls
and related items on eBay at any given time,
you will rarely find the studio dolls there—
for studio dolls, auction houses and dealers
are the best sources. Manufactured dolls can
be found from all sources. Prices and availability are similar, with bargains on eBay for
the latest of the Götz Sasha dolls.

Prices and Characteristics: The Sasha Studio dolls are made of gypsum, with all-cloth
or gypsum bodies. All other dolls are made
of vinyl with 5-piece vinyl bodies. Eyes are
painted, and hair synthetic.

SASHA

Sasha Studio Doll

Date: 1940s–1975

Price: $5,000+
Condition: Ex
Made by Morgenthaler.

Artist character dolls by Sasha Morgenthaler. Gypsum socket heads, "Type B" cotton tricot body jointed at hips, shoulders. 20", c. 1940s. Unmarked. Courtesy Theriault's.

Artist character doll by Sasha Morgenthaler. Gypsum socket head, firmly stuffed cloth body jointed at hips, shoulders. Type B-I. 20", c. 1950. Courtesy Theriault's.

Sasha Studio Doll

Date: 1950s
Price: $2,000+　　　Internet: $1,900+
Condition: Ex
Cloth body, made in studio.

Götz, Sasha Serie

Date: 1964–1970
Internet: $650
Condition: VG
Mark: Sasha Serie (in circle, head and torso).

Götz, Sasha Serie

Size: 16"　　　Date: 1964–1970
Internet: $800–$1,000
Condition: Ex
Mark: Sasha Serie (stamped, head and back).

Frido/Trendon, Sasha

Size: 19"　　　Date: late 1960s–early 1970s
Internet: $500–$600
Condition: MIB
For rarer cylinder box.

Frido/Trendon, Sasha

Size: 17"　　　Date: late 1960s–early 1970s
Internet: $300
Condition: MIB
For basic Frido/Trendon Sasha.

Frido/Trendon, Sasha Dungarees

Size: 17"　　　Date: 1969
Internet: $1,400
Condition: Ex
Rarer model. Made in England (Frido/Trendon Ltd).

Trendon Limited, Boy, Sexed

Size: 12"　　　Date: 1970s
Price: $100–$120　　　Internet: $80–$100
Condition: Ex

Trendon Limited, Boy, Unsexed

Size: 12"　　　Date: 1980s
Price: $100–$120　　　Internet: $80–$100
Condition: Ex

Trendon Limited, Sasha or Gregor

Size: 16"　　　Date: 1980s
Price: $175　　　Internet: $200
Condition: Ex
Made in England by Trendon Limited, Stockport, England.

Trendon Limited, Black Caleb

Size: 16"　　　Date: 1980s
Price: $115
Condition: Ex

Trendon Limited, Princess Sasha

Date: 1986
Internet: $1,600
Condition: MIB
Only 400 of edition of 3,500 actually made (company closed).

Trendon Limited, Sasha, Kiltie

Date: 1983
Internet: $500
Condition: MIB

Götz, Sasha

Size: 16"　　　Date: 1990s
Price: $150–$300　　　Internet: $150–$225
Condition: Ex

Sasha girl by Frido / Trendon Ltd., England. Hard vinyl. 17", c. 1970s. Unmarked doll, wrist tag: MADE IN / SERIE /ENGLAND in circle on one side, Sasha in double circle on other side. Courtesy Helen Simms Collection.

Sasha boy and girl by Götz. Hard vinyl head, 5-piece bodies with seam at waist. 17", c. 1960s. Boy is known as "No-Nose" model. Mark: Sasha Serie (in circle, on head and torso). Courtesy Theriault's.

Dolls sometimes named other female names such as "Alice," etc.
Mark: Sasha Götz 94 306 (back of neck) or similar.

Götz, Gregor
Size: 16"   Date: 1990s
Price: $110–$200   Internet: $150–$225
Condition: Ex

Götz, Sasha or Gregor
Size: 16"   Date: 1995 on
Price: $200–$260
Condition: MIB

Götz, Ruth
                   Date: 1999
                   Internet: $400
Condition: MIB
Limited edition of 400, tube.

Götz, Sasha, Black, Cora
Size: 16"   Date: 1990s
Price: $100–$120
Condition: Ex

Shirley Temple

Although there were certainly celebrities and celebrity dolls before her, Shirley Temple and her dolls can well be named as the starting point for the cult of celebrity that developed in the 20th century. Shirley Temple hit the market in 1934, and no celebrity dolls before or since have captured the imagination of the doll-buying public in the same way.

The first Shirley Temple dolls were produced by Ideal in 1934. At that time, Shirley Temple was a mega-star, headlining movies to brighten up a society that was going through the Great Depression. She was an absolute icon to little girls everywhere.

The doll was designed by Bernard Lipfert, who designed many of the most popular dolls of the early- to mid-20th century.

Shirley Temple as Snow White.
Composition head, 5-piece body.
11", c. 1939. Mark: SHIRLEY TEM-
PLE / 11. Courtesy Theriault's.

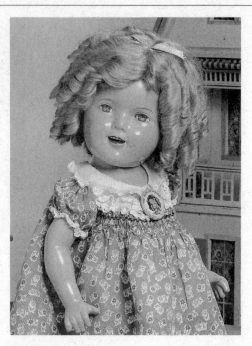

***Shirley Temple in* Captain Janu-**
ary dress. *Composition head, 5-*
piece composition body. 20", c.
1936. Mark: SHIRLEY TEMPLE /
Cop /IDEAL / N & T Co. (head)
SHIRLEY TEMPLE 20 (torso).
Courtesy Theriault's.

Shirley Temple composition dolls were pro-duced until 1939, and during her reign there were many imitators and "Shirley-type" dolls produced by other companies. In 1957, Ideal reintroduced the Shirley dolls, this time in vinyl. The dolls were produced by Ideal, again in vinyl in the 1970s and also in the early 1980s, just before Ideal ceased doll production. Various licensees have produced Shirley Temple dolls since.

Market Report: I think these dolls have been a hot collectible since their release! They are sought after not only by doll collectors, but also by collectors of Hollywood memorabilia and collectors of all things Shirley.

Prices for truly-mint composition dolls are higher than they have ever been, as are prices for dolls in rare outfits and dolls in rare sizes.

The composition dolls are the most sought after, with the 1950s vinyl dolls not far be-hind. Prices are not as high for 1970s and 1980s vinyl dolls and later dolls in vinyl and porcelain, but such dolls are still easily sold to collectors and eagerly sought.

When collecting early Shirley Temple dolls, familiarize yourself with her outfits (there are several books on the market with photos and information on the various outfits) since outfits can often determine the price of the doll. Beyond that, try to find early Shirleys with non-clouded eyes and as minimal craz-ing as possible.

Online/Offline Report: Fine dolls will bring similar prices online or offline. Online, prices are high thanks to strong international interest in Shirley. Offline, there are many

Shirley Temple in Hurricane costume. *Composition, 5-piece body. 18", c. 1940. Courtesy Theriault's.*

Shirley Temple in "Texas Ranger" outfit. *Composition, 5-piece body, flirty eyes. 27", c. 1939. Mark: Shirley Temple Ideal N & T Co. $1,800, auction. Courtesy Theriault's.*

Shirley Temple in "Rebecca of Sunnybrook Farm" outfit. *Vinyl. 11.5", c. 1983. Mark: same as previous doll. $40 MIB, dealer.*

knowledgeable dealers who trade Shirley as well. As with nearly all other vintage dolls, bargains can be found online for fixer-uppers and lesser-quality dolls. Beware of composition Shirleys online that have been restored with composition craze concealer or using other methods that are not fully disclosed.

Composition Shirley Temple

Dolls have 5-piece jointed composition bodies, mohair wigs, sleep eyes, and open mouths with teeth. Dolls are from 1934 into the 1940s and are made by Ideal except as noted.

SHIRLEY TEMPLE, COMPOSITION

Baby Shirley
Size: 16"   Internet: $1,000
Mint.

Baby Shirley
Size: 16–23"   Internet: $400–$500
Dolls with major flaws, restoration.

Baby Shirley
Size: 21–23"
Price: $1,600   Internet: $1,900
Flirty eyes, for dolls in original outfit, minor crazing.
Mark: SHIRLEY TEMPLE

Shirley Temple
Size: 11"
Price: $250–$400   Internet: $300–$400
VG; dolls with crazing, eye cracks.

Shirley Temple
Size: 11"
Price: $500+   Internet: $500–$700+
Excellent; 11" size very hard to find mint.

Shirley Temple
Size: 13"   Internet: $150–$200
Good; dolls with serious flaws (facial fading, blown eyes, some cracking/crazing.
Mark: 13 SHIRLEY TEMPLE (head & body)

Shirley Temple
Size: 13"
Price: $350   Internet: $250–$400
VG, crazing.
Mark: SHIRLEY TEMPLE (head) SHIRLEY TEMPLE 13 (back)

Shirley Temple
Size: 13"   Internet: $500–$600
Mint, wearing original tagged outfit.
Mark: same as above

Shirley Temple
Size: 15–16"
Price: $600   Internet: $650
Mint, wearing original tagged outfit.
Mark: Shirley Temple (neck) Shirley Temple-16 (back)

Shirley Temple
Size: 18"
Price: $450–$600   ·   Internet: $350–$500

Shirley Temple in different **Poor Little Rich Girl** *dress. Composition head, 5-piece body. 13", c. 1936. Mark: SHIRLEY TEMPLE (head) SHIRLEY TEMPLE / 13 (back). $415, eBay.*

Shirley Temple with trunk and tagged outfits. 12.5", c. 1930s. Mark: SHIRLEY TEMPLE / Cop / IDEAL / N & T Co. (head) SHIRLEY TEMPLE.

Shirley Temple. Vinyl, dress with original Shirley Temple banner. 12", c. 1957. Mark: IDEAL DOLL / ST-12 (head) ST –12-N (body). Courtesy Ellen Johnson.

VG, crazing, other small flaws.
Mark: Shirley Temple-Ideal-Corp (head) Shirley Temple-18 (back)

Shirley Temple
Size: 18"
Price: $700–$1,000　　　Internet: $600–$800
Excellent to mint, original dress; more for desirable outfits such as *Captain January* (see below).

Shirley Temple
Size: 18"
Price: $1,150　　　Internet: $1,000–$1,300
MIB.

Shirley Temple
Size: 20–22"
Price: $400–$650　　　Internet: $400–$700
VG.

Shirley Temple
Size: 20–22"
Price: $900–$1,200　　　Internet: $900–$1,100
Excellent or mint.
Mark: Shirley Temple-Ideal-N&TC (head) Shirley Temple-Ideal (back)

Shirley Temple
Size: 22"　　　Internet: $1,500
Pristine mint and all original.
Mark: SHIRLEY TEMPLE/22

Shirley Temple
Size: 27"
Price: $900　　　Internet: $1,100
Excellent or mint.
Mark: SHIRLEY TEMPLE IDEAL N & T CO. BROOKLYN

SHIRLEYS IN DESIRABLE OUTFITS AND SHIRLEY PRODUCTS

Shirley Temple, in Scottie Dress
Size: 13"
Price: $850
Desirable outfit, flaws to doll.
Mark: Shirley Temple (head) Shirley Temple/13 (back)

Shirley Temple, in *Our Little Girl* Outfit
Size: 18"
Price: $1,500
MIB, pin.
Mark: Shirley Temple 18 Copr. Ideal N & T Co. (head) 18 Shirley Temple (back)

Shirley Temple, in Texas Ranger Outfit
Size: 27"
Price: $1,800
VG; rare model with flirty eyes, rare outfit (missing hat).
Mark: Shirley Temple Ideal N & T Co.

Shirley Temple, in Cowboy Outfit
Size: 27"　　　Internet: $1,275
VG; original cowboy outfit including leather pants and vest, red scarf with Shirley Temple pin.
Mark: Shirley Temple-Ideal (head) Shirley Temple (back)

Shirley Temple, Make-Up Doll
Size: 25"
Price: $800
VG.

Shirley Temple. Vinyl. 12″, c. 1957. Same mark as previous doll.

Shirley Temple. Vinyl. 15″, c. 1972. Mark: © 1972 / IDEAL TOY CORP / ST-14-N-2 33 /HONG KONG (head) IDEAL (in circle) / © 1972 / 2M-5024 / 2.

Shirley Temple in Poor Little Rich Girl *dress.* Vinyl. In 1982, dolls had pink box, in 1983, blue box (as shown). 12″, c. 1983. Mark: IDEAL / c. 1982 Gabriel, Ind. / A Division of CBS Inc. $25 MIB, eBay.

Shirley Temple, Animated Promo Doll
Size: 27″   Internet: $3,500
Promotional doll for movie theatre, advertising Shirley Temple movie. Wooden base with electric motor; doll twirls and arms move, eyes move and doll bends at waist.
Mark: Shirley Temple Ideal N&T (head) Shirley Temple (back)

Shirley Temple, With Wardrobe, Trunk
Size: 16″   Internet: $975
With flaws, tagged outfits.

Outfit, Cherry Dress
Size: 18″   Internet: $400
For dress only.

Outfit, *Poor Little Rich Girl* Sailor Dress
Size: 18″   Internet: $300
For dress only.

Outfit, *Our Little Girl* Scottie Dress
Size: 20″   Internet: $300
For 3-dog dress only.

Carriage
Price: $400

Tea Set
Price: $500

Trunk, for 13″ Shirley
Size: 14″   Internet: $150
With flaws; Ideal trunk.

Look-Alike, Composition Body
Size: 19–20″
Price: $120–$200   Internet: $150–$200

Appropriately dressed, tin sleep eyes, mohair wig, minor crazing.
Mark: unmarked

Look-Alike, Cloth Body
Size: 24″
Price: $140
Unknown maker.
Mark: unmarked

Vinyl Shirley Temple

Prices are for dolls in excellent condition, with 5-piece bodies and sleep eyes, made by Ideal except as noted. Prices are organized by date, then doll size. For prices on Shirley Temple dolls produced by other companies in the 1980s and 1990s, see the Celebrity Dolls section in the Modern Dolls chapter.

SHIRLEY TEMPLE, VINYL

Shirley Temple
Size: 12″   Date: 1957
Price: $80 to $120   Internet: $70–$100
Average doll, VG.

Shirley Temple
Size: 12″   Date: 1957
Price: $155–$300   Internet: $150–$200
Mint or MIB: for most dolls in common outfits.
Mark: Ideal Doll/ST-12 (back of head) ST-12-N (back)

Shirley Temple in **Poor Little Rich Girl** *dress.* Composition, 5-piece body. 18", c. 1936. Mark: SHIRLEY TEMPLE / Cop / IDEAL / N & T Co. (head) SHIRLEY TEMPLE / 18 (back).

Shirley Temple, With Trunk, Clothes
Size: 12"   Date: 1957
Price: $600
Mint doll, trunk, extensive clothes.
Mark: Ideal Doll/ST-12 (head) ST-12 (back)

TV Wardrobe Gift Set
Size: 12"   Date: 1957
Price: $350
VG; TV window box; doll, school dress, party dress, script purse, pearl necklace.

Shirley Temple
Size: 17–19"   Date: 1957
Price: $200–$300   Internet: $150–$200
VG; average doll.

Shirley Temple
Size: 17–19"   Date: 1957
Price: $300–$400   Internet: $300
Mint.

Shirley Temple, Flirty Eyes
Size: 17–19"   Date: 1957
                     Internet: $320
Excellent.
Mark: Ideal Doll/ST-19 (neck, torso)

Shirley Temple, Flirty Eyes
Size: 17–19"   Date: 1957
Price: $400   Internet: $425
MIB pristine, hang tags.

Shirley Temple, Playpal
Size: 36"   Date: 1959
Price: $900   Internet: $700–$900
VG; average doll.

Mark: Ideal Doll/ST-35-38-2 (head) Ideal (in oval)/35-5 (back)

Shirley Temple, Playpal
Size: 36"   Date: 1959
                   Internet: $1,000–$1,200
Mint.

Shirley Temple, Playpal
Size: 36"   Date: 1959
                   Internet: $1,800+
MIB.

Shirley Temple, Montgomery Ward
Size: 15"   Date: 1972
Price: $125
Exclusive for Montgomery Ward in 1972; uses 1957 mold.

Shirley Temple
Size: 16"   Date: 1973
                   Internet: $100
MIB; box has movie photos. In white dress with red polka dots.

Shirley Temple
Size: 8"   Date: 1982
                  Internet: $15–$25
MIB; for most outfits.

Shirley Temple in Common Outfits
Size: 12"   Date: 1982
                   Internet: $20–$30
Poor Little Rich Girl, Heidi, farmer, similar dolls.

Shirley Temple in Popular Outfits
Size: 12"   Date: 1982
                   Internet: $30–$50

For popular outfits including *Captain January,* Pretty in Pink, sailor outfit.

Shirley Temple in *Stand Up and Cheer!*

Size: 12″   Date: 1982
                    Internet: $50+
Stand Up and Cheer! or *Rebecca of Sunnybrook Farm.*

Skookum Indian Dolls

Mary McAboy, from Montana, received a patent for the dolls that became the Skookum Indian dolls in 1913. The very first dolls were made with shrunken-apple heads. In approximately 1917, the H.H. Tammen Co. started to distribute the dolls, followed by the Arrow Novelty Company in 1920. The dolls went from apple heads to composition and, finally, to plastic. The majority of the dolls were made from composition. Babies, male, and female dolls were made, in a wide variety of styles. Most Skookum dolls were distributed to the tourist trade. The dolls were generally unmarked except for paper labels on the feet, with 1950s and later dolls having the trademark embossed on the bottom of their molded plastic feet.

Many people have asked what "Skookum" means. The website www.skookumgal.com (a fantastic site with historical information about these dolls) quotes a 1920 *Playthings* magazine article by Mary McAboy: "Skookum is the Siwash word for 'Bully Good.' They are 'Bully Good Indians.'" Although I've found it hard to pin down the end of production for these dolls, I believe they were produced through the early 1960s.

Market Report: A few years ago no one wanted a Skookum! You could find one at a flea market for a few dollars, or thrown in a box under a table at a doll show. Today, Skookum Bully Good dolls are hot, and large sizes and rarer examples can trade for several hundred dollars.

I'm not sure if the popularity of Skookum dolls is tied to the popularity of Native American dolls in general (all categories of Native American dolls are selling well through my doll business, from modern porcelain dolls to Armand Marseille Native Americans to Skookum dolls) or if the dolls are finally coming into their own as a well-costumed mid-20th-century composition doll. Whatever the reason, the dolls are certainly desirable, and you won't find them thrown in a box at a doll show any longer.

Online/Offline Report: Prices and availability online and off are similar, with choice examples from dealers and auctions priced somewhat higher.

Prices and Characteristics: All Skookums are composition with non-jointed bodies, which actually don't have arms (a Native American blanket surrounds each doll and gives it the illusion of arms). All Skookums are in Native American dress, often with headband, beads, and ankle wraps. These dolls were sold for nearly 50 years and they can be hard to date; prices quoted are generally for earlier, more desirable dolls. Prices are for dolls in excellent condition; higher prices in a range often indicate a doll with a label or box, an earlier doll, or more intricate or unusual costuming. Sometimes a foot label will indicate the tourist site the doll was sold at. Dolls with plastic feet (from 1950s and 1960s) sell for considerably less than quoted prices. Dolls are organized by size.

Marks: Dolls are unmarked except for box labels and paper labels on the foot of the doll (which are often gone). A typical label: "Skookum / Bully Good Indian / Pat. Pending / Trademark Registered" (paper label, foot) or "Skookum / Indian / Patented / February 17 / 1914," with circle around "The HH Tammen Co, New York, Denver."

SKOOKUM DOLLS

Brave

Size: 10–11″
Price: $80–$160   Internet: $75–$100
Higher price for mint doll with label.

Older Woman, Early Model

Size: 11″
Price: $1,100
Unusual modeling.

Skookum Native American man. *Composition mask face, straw-stuffed unjointed body. Unusually large size. 34″, c. 1920. Unmarked. $1,600, auction. Courtesy Theriault's*

Pair of Skookum Native Americans. *Composition mask faces, straw unjointed bodies. 14″, c. 1920. Unmarked. $450 pair, at auction. Courtesy Theriault's.*

Skookum Native American with Papoose. *Composition mask face, straw unjointed body. 11″, c. 1937. Unmarked. $140, dealer.*

Brave
Size: 12″
Price: $250   Internet: $315

Woman and Papoose
Size: 12″
                 Internet: $180

Woman and Papoose
Size: 13–14″
Price: $425–$600   Internet: $200–$300

Brave
Size: 15″
Price: $400   Internet: $300

Woman and Papoose
Size: 15–16″
Price: $500–$525   Internet: $250–$415

Brave or Chief
Size: 17″
Price: $425   Internet: $250–$400

Brave or Chief
Size: 21″
Price: $500–$700   Internet: $400

Woman With Papoose
Size: 21″
Price: $330
Original box.

Brave With Feathered Headdress, Studio-Size
Size: 34″
Price: $3,400

Brave, Studio-Size
Size: 34″
Price: $1,500–$1,600

Native American Female, Seated Display With Papoose
Size: 34″   Internet: $2,500
Flat wood base so large Skookum sits.

Brave, Studio-Size, Kidskin Costume
Size: 36″
Price: $2,300

Steiff

Of course, Steiff is best known for its bears and plush animals, but Steiff has also made dolls on and off throughout its history. In fact, the first Steiff dolls were made before the first Steiff bears.

The Steiff company was founded by Margarete Steiff of Germany. Margarete Steiff started making toys, including dolls, in 1893. The dolls were cloth, and the first dolls included dolls with themes taken from daily life—policemen, circus performers, and many others. By 1905, Margarete had founded the Steiff company. She brought her nephews in to help her run the company in 1908, and she died in 1909.

The first play dolls fashioned to look like children were made by Steiff in 1913. Both

Steiff girl. *All felt, swivel head, jointed at shoulders and hips. 14", c. 1912. Unmarked. Courtesy Theriault's.*

Steiff Professor. *All felt, swivel head, jointed shoulders and hips. Suit part of doll. 16", c. 1911. Mark: Steiff (button in ear). Courtesy Theriault's.*

Steiff Soldier. *Felt swivel head, stuffed cloth body, felt hands and feet, jointed arms and legs. 18", c. 1911. Mark: Steiff (button in ear). Courtesy Theriault's.*

the character "real life" dolls and children dolls were made with a vertical seam in the center of the face until 1930. The dolls also had glass set eyes and often mohair for hair. In 1930, Steiff ceased making its character line of dolls and made only children, and the dolls now had heads made of pressed felt (with no center seam).

Steiff dolls have continued to be made nearly continuously until today, with the last group made in 2001 with vinyl heads for distribution by Götz. Steiff dolls have been made out of nearly every type of material—in the early 20th century, some dolls were bisque and celluloid, later dolls have been mostly vinyl, with some cloth. However, Steiff is still best known for its mid-20th-century cloth dolls.

Market Report: As with all early to mid-20th-century cloth dolls, there is a strong demand right now. Also Steiff dolls are eagerly collected by plush collectors focusing on Steiff who wouldn't necessarily include dolls in their collections otherwise.

Online/Offline Report: Most of the earlier Steiff dolls are found most easily at auction houses and through dealers, although they do turn up occasionally on eBay. Prices for the better dolls are similar through all venues. On eBay, many vinyl and later Steiff dolls can easily be found.

Prices and Characteristics: All dolls are made of felt cloth with bead glass or steel eyes, with jointed arms and legs, in excellent condition except as noted. Dolls are unmarked or have a Steiff button in the ear.

STEIFF DOLLS

Child, Various
Size: 11–17"   Date: 1910–1930s
Price: $1,200–$1,400+ Internet: $1,000–$1,800
Higher prices for larger sizes or mint. Center seam face, stitched mouth.

Adult, Various
Size: 12–18"   Date: 1910–1930s
Price: $1,600+   Internet: $1,600+
More for mint dolls, unusual characters.

Fat Captain
Size: 15"   Date: 1910
Price: $1,400
Flaws.

Military Man
Size: 11"   Date: 1911
                      Internet: $1,300+
Gray uniform and hat; button in ear.

Soldier
                      Date: 1910s
Price: $2,000
Mint.

Bertha
                      Date: 1989
                      Internet: $210

NRFB, limited edition of 1,000, all paperwork in German.

Little Red Riding Hood
Date: 1989
Internet: $235
MIB, limited edition of 1,000 certificate, box in German.

Strawberry Shortcake

Strawberry Shortcake dolls were created based on the Strawberry Shortcake characters that initially were part of the American Greeting Cards line in 1979. Kenner (see Kenner section) licensed the rights to Strawberry Shortcake, and produced the dolls starting in 1980. The initial line of dolls included Strawberry Shortcake, Huckleberry Pie, Blueberry Muffin, and Apple Dumpling. Other characters were released later. The early dolls did not come with pets (except for Apple Dumpling who came with Tea Time Turtle).

Starting in 1981, the dolls included pets—Strawberry Shortcake came with Custard the Cat, Huckleberry Pie with Pupcake the Dog, Blueberry Muffin with Cheesecake the Mouse, Apple Dumpling again with Tea Time Turtle (in vinyl this time; the earlier doll came with a hard plastic Tea Time Turtle). All additional characters also came with pets. Through the years that followed, the popular Strawberry Shortcake line was produced with many variations. There were "international" dolls in 1983, miniatures in the early 1980s, and Berrykins in the mid-1980s. Along with the dolls came a plethora of licensed products and play toys. The Berrykins, released in 1985, were the last Strawberry Shortcake dolls produced by Kenner. Another company, Toy Headquarters (THQ), licensed the rights to the dolls for a short time, but the dolls never regained their initial popularity at the end of the 20th century.

Fast forward to the 21st century, to the nostalgia craze which swept the toy industry in 2003 and 2004. Care Bears, My Little Pony, and Strawberry Shortcake all went back into production during this time. Bandai currently produces a large variety of Strawberry Shortcake dolls and toys.

Market Report: There is an unbelievably strong market for vintage Strawberry Shortcake dolls, given that the dolls are only 20 or so years old. At any given time on eBay, there are several thousand listings for Strawberry Shortcake dolls and related items. MIB and NRFB rarer dolls and accessories can easily bring $200 to $400. Some favorites with collectors include the Party Pleasers from 1984, Berrykins (especially Banana Twirl, produced for one year only), and some of the rarer rag dolls.

Online/Offline Report: The widest variety of Strawberry Shortcake items—literally thousands of items—will be found on eBay. Doll dealers who deal in later dolls also will carry Strawberry Shortcake items. Prices are generally similar; however online bidding wars can sometimes bring prices higher than you would pay from a dealer or shop.

Prices and Characteristics: All dolls are vinyl except as noted. Classic-size Strawberry Shortcake dolls are 5.5 inches tall. For loose dolls, assume approximately half the MIB price if mint; much less if played with, but more for the rarest loose dolls.

STRAWBERRY SHORTCAKE

Various Characters With Pet: Cafe Ole, Blueberry Muffin, Mint Tulip, Purple Pie Man, Cherry Cuddler, Almond Tea, Lime Chiffon, Others
Date: 1982
Internet: $35–$55
Condition: MIB
With pet; square-celloed box.

Baby Apricot
Date: 1991
Internet: $110–$140
Condition: MIB
12″ tall; squeeze tummy and she blows an apricot-scented kiss.

Banana Twirl Berrykin With Her Berrykin Critter
Date: 1984
Internet: $320–$400
Condition: MIB, or NRFB
Produced for 1 year only; banana scent.

Crepe Suzette with Eclair (pet).
*Vinyl, scented. 5.5", c. 1982. $50
NRFB, eBay.*

Strawberry Shortcake. *Vinyl,
strawberry scented. 1st edition, no
pet. 5", c. 1980. $55 NRFB, eBay.*

Berry Happy Doll House
Date: 1983
Internet: $255–$300
Condition: VG
With some furniture, gently played with.

Berry Happy Doll House
Date: 1983
Internet: $500
Condition: MIB
Nearly complete with furniture.

Berry Princess
Date: 1985
Internet: $90
Condition: MIB

Blueberry Muffin
Date: 1980
Internet: $70
Condition: NRFB
With pet Cheesecake, earlier box (round cello
window).

Blueberry Muffin
Date: 1982
Internet: $35
Condition: NRFB
With pet Cheesecake, later box (square cello
window).

Crepe Suzette
Date: 1982
Internet: $65–$75
Condition: NRFB
With pet Éclair (dog).

Huckleberry Pie
Date: 1979
Internet: $45–$65
Condition: NRFB
With pet Pupcake (dog).

Huckleberry Pie, Rag Doll
Date: 1980
Internet: $200
Condition: MIB
Cloth doll.

Lemon Meringue

Date: 1980
Internet: $50–$70

Condition: NRFB
With pet Marmalade.

Lemon Meringue

Date: 1982
Internet: $130

Condition: NRFB
With pet Frappe.

Orange Blossom

Date: 1980
Internet: $40

Condition: NRFB

Orange Blossom With Orange Berrykin

Date: 1985
Internet: $250

Condition: MIB
Black doll, with Berrykin friend. Produced for 1 year only.

Orange Blossom, Rag Doll

Size: 14.5″   Date: 1982
Internet: $55

Condition: Mint
14.5″.

Party Pleaser, Peach Blush

Date: 1981
Internet: $120–$160

Condition: MIB
With Melonie Bell.

Party Pleaser, Plum Pudding

Date: 1981
Internet: $95–$165

Condition: MIB
With Elderberry Owl.

Party Pleasers, Various

Date: 1982
Internet: $40–$60

Condition: MIB
Angel Cake, Mint Tulip, Orange Blossom, others.

Plum Berrykin

Date: 1980s
Internet: $355

Condition: MIB
With all accessories.

Plum Pudding Deluxe Mini

Date: 1984
Internet: $250

Condition: MIB

Raspberry Tart

Date: 1980
Internet: $70

Condition: NRFB
With pet Rhubarb, earliest box (round cello window).

Raspberry Tart

Date: 1982
Internet: $35

Condition: NRFB
With pet Rhubarb, later box (square cello window).

Strawberry Shortcake

Date: 1980
Internet: $50–$60

Condition: MIB
Early version, no pet.

Strawberry Shortcake

Date: 1982
Internet: $50

Condition: MIB
With Custard (cat).

Strawberry Shortcake

Date: 1982
Internet: $75

Condition: NRFB
With Custard (cat).

Strawberry Shortcake With Berrykin

Date: 1985
Internet: $230

Condition: MIB
Produced for 1 year only.

Strawberry Shortcake, Cookie Jar

Date: 1980s
Internet: $230

Condition: Mint
Porcelain.

Strawberry Shortcake, Rag Doll

Date: 1981
Internet: $130

Condition: MIB

Strawberry Shortcake, Baby Blow Kiss

Date: 1991
Internet: $110–$135

Condition: MIB
Squeeze tummy and she blows a kiss.

Sweet Sleepers, Various

Date: 1980
Internet: $40–$60

Condition: MIB
Sleep eyes.

Sunshine Family

At the very end of the Barbie era, the Sunshine Family delighted late baby boomers and early Gen-X children. Heavily promoted on television, the Sunshine Family consisted of a Mom (Steffie), Dad (Steve), and baby (Sweets). Later on, Baby Sweets grew into a little girl and got a little brother. Even later, Grandma and Grandpa joined the family, and a Black version of the family called the Happy Family was released. The dolls were vinyl, and although not costumed in high-quality clothing, the dolls and their world held definite charm for children looking for an alternative to Barbie and friends. In fact, for new moms coming out of the 1960s "hippie" era, these dolls held a charm quite different from Barbie, as the dolls seemed environmentally conscious (their Idea Books often held recycling ideas) and quite outdoorsy (one accessory set, for instance, was the "River Trip Craft Kit").

Available separately for the dolls was a well-designed foldout house, as well as clothing kits which contained a craft component for play (beading, yarn crafts, stickers, etc.). In fact, crafting was a large part of the Sunshine Family philosophy and crafting Idea Books were sold with many items. Besides the main line of dolls, the dolls were produced in historical varieties, including an Indian Maiden, a Pioneer Girl, and a Star-Spangled Southern Belle. The Sunshine Family was produced from 1974 to 1978.

Market Report: Not an especially hot market, nor a terribly expensive doll. You can find mint NRFB Sunshine Family items quite reasonably from eBay and dealers. It's a wonderful vintage doll with nearly all items available priced at under $100.

Online/Offline Report: Thanks to people cleaning out their attics and easily being able to recognize the Sunshine Family, you'll find the widest variety of dolls and accessories on eBay, although many are heavily played with.

Prices and Characteristics: All dolls are vinyl; adult Sunshine Family dolls are 9 inches to 9.5 inches tall. Dolls are marked on back: © 1973 / MATTEL, INC.; on heads: © 1973 / MATTEL, INC. / TAIWAN.

SUNSHINE FAMILY

Sunshine Family

Date: 1974–1978
Internet: $5–$10

Condition: Av
For set of 3 loose, average dolls in original clothing.

Sunshine Family

Date: 1974–1978
Internet: $30–$50

Condition: Mint
For set of 3 loose dolls in original clothing.

Sunshine Family

Date: 1974
Internet: $60–$80

Condition: MIB
Set of 3, Steve, Steffie, 9″, and Baby Sweets, 3″.

Sunshine Fun Family, Later Family

Date: 1978
Internet: $45–$75

Condition: NRFB
Later Sunshine Family box and family includes 4 (not 3) dolls, with rarer older girl. Yellow box.

Sunshine Family Grandparents

Date: 1975
Internet: $40–$50

Condition: MIB
Grandma and Grandpa.

Baby Room

Date: 1976
Internet: $35

Condition: MIB

Dress Up Kit

Date: 1976
Internet: $8

Condition: MIB
Dress for Mom, shirt for Dad, and playsuit for baby, pack of beads and Idea Book.

Green House

Internet: $75

Condition: NRFB

Happy Family (Black Dolls)

Date: 1975
Internet: $20

Condition: Ex
Mom (Hattie), Dad (Hal), and Baby Hon.

Indian Maiden

Date: 1975
Internet: $75

Condition: Mint

Sunshine Family (Steve, Stephanie, Baby Sweets). All vinyl. c. 1973. $60 NRFB, eBay. Courtesy Marsha L. Cumpton.

River Trip Craft Kit

Internet: $30

Condition: NRFB

Sears Exclusive, Barbie Baby-Sits

Date: 1974

Internet: $45

Condition: Mint

Star-Spangled, Pilgrims

Date: 1976

Internet: $50

Condition: MIB

Steve and Steffie dressed as pilgrims.

Star-Spangled, Pioneer Girl

Date: 1976

Internet: $30

Condition: Mint

Sunshine Family Home

Date: 1975

Internet: $75

Condition: NRFB

Unassembled.

Sunshine Family World

Date: 1970s

Internet: $65

Condition: MIB

For house and dolls.

Surrey

Internet: $40

Condition: NRFB

"Bicycle" for 3 with roof.

Young Sweethearts

Date: 1975

Internet: $30

Condition: MIB

12" Michael and Melinda.

Tammy Family

In the 1960s, many mothers objected to Barbie dolls and their oh-so-grown-up bodies. These mothers were looking for an alternative doll, and the very wholesome (and somewhat flat-chested) Tammy from Ideal fit the bill.

Tammy was presented as a teenage fashion doll, just like Barbie, and, in fact, was Ideal's "answer" to the Barbie doll. In spite of her flatter measurements (or because of them?) many little girls felt that Tammy was an "older" doll than Barbie, and often, little girls who owned both Barbie and Tammy would have Tammy with her sensible fashions be the "mother" of the Barbie family.

Nevertheless, Tammy was a beautifully made vinyl fashion doll in her own right. The clothing and accessories produced for Tammy were well-made and detailed. Tammy was a success and soon she had a freckled little sister (Pepper), a boyfriend (Bud), a brother (Ted), a Mom and Dad, plus other friends.

Glamour Misty. 12", c. 1965. Mark: © 1965 / IDEAL TOY CORP / V12 –3 (head) © 1965 / IDEAL (in circle) / M-12 (lower back). $30–$50, eBay.

Tammy. Vinyl. 12", c. 1962. Mark: © IDEAL TOY CORP / BS-72 (head) ©IDEAL TOY CORP / BS-12 / 4 (body). Original jumpsuit. $75 MIB, eBay.

Unfortunately, Tammy was never as popular as Barbie, and she was only on the market from 1962 to early 1966.

Market Report: There hasn't been any significant movement in prices for Tammy dolls, either up or down, since the late 1990s. Tammy shouldn't be overlooked, however, by fashion doll collectors or collectors of 1960s dolls because of her quality and her detailed clothing.

Online/Offline Report: As with all baby boomer toys, the selection of Tammy family items on eBay is overwhelming, with hundreds of items available at any given time. Most items, however, are not mint. You can also find a fine selection of vintage Tammy items from vintage Barbie doll dealers, often with an emphasis on mint and rare items. Prices and availability for mint items is similar from all venues.

Prices, Characteristics, and Marks: All dolls are vinyl with painted eyes, produced between 1963 and 1966. Most dolls are marked ©IDEAL TOY CORP or © (date) IDEAL (in oval), with letters and numbers on the head and back.

TAMMY FAMILY

Bud
Size: 12"   Internet: $20–$40
Condition: Ex

Dad
Size: 13"   Internet: $15–$30
Condition: Ex

Dad
Size: 12"   Internet: $60
Condition: MIB

Dodi (Pepper's Friend)
                             Internet: $30–$50
Condition: Ex

Pepper, Tammy's little sister.
*Vinyl. 9.5", c. 1963. Mark: ©1955 /
IDEAL TOY CORP / P9-3 (head)
1964 © / IDEAL (in circle) / DO-9
(lower back). $40 MIB, eBay.*

Tammy accessory pak #9187-80.
$25 MOC, dealer.

Pepper's Outfit, "Teacher's Pet."
*On box: © 1964 IDEAL TOY
CORPORATION / MADE IN
JAPAN. $60 NRFB, dealer.*

Glamour Misty
Size: 12" Internet: $20–$40
Condition: Ex

Glamour Misty, Original Set
Size: 12" Internet: $300
Condition: MIB
With robe, 3 applicators for hair color, comb.

Mom
Size: 12.5" Internet: $100
Condition: MIB

Mom, Black Hair
Size: 12.5" Internet: $200
Condition: MIB
With rarer black hair.

Patti (Pepper's Friend)
          Internet: $285
Condition: MIB

Pepper (Sister)
Size: 9" Internet: $45–$65
Condition: MIB

Pepper, Pos'n
Size: 9" Internet: $75–$125
Condition: MIB
Pos'n dolls have flexible, bendable limbs.

Pepper and Dodi Gift Set
          Internet: $430
Condition: NRFB
Montgomery Ward exclusive.

Pepper and Dodi Hatbox Case
          Internet: $35–$50
Condition: Ex

Yellow vinyl hatbox case, 10.5", with Pepper and
Dodi graphics dancing to music of MOPS band.

Pete, Pos'n (Little Brother)
Size: 9" Internet: $125
Condition: MIB
Hard to find; same doll as Salty, dressed and
boxed differently.

Salty, Pos'n (Pepper's Friend)
Size: 8" Internet: $100–$140
Condition: MIB
For mint doll with all accessories.

Tammy
Size: 12" Internet: $25–$35
Condition: Gd, VG
Oversupply on Internet.

Tammy
Size: 12" Internet: $100–$125
Condition: MIB

Tammy (Japanese)
Size: 12" Internet: $40+
Condition: Ex

Tammy Outfit, Beauty Queen
          Internet: $275
Condition: Mint
No box.

Tammy, Grown Up
Size: 12" Internet: $20–$50
Condition: Ex
More slender and shapely.

Tammy, Outfits

Internet: $25–$30
Condition: VG to Ex
For complete and near complete outfits.

Tammy, Outfits

Internet: $60–$100
Condition: Mint
For most Tammy outfits, mint and complete; slightly higher for rare items or MOC items.

Tammy, Pos'n

Size: 12″   Internet: $85–$125
Condition: MIB

Tammy, Redhead

Size: 12″   Internet: $100–$150
Condition: MIB

Ted (Brother)

Size: 12.5″   Internet: $25–$50
Condition: Ex, MIB

Ted, Pos'n

Size: 12.5″   Internet: $100+
Condition: MIB

Terri Lee

Okay—I'll admit it. As a beginning collector, I thought Terri Lee dolls were just the homeliest things I had ever seen. Collectors who grew up in the 1940s or 1950s and who owned and loved a Terri Lee, as well as the multitudes that collect them today, I am sure, would strongly disagree with me.

Terri Lee dolls were born in 1946 when Violet Lee Gradwohl decided she wanted to create a doll. She had her niece, Maxine Stevens Runci, sculpt the doll, and together they introduced Terri Lee at Toy Fair. The doll was based on Maxine's 4-year-old daughter. The first dolls were made of composition (marked TERRI LEE / PAT. PENDING on their backs). The composition dolls were produced for only two years since the creators of the doll wanted to make them more durable.

In 1948, Terri Lee, a 16-inch doll, was made in hard plastic (the earliest dolls were still marked TERRI LEE / PAT. PENDING on their backs). From 1948 to 1950, the dolls had painted flesh tones and they are called "painted plastic dolls" by collectors. Soon after, from 1950 to 1952, the dolls were made in hard plastic with the flesh tones mixed into the plastic. The mark on the doll changed in 1952 when the patent for it was granted, and it became only "TERRI LEE" from this point on. The majority of Terri Lee dolls were made of hard plastic, although briefly, in 1950, they were made of soft vinyl. This soft vinyl deteriorated quickly and there are not many soft vinyl Terri Lee dolls left in good condition today.

Terri Lee had an extensive wardrobe produced for her—everything from Campfire Girl outfits to formal gowns. As her popularity grew, she also had a family—a brother, Jerri Lee, baby dolls, Connie Lynn and Linda Baby (originally Linda Lee). Patti Jo, a Black doll, was produced starting in the late 1940s. The baby dolls were also sculpted based on members of the Gradwohl and Runci families. In the mid-1950s, a Tiny Terri Lee and Jerri Lee, 10-inch tall walking dolls, were produced.

The dolls were made until 1958 by the family-owned company, when legal problems and a factory fire caused its demise. Various companies received rights to the molds, including Mar-Fan, Magna, and I & S Industries, and they continued to produce walking, talking, and other versions of Terri Lee into the 1960s. Many collectors feel that these later dolls and their fashions are not of the same high quality as the earlier dolls and fashions. The final Terri Lee dolls were produced by these companies in 1962.

In 1999, Knickerbocker began to produce good-quality reproductions of the Terri Lee dolls until they went out of business in 2002. Currently, Terri Lee Associates, a company created by the original members of the Lee family, owns all the rights to the Terri Lee family of dolls, and they are producing high-quality, very limited-production editions of these dolls for the collector market.

Market Report: Terri Lees are another hot market, with anything in excellent or better condition from the 1950s doing extremely well. Terri Lee is also a doll with highly identifiable outfits, and dolls in rarer outfits can bring several hundred dollars more than dolls in the most common or mother-made outfits. Even the prices for the now-retired Knickerbocker reproductions are rising, since not that many reproduced dolls were made, and they are quite nicely done. Terri Lee Associates is currently selling out of all of its limited-edition Terri Lees.

Online/Offline Report: Again, as with many baby boomer dolls, the online market is exceptionally strong. This makes sense, because the baby boomers are computer literate, and they have embraced eBay and all things Internet as quickly and totally as they originally embraced their playthings in the 1950s and 1960s. However, don't overlook dealers or auction houses for Terri Lee dolls, where you always have the advantage of inspecting quality and condition personally.

Prices and Characteristics: All dolls have painted eyes and jointed 5-piece bodies except as otherwise noted. Composition dolls were produced from 1946 to 1947, painted hard plastic from 1947 to 1950, and hard plastic from 1951 to 1962, with hard plastic dolls marked "Pat. Pending" only made through 1951. Soft vinyl dolls were only made in 1950.

Marks: Composition dolls are marked on back TERRI LEE / PAT. PENDING or TERRI LEE PATENT PENDING. Painted plastic and hard plastic dolls through 1951 are marked TERRI LEE / PATENT PENDING, and dolls 1952 and after are marked TERRI LEE.

TERRI LEE, COMPOSITION

Jerri Lee
Size: 16″
Price: $210   Internet: $300–$400
Condition: Ex
Lower prices for dolls with flaws.

Terri Lee
Size: 16″   Internet: $200–$300
Condition: VG
Crazing, other flaws.

Terri Lee
Size: 16″
Price: $500   Internet: $500–$600
Condition: Ex
In desirable outfit.

Terri Lee
Size: 16″
Price: $700   Internet: $1,000–$1,200
Condition: Mint
Original, fresh face color, no crazing.

TERRI LEE, HARD PLASTIC

Terri Lee, Painted Plastic
Size: 16″   Internet: $1,300
Condition: MIB
Pristine.

Terri Lee, Patent Pending
Size: 16″
All Markets: $400–$500+
Condition: Ex
In common outfit.

Terri Lee, Patent Pending, Cowgirl
Size: 16″   Internet: $700
Condition: VG
With flaws, more common cowgirl outfit.

Terri Lee, Patent Pending, Cowgirl
Size: 16″   Internet: $1,700
Condition: Mint
Fringed white cowgirl outfit; sold with added outfits.

Terri Lee
Size: 16″   Internet: $175–$225
Condition: VG
Played with, flaws.

Terri Lee
Size: 16″   Internet: $300–$400
Condition: Ex
Doll in original clothing.

Terri Lee, Black
Size: 16″   Internet: $1,100+
Condition: Ex

Terri Lee, Campfire Girls, Bluebird Outfit
Size: 16″   Internet: $450
Condition: Ex
Desirable platinum blonde in sought-after outfit.

Terri Lee, Platinum Blonde, *Alice in Wonderland* Outfit
Size: 16″   Internet: $700
Condition: Ex
Fancy outfit tagged "Alice in Wonderland/Terri Lee."

Terri Lee, Side Braids
Size: 16″   Internet: $325
Condition: Ex

Terri Lee in formal. Hard plastic. 16″. Mark: TERRI LEE (back).

Terri Lee, Campfire Girls Bluebird outfit. Hard plastic. 16″. Mark: TERRI LEE and outfit tagged "Terri Lee" in script. eBay, $455. Courtesy Karen Cvitkovich.

Terri Lee, Girl Scout Uniform. Hard plastic. 16″. Mark: TERRI LEE and outfit tagged "Terri Lee" in script. Courtesy Helen Simms Collection.

Jerri Lee, Patent Pending, Cowboy, Wardrobe
Size: 16″   Internet: $1,995
Condition: Mint
Earliest patent pending model; with wardrobe.

Jerri Lee
Size: 16″   Internet: $200–$300
Condition: VG
Played with, flaws.

Jerri Lee
Size: 16″   Internet: $400–$500
Condition: Ex
Caracul wig, original clothing.

Outfit, Jerri Lee, Drum Major
                   Internet: $585
Condition: MIB

Tiny Terri Lee
Size: 10″   Internet: $50–$100
Condition: VG
Played with, flaws.

Tiny Terri Lee
Size: 10″   Internet: $150–$200
Condition: Mint

Tiny Terri Lee, Trunk, Clothes
Size: 19″   Internet: $455
Condition: Mint
With small Steiff Snobby dog, several vintage tagged outfits, trunk.

Connie Lynn
Size: 18″   Internet: $350
Condition: MIB
Baby, 1955.

TERRI LEE, VINYL

Linda Baby
Size: 10.5″   Internet: $100
Condition: Av

Linda Baby
Size: 10.5″   Internet: $195
Condition: Ex
In kimono.

Terri Lee
Size: 16″   Internet: $220
Condition: VG

Terri Lee, Knickerbocker Reproductions
Size: 16″   Internet: $75–$125
Condition: MIB
Late 1990s and early 2000s reproductions. Hard vinyl.

Tiny Town

As mentioned in the section on BAPS dolls, there has been an upswing in interest in small metal-footed cloth dolls, particularly the dolls of Tiny Town from California and BAPS from Germany. Most collectors that collect BAPS collect Tiny Town, and vice-versa. Tiny Town dolls were made in the 1940s and 1950s by Alma LeBlanc, who was a former employee of the Nancy Ann Storybook Doll Company. Just like the Nancy Ann Storybook dolls, the dolls came boxed, with a small wrist tag and a pamphlet which highlighted other dolls available in the Tiny Town series.

As with BAPS dolls, the production of Tiny Town dolls was a small cottage industry, and all the dolls were hand-done.

The dolls portray children, international themes, and storybook characters; among themes that have been documented are couples from foreign lands. Like BAPS dolls, their faces are hand-painted, and their bodies are made of cloth-covered wire armature. Most dolls are unmarked, as they originally came only with their paper labels for identification.

Market Report: Prices are trending up as more collectors become aware of this genre of dolls.

Online/Offline Report: It is easier to find Tiny Town dolls than to find BAPS dolls, but they are still hard to find. Again, your best sources are knowledgeable dealers. Just as with BAPS, educate yourself about Tiny Town dolls and you may find them improperly marked or unmarked, and also sometimes misidentified at online auctions. Tiny Town dolls are scarce on eBay.

Prices and Characteristics: Most Tiny Town dolls are unmarked, but sometimes the character is marked on the bottom of the foot. All dolls are cloth, with cloth-wrapped wire bodies, hand-painted cloth faces, and metal shoes. All are from the 1940s and 1950s. Prices are for excellent dolls and are similar from all venues.

TINY TOWN

Boy, Girl, or International Character
Size: 3–5″
Price: $65–$100
More for rarer dolls.

Blondie, Series 1
Size: 4″
Price: $210
MIB, with pamphlet describing other dolls available. White metal shoes, shoe stamped "Blondie."

Bride and Groom
Size: 4″
Price: $270
Series 5, for pair.

Brother
Size: 5″
Price: $100
White metal shoes, red corduroy outfit.

Cowgirl
Size: 4″
Price: $125
Wrist tag.

Irish Boy or Irish Coleen
Size: 4″
Price: $85+
Mint; black painted metal shoes, wrist tag.

Little Artist
Size: 4.5″
Price: $50
Wrist tag.

Pat, Schoolgirl
Size: 4″
Price: $95
Metal shoe stamped "Pat," red hair.

Schoolgirl
Size: 4″
Price: $155
Mint.

Spanish Couple
Size: 4″
Price: $215
For pair.

Tressy

Tressy dolls, the original grow-hair dolls, came out in 1964 to directly compete with Barbie dolls. Tressy was a fashion doll with a twist—when you turned a key in Tressy's tummy, her hair would grow! The hair could also be retracted using the same device, to be grown again and again by her owner. Tressy was one in a long line of "gimmick dolls" that goes back to the early patented Brus (look—a doll that can nurse!) to the walking and wetting dolls of the mid-20th century to today, when nearly every doll made for children, it seems, has a gimmick (talking, singing, eating, dancing, learning, you name it).

Although very popular when first introduced thanks to widespread advertising on children's television shows, Tressy never achieved the popularity of Barbie, and she was produced by American Character only

Tressy. *Vinyl doll, turn key in back, hair ponytail at top of head goes in. Push button and pull, hair grows. Ponytail on this doll put up by original "mother." 12", c. 1964. Mark: AMERICAN CHARACTER / 19©63 / COPR. (in circle). $35, eBay, more in better condition.*

from 1963 to 1966. Several variations of Tressy, including Cricket (a younger doll) and Mary Make-Up, were also produced.

Tressy has left a legacy of grow-hair dolls that continue to come in and out of the market today. It can be assumed that Tressy was the inspiration for the much larger and very popular Crissy by Ideal in 1969. In 2004, Fisher-Price produced a Dora the Explorer doll with hair that "magically" grows and retracts by touching a magic wand to a crown on the doll's head. This Dora could be considered Tressy's granddaughter!

Market Report: Tressy is eagerly collected, especially by collectors of 1960s fashion dolls and by collectors of American Character dolls, but she has not inspired a collector following as strong as Barbie or even Tammy by Ideal.

Online/Offline Report: The best selection of Tressy items is online, but Tressy dolls and outfits are carried by many vintage Barbie and 1960s doll dealers.

Prices, Characteristics, and Mark: Tressy was made by American Character (see the American Character section). All Tressys are vinyl with painted eyes and hair that grows, and they are 11.5" tall. All Tressy dolls and items are from 1964 to 1966. Prices are similar from all venues; price results are predominantly from the Internet. **Mark:** "Amer. Char. 1963" (in circle, head).

TRESSY

Mary Make-Up
Internet: $275
Condition: MIB
With all accessories.

Tressy
Internet: $40–$60
Condition: Mint
Uncut hair, original red dress and key.

Tressy, Basic Box
Internet: $100–$150
Condition: MIB

Tressy, Special Carry Trunk
Internet: $200
Condition: MIB
In unusual purple carry trunk from Jewel Home Shopping Service.

Tressy, Black
Internet: $200–$300+
Condition: Av
Played-with condition.

Tressy, Black
Internet: $800
Condition: Mint
Pristine mint.

Sailing Outfit
Internet: $240
Condition: NRFB

Dam Troll. *Vinyl 1-piece. 7.25", c. late 1960s. Mark: Thomas/Dam/Danmark (back) © / 1964 / DANMARK (foot). $40, eBay.*

Reisler Troll. *Vinyl 1-piece, mohair on head and also as "skirt." 4", c. late 1960s. Mark: Reisler/MADE IN / DENMARK (in circle). $40, eBay.*

Totally Troll by Playmates. *Vinyl, 1 piece. Hans V. Fefferdane. 5", c. 2001. $5, eBay.*

Tressy, Outfits (Carded)

Internet: $50–$100

Condition: MOC

Tressy, Outfits (Boxed)

Internet: $100–$200

Condition: NRFB

For most common outfits.

Trolls

Okay, admit it—somewhere, in the past, there has been a troll in your life. Perhaps you were a child during the 1960s and you found a troll doll hanging out of your Christmas stocking on Christmas morning. If you were in college during the 1960s, you may have had a groovy troll decorating your dorm room. Or perhaps you bought one of the more recently made trolls—either as a souvenir, or out of simple baby boomer troll nostalgia.

However that troll got there, you are in good company—trolls have been immensely popular dolls, and there seems to be a troll or two in almost any household you come across. There have literally been thousands of varieties of troll dolls produced by many manufacturers. In fact, trolls were the second-biggest-selling doll of the sixties (the troll heyday!) right after Barbie!

Trolls have been a part of folklore forever. They have long been described as bad and

mischievous creatures who live in caves, in logs, and under bridges. Trolls are believed to be good luck, which certainly has helped the sale of troll dolls, since troll dolls can be found in houses, in cars, even at work, purchased with the hope that they will bring luck to their owners.

Trolls in their collectible form were first created by Thomas Dam and his family, in Denmark in the 1950s. The first Dam trolls were carved in wood. Later they were made of soft rubber, and finally, vinyl. The trolls made by Thomas Dam's company became known as "Dam Things," and these are the most popular trolls with collectors today. However, Trolls by Uneeda (Wishnik Trolls) and Reisler from Denmark are also well-made and considered highly collectible.

Although Dam Things made the best-known and most collectible trolls, many companies got on the troll bandwagon and began to produce trolls in the mid-1960s. Most of these trolls are unmarked, so it is often difficult to identify trolls from any of the "clone" troll makers. Many of the clone troll manufacturers were from Hong Kong and Taiwan, and the trolls they made were cheap imitations and of low quality. These low-quality trolls flooded the market in the mid-1960s, which caused trolls to become less popular—troll popularity peaked in approximately 1966.

Norfin Bank Troll by Dam. *Vinyl 1-piece with slot in back for coins. 3.75″ tall, 6.5″ long. Mark: © DAM (1 side) and 1984 (other side). Tag: "ADOPT A / NORFIN" (one side) and "MADE IN DENMARK by / DAM THINGS APS." Courtesy Ellen Johnson.*

Trolls went downhill from there, and became almost invisible by the 1980s. However, starting in 1989, troll production started in earnest again, when troll nostalgia hit big, causing the second boom period for trolls in the early 1990s. Trolls became ubiquitous again, and were found in nearly every toy shop and gift shop. Today, trolls are not as common as in the early 1990s, but can still be found. Today's trolls are made by several manufacturers, including Dam Trolls which sells their current trolls only in Denmark.

Market Report: The variety of trolls that have been produced is amazing. There have been ugly, pretty, mean, strong, fat, and skinny trolls. Some people think troll dolls are cute, others think them outrageously ugly. There have been Rasta trolls, and pencil-topper trolls, and numerous holiday-themed trolls (Santas, elves, reindeer). There are ballerina trolls, college trolls, and "shapely" female trolls with molded breasts. Trolls have been made out of vinyl, wood, hemp, rubber, glass, porcelain, and ceramic. Even the hair on trolls heads have been varied—mohair, fur, nylon, straw—nearly anything you can think of. The nicest troll hair—often mohair—was found on the early 1960s Dam Things trolls.

Some of the rarest and most sought-after vintage trolls include animal trolls (trolls made to resemble various animals—lions, giraffes, cats, etc.), moon trolls, 2-headed trolls (extremely rare!), and black trolls (also very rare). Large Dam trolls (12″ and over) are extremely desirable.

In addition to the rare trolls mentioned above (animal, moon, 2-headed, and black), look for original 1960s Dam trolls in their original costumes, with their hair and bodies in good condition. Dam trolls had felt clothing that was often riveted to the body (very different than the clothing on the later Russ trolls, which often is made of synthetic fiber and has Velcro closures). Many older trolls are found naked today because the felt from the clothing was fragile and often disintegrated.

Prices on trolls range from only a few dollars ($1 to $5) for late, common Russ trolls, to $200 and up for rare 1960s Dam Things animal trolls (like giraffes and lions). Smaller, more common animals can be $25 to $50. Non-Dam troll animals can be much cheaper, especially if their tags are not attached. Small 1960s trolls can be found for $15 to $30.

Online/Offline Report: You'll find truckloads of trolls on the Internet. Learn about the different varieties and what makes a troll desirable before plunging in too deeply. Many doll dealers don't carry trolls (some don't even consider them dolls), so your best sources will probably be the Internet, specialty troll dealers and vintage toy dealers.

Prices and Characteristics: All trolls are vinyl, and prices are for trolls in excellent condition. Most trolls sell on eBay in the $10 to $30 range; included below are some examples which bring higher prices.

TROLLS

Anri Troll
Size: 3–6″   Internet: $100–$220
Troll from Italy.
Mark: ANRI. Italy (sticker)

Dam Troll, Various
Size: various   Date: 1960s–1970s
                       Internet: $40–$100
Basic vintage Dam troll, mint and original clothing.

Dam Troll
Size: various   Date: 1970s and later
                       Internet: $20–$40
Played with and more common later models.

Dam Troll, Hula Girl
Size: 3″   Date: 1970s
                  Internet: $175
Unmarked; marked clear box.

Dam, Tailed Troll
Size: 3–7″   Date: 1960s–1970s
                    Internet: $70–$100
Played with, no clothing.
Mark: DAM THINGS EST 1965

Dam, Tailed Troll
Size: 3–7″   Date: 1960s–1970s
                    Internet: $175–$375
Mint original clothing, depends on rarity.
Mark: DAM THINGS Est. C 1965

Dam Troll, Uncommon Face, Original Clothes
Size: 8+″   Date: 1965
                   Internet: $335
For very large sizes with unusual face modeling.

Dam Trolls, Animals
                   Date: 1960s and later
                   Internet: $150–$300
Price depends on rarity of animal troll; monkey $300, giraffe $150, etc.

Dam Troll, Donkey
Size: 8.5″   Date: 1960s
                    Internet: $180
Mark: Dam Things EST. 1964

Dam Troll, Turtle
Size: 4.5″   Date: 1960s
                    Internet: $220

Orange hair.
Mark: Design Dam, c. Dam Things Est. 1964

Moon Troll, Purple
Size: 4″   Date: 1960s
                  Internet: $170
Little alien-like troll.
Mark: JAPAN (foot)

Nyform Troll, Golf Player
                  Date: 1960s
                  Internet: $150–$300
For vintage 1960s golf players. Nyform has made hard resin trolls in Norway since 1964; they still make trolls today.

Nyform Troll
                  Date: 1960s–1970s
                  Internet: $30–$60
More for hard-to-find characters; less for newer trolls.

Reisler Troll
Size: 3–6″   Date: 1960s–1970s
                    Internet: $10–$30
Made in Denmark, often wearing feathers for clothing.
Mark: REISLER-Made in Denmark-J.N (foot)

Uneeda Wishnik Trolls
Size: 3–6″   Date: 1960s
                    Internet: $5–$15
Various basic models.

Uneeda Wishnik Hula Girl Troll
Size: 5.5″   Date: 1970s
                    Internet: $330
Blonde hair rooted as skirt and in head; green skin.

Uneeda Wishnik "Sock It To Me" Laugh-In Troll
Size: 6″   Date: 1960s
                  Internet: $40

Uneeda, 2 Heads
                  Date: 1965
                  Internet: $30–$50

Uneeda

Uneeda Dolls is such an interesting company because it's so average. Formed in 1917, it has been making dolls for little girls ever since. For the most part, you haven't heard much about its dolls, since Uneeda dolls have never been about big names, celebrities, innovation, or licensed properties. Instead, Uneeda has, throughout its entire history, focused on making a good-quality (if somewhat aver-

Dollikins. *Vinyl, jointed at neck, shoulders, elbows, wrists, waist, hips, knees, ankles. 19". Mark: UNEEDA / 28. $200, eBay. Courtesy Ellen Johnson.*

Pee Wee, Debutante. *Vinyl, jointed at neck. 4", c. late 1960s. Mark: © UD.CO.INC. / MCM-LXXVII / MADE IN HONG KONG (head and back). $15 MIB, eBay.*

Baby Jennifer. *Vinyl, 5-piece body. 12", c. 1978. $30, eBay. Courtesy Marsha L. Cumpton.*

age) doll at a good price—good play value for the money. One of the only "shining stars" in the Uneeda universe has been its multi-jointed Dollikin doll from the late 1950s.

Many early Uneeda dolls are unmarked and cannot be identified today unless accompanied by their original packaging or tags, but Uneeda did make many composition and hard-plastic dolls. Uneeda was also known for clever (and cheaper) clones of dolls such as Cissy and Barbie (Miss Suzette).

Uneeda still makes toys today, and a visit to its showroom at Toy Fair in New York shows vinyl play dolls which are sold at excellent prices by many mass marketers.

Market Report: Dollikin dolls are very popular with fashion doll collectors, although they are not bringing the high prices of just three or four years ago. Nevertheless, mint, identified vintage Uneeda dolls do have collectors searching for them.

Online/Offline Report: Dollikins are found via dealers and eBay alike, at similar prices. More "offbeat" Uneeda dolls often will have better representation on eBay, although they are plentiful at doll shows as well. Prices are slightly higher for most Uneeda items at shows and shops.

UNEEDA DOLLS, COMPOSITION

Uneeda Kid
Date: 1910
Price: $725
Condition: Mint
Advertising Uneeda Biscuits, Nabisco.

Sweetums
Size: 11"   Date: 1936
Price: $250
Condition: MIB

Prices and Characteristics: All dolls listed below are vinyl, except as noted.

UNEEDA DOLLS, VINYL

Baby Dollikin
Size: 20"   Date: 1960
             Internet: $160–$260
Condition: Ex
Multijointed.
Mark: UNEEDA (head) UNEEDA DOLL CO INC. (back)

Betsy McCall
Size: 12"   Date: 1963
             Internet: $120–$150
Condition: MIB
Older-looking Betsy McCall fashion doll.

Cissy Look-Alike
Date: 1960s
Internet: $150
Condition: Ex
Hair grows.

Disney's Pollyanna

Size: 31″   Date: 1960s
                      Internet: $100
Condition: Ex
Mark: Walt Disney Prod./MDF by Uneeda

Dollikin

Size: 19″   Date: 1957–1960s
                      Internet: $150–$190
Condition: Gd
For dolls with splits and other flaws, but original clothing. Dollikins have 16 joints and high-heeled feet.
Mark: Uneeda 2 S

Dollikin

Size: 19″   Date: 1957–1960s
                      Internet: $185–$220
Condition: Ex
Holds all positions, no split seams.

Dollikin

Size: 19″   Date: 1957–1960s
                      Internet: $300–$350+
Condition: Mint
MIB or pristine mint.

Fairy Princess, Bride

Size: 32″   Internet: $100–$120
Condition: Mint
Similar to Pollyanna, but eyes tilt up, and mouth is closed with smile.

Hee Wee

Size: 4″   Date: late 1960s
                      Internet: $10 to $20
Condition: MIB

Little Sophisticates

Size: 8.5″   Date: 1967
                      Internet: $20–$40
Condition: VG
Played with, redressed.

Little Sophisticates

Size: 8.5″   Date: 1967
                      Internet: $100
Condition: Mint
Mint, in tagged dress.

Little Sophisticates

Size: 8.5″   Date: 1960s
                      Internet: $300
Condition: MOC
Mark: UNEEDA DOLL CO. 1967/MADE IN JAPAN (head)

Little Sophisticates Reproduction

Size: 8.5″   Date: 2001
                      Internet: $25–$40
Condition: MIB

Little Miss Dollikin

Size: 6.5″   Date: 1971
                      Internet: $25–$50
Condition: NRFB

Miss Suzette, Barbie Clone

Size: 11.5″   Date: 1960s
                      Internet: $150
Condition: Ex
Mark: Uneeda Doll Co. Inc. 1962

Mommy Dollikin

Size: 20″   Date: 1957–1960s
                      Internet: $170
Condition: Ex
Missing baby, other flaws, but with box.

Pee Wee

Size: 3–4″   Date: 1960s
                      Internet: $20–$30
Condition: MIB

Pollyanna

Size: 31″   Date: 1960s
                      Internet: $100
Condition: Ex

Tickin' Tot

                      Date: 1986
                      Internet: $30
Condition: MIB
Black or Caucasian baby, vinyl; press heart, feel heartbeat.

Tiny Teen

Size: 5″   Date: 1967
                      Internet: $20
Condition: Ex
Tiny fashion doll.

Tiny Teen

Size: 5″   Date: 1967
                      Internet: $65
Condition: MOC

Troll With 2 Heads

                      Date: 1970s
                      Internet: $30–$50
Condition: Ex

Wee Three

Size: 19″   Date: 1960s
                      Internet: $100
Condition: MIB
Mother, daughter, and baby son.

Vinyl

This section includes some notable vinyl dolls which did not easily fit into other sections of this book. Of course, listings of un-

Vinyl ballerina. *Walker, jointed at neck, shoulders, waist, hips, knees, and ankles. 19", c. late 1950s. Mark: 20HH. $50, eBay.*

Eegee fashion doll, Miss Revlon Clone. *All vinyl, original outfit. 17", c. 1950s. Mark: EEGEE (head). $40, dealer.*

Furga "Modestino" boy. *All vinyl. 15", c. 1966. Mark: FURGA (head) FURGA / ITALY (back).*

marked vinyl dolls and vinyl dolls from lesser-known makers could fill this entire book. Vinyl became the material of choice for play dolls from the late 1950s through today, thanks to a combination of unbreakability, a soft feel unlike dolls made of hard plastic, composition, or bisque, low cost, and relatively good durability.

Market Report: The market varies completely depending on the doll. Dolls with some name recognition such as Poor Pitiful Pearl do very well, as do the Furga fashion dolls of the 1960s; however, the nearly unlimited amounts of vinyl play dolls by lesser manufacturers do not.

Online/Offline Report: Again, this will completely vary by doll, but there is a huge availability of generic vinyl play dolls on eBay, often for only a few dollars.

Prices and Characteristics: Prices listed are for dolls in excellent condition, unless otherwise noted. Prices are similar for all markets, except as noted, and dolls tend to have 5-piece bodies.

VINYL DOLLS, VINTAGE

Allied Doll & Toy Co., Bonnie's Fashion Show

All Markets: $30
In box. Doll and 4 extra outfits on paper mannequins.

Amanda Jane Ltd., Amanda Jane

Size: 8"   Date: 1950s–1960s
Price: $110
Made in England.

Beehler Arts, Howdy Doody

Size: 8"   Date: 1952
Price: $100

Brookglad Corporation, Poor Pitiful Pearl

Size: 18"   Date: 1958
Price: $230–$250
Mint.

Brookglad Corporation, Poor Pitiful Pearl

Size: 13"   Date: 1958
Price: $225–$250
For MIB; jointed doll (some have unjointed soft vinyl bodies).

Creative Playthings, Little Brother or Little Sister

Size: 20"   Date: 1967–1970s
Price: $30
First anatomically correct dolls in the United States.

Dennis The Menace

Size: 13.5"   Date: 1958
Price: $125
Cloth body.

Eegee, Bride, Li'l Susan

Size: 20"   Date: 1950s
All Markets: $130
MIB.

Furga girl. All vinyl, mama crier. 14", c. 1968. Mark: FURGA. Courtesy Helen Simms Collection.

Furga girl. All vinyl, mama crier. 13.5", c. 1960s. MADE / ITALY / FURGA (back).

Jane West by Marx. All soft vinyl. 11", c. 1966. Comes with many vinyl Western accessories. Mark: LOUIS MARX & CO / © /... (in circle, back). $20 with accessories, eBay.

Eegee, Little Debutante
Size: 15" or 17"　　　Date: 1957
All Markets: $110
MIB. Jointed only at the neck.
Mark: Eegee or E

Eegee, Little Miss Debutante
Size: 10.5　　　Date: 1958
Price: $25
VG.
Mark: 20 HH/Eegee

Eugene Co., Your Dream Bride
Size: 18"　　　Date: late 1950s
Price: $90
MIB; jointed, sleep eyes, in original cello and box.

Evergreen, Miss Teenage USA
Size: 11.5"　　　Date: 1960s
Price: $95
MIB. Barbie clone.
Mark: Evergreen/BRITISH COLONY/OF HONG KONG/1011½.

Fisher-Price, Baby Ann
　　　Date: 1973
Price: $100
NRFB.

Fisher-Price, My Friend Mandy
Size: 14"　　　Date: 1977–1982
Price: $40–$100
MIB; for Mandy or a friend of Mandy (Becky, Jenny, Joey). Higher prices for earliest Mandys.

Furga, Alta Moda Fashion Doll, Sylvie, Sheila, Suzanna, Simona
Size: 17"　　　Date: 1960s
Price: $60–$100
For redressed or played-with dolls. These dolls have exaggerated eyelashes.

Furga, Alta Moda Fashion Doll, Simona
Size: 17"　　　Date: 1960s
Price: $115
MIB. Furga dolls were made in Italy.

Furga, Alta Moda Fashion Doll, Sylvie
Size: 17"　　　Date: 1960s
Price: $260
Mint with 5 original outfits. Fashion dolls in this series include Sheila, Sylvie, and Susanna.

Furga, Alta Moda Fashion Outfits
　　　Date: 1960s
Price: $75–$125
MIB.

Furga, Sylvie, #8501
Size: 17"　　　Date: 1960s
Price: $290
MIB.
Mark: Furga Italy (head).

Furga, Sophia
Size: 17"　　　Date: 1960s
Price: $100–$130
MIB; elaborate dress, velvet, feathers, fur.
Mark: Furga Italy (head, body).

Gay Bob Trading Company, Gay Bob
Size: 11.5"　　　Date: 1977
All Markets: $105–$155

Unmarked vinyl girl. 15", c. 1970s. $10, eBay.

Berenguer Mini doll. 9", c. 1980s. Vinyl head and lower limbs, cloth body. Mark: Berenguer ©. $5–$10, eBay.

My Friend Mandy by Fisher Price. In separately available jogging suit. Cloth body with vinyl head and limbs. 15.5", c. 1979. Mark: 28/20141 / © 1970 / FISHER PRICE. $30–$40 loose, mint, eBay; $7–$15 good condition, eBay.

MIB. Comes in "closet," anatomically correct, with single earring.

Girl Scout, Walker
Size: 8"   Date: 1950s–1960s
Price: $100
Full outfit including beret, shoes, socks.

Judith Corporation, Judith, The Mommy-to-Be Doll, Black
                    Date: 1991
All Markets: $20
MIB. Baby inside the "mommy's" tummy.

Jus Toys, Flatsys
Size: 2.5"   Date: 1969
Price: $5
MOC only; no value at all otherwise. Generally 2.5".

Libby Majorette Doll Corp., *I Dream of Jeannie* **Doll**
Size: 20"   Date: 1966
Price: $310
In original harem outfit.

Libby Majorette Doll Corp., *I Dream of Jeannie*
Size: 19"   Date: 1966
Price: $745
NRFB. For doll in very-hard-to-find green outfit.

Marx Toy Co., Jane West
Size: 11"   Date: 1966
Price: $20–$30
Rubbery vinyl.

Marx, Sindy
Size: 11"   Date: 1978
Price: $20–$50
MIB

Marx, Gayle, African American
Size: 11"   Date: 1978
Price: $75–$100
Sindy's friend.

MY-TOY, H.R. Pufnstuf, Witchiepoo
Size: 21"   Date: 1970
Price: $295
Mint. From the TV series.
Mark: 1970 MY TOY INC.

Nancy Nurse
Size: 24"   Date: 1957
Price: $70–$100
In full nurse's uniform with hat.
Mark: A E 554/13

Nancy Nurse
Size: 24"   Date: 1957
Price: $300
MIB; with many nursing accessories.

Nun, White Habit
Size: 19"   Date: 1960s
Price: $85

Playmates, Corky, Cricket's Brother
                    Date: 1987
Price: $145
MIB. With extra accessories.

Little Bill "My Talking Friend" by Fisher Price. Says phrases like "we're space explorers," "let's play dinosaurs." 13", c. 2001. Courtesy Ellen Johnson.

Playmates, Cricket, Talking
Size: 25"   Date: 1985
Price: $215
NRFB. Eyes and mouth move when she talks; cassette player in body.

Reliable, Bonnie Braids, Baby
Size: 13"
Price: $70
Soft vinyl.

Reliable, Queen's Guard
Size: 16"   Date: 1950s
All Markets: $50

Royal Doll Company, Miss Revlon Clone
Size: 19"   Date: 1950s
Price: $300
MIB. Company bought blank dolls and dressed them.

Sayco, Baby Beautiful
Size: 19"
Price: $50
Replaced clothing.

Sayco, Glamour Girl
Size: 21"   Date: 1950s
Price: $50
Soft vinyl. Made with Flexi-tex vinyl so you can pose her to sit, kneel, or cross legs.

Sayco, Miss America
Size: 11"   Date: 1950s
Price: $50
Original outfit, mint.

Sayco, Playpal
Size: 36"   Date: 1960s
Price: $65–$105
Patti Playpal "clone."
Mark: SAYCO CO.

Sayco, Toddler
Size: 28"   Date: 1950s–1960s
Price: $60
Large toddler, rooted hair, sleep eyes.
Mark: MADE IN THE USA/750.

Unmarked, Bride, Fashion Doll
Size: 20"   Date: 1958–1960
Price: $125
Sleep eyes.

Whitman, Peepul Pals
Date: late 1960s
Price: $25–$40
Various characters—Brenda Bride, Cinderella, Goldilocks, in hard plastic play box.

Vogue

The history of The Vogue Doll Company is so intertwined with the fate of its most famous doll, Ginny, that the basic history of the company can be found in the Ginny section. However, Vogue is known for many other dolls besides Ginny. The company began with various bisque dolls imported from Germany, including the Just Me from Armand Marseille, which were dressed by company founder Jennie H. Graves and sold with her Vogue label in the 1920s and 1930s.

Other dolls in celluloid, rubber, composition, and hard plastic followed.

The first notable doll developed and manufactured by Vogue was the 8-inch composition Toddles, sculpted by Bernard Lipfert. Toddles was the predecessor to Ginny. Toddles was in production from 1937 to 1948. Toddles was also sold with curved legs in a baby version called Sunshine Babies. The hard-plastic Crib Crowd followed in 1948 (through 1952), concurrent with the "transitional" dolls which were produced just before Ginny's debut. These dolls were hard plastic with painted eyes, and were made from 1948 through 1950. Finally, Ginny was officially born in 1952. She had sleep eyes and was strung, with painted lashes.

Ginny was so popular that she basically took over the entire Vogue line for the early 1950s. In 1955, Ginnette, her baby sister, was born. Ginnette was 8 inches tall and made for many years until approximately 1970. In 1957, Ginny got a big sister, the fashion doll Jill. Jill was produced through the late 1950s and early 1960s—as a hard-plastic doll until 1961, and as a vinyl doll thereafter. Jill had a friend, Jan, introduced in 1959 and always with a vinyl head, and also a vinyl boyfriend, Jeff, introduced in 1958.

Other dolls followed in the early 1960s, including Brikette, Li'l Imp, Baby Dear, Littlest Angel, Wee Imp, Ginny Baby, Miss Ginny, and many others.

In 1995, a reformed company, The Vogue Doll Company, Inc., acquired the Ginny name, molds, and all other intellectual property from Dakin, Inc. Owners of the new company included Linda Smith and Wendy Lawton. This company set out to recapture the spirit and quality of the 1950s dolls. The company and the new Ginny dolls (plus, newly reissued and reproduced Wee Imps, Just Mes, and Crib Crowd dolls) have been highly successful.

Market Report: Vogue dolls made through the early 1960s are eternally popular, although dolls such as Jill, Li'l Imp, Littlest Angel, and the others don't bring prices anywhere near the prices of the earliest Ginny

dolls. Even the earlier Toddles doesn't have the following (or prices, except for the most mint examples!) of Ginny. Overall, prices for many of the Vogue dolls have declined some in the last few years.

Online/Offline Report: There is a huge selection of Vogue dolls online, and the competition for the best early examples is strong. Because of this, expect to spend roughly the same amount at all venues for the best Vogue dolls. Bargains can be found on eBay for fixer-up and played-with Vogue dolls.

Prices and Characteristics: All dolls are in excellent condition, except as noted, with 5-piece bodies. For Ginny prices, see the Ginny section.

VOGUE DOLLS, COMPOSITION

Sunshine Baby
Size: 8″   Date: 1930–mid-1940s.
                            Internet: $110
Same head, body as Toddles but curved baby legs, molded painted hair.
Mark: VOGUE (head) DOLL CO (back)

Toddles, Various
Size: 8″   Date: 1937–1948
                            Internet: $100–$150
VG; dolls with soiled outfits, crazing. Toddles have painted eyes.
Mark: VOGUE (back of neck) or VOGUE or DOLL CO (back)

Toddles, Various
Size: 8″   Date: 1937–1948
Price: $150–$160   Internet: $250
Excellent; dolls with minor crazing and outfit flaws.

Toddles, Various
Size: 8″   Date: 1937–1948
Price: $380–$415   Internet: $350
MIB or pristine mint, with marked shoes, either character or "Toddles."
Mark: Example: Robin Hood or Toddles (shoes)

Toddles, Alice in Wonderland
Size: 8″   Date: early 1940s
Price: $425
MIB.
Mark: VOGUE

Toddles, Bo Peep
Size: 8″   Date: early 1940s
Price: $540
Mint.
Mark: VOGUE

Toodles Hansel and Gretel. *All composition, 5-piece bodies. 8", c. early 1940s. Mark: Doll Co (back) and red shoes have name of doll (Hansel, Gretel) on left sole. $350 each, dealer.*

Toodles bride. *All composition, 5-piece body. 7.5", c. 1940s. Mark: VOGUE (back and head) and tagged gown: Vogue Dolls, Inc., (script) / Medford Mass. $275, dealer.*

Littlest Angel. *Vinyl, 7-piece body (jointed at knees). 10.5", c. 1961–1963. R & B / 24 (head) R & B DOLLS (back). $100, eBay.*

Toodles, Draftee

Date: early 1940s
Price: $600
MIB.
Mark: VOGUE (head) DOLL CO (back)

Toodles, Wee Willie Winkie

Size: 8"   Date: early 1940s
Price: $300
Excellent; minor crazing.
Mark: VOUGE (head) DOLL CO (back)

WAV-ette, Lieutenant

Size: 13"   Date: 1943–1944
    Internet: $400
Purse has metal USA insignia; officially sanctioned by U.S. armed services.

VOGUE DOLLS, HARD PLASTIC

Jills have bent-knee walker hard-plastic bodies and sleep eyes.

Jill, Various

Size: 10"   Date: 1957–1960
    Internet: $75–$100
Average, played with, mussy hair.

Jill, Various

Size: 10"   Date: 1957–1960
Price: $150   Internet: $140–$200
Excellent; more for mint. For friends of Jill and vinyl Jill (1962–1963) see below.

Jill, Various

Size: 10"   Date: 1957–1960
Price: $300+   Internet: $200–$300
MIB; higher prices for more desirable outfits.

Jill, Bride, #3192

Size: 10"   Date: 1958
    Internet: $150
Mark: JILL/VOGUE DOLLS INC./MADE IN USA/© 1957

Jill, Common Outfits

Size: 10"   Date: 1957–1960
    Internet: $100–$150
MIB.

Jill, Rarer Outfits

Size: 10"   Date: 1958
    Internet: $225
Mark: VOGUE DOLLS/INC.

Wee Imp

Size: 8"   Date: 1960
    Internet: $70–$100
Average, bright red hair and freckles; for played-with dolls.
Mark: VOGUE (head) GINNY/VOGUE DOLLS/INC/Pat. No. 2687594/MADE IN U.S.A.

Wee Imp

Size: 8"   Date: 1960
Price: $175   Internet: $150–$200
MIB or pristine mint.

Littlest Angel

Size: 10.5"   Date: 1950s
    Internet: $230
Excellent; bendable knees. For vinyl dolls, see below.
Mark: R & B (back)

Littlest Angel. *Vinyl, 7-piece body (jointed at knees). 10.5", c. 1961–1963. R & B / 24 (head) R & B DOLLS (back). $100, eBay.*

Li'l Imp. *Vinyl head, 7-piece hard plastic body (jointed at knees), original sailor outfit. 11", c. 1959. Unmarked doll, original shoes correctly marked: FAIRYLAND TOY PRCD. / NO. 60 / MADE IN U.S.A. $125, dealer.*

VOGUE DOLLS, VINYL

Note that Baby Dear (1st edition) has been reissued by Ashton Drake in 2004.

Baby Dear, 1st Edition
Size: 18″   Date: 1960–1964
                             Internet: $265
Mint. Vinyl head and limbs, cloth body, topknotted hair. Designed by popular children's author, Eloise Wilkin.
Mark: VOGUE DOLLS/INC.

Baby Dear, 1st Edition
Size: 18″   Date: 1960–1964
                             Internet: $50–$75
Average, played with, wear, replaced clothing.

Baby Dear, 1st Edition
Size: 18″   Date: 1960–1964
                             Internet: $100–$150
Excellent, original clothing.

Baby Dear, 2nd Edition
Size: 18″   Date: 1964
                             Internet: $300
MIB, no crier. Much less for later dolls.
Mark: VOGUE DOLL/© 1964

Baby Dear, 2nd Edition
Size: 18″   Date: 1965–1970s
                             Internet: $30–$50
VG; redesigned head, rooted hair all around, crier.
Mark: VOGUE DOLL/© 1964

Baby Dear One
Size: 23″   Date: 1962–1963
                             Internet: $125
Mark: ©/1961/E. Wilkin/Vogue Dolls/Inc.

Brikette
Size: 22″   Date: 1959–1961
                             Internet: $100–$150
Rarer size with flirty eyes.
Mark: VOGUE INC./19©60

Jill in tagged outfit. Hard plastic, swivel neck, jointed at shoulders, hips, and knees. 10", c. 1957. Mark: VOGUE (head) JILL / VOGUE DOLLS, INC. / MADE IN U.S.A. / © 1957. $100, eBay.

Brikette

Size: 16"	Date: 1960–1961
	Internet: $50–$75

Excellent.

Brikette, New

Size: 16"	Date: 1979–1980
	Internet: $25–$50

MIB.
Mark: Lesney Prod. Corp.

Ginnette

Size: 8"	Date: 1957–1968
	Internet: $40–$60

VG, played with, no box.

Ginnette

Size: 8"	Date: 1957–1958
	Internet: $125–$225

MIB. Less for later 1960s dolls in later boxes and outfits.

Ginnette

Size: 8"	Date: 1957–1958
	Internet: $175

Mint; original maize yellow outfit.

Ginnette, Black

Size: 8.5"	Date: 1957–1958
	Internet: $540

Sleep eyes.
Mark: Vogue Dolls/Malden Mass

Ginnette, Painted Eye

Size: 8"	Date: 1955–1956
	Internet: $135–$200

Excellent.
Mark: Vogue (waist)

Jan, Various

Size: 10"	Date: 1958
	Internet: $50–$75

Excellent.

Jan, Various

Size: 10"	Date: 1958
	Internet: $125

MIB, in desirable outfit.

Jan, Outfit, #7507

Size: 10"	Date: 1959
	Internet: $80

Jeff, Various

Size: 10"	Date: 1957
	Internet: $50–$60

MIB.

Jeff, Cowboy

Size: 10"	Date: 1959
	Internet: $100

In cowboy outfit.

Jeff, Dinner Jacket Outfit

Size: 10"	Date: 1957
	Internet: $50

With bow tie; holds round box with flowers.
Mark: Vogue (back of neck) Vogue Dolls (back)

Jeff, Groom, #6165

Size: 10"	Date: 1958
	Internet: $50

Jeff in tuxedo.
Mark: Vogue (head) Vogue Dolls (back)

Jill, Vinyl

Size: 10"	Date: 1962–1963
	Internet: $140

MIB, box worn; much less for loose.
Mark: VOGUE

Jimmy, Painted Eyes
Size: 8″   Date: 1950s
                    Internet: $150
Tagged Jimmy outfit, Ginnette shoes.

Li'l Imp
Size: 11″   Date: 1959–1960
                    Internet: $50
Sometimes unmarked; shoes properly marked
"Fairyland Doll Company" on bottom.
Mark: R and B/44 (head); R and B Doll Co. (back)

Littlest Angel, Travel Set
                    Date: 1960s
                    Internet: $155
MIB.

Littlest Angel
Size: 10.5″   Date: 1960s
                    Internet: $50–$100
Excellent; gently played with, minor flaws. Lit-
tlest Angel was also produced in a hard plastic
version.
Mark: R and B (head) R & B Doll Co. (back)

Littlest Angel
Size: 10.5″   Date: 1960s
                    Internet: $200
Mint.
Mark: R & B (back)

Too Dear Baby
Size: 17″   Date: 1963–1964
                    Internet: $70–$100
Rooted hair, toddler type. All-vinyl body that
can stand.
Mark: ©/1963/E. WILKIN/VOGUE DOLLS

Wellings, Norah

Norah Wellings was born in 1893 in Shrop-
shire, England. She was the main designer of
dolls for Chad Valley from 1919 to 1926. In
1926, she left Chad Valley to form her own
doll company with her brother Leonard
Wellings. The factory, named The Victoria
Toy Works, produced dolls of velvet, plush,
and felt, including molded felt doll heads.

Among the many dolls made by Norah
Wellings were dolls for the tourist trade.
Her company supplied souvenir dolls for
ship lines such as Cunard and rail lines such
as Pacific Railway Co. These were dolls of
people employed by the various transporta-
tion or travel lines, cast as bellmen or sailors,
and the dolls would have the name of the
ship or company embroidered on the hat.
Other dolls made by the company included
international dolls, dolls representing the
various armed services, pajama bags, Black
dolls, fantasy figures, and many others.
Norah also made children and baby dolls.

During World War II Norah's work was so
well-known and loved that she was named
Doll Maker to the British Commonwealth.

The Wellings company made dolls until the
death of Leo Wellings in 1959. Leo had handled the majority of the business dealings for
the company, and Norah didn't want to continue after his death. She closed the factory
in 1960, retired, and lived in England until
her death in 1975.

Market Report: Norah Wellings dolls are
another example of fantastic vintage dolls
that can be collected on a reasonable budget.
Even the best, mint examples rarely trade for
more than several hundred dollars (with a
few exceptions for very rare dolls such as
very large children or children with glass
eyes). Many lovely Norah Wellings dolls can
be found in the $100 to $300 range, and even
for less if the doll has been played with or is
worn. The market for these dolls is mostly
static, with prices declining slightly in the
last few years from the eBay effect.

Online/Offline Report: At any one time,
there are only a few dozen Norah Wellings
dolls on eBay. This may change as more and
more auctions are started from eBay UK.
For the best selection of Norah Wellings
dolls, dealers and shows are the surest bet.
Prices are similar at all venues, with some
lower pricing on eBay, but beware of wear
and moth holes since they don't always show
up in photos (or descriptions) on eBay, which
accounts for some of the lower pricing.

Prices and Characteristics: The dolls are
from the 1930s to 1960s, and it can be difficult
to individually date the dolls, but a great
number seem to be from the 1930s and 1940s.
All dolls are made of cloth with stitched
joints and various styles of molded faces with
painted features (rarely, with glass eyes).

Royal Canadian Mounty by Norah Wellings. All cloth. 9". Mark: Tag on bottom of foot: MADE IN ENGALND / BY / NORAH WELLINGS. Courtesy Marsha L. Cumpton.

Norah Wellings old man and woman. All cloth, pressed-felt faces, muslin torsos, felt-jointed limbs. 24", c. 1930. Mark: Made in England Norah Wellings (cloth tags). $1,600 pair, at auction. Courtesy Theriault's.

Three Norah Wellings dolls, for I. Magnin. All pressed-felt faces, one with glass eyes, muslin bodies. 14" to 17". Marks: Made in Great Britain for I. Magnin Co., California, Seattle, 1937. Courtesy Theriault's.

Marks: The dolls are generally marked with a tag on the foot or wrist: Made in England / By / Norah Wellings.

NORAH WELLINGS DOLLS

Baby
Size: 11"
Price: $90
Excellent.

Black Doll, Mammy
Size: 9–13"
Price: $150　　　　Internet: $170
Excellent. Exaggerated features.

Islander, Black
Size: 14–17"
Price: $150–$300　　　Internet: $75
Excellent, except Internet price for worn doll. In grass skirt.

Islander, Black
Size: 36"
　　　　　　　　　Internet: $460
Excellent.

Boy
Size: 14–15"
Price: $300　　　　Internet: $175
Excellent; brown felt shorts, sweater, and knit cap, swivel head; Internet price with flaws.

Child
Size: 9"
Price: $45　　　　Internet: $30 to $60
For average dolls with soiling, flaws.

Child, English Schoolgirl
Size: 8–16"
Price: $300–$600
Mint.

Dutch Boy
Size: 15"
Price: $730
Mint.

English Royal Guard
Size: 18"
Price: $200
All cloth, glass inset eyes, muslin body with jointed shoulders and hips.

Sailor
Size: 7–8"　　　　Internet: $40–$60
Average, often sold as cruise ship souvenirs, often with name of ship on hat.

Policeman
Size: 8"
Price: $105

Scarlett O'Hara
Size: 14"　　　　Internet: $225
With note, for Christmas 1939.

Older Man and Woman, Pair
Size: 24"
Price: $1,600
Mint, 1930s.

6 MODERN DOLLS

American Girl

I don't think there are any mothers of little girls born since the late 1980s who aren't aware of the American Girl dolls. The Pleasant Company, founded by Pleasant T. Rowland, a former educator, created the American Girl dolls in 1986. In 1998, Mattel, Inc. (creator and producer of the Barbie doll), acquired the Pleasant Company. The dolls have been a huge hit with mothers and little girls alike thanks to their educational aspects (there is an entire series of historical adventure books sold about the dolls) and their detailed clothing and accessories. Over 5 million American Girl dolls have been sold, and over 60 million American Girl doll books.

Market Report: The American Girl dolls by Pleasant Company/Mattel were a late-20th-century breakthrough in play dolls. By the 1990s, most dolls were either play dolls of very low quality, or "special occasion" dolls like Madame Alexanders. American Girl dolls filled a void in the market, by providing dolls that were meant for play, but of a very high quality. I think these dolls will endure well into the 21st century.

A secondary market for these dolls is just developing as more dolls and accessory items are retired by Pleasant Company/Mattel. Look for earlier Pleasant Company items to increase in value as time goes on, and as little girls who had these dolls as children grow up and become nostalgic for them.

Online/Offline Report: Most dealers are not yet handling these dolls or the rare retired accessories, so the greatest selection is found on the Internet.

Prices and Characteristics: Dolls are vinyl with jointed limbs and cloth torsos.

AMERICAN GIRL DOLLS

Coconut, Dog
Size: 28″   Internet: $300
Condition: Ex
Large plush version of smaller dog

Felicity, Town Fair Outfit With Windmill
                        Internet: $200
Condition: Ex
1997.

Felicity's Plantation Play, Accessories
                        Internet: $215
Condition: Ex
1997.

Josefina's Piano in Box
All Markets: $660–$810
Condition: MIB
Retired. Tiny keys play, original sheet music.

Kristen, With Trousseau
Size: 18″
All Markets: $920
Condition: Ex
With many accessories.

Lindsey
Size: 18″   Internet: $220
Condition: MIB
Retired.

Lindsey, Limited Edition
                        Internet: $260
Condition: MIB

Mini Room, Lil's Diner
                        Internet: $445
Retired. With all accessories.

American Girl, Samantha. Vinyl head and limbs, cloth torso. 18″, c. 2004. Mark: PLEASANT COMPANY.

Minis, Diner Counter Set
Internet: $260
Condition: Ex

Minis, Purple Room, Complete
Internet: $265
Condition: Ex

Molly, With Many Accessories
Size: 18″
All Markets: $800
Condition: Ex

Samantha, With Many Accessories
Size: 18″
All Markets: $830
Condition: Ex

Artist Dolls

As a group, these dolls have had an amazing influence. Most artist dolls have been made in the last 40 years or so, with their influence and acceptance picking up considerable steam in the last 15 years. Artist dolls have made dolls more than just a plaything for children—they have made dolls acceptable as true art.

There has been a great debate about exactly what constitutes an artist doll. For purposes of this book, I am defining an artist doll as a doll made in a very limited edition—either one-of-a-kind, or a small, handmade edition of dolls made directly by the artist (not man-

ufactured or handmade overseas). An artist doll is made for an adult collector and not for a child for play. Finally, an artist doll is mostly made to be a piece of artwork, for viewing and aesthetic pleasure, and not as a plaything for an adult.

Market Report: Collectors of one-of-a-kind and artist dolls will often collect only that type of doll. Also, most artist dolls sell for many hundreds or thousands of dollars. The market is very specialized, and sales on the secondary market can be difficult, although certain pieces by desirable artists with limited output will always bring high prices.

Online/Offline Report: Because this market is so specialized, you will rarely find true artist dolls on eBay—first, because these dolls generally change hands privately, and second, because the market is so specialized, these dolls could potentially sell far below their actual market potential on eBay. Collectors seeking artist dolls generally deal directly with either a specialized dealer or the artist.

Prices and Characteristics: Due to space considerations, the prices for artist dolls for this edition will focus on some of the classic artist dolls from the earlier periods. Look for prices for later artists in later editions of this book. All prices are for dolls in excellent con-

Portrait of Queen Elizabeth II by Martha Thompson. *Porcelain shoulder head, muslin body, porcelain lower limbs. 22", c. 1953. Mark: Martha Thompson Elizabeth II 1953. Courtesy Theriault's.*

Elise portrait doll by Kathy Redmond. *Hand-pressed porcelain heads, sculpted hair, muslin bodies, porcelain limbs. 15". Mark: Elise and Redmond logo. Courtesy Theriault's.*

dition or better. All prices are dealer, show, and auction prices except as indicated.

ARTIST DOLLS

Gibbs, Ruth, Child
Size: 7"   Date: 1940s
All Markets: $50
Material: bisque
Porcelain shoulder head, arms, legs, cloth body.
Mark: RG

Lillian Smart, Various Members of Blackfoot Tribe
Size: 10–12"   Date: early 1900s
All Markets: $350
Material: apple
From the early 1900s, Seattle, Washington.
Mark: Ta-Nuk Studio, Lillian M. Smart, Seattle Wa, Pat Applied For (label on foot)

Redmond, Kathy, Heads of Elderly Ladies
Price: $275
Material: bisque
Decorated hats.

Sorenson, Lewis, Gibson Girl
Size: 24"
Price: $175
Material: wax
Charter member of NIADA.

Sorenson, Lewis, St. Nicholas
Size: 24"
Price: $1,500
Material: wax

Sorenson, Lewis, Toymaker
Price: $450
Material: wax

Thompson, Martha, Little Women, Meg, Amy, Jo, or Beth
                          Date: 1950s
Price: $300–$470
Artist dolls, c. 1950s and 1960s. Most dolls marked MDT on back of head or shoulder plate. Charter member of NIADA, 1903–1964.
Mark: 53 AMY M.D.T. (shoulder plate), MDT (cloth body) or similar.

Thompson, Martha, Betsy, Young Girl
Size: 14"   Date: 1950s–1960s
Price: $345
Material: bisque

Thompson, Martha, Child
Size: 13"   Date: 1959
Price: $425
Material: bisque
Mark: M. Thompson 1959

Thompson, Martha, Child, Girl
Size: 6"   Date: 1950s–1960s
Price: $200
Material: pottery
Cloth body, lower arms and legs of pottery; molded and painted socks and shoes.
Mark: MT (bottom of shoe)

Thompson, Martha, George or Martha Washington
                          Date: 1950s–1960s
Price: $400
Material: bisque

Thompson, Martha, Jenny Lind
Size: 20″   Date: 1950s–1960s
Price: $400
Material: bisque

Thompson, Martha, Lace Maker
                             Date: 1950s
Price: $1,400

Thompson, Martha, Lady, Upswept Hair
Size: 12″   Date: 1950s–1960s
Price: $345
Material: bisque

Thompson, Martha, Lady, Black Curls
Size: 18″   Date: 1950s–1960s
Price: $175
Material: bisque

Thompson, Martha, Princess Carlotta
Size: 18–20″   Date: 1950s–1960s
Price: $500–$630
Material: bisque
Princess Carlotta, Princess Margaret Rose,
Queen Elizabeth II. Queen Victoria: $375.

Thompson, Martha, Victorian Bonnet Girl
Size: 15″   Date: 1953
Price: $725
Material: bisque
Sculpted bonnet.
Mark: M.D. Thompson '53

Thompson, Martha, Young Girl, Molded Hair
Size: 9″   Date: 1950s
Price: $1,800
Material: bisque
Girl seated in chair, 1820s style, holding doll.
Mark: M.D.T. 56

Tuttle, Eunice, *Alice in Wonderland* Set
                             Date: 1970s
Price: $900
Material: all-bisque
NIADA member from 1968–1979. Alice, Twee-
dle Dee and Tweedle Dum, Mad Hatter, Queen
of Hearts, Walrus and Carpenter.

Tuttle, Eunice, Angel Baby
                             Date: 1970s
Price: $175
Material: all-bisque
All Tuttle dolls are fully jointed all-bisque, with
background, base, and accessories in Plexiglas
cube.

Tuttle, Eunice, Black Boy or Girl
                             Date: 1970s
Price: $230
Material: all-bisque
Chet or Candy.

Tuttle, Eunice, Girl
                             Date: 1970s
Price: $170–$200
Material: all-bisque

Tuttle, Eunice, Girl With Prop
                             Date: 1970s
Price: $345–$430
Material: all-bisque
Girl with cat, hoop, doll, or doll and stroller.

Tuttle, Eunice, Infant Marguerita
                             Date: 1970s
Price: $290
Material: all-bisque

Tuttle, Eunice, Mary Ellen Cassat
                             Date: 1970s
Price: $175
Material: all-bisque

Tuttle, Eunice, Miss Hatch With Baby
                             Date: 1970s
Price: $345
Material: all-bisque

Tuttle, Eunice, Prince Edward
                             Date: 1970s
Price: $320
Material: all-bisque

Tuttle, Eunice, Renoir Girl
                             Date: 1970s
Price: $345
Material: all-bisque

Ashton Drake

Ashton Drake has produced hundreds of porcelain and vinyl collector dolls since its inception in 1985. Ashton Drake sells many of its dolls through direct-response mail and magazines, and it is responsible for introducing many people to the concept of the modern collector doll. The majority of its collector dolls have been in porcelain by such well-known artists as Yolanda Bello, but it is also known for its vinyl collector dolls, especially Gene Marshall, a fashion doll which singlehandedly created the renaissance in large-size collector fashion dolls in 1995. Recently, Ashton Drake's vinyl Emily baby doll series has been all the rage with reborn artists.

Also relatively new for Ashton Drake has been its high-quality reproductions of baby

Gene, Coca-Cola Girl Holiday Shopper. *Vinyl, swivel neck, jointed at shoulders, elbows, waist, hips, knees. Earlier Genes are only jointed at the shoulders and hips. Limited edition of 3,000. 15.5", c. 2002. $100–$125, dealer.*

boomer dolls. In recent years, the company has done excellent reproductions of Thumbelina, Patti Playpal, Mrs. Beasley, and others. New collectors should take care when purchasing dolls that have been reproduced, and should carefully check clothing and doll markings, etc., when purchasing dolls in the reproduced categories.

- **Gene:** When Gene came onto the scene in the mid-1990s, the only serious fashion doll was Barbie. Gene started a renaissance in fashion dolls for collectors. Thanks to Gene, doll manufacturers saw that there was a market for top-quality fashion dolls with changeable clothing aimed at the adult collector market. Gene was the initial catalyst for the revival of the Madame Alexander Cissy, and for the development of later fashion dolls such as Sommers &

Field, Tyler Wentworth, Brenda Starr, Alex by Madame Alexander, and countless others. Gene even inspired some glamour in the Barbie Collectibles line with such dolls as the Silkstone Barbie dolls and the Gene-inspired Fabulous 40s Barbie. Although the Gene line has shrunk somewhat since its 1990s heyday, I think that Gene's influence on fashion dolls will endure for a long time.

Market Report: Thanks to the market conditions created by Internet auctions, secondary market prices are down for many Ashton Drake categories, including Gene dolls and the Yolanda Bello babies. Look for prices on Gene dolls to steadily rise as the company produces fewer products in this line and as more and more of the original dolls are "cannibalized" by both repaint

Gene, Winter's Romance, dressed in separately available Gene outfit "Press Conference." Vinyl, jointed at neck, shoulders, elbows, waist, hips, knees. Doll $100–$125, dealer; outfit $20 NRFB, eBay.

Priceless Gene and Top of the Morning Trent. Gene is a 1999 FAO Schwarz exclusive. Trent issued in a limited edition of 3,750 in 2002. Vinyl. 15.5" and 17". Gene $75, eBay; Trent $80, eBay.

Scarecrow by Mary Tretter. Porcelain, cloth body, jointed, with part of yellow brick road that fits into rest of dolls in series. 16", c. 1994–1995. $150 MIB, dealer.

artists and collectors selling dressed dolls in separate pieces (nude dolls and the clothing). Look for prices on the porcelain dolls such as the Yolanda Bello babies to stabilize.

Online/Offline Report: Prices are down at shows, through Internet auctions, and through dealers. One example is the Gene Premiere doll, which sold for many years for $500 plus. This doll can now be found for $200 on eBay, and for between $300 and $400 from dealers. Some very limited editions of Gene are increasing in value.

Prices and Characteristics: All dolls are vinyl except where noted. Genes are made of hard vinyl and are 15.5 inches tall. Later dolls have more jointing (waists, elbows) than earlier dolls. All prices are for dolls MIB, and all prices are Internet prices except where noted. "LE" means "limited edition."

ASHTON DRAKE

Grace, Little House on the Prairie
Date: early 1990s
Internet: $165
Bisque doll.

Jason, Yolanda Bello's Babies
Size: 14"   Date: 1986
Internet: $205
Bisque doll, first in Picture Perfect Babies series.

Little Rascals, Set of 5 Dolls
Size: 8"   Internet: $150

Mrs. Beasley
Size: 20"   Date: 2002
Internet: $65–$95
Reproduction of 1960s Talking Mrs. Beasley. Cheryl Ladd is the voice.

Patti Playpal
Size: 35"   Date: 2003
Price: retail

Snow White and the Seven Dwarfs
Internet: $200

Speedee, First McDonald's Advertising Figure
Size: 16"   Date: 1998
Internet: $55
Bisque, commemorating McDonald's 40th anniversary.

Thumbelina, Classic, Reproduction
Size: 20"   Date: 2001
Internet: $125
Reproduction of 1960s Thumbelina.

GENE DOLLS

Gene, A Toast at Twelve
Date: 2000
Internet: $190
LE 700, Gene Convention Doll 2000.

Gene, Bon Bon
Date: 2003
Internet: $300–$350
Fan Appreciation Doll 2003.

Gene, Broadway Medley
Date: 1998
Internet: $180
Gene Convention Doll.

Gene, Champagne Flight
Date: 2002
Internet: $200–$255
LE 200; Las Vegas FAO Schwarz exclusive.

Gene, Derby Dreams
Date: 2003
Internet: $170
LE 425, Gene Convention Doll 2003.

Gene, Diamond Evening
Date: 2001
Internet: $265

Gene, Holiday Magic, Outfit
Date: 1996
Internet: $125–$200
LE 2,000.

Gene, King's Daughter
Date: 1997
Internet: $100
LE 5,000.

Gene, Meet Me in Paris
Date: 2000
Internet: $285–$375
LE 500 for Paris Fashion Doll Festival 2000.

Gene, Moments to Remember
Date: 2000
Internet: $180
FAO Schwarz exclusive; pink outfit. Blue outfit issued for Modern Doll Collectors Convention.

Gene, My Favorite Witch
Date: 1997
Internet: $525
2nd Gene Convention Doll, artist proof.

Gene, Night at Versailles
Date: 1997
Internet: $150–$285
LE 5,000 for FAO Schwarz.

Gene, Premiere
Date: 1995
Internet: $175–$225
First Gene doll produced.

Gene, Regular Dressed Doll Releases
Date: 1995–now
Internet: $50
Incognito, White Hyacinth, Monaco, Red Venus, Iced Coffee, Midnight Gamble, Tea at the Plaza, Twilight Rumba, others.

Gene, Spotted in the Park
Date: 2000
Internet: $100–$140
Limited edition for FAO Schwarz.

Gene, Unforgettable
Date: 1999
Internet: $100–$200
Dolly Cipolla design.

Madra, Black Widow
Date: 2000
Internet: $150–$225
LE 2,500.

Madra, First Encounter
Date: 2000
Internet: $100

Trent, Lover in Disguise
Date: 2001
Internet: $100
Costume Ball series.

Violet Waters, Torch Song
Date: 2002
Internet: $155

Barbie, Modern

For pre-1980 Barbie, please see the Vintage Dolls chapter.

NOTE: *All photos of Barbie dolls in this section, unless noted, are 11.5" tall and all-vinyl, jointed at the neck, shoulders, hips, and waist. Dolls have various Mattel markings, but since it is the custom of most collectors to keep these dolls NRFB, marks will not be included in this section.*

Modern collectible Barbie dolls are in a class all their own. Whereas other collectible dolls are produced in limited editions from a few hundred to a few thousand dolls, so many people collect Barbie dolls that a limited-edition doll can be produced in an edition of 45,000 and that edition can still sell out in a very short period of time. Part of the modern collector doll craze can be traced back to the Happy Holiday Series of Barbie dolls which began in 1988.

Barbie Making Her Grand Entrance as Scarlett O'Hara (Scarlett #3) and Ken as Rhett Butler. *Ken 12″, all vinyl. These dolls were sold via infomercials in the mid-1990s by Mattel. c. 1994. Barbie $35–$50 NRFB, eBay; Ken $20–$30 NRFB, eBay.*

Barbie doll as Eliza Doolittle, *Ascot Scene, from the Hollywood Legends collection. c. 1995. $40–$55 NRFB, eBay.*

Pink Box and Modern Collectible Barbie: There are two types of modern Barbie dolls that collectors seek. Some collectors seek MIB or NRFB play Barbie dolls, also called "pink box" dolls that have been sold for children's play. Other Barbie collectors seek Collectible Barbie dolls (Barbie Collector dolls since 2004), which are Barbie dolls produced specifically for adult collectors since the late 1980s; these are the dolls that most collectors think of when they think of modern Barbie dolls.

Pink Box: Pink-box Barbie dolls come in endless varieties—career Barbies, Barbies in ball gowns, Barbies ready for swimming in pools, Barbies pushing baby carriages, and Barbies going on dates. There are also fantasy and movie-inspired pink-box Barbie dolls—everything from *The Wizard of Oz* characters, to Rapunzel to the *Nutcracker* ballet characters. Pink-box dolls are generally sold by stores such as Toys "R" Us, Target, and Wal-Mart.

Collectible Barbie: As for the Collectible Barbie dolls, they are generally done in series. Again, we see movie themes, such as *My Fair Lady* and *Gone With the Wind*. There are Barbie dolls (and related dolls by Mattel) that commemorate great and notable movie and TV stars and TV shows—Lucille Ball, Audrey Hepburn, The Munsters. Finally, there are collectible Barbies by great fashion designers such as Bob Mackie, Nolan Miller, and Escada. Collectible Barbie dolls are generally sold by specialty doll shops.

Harley Davidson Ken. *Second Harley Ken. Vinyl. 12", c. 1999. $40–$60 NRFB, eBay.*

Harley Davidson Barbie. *Second Harley Barbie. c. 1998. $70–$90, eBay.*

Millennium Princess Teresa. *c. 1999. $25, eBay.*

Collectible modern Barbie dolls often harken back to their vintage Barbie roots. In addition to reproductions of early Barbie dolls in vintage Barbie outfits, the Silkstone dolls with their retro painting, high-fashion outfits, and porcelain-like vinyl have been very popular with collectors.

Market Report: As with many popular modern dolls, the eBay marketplace has brought prices down considerably in the last five years, for both Internet sales and dealer sales. Bob Mackie Barbies which would regularly sell in the $500 to $1000 range now sell for considerably below that, although both the Neptune Fantasy and Empress Bride Bob Mackie dolls still regularly bring over $500 each. Many other modern Barbie dolls have seen their prices hover at or below retail. However, there are still strengths in the market—1988 Happy Holiday Barbies are again selling for over $500, and the earliest Silkstone dolls are eagerly sought after. In 2004, Barbie Collectibles, the doll division that produces collectible Barbie dolls, announced that its collectible dolls will be produced in smaller editions than in years past. The effect that this will have on the secondary market of these dolls is unknown as this book goes to press.

Online/Offline Report and a Note on Barbie Doll Boxes: Prices are weakest on Internet auction sites; dolls generally cost more from dealers but with good reason—the condition of the box for pink-box and modern collectible Barbie MIB and NRFB dolls is paramount to the value, and collectors appreciate getting a perfect box from a dealer whom they know, or a local shop where shipping damage to the doll's box is not a concern. Although boxes are a part of the value of many modern dolls, a Barbie doll's box can be 50% or more of the value of a doll, due to the intricate graphics on the boxes and the way the dolls are presented in the box. Look for mint boxes with little wear and no major flaws for best value.

Prices and Characteristics: All dolls are vinyl, generally with 5-piece bodies that swivel at the waist and knees that bend. Barbies have painted features and are 11.5 inches tall, with rooted vinyl hair. "CE" means "Collector's Edition" and "LE" means "Limited Edition." All prices are for NRFB dolls except as noted.

BOB MACKIE BARBIE DOLLS

Bob Mackie #1, Gold

Date: 1990
Internet: $275–$400
First in original Bob Mackie Series.

The Flamingo Barbie. *Second in the Birds of Beauty Series. c. 1999. $50 NRFB, eBay.*

Cool Collecting Barbie. *Comes with mini Magic 8-Ball, View Master, and Barbie Queen of Prom Game. c. 2002. $25–$35 NRFB, eBay.*

Holiday Memories Barbie. *Hallmark, c. 1995. $20 NRFB, eBay.*

Bob Mackie #2, Starlight Splendor
Date: 1991
Internet: $255–$300
Black doll.

Bob Mackie #3, Platinum
Date: 1991
Internet: $175–$225

Bob Mackie #4, Neptune Fantasy
Date: 1992
Internet: $350–$375

Bob Mackie #4, Neptune Fantasy
Date: 1992
Internet: $255
For mint doll, no box.

Bob Mackie #5, Empress Bride
Date: 1992
Internet: $380–$425

Bob Mackie #5, Empress Bride
Date: 1992
Internet: $250
For mint doll, no box.

Bob Mackie #6, Masquerade Ball
Date: 1993
Internet: $140–$200

Bob Mackie #7, Queen of Hearts
Date: 1994
Internet: $75–$100

Bob Mackie #8, Goddess of the Sun
Date: 1995
Internet: $75–$100

Bob Mackie #9, Moon Goddess
Date: 1996
Internet: $75–$125

Bob Mackie #10, Madame Du Barbie
Date: 1997
Internet: $380–$480
Final doll in series.

Bob Mackie, Jewel Essence #1, Amethyst Aura
Date: 1997
Internet: $50–$75
Jewel Essence Collection.

Bob Mackie, Jewel Essence #2, Diamond Dazzle
Date: 1997
Internet: $60–$80
Jewel Essence Collection.

Bob Mackie, Jewel Essence #3, Emerald Embers
Date: 1997
Internet: $50–$60
Jewel Essence Collection.

Bob Mackie, Jewel Essence #4, Ruby Radiance
Date: 1997
Internet: $50–$70
Jewel Essence Collection.

Bob Mackie, Jewel Essence #5, Sapphire Splendor
Date: 1997
Internet: $50–$70
Jewel Essence Collection.

Christian Dior Barbie II. Commemorating the 50th anniversary of Christian Dior. 1997. $50–$70, eBay.

Holiday Sensation Barbie. Hallmark. Third in Holiday Homecoming Series. c. 1998. $30 NRFB, eBay.

Yankees Barbie (part of series of Baseball Team Barbies).

Bob Mackie, Fantasy Goddess #1, of Asia
Date: 1998
Internet: $60–$75
International Beauty Collection.

Bob Mackie, Fantasy Goddess #2, of Africa
Date: 1999
Internet: $240–$280
International Beauty Collection.

Bob Mackie, Fantasy Goddess #3, of the Americas
Date: 2000
Internet: $90–$120
International Beauty Collection.

Bob Mackie, Fantasy Goddess #4, of the Arctic
Date: 2001
Internet: $75–$90
International Beauty Collection.

Bob Mackie, Lady Liberty
Date: 2000
Internet: $120–$140
Limited edition of 15,000; FAO Schwarz exclusive.

Bob Mackie, Papillion
Date: 1999
Internet: $90–$115
FAO Schwarz exclusive; for Barbie's 40th Anniversary.

Bob Mackie, Tango
Date: 1999
Internet: $300–$350
Porcelain. Dance Collection Series.

Bob Mackie, Charleston Barbie
Date: 2001
Internet: $125–$140
Porcelain. Dance Collection Series.

Bob Mackie, Radiant Redhead
Date: 2002
Internet: $90–$110
First doll in The Red Carpet Collection.

Bob Mackie, Brunette Brilliance
Date: 2003
Internet: $150–$200
Second doll in The Red Carpet Collection.

Bob Mackie, Sterling Silver Rose
Date: 2002
Internet: $30–$50
Avon Exclusive, Collector Edition.

Bob Mackie, Sterling Silver Rose, Black
Date: 2002
Internet: $30–$50
Avon Exclusive, Collector Edition.

BYRON LARS BARBIE DOLLS

Byron Lars #1, In the Limelight
Date: 1997
Internet: $110–$130
First doll in the Runway Series.

Byron Lars #2, Cinnabar Sensation, Black
Date: 1998
Internet: $70–$100
Second doll in the Runway Series.

Barbie Fashion Avenue Outfit, with outfit for Kelly. *c. 1996. $10 NRFB, eBay.*

Barbie Fashion Avenue outfit. *Toys "R" Us Exclusive Coat Collection. One of the popular Fashion Avenue outfits from the play line in the late 1990s. c. 1999. $10 NRFB, eBay.*

Walt Disney World 25th Anniversary Barbie. *c. 1996. $15, eBay.*

Byron Lars #2, Cinnabar Sensation, Caucasian
> Date: 1998
> Internet: $30–$50

Byron Lars #3, Plum Royale
> Date: 1999
> Internet: $200–$225

Third doll in the Runway Series.

Byron Lars #4, Indigo Obsession
> Date: 2000
> Internet: $175–$200

Fourth and final doll in the Runway Series.

Byron Lars, Treasures of Africa #1, Moja
> Date: 2001
> Internet: $200–$230

Byron Lars, Treasures of Africa #2, Mbili
> Date: 2002
> Internet: $150–$200

Byron Lars, Treasures of Africa #3, Tatu
> Date: 2003
> Internet: $120–$150

Byron Lars, Treasures of Africa #4, Nne
> Date: 2004
> Internet: Retail

GREAT ERAS BARBIE DOLLS

Great Eras, 1920s Flapper
> Date: 1993
> Internet: $40–$50

CE.

Great Eras, Gibson Girl
> Date: 1993
> Internet: $40–$50

CE.

Great Eras, Egyptian Queen
> Date: 1994
> Internet: $50–$60

CE.

Great Eras, Elizabethan Queen
> Date: 1995
> Internet: $25–$45

CE.

Great Eras, Medieval Lady
> Date: 1995
> Internet: $20–$30

CE.

Great Eras, Grecian Goddess
> Date: 1996
> Internet: $30–$40

CE.

Great Eras, Victorian Lady
> Date: 1996
> Internet: $25–$30

CE.

Great Eras, Chinese Empress
> Date: 1997
> Internet: $25–$35

CE.

Great Eras, French Lady
> Date: 1997
> Internet: $25–$35

CE.

Fashion Editor Barbie, a Silk-stone Fashion Model Barbie doll. *Limited edition for FAO Schwarz. $100–$130 NRFB, eBay.*

Hollywood Nails Barbie. *Play line doll. c. 2000. $10 NRFB, eBay.*

Special Collection Barbie Bakeware accessory set. *One of several fun accessory sets issued in the play line in the late 1990s. c. 1997. $6 NRFB, eBay.*

HAPPY HOLIDAYS BARBIE DOLLS

Happy Holidays #1

Date: 1988
Internet: $300–$400
Red dress.

Happy Holidays #2

Date: 1989
Internet: $100–$150
White dress.

Happy Holidays #3

Date: 1990
Internet: $35–$45
Pink dress.

Happy Holidays #4

Date: 1991
Internet: $25–$50
Green dress.

Happy Holidays #5

Date: 1992
Internet: $25–$50
Silver and white dress.

Happy Holidays #6

Date: 1993
Internet: $25–$45
Red and gold dress.

Happy Holidays #7

Date: 1994
Internet: $25–$50
Gold dress.

Happy Holidays #7, Brunette

Date: 1994
Internet: $350
LE 340 for 1994 Barbie Festival in Orlando.

Happy Holidays #8

Date: 1995
Internet: $15–$30
Green dress.

Happy Holidays #9

Date: 1996
Internet: $20–$30
Burgundy and gold dress.

Happy Holidays #10

Date: 1997
Internet: $25–$30
Red and white "ribbons" dress.

Happy Holidays #11

Date: 1998
Internet: $15–$20
Black and pink dress.

HARLEY DAVIDSON BARBIE DOLLS

Harley Davidson #1, Blonde

Date: 1996
Internet: $250–$350
LE.

Harley Davidson #2, Redhead

Date: 1998
Internet: $50–$70
CE.

In the Pink, a Silkstone Fashion Model Barbie doll. *c. 2001. $100–$120, eBay.*

Lingerie (or Fashion Model) Barbie #6. *This line of dolls has the Silkstone hard-vinyl doll bodies. This was the last doll in the series to be issued in lingerie because of a big hullabaloo caused in the media by conservative Christian family groups that didn't understand that this was a doll issued for adult collectors. c 2003. $35–$45, eBay.*

Harley Davidson #3, Black Hair
Date: 1999
Internet: $30–$50
CE.

Harley Davidson #4, Brunette
Date: 2000
Internet: $30–$50
CE.

Harley Davidson #5, Redhead
Date: 2001
Internet: $60–$80
CE, red flames on black outfit. Caucasian and Black available.

Harley Davidson #5, Black
Date: 2001
Internet: $80–$100
CE.

Ken, Harley Davidson #1
Date: 1999
Internet: $40–$65
CE, dark hair pulled back in ponytail, goatee.

Ken, Harley Davidson #2
Date: 2000
Internet: $30–$50
CE, light blue denim and black leather outfit, beard.

Fatboy Motorcycle
Date: 1999
Internet: $40–$60
Produced for display with the Harley Davidson dolls.

PORCELAIN (BISQUE) BARBIE DOLLS

Fabergé Porcelain #1, Imperial Elegance
Date: 1997
Internet: $300–$400
LE 15,000.

Fabergé Porcelain #2, Imperial Splendor
Date: 2000
Internet: $175–$200

Tommy as Munchkin Mayor. *Several Kelly and Kelly-size dolls have been issued as Munchkins in the Wizard of Oz series. Vinyl. 4.5", c. 1999. $5–$9 NRFB, eBay.*

Jenny (Kelly's friend) as a Pumpkin. *Halloween Party Target Exclusive. 4.5", c. 2000. $5 NRFB, eBay.*

Kelly and Tommy as Raggedy Ann and Andy. *First in Storybook Favorites Series. Vinyl. 4.5", c. 1999. $20–$30 NRFB, eBay.*

Fabergé Porcelain #3, Imperial Grace
Date: 2001
Internet: $180–$200

Holiday Porcelain #1, Holiday Jewel Barbie
Date: 1995
Internet: $50

Holiday Porcelain #2, Holiday Caroler Barbie
Date: 1996
Internet: $35–$45

Holiday Porcelain #3, Holiday Ball Barbie
Date: 1997
Internet: $30–$50

Holiday Porcelain #4, Holiday Gift Barbie
Date: 1998
Internet: $50–$75

Porcelain Treasures #1, Blue Rhapsody Barbie
Date: 1986
Internet: $100
The very first collectible Barbie issued for adult collectors.

Porcelain Treasures #2, Enchanted Evening
Date: 1987
Internet: $30–$40

Porcelain Treasures #3, Benefit Performance Barbie
Date: 1987
Internet: $100–$140

Porcelain Treasures, Wedding Party
Date: 1989
Internet: $65–$85

Porcelain Treasures, Solo in the Spotlight
Date: 1990
Internet: $40–$50

Porcelain Treasures, Sophisticated Lady
Date: 1990
Internet: $50–$70

Porcelain Treasures, 30th Anniversary Ken
Date: 1991
Internet: $50–$70

Porcelain Treasures, Gay Parisienne
Date: 1991
Internet: $50–$70

Porcelain Treasures, Plantation Belle, Redhead
Date: 1992
Internet: $60–$90

Porcelain Treasures, Silken Flame
Date: 1993
Internet: $45–$65
Porcelain Treasures Collection.

Porcelain Treasures, 30th Anniversary Midge
Date: 1993
Internet: $45–$60

Porcelain Treasures, 30th Anniversary Skipper
Date: 1994
Internet: $45–$65

Porcelain, WOZ #1, Dorothy and Toto
Date: 2000
Internet: $60–$90

Porcelain, WOZ #2, Wicked Witch
Date: 2000
Internet: $125–$135

Porcelain, WOZ #3, Scarecrow
Date: 2001
Internet: $80–$100

Porcelain, WOZ #4, Tin Man
Date: 2001
Internet: $80–$100

Porcelain, WOZ #5, Winged Monkey
Date: 2001
Internet: $100–$120

Porcelain, WOZ #6, Cowardly Lion
Date: 2002
Internet: $75–$150

Presidential Porcelain #1, Crystal Rhapsody, Blonde
Date: 1992
Internet: $75–$95
First doll sold directly to consumers by Mattel.

Presidential Porcelain #2, Royal Splendor Barbie
Date: 1993
Internet: $45–$60

Presidential Porcelain #3, Evening Pearl
Date: 1996
Internet: $70–$90

SILKSTONE BARBIE DOLLS

Silkstone Barbie dolls are made of Silkstone, a very hard vinyl that mimics porcelain. They have swivel waists, but non-bending knees. Painting of the dolls is nostalgic, with some resemblance to the 1960s Barbie dolls. All are limited editions.

Accessory Pak
Date: 2002
Internet: $25–$30

Capucine
Date: 2003
Internet: $120–$135

Chataine
Date: 2002
Internet: $400–$550
LE 600, brunette Capucine produced for FAO Schwarz.

City Smart
Date: 2003
Internet: $450–$600

LE 600, promotional doll for Japan, only 200 sold in the USA.

Continental Holiday Gift Set
Date: 2002
Internet: $50–$60

Delphine
Date: 2000
Internet: $90–$120

Dusk to Dawn Gift Set
Date: 2001
Internet: $120–$145

Fashion Designer
Date: 2002
Internet: $45–$55

Fashion Editor
Date: 2001
Internet: $70–$100

In the Pink
Date: 2001
Internet: $100–$125

Joyeux, Redhead
Internet: $420
Limited edition for FAO Schwarz.

Ken, Fashion Insider Gift Set
Date: 2003
Internet: $65–$75

Limited Edition Display Case
Date: 2001
Internet: $600
Rarer case says "Limited Edition" on top, sides. Only 100 produced.

Lingerie #1, Blonde
Date: 2000
Internet: $200–$250
First Silkstone doll ever issued.

Lingerie #2, Brunette
Date: 2000
Internet: $220–$275

Lingerie #3, Raven Hair
Date: 2001
Internet: $110–$130
Black lingerie.

Lingerie #4, Blonde, Short Hair
Date: 2002
Internet: $50–$60
Marilyn Monroe-type hairstyle.

Lingerie #5, Black Doll
Date: 2002
Internet: $40–$50

Lingerie #6, Red Hair
Date: 2003
Internet: $40

Lisette
Date: 2001
Internet: $80–$100

Maria Therese
Date: 2002
Internet: $50–$65

Model Life Gift Set
Date: 2003
Internet: $60–$75

Outfit, Black Enchantment
Date: 2002
Internet: $30

Outfit, Blush Becomes Her
Date: 2001
Internet: $35–$45

Outfit, Boulevard
Date: 2001
Internet: $45–$65

Outfit, Country Bound
Date: 2002
Internet: $25

Outfit, Garden Party
Date: 2000
Internet: $100–$125

Outfit, Lunch at the Club
Date: 2000
Internet: $70–$85

Outfit, Midnight Mischief
Date: 2003
Internet: $35–$40

Provençale
Date: 2002
Internet: $80–$100

Ravishing in Rouge
Date: 2001
Internet: $70–$80

Sunday's Best, Black Doll
Date: 2003
Internet: $35–$45

Wardrobe Case
Date: 2003
Internet: $70–$80
With room for doll, hanging outfits, and accessories.

VINTAGE REPRODUCTION BARBIE DOLLS

35th Anniversary, Blonde
Date: 1994
Internet: $35–$40

35th Anniversary, Brunette
Date: 1994
Internet: $25–$40

35th Anniversary Gift Set
Date: 1994
Internet: $60–$70

Busy Gal
Date: 1995
Internet: $30

Commuter Set
Date: 1999
Internet: $40–$50
Collector's Request Series.

Enchanted Evening, Blonde
Date: 1996
Internet: $20–$25

Enchanted Evening, Brunette
Date: 1996
Internet: $20–$25

Fashion Luncheon
Date: 1997
Internet: $30–$40

Francie, 30th Anniversary
Date: 1996
Internet: $30–$35

Gay Parisienne
Date: 2003
Internet: retail
Collector's Request Series.

Gold and Glamour
Date: 2002
Internet: $30
Collector's Request Series.

Poodle Parade
Date: 1996
Internet: $25

Silken Flame, Blonde
> Date: 1998
> Internet: $20–$30

Silken Flame, Brunette
> Date: 1998
> Internet: $20–$30

Solo in the Spotlight, Blonde
> Date: 1995
> Internet: $20

Solo in the Spotlight, Brunette
> Date: 1995
> Internet: $20

Sophisticated Lady
> Date: 2000
> Internet: $30–$60

Collector's Request Series.

Suburban Shopper
> Date: 2001
> Internet: $40–$50

Collector's Request Series.

Twist 'N Turn, Brunette
> Date: 1999
> Internet: $30

First doll in the Collector's Request Series.

Twist 'N Turn, Redhead
> Date: 1999
> Internet: $30

Wedding Day, Blonde
> Date: 1997
> Internet: $20–$25

Wedding Day, Redhead
> Date: 1997
> Internet: $20–$30

Wild Bunch Francie
> Date: 1997
> Internet: $50–$60

Midge, 35th Anniversary Gift Set
> Date: 1997
> Internet: $30–$50

Reproduction of 1963 Midge, in bathing suit; Senior Prom dress.

MODERN BARBIE DOLLS, VARIOUS

Angel Face
> Date: 1982
> Internet: $30

Pink box play line doll.

Barbie, Lovin' You
> Date: 1983
> Internet: $30

Pink box play line doll.

Bill Blass
> Date: 1996
> Internet: $40–$60

Crystal Jubilee
> Date: 1999
> Internet: $100–$140

For Barbie's 40th Anniversary.

Crystal Jubilee, Pink
> Date: 1999
> Internet: $150–$190

An FAO Schwarz special; original retail $300.

Dream Date
> Date: 1982
> Internet: $40

Pink box play line doll.

Gold Jubilee
> Date: 1994
> Internet: $395

For Barbie's 36th Anniversary. LE 5,000 USA and 2,000 international.

Golden Anniversary
> Date: 1995
> Internet: $45–$75

For 30th Anniversary of Mattel. LE 25,000, TRU Store special.

King Arthur and Guinevere, Barbie & Ken Gift Set
> Date: 1999
> Internet: $100–$120

Life Ball Barbie Styled by Vivienne Westwood
> Internet: $550

Made to benefit a European charity. LE 1,000.

Midnight Tuxedo, Blonde
> Date: 2001
> Internet: $50–$60

2001 Barbie Collector Club doll.

Midnight Tuxedo, African American
> Date: 2001
> Internet: $450

Munsters, Barbie & Ken Gift Set
> Date: 2001
> Internet: $175–$350

My Size Barbie

Date: 1992
Internet: $100

36″, pink gown.

My Size Bride

Internet: $155

36″, MIB.

My Size, Rapunzel

Internet: $120

36″, MIB.

Pink Splendor

Date: 1996
Internet: $250–$350

Princess of the French Court

Date: 2000
Internet: $100

Dolls of the World series.

Romantic Rose Bride

Date: 1995
Internet: $85

Second in the Wedding Flower Series.

Romeo and Juliet

Date: 1998
Internet: $65–$85

See's Candies #1

Date: 1999
Internet: $18–$25

See's Candies #2, I Left My Heart in San Francisco

Date: 2000
Internet: $18–$25

See's Candies #2, I Left My Heart in San Francisco, Black

Date: 2000
Internet: $25–$35

Star Lily Bride

Date: 1994
Internet: $85

First in the Wedding Flower Series.

Stardust (Erté Inspired)

Date: 1994
Internet: $195

Superstar Barbie

Date: 1977
Internet: $100

Pink box play line doll.

Talking Spanish Teacher Barbie

Date: 2000
Internet: $20

Speaks 60 words and phrases in Spanish and English.

Tango, Barbie & Ken Gift Set

Date: 2002
Internet: $65–$75

FAO Schwarz exclusive gift set.

Treasure Hunt, Redhead

Date: 2003 *
Internet: $100–$125

Many fewer Treasure Hunt redheads were made.

UNICEF

Date: 1989
Internet: $20

Pink box play line.

Victorian Barbie & Cedric Bear, Blonde

Date: 2000
Internet: $100

Club edition, LE 5,000; individually numbered boxes.

Water Lily

Date: 1997
Internet: $45

First in the Artists Series, Claude Monet.

Wedgwood #1

Date: 2000
Internet: $85–$140

Blue dress.

Wedgwood #2

Date: 2001
Internet: $40–$50

Pink dress.

Berenguer and Other Reborn Babies

Reborn dolls are simply customized baby dolls. These dolls are "reborn" by artists redoing them so they have a more hand-done, customized baby look—the dolls are repainted, the hair rewigged or reapplied completely, the doll is recostumed, the inside of the doll's body can be retinted for skin shading, bodies are reweighted, and more. The most popular baby dolls that are reborn are the dolls by Berenguer, but other dolls, including Ashton Drake's Welcome Home Baby Emily, are also popular.

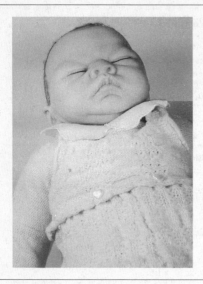

***Welcome Home Baby Emily by
Ashton Drake.*** *Represents newborn baby. Very soft Magic Skin-
like skin head, lower arms and
legs, weighted stuffed body,
scented with baby powder. Designed by Linda Webb. 19.5″, c.
2003. Mark: LW; ©A.D.G.*

Market Report: This area is so new, it's hard
to predict a trend. Are reborn babies a passing craze, or are the reborn dolls done by talented artists dolls that will maintain or
increase their value over time? No one
knows for sure, except that the highest
priced reborn dolls currently bring between
$500 and $800.

Online/Offline Report: Reborn dolls are almost solely an Internet item. Most reborn
dolls are sold via Internet auctions and websites, or through special orders with known
artists.

Prices and Characteristics: Dolls are vinyl
or soft vinyl, generally 21 to 22 inches tall,
and the dolls listed were "reborn" in 2004.

REBORN DOLLS

Reborn Dolls, Established Artists
                    Internet: $400–$900
The majority of completely reborn Berenguer
and other similar dolls (Welcome Home Baby
Emily from Ashton Drake, certain Lee Middleton and Zapf baby dolls, others) by well-known
artists trade in this range on eBay.

Abigail, a Berengeur Reborn by Artist Kathy McLeod
                    Internet: $800
All factory coloring removed, color washed inside and out in a custom blend of paints,
blushed, mohair individually rooted, nose

opened, new body, outfit of vintage fabric and
lace.

Brady, an Emily Reborn, Artist, Heaven Sent Nursery
                    Internet: $785
Color washed, nostrils opened, fingernails done,
blushed, etc. Made from Welcome Home Baby
Emily by Linda Webb.

Welcome Home Baby Emily
Price: retail
Popular realistic baby doll, also often used by Re-
born artists. Doll retails for approximately $169.

Celebrity Dolls

As discussed in the section on vintage
celebrity dolls, celebrity dolls have been with
us in some form since the 1800s. However,
with the modern cult of celebrity that has developed along with the baby boomer generation, celebrity dolls have huge popularity
today. Some companies have made their
mark with a variety of celebrity dolls, including the Danbury Mint and the Franklin
Mint, generally by selling their dolls to the
mass market via inserts in magazines as diverse as *Good Housekeeping* and the *National
Enquirer.* Other companies such as GADCO
(Great American Doll Company) and Mego
flourished by making low-cost vinyl
celebrity dolls for general toy departments.
Of course, celebrity dolls have been pro-

Scarlett O'Hara by World Dolls. *Vinyl. 18.5", c. 1985. Mark: WORLD DOLLS, INC /©SELZNICK KREN 1967 and clothing tag. $25, eBay. Courtesy Ellen Johnson.*

Rhett by World Dolls, Inc. *Vinyl. 22", c. 1985. Same Mark as World Dolls Scarlett, left. $35 MIB, eBay. Courtesy Ellen Johnson.*

Marilyn Monroe #5023 in Don't Bother to Knock. *Vinyl, can share clothing with Barbie-size dolls. 11.5", c. 1983. Authorized by 20th Century Fox. Mark: Tristar © 1982 (box). $60 NRFB, eBay.*

duced in nearly every price range and in nearly every modern doll genre—from $10 dolls by Mego of 1970s television stars to wax dolls priced at several thousand dollars by Crees & Coe.

Market Report: Because celebrity dolls are collected by Hollywood memorabilia collectors as avidly as by doll collectors, the dual market generally means that a buyer can be found for even the most basic vinyl celebrity doll. This effect can be seen in the collectible dolls produced by the Danbury Mint and the Franklin Mint (among others)—most of their dolls produced in the past 20 years or so have languished on the secondary market, with a much stronger secondary market and secondary market prices for their celebrity dolls.

Online/Offline Report: So many celebrity dolls have been produced in the modern collectible doll era that they are easily found (in great quantities) on eBay and otherwise on the Internet. Dolls without their original boxes can often be found at considerable discounts.

Prices and Characteristics: Prices are for dolls MIB or NRFB. For earlier composition and hard-plastic celebrity dolls produced prior to 1980, see the Celebrity Dolls section in the Vintage Dolls chapter.

CELEBRITY DOLLS, MODERN

Alexis From *Dynasty*
Size: 19"   Date: 1985
                 Internet: $70
Manufacturer: World Dolls
Material: vinyl

Audrey Hepburn, *Breakfast at Tiffany's*
Size: 11.5"   Date: 1999
                 Internet: $60–$80
Manufacturer: Mattel
Material: vinyl
As Holly Golightly in *Breakfast at Tiffany's*. First doll to be authorized by the Hepburn estate. Black gown.

Beatles, Set
Size: 17"   Date: 1997
                 Internet: $180
Manufacturer: Applause
Material: cloth
Set of 4.

Beatles, Set
Size: 11"   Date: 1991
                 Internet: $270–$290
Manufacturer: Hamilton Collection
Material: plastic
Set of 4. With their instruments.

Betty Boop
Size: 10.5"   Date: 1982
                 Internet: $100
Manufacturer: King Features
Material: bisque
No box.

Michael Jackson from American Music Awards. *Vinyl. 11.5", c. 1985. Includes "Glittering Magic Glove." Mark: © 1984 M.J. Productions (box). $15 NRFB, eBay.*

George Burns. *Vinyl, edition of 18,000, poseable vinyl, includes mike. 8", c. late 1990s. Mark: © 1997 Hollywood Chamber of Commerce by Exclusive Toy Products Inc., LA CA (box). $10, eBay.*

Shirley Temple Doll by Danbury Mint. *A reproduction of a 1930s composition Shirley Temple, done in bisque. 15". For more modern Shirley Temple dolls, see the section on Danbury Mint dolls.*

Bob Hope
Size: 19″   Internet: $195
Manufacturer: Franklin Mint
Material: bisque
Microphone, golf club, and coin with recording of Hope.

Elton John, Sings "Crocodile Rock"
Size: 12″   Internet: $135–$175
Manufacturer: Yaboom
Material: vinyl
Press doll's tummy and he sings (via cassette) a 20-second intro and a full-length version of Elton John singing "Crocodile Rock."

Elvis Presley, Gold and Platinum
Size: 19″   Date: 1984
     Internet: $100
Manufacturer: World Doll Co.
Material: bisque

Elvis Presley
Size: 18″   Date: 1987
     Internet: $120–$150
Manufacturer: Danbury Mint
Material: bisque
In white jumpsuit, 300 rhinestones.

Frank Sinatra, Sings "Because It's Witchcraft"
Size: 17″   Internet: $200
Manufacturer: Franklin Mint
Material: bisque

I Love Lucy, as Sally Sweet
Internet: $180
Manufacturer: Hamilton Collection
Material: bisque
From "The Diet" episode.

I Love Lucy, America's Favorite Redhead
Date: 1990
Internet: $150
Manufacturer: Hamilton Collection
Material: bisque
First in series; only Lucy doll Lucy saw before her death. Polka-dot dress.

I Love Lucy, Carmen Miranda
Size: 18″   Date: 1996
     Internet: $120
Manufacturer: Hamilton Collection
Material: bisque

I Love Lucy, Grape Stomp
Date: 1990s
Internet: $120
Manufacturer: Hamilton Collection
Material: bisque

Jacqueline Kennedy
Date: 1996
Internet: $200
Manufacturer: GADCO
Material: vinyl
Bruno Rossellini designed many GADCO dolls. Jackie O as a child.

Jacqueline Kennedy, Memories of Camelot
Size: 16″   Internet: $450
Manufacturer: Franklin Mint
Material: bisque
Limited edition of 950. Wearing pink ball gown by Oleg Cassini that Jacqueline wore to the unveiling of the *Mona Lisa*.

Dorothy from The Wizard of Oz.
Vinyl, multijointed. 8", c. 1974.
Mark: © MEGO CORP / MCM-
LXXII / PAT PENDING / MADE
IN / HONG KONG. $20 MIB
with Toto, $10 loose, eBay.

John F. Kennedy. *Vinyl head and*
arms, cloth and cardboard body.
12.5". Mark: TKR in trapezoid
shape. $10, eBay. Geneva Wallen
collection.

John Wayne "American Guardian
of the West" by Effanbee. *Third in*
the Legends series. Vinyl, 17.5", c.
1982. Mark: EFFANBEE / © 1982
/ WAYNE EMT. $50 MIB, eBay.
Courtesy Ellen Johnson.

John Kennedy, Wedding Suit
Size: 16.5"   Internet: $200
Manufacturer: Franklin Mint
Material: bisque

Elizabeth Taylor
Internet: $125
Manufacturer: Franklin Mint
Material: bisque
Green dress.

Marilyn Monroe
Size: 17"   Date: 1983
Internet: $225
Manufacturer: World Dolls
Material: bisque

Marilyn Monroe, The Ultimate
Size: 24"   Date: 1996
Internet: $250–$400
Manufacturer: Franklin Mint
Material: bisque
Vicky from 1954's *There's No Business Like Show Business*.

Marilyn Monroe, Love Marilyn
Internet: $100
Manufacturer: Franklin Mint
Material: bisque

Marlene Dietrich, as Young Girl
Size: 34"   Internet: $200
Manufacturer: GADCO
Material: bisque
Bruno Rossellini.

Mary Kate/Ashley Olsen as Michelle in *Full House*
Size: 15"   Date: 1990
Internet: $80
Manufacturer: Meritus Industries.
Material: vinyl
Talking doll.

Mary Kay Ash, 25th Anniversary
Size: 17"   Date: 1988
Internet: $200
Material: bisque

Mary Kay Ash, 30th Anniversary
Size: 18"   Date: 1993
Internet: $235
Material: bisque
Black evening dress trimmed with gold lace, rhinestones, pearls. Doll has added wig.

Princess Diana, Portrait of a Bridal Princess
Internet: $150
Manufacturer: Franklin Mint
Material: bisque

Princess Diana, Blue and Gray Suit, Outfit
Internet: $150
Manufacturer: Franklin Mint

Princess Diana, Bride Doll
Internet: $300
Manufacturer: Franklin Mint
Material: bisque

Ronald Reagan by Horsman.
Vinyl, 17.5", c. 1987. Mark: HORS-
MAN (in parallelogram in circle) /
19©87. $30 MIB, dealer. Courtesy
Ellen Johnson.

Princess Diana, Fashion Doll, Trunk and Outfits

Internet: $250–$400
Manufacturer: Franklin Mint
Material: vinyl
Prices higher with more outfits; range from 6 to 11 outfits.

Princess Diana, Holiday Tribute

Size: 34"   Date: 1997
Internet: $225
Manufacturer: GADCO
Material: vinyl
Limited edition of 750.

Princess Diana, Navy Blue Ball Gown

Size: 18"   Internet: $265
Manufacturer: Franklin Mint
Material: bisque

Princess Diana, President's Premier Edition

Size: 16"   Internet: $270
Manufacturer: GADCO
Material: hard vinyl
Limited edition of 1,500. Includes trunk of clothes/gowns.

Princess Diana, Princess of Charm

Size: 18"   Date: 2001
Internet: $250
Manufacturer: Franklin Mint
Material: bisque

Princess Diana, Princess of Radiance

Size: 16"   Date: 2001
Internet: $440
Manufacturer: Franklin Mint

Material: bisque
Limited edition of 750.

Princess Diana, Princess of Sophistication

Size: 18"   Date: 2001
Internet: $320–$340
Manufacturer: Franklin Mint
Material: bisque

Princess Diana, Wedding

Size: 11.5"   Date: 1982
Internet: $100
Manufacturer: Goldberger Doll Co.
Material: vinyl

Princess Diana, White Chiffon Gown Outfit

Internet: $80
Manufacturer: Franklin Mint

Ramones

Internet: $120
Manufacturer: Unknown
Material: vinyl
Set of 4.

Ricky Ricardo, "Babaloo"

Size: 19"   Date: 1997
Internet: $115
Manufacturer: Hamilton Collection
Material: bisque

Rose, *Titanic,* Jumping Scene

Size: 11.5"   Date: 1998
Internet: $25
Manufacturer: Galoob Toys
Material: vinyl

Vivian the Volunteer, from Nana's Family by Annie Wahl. *Resin, stationary. 9" seated, c. 2002. Retail, $99.*

Smooth the Elf from the Twelve Elves of Christmas by Jodi and Richard Creager. *Resin. c. 2002. Retail, $99.*

Snoop Doggie Dog, "Snoopafly"
Size: 12"   Internet: $35
Manufacturer: Vital Toys
Material: vinyl

Twiggy Fashion Doll, Trunk, Clothes
                    Internet: $200
Manufacturer: Franklin Mint
Material: vinyl

Collection of the Masters

Collection of the Masters was started by celebrity and doll collector Richard Simmons in 2000. Richard collected one-of-a-kind artist dolls, and he wanted to bring the art of the artists to a wider audience. So Richard teamed up with Goebel, the well-known collectible company (home of Hummels) to produce and distribute the work of these artists to a broader audience. Often, the dolls selected for production were from Richard's own collection. Most of the dolls have been produced in resin.

Dolls of artists such as Annie Wahl (Nana's Family, Reminder Angels), Stephanie Blythe, Marree Masey, and others were produced, generally in resin. Before his association with Goebel, Richard was involved with a line of dolls for Knickerbocker.

Market Report: The dolls from this company are beautiful, well-made, and unusual.

The company, however, struggled to get the general buying public to understand the beauty of these dolls and the resin material that they were made from, since the public is much more familiar with collectible dolls made from bisque or vinyl. In 2003, the company produced very few new releases. Richard's contract with Goebel expired in 2004, and the dolls are no longer being produced.

The market is sleepy for these dolls right now, but as later collectors discover them and try to add them to their collections, they should increase in price over time. The dolls were not produced in huge numbers (except, perhaps, for the Reminder Angels line, which was sold in many general gift shops). Some of the rarer Nana's Family pieces are already highly sought after.

Online/Offline Report: Some dealers still have these dolls in stock, and you can find them at issue price. However, you can also find these dolls on eBay, often at a discount from original retail prices.

Prices and Characteristics: Prices are for dolls MIB; most are still available at retail. Many of the resin pieces have some wire ar-

Dimples, Shirley Temple by Elke Hutchens. Bisque shoulder plate, cloth body and bisque limbs, 10.5", c. 2002. Mark: (in script) Shirley Temple / Elke Hutchen /(Danbury Mint symbol) / ©MBI. $50 MIB, eBay. Courtesy Ellen Johnson.

Danbury Mint, "Friend or Foe" Goebel Hummel Doll in Expressions of Youth series. Bisque with cloth torso, 9" sitting. Courtesy Carol Mordock.

mature for posability, but the dolls are not traditionally jointed.

COLLECTION OF THE MASTERS

Various Dolls by Artists: Cynthia Malbon, Maree Massey, Jodi and Richard Creager, Annie Wahl, Rosemary Volpe, and Others
Price: retail
Material: resin
Most dolls still available at retail. Series include Reminder Angels, Nana's Family, The Twelve Elves of Christmas (only 4 produced), Memories of Childhood, and Beloved Babies.

Nana's Family, Eddie
Price: $435
Material: resin
Nana's Family is by artist Annie Wahl.

Nana's Family, Nicky
Price: $350
Material: resin
Limited edition of 750. Nicky is a turkey farmer.

Danbury Mint

The Danbury Mint is a general direct-market collectibles company with a division devoted to dolls. They have been in business for 30 years, since the mid-1970s. The company is owned by MBI, a privately owned direct-marketing company that creates and markets products under various names. All of its dolls are handled through the Danbury Mint label.

Although the Danbury Mint sells dolls of other companies through its direct-marketing catalogs, the Danbury Mint also produces and licenses dolls under its label. These dolls have been sold through magazines as well as direct mail.

Market Report: A strong secondary market has not developed for most Danbury Mint dolls, with the exception of some celebrity

Shirley and Her Doll, from the "Two of a Kind" collection. Based on a photo of Shirley holding a Shirley Temple doll. Bisque. Sitting 15″, c. 2001. Courtesy Carol Mordock.

dolls (Princess Diana, Shirley Temple) produced by the firm. However, even a celebrity doll from this firm may not bring the original retail value today due to the opening up of the secondary market caused by eBay and other online outlets.

Online/Offline Report: Most Danbury Mint dolls trade from collector to collector on eBay—dealers rarely handle the dolls except for some of the celebrity dolls.

Prices and Characteristics, Marks: For dolls MIB. All dolls are bisque unless otherwise noted. Most Danbury Mint dolls can be found at or below retail. Marks: Danbury Mint dolls have "Copyright" or "© MBI" on their backs, sometimes also an artist's signature, or "Shirley Temple Copyright MBI." This is helpful if you find a doll without the box or tags. Danbury Mint dolls without box and tags are worth a fraction of the prices quoted here.

DANBURY MINT

Baby Annie and Baby Andie
Date: 1998
Internet: $120

Betty Boop, Coca-Cola
Size: 11″   Date: 2000
                              Internet: $80–$100

Cabbage Patch, Olympikids
Size: 14″   Date: 1996
                              Internet: $75–$100
Set of 2.

Crissy, Bisque
Size: 16″   Date: 2003
                              Internet: $300–$325
Reproduction of a 1970s favorite with hair that grows.

Mother and Daughter, Bride Set
Size: 17″   Internet: $75–$120 per set
Series of 4 sets, mother and daughter on wedding day.

Prince Andrew, Bridegroom
Size: 20″   Internet: $75–$100
Royal Wedding Series.

Princess Diana, Bride
Size: 18″   Date: 1985
                              Internet: $160–$195

Sarah Ferguson, Bride
Size: 20″   Internet: $100
Royal Wedding Series.

Shirley and Her Doll
                              Internet: $85–$100
Shirley with Shirley doll.

Shirley Temple, Bright Eyes
Size: 16″   Date: 1991
                              Internet: $60–$75
In red gown.

Patsy, Summer reproduction.
*Vinyl, 4 dolls in Seasons series. 13″,
c. 2002. $50 NRFB, eBay.*

Patsyette "June" reproduction.
*Vinyl, Calendar Girl Series. 9″.
c. 2002. Distributed by Ashton
Drake. $30 MIB, eBay.*

Little Miss Muffet. *Vinyl. 12″, c.
1980s. Courtesy Cathy Messenger.*

Shirley Temple, Dress-Up Doll
Size: 16″   Date: 1991
                       Internet: $60–$100
Vinyl doll; separate outfits available.

Shirley Temple, Caroler
Size: 16″   Internet: $125
With songbook.

Shirley Temple, Dimples
Size: 18″   Date: 1996
                       Internet: $150
Portrait Collection.

Shirley Temple, First Vacation
Size: 17.5″   Date: 1998
                       Internet: $100

Shirley Temple, Heidi
Size: 14″   Date: 1995
                       Internet: $50–$70

Shirley Temple, La Belle Diaperina
Size: 14″   Internet: $80–$100
Shirley in her first role.

Shirley Temple, Little Princess
Size: 17″   Date: 1980
                       Internet: $115–$130
Doll in crown, scepter, and cape.

Shirley Temple, Sunday's Best
Size: 18″   Date: 1996
                       Internet: $65–$75
Toddler type.

Sleeping Beauty, Bisque
Size: 19″   Internet: $155
By Judy Belle.

**Princess Diana, Prince Charles, Flower Girl,
Royal Wedding**
Size: 12–20″   Date: 1981
                       Internet: $300+
The first Princess Diana wedding dolls by Danbury Mint, as a set.

Thumbelina Reproduction
                       Date: 2000
                       Internet: $150

Tiny Tears, Bisque, With Layette
Size: 11″   Internet: $100–$160

Effanbee, Modern

For the early, successful history of the Effanbee Doll Co., plus prices for dolls through 1980, see the Effanbee section in the Vintage Dolls chapter. The original Effanbee Doll Co. got into financial troubles during World War II and was sold in 1946. The company has had a series of owners since then.

Effanbee's Varied Past; Trouble in the 1970s and 1980s: Effanbee, overall, has had a long and varied past which has gone up and down with the fortunes of the doll industry. The company shone in the eras of composition and hard plastic, with classic dolls such as Patsy, Honey, and Tintair. But

Brenda Starr, Reporter in Red. *Vinyl, jointed neck, shoulders, elbows, hips, knees. 16″, c. 2003. $80, eBay.*

Brenda Starr, Bathing Beauty. *Effanbee (after purchase by Tonner Doll Company). Hard vinyl, first Brenda Starr, limited edition of 1,000. 16″, c. 2003. $95 MIB, eBay.*

during the 1970s and 1980s the company tried to imitate Madame Alexander with vinyl collector dolls. These vinyl dolls were made with cheap costuming and flat faces, and they are not favorites of collectors today. In the 1980s, Effanbee also did a series of celebrity vinyl dolls, The Legend Series, including notables such as Liberace, Groucho Marx, and John Wayne, and a Presidents Series, also not a collector favorite.

Tonner Doll Company Acquires Effanbee: Effanbee Dolls nearly found its way again in the 1990s, with some charming Patsy reproductions, a Cindy (Dewees Cochran) reproduction, vinyl Kewpie dolls, and a 16-inch soft vinyl Brenda Starr fashion doll. However, the company faced further financial problems and went bankrupt in 2001. Luckily for doll collectors, the Tonner Doll Company purchased the assets of Effanbee

(including molds) and started to produce high-quality updated versions of many Effanbee dolls in 2002.

The Tonner Doll Company has completely revitalized the company, with Effanbee Dolls again the darling of modern doll collectors and also vintage collectors looking for quality updates of their favorite vintage dolls. Patsy was given a new look, with dolls based on the old molds but with rooted hair (in some cases) and with less-glossy vinyl skin. The new Brenda Starr was remade to share clothing with the Tyler Wentworth series of fashion dolls, and the face is now in the hard vinyl that collectors prefer. Additional characters have recently joined the line, including the well-received Daphne Dimples. Most dolls are now produced in very limited editions of 1,000 or fewer, which has been well-received by collectors.

Dewees Cochran's Angela Apple-seed Tea Party, Reproduction.
Vinyl, limited edition of 3,000. 13",
c. 2000. $59 MIB, eBay.

Market Report: The market for the modern 1970s and 1980s Effanbee vinyl dolls has prices trending down. The latest Effanbee dolls from the Tonner Doll Company are very new, and the secondary market is still developing for them.

Online/Offline Report: More of the modern, vinyl dolls will be found on eBay than from any other source, with prices similar from all venues.

Prices and Characteristics: All dolls are vinyl, and prices are for dolls MIB or NRFB. Most modern Effanbee dolls (now produced by the Tonner Doll Company) are available at retail from authorized Effanbee dealers.

EFFANBEE DOLLS, MODERN

Babe Ruth
Size: 18"   Date: 1985
     Internet: $75
Famous Legends Series, Great Moments in Sports.

Basil St. John, Suit
Size: 17"   Date: 1990s
     Internet: $115

Brenda Starr, Bathing Beauty
Size: 16"   Date: 2003
     Internet: $100
Limited edition of 1,000. First Brenda Starr from Robert Tonner's Effanbee.

Brenda Starr, Maharaja's Ball
Size: 16"   Date: 2001
     Internet: $85
Limited edition of 1,000.

Brenda Starr, Mandarin Mystery, Modern Doll Collector's Convention
Size: 16"   Date: 2000
     Internet: $60
Limited edition of 250. Brown version of Mandarin Mystery, Modern Doll Collectors Convention.

Brenda Starr, Marie Antoinette
Size: 26"   Date: 2001
     Internet: $110

Brenda Starr, Tonner version
Size: 16"   Date: 2003–present
Price: retail
Most varieties.

Judy Garland, as Dorothy in *The Wizard of Oz*
Size: 14"   Date: 1984
     Internet: $100
Sixth doll in the Famous Legends Series.

Kewpie, Black
Size: 16"   Date: 1990
     Internet: $160

Kewpie, Millennium Set (2 dolls)
Size: 16"   Date: 1999
     Internet: $150
8" New Year's baby and 16" guardian angel.

Kewpies, 7 Dwarfs

Size: 8″   Date: 1999
                          Internet: $100
For set; Snow White also produced.

Patsy and Patsyette Reproductions

Size: various   Date: 1990s–present
                          Internet: retail
Various vinyl reproductions of Patsy, Patsyette,
Patsy Joan, and Wee Patsy.

Suzy Sunshine

Size: 18″   Date: early 1980s
                          Internet: $20

Vinyl Dolls

Size: 6–24″   Date: 1970s–1980s
                          Internet: $15–$30
For most vinyl child/lady dolls from the 1970s
and 1980s, including Storybook Series, Enchanted Garden, Just Friends, Historical Collection, various fancy-dressed ladies, and others.

Fashion Doll Makeover (Repaint) Artists

Fashion doll makeover artists are a fairly
new phenomenon. Makeover artists take a
fashion doll—generally, a Barbie, Gene,
Tyler, or similar doll, and they remove the
clothing and face paint. They then repaint
the doll, giving it a whole new look. Many
artists also restyle the hair or reroot or rewig
the doll. For a fully made-over doll, the costuming is also redone. Some artists also will
paint the breast, neck, and other areas of the
doll's body for more realism, and also will
give the dolls new manicures and pedicures.
This process is also referred to by some
artists as doll customization, or doll repainting (where the doll is repainted but not redressed).

Although Barbie dolls were probably the
first dolls to be made over in this manner,
makeover artistry really took off with the ascendancy of the 16-inch larger-size fashion
dolls in the late 1990s to early 2000s. At first,
companies frowned upon makeover artists
and their work, but as the market for this
work has grown (with the market to sell
dolls to these artists as well) the practice has
been widely accepted, as long as the
makeover artists do not infringe on the copyright or other intellectual property right of
the manufacturers of the dolls.

Market Report: Many makeover artists do
this for their own enjoyment, but there are
also makeover artists who have become quite
well known and who sell their work for
many hundreds of dollars. Most of the remade dolls produced are one-of-a-kinds, and
they can sell for over $1,000 per doll at the
upper end from the best-known artists. The
majority of the well-remade dolls by the
well-known artists, however, sell closer to
the $300 to $500 range, while new and strug-
gling artists' remade dolls will sometimes
barely sell for the original price. Also note
that repainted 16-inch fashion dolls are
much more popular than repainted Barbie
dolls or other small fashion dolls.

When searching for remade dolls on eBay,
be aware that many artists and collectors also
refer to the dolls as "repaints" and you need
to search the term "repaint" as this is the
more commonly used eBay term. Artists also
frequently use the term OOAK, for "one-of-
a kind."

Repainted (or remade) dolls are hot—many
collectors who own fashion dolls enjoy owning original work and unique dolls that cannot be obtained anywhere else. However, the
future market potential for these dolls is un-
clear, and the market varies greatly depending on the artists and their individual output
and following.

Online/Offline Report: The majority of repainted dolls sell on eBay and on the websites of the individual artists. The dolls are
rarely handled by dealers. Sometimes the
artists will also sell their work at doll shows,
especially shows specializing in fashion dolls.

Prices and Characteristics: Prices are for
dolls in excellent condition, and repainted
dolls listed here are hard vinyl. Most dolls are
sold nude by the artists, except as noted.

REPAINT ARTISTS, DOLLS

American jeZebel, Various

Size: 16″   Date: 2004
                          Internet: $500–$700

AnnaKelly by Jewlianne. Re-painted fashion doll, 16". Courtesy Jewlianne.

Marika by Jewlianne. Repainted fashion doll, 16". Courtesy Jewlianne.

American jeZebel, Shiloh
Size: 16"   Date: 2004
                   Internet: $685
RTW Sensational Sydney repainted and re-rooted.

CES, Carole Stimac, Agata
Size: 16"   Date: 2004
                   Internet: $800
Repainted Platinum Gene.

CES, Carole Stimac, Malia
Size: 16"   Date: 2004
                   Internet: $1,900
Repainted Simply Gene Raven.

CES, Carole Stimac, Michelina
Size: 16"   Date: 2004
                   Internet: $660
Repainted Simply Gene Raven.

DAO, Dawn Aldous Originals, Sora II
Size: 16"   Date: 2004
                   Internet: $660
Mei Li repainted and rerooted.

Faces by Adrian, Various
Size: 16"   Date: 2004
                   Internet: $300–$400
Various Gene and Tyler repaints and/or reroots.

Faces by Adrian Alicante, Repainted RTW Elegance Sydney
Size: 16"   Date: 2004
                   Internet: $750
Repainted RTW Elegance Sydney, also rerooted.

JACS Designs, Various
Size: 16"   Date: 2004
                   Internet: $800–$1,000
Full repaint and reroot.

JACS Designs, Marcus
Size: 17"   Date: 2004
                   Internet: $400

Jewlianne
Size: 16"   Date: 2004
                   Internet: $460
Repainted Satin Sydney.

Jewlianne, Shyla, Tyler Repaint
Size: 16"   Date: 2003
                   Internet: $550
Repainted Raven Sensational Sydney (repainted, hair redone, realistic built-up nipples).

Laurie Leigh Art, Various
Size: 16"   Date: 2004
                   Internet: $400–$600

Laurie Leigh Art, Neil in the Romance Cover Model Series
Size: 16"   Date: 2004
                   Internet: $575
Matt O'Neill repaint and reroot.

Laurie Leigh, Ivy
Size: 16"   Date: 2003
                   Internet: $775
Repainted Firebird Sydney.

One and Only, Romany Princess Gene Repaint
Size: 16"   Date: 2003
                Internet: $900
Renée Coughlan. Repainted black haired Simply Gene.

Repaints by Ann, Matt Repaints
Size: 16"   Date: 2004
                Internet: $400–$500
For repainted/rerooted Matt O'Neills, fully costumed as a character.

Wright, Adrian, "Blaze" Tyler Repaint
Size: 16"   Date: 2003
                Internet: $475
Repainted Pink Champagne Tyler.

Franklin Mint

The Franklin Mint started producing dolls for collectors in the 1980s. Along with the Danbury Mint and Ashton Drake, Franklin Mint dolls are commonly advertised in magazines. Franklin Mint was most successful during the late 1980s and early 1990s, when collecting anything was all the rage, and when the concept of producing collectible dolls for adults was first taking hold.

The company was battered by the realities of the post-9/11 world and its effect on the collectibles market, and they never fully recovered. In late 2003, the company downsized and announced that it would no longer produce collectible dolls.

Market Report: Many people who bought Franklin Mint dolls in the 1980s and early 1990s were convinced that, since the dolls were limited editions, their value would only increase. Unfortunately, this has not proven to be the case. Except for celebrity dolls, the majority of the Franklin Mint dolls have not increased in price at all, and many can be found below original issue price on eBay. However, certain rarer dolls can trade for several hundred dollars, and with the company's decision to quit production of dolls in late 2003, prices for some dolls may rise.

Online/Offline Report: Dealer's don't generally carry Franklin Mint dolls in great numbers. The dolls are plentiful on eBay and on private websites on the Internet (often being sold from private collections) and, as mentioned in the market report, you can often find the dolls at below-issue prices there.

Prices and Characteristics: Prices are for dolls MIB or NRFB. Many of the Franklin Mint dolls were produced over a period of years from the late 1980s through the early 2000s, so dating individual dolls can be difficult.

FRANKLIN MINT

April in Paris
Size: 22"   Internet: $300
Material: bisque

Aunt Pittypat, *Gone With the Wind*
Size: 20"   Date: 1994
                Internet: $330–$350
Material: bisque
Dolls in this series are likenesses of the actors and actresses in movie.

Bébé Bru, Victorian Bride
Size: 19"   Internet: $250
Material: bisque
Doll does not resemble an antique Bru.

Belle Watling, *Gone With the Wind*
                Date: 1991
                Internet: $560
Material: bisque

Bonnie Blue Butler, *Gone With the Wind*
                Internet: $360
Material: bisque
As portrayed by Cammie King in *Gone With the Wind*.

Butterfly McQueen, *Gone With the Wind*
Size: 12"   Internet: $325
Material: bisque

Cleopatra
                Internet: $100
Material: bisque

Cowardly Lion, *The Wizard of Oz*
Size: 21"   Date: 1989
                Internet: $300
Material: bisque

Doreen, From Donegan County
                Internet: $500
Material: bisque
Plays "Sweet Rosie O'Grady."

Catherine and the Poetry of the Fan. Bisque shoulder head, cloth body, bisque limbs. 17.5", c. 1983. Mark: SHD. $65, dealer. Courtesy Marsha L. Cumpton.

Jackie Kennedy in wedding dress. Bisque, cloth body, bisque limbs. 17", c. 1980s. Mark: Only wrist tag and LE number on back of neck (many Franklin Mint dolls are poorly marked). $130 MIB, eBay. Courtesy Ellen Johnson.

Dorothy, *The Wizard of Oz*
Size: 17"   Date: 1986
           Internet: $95
Material: bisque

Ellen O'Hara, *Gone With the Wind*
Size: 21"   Internet: $425
Material: bisque
Rare *Gone With the Wind* character.

Erté, *Symphony in Black*
Size: 19"   Date: 1989
           Internet: $700
Material: bisque
With greyhound dog.

Glinda, *The Wizard of Oz*
           Date: mid-1990s
           Internet: $100
Material: bisque

I Love Lucy, Fashion Doll, Trunk
           Internet: $350
Material: vinyl
Doll with trunk and 9 outfits.

I Love Lucy, Vitameatavegamin
Size: 18"   Internet: $120
Material: vinyl

I Love Lucy Baby Ballet
           Internet: $150–$220
Material: bisque

I Love Lucy Candy Factory
           Internet: $100
Material: vinyl

I Love Lucy Sales Resistance
Size: 16"   Internet: $80–$150
Material: vinyl

Lady of the Lake
Size: 17″   Internet: $145
Material: bisque

Mammy (Hattie McDonald), *Gone With the Wind*
Size: 18″   Internet: $320
Material: bisque

Mammy, *Gone With the Wind*
Size: 20″   Internet: $150
Material: bisque

Marilyn Monroe, Happy Birthday, Mr. President
Size: 22″   Internet: $150
Material: vinyl

Marilyn Monroe, Love, Marilyn
Size: 18″   Internet: $140–$170
Material: bisque

Moonlight Masquerade, Fabergé
Size: 22″   Internet: $250
Material: bisque

Pearl, the Gibson Girl
                       Internet: $400
Material: bisque

Princess Alexandra
Size: 19″   Date: 1991
                       Internet: $200–$300
Material: bisque

Prissy, *Gone With the Wind*
Size: 18″   Internet: $450
Material: bisque

Queen Galadriel
Size: 22″   Internet: $310
Material: bisque
First collector doll issued under license from the estate of J.R.R. Tolkien; artist is Greg Hildebrandt.

Rose, *Titanic,* The Night Rose Meets Jack, Extra Outfits
Size: 15.5″   Internet: $225
Material: vinyl
Authorized by 20th Century Fox. Rose doll in her dinner dress, with flying dress, dress from opening scene, safe with heart of the ocean necklace.

Rose, *Titanic,* Flying Scene
Size: 17″   Date: 2000
                       Internet: $150
Material: bisque

Rose, *Titanic,* Opening Scene Ensemble
Size: 15.5″   Internet: $100
Material: vinyl

Rose, *Titanic,* Reunited
Size: 17″   Internet: $155
Material: bisque
From final dream sequence in movie.

Rose, *Titanic,* Ship Struck Iceberg
Size: 15.5″   Internet: $110
Material: vinyl

Rose, *Titanic,* Tea Dress
Size: 15.5″   Internet: $100
Material: vinyl

Sandy, *Grease,* With Trunk and Dresses
                       Internet: $175
Material: vinyl

Scarecrow, *The Wizard of Oz*
Size: 22″   Date: 1989
                       Internet: $200
Material: bisque

Scarlett O'Hara, Fashion Doll
Size: 15.5″   Internet: $100
Material: vinyl

Scarlett O'Hara, Fashion Doll, Blue Gown Outfit
Size: 15.5″   Internet: $200
NRFB; fits Scarlett fashion doll, Gene, and other 16″ dolls. Rarest Scarlett outfit. For outfit only.

Scarlett O'Hara, Fashion Doll, Trunk
Size: 15.5″   Internet: $115
Material: trunk
Shaped like Parisienne Hatbox.

Scarlett O'Hara, Fashion, Doll, Various Outfits
Size: 15.5″   Internet: $30–$100
NRFB; depends on rarity of outfit.

Scarlett O'Hara, Honeymoon Doll
Size: 22″   Internet: $250
Material: bisque

Scarlett O'Hara, Bride
Size: 22″   Internet: $450
Material: bisque
With original case. Gold Standard series.

Wicked Witch, *The Wizard of Oz*
Size: 21″   Date: 1991
                       Internet: $260
Material: bisque

Typical Götz vinyl doll. *Vinyl swivel head, arms, legs, cloth body. 17", c. early 2000s. Courtesy Mary Turkel.*

Götz Kinderland doll by Hildegard Günzel. *Vinyl head, arms, legs, cloth body. Doll carrier and book inside box. 12", c. early 2000s. Courtesy Mary Turkel.*

Götz

The Götz (or Goetz in English) Doll Company produced quality children's and collectors' dolls for 50 years. Known mainly as a producer of Sasha dolls (see the Sasha Dolls section in the Vintage Dolls chapter for pricing and information), Götz also produced baby dolls and manufactured renditions of artist dolls. Hurt badly by the general economy and slowness in the high-end collectible dolls market after 9/11, the company closed its doors in early 2004.

Market Report: The market for Sasha dolls by Götz is very strong, with general weakness for the majority of other dolls produced by this company at this time. Many stores still have discounted dolls in stock from the company's going-out-of-business sale.

Online/Offline Report: Dealers carry a good selection of the Götz Sasha dolls, as does eBay, but you'll find the greatest selection of the Götz play dolls and other collector lines on eBay, except for the latest released dolls which are still in stock at some doll shops.

Prices and Characteristics: Both the play line and artist dolls from Götz are vinyl. Most Götz dolls trade at or near retail.

Günzel, Hildegard

Hildegard Günzel is one of the best-known doll artists working today, one of the artists at the forefront of the creation of the market for art dolls, and one of the earliest "names" for collectors gravitating toward artist-made dolls in the 1980s. Hildegard was born in Germany in 1945, and was trained at the German Master School of Fashion in Munich. Hildegard made her first dolls in the 1970s, using cloth and polymer clays. In 1980, she started to work in porcelain. Her dolls were exhibited at a few European stores and shows, until Hildegard exhibited her dolls at Toy Fair in 1986. By 1988, her dolls were part of the Classic Children collection of the Wanke Company, a company that did much for the development of artist dolls.

Although Hildegard has her own doll company, where she produces small editions of generally 10 to 100 porcelain and wax-over-porcelain dolls, she has worked to produce vinyl and other dolls for collectors and play dolls with many well-known companies, including Waltershausen, Götz, and others. She has also designed collector teddy bears. Additionally, Hildegard has taught doll-making to many artists worldwide through seminars and classes. Her book, *Creating*

Odile, The Lifetime Award Collection. *Wax-over-porcelain. 40″, c. 2004. Limited edition of 10. Courtesy Porzellanpuppenmanufaktur Hildegard Günzel.*

Danette, Whispering Island Collection. *Wax-over-porcelain. 38″, c. 2003. Limited edition of 20. Courtesy Porzellanpuppenmanufaktur Hildegard Günzel.*

Original Porcelain Dolls: Modeling, Molding, and Painting (first released in 1988) was one of the first books on original (not reproduction) dollmaking that many artists owned, and it was an inspiration to many.

In 2003, Hildegard received a Lifetime Achievement Award from Jones Publishing, USA. She was the first individual doll artist to receive this award (the Steiff company has also received this award).

Market Report: There is always a strong demand for the very limited editions of Hildegard Günzel dolls. Many celebrities, including Demi Moore, have collected Hildegard's dolls though the years.

Because of the specialized nature and high original retail prices of the limited dolls, they generally don't trade well on eBay (reserve prices are often not met, and it is hard to find a buyer within the one-week time frame that the eBay format allows). That doesn't mean that the dolls aren't desirable, just that it is easier and more successful, generally, to buy and sell these dolls through knowledgeable dealers with developed clienteles.

Online/Offline Report: As mentioned in the market report, the best venue for buying and selling the limited-edition Hildegard Günzel dolls is through dealers. Collectors wishing to purchase dolls when released should develop a relationship with dealers who carry her dolls at retail. Play vinyl dolls and collector bears designed by Hildegard for other companies are easily found on eBay.

Prices and Characteristics: Hildegard Günzel has made dolls in vinyl (distributed

Innocence, Masterpieces of the World. Wax-over-porcelain, leather apparel. 36", c. 1997. One of a Kind. Courtesy Porzellanpuppen-manufaktur Hildegard Günzel.

through Götz), porcelain, and wax-over-porcelain. Most of her latest dolls have been wax-over-porcelain, a process that gives an ethereal glow to the doll's skin. Doll editions for the wax-over-porcelain dolls are generally very small, ranging from 10 to 50 pieces only. Most Hildegard Günzel dolls trade at or near retail.

Himstedt, Annette

Annette Himstedt is one of the best-known current doll artists in the world. Collectors feel that her dolls capture children so well that they are some of the most realistic dolls of children ever made. Annette Himstedt made her first doll 20 years ago, in 1975. Her first dolls were crude, but by 1979 she was making porcelain dolls. She exhibited her first dolls in Germany in 1982, but only made one-of-a kind dolls at this time. In 1986 she opened a workshop in Spain that produced vinyl versions of her one-of-a-kind dolls. These first vinyl dolls were distributed in the United States by Mattel and by the artist in Europe, but today, Annette Himstedt distributes her own dolls worldwide. She still makes porcelain dolls (in very small editions) as well as larger, but still limited, editions in vinyl, which are generally a few hundred pieces each.

Market Report: Annette Himstedt has a devoted following of doll collectors worldwide. Her editions sell out quickly, often being sold out to doll retailers as early as Toy Fair in February. That said, a strong secondary market has not yet developed for many of her dolls, especially the very expensive porcelain editions. Some of the collectors' favorites and the aforementioned porcelain dolls rarely make it to the secondary market, and at the same time, the same dolls tend to come up on eBay again and again, sometimes not reaching their original suggested retail price. However, her current Puppen Kinder vinyl dolls are quite hot, and many of those dolls are selling for considerably over original retail.

Online/Offline Report: Your best bet to get current, hard-to-get Annette Himstedt dolls is to develop a strong relationship with a doll store. For older, harder-to-find dolls, check online often, and also check with dealers. You can occasionally find bargains on eBay for Annette Himstedt dolls that are a few years old.

Prices and Characteristics: All dolls priced here are hard vinyl, with glass eyes and hand-knotted human hair wigs. Prices are for dolls MIB except as noted. "LE" means "limited edition."

Fina & Sina. Vinyl, 2004 Club Dolls (with club miniatures). 38". Limited edition of 713 each. Courtesy Annette Himstedt Puppenmanufaktur.

Freddie. Vinyl. 38", c. 2004. Limited edition of 377. Courtesy Annette Himstedt Puppenmanufaktur.

ANNETTE HIMSTEDT DOLLS

Aura
Size: 24"   Date: 1996
                             Internet: $600
8-year-old gypsy girl.

Baby Lieschen, Collectors Club
Size: 23"   Date: 1998
Price: $300

Barefoot Children, Bastian
Size: 26"   Date: 1986
Price: $400   Internet: $350
First series of Barefoot Children. Barefoot Children were issued through Timeless Creations, a division of Mattel.

Barefoot Children, Ellen
Size: 26"   Date: 1986
Price: $350
First series of Barefoot Children.

Barefoot Children, Fatou
Size: 26"   Date: 1986
Price: $600
First serie of Barefoot Children.

Barefoot Children, Käthe
                             Date: 1987
                             Internet: $350

Barefoot Children, Lisa
Size: 26"   Date: 1986
Price: $225–$350
First series of Barefoot Children.

Barefoot Children, Paula
Size: 26"   Date: 1986
Price: $275–$350   Internet: $800
First series of Barefoot Children.

Barefoot Children, Sanga
Size: 21"   Date: 1992–1993
                             Internet: $350

Linn. Vinyl. 38", c. 2004. Limited edition of 277. Note open mouth. Courtesy Annette Himstedt Puppenmanufaktur.

Bina, Masterpiece Collection
Size: 32.5"   Date: 2002
                     Internet: $2,500
Limited edition of 25. Hand sculpted, kid torso.
Masterpiece Kinder Aus Porzellan Collection.

Frederike, World Child Collection
Size: 30"
Price: $500–$750   Internet: $850

Images of Childhood Collection, Lona
Size: 30"   Date: 1993
Price: $275–$350

Images of Childhood Collection, Tara
Size: 27"   Date: 1993
Price: $400

Li'l Fan Fan, Asian Girl
Size: 33"   Date: 2003
                     Internet: $875
LE 277.

Linn, Himstedt Kinde Collection
Size: 37.5"   Date: 2004
                     Internet: $900+
Only open-mouth doll in collection.

Makimura
Size: 31.5"   Date: 1988
                     Internet: $900
Asian doll; Puppen Kinder vinyl series.

Malin (Red-Blonde Hair)
Size: 29"   Date: 1988–1989
                     Internet: $1,300

Marlene
Size: 33"   Date: 2003
                     Internet: $875
LE 277.

Mascha
Size: 32"   Date: 2003
                     Internet: $875

Max and Klarchen
Size: 31.5"   Date: 2002
                     Internet: $1,150
Anniversary Club piece. LE 713.

Midori
Size: 35"   Date: 2002
                     Internet: $800–$900
LE 277.

Neblina, Faces of Friendship Series
Size: 27"   Date: 1991
Price: $400   Internet: $1,200
Hand-knotted wig.

Puppen Kinder Collection, Amanda
Size: 34"   Date: 2003
                     Internet: $1,200
LE 277.

Puppen Kinder Collection, Annika
Size: 28"   Date: 2002
                     Internet: $1,400
LE 277.

Puppen Kinder Collection, Kersti
Size: 28"   Date: 2002
                     Internet: $1,800
LE 277.

Grace. *Vinyl, seated (also pro-duced in standing version 21″ tall). 12″, c. 2001. Limited edition of 3500. Courtesy Jan McLean De-signs.*

Cissy, Lollipop series. *Vinyl. 26″, c. 2001. Limited edition of 5,000. Courtesy Jan McLean Designs.*

Tinka

Size: 24″   Date: 1997
                             Internet: $1,000
LE 620.

Jan McLean Designs

In 1999, my husband and I took a cruise around New Zealand. About halfway through the cruise, we stopped in Dunedin, on the south island of New Zealand. When you take a cruise, you *do* get to see quite a lot, but you normally are in any given port of call for about eight hours or so, tops. So you make your choices about what to see in each port of call very carefully. Well, the penguins near Dunedin were intriguing, but what I really wanted to see was the charming Dunedin doll studio of Jan McLean Designs.

If you've ever seen a Jan McLean doll you would remember it—Jan McLean dolls are very distinctive—impossibly tall beautiful women, and chubby, angelic children with pigtails and old-fashioned dresses. The dolls are made out of vinyl, resin, or porcelain. And, of course, there are Jan's signature Lollipop dolls—dolls so tall and thin, with big eyes and in such a rainbow of colors, that they actually resemble lollipops! Jan definitely makes them with great attention to detail—she spares no expense, employing jewelers, milliners, and even cobblers to finish her creations.

Jan McLean started dollmaking in 1983 when she wanted to make reproduction dolls, as heirlooms, for her daughter. In 1985, Jan became inspired by the work of the German doll artist Hildegard Günzel when Ms. Günzel visited New Zealand, and Jan saw her dolls there. Jan was so inspired that she began to sculpt her own dolls. Her very first original dolls, Chloe and Phoebe, were "born" in 1987 and were followed by Poppy and Pansy. In 1991, Jan McLean exhibited her dolls at the New York Toy Fair where she became an overnight success when she won her first *DOLLS* Award of Excellence for Pansy.

Although as many dolls as possible are produced in-house in New Zealand, some of Jan's larger production runs are produced overseas (with tight quality controls), to make the dolls affordable to a wider audience. Jan produces limited-edition dolls in porcelain, as well as vinyl and resin. Jan even ventured into the world of mass marketing in 2002 with her mini Lollipop Girls (which were only produced by a contracted company for two years—Jan took production of the mini Lollipop Dolls back in-house in 2004). The mini Lollipop Girls are 12-inch vinyl play doll versions of Jan's larger, 26-inch Lollipop Girl porcelain dolls.

Market Report: Since Jan's dolls have been on the market for only 14 years, the secondary market is very young. Many dolls can still be found at original retail.

Online/Offline Report: Many dealers and doll shops carry a nice range of Jan's dolls, including some dolls from past years. You can also easily find the dolls online. Prices vary in both venues, with most later editions still available at retail prices.

Prices and Characteristics: Jan's dolls can be bisque, resin, or vinyl. Most dolls can still be found at original retail prices.

Kish, Helen

Helen Kish has inspired a nearly fanatical devotion in her fans. Helen studied art and design at the University of Colorado, and has made dolls for over 20 years. She was one of the first well-known American doll artists, making both one-of-a-kind porcelain and small-edition dolls. She added manufactured vinyl dolls to her lineup in 1994, which have brought her dolls to a wider audience.

Helen continues to work in her studio in Denver, Colorado, where she continues to produce porcelain dolls (her Signature Edition) in editions of 75 to 100 dolls. Her vinyl dolls are still also limited, either to one year of production or editions running from 350 to 500 dolls. Currently, the popular vinyl child doll Riley is in the line, as well as Bethany and two 16-inch fashion dolls, Electra and Rio. Helen also produces outfits for her dolls. Riley is so popular that the doll is currently being repainted by doll artists, an honor usually reserved for adult fashion dolls.

Market Report: The market for Helen Kish dolls is growing and very strong. Early editions of her dolls can bring several hundred dollars over original retail. As with most modern artists, later editions can vary greatly on the secondary market, and some can be found at or below retail online.

Online/Offline Report: For a relatively new company, Helen's vinyl dolls trade well on eBay. Her more limited-edition porcelain dolls are generally found via dealers and not through eBay. For hot new Kish releases, collectors should establish relationships with authorized dealers.

Prices and Characteristics: All dolls are vinyl, prices for MIB or NRFB. Most recent Helen Kish dolls are available from authorized Helen Kish dealers at retail prices. "LE" means "limited edition."

HELEN KISH DOLLS

Baby Teddy Waldorf
Size: 8″   Internet: $360
From Tea at the Waldorf Collection.

Cara and Her Trunk
Size: 10.5″   Date: 1994
                     Internet: $500–$700
With trunk of clothing.

Hansel and Gretel, Pair
Size: 11.5″   Internet: $480

Kiki, French Girls Collection
Size: 12″   Date: 2002
                   Internet: $225
LE 75.

Mary Kate in 1950 by Helen Kish. Vinyl. 10.5". Limited edition of 1,500. Courtesy Mary Turkel. $199 issue price.

Margarete by Helen Kish. Vinyl. 12", c. 1999. Courtesy Mary Turkel.

Matty Quint

Size: 7"   Internet: $300
LE 100.

Meredith, Sunday Best Collection

Size: 16"   Date: 1996
                            Internet: $300
LE 950.

Milly Quint

                            Internet: $400–$500
Blonde hair.

Molly Quint

                            Internet: $400–$500
Red hair.

Molly, Sunday Best Collection

Size: 16"   Date: 1996
                            Internet: $275
LE 950.

Riley, for UFDC New Orleans Convention

Size: 7.5"   Date: 2003
                            Internet: $225–$350
In multicolored dress and braids.

Riley, Kish Club Doll

Size: 7.5"   Internet: $200
In light blue dress.

Snow White

Size: 16"   Date: 1997
                            Internet: $350
LE 500.

Taffy

Size: 12"   Date: 1999
                            Internet: $300
LE 300.

Knickerbocker

Knickerbocker's modern collectible doll production has included important lines such as Marie Osmond Dolls and modern reproductions of Terri Lee, until the company's end in 2001 (for more information and company history, see the Knickerbocker section in the Vintage Dolls chapter and the Marie Osmond Dolls section in this chapter).

Willow and Daisy (a.k.a. Somers and Field): Willow Somers and Daisy Field are 16-inch fashion dolls created by Doug James and Laura Meisner. Known as "The Mod British Birds," the dolls were created during the ascendancy of the large-size fashion doll on the doll scene in the late 1990s to early 2000s, and they entered the market in 1999. These original dolls had a separately available wardrobe of mod fashions, and were loved by a small but devoted following of collectors. Unfortunately, creative differences with Knickerbocker as well as Knickerbocker's financial troubles doomed the line to only 3 years of production, with a very short production run in the final year, 2001.

Daisy in Jazz Club outfit. Somers & Field. 16", c. 1999. Doll $30 (and under), eBay; outfit $50+ NRFB.

Willow Go-Go Girl doll in Poor Boy outfit. Somers & Field. All vinyl 5-piece body. 16", c. 2000. Doll $30 (and under); outfit $50+ NRFB, eBay.

The "back story" for the dolls is that Willow Somers and Daisy Field are best friends in 1960s England. Willow is British and Daisy is Anglo-Indian, and the girls' fathers co-own the British department store, Somers & Field. The extensive wardrobe for the dolls is "from" their fathers' department store.

Market Report: Collectors still haven't found most Knickerbocker dolls. With the exception of the last, very limited year of production in 2001 when the full editions of the dolls and outfits weren't produced, most Somers and Field items can be found very reasonably on eBay.

Online/Offline Report: The majority of the secondary market for these dolls exists on eBay and with dealers specializing in fashion dolls.

Prices and Characteristics: All dolls are vinyl with 5-part bodies and are 16 inches tall; the Terri Lee reproductions are made of hard vinyl. Prices are for NRFB dolls and outfits.

KNICKERBOCKER

Somers & Field, Daisy in an Art Opening With Andie and Edie

　　　　　　Date: 2001
　　　　　　Internet: $180

Somers & Field, Daisy, Trafalgar Square

　　　　　　Date: 1999
　　　　　　Internet: $100

Somers & Field, Outfit, Kings Road

　　　　　　Date: 2000
　　　　　　Internet: $45

Kings Road outfit for Somers & Field. c. 2000. $55 NRFB, eBay.

Somers & Field, Outfit, Lunar Landing
> Date: 2001
> Internet: $110

Less than 100 of the projected edition of 1,500 were produced

Somers & Field, Outfit, Black and White
> Date: 2001
> Internet: $100

Dolls and outfits from the final year of production (2001) are hard to find; few were produced before Knickerbocker declared bankruptcy.

Somers & Field, Outfit, Chelsea Fashion Show
> Date: 2001
> Internet: $110

2001; fewer than 300 were made.

Somers & Field, Outfits Through 2000
> Date: 2000
> Internet: $15–$30

Most of these outfits, although produced in small quantities, are in ample supply.

Terri Lee, 50th Anniversary
> Date: 1999
> Internet: $100

Terri Lee, 50th Anniversary
> Date: 2000
> Internet: $95

Limited edition of 5,000.

Terri Lee, Garden Party
> Date: 2000
> Internet: $75

Limited edition of 5,000.

Terri Lee, Millennium Bride
> Date: 2000
> Internet: $120

Lawton, Wendy

The Lawton Doll Company is the last large-scale manufacturer of porcelain dolls left in the United States. This is sad news to collectors, but a testament to the popularity and uniqueness of the dolls of Wendy Lawton.

Wendy Lawton has been a dollmaker for over 25 years, since founding her company in 1979. One of the first American doll artists to become popular in the late-20th-century artist doll movement, Wendy's company has created more than 250 original dolls, all in porcelain and in limited editions. Besides her limited-edition porcelain dolls, Wendy also designed dolls for the Ashton Drake Galleries and also offered more affordable dolls through her company's Gallery Editions, which were designed by Wendy but manufactured in Asia. These dolls were discontinued in 2002, and now all the dolls of The Lawton Doll Company are made completely in its Turlock, California, workshops.

Claire Jolie, UFDC souvenir doll for Wendy Lawton dinner at UFDC National Convention in New Orleans. Limited edition of 300. $700 with companion trousseau, eBay.

Flora McFlimsey, 1993 special edition. Bisque. Limited edition of 250. Original retail $895. Courtesy The Lawton Doll Company.

Popular themes for dolls by The Lawton Doll Company have included classic children's literature, especially *Little Women,* playthings of past eras, immigrants, American history, and much more. Wendy's current porcelain dolls are created in small editions, generally from 175 to 250 dolls each, and retail in the $600 to $900 range.

Market Report: The secondary market for Wendy Lawton dolls is not yet fully developed. However, her dolls have a fanatical following and her small editions generally sell out. Look for the latest dolls from retailers at retail; earlier editions can sometimes be found on eBay or through dealers. Most collectors won't part with a Wendy Lawton doll unless they can get their "price" for her; therefore many dolls that do find their way to eBay don't tend to meet reserve.

Online/Offline Report: Check with authorized retailers for the latest dolls; some earlier editions can be found on eBay.

Prices and Characteristics: All prices are for dolls MIB. Most of Wendy's dolls are bisque with jointed, wood bodies, except as noted below. Wendy's most recent dolls are

generally available at retail from authorized dealers. "LE" means "limited edition."

WENDY LAWTON DOLLS

Alice in Wonderland
Size: 9″   Date: 2001
                            Internet: $475–$650

Alice, Lawton Guild Convention
Size: 16″   Date: 1995
                            Internet: $825–$1,000
LE 180. 1995 Convention Guild Collector's doll.

Claire Jolie, With Wardrobe Set
Size: 7″   Date: 2003
                            Internet: $1,000
LE 300. For UFDC 2003 Moonlight and Magnolia dinner, New Orleans.

Josephine
Size: 12″   Date: 1995
                            Internet: $1,000
LE 360. For UFDC Region 2N Conference, 1995.

Joy For Your Journey
Size: 9″   Date: 1999
                            Internet: $450–$600
LE 250. Travel doll.

Josephine, 1995 special edition for UFDC Region 2 North Conference. Bisque. Limited edition of 360. Courtesy The Lawton Doll Company

Orphan Annie

Size: 14″   Internet: $235
LE 500. Classic Children's Collection.

Shirley Temple Reproduction

Size: 16″   Date: 1980s
                       Internet: $400–$500
Composition, LE 250 in Stand Up and Cheer.

Snow White

Size: 14″   Date: 1993
                       Internet: $225
LE 500; Folk Tales & Fairy Stories Series.

Travel Doll, Lawton Collector's Guild

Size: 9″   Date: 1997
                       Internet: $775–$900
Wendy's first travel doll; special doll for Guild members only. White dress with black trim, red coat, hat. Has suitcase and travel journal.

Lee Middleton Original Dolls

Lee Middleton, from Springfield, Ohio, started crafting dolls in her home in 1978. She was a self-taught artist, and her most successful work was the creation of lifelike baby dolls, and the creation of some of the first "porcelain-look" vinyl dolls.

Her dolls were very popular and her business grew and grew, first becoming a cottage industry, and eventually becoming a full-fledged manufacturing facility located in

Belpre, Ohio. Made by a woman with strong Christian values, each Lee Middleton doll, to this day, comes with a tiny doll-size Bible.

Lee's first dolls were made in porcelain, and finally in then-revolutionary porcelain-look vinyl in 1984. Her vinyl dolls were considered some of the very first vinyl collectible dolls ever produced. Lee was known also for the lifelike expressions on her baby dolls, and their "real" feel—if you put them in your arms, it's like holding a real baby.

Sadly, Lee Middleton died in 1997. However, talented artists including Reva Schick and Reva Helland have kept the company going with their original baby sculptures. The Lee Middleton Doll Company carried dolls originally sculpted by Lee through 2003. Some of the dolls are sold through Newborn Nursery Adoption Centers, attended by a live "nurse," and the baby dolls can be selected by their new owners in a hospital nursery setting. The company also currently produces several play lines of baby dolls, including the Treasured Children collection in which the vinyl babies are fully armatured, yet still soft to hold.

Battered by the economy and changes to the collectible dolls market, the Lee Middleton Doll Company made several changes to its Artist Studio Collection (collector) dolls in

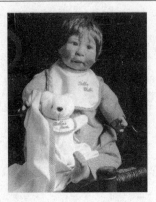

Bubba Chubbs by Lee Middleton.
*21", c. 1986. First limited edition,
5,550. $200, dealer. Courtesy Lee
Middleton Original Dolls.*

First-Generation African-American by Reva Schick. *c. 2003. Limited edition of 2,000. $199 issue price.*

2003, including reducing the number of dolls in each edition (often to only 500 to 1,000 dolls) and also reducing the price of the dolls. In 2004, the company ended its production at its Belpre, Ohio, plant and sent production overseas to Asia.

Market Report: The secondary market for Lee Middleton dolls is very slow, with the highest prices for some of the earliest Lee Middleton dolls as well as for "reborn" dolls. The secondary market was definitely affected by the company's overall price reduction on new dolls in 2003, and may recover somewhat from that in the next few years.

Online/Offline Report: The latest editions of the Artist Collection Lee Middleton baby dolls often sell out to dealers within a few weeks of their release because of the very small editions. To obtain these dolls, you need to be a customer of an authorized Lee Middleton retailer, and you must often pre-order the doll (order the doll when the line is announced, before the dolls arrive in the store). Older Lee Middleton dolls are plentiful on the secondary market on eBay and through other online sources; you can sometimes also find old stock through retailers.

Prices and Characteristics: All Lee Middleton dolls are vinyl with vinyl limbs and soft bodies—some of the dolls have full vinyl limbs (which makes it easier to dress the dolls in various outfits) and others have only lower limbs of vinyl, for better "hugability." Some of the latest standing toddler dolls are full vinyl. Almost all the baby dolls are between 20 inches and 24 inches. Prices for most Lee Middleton dolls at this time are at retail, (generally $125 to $300) with some of the rarest earlier dolls higher.

Christmas Angel 1991 by Lee Middleton. 14", c. 1991. Limited edition of 5,000. $190, dealer. Courtesy Lee Middleton Original Dolls.

Living Dead Dolls

Living Dead dolls are, for sure, an acquired taste, but they have a small-yet-fanatical following. Currently manufactured by Mezco Toys, these horrific creations are accompanied not by a birth certificate, or a certificate of authenticity, but by a death certificate.

The Living Dead dolls were created by Ed Long and Damien Glonek and entered the market in 1998, sold exclusively through Damien's horror movie memorabilia company, Unearthly Possessions. In 2000, Mezco Toys took over manufacturing and distribution of the dolls. Mezco Toys was started in 2000 by Michael Markowitz.

As for the Living Dead dolls, they are vinyl dolls caught in an eternal horror movie. You cannot help but enjoy the sense of humor of these dolls, even if you don't appreciate their design or unique look (my favorite is the Fashion Victim series!). Themes include scary clowns, devils, dead children (I never said these dolls were meant for a plaything…), and dead brides and grooms.

Besides the Living Dead dolls, Mezco also produces lines of The Osbourne Family figures/dolls and Popeye figures and dolls and other licensed products.

Market Report: The dolls are enjoying a healthy secondary market on eBay, especially for Series 1 and 2 dolls (the dolls are currently in Series 6). Suggested retail for the current releases runs from about $25–$50 for most dolls. Living Dead dolls made prior to Mezco's production are highly sought after.

Online/Offline Report: When searching for Living Dead Dolls on eBay, be sure to search many categories including Action Figures, Entertainment, and Dolls. Most traditional doll dealers don't carry these dolls, although you will see them pop up at some doll shows. As for current releases, you're more likely to find them at stores such as Hot Topic and Spencer Gifts than at doll shops or traditional toy shops.

Prices and Characteristics: All dolls are vinyl, and prices are for dolls NRFB. Priced dolls are 10 to 12 inches tall. Mini Living Dead dolls are 4 inches tall and generally sell for retail, as do the recently released porcelain series which includes Posey and Abigail, which are 18 inches tall.

LIVING DEAD DOLLS

Damien, Series I

Internet: $65

Living Dead Dolls "Mausoleum" gift set. Spencer Gifts exclusive. All vinyl. 4″, c. 2003. $25 NRFB, eBay. Courtesy Ellen Johnson.

Died & Doom, Bride & Groom, Series 1

Date: 2001
Internet: $150–$200
Tower Records exclusive.

Eggzorcist

Internet: $150

Eggzorcist, Series 1

Internet: $150–$160
In bunny costume, noose around neck.

Fashion Victims

Date: 2004
Internet: retail
Fashion Victims are 13″ fashion dolls, with extra outfit.

Hazel & Hattie

Internet: $150
Siamese twins. Tower Records exclusive. Limited edition of 3,000.

Lulu, Series 4

Internet: $90
Demented skater in tutu.

Posey, Handmade and Signed (Pre-Mezco), No Eyes

Date: 1998
Internet: $600
Doll handmade and signed before dolls sold to Mezco. Came in black coffin with no cello window (unlike the Series 1 Mezco Poseys). The handmade dolls came with and without eyes; with eyes is rarer.

Posey, Series 1

Internet: $120–$155

Sinister Minister & Bad Habit

Internet: $225
Limited edition of 999.

Tragedy

Internet: $100
Boyfriend of Misery. Hot Topic exclusive.

Madame Alexander

For the full history of the Madame Alexander Doll Company, including the modern era as well as the market report on modern Madame Alexander dolls, see the Madame Alexander section in the Vintage Dolls chapter.

NOTE: *All photos of Madame Alexander dolls in this section, unless noted, are made of hard vinyl, and jointed at the neck, shoulders and hips. All dolls have a clothing tag with the name of the doll sewn into the clothing. Most dolls are marked "ALEX" or "Alexander," but most modern Madame Alexander dolls are virtually worthless without the clothing, so marks are omitted here. All prices are for dolls MIB.*

Although Madame Alexander dolls have been play dolls (albeit premium play dolls) for most of their history, starting in the 1970s and strongly into the 1980s, its dolls became primarily dolls for adult collectors, except for its baby dolls and certain lines aimed at children. Therefore, we have included the post-1970 Madame Alexander dolls here in the Modern Dolls chapter.

Prices and Characteristics: All dolls are vinyl (generally hard vinyl), and all prices for modern Madame Alexander dolls are for MIB dolls, with tag. Prices are significantly lower without the box and tag. Prices are predominantly Internet prices, with dealer and other prices noted. Dolls are organized by theme.

MODERN MADAME ALEXANDER, 1970S–NOW

BABY DOLLS, VARIOUS, 1970S–1990S
Size: 14–22″   Date: 1970s–1990s
   Internet: $55–$100
Most have cloth torsos. Includes most Puddin, Pussy Cat, and Victoria babies.

Baby Sister or Baby Brother
Size: 20″   Date: 1989
   Internet: $35–$45

CISSETTE, VARIOUS, LATE 1980S–1990S
Size: 10″   Date: 1990s
   Internet: $65–$100
Many themes. Dolls have feet posed for high heels; lady-style bodies.

Cissette, *Grease*, Pair
Size: 10″   Date: 1990s
   Internet: $175
Limited edition for FAO Schwarz.

Cissette, Show Girl
Size: 10″   Date: 1996
   Internet: $175
1996 National Convention Doll, limited edition of 910; several costume colors.

Cissette, Samantha, From *Bewitched*
Size: 10″   Internet: $255

Cissette, Portrettes
See Hard Plastic Dolls in the Madame Alexander section in the Vintage Dolls chapter.

CISSY, MODERN, VARIOUS
Size: 21″   Date: 1996–now
   Internet: $300–$500+
Most dolls have high-fashion themes, some have historical costume themes.

Cissy, Budapest
Size: 21″   Date: 1998
   Internet: $500
Limited edition of 1,500.

Cissy, Cocktails, by Mel Odom
Size: 21″   Date: 2003
   Internet: $500
Limited edition of 200.

Cissy, Madame Du Pompadour
Size: 21″   Date: 2001
   Internet: $1,725
First by Tim Alberts, limited edition of 100.

Cissy, Pompadour Spring
Size: 21″   Date: 2002
   Internet: $400
Limited edition of 200.

FIRST LADIES (PRESIDENTS' LADIES), VARIOUS, SERIES I THROUGH V
Size: 14″   Date: 1976–1980s
   Internet: $40–$75
Per doll. Six series of 6 dolls, 36 dolls in all, in gowns.

First Ladies, Series VI
Size: 14″   Date: 1980s
   Internet: $80–$100
Fewer dolls were produced in Series VI.

GONE WITH THE WIND, VARIOUS, 1970S–1990S

Ashley, Pittypat, Bonnie Blue, 600 Series
Size: 8″   Date: 1990—1991
   Internet: $50–$60
More for Confederate Officer Ashley.

Mammy, 635
Size: 8″   Date: 1980s
   Internet: $85

Mammy 402, Jubilee II, Others
Size: 8″   Date: 1980s
   Internet: $35–$55

Melanie, 8, 10, or 12″
Size: various   Date: 1970s–1990s
   Internet: $25–$40
Nearly all smaller styles.

Melanie, Portrait, Peach Gown
Size: 21″   Date: 1989
   Internet: $150–$200

Melanie, Portrait, Red and White Gown
Size: 21″   Date: 1974
   Internet: $200–$250

Elise Bridesmaid #1655. Vinyl. 17″,
c. 1982–1985. $65, eBay.

Elise Ballerina #1640. Vinyl. 17″,
c. 1970s–1980s. $65, eBay.

Prissy 630

Size: 8″	Date: 1990
	Internet: $85

Produced for only one year.

Rhett, 8, 10, or 12″

Size: various	Date: 1970s–1990s
	Internet: $25–$40

Nearly all smaller styles.

Scarlett, Any 8″ Size

Size: 8″	Date: 1970s–1990s
	Internet: $30–$50

Certain rarer models more.

Scarlett, Any 10″ Cissette

Size: 10″	Date: 1970s–1990s
	Internet: $60–$100

More for certain rare models.

Scarlett, Cissette, in Green Gown

Size: 10″	Date: 1970
	Internet: $120

Scarlett, #1385, 12″, Green Gown

Size: 12″	Date: 1981–1985
	Internet: $40–$50

Scarlett, Any 21″ Size

Size: 21″	Date: 1975–1995

All Markets: $125–$175
Includes #2252, #2210, #2247, #2292. Jacqueline
face. Includes Mourning Scarlett.
Mark: Alexander 1961 (c).

INTERNATIONAL DOLLS, VARIOUS, 1970S–1990S

Size: 8″	Date: 1970s–1990s
	Internet: $20–$40

The vast majority of the international dolls
sell in this price range, with a few exceptions.
Dolls have the name of the country on the
box/clothing tag. Many dolls have 400 or 500
series numbers.

Arriving in America, #326

Size: 8″	Date: 1992
	Internet: $40

Rebecca #1585. Mary Ann face. Vinyl. 14", c. 1970s–early 1980s. $35, eBay.

Anne of Green Gables #1570, Arrives at Station. Vinyl. 14", c. 1993. $70, eBay.

Baby Victoria #3750. Vinyl. 14". $50, eBay.

Egypt, With Sarcophagus
Size: 8"   Internet: $130–$150

Irish, Green Glory
Size: 8"   Internet: $85+

Italy, Venice Gondolier
Size: 8"   Date: 1998
                  Internet: $80

Latvia
Size: 8"   Date: 1987
                  Internet: $50–$60

LITTLE WOMEN, VARIOUS, 1970S—1990S

Series 405–410: Amy, Beth, Jo, Meg, Laurie, Marme, Each
Size: 8"   Date: 1975
                  Internet: $20–$25

Series 411–416: Amy, Beth, Jo, Meg, Laurie, Marme, Each
Size: 8"   Date: 1970s
                  Internet: $30–$40

Series 1220s and 1300s: Amy, Beth, Jo, Meg, Laurie, Each
Size: 12"   Date: 1970s
                  Internet: $20–$35

Series 18500s: Amy, Beth, Jo, Meg, Laurie, Each
Size: 16"   Date: 1997–1999
                  Internet: $80–$100
Little Woman Journal Series.

Amy Goes to Paris Gift Set, #14635
Size: 8"   Date: 1996
                  Internet: $150
Trunk, clothing, all accessories.

Jo Goes to New York Trunk Set
Size: 8"   Date: 1995
                  Internet: $160
Produced for only one year.

STORYLAND DOLLS, VARIOUS, 400S SERIES (WENDY TYPE)
Size: 8"   Date: 1980s–1990s
                  Internet: $20–$35
Hansel, Gretel, Bo Peep, Red Riding Hood, Daffy Down Dilly, Huckleberry Finn, Jack and Jill, Little Maid, Mary, Mary, Miss Muffet, Mother Goose, many others.

Captain Hook, *Peter Pan*, #478
Size: 8"   Date: 1992
                  Internet: $50–$75

Columbus
Size: 8"   Date: 1992
                  Internet: $90

Curly Locks, #421
Size: 8"   Date: 1987
                  Internet: $45

Michael, *Peter Pan*
Size: 8"   Date: 1992
                  Internet: $70

Peter Pan
Size: 9"   Date: 1992
                  Internet: $45–$60

McGuffey Ana #496. *8", c. 1989. $40, eBay.*

Mrs. Darling (from Peter Pan). *Cissette Portrette. 10", c. 1993–1994. $90, eBay.*

Tinker Bell #467. *Peter Pan, Storyland Collection With Ann Rast Stand. 8", c. 1991. $40, eBay.*

Laurie #410. *Little Women. 8", c. 1989. $35, eBay.*

Jo #14523. *Little Women. 8", c. 1995. One in an extensive series of Little Women dolls that Madame Alexander has produced over the years. $55, eBay.*

Russia #110540. *8". Produced for 1 year only: 1994. One in an extensive series of international dolls that Madame Alexander has produced over the years. $55, eBay.*

Amy Goes to Paris Trunk Set #14635. *8", c. 1996. Doll, trunk, and outfits for Paris trip. $140, eBay.*

Netherlands boy #577. *8", c. 1970s. $25, eBay.*

Scotland #596. *8", c. early 1990s. $45, eBay.*

Arriving in America #326. 8″, c. 1993. $40, eBay.

Wendy 1893. *Exclusive for Shirley's Dollhouse, limited edition of 3,600. Commemorates 1893 Chicago World's Fair Columbian Exhibition. 8″, c. 1893. $75, eBay. Courtesy Janet Lawrence.*

Snow White, #455

Size: 8″   Internet: $75

Tiger Lily, *Peter Pan,* #469

Size: 8″   Date: 1992
                            Internet: $65–$85

Peter Pan character.

Wendy, *Peter Pan*

Size: 9″   Date: 1992
                            Internet: $50

STORYLAND DOLLS, VARIOUS, 1500S SERIES

Size: 14″   Date: 1970s–1980s
                            Internet: $30–$40

Dolls include Sleeping Beauty, Fairy Godmother, Snow White, Heidi, Goldilocks, Cinderella, Alice, Anne of Green Gables, others.

Anne of Green Gables, Anne Goes to School Trunk Set

Size: 14″   Date: 1992–1994
                            Internet: $200–$240

Isolde

Size: 14″   Date: 1985
                            Internet: $50

Produced for only one year.

SPORTS SERIES, VARIOUS, 1990S

Size: 8″   Date: 1990s
                            Internet: $30–$40

Baseball, Tennis, Soccer, Ice Skating Girl, others in 1600s series.

WENDY-STYLE DOLLS, 8″, VARIOUS

Size: 8″   Date: 1970s–1990s
                            Internet: $20–$40

Many themes. Most dolls in this price range;
some higher; see examples.

Addams Family

Size: 8″   Internet: $175
Set of 4 dolls.

Christine, *Phantom of the Opera*

Size: 8″   Date: 1998
                            Internet: $100

Best Friend #26090. *Blue variety. 8", c. 2000. $50, eBay.*

Little Shaver #26825. *All cloth. 10", c. 2000. $25, eBay.*

Emerald City Dorothy #94-2. *One of many dolls in the extensive Wizard of Oz series that Madame Alexander has produced over the years. 8", c. 1994. $65, eBay.*

Scarecrow #430. *8", c. 1993–1995. $40, eBay.*

Winged Monkey #140501. *8", c. 1994. $200, dealer.*

Wizard of Oz. *8", c. 1994.*

Peasant Munchkin #140444. *8", c. 1993–1995. $130, dealer.*

Lollipop Munchkin #14513. *8", c. 1995. $100, dealer.*

Munchkin Herald #140445. *8", c. 1994–1995. $110, dealer.*

Dorothy #464. 8″, c.1991–1993.
$55, eBay; $65, dealer.

Wicked Witch; 8″ Wendy. c. 1995.
Rarest of all the mid-1990s Wizard
of Oz set; because doll was unattractive with green skin, few were
sold. $250+, dealer.

Christopher Columbus
Size: 8″   Date: 1992
                            Internet: $85

Daniel Boone, #315
Size: 8″   Date: 1990
                            Internet: $50

Frankenstein and Bride
Size: 8″   Date: 1990
                            Internet: $215
Legends Series.

Harley Davidson Wendy, #17420
Size: 8″   Date: 1997
                            Internet: $65

***I Dream of Jeannie* Set**
Size: 8″   Internet: $250–$300
With Major Nelson, astronaut outfit.

***I Love Lucy* Set**
Size: 8″   Date: 1995
                            Internet: $250

4 dolls, 1 box, Ethel, Lucy, Ricky, and Fred.
FAO Schwarz exclusive.

***I Love Lucy,* Candy Factory**
Size: 8″   Date: 1997
                            Internet: $200
Lucy and Ethel, set, FAO Schwarz exclusive.

Maid Marion, #492
Size: 8″   Date: 1990
                            Internet: $45

Mother Superior, *Sound of Music*
Size: 8″   Date: 1992
                            Internet: $105

Nurse, #308
Size: 8″   Date: 1989
                            Internet: $115

Queen Isabella, #329
Size: 8″   Date: 1992
                            Internet: $55

Modern Romance Alex wearing Alex outfit. *Madame Alexander's modern fashion doll. This doll was a limited edition of 200 for the Modern Doll Collector's convention. 16", 2000.*

Renoir, #1578

Size: 8"	Date: 1970s
	Internet: $45

Scouting

Size: 8"	Date: 1994
	Internet: $85–$125

Girl Scout.

Vatican City Priest

Size: 9"	Date: 1990s
	Internet: $100

Welcome Home, Desert Storm

Size: 8"	Date: 1991
	Internet: $25

WIZARD OF OZ, VARIOUS, 1970S–1990S

Apple Tree

Size: 8"	Date: 1990s
	Internet: $75–$100

Auntie Em, #14515

Size: 8"	Date: 1995
	Internet: $400

Hard to find, from *Wizard of Oz* series.

Dorothy

Size: 8"	Date: 1990s
	Internet: $30–$40

Dorothy

Size: 14"	Date: 1990
	Internet: $30

Dorothy

Size: 21"	Date: 2003
	Internet: retail

Cissy face.

Glinda, The Good Witch

Size: 8"	Date: 1994
	Internet: $100

Glinda, The Good Witch

Size: 14"	Date: 1994
	Internet: $125

Dorothy, Emerald City, #942

Size: 8"	Date: 1994
	Internet: $150

Lullaby Munchkin, #14512

Size: 8"	Date: 1995
	Internet: $100

Produced for only one year.

Mayor of Munchkin Land, #140443

Size: 8"	Date: 1990s
	Internet: $50

Munchkins, Flower, Peasant, or Herald

Size: 8"	Date: 1994–1995
	Internet: $60–$85

Scarecrow, Tin Man, Lion

Size: 8"	Date: 1990s
	Internet: $40–$50

Wicked Witch

Size: 8"	Date: 1990s
	Internet: $250+

Green face.

Wicked Witch

Size: 10″   Date: 1992
           Internet: $100+
Green face.

Wicked Witch

Size: 21″   Internet: $175

OTHER DOLLS

Historic Figures, 1300 Series

Size: 12″   Date: 1970s–1980s
           Internet: $30–$45
Cleopatra, Marc Antony, Blue Boy, Josephine, Napoleon, others.

Suzy, Straw Bonnet and Pinafore, #1150

Size: 12″   Date: 1970
All Markets: $75
Mark: Mark: Alexander 1964 (c).

Maggie, Green Jacket, #1720

Size: 17″   Date: 1972
All Markets: $50
Mark: Alexander 1968.

McGuffey, Ana, #1525

Size: 14″   Date: late 1970s
           Internet: $30

Millennium Spectacular Cissy

Size: 16″   Date: 1999
           Internet: $275
Limited edition of 1,000; commemorates the millennium.

Mimi, #1411

Size: 14″   Date: 1984
           Internet: $35
Mary Ann face.

Coco & Cleo Travel Abroad

Size: 16″   Date: 1999
           Internet: $200
Produced for only one year; company was forced to stop using Coco name by Chanel company. Also Coco Belle Époque.

Elise, Bride, Bridesmaid, Ball Gown, or Ballerina

Size: 17″   Date: 1975–1980s
All Markets: $50–$90
All vinyl Elise.

Various 21″: Godey, Mary, Queen of Scots, Agatha, Cornelia, Others

Size: 21″   Date: 1977–1989
           Internet: $100–$125
$200+ for Gainsborough.

Wicked Stepmother

Size: 21″   Date: 1996
           Internet: $180
Sleeping Beauty Series.

Marie Osmond Dolls

During Marie Osmond's long entertainment career, she was always also a doll collector. The only girl in a family with eight brothers, Marie's mother would always bring her a doll from each location where the Osmond Brothers performed.

Marie became a celebrity in her own right, but never lost her love of dolls. In 1990, she joined forces with the L.L. Knickerbocker Company, Inc. (see Knickerbocker section) to create a line of porcelain dolls. Marie took part not only in the marketing of the dolls, but also in the creation—she became involved in the doll design process, everything from choosing themes to costuming.

Since 1991, Marie has been very successful in selling her dolls through the cable shopping channel QVC; she also sells her dolls through a network of doll dealers and gift shops.

Eventually, Marie began to sculpt dolls for the line and her personal creations include the highly stylized and very successful Adora Belles. Her first doll sculpted for Marie Osmond Dolls was Olive May, in 1995. One of her most popular lines of dolls has been the Tiny Tots, small porcelain dolls in a sitting position that retail for approximately $40–$50. Tiny Tots are often created to go with larger toddler dolls in the line—for instance, the highly popular *Wizard of Oz* dolls were done both in a large toddler size doll and also as Tiny Tots. Most of the Marie Osmond Dolls are porcelain, although certain lines such as the Adora Belles are vinyl.

Marie Osmond Dolls remained part of Knickerbocker until Knickerbocker went out of business in 2002. At that time, Marie and her husband, Brian, decided to buy certain lines of dolls from Knickerbocker, including Marie Osmond Dolls and Magic Attic Dolls. They renamed their new com-

Mopsy & Rags. *Bisque head, cloth bodies. Limited edition of 5,000. Marie Osmond's original bisque Raggedy-Ann inspired dolls. 19", c. 1994. $100 each, dealer. Courtesy Janice Justis.*

Olive May. *Bisque, cloth body. Limited edition of 20,000. 24", c. 1995. $150, dealer. Courtesy Janice Justis.*

Adora Beau. *All bisque, limited edition of 1,000. 13", c. 2000. $90, eBay.*

pany Marian LLC. In 2004, the company changed its name to Charisma Dolls, and the line expanded to include vinyl Kewpie (formerly produced by Cameo) dolls as well as Saddie Gladdies, a topsy-turvy type rag doll.

Market Report: Marie's dolls have a devoted following, with many women discovering her dolls (and doll collecting in general!) from QVC. Until recently, however, most editions of Marie's dolls have been quite large, so that secondary market demand is still developing.

That said, some of Marie's earliest dolls are quite scarce and prices for them have risen as later collectors have tried to find some of these dolls for their collections. The secondary market may also take off at some point for some of the very small editions of dolls released in the last three years—sometimes, fewer than 1,000 dolls. Current releases often sell out very quickly. Now that the Magic Attic dolls are no longer being produced, look for these retired dolls and outfits to increase in price.

Online/Offline Report: For the latest releases of Marie's dolls, either develop a relationship with an authorized doll dealer, or catch Marie's appearances on QVC, where her dolls often sell out during their first appearance on a show. For retired dolls, eBay generally has a good selection with hundreds of dolls available at any time.

Prices and Characteristics: Prices are for dolls MIB or NRFB. Most dolls are traded MIB or NRFB, hence marks on the dolls are not given; however, all Marie Osmond dolls are clearly marked on the vinyl or porcelain. "LE" means "limited edition."

MARIE OSMOND DOLLS

Adora Beau
Internet: $150
Material: bisque
LE 1,000. Male companion to Adora Belle.

Adora Beau, Mouseketeer
Size: 15"   Internet: $250–$250
Material: bisque
LE 300. 2002 Disneyana Mystery Event.

Adora Belle, Holiday 2001
Size: 15"   Date: 2001
                            Internet: $125
Material: vinyl

Adora Belle, Disneyland Hostess, Gondolier
Size: 15"   Date: 2002
                            Internet: $300
Material: vinyl
Exclusive to Disneyland.

Adora Belle, Disneyland Hostess, Haunted Mansion
Size: 15"   Date: 2002
                            Internet: $185–$250
Material: vinyl

Remember Me Rose. *First doll in the Rose series. Limited edition of 20,000. 17.5″ seated, c. 2001. $150, dealer. Courtesy Janice Justis.*

Glinda the Good Witch Tiny Tot. *5″ seated, c. early 2000s. $50, eBay.*

American Classic Rose, Coming Up Roses Series
Size: 12″   Date: 2002
                    Internet: $180–$150
Material: bisque
LE 3,000. The most limited of the Rose series and second in the 12-doll Coming Up Roses Series. 12″ in seated position.

Barbie, Dawn
                    Internet: $300
Material: porcelain
Somewhere in Time series. Poodle skirt, 1950s outfit.

Beauty Bug Ball
Size: 10″   Date: 2000
                    Internet: retail
Material: bisque
For most characters.

Beauty Bug Ball, Miss Quito
Size: 10″   Internet: $225
Material: bisque

LE 7,500. Last character in series; rarer than other dolls.

Beauty Bug Ball
Size: 12″   Date: 1999
                    Internet: $20
Material: vinyl

Cruella DeVille
                    Internet: $250
Material: bisque
LE 500.

Disney Baby Tinker Bell
                    Date: 1997
                    Internet: $160
Material: bisque

Elise
Size: 32″   Internet: $350
Material: bisque
LE 2,500. Somewhere in Time series, gay 90s-type outfit.

Georgette

Date: 2001
Internet: $285

Material: bisque
LE 2,500. Sculpted by Marie's father, George.

Hansel and Gretel

Size: 18″   Date: 1996
Internet: $275

Material: bisque
LE 5,000; also done later as Tiny Tots.

Lolli

Internet: $210

Material: bisque
First in series.

Rachel, Toddler

Size: 20″   Internet: $200
Material: bisque
LE 5,000.

Remember Me Rosebud

Size: 16″   Date: 2001
Internet: $195

Material: bisque
16″ seated; First in the Rose series.

Rudy, Ellis Island Series

Size: 15″   Date: 2002
Internet: $80

Material: bisque
LE 2,500. Second in Ellis Island Series.

Wizard, Tiny Tot

Size: 6″   Date: 2001
Internet: $200

Material: bisque
Final doll released in *Wizard of Oz* Tiny Tot series; hardest to find.

Miniature Dolls

Miniature dolls are dolls sized for dollhouses—generally, in 1/12 scale, which is one inch equals one foot in the real world (so that a 5.5-inch doll is a 5-foot, 6-inch woman). Well-made artist miniature dolls are nearly miraculous—scale is everything, and when a miniature doll is perfectly scaled, the dolls are enchanting and can transport you to a Lilliputian world.

Miniature dolls by some of the best-known miniature doll artists can be very difficult to collect. Often the output of the best-known artists is limited, and you can obtain the dolls only from the artist, at doll shows. The

artists tend to not even have websites and their dolls rarely show up on eBay, if at all.

Although only the dolls of a few very well-known artists are included here, there are many other artists who can be discovered at your local miniatures show—these artists sometimes show their work at general doll shows, but only rarely.

Briefly, Marcia Backstrom is world-known for her fantastic, detailed, original miniature dolls done mostly in resin. Cathy Hansen's work is mostly reproduction, but her miniature French fashion ladies, Brus, and other antique dolls are incomparable. Not all of her work is done to dollhouse scale. Gina Bellous is another artist who has worked for years making miniature porcelain dolls. Her current offerings include celebrity dolls (one-of-a-kind) as well as molds and kits for other dollmakers. Finally, Stephanie Blythe makes dolls of all sizes, but she has done some outstanding small dolls, including fairy dolls.

Market Report: Original miniature dolls from well-known miniature doll artists such as Marcia Backstrom and Gina Bellous will easily cost several hundred dollars. High-quality miniature reproduction dolls from artists such as Cathy Hansen generally cost in the $200 to $300+ range. If you are looking for these dolls on the secondary market, you will have a hard time finding them. Occasionally, they come up for sale on eBay, but in small numbers, rarely more than a half dozen at any time from all artists combined.

Online/Offline Report: Miniature shows are the best place to obtain these dolls directly from the artists. Occasionally, they can also be found from miniature or doll dealers. Private collectors selling collections are often the best source. Online, as mentioned above, the dolls are scarce. Out of the artists listed here, only Gina Bellous and Stephanie Blythe have their own websites with limited offerings directly to collectors.

Prices and Characteristics: All dolls are bisque, in excellent condition, with dolls from Stephanie Blythe being all-bisque. Bodies may be made from various materials, some

*Lisette by Cathy Hansen. 4″.
1998 UFDC National Convention
doll. With original trunk and separately purchased outfit. $350,
dealer.*

*Reproduction Bru by Cathy
Hansen. Bisque head on shoulder
plate, leather body, bisque lower
arms, legs. Unmarked doll, outfit
by Christine Johnson (tag). 8″, c.
2000. $365 original retail.*

*Bru French fashion reproduction
by Cathy Hansen. 8″, bisque head
on shoulder plate, leather body,
bisque lower limbs. Mark: Cathy
Hansen 1999 (in script under
leather on shoulder plate). Outfit
by Christine Johnson (tag). $335 re-
tail.*

have wired armatures. Cathy Hansen dolls listed here are generally from the late 1980s to now; Stephanie Blythe has been making dolls since 1977. Dolls from the other artists are from the past 15 years. For Cathy Hansen UFDC pieces, see the UFDC section.

CATHY HANSEN

All-Bisque, Child, Antique Reproduction
Size: 3.5–5″
Price: $185–$300
With glass or well-painted eyes.

Creole French Fashion Doll
Size: 6″
Price: $325–$400
Dressed; leather body, glass eyes, bisque feet.

Girl and Her Doll
Size: 3.5″
Price: $270

Huret and Wardrobe
Size: 8″
Price: $375
From eBay auction, 2 outfits.

Smiling Bru French Fashion Doll
Size: 8″
Price: $200–$300

Tiny Huret Reproduction
Size: 3″
Price: $200+
Small leather body with bisque feet.

STEPHANIE BLYTHE

Fairy or Mermaid
Size: 4–6″
Price: $500+
For limited editions; one-of-a-kind dolls from this artist sell for much more.

Sewing Box Fairy
Price: $1,000+
Fairy in luxurious small sewing box.

Sweet Peas, Snail Persons, Babes in Woods, or Bee Boys
Size: 2–4″
Price: $400+

OTHER ARTISTS

Viola Williams, Child or Lady
Size: 4–6″
Price: $200+

Jill Nemirow-Nelson, Lady
Size: 5–6″
Price: $150+
Various styles, many humorous.

Marcia Backstrom, Child or Adult
Size: 4–6″
Price: $300–$500+
Very hard to find on the Internet; mostly from shows and private collections.

Michelle Geoffrion-Mahler, Adult or Fairy
Size: 5–6″
Price: $200+

Various pieces by Australian artist Maree Massey. All-bisques, largest piece 5.5", c. 2002. Prices from $55–$300+, retail.

Reproduction Antique Dolls

People have been reproducing antique dolls for nearly as long as people have been collecting them. Some antique doll reproducers are unscrupulous, trying to pass off their reproductions as the real thing, but the majority of reproduction artists are true artists who make their dolls for the love of antique dolls and their artistry. Reproduction dolls fill a real need for collectors, many of whom admire the artistry and the look of the antique dolls, but who cannot afford an original Bru, Jumeau, or German character doll. Also, some collectors of antique dolls enjoy learning how the dolls were created and they enjoy creating their own interpretations of the antiques.

Reproduction Dollmaking as a Hobby: Antique doll reproduction as a hobby was popularized by the late Mildred Seeley, founder of Seeley's (a doll reproduction mold and supply company) and the Doll Artisan Guild (an organization for doll reproduction artists). Seeley's was founded in 1946, and the hobby of doll reproductions took off in the 1970s, gaining popularity in the 1980s and 1990s. As more and more women have less and less time to pursue creative hobbies, there has been some retraction in the popularity of reproduction doll art as a hobby, but

thousands of people still enjoy this hobby worldwide.

Legitimate Reproductions Are Clearly Marked: All legitimate doll reproduction artists clearly incise, into the bisque head or back of the doll, their name or mark and date, so that the reproduction cannot be confused with the original by later purchasers of the doll. The artistry of some of the antique reproduction dollmakers can be astounding, and some of their dolls may be confused with the real thing, so proper marking is quite important.

How to Tell an Antique from a Reproduction: If you are considering buying an antique bisque or china doll and you are concerned that the doll is an unmarked reproduction, you can check several things. First, antique bisque tends to be rougher in feel than newer bisque. When you study antique dolls, feel their cheeks with your fingers and compare that, if possible, with the feel of reproductions. The reproduction cheeks almost always feel glassier and smoother than antique cheeks. Second, check inside the head. There is a different look to the inside of the head of the antiques versus the newer reproductions. If the doll is an all-bisque, look at the stringing—most reproductions are strung with metal loops held in place by plaster, a method that was used only by the latest of the antique all-bisques. Finally, the body on all but intentionally deviously-made reproductions should be a dead giveaway, since modern composition and leather bodies look and feel nothing like the antiques. Of course, a reproduction head can be placed on an older body. Your best way to avoid inadvertently buying a reproduction is to buy from a knowledgeable antique doll dealer whom you trust, and to buy dolls in person so you may examine them. It is often impossible to tell from an Internet photo whether or not a doll is a true antique, so if you buy antique dolls from the Internet, make sure you get a money-back guarantee and/or know the seller.

Market Report: Even with all the caveats in this section, there is a healthy, independent market for beautifully made antique reproduction dolls. As mentioned, some of the reproduction dollmakers making dolls today are true artists, and their dolls are highly sought after by collectors. Many collectors want the look of a Triste Jumeau or a Bébé Bru in their collection, but they cannot afford the several thousand dollars for the "real thing." So these collectors instead add a beautifully made reproduction of that Jumeau or Bru to their collection.

As with purchasing an actual antique doll, look for well-painted features and good-quality, translucent bisque. Stay away from dolls with heavy, opaque bisque. Also look for dolls with properly color-washed skin as opposed to dolls made with pre-tinted bisque. Cheek blush can also give away a poorly made reproduction—is the blush done smoothly, with good blending, or is the blush abrupt at the edges and patchy?

When buying a reproduction of a particular doll, make sure you are familiar with the style and painting of the features on the original. If you are buying a Tête Jumeau reproduction, make sure that the paint colors used are true to the original, that the features are painted to look like the original, and the body used is the proper antique style. Clothing made from antique fabrics is a bonus—at minimum, the clothing style should copy the style of the clothing that the original dolls wore. Expect to pay several hundred dollars for the finest reproduction dolls.

Online/Offline Report: One of my pet peeves is when sellers on eBay *don't* tell you a doll is a reproduction until you click on the auction. This is misleading at best, and slightly fraudulent at worst. Additionally, some eBay sellers are simply not educated enough to know the difference, and will list reproductions as the real thing. With a very good reproduction, it may be impossible to tell that the doll is a reproduction from a blurry eBay photo, or even from a decent eBay photo, so beware.

You can find dealers who specialize in antique reproduction dolls at doll shows—most antique doll dealers do not carry them. You can also find properly listed reproductions easily on eBay and other Internet auction sites, but remember it can be just as hard to judge the quality of a reproduction as an original antique doll from just Internet photos. Only the best reproduction antique dolls bring the prices quoted below.

Prices and Characteristics: All prices are for bisque dolls in excellent condition. These prices are for reproductions that *accurately* reproduce the antique, with clothing appropriate to the time period of the antique. Allow more for clothing made from extra-fine or vintage materials. Prices are mixed from all venues.

REPRODUCTION DOLLS

All-Bisque Reproduction
Size: 4–6"
Price: $150–$250
For dolls with glass eyes, fully jointed, mohair wigs, well dressed.

French Bébé Reproduction
Size: various
Price: $200–$500
For reproductions of Bru, Jumeau, Steiner, and similar French bisque bébé dolls. For dolls with glass eyes, appropriate bodies, mohair or human hair wigs, well dressed.

Tête Jumeau reproduction by author. *Made under the tutelage of Margaret Anne Wolfe, Seeley instructor, from a Seeley mold. 20", c. 1998.*

Kestner XI reproduction by Margaret Anne Wolfe. *14", c. 1990s.*

Reproduction Nippon doll. *5.5". You can tell that it is a reproduction because of large, irregularly shaped holes in feet to drain slip and ultra-smooth bisque, as well as style of painted features. Mark: NIPPON. $20, eBay.*

French Fashion Reproduction

Size: 15–20"
Price: $250–$600
Highest prices for dolls with elaborate outfits from vintage material and trims, with fine hats, well-made leather shoes, and other accessories. Lower price range for nude dolls or dolls in simple outfits. Glass eyes, mohair wigs.

German Bisque Reproduction

Size: various
Price: $200–$400
For dressed reproductions of Kestner, Simon & Halbig, K * R, other character and child dolls. Glass eyes, human hair or mohair wigs.

Bleuette Reproduction

Price: $200–$300
For accurate reproductions, well-dressed.

Garnett, Neva Wade, Jumeau Portrait Fashion

Size: 19"
Price: $250–$350
Beautifully done, mohair wig, gusset-jointed kid body with bisque hands.
Mark: 1981 Calli-Lou. Dolls from Ms. Garnett (author of several books on reproduction doll-making) can sell for several hundred dollars.

Takara

Takara's most famous doll is the Jenny doll. Jenny actually started out as the Japanese Barbie doll, under license from Mattel. Takara used the "Barbie" name on the doll that would become Jenny, but she wasn't much like the American Barbie doll—the Japanese Barbie had a more innocent schoolgirl look. She was flat-chested with large Westernized eyes—much more of an "anime" look overall. This was done on purpose, to create a Barbie doll that would appeal to Japanese children. However, in 1985, Takara lost the rights to use the Barbie name, and their "Barbie" became Jenny. Jenny represents a 17-year-old high school student not from Japan, but from Los Angeles. Jenny is still made today.

Before they produced the Japanese Barbie, Takara produced a fashion doll called Licca. Licca hit the market in 1967 and was supposed to represent a 10-year-old girl, and she was billed as "a little girl's best friend." Licca has an entire family of dolls, as well as her own friends, and has been produced for over 30 years. Licca even starred in her own animated series in Japan, *Super Doll Licca-chan,* in 1998. Licca is also still made today.

Takara has also produced the new releases of the Blythe doll for the Asian market since 2000. For Blythe prices and informa-

School Uniform Jenny. Vinyl.
10.5", late 1990s. $30 NRFB,
dealer.

**FIFA World Cup France gift set,
Jenny and boyfriend Jeff.** Vinyl.
10.5" and 11", 1998. $50 NRFB,
dealer.

tion, see the Blythe section in the Vintage
Dolls chapter.

Market Report: There was more of a
craze, and higher prices, for these dolls five
years ago. As their availability has increased due to international Internet auctions from Asia, prices have definitely
declined. This makes sense, as the general
play-line Jenny and Licca dolls have been
released in very large numbers. However,
there are special collector and limited-edition sets that are harder to find and which
have higher prices. Also, with the popularity of the new Volks dolls, fashion dolls in
general, and other Japanese "look" dolls,
there is the potential for price appreciation
in the future.

Vintage early Licca dolls from the 1960s and
early 1970s are harder to find in the United

States and also on eBay, and also bring
higher prices.

Online/Offline Report: There are several
Internet dealers who deal almost exclusively
in Japanese fashion dolls, and you can also
find the dolls being offered on eBay both
from international and American dealers
and collectors. Specialized dealers will have
the best selection of the vintage Jenny and
Licca dolls. Remember when bidding on
Jenny, Blythe, and Licca from overseas to
note shipping charges, which can be considerable and which may add up to 50% or
more to the price of some dolls.

Prices and Characteristics: All dolls are
vinyl and prices are for NRFB dolls. All
dolls are approximately 10 inches tall. For
Takara Blythe dolls, see the Blythe section in
the Vintage Dolls chapter. The most recent

Ski Fan Jenny. *Vinyl. 10.5", c. 1992. $40 NRFB, dealer.*

Schoolgirl Olive (friend of Jenny). *Vinyl. 10", c. 1990s. $30 NRFB, dealer.*

Jenny and Licca dolls can be found at or below retail.

TAKARA DOLLS

Jenny or Licca
Date: 1990s–2000s
Internet: $30–$70
For most regular-line dolls; more for rarer and earlier models; see examples below.

1st Generation Licca Reproduction
Internet: $70
From Licca Club.

Excelina Barbie
Internet: $175
Excelinas have rare blue eyes.

Jenny Club Friend, Marine
Date: 1986
Internet: $165
Rarer Jenny Club friend.

Jenny Club Friends
Date: 1986
Internet: $50–$70
Flora, Julia, others.

Jenny Trendy
Date: 1986
Internet: $70

Jenny, Friend, Schoolgirl, Olive
All Markets: $30

Jenny, Yves St. Laurent
Date: 1986
Internet: $75–$90

Macko-Chan, Friend of Licca
Date: 1970
Internet: $500+
Rare vintage Takara doll.

Takara Barbie in Kimono
Date: early 1980s
Internet: $55–$75

Tonner Doll Company, Inc.

The Tonner Doll Company is one of the pre-eminent doll companies designing and producing dolls in the world today. Robert Tonner, the company founder and the artistic force behind the company, started the company in 1991 (as The Robert Tonner Doll Design, then Robert Tonner Doll Company, and Tonner Doll Company, Inc., since 2001). Tonner started his career by studying fashion at the Parsons School of Design in New York, and he was later a head designer for Bill Blass. After beginning a doll collection in 1979, he first attempted doll sculpting in 1981 and the rest, as they say, is history.

Known for his fashion dolls and children's dolls alike, Tonner's first big success was with the 19-inch vinyl American Model dolls in 1994, a doll that was a forerunner and a foreshadowing of the 16-inch fashion doll craze which was opened up by Gene from Ashton Drake in 1995. His first highly successful child doll was the Magic Attic doll, an 18-inch vinyl play doll with a line of books, first done for Georgetown Dolls in 1995 (then by Knickerbocker, and then by Marian, LLC).

Well-known dolls then came fast and furiously from the fertile mind of this doll designer: a newly sculpted 14-inch Betsy McCall doll in 1996, then the Tyler Wentworth fashion doll and Mary Engelbreit's Ann Estelle in 1999, Kitty Collier and Tiny Betsy McCall in 2000, and many more dolls since. In 2003, the Tonner Doll Company purchased the assets of the bankrupt Effanbee Doll Company, and they now produce Effanbee dolls as well (see the Effanbee section in this chapter for more information).

Market Report: Although affected by the general market weaknesses caused by the economy and the Internet doll deluge, Robert Tonner Dolls are very hot and sought after by collectors. Look for prices on individual Tyler Wentworth releases to increase as more and more original dolls are repainted by repaint artists, and as original dressed dolls are resold on the secondary market in parts—nude dolls to repaint artists and their outfits to collectors. Very limited editions of Tonner Doll Company dolls done for UFDC, Collectors United, and other organizations and special events are especially sought after today, and dolls that quickly sell out include Sydney Chase dolls (a character in the Tyler Wentworth line) and Tiny Kitty dolls (a small 10-inch version of the 18-inch Kitty Collier).

Online/Offline Report: You can find some real bargains on retired dolls on eBay right now, but your best bet to obtain the hot and hard-to-get current releases is to establish a good relationship with one of the company's authorized retailers.

Prices and Characteristics; Marks: All dolls are made of hard vinyl except as noted, generally with rooted hair. Marks generally:

TONNER on head; ©1999 /ROBERT TONNER/DOLL CO. INC. on back torso or ROBERT TONNER / DOLL CO. INC. (head) and ©1999 /ROBERT TONNER/ DOLL CO. INC. (back). All prices are for dolls MIB or NRFB; prices will be slightly higher for NRFB dolls. "LE" means "limited edition."

ROBERT TONNER DOLLS

American Model, Bailey
Size: 19″   Date: 1998
                             Internet: $125
LE 500.

American Model, Collette
Size: 19″   Date: 1997
                             Internet: $225
There are more than 25 dolls in the American Model series, plus separate outfits and additional special-event issues. Most are a limited edition of 500.

American Model, Daphne
Size: 19″   Date: 1998
                             Internet: $125
LE 500.

American Model, Deborah
Size: 19″   Date: 1996
                             Internet: $440
LE 50, for Doll and Teddy Bear Expo East.

American Model, Eric
Size: 20″   Date: 1999
                             Internet: $280
LE 500.

American Model, Gillian, Bride
Size: 19″   Date: 1995
                             Internet: $160
LE 500. Tonner's first bride doll.

American Model, Michelle
                             Date: 1997
                             Internet: $425
LE 100. A special edition for the 1997 Doll and Teddy Expo West.

American Model, Paige
Size: 19″   Date: 1995
                             Internet: $160
LE 500.

American Model, Regina
Size: 19″   Date: 1999
                             Internet: $175
LE 500.

Tyler Wentworth Signature Style.
*First Tyler Wentworth doll, also
available as brunette and redhead.
The early Tyler Wentworth dolls
were jointed only at the neck, hips,
knees, and shoulders. The dolls
have gained more articulation over
the years, and some of the latest
models even have jointed upper
ribcages and wrists. These early
dolls also had paler skin and simpler and lighter makeup than later
models. This doll is a "Second
Generation" of the Signature series, with darker coral lips. 16.5", c.
1999. $80, dealer.*

Debut Sydney Chase. *First regular-line Sydney Chase doll. 16.5", c.
2001. $525, eBay. Courtesy Tonner
Doll Company, Inc.; photograph
supplied by Storm Photo,
Kingston, NY.*

Ava Gardner

Size: 14″   Date: 2002
                      Internet: $415
Bisque doll, LE 260, UFDC Region 8 Conference 2002.

Betsy McCall

Size: 14″   Date: 1996–2003
                      Internet: $80–$100
For harder-to-find and special-event dolls; less
for most regular-line dolls.

Betsy McCall, Betsy Loves Bunnies

Size: 7.5″   Date: 2003
                      Internet: $200–$250

Betsy McCall, Favorite Teddy

Size: 7.5″   Date: 2001
                      Internet: $260
LE 500, Epcot Teddy Bear and Doll Weekend
2001.

Betsy McCall, Just Peachy Gift Set

Size: 7.5″   Date: 2002
                      Internet: $275
For Collectors United 2002.

Cloudland Genevieve, by Shelley Thornton

Size: 24″   Date: 2002
All Markets: $140–$200
Quality play line of dolls by renowned cloth doll
artist.

Edith Head, Carole in Gable & Lombard

Size: 17″   Date: 1998
                      Internet: $110
Bisque.

Edith Head, Jane in *This Way, Please*

Size: 17″   Date: 1998
                      Internet: $75
Bisque.

Angelina, C'est Si Bon Masquerade for UFDC 2003 Tonner Dinner at National Convention in New Orleans. Vinyl, 16.5". Limited edition of 400. $250 NRFB, eBay.

Tyler Wentworth, Precious Metal. Vinyl, 16.5", c. 2001. Limited edition of 2,000. $135 MIB, dealer.

RTW (Ready-To-Wear) Sydney Chase. Shown in the tube packaging for Tonner RTW dolls, 2003–2004. Vinyl. 16". $80, eBay.

Edith Head, Lady Lou in *She Done Him Wrong*

Size: 17"

Date: 1998

Internet: $75

Bisque. Resembles Mae West.

Linda McCall, Travel Time

Size: 10"   Internet: $150

Merilee

Size: 16"

Date: 1977

Internet: $100

Very early Tonner child doll. LE 500; Christmas doll.

Rose, *Titanic,* Rose Boards the Titanic

Size: 18"   Date: 1998

All Markets: $600

FAO Schwarz exclusive.

Rose, *Titanic,* Rose's Evening With Jack

Size: 18"   Date: 1998

All Markets: $600

FAO Schwarz exclusive.

Sophie, Caroling Girl (Mary Engelbreit)

Size: 10"

Date: 2002

Internet: $150–$180

LE 1,000. Sophie is a Mary Engelbreit character.

Tinker Bell

Size: 7.5"

Date: early 1990s

Internet: $250

LE 250; bisque.

ROBERT TONNER, TYLER WENTWORTH COLLECTION

All Tyler Wentworth dolls are 16 inches; male dolls are slightly taller. They are made of hard vinyl, and have various jointing, with later dolls tending to have more jointing than earlier dolls. Features are painted and hair is rooted. Many Tyler Wentworth dolls are still available from retailers at retail prices except for event dolls, very limited dolls, and many of the Sydney Chase dolls and the now-retired Mei Li.

Angelina, C'est Si Bon Masquerade

Date: 2003

Internet: $175–$300

First Hispanic doll in Tyler Wentworth collection.

Esme

Date: 2002

Internet: $40–$45

Basic doll, in lingerie; sold in a tube. Knees bend, but not elbows. First Esme Ready-to-Wear (RTW) doll.

Esme, Wild Orchard

Date: 2002

Internet: $140

LE 1,500.

Mei Li, First Appointment

Date: 2001

Internet: $100

LE 1,000.

Betsy McCall as Wendy from Peter Pan. Vinyl. 14″, c. 2002. Limited edition of 500. $100, dealer.

Sophie, Caroling Girl. From Mary Engelbreit series. 10″, c. 2002. $200 NRFB, eBay.

Mei Li, Embassy Dinner
> Date: 2002
> Internet: $130–$145

Mei Li, RTW
> Date: 2002
> Internet: $100

Sold in a tube. Knees bend, but not elbows.

Sydney Chase, Debut
> Date: 2001
> Internet: $525

First regular-line Sydney Chase released.

Sydney Chase, Focus on Fashion
> Date: 2001
> Internet: $400

LE 500. Exclusive for UFDC's Starry, Starry Night Convention in Atlanta, Georgia, 2001. For more UFDC Tonner dolls, see UFDC Section, below.

Sydney Chase, Mover & Shaker
> Date: 2002
> Internet: $150

LE 1,500.

Sydney Chase, Night at the Opera
> Date: 2003
> Internet: $400

Limited edition for Collector's United.

Sydney Chase, RTW, Satin
> Date: 2004
> Internet: $130–$170

Sydney Chase, Sheer Glamour
> Date: 2002
> Internet: $285–$350

LE 2,000.

Sydney, Black and White Ball
> Date: 2002
> Internet: $450

Sandy McCall as Peter Pan.
*Vinyl. 14", c. 2002. Limited edition
of 500. $100, dealer.*

Linda McCall as Tinker Bell.
*Vinyl. 10", c. 2002. Limited edition
of 500 $65, eBay.*

Sydney, RTW
Date: 2002
Internet: $75–$110
Basic doll, in white lingerie; sold in a tube.
Knees bend, but not elbows.

Sydney, RTW Elegance
Date: 2003
Internet: $150–$200
Jean's Dolls exclusive.

Tyler Wentworth, Champagne & Caviar
Date: 2001
Internet: $120–$150

Tyler Wentworth, Blush
Date: 2003
Internet: $225–$300
LE 300. Theatre de la Mode, 2003 Paris Convention.

Tyler Wentworth, Fleurs de Mal
Date: 2001
Internet: $135
LE 3,000. Theatre de la Mode.

Tyler Wentworth, Florentine
Date: 2002
Internet: $100–$130
LE 1,500.

Tyler Wentworth, Framboise Robe du Grande Soir
Date: 2001
Internet: $150
LE 3,000. Theatre de la Mode.

Tyler Wentworth, Glamour RTW
Date: 2003
Internet: $50
Basic doll, in black lingerie; pale blonde hair in
upswept hairdo. Sold in a tube. Knees and el-
bows bend.

Tyler Wentworth, Hope
Date: 2002
Internet: $270–$420
LE 500; exclusive for Rosalie Whyel Museum of
Doll Art to benefit Teen Hope (Victorian).

Tyler Wentworth, Look of Luxe
Date: 2001
Internet: $225–$325
LE 2,000.

Tyler Wentworth, Masquerade
Date: 2001
Internet: $125–$200
LE 325, Modern Doll Collectors Convention
2001.

Tyler Wentworth, Midnight Garden
Date: 2001
Internet: $120–$150

Tyler Wentworth, Outfit, Market Week
Date: 2000
Internet: $125
LE 1,000, outfit for 2000 Toy Fair Event.

Tyler Wentworth, Outfit, Prêt a Porter
Date: 2001
Internet: $90
LE 500, outfit for 2001 Toy Fair Event.

Kitty Collier, My Blue Heaven.
Vinyl. 18", c. 2001. $150 retail.

Emme Elegance. Vinyl, in likeness
of the large-size fashion model
Emme. 16.5", c. 2002. $99 retail.

Tyler Wentworth, Opera Gala.
Jointed at neck, shoulders, hips,
and knees. Limited edition of
3,000. 16.5", c. 2000. $169 issue
price.

Tyler Wentworth, Outfit, Cosmetics Campaign
Date: 2002
Internet: $90
LE 550, outfit for 2002 Toy Fair Event.

Tyler Wentworth, Outfit, Sketchbook Savvy
Date: 2003
Internet: $75
LE 750, outfit for 2003 Toy Fair Event.

Tyler Wentworth, Palm Beach Nights
Date: 2000
Internet: $150
LE 500. 2000 Walt Disney World Bear and Doll
Convention.

Tyler Wentworth, Papillion
Date: 2002
Internet: $120–$155
LE 1,500.

Tyler Wentworth, Queen of Hearts
Date: 2002
Internet: $150
LE 300. Collector's United, Nashville.

Tyler Wentworth, Reflet D'Argent
Date: 2002
Internet: $150
LE 3,000. Theatre de la Mode.

Tyler Wentworth, RTW Career
Date: 2003
Internet: $50
Basic doll, in lingerie; short cropped red hair,
sold in a tube. Knees and elbows bend.

Tyler Wentworth, RTW Fall
Date: 2002
Internet: $50
Basic doll, in lingerie; long brown hair. Sold in a
tube. Knees bend, not elbows.

Tyler Wentworth, RTW Sport
Date: 2003
Internet: $55–$70
Basic doll, in sporty lingerie; blondish/brown
curls. Sold in a tube. Knees and elbows bend.

Tyler Wentworth, RTW Spring
Date: 2002
Internet: $90–$105
Basic doll, in lingerie; curly light brown hair.
Sold in a tube. Knees bend, not elbows.

Tyler Wentworth, RTW Summer
Date: 2002
Internet: $60
Basic doll, in lingerie; long honey blonde hair.
Sold in a tube. Knees bend, not elbows.

Tyler Wentworth, RTW Winter
Date: 2002
Internet: $90
Basic doll, in lingerie; black hair in ponytail.
Sold in a tube. Knees bend, not elbows.

Tyler Wentworth, Very Valentine
Date: 2004
Internet: $250
LE 500 for AIDS benefit, Toy Fair 2004.

Tyler Wentworth, Vienna Waltz
Date: 2001
Internet: $375

Katrena by Wendy Lawton. *8″ Convention Doll for 53rd UFDC National Convention, Denver, Colorado, 2002. $250+, dealer.*

Just Me reproduction by Vogue. *All bisque. 10″, Convention Doll, 2003 Modesto Regional 2N Convention 2002. Limited edition of 280. Mark: VOGUE DOLLS® / Just ME® / #196 / 280.*

At Home in a Shoe by Rosemary Snyder. *Dolls are porcelain and cloth. 2.5″ high, 5″ long. For 2002 UFDC National Convention luncheon.*

LE 350. Collector's United Exclusive, 2001, Nashville.

Tyler Wentworth, Weekend in DC Gift Set
> Date: 2001
> Internet: $225

Tyler Wentworth, White House Dinner
> Date: 2000
> Internet: $150–$200

Smaller number than planned edition were produced due to production problems (650 produced).

UFDC Dolls

An entire collection could be based on the dolls produced for the UFDC, the United Federation of Doll Clubs. Through the years, the UFDC has had special limited-edition dolls produced as convention favors and luncheon and dinner favors for events held at conventions. They also have limited-edition dolls produced as companion pieces and for fund-raising for the organization. The dolls produced for the UFDC are from a virtual who's who of the modern doll world, and include dolls from Madame Alexander, Robert Tonner, Vogue, Helen Kish, Wendy Lawton, R. John Wright, Käthe Kruse, and many others. Most of the dolls are produced in very limited editions, ranging from fewer than 100 up to 2,000 or so dolls for National Convention favors.

The UFDC was created in 1949, and today has over 700 member clubs from 17 countries. A nonprofit corporation, the UFDC exists to stimulate and maintain an interest in all matters regarding doll collecting, and they aid in historical preservation, research, and exhibition of dolls. For more information on the UFDC, visit www.ufdc.org.

Market Report: Many UFDC members treasure these dolls as mementos from their UFDC conventions and events, and therefore fewer of these dolls are offered for sale than similar dolls. Earlier UFDC dolls can be especially hard to find. The market for these dolls is very strong, with some collectors starting to base collections on them, and with collectors of various modern categories of dolls often needing these dolls to complete a collection of, say, Tyler Wentworth or Cissy dolls.

Online/Offline Report: UFDC dolls are relatively rare on eBay, with maybe 10 to 30 dolls up for auction at any one time. Prices from dealers may be a bit higher, but the few dealers who specialize in UFDC dolls and merchandise will have a much wider selection than either eBay or other online sources can provide.

Prices and Characteristics: All prices are for dolls MIB. "LE" means "limited edition."

Girl by R. John Wright. Doll is all felt, has candy box container in middle (doll pulls apart at waist to reveal container). Limited edition of 1,600, Convention Doll for 54th UFDC National Convention, New Orleans, 2003. $400–$500, eBay.

Crib Crowd by Vogue. For UFDC New Orleans National Convention luncheon, 2003. 8". $160, eBay.

UFDC DOLLS, BY MANUFACTURER

Cathy Hansen, Lisette
Size: 4"   Date: 1998
All Markets: $285–$325
Material: all-bisque

Cathy Hansen, Lisette with Trusseau
Size: 4"   Date: 1998
     Internet: $470
Material: all-bisque
Souvenir of 1988 New Orleans National Convention, with limited edition wardrobe and accoutrements.

Cathy Hansen, Marie Louisette
Size: 3.5"   Date: 1989
     Internet: $325
Material: all-bisque

Ginny, Crib Crowd Bunny
Size: 8"   Date: 2003
     Internet: $230–$270
Material: vinyl
LE of 275 for Vogue New Orleans National Convention luncheon.

Kish, Helen, Riley
Size: 7.5"   Date: 2003
     Internet: $200–$350
Material: vinyl
LE of 500 for 2003 New Orleans National Convention.

Lawton, Wendy, Claire Jolie, with Wardrobe
Size: 7"   Date: 2003
     Internet: $875–$1,000
Material: bisque
LE of 300 for New Orleans National Convention Lawton dinner, Moonlight and Magnolias.

Mary Hoyer, pair of dolls

Size: 14″   Date: 1999
                             Internet: $150
Material: hard plastic
Set of male and female. LE of 200 for 1999
UFDC luncheon, price for 1 of pair.

The Virginia Atelier, All-Bisque Lady

Size: 6″   Date: 1966
All Markets: $95
Material: all-bisque
Souvenir of Richmond UFDC Regional Confer-
ence.

Tonner, Robert, Ava Gardner

Size: 14″   Date: 2002
                             Internet: $415
Material: bisque
LE 260. Souvenir for Region 8 Conference 2002.

Tonner, Robert, Betsy McCall, Ready to Travel (1st)

Size: 8″   Date: 2000
                             Internet: $325
Material: hard vinyl
LE 500. First ever issued, Betsy Visits the Windy
City meal souvenir, National Convention,
Chicago 2000.

Tonner, Robert, Sean, C'est Si Bon Masquerade

Size: 18″   Date: 2003
                             Internet: $500
Material: hard vinyl
LE 300. C'est Si Bon Masquerade Companion
doll to Angelina; UFDC Tonner dinner 2003,
New Orleans. This face mold will not be pro-
duced again.

Tonner, Robert, Sydney Chase, Focus on Fashion

Size: 16″   Date: 2001
                             Internet: $400–$450
Material: hard vinyl
LE of 500 for Atlanta National Convention din-
ner.

Tonner, Robert, Tyler Wentworth, C'est La Fete

Size: 16″   Date: 2002
                             Internet: $225
Material: hard vinyl
Limited edition for Denver National Conven-
tion dinner.

Tonner, Robert, Tyler Wentworth, Chicago So-phisticate

Size: 16″   Date: 2000
                             Internet: $240–$275

Material: hard vinyl
LE of 500 for Fin du Millenaire Chicago Convention.

Wright, R. John, Musette

Size: 12″   Date: 2003
                             Internet: $400–$450
Material: cloth, felt
LE 1,600. New Orleans 2003 National Conven-
tion Souvenir.

Wright, R. John, Peppermint Scootles

Size: 6″   Date: 2003
                             Internet: $400
Material: cloth
LE of 300 for New Orleans National Conven-
tion luncheon.

Wright, R. John, Scout & Theo

Size: 15″, 9″   Date: 2002
                             Internet: $2,400
Material: cloth
LE of 100 for UFDC Denver luncheon 2002.

Wakeen, Susan

Susan Wakeen is a well-known American
doll artist, and was the co-owner (with her
husband) of Susan Wakeen Dolls. All dolls
from the Susan Wakeen doll company were
sculpted by Ms. Wakeen, who made dolls
from 1985 to 2005. Ms. Wakeen is especially
known for her baby doll sculpts, and she has
won numerous industry awards. Susan Wakeen Dolls produced baby dolls in both small
editions (750 to 1,250 dolls, the Signature
Collection) as well as a larger lines of dolls
produced for children and collectors (such as
the Mommy Loves Me babies). Susan also
has an 8-inch line of dolls with themes such
as Days of the Week and Storybook. Finally,
Susan Wakeen Dolls also made a 15.5-inch
fashion doll named Eve.

Market Report: The market for Susan Wakeen dolls is still young, with Susan Wakeen
dolls on the market for only about 10 years.
So far there is only minimal secondary market action.

Online/Offline Report: Pricing is at or near
retail for most venues.

***Millennium Eve by Susan Wakeen,** wearing Tyler Wentworth's Fashion Design Weekly Award outfit. Vinyl. 16", c. 2000. Doll MIB in original gray evening gown. $40, eBay.*

Prices and Characteristics: Susan Wakeen dolls are made from high-quality vinyl. Most Susan Wakeen dolls can still be found at retail prices.

R. John Wright Dolls

R. John Wright has been making cloth dolls since 1976 in his workshop in upstate New York with his wife, Susan. His dolls are legendary among collectors, and they have included such well-loved characters as Winnie the Pooh (and most of the other characters from the Hundred Acre Wood), Paddington Bear, Kewpie, The Little Prince, and many others. The dolls are still completely made at the New York workshop, and they are generally created in small editions ranging from several hundred up to 2,000 pieces. R. John Wright dolls appeal to doll collectors, teddy bear collectors, and art collectors alike.

Market Report: The market for R. John Wright dolls is very strong, with high worldwide demand for the editions produced. The dolls tend to maintain their value on the secondary market, and most dolls change hands through private collectors or through doll dealers.

Online/Offline Report: R. John Wright dolls are somewhat hard to find on eBay, with usually only a page or so of his dolls on sale at any time. The earlier dolls are hardest to find, and prices on eBay can be very strong for smaller-edition dolls in all categories—for instance, a Gepetto and Pinocchio II Traditional from 1995 recently sold for over $2,500.

Prices, Characteristics and Marks: R. John Wright dolls are made of wool felt, with molded faces. Most of the current releases are available at retail from authorized R. John Wright dealers. Marks: Dolls are tagged, for example: R. John Wright Dolls, Inc. / Christopher Robin / Series II / No. 041500 / Walt Disney Company (clothing tag). Prices for dolls MIB; also see the section in this chapter on UFDC dolls. "LE" means "limited edition."

R. JOHN WRIGHT DOLLS

Children, Various
Size: various   Internet: $600–$1,000
Rarer dolls more.

Bedtime Christopher Robin and Pooh
Size: 17.5"   Date: 1999
                  Internet: $1,350
LE 500; Pooh is 7.5".

Christopher Robin II
Size: 18"
Price: $850

Rosemary & Timothy. *All felt, hand painted; fully jointed. 17". Limited edition of 1,000. Courtesy R. John Wright Dolls, Inc.*

Fleur. *All felt, hand painted, fully jointed. 6", c. 1999. Limited edition of 250. Courtesy R. John Wright Dolls, Inc.*

Alice in Wonderland. *All felt, hand painted, fully jointed. 17", c. 2004. Limited edition of 750. Courtesy R. John Wright Dolls, Inc.*

Raggedy Ann. *All felt, hand painted, fully jointed. 17", c. 2004. Limited edition of 1,000. Courtesy R. John Wright Dolls, Inc. © Simon & Schuster, Inc. Licensed by UNITED MEDIA. Raggedy Ann and Andy and associated characters are trademarks of Simon & Schuster.*

Gepetto
Size: 18"
Date: 1996
Internet: $1,150
LE 250.

Gepetto and Pinocchio
Size: 17"
Date: 1994–1995
Internet: $2,100
Pinocchio is 10".

Gepetto and Pinocchio II
Size: 18", 9"
Date: 1995
Internet: $2,550
LE 500. Includes limited edition chair.

Heidi and Snowflake
Date: 2000
Internet: $1,500
Snowflake is a goat.

King Christopher Robin
Size: 12"
Date: 1998
Internet: $3,500
LE 50. With toy soldiers.

Lillian
Size: 17"
Price: $850
Date: 1983
LE 250. Little Children Series 1.

Lindsay
Size: 16"
Price: $750

Little Bo Peep
Size: 17″
                    Internet: $1,750
LE 100; doll shop exclusive.

Little Miss Muffet
Size: 17″   Date: 1992–1993
                    Internet: $900–$1,000
LE 100 for Dee's House of Dolls.

Michael
Size: 16″
Price: $850

Peter
Size: 17″   Date: 1983
Price: $750
LE 250. Little Children Series 1.

Snow White and Seven Dwarfs
Size: various   Date: early 1990s
Price: $4,000+

St. Nicholas
Size: 18″   Date: 1979–1981
                    Internet: $1,200
LE 250.

The Little Prince
                    Date: 1985
                    Internet: $1,200
LE 250. Exclusive for The Toy Shoppe.

William, Series I
Price: $1,200

APPENDIX I: DOLL-COLLECTING TERMS AND DEFINITIONS

For definitions of various doll conditions (MIB, excellent, fair, etc.), please see the introduction to this book.

All-bisque: Doll, usually quite small (under eight inches) that is made entirely of bisque parts. Most all-bisque dolls are from the late 1800s and early 1900s, to about 1930.

Applied ears: Applied to a doll after the mold for the head has been poured. The ears are molded separately, then applied to the doll's head before the head is put in the kiln.

Ball jointed: Common method of jointing composition bodies; uses little wood "balls" at joints for movement.

Basic doll: Fashion or other doll that is sold dressed in a swimsuit or lingerie. The new owner can then dress the doll in separately purchased outfits, or sew an outfit for the doll. See also Dressed Doll.

Bébé: Term commonly used to describe French dolls representing small children.

Belton: Sometimes used to describe early German bisque dolls with a solid dome bisque head with two or three holes in the pate for stringing. The dolls are unknown as to maker.

Bent-limb baby body: Generally a composition body for antique dolls jointed at the shoulders and hips, with arms bent at the elbows and legs bent at the knees. Intended to sit, not stand.

Bisque: Unglazed porcelain that is usually molded into shape, then fired at high temperatures in a kiln to form doll heads and doll body parts. Most German and French dolls from the late 1800s and very early 1900s had heads made of bisque.

BLW: Bent-limb walker, especially used to describe eight-inch 1950s dolls like Ginny and Alexander-kins.

Book value: The value of your doll in a price guide such as this one, but not the value you can expect when you sell your doll to a dealer (expect, generally, 40% to 60% of "book value" in such a sale).

Breveté: The French word for "patented." Sometimes abbreviated to Bte. or B.T.E.; can be found stamped on antique dolls.

CE: Collector's edition.

Celluloid: The first plastic used to make dolls; highly flammable and usually quite thin. Used for dollmaking from the late 1800s thorough approximately the 1940s (generally until hard-plastic dolls were introduced).

Character doll: Doll made to look like a living child or adult (and not stylized like most earlier dolls from the 1800s); these dolls were popular from approximately 1910.

China: Glazed porcelain used for making dolls' heads, very popular in the mid-1800s.

Clone: Doll made by another doll manufacturer, and usually sold at a lower price, to "copy" and take advantage of part of the market created by a popular doll. For instance, there were many Ginny clones in the 1950s, and Barbie clones in the 1960s, and there are American Girl doll clones today.

Closed-mouth doll: Doll sculpted so that the mouth is closed with no teeth showing. Prized by collectors of bisque antique dolls, who prefer the closed-mouth dolls to the open-mouth dolls.

Collectible Barbie: Barbie doll made for adult collectors of fashion dolls, as opposed to play "pink-box" Barbie dolls.

Composition: A mixture of wood pulp, sawdust, glue, and similar items that is used to make bodies for antique dolls and for entire dolls (head and body) during the twentieth century until the advent of hard plastic dolls.

Composition body: Common-style body for antique dolls, made of composition parts and often wood ball joints or other wood parts as well.

Conservation: Treatment of something that has already happened to a doll to stop the problems (i.e., stringing a doll, treating an insect infestation, resetting eyes that have fallen out, stopping further melting of silks, etc.).

Crazing: Little crisscross cracks that sometimes form, with age, over the surface of a composition or china doll. Most composition dolls found today have some crazing.

Deboxing: Taking collectible fashion dolls (especially Barbie!) out of their boxes, which is not normally done for fear that the dolls will lose most of their value.

DEP: Often found on French and German dolls; an abbreviation for the French and German words for "patent."

Dollhouse doll: Doll generally scaled one inch to one foot for use in dollhouses (although antique dollhouse dolls do not hold to these proportions and are generally larger).

Dolly-faced: Term used for late 1800s and early 1900s bisque dolls representing an idealized version of a doll; not as realistic as portrait-faced or character dolls (see below).

Dome head: Doll head that is made with a closed, or domed, top (as opposed to an open head); may have sculpted or painted hair.

Dressed doll: Fashion doll that is available predressed in a complete outfit, as opposed to a basic doll (see above), which is dressed in a swimsuit or lingerie, ready for the owner to dress.

Flange neck: A doll head where the edge of the neck flares out for attachment to a cloth doll body.

Fashion doll: Doll with a lady-type body, usually made with additional wardrobe clothing available.

Flirty eyes: Doll eyes that can move from side to side.

Fully jointed composition body: Generally, an antique doll body with jointing at the shoulders, elbows, hips, and knees. May or may not have jointing at wrists (many earlier French and German dolls do not have jointing at the wrists).

GES: Abbreviation for "Gesch," which is the German word for "patent."

Googly eyes: Big, round, side-glancing eyes, very popular on dolls from the 1910s through the 1920s.

Green ear: A condition that occurs in early 1960s vintage Barbies—the metal in the earrings that came with the dolls oxidizes and turns the ears "green."

Gusset joint: Type of joint sewn into leather and cloth bodies that can allow the joint to bend.

Hairline: Type of crack in bisque dolls that can often be seen only upon close examination, usually with the assistance of a light. Hairlines *can* also be seen with the naked eye; not considered as bad a flaw as a crack that has been repaired or one that has bisque missing.

Hard plastic: Type of durable, very hard plastic used to make dolls in the 1940s and 1950s.

HTF: Hard to find.

Intaglio eyes: Eyes that are molded into the head and are meant to be painted.

Inset eyes: Eyes that are set into the doll's head that do not move (generally glass); common setting for eyes in dolls from the 1800s and earlier and for large-size modern fashion and artist dolls.

Incised: Marks that are "incised" are actually scratched into the bisque on a doll's head or shoulder plate.

Kid: Common term for soft leather used to make French and German fashion doll bodies.

LE: Limited edition.

Limited-edition doll: Any doll with a limited number of dolls produced. Can range from ten to many thousands of dolls. Limited-edition dolls are often marked with their numbers of production; for example, "542/2000" (#542 out of 2,000 dolls produced in that edition).

Market value: As opposed to the book value (see above), this is the actual price you can expect your doll to sell for. This book has attempted to close the gap between market and book values.

Mark or markings: Letters and numbers and symbols placed by the manufacturer of a doll on the doll's head or body, which are invaluable for identifying dolls today. It is often impossible to identify an antique or vintage doll without a mark.

MIP: Mint in package; generally used when the packaging is not a traditional doll box.

MOC: Mint on card; generally used for items sold packaged with plastic blister packaging or for items shrink-wrapped to a card.

Mohair: Hair of the angora goat, used for antique doll wigs. Very desirable; very soft and natural-looking wigs are made of mohair.

Molded ears: Ears that are molded right in with the doll's head, as opposed to applied ears (see above).

Mold number: See "mark." The mold number designates the mold that was used to make the doll's head and can be an invaluable part of the markings for doll identification.

OOAK: One of a kind.

Open/closed mouth: Mouth molded to appear open, but which does not actually have an opening in the bisque.

Open head: Doll head with the crown cut out so that eyes can be inserted. The crown opening is usually covered with a "pate" so that the wig can be put on the doll.

Open mouth: Generally, a mouth molded open to reveal teeth inside. Can also reveal tongues on bisque baby dolls.

Parian doll: Doll made of unglazed bisque that is also finished without a wash of color; generally bisque appears pure white.

Pate: Covers the crown hole in an open-head doll; can be made of cardboard, cork, plaster, or other materials.

Portrait doll: Term used for late 1800s and early 1900s bisque dolls representing people, generally with more in-depth modeling than dolly-faced dolls.

Poupée: Term used for antique French fashion dolls; also means "doll" in French.

Preservation: Protection of a doll from destructive forces—heat, light, insects, dust, and dirt.

Presentation box: Original presentation of antique dolls, doll furniture, clothing, and accessories (sometimes in combination), as found in the original retail stores.

Provenance: An antique doll with a genuine provenance is hard to find; a provenance usually consists of historical information regarding the original and subsequent owners of the doll.

Reproduction: Doll made to look like antique bisque, china, or parian dolls. These are not fakes, since most reproduction artists are meticulous about marking their dolls as reproductions. The term can also apply to rereleases of earlier dolls by modern doll companies.

Restoration: The fixing of a problem or "improvement" of a doll; may include the adding of new components to a doll (new wig, replaced dress, repaired finger, new paint).

Retail price: When modern dolls are currently in production and being shipped, you can get them from dealers or at toy stores for the "retail" price (suggested by manufacturer).

Secondary market: Once a modern doll is no longer available at the retail level, this is the only place you can obtain the doll. Doll shows, collector-to-collector sales, dealers, doll shops specializing in vintage and antique dolls, and on-line and bricks-and-mortar auction houses comprise the secondary market.

Series: Set of modern Barbies or other fashion dolls produced along a theme, usually released once per year; for example, the Happy Holidays Barbie series, which ran from 1988 to 1998.

Shelf wear: Condition afflicting in-box dolls after years of sitting on a store shelf or going to shows; usually evidenced by small creases, box rubs in various spots, etc.

Shoulder-head: A doll with the head and shoulders molded together in one piece; usually attached to a kid or cloth body.

Shoulder plate: The shoulder portion of a shoulder-head, or the bisque shoulders used with a swivel head.

Sleep eyes: Dolls' eyes that are open when the doll is upright, but closed when the doll is put prone.

SLW: Straight-leg walker; especially used to describe eight-inch 1950s dolls like Ginny and Alexander-kins.

Socket head: A doll's head that is molded with a neck that is placed into the doll's body with a cup-and-saucer-like arrangement so that the doll's head can turn—the most common type of doll head, used in antique composition doll bodies and modern five-piece composition, hard plastic, and vinyl bodies.

SS: Abbreviation for "swimsuit"; especially used when discussing vintage Barbie dolls.

Strung: Strung with elastic to hold a doll's limbs together.

Swivel head: A socket head using a separate shoulder plate.

Titian: Red hair, often used to describe red Barbie doll hair.

UFDC: United Federation of Doll Clubs.

Toddler body: Generally a composition body for antique dolls that is jointed at the hips and shoulders; unlike a bent-limb baby body (see above), the body is made to stand, with side-hip jointing for the legs.

Vinyl: Plastic developed in the late 1940s that has become the dominant type of plastic used to make dolls since the 1960s; can be hard or soft.

APPENDIX II: RESOURCES

KEY DOLL RESOURCES
Official Price Guide To Dolls.com
www.officialpriceguidetodolls.com
The website for this book—sign up for our Official Price Guide Newsletter, which will keep you up-to-date on price updates, doll news, and new editions of this book. Also you can purchase additional, autographed copies of this book at this site. You'll also find new and updated Web links—it is your key to this book and to the Internet world of dolls.

Doll Collecting at About.com
www.collectdolls.about.com
With guide Denise Van Patten (author of this book). Largest information-only website on dolls in the world.

Theriault's
www.theriaults.com
World-famous auction house for dolls; contributor of over 300 photos for this book.
PO Box 151
Annapolis, MD 21404
Tel: 410-224-3655

UFDC (United Federation of Doll Clubs)
www.UFDC.org
"The World's Leading Organization for Everyone Interested in Dolls" for over fifty years. Nonprofit organization of doll clubs and collectors worldwide. Newsletter, full-color quarterly magazine and organizer of doll conventions, plus a doll museum at the headquarters in Kansas City.
10900 North Pomona Ave.
Kansas City, MO 64153
Tel: 816-891-7040
Fax: 816-891-8360

ADDITIONAL DOLL RESOURCES
This is only a small selection of the available doll companies and doll websites—for more information, additional contact information, and links, visit www.officialpriceguidetodolls.com.

eBay
www.eBay.com
Leading online auction house for everything, including dolls.

DOLL AUCTION HOUSES
Cobbs Doll Auction
www.cobbsdolls.com
1909 Harrison Rd.
Johnstown, OH 43031
Tel: 740-964-0444

Frasher's Doll Auctions
23232 South Mecklin School Rd.
Oak Grove, MO 64075
Tel: 816-625-3786

McMasters Harris
www.mcmastersharris.com
P.O. Box 1755
Cambridge, OH 43725
Tel: 740-432-7400

Theriault's
www.theriaults.com
P.O. Box 151
Annapolis, MD 21404
Tel: 410-224-3655

DOLL COMPANIES
Barbiecollector.com
www.barbiecollector.com
Official website and Barbie doll-collecting club.

Effanbee Dolls
www.effanbeedoll.com
Long-standing doll company, home of Patsy and Brenda Starr.

Lee Middleton Dolls
www.leemiddletondolls.com
Leading manufacturer of baby dolls.

Madame Alexander Dolls
www.alexanderdoll.com
American doll company for eighty years.

Tonner Doll Company, Inc.
www.tonnerdoll.com
Modern doll company; dolls include Tyler Wentworth and Betsy McCall.

Vogue Dolls
www.voguedolls.com
Home of Ginny dolls.

R. John Wright Dolls

www.rjohnwright.com
Modern cloth artist dolls.

DOLLMAKING

Seeley's

www.seeleys.com
Doll Artisan Guild, dollmaking classes, molds, and supplies.

MAGAZINES

Antique Doll Collector

www.antiquedollcollector.com

Barbie Bazaar

www.barbiebazaar.com

Contemporary Doll

www.scottpublications.com/cdcmag

Doll Artisan Guild/Dolls Beautiful

dollartisanguild.org/html/magazines.html

Doll Crafter

www.jonespublishing.com/index-crafter.htm

Doll Reader

www.dollreader.com

Dolls

www.jonespublishing.com/dolls/dollshome.html

Haute Doll

www.barbiebazaar.com/hautedoll.htm
Devoted to fashion dolls.

MUSEUMS

Arizona Doll and Toy Museum

www.artcom.com/museums/nv/af/85004-23.htm
Exhibits include a turn-of-the-century schoolroom with antique dolls as students and teacher.
602 East Adams St.
Phoenix, AZ 85004

Bethnal Green Museum of Childhood

www.vam.ac.uk/vastatic/nmc
Wonderful collection of antique dolls and baby houses (miniatures), games, puppets, trains, and a gift shop.
Cambridge Heath Rd.
London E2 9PA, U.K.
Tel: 020-208-980-2415
Tube: Bethnal Green U.K.

The Children's Toy & Doll Museum

www.tourohio.com/TOYDOLL
Antique and contemporary dolls and a children's activity room.
206 Gilman St.
PO Box 4034
Marietta, OH 45750
Tel: 740-373-5900

Denver Museum of Miniatures, Dolls & Toys

www.coloradokids.com/miniatures
Housed in a historic building, features exhibits including miniatures, dolls, dollhouses, toys, and teddy bears.
1880 Gaylord St.
Denver, CO 80206
Tel: 303-322-1053

Doll & Toy Museum

www.home.att.net/~dollmuseum
Features thousands of dolls, antique to modern, and toys.
700 Winchester Pike Canal
Winchester, OH 43110
Tel: 614-837-5573

Doll and Toy Museum of the City of New York

www.dollandtoymuseumofnyc.org
Located in Public School 142 in Brooklyn. 1,200 feet of display space, including twelve separate exhibits and two large dollhouses.
610 Henry St., Room 103
Brooklyn, NY 11201
Tel: 718-243-0820 (to schedule an appointment)

The Doll Museum

www.dollmuseum.com
Antique and modern dolls, museum shop, repairs.
520 Thames St.
Newport, RI 02840
Tel: 610-670-6868

The Enchanted Doll World Museum

www.compalace.org/dollmuseum.html
Set in an English-style castle, the museum has over 4,000 dolls set in 400 scenes.
615 North Main
Mitchell, SD 57301
Tel: 605-996-9896

The Enchanted Mansion

www.angelfire.com/la2/enchantedmansion
Doll museum and shop.
1900 Lee Dr.
Baton Rouge, LA 70808
Tel: 225-769-0005

The Fennimore Doll & Toy Museum and Gift Shoppe

www.fennimore.com/dolltoy
1140 Lincoln Ave.
Fennimore, WI 53809
Tel: 608-822-4100

The Jacksonville Museum of Dolls and Collectibles

www.jmdc.org
Doll exhibits and doll museum
1776 Canterbury St.

Jacksonville, FL 32205
Tel: 305-322-6077

La Crosse Doll Museum

www.dollmuseum.org
6,500 dolls dating from the pre-Columbian era to
the present-day
1213 Caledonia St.
La Crosse, WI 54603
Tel: 608-785-0020

The Lois Luftin Doll Museum

www.beau.lib.la.us/doll.html
Lois and Albert "Dutch" Luftin devoted over
forty-eight years to collecting the over 3,000 dolls
on display at the old Kansas City Southern Railway Depot.
120 South Washington Ave.
DeRidder, LA 70634

Mary Meritt Doll Museum

www.merritts.com/dollmuseum/default.asp
Opened in 1963, collection spans the expanse of
time from ancient Egypt to the twentieth century.
843 Ben Franklin Hwy
Douglassville, PA 19518
Tel: 610-385-3809

McCurdy Historical Doll Museum

www.utahvalley.org/visguide/ATTRACTS/
Mccurdy.htm
Located in a restored historic carriage house, with
over 4,000 dolls on display.
246 North 100 East
Provo, UT 84606
Tel: 801-377-9935

Musee de la Poupée et du Jouet Ancien

23 rue de Saille
44350 GUERANDE, France

Museum of Childhood

www.edinburgh.gov.uk/CEC/Recreation/Leisure/
*Data/Museum_Of_Childhood/Museum_Of_*
Childhood.html
Five galleries of childhood memorabilia, includ-
ing toys and games.
42 High St.
Edinburgh EH1, Scotland
Tel: 0131-529-4142

Museum of the City of New York

www.mcny.org/toy.htm
The toy collection of this museum contains over
10,000 toys and amusements used by New York-
ers from the colonial period to the present.
1220 Fifth Ave. (at 103rd St.)
New York, NY 10029
Tel: 212-534-1672

Oken's House and Doll Museum

www.warwick-uk.co.uk/places-of-interest/
okens-house.asp
Museum and shop.
Castle Street
Warwick, U.K.
Tel: 440-192-649-5546

Prairie Museum of Art & History

www.prairiemuseum.org
Dollhouse Dreams gallery has over 1,500 dolls
from around the world.
1905 S. Franklin
Colby, KS 67701
Tel: 785-462-4590

Rosalie Whyel Museum of Doll Art

www.dollart.com/index.htm
Internationally known doll museum near Seattle.
1116 108th Ave. N.E.
Bellevue, WA 98004
Tel: 425-455-1116

Shelburne Museum

www.shelburnemuseum.org
Museum with a large collection of dolls and
miniatures.
U.S. Route 7, P.O. Box 10
Shelburne, VT 05482
Tel: 802-985-3346

Strong Museum

www.strongmuseum.org
Large collection focusing on American dolls.
1 Manhattan Square
Rochester, NY 14506
Tel: 716-263-2600

Yokohama Doll Museum

www.city.yokohama.jp/me/ycvb/english/doll/
archive
Dolls from 130 countries, including Japan.

REPAIR AND RESTORATION
Gaylord

www.gaylord.com
Archival supply house; products for doll preservation and restoration.

Restore Products, UK

www.restore-products.co.uk
Source for products for doll costume preservation.

Twin Pines of Maine

www.twinpines.com
Products for doll restoration.

APPENDIX III: REFERENCE LIBRARY AND BIBLIOGRAPHY

I have over 300 books on dolls. Since I have about 2,000 dolls in my collection, that works out to one book for every six or seven dolls I have! You may not want or need that many doll books, but you may well need more information on dolls than can be included in *The Official Price Guide to Dolls*.

I'm glad that you have started with this book—it's a wonderful reference, price guide, and starting point to explore the world of dolls. However, you may well have become intrigued with a particular type of doll after reading this book, or your collection might be specialized to one era or type of dolls, so that you require more in-depth information on that type of doll than this book can provide. Since this book cannot cover in deep detail each of the hundreds of categories of dolls produced in the last 200 years, you may want additional references. This reference library will help you find what you need. Some of these books are out of print, but available at online auctions or through secondhand book sellers, including those online. Due to space limitations, I have carefully selected 175 books to include.

I have organized these books by type of doll to assist you in finding further information for dolls in any category. In some way, nearly all of these books have contributed to *this* book on dolls—all of them have been invaluable references to me over the years.

Advertising Dolls

Outwater, Myra Yellin. *Advertising Dolls: The History of American Advertising Dolls from 1900–1990* (Atglen, PA: Schiffer Publishing, Ltd., 1997).

Robison, Joleen Ashman, and Kay Sellers. *Advertising Dolls: Identification & Value Guide* (Paducah, KY: Collector Books, 1992).

All-Bisque and Miniature Dolls

Ackerman, Evelyn. *Dolls in Miniature* (Annapolis, MD: Gold Horse Publishing, 1991).

Angione, Genevive. *All-Bisque and Half-Bisque Dolls* (Exton, PA: Schiffer Publishing Ltd., 1969).

Heritier, Mathilde, and Samy Odin. *Mignonette: Her History, Wardrobe and Miniature World, 1878–1917* (Paris, France: Musée de la Poupée-Paris).

Seeley, Mildred. *The Complete Book of All-Bisque Dolls* (Livonia, MI: Scott Publications, 1992).

Smith, Patricia. *Patricia Smith's Album of All-Bisque Dolls* (Paducah, KY: Collector Books, 1992).

Theriault, Florence. *In the Palm of One's Hand: Small Bisque Dolls, 1977–1920* (Annapolis, MD: Gold Horse Publishing, 1999).

Theriault, Florence. *The Little Ones: French and German All-Bisque Dolls* (Annapolis, MD: Gold Horse Publishing, 1999).

Automata

Theriault, Florence. *Dolls in Motion, 1850–1915* (Annapolis, MD: Gold Horse Publishing, 2000).

Barbie Dolls

Arend, Scott, Karla Holzerland, and Trina Kent. *Skipper: Barbie Doll's Little Sister* (Paducah, KY: Collector Books, 1998).

Barbie Bazaar, Mattel, and Christmas Catalog Reprints, 1969–1972 (Special edition) (Kenosha, WI: Murat Caviale Inc.).

Barbie Bazaar, Mattel, and Christmas Catalog Reprints, 1959–1965 (Special edition II) (Kenosha, WI: Murat Caviale Inc.).

Blitman, Joe. *Barbie Doll's Cousin Francie & Her Mod, Mod, Mod, Mod World of Fashion* (Grantsville, MD: Hobby House Press, Inc., 1996).

Blitman, Joe. *Barbie Doll & Her Mod, Mod, Mod, Mod World of Fashion, 1967–1972* (Grantsville, MD: Hobby House Press, Inc., 1996).

Davidson, Marl B. *Barbie Doll, Structure & Furniture* (Grantsville, MD: Hobby House Press, Inc., 1997).

Deutsch, Stefanie. *Barbie, the First 30 Years: 1959 Through 1989* (Paducah, KY: Collector Books, 1996).

DeWein, Sibyl, and Joan Ashabraner. *The Collector's Encyclopedia of Barbie Dolls and Collectibles* (Paducah, KY: Collector Books, 1977).

Eames, Sarah Sink. *Barbie Doll Fashion: Volume I, 1959–1967* (Paducah, KY: Collector Books, 1990).

Eames, Sarah Sink. *Barbie Doll Fashion, Volume II: 1968–1974* (Paducah, KY: Collector Books, 1997).

Gaskill, Cynthia. *Barbie Retro* (Annapolis, MD: Gold Horse Publishing, 2000).

Gaskill, Cynthia. *Exclusively Barbie* (Annapolis, MD: Gold Horse Publishing, 1998).

Kaplan, Connie Craig. *Collector's Guide to Barbie Doll Vinyl Cases* (Paducah, KY: Collector Books, 1999).

Long, Patricia. *The Barbie Closet* (Iola, WI: Krause Publications, 1999).

Manos, Paris and Susan. *The Wonder of Barbie Dolls and Accessories, 1976–1986* (values updated) (Paducah, KY: Collector Books, 1996).

Manos, Paris and Susan. *The World of Barbie Dolls* (values updated) (Paducah, KY: Collector Books, 1994).

Melillo, Marcie. *The Ultimate Barbie Doll Book* (Iola, WI: Krause Publications, 1996).

Mieszala, Lorraine. *Collector's Guide to Barbie Doll Paper Dolls* (Paducah, KY: Collector Books, 1997).

Neenan, Cynthia. *Barbie a Go-Go* (Annapolis, MD: Gold Horse Publishing, 2000).

Olds, Patrick C. and Joyce L. *The Barbie Doll Years.* 4th edition (Paducah, KY: Collector Books, 2001).

Shibano, Keido Kimura. *Barbie in Japan* (Kenosha, WI: Murat Caviale Inc., 1994).

Steele, Valerie, and David Levinthal. *Barbie Millicent Roberts, an Original* (New York: Pantheon, 1998).

Varaste, Christopher. *Face of the American Dream, Barbie Doll, 1959–1971* (Grantsville, MD: Hobby House Press, Inc., 1999).

Westenhouser, Kitturah. *The Story of Barbie* (Paducah, KY: Collector Books, 1994).

Celluloid Dolls

Fainges, Marjory. *Celluloid Dolls of the World* (Sydney, Australia: Kangaroo Press, 2000).

Celebrity Dolls

Axe, John. *Collectible Sonja Henie* (Riverdale, MD: Hobby House Press, Inc., 1979).

Axe, John. *The Encyclopedia of Celebrity Dolls* (Cumberland, MD: Hobby House Press, Inc., 1983).

Axe, John, and A. Glenn Mandeville. *Celebrity Doll Price Guide & Annual* (Cumberland, MD: Hobby House Press, Inc., 1984).

Kraus-Mancuso, Suzanne. *Shirley Temple Identification & Price Guide to Shirley Temple Collectibles* (Grantsville, MD: Hobby House Press, Inc., 2002).

Kraus-Mancuso, Suzanne. *Shirley Temple Identification & Price Guide to Shirley Temple Collectibles, Volume II* (Grantsville, MD: Hobby House Press, Inc., 2003).

China Dolls

Borger, Mona. *China Dolls for Study & Admiration* (San Francisco: Borger Publications, 1983).

Krombholz, Mary Gorham. *Identifying German Chinas, 1840s–1930s* (Grantsville, MD: Hobby House Press, Inc., 2004).

Richter, Lydia. *China, Parian & Bisque German Dolls* (Grantsville, MD: Hobby House Books, Inc., 1993).

Seeley, Mildred. *Beloved China Dolls* (Livonia, MI: Scott Publications, 1996).

Cloth Dolls

Avery, Kim. *The World of Raggedy Ann Collectibles* (Paducah, KY: Collector Books, 1997).

Bertrand, Shirley. *Characters of R. John Wright* (Grantsville, MD: Hobby House Press, Inc., 2000).

Bradshaw, Marjorie A. *The Doll House Story of the Chase Doll* (1986).

Coleman, Dorothy S. *Lenci Dolls* (Riverdale, MD: Hobby House Press, 1977).

Edward, Linda. *Cloth Dolls from Ancient to Modern* (Atglen, PA: Schiffer Publishing, Ltd., 1997).

Goddu, Krystyna Poray. *R. John Wright: The Art of Toys* (Cumberland, MD: Reverie Publishing, 2004).

Hall, Patricia. *Raggedy Ann and More* (Gretna, LA: Pelican Publishing Company, Inc., 2000).

Lindenberger, Jan. *Raggedy Ann & Andy Collectibles* (Atglen, PA: Schiffer Publishing, Ltd., 1995).

Richter, Lydia. *The Beloved Käthe Kruse Dolls, Yesterday and Today* (Cumberland, MD: Hobby House Press, Inc., 1991).

Composition Dolls

Judd, Polly and Pam. *Composition Dolls 1928–1955* (Cumberland, MD: Hobby House Press, Inc., 1991).

Judd, Polly and Pam. *Composition Dolls, Volume II: 1909–1928* (Cumberland, MD: Hobby House Press, Inc., 1994).

Lutterman, LaVonne. *Complete Composition Repair* (Worthington, MN: Aurore Publishing, 1990).

Mertz, Ursula R. *Collector's Encyclopedia of American Composition Dolls 1900–1950* (Paducah, KY: Collector Books, 1999).

Doll Costuming

Ackerman, Evelyn. *My Favorite Patterns for Dressing Antique Dolls 1865–1925* (Annapolis, MD: Gold Horse Publishing, 1993).

Ackerman, Evelyn. *My Favorite Patterns for Dressing Antique Dolls 1865–1925, Volume II* (Annapolis, MD: Gold Horse Publishing, 1994).

Anderton, Johana Gast. *Sewing for 20th-Century Dolls* (Grantsville, MD: Hobby House Press, Inc., 1972).

Atkinson, Sue. *Making & Dressing Dolls' House Dolls* (London: David & Charles, 1992).

Blum, Stella. *Victorian Fashions & Costumes from Harper's Bazaar, 1867–1898* (New York: Dover Publications, Inc., 1974).

Coleman, Dorothy S., Elizabeth A., and Evelyn J. *The Collector's Book of Dolls' Clothes: Costumes in Miniature, 1700–1929* (New York: Crown Publishers, Inc., 1975).

Dodge, Venus A. *The Dolls Dressmaker: The Complete Pattern Book* (London: David & Charles, 1987).

Henry, Maxine. *Dressing Porcelain Dolls* (London: B.T. Batsford Ltd., 1995).

Hoyer, Mary. *Mary Hoyer and Her Dolls: Patterns to Crochet, Knit and Sew* (Cumberland, MD: Hobby House Press, Inc., 1982).

McMahon, Hazel. *Famous Couples Fashion Doll Patterns* (Cumberland, MD: Hobby House Press, Inc., 2003).

Olian, JoAnne. *Children's Fashions 1860–1912* (New York: Dover Publications, Inc., 1994).

Seeley, Mildred and Colleen. *Doll Costuming: How to Costume French & German Bisque Dolls* (Livonia, MI: Scott Publications, 1989).

Theimer, François. *La Poupée Modele: Les Patrons de Robes et Accessoires pour la Poupée LILY* (Editions Polichinelle, 1997).

Theriault, Florence. *Perfectly Fitting: Antique Doll Costumes and Accessories, 1840–1925* (Annapolis, MD: Gold Horse Publishing, 2001).

Theriault, Florence. *Stitches in Time: Doll Costumes and Accessories, 1850–1925* (Annapolis, MD: Gold Horse Publishing, 1995).

Theriault, Florence. *The Way They Were: Doll Costumes and Accessories, 1850–1925* (Annapolis, MD: Gold Horse Publishing, 1993).

Theriault, Florence. *What Dolls Wore Before: Doll Costumes and Accessories, 1850–1925* (Annapolis, MD: Gold Horse Publishing, 1997).

Ulseth, Hazel, and Helen Shannon. *Antique Children's Fashions 1880–1900* (Cumberland, MD: Hobby House Press, Inc., 1991).

Dolls of the 1960s and 1970s

Axe, John. *Tammy and Her Family of Dolls* (Grantsville, MD: Hobby House Press, Inc., 1995).

Cross, Carla Marie. *The Crissy Family Doll Encyclopedia* (Cumberland, MD: Hobby House Press, Inc., 1998).

Gaskill, Cynthia. *Classic Plastic Dolls 1945–1965* (Annapolis, MD: Gold Horse Publishing, 1996).

Gaskill, Cynthia. *More American Dolls from the Post-War Era, 1945–1965* (Annapolis, MD: Gold Horse Publishing, 1993).

Johnson, Joedi. *Dawn & Her World, A Collector's Guide* (Billings, MT: Cattpigg Press, 1995).

Langford, Paris. *Liddle Kiddles* (Paducah, KY: Collector Books, 1996).

Mandeville, A. Glenn. *Sensational '60s Doll Album* (Grantsville, MD: Hobby House Press, Inc., 1996).

Sabulis, Cindy, and Susan Weglewski. *Collector's Guide to Dolls of the 1960s and 1970s* (Paducah, KY: Collector Books, 2000).

Sabulis, Cindy, and Susan Weglewski. *Collector's Guide to Tammy* (Paducah, KY: Collector Books, 1997).

Effanbee

Axe, John. *Effanbee: A Collector's Encyclopedia 1949–1983* (Cumberland, MD: Hobby House Press, Inc., 1983).

Schoonmaker, Patricia N. *Effanbee Dolls, the Formative Years 1910–1929* (Cumberland, MD: Hobby House Press, Inc., 1984).

Smith, Patricia R. *Effanbee* (Paducah, KY: Collector Books, 1983).

Fashion Dolls, Antique

MacNeil, Sylvia. *The Paris Collection* (Grantsville, MD: Hobby House Press, Inc., 1992).

Seeley, Mildred and Colleen. *Study of the Fashion Dolls of France,* revised edition (Livonia, MI: Scott Publications, 1995).

Tarnowska, Maree. *Fashion Dolls* (Cumberland, MD: Hobby House Press, Inc., 1986).

Theriault, Florence. *French Dolls in Folklore Costume 1835–1917* (Annapolis, MD: Gold Horse Publishing, 1999).

Theriault, Florence. *A Fully Perfected Grace: The World of the French Fashion Doll, 1850–1880* (Annapolis, MD: Gold Horse Publishing, 1996).

Theriault, Florence. *Lady Dolls of the 19th Century and the Costumes They Wore* (Annapolis, MD: Gold Horse Publishing, 2002).

Theriault, Florence. *The Trousseau of Blondinette Davranches* (Annapolis, MD: Gold Horse Publishing, 1994).

Fashion Dolls, Vintage and Modern

Augustyniak, J. Michael. *Thirty Years of Mattel Fashion Dolls* (Paducah, KY: Collector Books, 1998).

Cook, Carolyn. *Gene* (Grantsville, MD: Hobby House Press, Inc., 1998).

Faraone, Jim. *4th Fashion Doll Makeovers* (Grantsville, MD: Hobby House Press, Inc., 2001).

Faraone, Jim. *Ultimate Fashion Doll Makeovers: Tips from the Experts* (Grantsville, MD: Hobby House Press, Inc., 2002).

Judd, Polly and Pam. *Glamour Dolls of the 1950s & 1960s*, revised edition (Cumberland, MD: Hobby House Press, Inc., 1993).

Judd, Polly and Pam. *Hard Plastic Dolls, II* (Grantsville, MD: Hobby House Press, Inc., 1994).

Mandeville, A. Glenn. *Doll Fashion Anthology & Price Guide,* 4th revised edition (Grantsville, MD: Hobby House Press, Inc., 1993).

Odom, Mel. *Gene Marshall, Girl Star* (New York: Hyperion, 2000).

Owens, Beth. *Contemporary Fashion Dolls: The Next Generation* (Grantsville, MD: Hobby House Press, Inc., 2000).

Simms, Grace L. *Darci Identification & Price Guide* (Grantsville, MD: Hobby House Press, Inc., 2000).

French Bisque

Koenig, Marie. *Musée de Poupées* (Paris: Librairie Hachette, 1909).

Polichinelle, La Gazette des Poupées, Jouets et Automates de Collection (Reprints 27–30) (1 rue Rossini, 75009 Paris, 1993).

Seeley, Mildred and Vernon. *How to Collect French Bébé Dolls* (Tucson, AZ: HP Books, 1985).

The S.F.B.J. Catalog of 1912 (Catalog Reprint Series) (Annapolis, MD: Gold Horse Publishing, 1997).

Theimer, François, and Florence Theriault. *The Jumeau Book* (Annapolis, MD: Gold Horse Publishing, 1994).

Theimer, François, and Danielle and Florence Theriault. *The Encyclopedia of French Dolls, Volume I: A–K* (Annapolis, MD: Gold Horse Publishing, 2003).

Theriault, Florence. *The Beautiful Jumeau* (Annapolis, MD: Gold Horse Publishing, 1997).

Whitton, Margaret. *The Jumeau Doll* (New York: Dover Publications, Inc., 1980).

General and History

Bristol, Olivia. *Dolls: A Collector's Guide* (New York: Stewart, Tabori & Chang, 1999).

Coleman, Dorothy, Elizabeth, and Evelyn. *The Age of Dolls* (Washington, D.C.: Dorothy Coleman, 1965).

Coleman, Dorothy S., Elizabeth A., and Evelyn J. *The Collector's Encyclopedia of Dolls* (New York: Crown Publishers, Inc., 1968).

Coleman, Dorothy S., Elizabeth A., and Evelyn J. *The Collector's Encyclopedia of Dolls, Volume Two* (New York: Crown Publishers, Inc., 1986).

Early, Alice K. *English Dolls, Effigies and Puppets* (London: B.T. Batsford Ltd., 1955).

Fawcett, Clara Hallard. *Dolls: A New Guide for Collectors* (Boston: Charles T. Branford Co., 1964).

Goodfellow, Caroline. *The Ultimate Doll Book* (London: Dorling Kindersley, 1993).

Goodfellow, Caroline. *Understanding Dolls* (Suffolk, UK: Antique Collectors' Club, 1983).

King, Constance Eileen. *The Collector's History of Dolls* (New York: St. Martin's Press, 1977).

Low, Frances H. *Queen Victoria's Dolls* (London: George Newnes, Ltd., 1894).

Starr, Laura B. *The Doll Book* (New York: The Outing Publishing Company, 1908).

St. George, Eleanor. *The Dolls of Yesterday* (New York: Bonanza Books, 1948).

German Dolls

Cieslik, Jurgen and Marianne. *German Doll Encyclopedia 1800–1939* (Cumberland, MD: Hobby House Press, Inc., 1985).

Cieslik, Jurgen and Marianne. *German Doll Marks & Identification Guide* (Cumberland, MD: Hobby House Press, Inc., 1990).

Foulke, Jan. *Simon & Halbig Dolls: The Artful Aspect* (Grantsville, MD: Hobby House Press, Inc., 1984).

Foulke, Jan. *Kestner, King of Doll Makers* (Cumberland, MD: Hobby House Press, Inc., 1989).

Krombholz, Mary Gorham. *The Story of German Doll Making 1530–2000* (Grantsville, MD: Hobby House Press, Inc., 2001).

Ladensack, Anita. *The History and Art of Googlies* (Grantsville, MD: Hobby House Press, Inc., 2002).

The Ladies of Hertwig (Annapolis, MD: Gold Horse Publishing, 2003).

Smith, Patricia R. *Armand Marseille Dolls* (Paducah, KY: Collector Books, 1976).

Theriault, Florence. *Hertwig & Co. Archives 1890–1937* (Annapolis, MD: Gold Horse Publishing, 2000).

Weintraub, Sharon Hope. *Naughties: Nudies & Bathing Beauties* (Grantsville, MD: Hobby House Books, Inc.).

Ginny and Similar Dolls

Gaskill, Cynthia. *Hi! I'm Ginny* (Annapolis, MD: Gold Horse Publishing, 2000).

Mandeville, A. Glenn. *Ginny,* 2nd revised edition (Cumberland, MD: Hobby House Press, Inc., 1994).

Roberts, Sue Nettleingham, and Dorothy Bunker. *The Ginny Doll Encyclopedia* (Grantsville, MD: Hobby House Press, Inc., 1994).

Stover, Carol J. *Small Dolls of the 40s and 50s* (Paducah, KY: Collector Books, 2002).

Identification and Pricing

Bach, Jean. *The Main Dictionary of Doll Marks* (Pittstown, NJ: The Main Street Press, 1985).

Foulke, Jan. *16th Blue Book* (Cumberland, MD: Hobby House Press, Inc., 2003).

Herlocher, Dawn. *Doll Makers & Marks* (Norfolk, VA: Landmark Specialty Books, 1999).

Moyer, Patsy. *Doll Values,* 1st through 7th editions (Paducah, KY: Collector Books, 2003).

Moyer, Patsy. *Modern Collectible Dolls,* Volumes I–IV (Paducah, KY: Collector Books, 1997–2000).

Shea, Ralph A. *Doll Mark Clues,* Volumes 1, 3–8 (Ridgefield, NJ: Ralph A. Shea Publisher, 1972–1981).

Smith, Patricia. *Modern Collectible Dolls,* Series 1–8 (Paducah, KY: Collector Books, 1973–1996).

Madame Alexander Dolls

An American Legend (Portfolio Press, 1999).

Mandeville, A. Glenn, and Benita Cohen Schwartz. *Cissy Identification & Price Guide* (Grantsville, MD: Hobby House Press, Inc., 2003).

Mandeville, A. Glenn, and Benita Cohen Schwartz. *Madame Alexander Dolls: 4th Collector's Price Guide* (Grantsville, MD: Hobby House Books, Inc., 2003). Over 2,000 Madame Alexander dolls are listed with their prices, including many exclusive and store specials.

Smith, Patricia. *The Collector's Encyclopedia of Madame Alexander Dolls 1965–1990* (Paducah, KY: Collector Books, 1991).

Smith, Patricia. *Madame Alexander Dolls* (Paducah, KY: Collector Books, 1978).

Theriault, Florence. *Vintage Alexander* (Annapolis, MD: Gold Horse Publishing, 2002).

Nancy Ann Storybook Dolls

Miller, Marjorie A. *Nancy Ann Storybook Dolls* (Grantsville, MD: Hobby House Press, Inc., 1980).

Pardee, Elaine M., and Jackie Robertson. *Encyclopedia of Bisque Nancy Ann Storybook Dolls, 1936–1947* (Paducah, KY: Collectors Books, 2003).

Other Twentieth-Century Dolls

Adams, Margaret. *Collectible Dolls and Accessories of the Twenties and Thirties from Sears, Roebuck and Co. Catalogs* (New York: Dover Publications, Inc., 1986).

Anderton, Johana Gast. *More Twentieth-Century Dolls from Bisque to Vinyl, Volume One: A–H* (Des Moines, IA: Wallace-Homestead Book Co., 1979).

Anderton, Johana Gast. *More Twentieth-Century Dolls from Bisque to Vinyl, Volume Two: I–Z* (Des Moines, IA: Wallace-Homestead Book Co., 1979).

Anderton, Johana Gast. *Twentieth-Century Dolls from Bisque to Vinyl* (Kansas City, MO: Trojan Press, Inc., 1971).

Casper, Peggy Wiedman. *Terri Lee Dolls* (Grantsville, MD: Hobby House Press, Inc., 2001).

Garrett, Debbie. *The Definitive Guide to Collecting Black Dolls* (Grantsville, MD: Hobby House Press, Inc., 2003).

Gibbs, Patikii. *Horsman Dolls* (Paducah, KY: Collector Books, 1985).

Izen, Judith. *American Character Dolls* (Paducah, KY: Collector Books, 2004).

Izen, Judith. *Collector's Guide to Ideal Dolls Identification & Values,* 2nd edition (Paducah, KY: Collector Books, 1999).

Izen, Judith, and Carol Stover. *Collector's Encyclopedia of Vogue Dolls* (Paducah, KY: Collectors Books, 1998).

Jensen, Don. *Collector's Guide to Horsman Dolls 1865–1950* (Paducah, KY: Collector Books, 2002).

Osborn, Dorisanne. *Sasha Dolls Through the Years* (Annapolis, MD: Gold Horse Publishing, 1999).

Van Patten, Joan F., and Linda Lau. *Nippon Dolls & Playthings* (Paducah, KY: Collector Books, 2001).

Paper Dolls

Ferguson, Barbara Chaney. *The Paper Doll, A Collector's Guide with Prices* (Des Moines, IA: Wallace-Homestead, 1982).

Theriault, Florence. *Dressing Dolls: Antique & Collectible Paper Dolls 1850–1965* (Annapolis, MD: Gold Horse Publishing, 2001).

Repair and Restoration

Caruso, Mary. *Care of Favorite Dolls: Antique Bisque Conservation* (Cumberland, MD: Hobby House Press, Inc., 1999).

Gaylin, Evelyn. *Doll Repair* (Riverdale, MD: Hobby House Press, 1971).

Hill, Nicholas J. *The Definitive Book on the Care and Preservation of Vinyl Dolls* (Scarborough, ME: Twin Peaks Press, 2000).

Koval, Barbara. *How to Repair & Restore Dolls* (Sydney, Australia: Kangaroo Press, 1991).

Perry, Doreen. *Restoring Dolls, A Practical Guide* (London: Bishopsgate Press Ltd., 1985).

Westfall, Marty. *The Handbook of Doll Repairs and Restoration* (New York: Three Rivers Press, 1979).

Reproduction Dollmaking

Seeley, Mildred. *Fabulous French Bébés for Collectors and Crafters* (Livonia, MI: Scott Publications, 1992).

Seeley, Mildred. *For the Love of Dolls and Roses* (Livonia, MI: Scott Publications, 1994).

Seeley, Mildred. *Judging Dolls* (Livonia, MI: Scott Publications, 1991).

APPENDIX IV: MOLD INDEX

Marks have been presented in the appropriate chapters throughout this book. However, to aid in identification of dolls, this index presents mold numbers for antique bisque dolls, symbols, and some harder-to-identify trademarks for both antique and vintage dolls. These numbers, trademarks, and symbols are presented with their corresponding doll companies.

Marks that include the actual name of the company (such as "Alexander" for Madame Alexander, or "Ideal" for Ideal), as well as marks that include the actual name of the doll (such as "Baby Sandy" or "Lori"), are not included here—those companies and doll names can be found in the regular index.

Also note that, generally, the mold numbers and other marks presented in this index appear with other letters and numbers—various numbers that denote the size of the doll, etc. If you are not familiar with doll marks, look through this book and the several thousand marks presented with the price listings. This will help you learn what such marks look like and which numbers represent the mold numbers versus the size numbers.

Also note the following number and letter marks:

1 (or any other single-digit number, with no letters or other numbers): Generally may be the mark of a French fashion doll, French bébé, an early German bisque doll, or an all-bisque. If with other letters/numbers, such a single digit is a size number only.

10 (or 11, 12, 13, 14, 17, or any other number in the teens, with no other letters or numbers): Generally may be the mark of a French fashion doll, French bébé, an early German bisque doll, or an all-bisque. If with other letters/numbers, such a single digit is a size number only.

Single letter (for example, C, D, E, F, J, K, L, etc., with no other number or other letters): Generally may be the mark of a French fashion doll, French bébé, Kestner doll, or an early German bisque doll.

Two-digit numbers: May be mold numbers (see below), but are more often size numbers.

Four-digit numbers: A wide variety of four-digit number marks were used on half dolls, bathing beauties, piano babies, and other similar items from 1900 to the 1930s. Also see the "Heubach" listings, where the beginning of a number series is shown with asterisks; for instance, "7***" indicates mold numbers falling between 7000 and 7999.

MARK	DOLL COMPANY	MARK	DOLL COMPANY
14	Schmidt, Bruno	115A	Kämmer & Reinhardt
16X	Kestner	116	Kämmer & Reinhardt
23	Recknagel	116A	Kämmer & Reinhardt
34	Kuhnlenz, Gebrüder	117	bisque, German, unknown
38	Kuhnlenz, Gebrüder		
39	Kuhnlenz, Gebrüder	117	Kämmer & Reinhardt
41	Kuhnlenz, Gebrüder	117A	Kämmer & Reinhardt
44	Kuhnlenz, Gebrüder	117N	Kämmer & Reinhardt
45	Recknagel	119	Handwerck, Heinrich
46	Recknagel	120	Simon & Halbig
47	Kuhnlenz, Gebrüder	121	Kämmer & Reinhardt
51	bisque, German, unknown	121	Recknagel
		121	Simon & Halbig
55	Kuhnlenz, Gebrüder	122	Kämmer & Reinhardt
60	S.F.B.J.	123	Kling
60	Unis, France	123	Kämmer & Reinhardt
61	Kuhnlenz, Gebrüder, all-bisque	124	Kämmer & Reinhardt
		125	Hertel, Schwab & Co.
62	bisque, German, unknown	126	Kämmer & Reinhardt
		127	Kämmer & Reinhardt
69	Handwerck, Heinrich	128	Kling
79	Handwerck, Heinrich	128	Steiner, Herm
89	Handwerck, Heinrich	128	Kestner
89	Kuhnlenz, Gebrüder	129	Kestner
92	Steiner	130	Kestner, all-bisque
98	König & Wernicke	131	Kling
99	Handwerck, Heinrich	131	Kämmer & Reinhardt
99	König & Wernicke	132	bisque, German, unknown
100	Alt, Beck & Gottschalck		
100	Heubach, Gebrüder	133	Steiner, Herm, Googly
100	Kämmer & Reinhardt	135	Kämmer & Reinhardt
101	Kämmer & Reinhardt	136	Kämmer & Reinhardt
101X	Kämmer & Reinhardt	136	bisque, German, unknown
102	Kestner		
102	Kämmer & Reinhardt	136	Hertel, Schwab & Co.
103	Kley & Hahn	137	bisque, German, unknown
103	bisque, German, unknown		
		142	Hertel, Schwab & Co.
106X	bisque, German, unknown	142	Kestner
		143	Kestner
107	Kämmer & Reinhardt	146	Kestner
109	Handwerck, Heinrich	147	Kestner
109	Kämmer & Reinhardt	148	Kestner
110	Wislizenus	149	Hertel, Schwab & Co.
111	all-bisque, Googly	149	Kestner
111	Kestner, all-bisque	150	Hertel, Schwab & Co.
112	Kämmer & Reinhardt	150	Kestner, all-bisque
114	Kämmer & Reinhardt	151	Hertel, Schwab & Co.
114A	Kämmer & Reinhardt	152	Hertel, Schwab & Co.
115	Kämmer & Reinhardt	152	Kestner

MARK	DOLL COMPANY	MARK	DOLL COMPANY
153	Kestner, all-bisque (attributed)	200	Marseille, Armand
		200	Kämmer & Reinhardt
154	Kestner	201	Bähr & Pröschild
154	Kley & Hahn	201	Catterfelder Puppenfabrik
155	Kestner	201	Kämmer & Reinhardt
156	all-bisque, German	201	Kestner, celluloid
157	Kley & Hahn	201	Schuetzmeister & Quendt
158	Kley & Hahn	203	Hertwig
159	bisque, German, unknown	203	Kling
		204	Bähr & Pröschild
160	Kley & Hahn	205	Hertwig
160	Kestner	208	bisque, German, unknown
161	Kestner		
162	Kestner	208	Kestner, all-bisque
163	Hertel, Schwab & Co.	210	Marseille, Armand
164	Kestner	211	Kestner
164	Simon & Halbig	214	Kestner
165	Hertel, Schwab & Co.	217	all-bisque Googly
165	Kuhnlenz, Gebrüder	218	all-bisque, Googly
166	Kestner	220	Kestner
166	Kley & Hahn	221	Kestner
167	Kestner	223	Marseille, Armand
167	Kley & Hahn	224	Bähr & Pröschild
167	Kling	226	Kestner
168	Kestner	226	S.F.B.J.
169	Kestner	227	S.F.B.J.
169	Kley & Hahn	230	S.F.B.J.
171	Kestner	231	Marseille, Armand
172	Hertel, Schwab & Co.	233	S.F.B.J.
172	Kestner	234	Kestner
174	Kestner	234	S.F.B.J.
176	bisque, German, unknown	235	S.F.B.J.
		236	S.F.B.J.
177	Kestner	237	Kestner
179	Hertel, Schwab & Co.	237	S.F.B.J.
180	Kestner	238	Kestner
182	Kestner	240	Marseille, Armand
183	bisque, German, unknown	242	S.F.B.J.
		243	Kestner
185	Kestner	244	Bähr & Pröschild
186	Kling	245	Kestner
189	Googly	246	Bähr & Pröschild
189	Kling	247	Kestner
191	Kämmer & Reinhardt	247	S.F.B.J.
192	Kämmer & Reinhardt	247	Unis, France
193	Kling	249	Kestner
195	Kestner	250	Kley & Hahn
196	Kestner	250	Heubach, Ernst
199	bisque, German	251	Heubach, Ernst
200	Arnold, Max Oscar		

MARK	DOLL COMPANY	MARK	DOLL COMPANY
251	Marseille, Armand	410	Marseille, Armand
251	S.F.B.J.	418	Heubach, Ernst
251	Schuetzmeister & Quendt	449	Marseille, Armand
251	Unis, France	452	Heubach, Ernst
252	Marseille, Armand	463	Heubach, Ernst
252	S.F.B.J.	485	bisque, German, unknown
253	Marseille, Armand	500	Marseille, Armand
257	Kestner	513	Schmidt, Bruno
260	Kestner	525	Kley & Hahn
261	all-bisque, German	526	Kley & Hahn
262	Heubach, Ernst	531	Kley & Hahn
264	Kestner	537	Schmidt, Bruno
267	bisque, German	542	Marseille, Armand
267	Heubach, Ernst	549	Kley & Hahn
275	Heubach, Ernst	550	Marseille, Armand
282	Kley & Hahn	560a	Marseille, Armand
292	all-bisque, Googly	570	all-bisque, German
296	bisque, German, unknown	585	Bähr & Pröschild
300	Heubach, Ernst	590	Marseille, Armand
300	Kling	592	Bähr & Pröschild
301	S.F.B.J.	604	Bähr & Pröschild
301	Unis, France	612	Bergmann, C.M.
302	Unis, France	620	Bähr & Pröschild
310	Marseille, Armand	624	Bähr & Pröschild
312	Heubach, Ernst	639	Alt, Beck & Gottschalck
314	Marseille, Armand	678	Bähr & Pröschild
320	Heubach, Ernst	687	Schmidt, Bruno
321	Heubach, Ernst	698	Alt, Beck & Gottschalck
323	Marseille, Armand	719	Simon & Halbig
328	Marseille, Armand	728	Kämmer & Reinhardt, celluloid or composition
329	Marseille, Armand	739	Simon & Halbig
329	all-bisque, German	740	Simon & Halbig
335	Marseille, Armand	769	Simon & Halbig
340	Bähr & Pröschild	817	Kämmer & Reinhardt, rubber
341	Marseille, Armand	833	all-bisque, German, baby
342	Heubach, Ernst	847	Averill, Georgene
345	Marseille, Armand	880	Alt, Beck & Gottschalck
351	Marseille, Armand	886	Simon & Halbig, all-bisque
352	Marseille, Armand	887	Simon & Halbig, all-bisque
353	Marseille, Armand	890	Simon & Halbig, all-bisque
355	Marseille, Armand	902	Simon & Halbig
370	Marseille, Armand	905	Simon & Halbig
371	Marseille, Armand	908	Simon & Halbig
390	Marseille, Armand	914	Schoenau & Hoffmeister
390N	Marseille, Armand		
399	Heubach, Ernst		
401	Marseille, Armand		
403	Kämmer & Reinhardt		

MARK	DOLL COMPANY	MARK	DOLL COMPANY
914	Porzellanfabrik Mengersgereuth	1361	Alt, Beck & Gottschalck
		1362	Alt, Beck & Gottschalck
924	Porzellanfabrik Mengersgereuth	1368	Simon & Halbig
926	Kämmer & Reinhardt, composition	1407	bisque, German, unknown
		1418	Simon & Halbig
929	Simon & Halbig	1428	Cuno & Otto Dressel
939	Simon & Halbig	1428	Simon & Halbig
949	Simon & Halbig	1469	Simon & Halbig
950	Simon & Halbig	1469	Cuno & Otto Dressel
969	Simon & Halbig	1488	Simon & Halbig
971	Marseille, Armand	1800	Schoenau & Hoffmeister
975	Marseille, Armand	1894	Marseille, Armand
979	Simon & Halbig	1896	Cuno & Otto Dressel
980	Marseille, Armand	1897	Marseille, Armand
985	Marseille, Armand	1900	Schoenau & Hoffmeister
990	Marseille, Armand	1900	Heubach, Ernst
996	Marseille, Armand	1902	Heubach, Ernst
996	Alt, Beck & Gottschalck	1906	Schoenau & Hoffmeister
1009	Simon & Halbig	1907	S.F.B.J.
1039	Simon & Halbig	1907	Jumeau
1040	Simon & Halbig	1909	Schoenau & Hoffmeister
1046	Alt, Beck & Gottschalck	1914	Cuno & Otto Dressel
1050	Simon & Halbig	1914	Simon & Halbig
1070	Kestner	1916	Bergmann, C.M.
1078	Simon & Halbig	1920	Cuno & Otto Dressel
1079	Simon & Halbig	2000	Marseille, Armand
1080	Simon & Halbig	2023	Schmidt, Bruno
1099	Simon & Halbig	2097	Schmidt, Bruno
1123	Alt, Beck & Gottschalck	3200	Marseille, Armand
1129	Simon & Halbig	3300	Marseille, Armand
1158	Simon & Halbig	4000	Schoenau & Hoffmeister
1159	Simon & Halbig	5636	Heubach, Gebrüder
1160	Simon & Halbig	5686	Heubach, Gebrüder
1199	Simon & Halbig	5700	Schoenau & Hoffmeister
1248	Simon & Halbig	5730	Heubach, Gebrüder
1249	Simon & Halbig	5800	Schoenau & Hoffmeister
1272	Schmidt, Franz	5896	Heubach, Gebrüder
1279	Simon & Halbig	69** (6970, 6996, etc.)	Heubach, Gebrüder
1294	Schmidt, Franz	7*** (7246, 7407, 7744, others)	Heubach, Gebrüder
1294	Simon & Halbig		
1295	Schmidt, Franz	8*** (8050, 8244, 8733, etc.)	Heubach, Gebrüder
1299	Simon & Halbig		
1303	Simon & Halbig	9487	Heubach, Gebrüder
1307	Simon & Halbig	9573	Heubach, Gebrüder
1322	Alt, Beck & Gottschalck	9578	Heubach, Gebrüder
1329	Simon & Halbig	9908	Heubach, Gebrüder
1349	Cuno & Otto Dressel	105** (10532, 10534, etc.)	Heubach, Gebrüder
1352	Alt, Beck & Gottschalck		
1358	Simon & Halbig	A 7	Steiner

MARK	DOLL COMPANY	MARK	DOLL COMPANY
A M	Marseille, Armand	H A	Alexandre, Henri
A SANITARY TOY	Knickerbocker	H C	bisque, German, unknown
A T	Thuillier		
A W	Wislizenus	Harriet Flanders	Averill, Georgene
ABG (intertwined symbol)	Alt, Beck & Gottschalck	HEbee-SHEbee	Horsman
		Heubach Koppelsdorf	Heubach, Ernst
Alex	Madame Alexander	Hygienic Toys	Chad Valley
American Doll & Toy Corp.	American Character	IV	Simon & Halbig
		J.I.O.	all-bisque, Orsini
B & O	bisque, German, unknown	J.K. Koge (in triangle)	Koge, celluloid dolls
		JDK	Kestner
B & P	Bähr & Pröschild	Joy Of A Toy (tag)	Knickerbocker
B F	Jumeau	Judy Ann	Nancy Ann Storybook
B L	Jumeau	Just Me	Marseille, Armand
BSW (in heart)	Schmidt, Bruno	Jutta	Cuno & Otto Dressel
Bte.	Schmitt et Fils, all- bisque	K	Kling
BTR	all-bisque, French	K & H	Kerr & Heinz
Buggrub	Schoenau & Hoffmeister	K & H (in banner)	Kley & Hahn
C P	Catterfelder Puppenfabrik	K & W	König & Wernicke
Calli-lou	reproductions; Garnett, Neva Wade	K * R	Kämmer & Reinhardt
		L.A.& S	Louis Amberg & Son
Cherie	Lanternier	Lambkins	Effanbee
D & C (intertwined)	Dewees Cochran	Le Parisien	Steiner
D.I.P.	Swaine & Co.	Limoges	Lanternier
Darling Dolly	Armand Marseille	M	Bébé Mascotte
Demalcol	Googly	M (shield symbol) F	bisque, German, unknown
DEP	DEP dolls (also part of mark for numerous French and German bisque dolls)	M B	Motherau
		M B (in a circle)	Morimura Brothers
		M.D.T.	Martha Thompson, Amy from *Little Women*
Duchess	Marseille, Armand	Madame Hendren	Averill, Georgene
E B	French fashion	Made in England (with elongated "g")	Pedigree
E D	Denamur, Etienne		
E J	Jumeau	MARION	Hertwig
E.1.H.Co.	Horsman	MBI	Danbury Mint
Elite	Handwerck, Max	MDT	Thompson, Martha
Excelsior (on body)	Kestner	Minerva	Buschow & Beck
F R	Falck & Roussel	MOA (in 8-point star)	Arnold, Max Oscar
F S & C	Schmidt, Franz	MT	Thompson, Martha
F S & Co.	Schmidt, Franz	My Girlie	George Borgfeldt & Co.
Fabrication Francaise A L & Cie	Lanternier	NEMS	Remco
		Nobbi Kid	Marseille, Armand
Favorite	Lanternier	OIC	Kestner
Fleur de lis	Royal (Japanese celluloid)	P D	Petit & Dumontier
Florodora	Marseille, Armand	P G	Pintel & Godchaux
FY	Yamato Importing	Paris Bébé	Danel et Cie; Jumeau
G K	Kuhnlenz, Gebrüder	Petite Française	Verlingue
G.B. & Co	George Borgfeldt & Co.	PM	Porzellanfabrik Mengersgereuth
Globe Baby	Hartmann, Karl		
Grace C. Rockwell	George Borgfeldt & Co.		
H	Halopeau		

MARK	DOLL COMPANY
Posey Pet	Madame Alexander
Poulbot	S.F.B.J.
Queen Louise	Marseille, Armand
R & B	Arranbee
R D	Rabery & Delphieu
R R	Jumeau
RA	Recknagel
RC	Radiguet & Cordonnier
Revalo	Ohlhaver, Gebrüder
RG	Gibbs, Ruth
S & Co	Swaine & Co.
S & H	Simon & Halbig
S ("P B" in star) H	Schoenau & Hoffmeister
S 1	Cuno & Otto Dressel
S H	Simon & Halbig
Santa	Heubach, Gebrüder
Santa	Simon & Halbig
Sch (in shield)	Schmitt et Fils
Sie C (with number)	Steiner
SQ (intertwined)	Schuetzmeister & Quendt
Storybook Doll	Nancy Ann Storybook Doll
Symbol: 8-point star	Arnold, Max Oscar
Symbol: anchor	Verlingue
Symbol: bell	Kling
Symbol: circle-dot	Bru
Symbol: circular rising sun containing an "H" superimposed over a "C"	Heubach, Gebrüder
Symbol: crossed swords	Bähr & Pröschild
Symbol: crown over "W"	Goebel

MARK	DOLL COMPANY
Symbol: eagle head	Petitcolin, celluloid
Symbol: heart	Ideal
Symbol: helmet	Buschow & Beck
Symbol: horseshoe	Heubach, Ernst
Symbol: shield	Schmitt et Fils
Symbol: star	Steiner
Symbol: star (P B inside)	Schoenau & Hoffmeister
Symbol: star (starburst) / DEP / Germany / 81	Heubach, Gebrüder
Symbol: sunburst	Heubach, Gebrüder
Symbol: swirly top over "9" (blue)	Dressel & Kister
Symbol: triple "M"s (stacked)	German, Mahr & Sohn (celluloid)
Symbol: turtle in diamond	Rheinische Gummi und Celluloid Fabrik Co. (Celluloid)
Symbol: wings and "LL"	Lois Aimee Le Jeune
Tee-Wee	Armand Marseille
Topper Corp	Deluxe Reading, Dawn
TR	bisque, German, unknown
V G	Verdier & Gutmacher
Vanta Baby	Louis Amberg & Son
Walkure	Kley & Hahn
Welsch	Arnold, Max Oscar
Wendy-Ann	Madame Alexander
Wendy-kin	Madame Alexander
WSK	Wiesenthal, Schindel & Kallenberg
XI	Kestner

ABOUT THE AUTHOR

Denise Van Patten is a longtime collector of dolls and a dealer of modern, vintage, and antique dolls through her doll shop in Northern California. She has been the guide to doll collecting on About.com (the world's largest information website for doll collectors) for over five years, and was the editor of the *Doll Reader* magazine website from 2001 to 2002. Her articles on dolls have been featured in many magazines. Look for Denise's schedule of doll lectures and appearances at www.officialpriceguidetodolls.com.

INDEX

HICKMANS